Domestic Transportation
Practice, Theory and Policy
SECOND EDITION

Roy J. Sampson
Professor of Transportation, University of Oregon

Martin T. Farris
Professor of Economics, Arizona State University

Houghton Mifflin Company / Boston
New York / Atlanta / Geneva, Illinois / Dallas / Palo Alto

Printed in the U.S.A.

Library of Congress Catalog Card Number: 71-141287

ISBN: 0-395-11965-0

Editor's Introduction

Publication of the second edition of *Domestic Transportation: Practice, Theory and Policy* is perhaps more timely than publication of the successful first edition just five years ago. Today, the study of transportation is more complex with demand and supply of transport larger and more diverse than ever. Yet the various combinations of passengers, shippers, and carriers have produced confusion, dismay, poor financial returns, and extreme concern for the future. Transport constitutes one-fifth of the economic activity in the United States and obviously affects most of the remaining four-fifths. The dynamics of technological and managerial change, inflation, politics, concern for ecology, domestic and international competition, and the simple desire to do better intensify the importance of the principles and issues in this book.

The second edition is offered as a refinement and enlargement of the first as well as an updated manuscript addressed to current and emerging dilemmas. As I consider the bankruptcy of the Penn-Central, the SST controversy, opening of the Arkansas River to barges and mini-freighters, the piping of solids, logistics, and conglomerates, I am delighted to see this thought-provoking book placed in the hands of those persons who offer the best hope of understanding and improving the world of transport.

Indiana University   L. LESLIE WATERS

Preface to the Second Edition

The study of transportation is a study of change—change in the locations and movements of goods and people as well as in the physical and institutional aspects of transportation itself. It has been said that change is the only constant. This is well illustrated in transportation.

Since our first edition, numerous physical changes have occurred in transportation. Old means of transport have expanded or declined, and new ones have been developed or proposed. Turbo trains, jumbo jets, supersonic aircraft, hydrofoils, surface-effect vehicles, passenger "pipelines," new types of automotive engines, and automated locomotives are being used commercially or are under consideration. The growing use of computers has brought new methods of physical and managerial transport control. Man has been transported to the moon and back. We cannot foresee what all these exotic changes may mean, but they demonstrate the dynamic character of the contemporary "transportation explosion."

On the institutional side, mergers have continued and conglomerates have arrived. Some old and established regulatory policies have been modified. The Department of Transportation has been created and plays a significant policy role. Legislation supporting urban transport has been enacted, and the "Railpax" program is underway. There is increasing concern about the effects of transportation on our environment and the "quality of life." Institutional change, our principal concern in this revision, has been as dynamic as physical change. But most of our old problems remain.

We have attempted to incorporate what we believe to be the most significant recent changes and trends in this revision, without sacrificing the basic premises and organization of our first edition. Two chapters have been added, several chapters have been rewritten, almost all chapters have been revised, and factual materials have been updated. We have tried to preserve and improve the best features of our first edition while presenting the most important new developments in a book of reasonable length.

We wish to express our gratitude to the many professors, students, and transportation practitioners throughout the country whose use of our first edition made this revised edition possible. Many of you have given us helpful comments, criticisms, and suggestions for revision, all of which are appreciated and many of which have been used. We hope that you will find this revised edition worthy of your continued use.

University of Oregon   Roy J. Sampson
Arizona State University   Martin T. Farris

Preface to the First Edition

Few students take more than one course in transportation. For only a handful does the initial course provide a foundation for a major or concentration in the field. As the first course is the limit of exposure for most, it should be both introductory and comprehensive, and suitable for both economics and business administration students.

Ideally, among other virtues, an introductory transportation text should be concise and stimulating. It should not burden the beginner with lengthy regulatory and legal doctrine and history, abstruse theory, or detailed practice. It should require as a minimum prerequisite only that basic knowledge of our business and economic system necessary for understanding the concepts and problems of transportation. But an introductory text must be comprehensive in the sense that it treats all modes of transportation as well as the basic principles of transportation economics and traffic management. It must develop an understanding of the evolution of transportation and its public regulation. It must build a strong foundation for further study, both in transportation and in other business and economics areas if it is to serve the terminal student as well as the potential major.

We have kept these requirements in mind in writing this book. We have used, experimented with, and refined this approach (including materials and sequence of presentation) in our own classes for several years where it has proved useful and teachable.

Two innovations are presented. First, this text offers an integrated approach to domestic transportation. The basic modes of transport are viewed as a whole rather than separately. Problems and practices are not segregated artificially into rail, motor, air, water, pipeline, forwarder, or shipper spheres. Secondly, the "traditional" sub-fields of transportation economics and industrial traffic management have been merged, since both are essential for transportation majors and obviously desirable for other students in economics and business. If the principles of traffic management are not presented until the economics and regulation of transportation are mastered, many beginning students will never be exposed to the managerial aspects of transportation. Rather than specializing in one area, we have favored a middle ground equally inhabitable by business administration and economics students.

We have organized our chapters into eight parts. Part One establishes the importance of our domestic transportation system and portrays its historical background and evolution. Part Two is a comprehensive overview of our present system and its general performance. In Part Three, the reader is introduced to the supply side of public transportation, that is, what service carriers sell, and under what conditions. Part Four brings demand and pricing into the equation by showing the interrelationships between demand, costs, and rates, and their influence upon the business and economic system. This part also stresses the interplay between transport and regional economic activity and development. Part Five deals with the regulatory structure within which transport operates. Part Six discusses transportation policy and the timely problems which are a part of the institutional environment. Part Seven brings the individual shipper and his problems of physical distribution management more clearly into the transportation picture. Finally, Part Eight, a single chapter, presents the authors' "educated guess" concerning future transport technology, regulation and public policy, and the future role of traffic management in physical distribution or business logistics. After studying these topics, the potential transportation major should be ready for advanced courses, while the non-major should have at least the minimum transportation background necessary for most general business activity.

This book is truly a joint and equal endeavor, both in conception and execution. There is no junior or senior author, either for the book as a whole or for any part of it. We do, however, wish to acknowledge our indebtedness and grateful appreciation to our own former transportation teachers, the late Professors Stuart Daggett, University of California, Berkeley, and Ralph L. Dewey, The Ohio State University; to many of our academic colleagues, both in our field of transportation and in other disciplines; to a number of carrier, regulatory, and industrial transportation practitioners; to many excellent transportation scholars and authors, past and present; and to dozens of our former students who have unknowingly shaped this text. We are, of course, fully responsible for any errors of omission or commission.

University of Oregon Roy J. Sampson
Arizona State University Martin T. Farris

Table of Contents

Part One

The Role of Domestic Transportation   1

  1 *The Significance of Transportation*   3
    General Significance of Transportation 3
    Economic Significance of Transportation 4
    Transportation and Business Logistics 13
    Additional Reading 15

  2 *The Development of Transportation*   16
    The Importance of Geography and Technology 16
    Water Transportation Came First 17
    Early Road Movement 20
    Canals 22
    Railroads and the Competitive Struggle 24
    Revival of Highway Transportation 29
    Air Transportation 32
    Revival of Water Transportation 33
    Pipelines: A Modern Giant 35
    Summary: The Political and Economic Impact of Transportation
      Development 37
    Additional Readings 37

  3 *Environmental and Sociological Aspects of Transportation*   39
    Environmental Aspects 39
    Sociological Aspects 44
    Economic Benefits Compared to Social Costs 45
    Summary 46
    Additional Readings 46

Part Two

Economic Characteristics and Performance of Domestic Transportation   49

  4 *Land Carriers*   51
    Railroads 51
    Trucks 59
    Busses 63
    Pipelines 64
    Additional Readings 66

5 Water, Air, and Other Forms of Carriage   6

Water Carriage   68
Air Carriage   74
Other Forms of Carriage and Related Services   79
Intermodal Carriage   82
Additional Readings   83

6 Transportation Geography: Routes and Commodity Movements   8

The Location of Transportation Routes   86
Commodity Movements   92
Changes in Interregional Relationships   98
Additional Readings   102

Part Three

Carrier Services in Domestic Transportation   10

7 Legal Service Obligations   10

Obligations in Common Carriage   104
Origin of Carrier Obligations   105
The Duty of Service   106
The Duty of Delivery   108
The Duty of Reasonable Rates   110
The Duty of Nondiscrimination   111
Contract Carrier Obligations   115
Conclusion 115
Additional Readings   115

8 Terminal and Special Line-Haul Services   11

Terminal Services   117
Accessorial Line-Haul Services   124
Conclusion   127
Additional Readings   128

9 Cooperative and Coordinated Service   12

Cooperative Carrier Service   130
Coordinated Carrier Services   136
Summary of Part Three   139
Additional Readings   140

Part Four

The Role of Costs and Rates in Domestic Transportation   14

10 The Economic and Legal Basis of Rates   14

Economic Functions of Rates   143
Regulation and Reasonable Rates   146
Definitions of Demand and Supply   148

The Demand for Transportation Services   150
Transportation Costs and Rate-Making   155
Additional Readings   159

11 Freight Classifications and Tariffs: Their Preparation and Use   161
The Preparation and Use of Classifications   162
Kinds of Tariffs and Their Use   165
How Rates Are Made or Changed   172
Additional Readings   176

12 Kinds of Freight Rates   177
The Terminology of Freight Rates   177
Additional Readings   186

13 Freight Rate Structures   187
The Postage-Stamp Rate Structure   187
Mileage Rate Structures   189
Basing Point and Fourth Section Rate Structures   194
Blanket Rate Structure   198
Additional Readings   205

14 Transportation Costs and Spacial Economic Activities   207
Competition, Transport Costs, and Spacial Activity   207
Transport Costs as Location Determinants   212
Transport Costs and Regional Economic Development   217
Additional Readings   222

15 Location Theory and Transportation   224
Agricultural Location: J. H. von Thunen   225
Industrial Location: Alfred Weber   227
The Location of Cities   231
Transport Costs and Natural Marketing Areas:
    Fetter, Losch, et al.   233
Summary   239
Additional Readings   239

Part Five
Regulation of Domestic Transportation   243

16 The Regulation of Transportation Monopoly   245
The Evolutionary Nature of Transport Regulation   245
The Essence of Monopoly Regulation   263
Additional Readings   265

17 Regulation of Transportation Competition: Beginnings   267
The Nature of Transportation Competition   267
Regulation of Intramodal Rail Competition   269
The Changing Character of the Transportation Market   271
Regulation of Motor Carriers   272
Additional Readings   280

18 Regulation of Transportation Competition: Evolution — 282
Air Transportation 282
Water Transportation 287
National Transportation Policy and "Inherent Advantage" 289
Freight Forwarders 292
The Reed-Bulwinkle Act 292
The Transportation Act of 1958 293
The Essence of Competition Regulation 295
Additional Readings 297

19 Regulatory Institutions — 299
Commissions and Boards 299
Courts 309
The Legislative Process 312
The Executive 313
Additional Readings 319

Part Six

Goals in Domestic Transportation Policy — 321

20 Unification, Integration, and Diversification — 323
Carrier Goals Leading to Conflict 323
Methods and Purposes of Unification and Integration 324
Effects of Unification and Integration 328
Obstacles to Unification and Integration 332
Public Policy on Unification and Integration 333
Diversification and Conglomerates 337
General Summary 339
Additional Readings 340

21 Society's Interest in Labor-Management Relations — 342
Conflicting Goals: Carrier, Employee, and Public 342
Institutional Environment 345
Mechanics of Labor-Management Conflict Settlement 347
Alternative Solutions 350
Conclusion 353
Additional Readings 353

22 Public Aids and Promotions of Transportation — 355
Nature of the Problem 355
Goals of Public Aid 359
Methods of Public Aids 361
Effects of Public Aids 369
Additional Readings 371

23 Passenger Transportation Policy Problems — 373
The Nature of Passenger Transportation 373
Social and Economic Problems 380

Policy Considerations   388
General Summary   389
Additional Readings   389

24 Conflicts in National Transportation Policy   *391*
Identification of Policy   391
Kinds of Conflicts   394
Proposed Solutions to Conflicts   402
Conclusions   406
General Summary of Transportation Policy   407
Additional Readings   407

Part Seven

Transportation Aspects of Physical Distribution Administration (Business Logistics)   411

25 Traffic Management's Role in the Decision-Making Mechanism   *413*
Physical Distribution and Industrial Traffic Management   413
Duties and Organization of the Industrial Traffic Department   421
Carrier Traffic Departments   426
Additional Readings   430

26 Traffic Control Decisions and Activities   *431*
Direct Day-to-Day Relationships With Carriers   431
Changing the Rates or Services Environment   441
Other "Routine" Activities   442
Summary   442
Additional Readings   443

27 Traffic Management's Relationship to Other Operating
Decisions   *444*
Legal Problems   445
Transportation Insurance   445
Purchasing and Sales Policies   448
Internal Warehousing and Materials Handling   450
Packing, Marking, and Loading   450
General Organizational and Personnel Policies   451
Summary   452
Additional Readings   453

28 Transportation Advice on Capital Decisions   *454*
Decisions on Transportation Equipment Expenditures   455
Containerization and Internal Materials Handling Equipment   458
Electronic Computer Equipment   459
Warehousing and Warehouse Location   460
Traffic Management and Plant Location   464
Traffic Management and Major Product Innovations   464
Summary   465
Additional Reading   465

Part Eight

Summary and Preview   467

    29 The Future of Domestic Transportation   469
        A Glance at the Past   469
        A View of the Present   471
        A Murky Glimpse at Marvels of the Future   472
        Additional Readings   477

Index   478

List of Figures

1. *Principal Land Transportation Routes of the United States* 90
2. *The Railroad Network of the United States* 91
3. *The National System of Interstate and Defense Highways* 94
4. *The Inland Waterways System of the United States* 95
5. *The Regional Airline Routes of the United States* 97
6. *The Crude Oil Pipeline System of the United States* 99
7. *The Product Oil Pipeline System of the United States* 101
8. *Demand and Supply Schedules and Changes in Demand* 149
9. *A "Zone" Concept of Demand and Supply* 150
10. *A Short-run Competitive Pricing Situation* 156
11. *Effects of Differing Terminal Costs* 158
12. *Page from the Uniform Freight Classification* 164
13. *Page from the National Motor Freight Classification* 166
14. *Portions of a Railroad Class Tariff* 168
15. *Page from a Railroad Commodity Tariff* 170
16. *Major Railroad Rate Territories* 173
17. *Illustrative Rate Profiles* 192
18. *A Basing Point Rate Situation, Showing a Fourth Section Deviation* 197
19. *A Rail Blanket Rate Profile: Lumber Rates in Cents per 100 lbs., to Various Points from Portland, Oregon, to the Gulf Coast, Via the Southern Route* 199
20. *A Rail Blanket Rate Map: Lumber Rates, in Cents per 100 lbs., from Western Oregon and Washington Origins to Various Transcontinental Destinations* 200
21. *Thunen's Zones* 227
22. *Weber's Locational Triangle* 230
23. *Natural Market Areas Under Various Transport Rates* 235
24. *Transportation and Location Theory* 240
25. *Organization of the Interstate Commerce Commission* 304
26. *Organization of the Civil Aeronautics Board* 306
27. *Origin Chart, Department of Transportation* 317
28. *Organization Chart, Department of Transportation* 318
29. *Segment of Organization Chart for Coordinating Physical Distribution Management* 419
30. *Functional Organization of an Industrial Traffic Department* 427
31. *Functional Organization of a Rail Carrier Traffic Department* 429

List of Tables

1. *The Nation's Estimated Freight Bill for 1968* 1(

2. *The Nation's Estimated Passenger Bill for 1968* 1.

3. *Net Investment in Privately Owned Transportation Facilities in 1965* 1.

4. *Total Miles of Railway Operated in U.S. by Decades* 2(

5. *Estimated Approximate Total Intercity Freight Ton-Mileage, and Per Cent Moved by Each Mode of Transport, Selected Years* 5.

6. *Approximate Percentage of Railroad Freight Tonnage of Manufactured and Miscellaneous Products Originated in Various Regions, 1940 and 1964* 10(

Part One

The Role of
Domestic Transportation

In order to appreciate the complexities of the domestic transportation system of the United States, it is necessary to understand three things: (1) the significance of transportation, (2) its environmental impact, and (3) its development.

A grasp of the significance of transportation, and its environmental effects, both general and specific, prepares us to understand why the specifics of the system are meaningful. An understanding of the past as well as the development and evolution of our transportation system prepares us to appreciate the position of domestic transportation today and to gain insight into its problems.

The first three chapters of this book are written with these three ideas in mind.

1

The Significance
of Transportation

Our American transportation system is so all-pervasive and so efficient that most of us rarely think about it unless we are inconvenienced by a breakdown of some of its parts. Instead, we tend to take transportation for granted. Every product we consume, however, has been transported, usually several times before it gets to us. Our daily journeys to and from work, shopping centers, or university classrooms involve transportation. Even the services we consume would be impossible without the transportation of tools, repair parts, or other means of producing services.

In a more general way, transportation is an important part of our culture and heritage. It played a pivotal role in the discovery, settlement, and development of our nation. The westward movement, discussed by historians and immortalized by folk songs about steamboating, railroading, and long cattle drives was a chapter in transportation development. The freedom and mobility of our people, literally a nation on wheels and a people ever curious to see new places and ever anxious to undertake new tasks, is based upon efficient transportation. Our lives are shaped by transportation much more than we realize.

This wonderfully complex and efficient transportation system, however, did not reach its present form without travail, nor does it operate without direction. Its past history is dwarfed only by its present immensity and its future prospects. Therefore, some understanding of this system—its general significance and its specific uses, its internal workings and its external relationships, its origins and its future paths, its problems and its accomplishments— is a necessary part of the education of every person aspiring to play a significant part in the economic, business, or political life of our country.

GENERAL SIGNIFICANCE OF TRANSPORTATION

Much of our social and cultural unity is based upon the existence of adequate transportation. Society is a blend of many regional and local viewpoints and traditions growing out of differing heritages, environments, and problems. Interregional contacts through travel and the exchange of good promote the interchange of ideas and the breakdown of parochialism, thu encouraging an upward uniformity in tastes, health, education, and way of life in general.

Likewise, efficient transportation makes it possible for large geographic areas to be politically unified. Cultural similarity, mutual understanding, and the economic interdependence brought about by large-scale interregional trade reduce tendencies toward isolationism, while the ability to communicat rapidly makes unification administratively feasible. Ancient Egypt was held together for many centuries by its Nile River and ancient Rome by its mag nificent system of highways. Ancient Greece, on the other hand, with a ter rain which hindered a well-developed system of internal transport, remained a group of independent and squabbling city-states until it fell victim to an outside conqueror.

One cause for our own country's secession from Britain, despite a common heritage, was the slow and inefficient transport which hampered political administration and mutual understanding. In more recent times, the United States government authorized and supported the building of the first trans continental railroad partly to encourage California to remain within the Union during the Civil War. The first Canadian transcontinental railroad was likewise built to encourage the Province of British Columbia to remain a political part of Canada. Australians built a railroad across the wide desert area of their continent to hold their country together politically. Railroad played a key role in Bismarck's unification of numerous small independent states and principalities into modern Germany during the late 1800's. Many other examples of this kind could be cited illustrating the cohesive force of transportation.

Good transportation is also vital to national defense. The ability to trans port troops and materials quickly and to mobilize industrial power is essen tial both in actual war and in international political bargaining. Transporta tion is both a weapon and a deterrent, and its importance to defense ha increased rather than diminished in this age of global conflict and potential push-button nuclear warfare.

ECONOMIC SIGNIFICANCE OF TRANSPORTATION

The economic significance of transportation can best be appreciated by considering transportation in five separate but interconnected roles. These are: (1) transportation and economic development, (2) transportation and production, (3) transportation and distribution, (4) transportation and prices and (5) transportation and economy. Each will be considered in turn.

Transportation and Economic Development

Several basic elements are necessary for substantial economic growth. Three of these are: an adequate transportation system, an adequate system of communication, and a flexible source of energy or power. Our primary concern is with adequate transportation.

The transportation system is an integral part of production and distribution. Both large-scale production and mass distribution are necessary for economic development. Neither are possible without efficient and relatively cheap transportation. Transportation is the very foundation of economic development. A study of investment and developmental loans for underdeveloped countries shows that one of the first and most necessary elements in any economy is that of an adequate transportation system. Without this, it is of little use to construct expensive plants or to hope for a broad distribution of economic goods.

Domestically, we are fortunate in possessing one of the most highly developed transportation systems in the world. Our present transportation system, however, is the result of great struggle over a period of many years. Much of it was financed by profit-seeking foreign capital as others helped us to develop the foundations of economic growth. Now we are doing the same for other areas, although generally not for direct profit-making purposes.

But the point is that the first, and often overlooked, economic significance of transportation is that it provides a foundation upon which the economic growth of a nation progresses. Those who make decisions affecting transportation, whether private transport company managers, public officials, or users of transport services, have great social responsibilities.

Transportation and Production

Transportation is an integral part of the process of production. This can be seen from several points of view. One traditional view is to note that transportation creates both "place" and "time" utility.

Basically, transportation means changing the place or the location of an item. The classical economists noted that "value" could be created by this process of changing location, thus they called this "place utility," or the creation of value by changing position or location. For productive purposes, raw materials or parts for assembly have no value unless they are transported to the place where they are needed. Production usually calls for the change of location of many items in order to bring them together in the right proportions to produce something. We rarely refer to "place utility" today, but the principle still exists. Transportation creates value by changing the location of things and people so that production may occur.

In addition, transportation takes time. Not only is movement itself time consuming, but the assembly of goods uses time. We generally think of delays in time as being costly and wasteful. Sometimes they are, but under some conditions they can be profitable and economical. Large-scale production involves the assembling of many items from diverse sources. All do not arrive at the same time, and storage (delay) is often necessary. However, having the necessary item so that the productive process moves smoothly can be most valuable. Some delay through storage of necessary components at times may avoid the greater delay of shortages. The matter of delay over time and its effect on production was called "time utility" by the classical economists. Again, transportation creates value by time utility.

It is easy to see that large-scale production depends on time and place utility and, hence, upon transportation. Often large-scale production is considerably cheaper than production on a smaller scale. Yet the huge output of our productive system would be impossible without adequate transportation and assembly facilities to bring tremendous amounts of raw materials to the place of production and to hold them until the exact time they are needed. Of course, the dependence on transportation as a foundation for large-scale production varies according to the characteristics of the product. Some products, like steel, require that tremendous tonnages of raw materials be transported and stored for the production process. Other items, such as electronic gear, require very small tonnages of materials. In the case of steel, it is a problem of mass movement of great weights. The problem in electronics may be just as perplexing; while the tonnages are very small, the materials are highly valuable and sometimes very fragile. In both cases, however, transportation is necessary in order to produce on a large scale.

When we consider the nation as a whole or the entire world, it is apparent that transportation stimulates regional specialization and division of labor. All areas and peoples are not equally endowed. Resources, climate, arts, and skills vary. Thus, the productive process in one region may be different from that in another. With adequate transportation, each area is able to specialize in the production which it does best. This is the principle of comparative advantage which is studied in basic economics. But this principle can be operative only when transportation is possible. If it is impossible to get the specialized goods produced elsewhere or to send the fruits of one region's production to others, an area finds it must devote most of its effort to satisfying its own needs. Little specialization or regional division of labor can take place without transportation.

Because of this regional specialization and division of labor, and because transportation allows large-scale production, the transportation system becomes a determining factor in the location of production facilities. Chapter 14 will analyze this locational factor in detail. It is necessary here only to point out that transportation furthers the productive process, helps determine where production is likely to take place, and permits the large concentration of foodstuffs and raw materials necessary to support densely populated manufacturing areas.

Finally, it should be noted that transportation is one of the costs of production. While transportation obviously creates value, it does so only at a ost. Everything one buys has a transportation cost within it. The amount aries, of course, according to the characteristic of the item and the produc-ve process. Yet the cost of transportation is there because transportation is n integral part of the productive process.

ransportation and Distribution

Transportation is also an integral part of distribution. Again, time and lace utility are involved. An item produced at one point has little value un-ss it is moved to the place where it is needed or demanded. Movement rough space creates value. The timeliness of marketing is most important.)elay in time can often increase value by preventing a market "glut" which wers value. Storage and delay allow us to enjoy production long after the hysical production has ceased. Hence, value is created by changes in time.

Large-scale production cannot exist in a vacuum. It is necessary to have ass distribution systems to move the items produced. The most efficient rge-scale production plant cannot operate unless the things produced are old. An adequate transportation system provides the means by which mass istribution takes place. Commonly, it is said that "transportation broadens ne market." All that this means is that transportation allows mass distribution o operate. Hence, transportation and distribution are closely interconnected.

Again, the results of regional specialization or division of labor are un-vailable without transportation. By having an efficient transportation system, he availability of goods is greatly increased. Perishable items are now avail-ble in areas where they were unheard of a few years ago because of the echnological advances of transportation. The whole country, indeed the vhole world, is now a market for production based on good transportation. 'ransportation indeed provides the means to distribute the results of produc-ion and makes a multiplicity of goods available from all corners of the earth.

The cost of transportation is likely to be a determining factor in the loca-ion of the market for a specific item. Just as transportation determines the ocation of production, it also determines the location of markets. If trans-ortation costs are low, more areas can sell their goods in a given market. If ransportation costs are high, a protected market area exists for a few pro-lucers just as effectively as if tariffs or import quotas existed. Often the deter-nining factor in the marketing decision is transportation.

Finally, transportation obviously is one of the costs of distribution just as t is a cost of production. In this sense, it has a marked effect on the price f most items. Naturally, the amount of transportation costs involved in dis-ribution varies with the characteristics of the item, but, on the whole, trans-ortation is a major cost of distribution just as it is of production.

ransportation and Prices

Enough has been said to make it apparent that transportation costs make p a substantial share of the price of any item. Estimates vary, of course, and lifferent physical characteristics of an item mean different amounts of transportation costs, but, on the average, approximately twenty cents out of ever consumer dollar goes to transportation. The Interstate Commerce Con mission makes various studies from time to time of the ratio of transportatic rates to wholesale prices. For some items, such as sand and gravel, transport tion makes up over half the price. On others, such as business machines, th ratio is less than one per cent. Most products, of course, fall somewhere b tween these ranges.

In addition to being a component of all prices, transportation plays oth roles in price. One of the more important of these is price stability. If lon; haul transportation were not available, each market would be dependent (the local production area for its supply. Most items are not produced equal during each month of the year. This is especially true of agricultural iten which have a long production cycle culminating in a harvest period. Und circumstances of isolation and without adequate transportation, the price an item would be low when it was available in large quantities and hig when it was scarce.

However, transportation allows other areas to compete in a given marke Therefore, if local supplies are unavailable, the price usually does not ri greatly. Supplies may be shipped in to meet the need. Theoretically, th price in any market in time of shortage of local supplies should rise no mo than the cost of transportation, processing, and storage. Actually, because the regional specialization and division of labor noted above, prices may ri considerably less than this since the supplying area often produces mo. cheaply than the local area due to economies of specialization. The point that because of transportation, a great deal of price stability exists in mo market areas.

In addition to price stability and the leveling out of supplies, transport tion also promotes lower prices. By allowing more producers to enter a giv market, more price competition is possible. Areas with the lowest productic costs *plus* transportation costs set the price. Others must meet this price lose their share of the market. Since regional specialization is possible, th may mean that suppliers some distance from a market are actually setting th price. Without transportation and more competitors in a given market, th price could be higher. Generally, adequate transportation promotes compet tion and lowers prices.

Economists have long pointed out the relationship between transportatic and the use and price of land. Good transportation allows land to be used . a number of ways. The value of land will depend on its productivity. Th productivity may be a matter of location or a matter of location plus th value of the yield from the land use. In either case, location is merely a co ceptualization of the transportation position of land in space, and the value the yield from land is primarily dependent upon the price in a given mark Thus, both of these factors are based upon transportation. The same pri ciples are involved for the value of other natural resources.

Enough has been said to make the points that all prices have transportation costs involved in them, that transportation promotes price stability, that transportation promotes competition and usually lower prices, and that transportation often determines the price of natural resources.

Transportation and the Economy

Another way to consider the economic significance of transportation is to relate the transportation industry to the total economy. This can be done by considering six points: (1) the nation's annual transportation "bill," (2) the amount and earnings of persons employed in transportation and transportation-related fields, (3) the amount of capital invested in the national transportation plant, (4) the importance of public expenditures to aid the transportation system, (5) the tax role of transportation, and (6) the pivotal role of the transportation industry as a buyer of the production of others. In all cases, we will be considering transportation in a rather broad context.

The Nation's Annual Transportation Bill

The Transportation Association of America periodically calculates the annual freight and passenger bills paid by the country as a whole. The latest figures available at the time of writing show that the nation paid more than $75 billion for freight transportation services during 1968, and almost $97 billion for passenger transportation during 1968. Note that this national transportation bill is about one fifth of Gross National Product ($865.7 billion in 1968). Tables 1 and 2 show how the nation's freight and passenger expenditures are distributed among the various modes of transportation.

The Amount and Earnings of Persons Employed in Transportation

Over-all employment in transportation and transportation-related industries was more than 10 million persons in 1968. This amounts to around 13 per cent of the total labor force in the United States. The Transportation Association of America studies show that this proportion of total employed has held fairly constant since 1940, even though there have been some changes in the numbers in various occupational classifications. The four subgroups involved in this more than 10 million figure are carrier personnel, transportation equipment manufacturing personnel, related industry personnel (which includes auto sales and service, highway construction and truck drivers in general industry) and transportation employees of federal and state governments. Thus, it should not be assumed from these figures that one out of every seven employed persons drives a truck, runs an engine, or flies a plane. Even so, all these people are directly related to domestic transportation; and it is, therefore, possible to say that transportation is one of the largest employers in the economy.

Additionally, the earnings of full-time employees working directly in transportation is rather high on the average. In 1968, full-time employees in

Table 1

The Nation's Estimated Freight Bill for 1968*
(in billions of dollars, rounded)

Highway	$55.1
Rail	10.6
Water	5.3
Oil Pipe Line	1.2
Freight Forwarder and Express	0.6
Air	1.1
Other Shipper Costs	1.4**
TOTAL	$75.3

*Figures include both regulated and nonregulated transportation, domestic as well as international.

**Includes loading and unloading of freight cars as well as the operation of traffic departments.

Source: Transportation Association of America, *Transportation Facts and Trends*, 7th ed., Washington, 1970.

the transportation industry earned an average annual wage of $9,666 as compared to an average of $8,341 in manufacturing, $8,164 in finance, insurance and real estate, and $8,538 in communications utilities. Of course, average can be very misleading, but the figures do tend to show that wages in transportation are superior to many employments.

Thus, not only are one out of every seven persons employed in transportation or transportation-related fields, but the direct transportation workers are paid a higher average annual wage. Transportation makes a substantial contribution to the total economy in both number employed and income generated by wages.

Capital Invested in Transportation

The fact that most types of transportation are heavy users of capital will be fully developed later in this book. However, if one will pause to consider the tremendous amount of equipment, terminals, trucks, pipes, ships, and planes in our transportation system, it will be readily apparent that the amount invested in transportation is substantial. Thus, more than $180 billion was privately invested in the domestic transportation system in 1965 (see Table for breakdown). During 1969, about $8.8 billion was spent for transportation equipment in this country.

Table 2

The Nation's Estimated Passenger Bill for 1968
(in billions of dollars, rounded)

Private Transportation	
Auto (including cost of new and used cars, gasoline, maintenance, tools, insurance, etc.)	$83.1
Air	2.0
Total Private Passenger Transportation	$85.1
For-Hire Transportation	
Local (including taxi and transit systems)	$ 3.7
Intercity (all modes)	6.2
International (air and water)	1.7
Total For-Hire Passenger Transportation	$11.6
GRAND TOTAL	$96.7

Source: Transportation Association of America, *Transportation Facts and Trends*, 7th ed., Washington, 1970.

Table 3

Net Investment in Privately Owned Transportation
Facilities in 1965
(in billions of dollars, rounded)

Highway Carriage, Including Automobiles	$113.4
Railroads	30.2
Air Carriers	4.9
Water Carriers	3.1
Oil Pipelines	3.0
Transit	2.7
Equipment Manufacturers	22.9
TOTAL	$180.2

Source: Transportation Association of America, *Transportation Facts and Trends*, 7th ed., Washington, 1970.

Public Expenditures for Transportation Facilities

In addition to the rather tremendous sums privately invested in transpo↑ tation facilities, large annual capital expenditures are made by Federal, stat and local governments on transportation facilities, especially highways. Whi Chapter 22 will develop the background of these public aids and promotion undertakings, it can be noted here that the total amounts are large. For i⸱ stance, during the decade of the 1960's, a total of more than $165 billion w⸱ spent by federal, state, and local governments in building and administerir domestic transportation facilities. It is clear that capital expenditures by th public through governmental projects is no small part of the government budgets each year. Again transportation is seen as an important part of th economy.

The Tax Role of Transportation

But transportation does more than merely spend public funds on facilitie⸱ it collects and pays a rather significant share of the total tax bill for the variou governments involved. Practically all highway expenditures are collected ⸱ the form of taxes on highway users, chiefly as gasoline taxes. Until recentl both passenger tickets and freight bills included an excise tax to the Feder⸱ government. Even now, airline tickets have an 8% Federal excise tax. In 196 for example, transport accounted for around 18 per cent of all Federal taxes, ⸱ a total of more than $26 billion. In regard to taxes collected by the states, th relative position is even larger although the total dollar figure is smaller. appears that around 35 per cent of all state taxes are levied on transportatio⸱ Thus transportation plays a major role as a collector and payer of taxes in th economy.

Transportation as a User of Industrial Products

Finally, it should be noted that the transportation industry is a majⸯ consumer of the industrial production of the nation. When one considers th⸱ transportation in its broadest sense includes the assembly of automobiles an⸱ trucks, this is almost self-evident. Yet students are often surprised to lear⸱ that transportation uses 75 per cent of all rubber produced, 56 per cent of a⸱ petroleum refined, 53 per cent of all lead, 35 per cent of all zinc, 27 per ce⸱ of all cement, 29 per cent of all steel, 19 per cent of all copper, and 20 p⸱ cent of all aluminum. Certainly, transportation is one of the major buyers ⸱ the economy's industrial production.

Summary

There may well be other means of illustrating the economic significance ⸱ transportation to the total economy. However, by noting the nation's annu⸱ transportation bill amounting to around 20 per cent of Gross National Produc⸱ the 13 per cent of the labor force employed in transportation at "superioⸯ annual income levels, the $180 billion or more of privately owned transportatio⸱

int, the large annual federal, state, and local government expenditures for
nsportation (estimated at $22.6 billion during 1970), the 18 per cent of
leral and 35 per cent of state revenues attributable to transportation, and
e significant role of transportation as a buyer of industrial production, one
i readily appreciate the pivotal importance of transportation in our total
onomy.

Having considered the significance of transportation in a general as well
in an economic sense, we are ready to review briefly the role of transporta-
n management in business.

ANSPORTATION AND BUSINESS LOGISTICS

As indicated above, the provision of transportation services is itself one
our leading forms of private business enterprise. Many transportation
npanies have assets of more than $1 billion each, and several are in the $2 or
billion class, or higher. But the most important aspect of transportation is
it it supplies essential business services to all other businesses. This aspect
transportation is our primary concern in this book.

finition of "Business Logistics" or "Physical Distribution nagement"

During recent years, the terms "business logistics" and "physical distribu-
n management" have become a part of our business vocabulary. These two
ms often are used interchangably, as they may be defined to include the
ne activities. Some persons do see differences in what these terms mean,
t the authors prefer to think of them as being the same.

Business logistics, or physical distribution management, may be defined
oadly as the management of the movement of goods through space (by
nsport) and through time (by warehousing, storage, production scheduling,
d related activities) from their *first origins* as raw materials to their *final
stinations* in consumers' hands.

The primary objective of physical distribution is the same as the overall
jective of any privately-owned business, namely to optimize cost-value ratios.
at is, it attempts to increase monetary values as much as possible, with the
st relative increases in monetary costs. From the firm's viewpoint, this
iximizes profits, while from society's viewpoint it increases economic effi-
ncy. These two viewpoints do not necessarily conflict in a private-enterprise
onomy.

Contrary to some authors, we do not view the physical distribution process
being a part of marketing. Rather, we prefer to think of marketing, as it
commonly conceived, as being a part of a larger distribution process. This
erall distribution process can be subdivided into *institutional* components
d *physical* components. Institutional distribution, comprising various buying,
ling, and related activities of wholesalers, jobbers, brokers, and retailers, as

well as advertising, marketing research, and the like, is what is known com
monly as marketing. Physical distribution, on the other hand, includes su
activities as the scheduling of purchasing, inventory control, storage, war
housing and materials handling, some aspects of manufacturing or processi
(as production scheduling and packaging) and, of course, transportation.

Average Costs of Physical Distribution

The aim of all economic activity involving goods is to transfer things fro
their present forms, places, and time references to more highly desired form
places, and time references. That is, the objective is to increase values I
increasing form utilities (by production) and space and time utilities (I
physical distribution). Value increases, of course, are accompanied by co
increases. It is worthwhile, therefore, to consider the relative magnitudes
production and distribution costs.

Many marketing students agree that about 41¢ of the average consum
dollar spent for goods goes for production costs, and 59¢ for distribution cos
(These costs include profits, of course.) The authors' own studies indica
that at least 30¢ or more of the 59¢ distribution costs go for what we ha
defined as *physical* distribution, leaving 29¢ or less attributable to institution
distribution (marketing). Further, around 15¢ of this 30¢ goes for *transport
tion,* leaving about 15¢ for the various other physical distribution costs.

This makes transportation costs the third largest single cost in the enti
economic process of production and distribution. For the "average" busine
(although there are many exceptions, both upward and downward) transport
tion costs are exceeded only by the costs of labor and of materials.

Business Management of Transportation and Physical Distribution

As transportation and other physical distribution expenditures requi
such a large part of the revenues of the average firm, it is apparent that the
expenditures must be well managed if the firm is to be most profitable.

The *industrial traffic manager,* who supervises the "buying" of his com
pany's transportation services, along with many other related transportatio
matters, has long been a key figure in the activities of most large or mediu
sized firms. He must be an expert in transportation, as well as a good manag
His performance directly affects both company profits and company services.

The *physical distribution manager* (known by various titles, dependi
upon the preferences of individual companies) is relatively new on the busine
scene, and is not yet as much a part of the scene as is the traffic manager. H
function is to supervise all physical distribution activities (and sometimes ev
marketing activities) and to coordinate these with other company functio
He must have a good working knowledge of transportation, but does not nece
sarily require the specialized knowledge of an industrial traffic manager—I
has a traffic manager under his supervision.

This book is concerned with basic transportation. That is, it deals with t
essential transport matters that every traffic manager and physical distributi

anager must know, and that every businessman and well-informed citizen
iould know. It does not delve deeply into the advanced areas of traffic man-
gement and physical distribution management, although Part Seven gives a
:neral overview of these specialized fields of management. Those choosing
ireers in these fields can move from this beginning into more advanced topics
˙ courses.

DDITIONAL READINGS

1. Bigham, Truman C., and Merrill J. Roberts, **Transportation Principles and Problems.** 2nd ed. New York: McGraw-Hill Book Co., Inc., 1952.
   Chapter 1. "General Significance of Transportation," pp. 1–13.
   Chapter 2. "Transportation and Production," pp. 14–28.
   Chapter 3. "Transportation and Exchange," pp. 29–48.
2. Daggett, Stuart, **Principles of Inland Transportation.** 4th ed. New York: Harper and Brothers, 1955.
   Chapter 2. "The Effects of Improved Transportation Upon Industrial Society," pp. 12–27.
3. Fair, Marvin L., and Ernest W. Williams, Jr., **Economics of Transportation.** Rev. ed. New York: Harper and Brothers, 1959.
   Chapter 1. "The Social Significance of Transportation," pp. 3–16.
   Chapter 2. "Transportation as an Economic Function," pp. 17–27.
   Chapter 3. "Transportation Development and National Economy," pp. 28–45.
4. Heskett, J. L., Robert M. Ivie, and Nicholas A. Glaskowsky, Jr., **Business Logistics.** New York: Ronald Press Company, 1964.
   Part I. "Scope and Importance of Business Logistics," pp. 3–42.
5. Locklin, D. Philip, **Economics of Transportation.** 6th ed. Homewood, Ill.: Richard D. Irwin, Inc., 1966.
   Chapter 1. "Economic Significance of Improved Transportation," pp. 1–17.
6. Mossman, Frank H., and Newton Morton, **Principles of Transportation.** New York: Ronald Press Company, 1957.
   Chapter 1. "Transportation in the Economy," pp. 3–12.
7. Norton, Hugh S., **Modern Transportation Economics.** Columbus, Ohio: Charles E. Merrill Books, Inc., 1963.
   Chapter 1. "Transportation, An Economic, Social and Political Function," pp. 3–17.
8. Pegrum, Dudley F., **Transportation: Economics and Public Policy.** Rev. ed. Homewood, Ill.: Richard D. Irwin, Inc., 1968.
   Chapter 1. "Transportation and the Economy," pp. 3–23.
9. Taff, Charles A., **Management of Traffic and Physical Distribution.** 4th ed. Homewood, Ill.: Richard D. Irwin, Inc., 1968.
   Chapter 1. "Conceptual Framework," pp. 1–21.
10. Troxel, Emery, **Economics of Transport.** New York: Rinehart & Company, Inc., 1955.
    Chapter 1. "The Shape of Things," pp. 1–17.
    Chapter 2. "Social Organization and Transportation," pp. 18–42.
11. Westmeyer, Russell E., **Economics of Transportation.** Englewood Cliffs, N.J.; Prentice-Hall, Inc., 1952.
    Chapter 1. "The Importance of Improved Transportation," pp. 3–22.

2

The Development
of Transportation

The history of transportation development and growth in the United
States is the history of the nation itself. In this respect, the necessity of an
adequate domestic transportation system is aptly illustrated. This chapter will
discuss the development of domestic transportation in this country and point
out the economic and political effects of that development.

THE IMPORTANCE OF GEOGRAPHY AND TECHNOLOGY

It is hard to overemphasize the importance of geography in the development of domestic transportation. The United States is a huge land mass with
a diversity of geographic forms. Some of these, such as mountains, prevent
transportation systems from penetrating various areas. Others, such as rivers
and lakes, promote transportation development with their natural "ways" or
their relatively favorable grades. Additionally, the size of the country is both
a deterrent and a stimulus to transportation development.

The continental land mass, with over 3 million square miles, held out a
challenge to be conquered. More than 3,000 miles from coast to coast and
1,500 miles from the Gulf of Mexico to Canada, the United States presented
a herculean task to man as he envisioned taming the virgin land. To meet the
challenge and to settle and civilize such a vast area meant that transportation
had to become a leading industry of the country, a necessary prerequisite, and
a vehicle of history.

In any given area, land forms present a series of alternatives to the necessary transportation system. Often it is less expensive to go around a hill
than to go over or through it, to go around a lake than to bridge it. Today's
transportation network, reflecting these geographic alternatives, is not always
based on the most direct line between two points. It was not until technology
allowed man to travel in the air that transportation began to break the fetters
of geography. And even here, the congestion of airways between some large
cities (often located relative to geographic landforms such as rivers and har-

ors) again threatens to saddle transportation development with another barrier, space.

Technology, too, has been important. In order to develop necessary speeds and carry weights of economic significance, rail transportation had to await the development of the steel rail and the steam locomotive. To have adequate domestic motor transportation, improved highways were necessary. To move highway traffic in a flexible and expedient manner, adequate motive systems such as the internal combustion engine were necessary. Engines awaited advances in petroleum technology. And so it goes. Numerous examples and innovations could be cited. It is impossible at times to indicate which came first or which development caused what, but it is clear that technology and transportation have been closely tied together.

Thus, as we trace the development of transportation, we must be alert to the forces of geography and the role of technology. Often a better understanding is gained by tracing development in terms of time. Hence, the development of transportation as presented here is in more or less chronological order. Although it is impossible to consider any one period or development in complete isolation, it does help to put first things first.

WATER TRANSPORTATION CAME FIRST

Water transportation came first in this country. While transportation by horse, on foot, by chariot and wagon had developed in early times, it was primarily the development of oceangoing vessels which led to real commerce between nations, states, and regions. Prior to the settlement of the New World by the white man, ocean transportation had become quite highly developed in many areas of the world. It was by means of ocean transportation, of course, that the New World was discovered.

When permanent settlement began in what is now the United States, the existing water transportation technology of Europe was imposed upon America. Parts of our coastline were indented by rivers, streams, and bays. Thus, a most active water transportation system naturally evolved in America, particularly between the various settlements or colonies and Europe.

Overland travel was slow and tedious. Roads of colonial America were merely widened Indian trails which lacked bridges, wandered about the countryside in a haphazard manner, and were usually impassable in poor weather. The trip from Philadelphia to New York took three days by the fastest overland means and necessitated several transfers to different wagons and boats. It is little wonder, then, that water transportation was first developed and remained the main type of domestic transportation for many decades.

It was often easier for the earlier settlers to send their products to Europe than to trade with each other. Regular shipping routes between Europe and the colonies were well established. Markets in Europe were highly developed and organized. Good means for handling shipments were readily available.

Most transportation, therefore, even as late as Revolutionary times, was between individual American points and Europe rather than between American ports.

With the many rivers on the American east coast, it was only natural that water transportation would develop first. Settlement typically proceeded inland from the coastline. The successful tobacco plantation of early America always included its own dock and warehouse facilities at riverside. In the northern colonies where the fall line (upper limit of navigation because of rapids or falls) was closer to the coast, commercial ports or cities developed. In the middle and southern colonies where the rivers and bays were numerous and the geographical barrier somewhat more distant from the coast, fewer ports were developed as each settlement could generally accommodate trade by its own facilities.

In certain areas coastal traffic did develop, of course. Small boats could go farther upstream and, hence, tap more territory. These same boats could call at the numerous coastal points. With roads so dangerous and expensive colonial America depended greatly on water transportation between its various settlements and colonies. Coastal water transportation was the accepted and in some cases, the only domestic transportation available. For example, when General George Washington traveled to the then capital of our newly independent country (New York City) to be inaugurated as our first President he traveled by boat from Virginia. Upon landing at the Battery on Manhattan Island, he paraded up Broadway on his stallion (which had also come by boat) to the capitol building on Wall Street (opposite the present site of the New York Stock Exchange).

Besides being naturally available and faster, coastal water transportation was generally cheaper than overland transportation. Even today water transportation remains one of the least expensive types of movement. The answer of course, is quite simple. Less energy and, hence, less expense is necessary to move a given weight on water than on land, provided that the movement is not at high speeds.

Above the fall line and on Western rivers where the fall line was many miles inland, a very active raft and river traffic grew up. Various vessels were constructed to float with the current and provide an efficient (although slow) transportation. It has been estimated, for example, that in 1790 over 150,000 bushels of grain were floated down the Susquehanna River to Philadelphia. Studies have shown that as late as 1818 some two-thirds of the market crops of the Piedmont plateau were raised within five miles of some river, and the remaining one-third not more than ten miles from navigable water. Commerce and economic activity were generally restricted to areas where transportation was adequate. In this case, inland water transportation was the key to settlement and development.

It was on the great rivers of the West that inland water transportation achieved its zenith. Timber was close at hand to make rafts and boats. The

Mississippi system extended almost across the entire continent and moved slowly to the sea. Here the flatboat was developed and played a significant role in the nation's development. These blunt-nosed boats with perpendicular sides were constructed of rough planks and propelled by the river current. Carrying large loads for that day and drawing but a foot or two of water, they were excellent vehicles for the movement of commodities from frontier farms to the markets of the world via the Port of New Orleans. Often the boat was sold for lumber at the end of its journey. The boatman, many times the farmer himself, merely walked back to his land, or if the journey was productive enough or urgency was required, he bought passage on the river steamers which likewise developed on the Mississippi system. This type of transportation was important for many decades. Students of history will recall that young Abe Lincoln made such a trip to New Orleans with cargo from Illinois.

This transportation was of considerable value to early America. A single flatboat might carry a cargo worth $2,000 or more. Such craft were readily constructed and required little skill to operate. A major share of the product of the Middle West was transported in this manner. The value of this transportation was large—one study estimates that $5,370,000 worth of cargoes floated down the Mississippi in 1807. By 1817 over 2,000 flatboats and barges a year were arriving at New Orleans, and that city had become the fourth most important seaport in the world. Unquestionably the flatboat provided one of the cheapest and most effective means of transportation in its day.

The application of the steam engine to transportation first took the form of steamboats. After Robert Fulton's first successful "Clermont" in New York in 1807, the steamboat provided upstream transportation on many of the country's rivers. Regular schedules were often established by the so-called packets, and the steamboat era commenced.

In the East, steamboats were principally used on the tidewater portions of rivers, with a few boats operating upstream on a few large rivers. It was principally in the West on the long Mississippi and Ohio Rivers where steamboating reached its full development. As early as 1809 steamboats appeared on the Ohio River, and the first trip from New Orleans to Pittsburgh was completed in 1811. It was not until 1814, however, that a distinctive type of shallow-draft boat was developed which could navigate in the shifting sand bars and silt of these great inland waterways.

Traffic developed rapidly, and along with flatboats and rafts, the steamboat made the Mississippi inland America's greatest transportation route of that time. This era continued for many years, and its romance is forever preserved in the writings of Samuel Clemens who chose a bit of steamboat slang, "Mark Twain" (meaning a sounding of two measures), as his pseudonym.

Costs to shippers varied according to water conditions and according to competition. Speed was generally slow as we think of transportation today —six miles an hour upstream and ten to twelve miles an hour downstream.

But the steamboat continued as the major transportation medium for many years. It was not until after the Civil War that it began to be displaced by the railroad as a leading mode of transportation. For half a century steam boating was the epitome of fast, efficient, and reliable transportation in America.

EARLY ROAD MOVEMENT

In colonial America, the provision of highways came very slowly. As noted above, early roads were merely the extension of primitive Indian trails called "traces." These early roads remained principally undeveloped because large amounts of capital and labor were necessary in constructing improved highways. Such large amounts of resources were not available for this type of internal improvement. Few roads worthy of the name were built prior to the end of the Revolutionary War.

Interestingly enough, the delivery of mail on so-called "post roads" was one of the first types of highway utilization. Even though the colonies had been developing for almost a hundred and fifty years, the first post roads did not come until the 1770's. These were generally restricted to the coastline and connected major cities. Very few interior post roads were built. During the Revolutionary War, the lack of overland transportation was a definite deterrent to the maneuverability of military forces. It was generally recognized that the nation would have to be concerned with internal transportation improvements if it was to grow and develop.

Our first improved roads were primarily private enterprise undertakings. These took the form of turnpikes or toll roads. Beginning in the 1790's, this new era of inland transportation was inaugurated. These turnpikes were generally of a relatively high quality for that time. Tolls were charged for travel over them. These tolls typically were collected at a way station with a pole or gate extending across the road to bar the passage of persons who had not paid. Upon payment the pole was swung open and the traveler was permitted to proceed. Since the barrier was mounted on an upright, often called a "pike," the derivation of the name "turnpike" is obvious.

The first and most famous privately owned turnpike in the new nation was constructed by the Philadelphia and Lancaster Company. Work began on this project, a distance of 62 miles between the cities of Philadelphia and Lancaster, Pennsylvania, in 1792. The road was completed in 1794, at a cost of almost a half-million dollars, and was a financial success almost immediately. The early success of the Lancaster Pike aroused the interest of other companies in this sort of development. By the early 1800's, there were hundreds of turnpike companies. Pennsylvania had chartered 86 companies which had completed 2,200 miles of turnpikes prior to the War of 1812; New York had 135 chartered companies and some 1,500 miles built during the same period. Most of these companies were joint stock companies, an organizational form developed somewhat earlier in England, and were forerunners of modern corporations. This form of organization was necessary due to the difficulty of raising large sums of capital by any other private device.

It was soon recognized that the Federal government would have to be involved in internal improvements. As early as 1797, therefore, a project known as the "National Pike" was authorized by the United States Congress. Many statesmen such as Thomas Jefferson, John C. Calhoun, and Henry Clay were most interested in the promotion of this type of national highway.

The National Pike, following the old Cumberland Road to the West, was envisioned as a connection to the frontier which then lay just across the Appalachian Mountains. The first segment of the road, completed in 1818, extended to Wheeling, West Virginia, with its eastern terminus at Cumberland, Maryland. Additional extensions were made from year to year, with construction continuing for another twenty years.

Much of our present highway policy had its beginning with the National Pike. The road was of high quality and extended literally from border to border, since it was to have its western terminus at St. Louis on the Mississippi, the then western boundary of the United States. Additionally, it was to touch the major cities and centers of population as well as the capitals of the inland states. Hence, it progressed through the old Northwest Territory, touching Columbus, Ohio; Indianapolis, Indiana; and Vandalia, Illinois; the then capital of that state. From 1806 to 1838, some $6.8 million was appropriated by Congress for its construction. An additional $1.6 million was appropriated for other Federal highways during the period.

With the election of Andrew Jackson in 1832, the matter of the constitutionality of the Federal government making internal improvements came to a head. Jackson, a champion of state's rights, felt strongly that the Federal government should not spend money on national roads or other internal improvements. Consequently, during his administration the National Pike was abandoned as a Federal project and turned over to the states through which it ran. The early road movement which had accomplished so much in assisting the settlement of the West came to a halt. The National Pike was never extended westward from Vandalia, Illinois, and thus never reached St. Louis.

With the growing interest in alternative means of transportation, principally canals and early railroads, there was little development of highways by the states after the Jackson administration. The remains of the National Pike are still to be seen in parts of the Midwest, and the role of the road was no small one. However, because of the question of its constitutionality and the development of other types of transportation, it was not until a later date that a revival of highway interest occurred.

CANALS

There was little more interesting and economically important to domestic transportation in the formative years of the United States than the canal During the 1780's and 1790's, some short canals had been built around rapids in rivers to improve inland water transportation. It was not until around the 1820's, though, that the canal came into its own as an important mode of transportation. The advent of the famous Erie Canal, completed in 1825 brought on a period of expansion that lasted until 1837.

The importance of the Erie Canal, lying wholly within the State of New York, can hardly be overemphasized. This project connected the Hudson River in the east with the mammoth chain of fresh-water lakes to the west and north of the nation, the Great Lakes. The canal was 364 miles long and cost approximately $7 million to construct, a rather gigantic sum in those days. However, the canal was well designed and proved to be an outstanding financial success.

The Erie Canal was a public works project of the State of New York It was one of Governor De Witt Clinton's favorite projects, and he worked diligently to get New York to construct this expensive internal improvement Indeed, for a period the project was referred to as "Clinton's Folly" by political opponents. Nevertheless, it rather quickly earned back all of its costs and proved a tremendous economic success to New York State.

Some historians feel that the development and the expansion of the Port of New York City is directly connected with the success of the Erie Canal. It provided a cheap and efficient method of bringing the produce from the vast western area which bordered upon the Great Lakes to one of the finest natural harbors on the eastern seaboard. The area traversed by the Erie was relatively flat and was easily canalized. Upstate New York was one of the few places where the Allegheny barrier did not prevent easy transportation. In this sense, the Erie was fortunately located. Likewise, New York as a city became, after the construction of the Erie Canal, the leading port on the eastern seaboard. From a financial point of view, tolls collected in the first seven years covered the entire construction costs of the canal.

The need for relatively cheap transportation plus the financial success of the Erie led many other states to consider canals and similar inland waterway projects. One of the most famous, the Pennsylvania Public Works System, was designed to rival the Erie and draw westward-moving immigrants and eastward-moving produce through the Port of Philadelphia. This project was a combination of canals and early rail transportation. The rail portion, necessary to cross the mountains, was made up of a series of inclined planes where canal boats were put upon wheels and drawn up and over the mountains by means of cables and stationary steam engines. The so-called "main line" of the Pennsylvania Public Works System from Philadelphia to Columbia on the Susquehanna River was completed in 1834 at a cost of $10 million. This was a rail section, since the topography of the area did not favor a canal. From this point, the Susquehanna was followed by a canal until the mountains were reached at Holidaysburg, where the portage railway took over the route. Across the mountains, another canal was built to the junction of the Allegheny and the Monongahela, at the then frontier town of Pittsburgh. This combination of rail and canal, however, did not prove to be a successful competitor with the Erie, although it probably did help Philadelphia to grow and develop. New York, having all-water transportation from the Great Lakes region, continued to draw the majority of the trade moving to the coast.

Other canals were attempted by other eastern seaboard areas. Two of these were the Chesapeake & Ohio Canal through Virginia and Maryland, which attempted to use part of the Potomac River and connect with the Ohio, and the James River Canal which again attempted to bridge the mountains and tap the productive area to the west. The James Canal was abandoned after the expenditure of over $10 million, and the Chesapeake & Ohio Canal never proved to be an outstanding financial success.

Inland, there was also an era of canal building in those states which bordered upon either the Great Lakes or one of the large inland rivers. Canals connected Lake Erie to the Ohio River in several places, with the Miami and Erie Canal and the Ohio and Erie Canal being outstanding examples. Additionally, the Wabash and Erie Canal from Evansville on the Ohio River extended upward and through Indiana to join with the Miami and Erie Canal somewhat south of Toledo. Further, the Illinois and Michigan Canal connected Lake Michigan and Chicago with the Illinois River, thus making a continuous waterway from the Mississippi into the Great Lakes via Lake Michigan.

Evidence of the extent of canal construction which took place during the 1820's and 1830's may be seen in figures on state indebtedness for internal improvement. Between 1820 and 1840, over $200 million of debt was incurred by various states for canals. During the financial panic of 1837, this indebtedness proved to be too heavy for many states. Some found it necessary to default on interest payments on their bonds, and a few completely repudiated their debt.

While these early canals were rather crude affairs technologically as compared to modern systems, they were marvels of their time. Typically, they were rather shallow. For example, the Erie Canal was but four feet deep, with widths of twenty-eight at the bottom and forty feet at the water line. They served a flat-bottomed vessel which was able to carry substantial tonnage when propelled by mule power along the canal towpath. An adequate water supply and locks to overcome land elevations were among the greatest difficulties. In many cases, aqueducts had to be constructed, large lakes had to be created, and locks had to be designed with little use of modern materials such as steel and cement. It is a wonder that canals were able to carry as much traffic as they did.

Rather substantial amounts of tonnage moved over canals during the early days and up to relatively modern times. As late as 1870, there were as many as 7,000 canal boats on the Erie and allied systems in New York causing a problem of congestion. Canal boats typically operated both day and night in continuous lines, one proceeding in one direction on the north bank and another proceeding in the other direction on the south. Historians have noted that it was possible to observe an almost continuous line of lanterns or torches moving across the New York plains at the height of the glory of the Erie Canal. From a tonnage point of view, the Erie reached its peak of over 4½ million tons annually in 1880 and declined thereafter. The economic importance of this is seen by the fact that New York State canals including the Erie, collected tolls averaging more than $4 million per year from 1825 to 1870. Obviously, even after the financial panic of 1837 had brought the rapid construction of canals to a halt, the better located canals continued to be a factor in the country's transportation system. Even today inland waterways continue to be an important part of our domestic transportation.

Canals, however, passed from supremacy on the transportation scene not only because more superior types of transportation became available, but also because of the inherent limitations of this type of transportation. The climatic factor was always a limiting one. Since many of the canals were in areas where water freezes during winter, they could be used only on a seasonal basis. Secondly, canals lacked the flexibility necessary to provide a complete transportation network. That is, they could go only along water courses and more or less parallel to rivers. Likewise, in many cases, canals ran in the wrong direction. With the exception of the Erie and a few others, many of them tended to run in a north-south direction, while the economic expansion of the nation has always been predominantly in an east-west direction. Coupling these factors with excessive promotions and high costs of construction of some of the marginal projects, it is easy to see why canals, although important in young America, had definite limitations.

RAILROADS AND THE COMPETITIVE STRUGGLE

Beginning with the Baltimore and Ohio Railroad in 1830, a new type of transportation emerged. Its outstanding feature was flexibility. The railroads were not tied to the rivers like the early inland water transportation. However, the technological and economic advantages of rail transportation were not immediately apparent. Indeed, the railroads were subjected to a stringent competitive struggle for the first twenty to thirty years of their existence, and it was impossible to predict which mode of transportation would prove supreme —rail, canal, highway, or river.

Early tramways had been used in Great Britain during the 1700's, principally for the transportation of coal. Likewise, simple types of railways had been used in America to do special jobs such as carrying coal down to docks for loading onto canalboats. The Baltimore and Ohio Railway, however, is generally considered as the first of the many great American general-purpose carriers of freight. This company, chartered by the State of Maryland in 1827, began construction in 1828, and opened the first portion of its road in 1830. This date, therefore, is used to mark the beginning of the railroad era in the United States. A few English railroads had operated on a general freight basis a few years earlier.

Technology has always been important in transportation, and it is particularly important in rail transport. Although the development of the steam engine had come at a somewhat earlier date, its application to transportation was not immediately apparent. Indeed, the lack of locomotives held back the development of the railroad as a mode of transportation in its early days. When the Baltimore and Ohio Railroad opened in 1830, there were less than five locomotives in the United States and most of those were experimental. The famous "Tom Thumb," constructed by Peter Cooper in New York during the 1820's, was an experimental model to demonstrate the practicability of locomotives and was used on the Baltimore and Ohio in 1830.

Early locomotives were primitive and developed such a small amount of horsepower that they were able to pull only extremely limited loads. The economic advantages inherent in railroad transportation had to await the development of better systems for converting energy into movement. Motive-power technology has steadily increased over the years, and today's diesel-electric units represent a delicate balance between economy in fuel use, horsepower developed, and weight of unit.

Likewise, the development of steel rails was necessary before railroads could become a highly practical type of transportation. Early tramways using horses or mules for motive power often had wooden rails over which the wheels of vehicles moved. These were supplemented by straps of iron bolted to the wood. Iron-covered rails caused considerably less resistance to the iron wheel than did wood rails, and had a longer service life. These straps became loose when heavy loads were propelled at any speed, however, causing a safety problem when the metal straps were thrown up through the bottom of the cars (these were known as "snakeheads"). It was a natural step to substitute the all-metal rail. The iron "T" rail was later displaced by imported steel rails, and rail weights increased so as to carry heavier loads. As American industry developed, local steel of heavier and heavier weights was used until the heavy continuous welded steel rail of today represents the most modern development in rail technology. Certainly over time, technology both in rail and in types of motive power has played a most important role in the development of domestic rail transportation.

The development of the rail network of the United States in the 19th Century can be compared to the development of the economy of the country.

Each decade saw more and more trackage. New companies were formed, new areas opened up, and new economic developments undertaken. Table 4 illustrates the total miles of railways by decades.

Table 4

Total Miles of Railway Operated in U.S. by Decades

1830	23
1840	2,818
1850	9,021
1860	30,626
1870	52,922
1880	93,262
1890	166,703
1900	192,556
1910	240,831
1920	259,941
1930	260,440
1940	245,740
1950	236,857
1960	230,169
1970	218,421 (preliminary estimate)

Source: Department of Commerce, *Historical Statistics of the United States* for 1830 to 1890, and Interstate Commerce Commission, various publications since 1900.

There was a marked growth of railroad mileage following 1830. Most of these early lines were local in character; however, they were often not interconnected, and could scarcely be called a system. Likewise, most early rail expansion was confined to eastern states, with but a few small roads in the middle west and south. To some degree, these early lines were considered supplemental to canals and rivers. Indeed, the vested interests of canal owners, operators, and workers involved in water transportation, plus the interests of persons concerned with highway transportation, caused great obstacles to early railway development. In some cases, legislatures required early railroads to invest part of their capital in canals or to build wooden fences where they paralleled canals so as not to frighten the tow animals. Also, some states required railroads to pay tolls to the state equivalent to what the freight hauled would have paid to state-owned canals.

But the flexibility of the railway and the economy that came with heavier rails, better motive power, and larger loads soon became evident. By 1850, the era of the trunk lines began; and by 1860, various systems had linked the east coast to the Mississippi River and a rather substantial network of railroads covered the whole eastern half of the nation. While more will be said about consolidations and mergers in Chapter 20, it should be noted here that much of this expansion came by connecting numerous rail companies end-to-end. By the end of the 1860's single-company service was available between New York and Chicago, and the basic trunk-line railroads had been established.

The Civil War and the tremendous economic advance of the 1860's provided a great impetus for railway expansion. The war proved the military and economic advantages of rail transportation. Some historians have given great weight to the role of the superior rail transportation network in the victory of the North. The war-accelerated business pace also led to more rail expansion; and in order to secure California and the West to the Union, the first transcontinental railroad was started during the hostilities. While the Union Pacific built westward from Omaha, the Central Pacific built eastward from Sacramento. Although these lines were not joined together on the plains of Utah until 1869, this first rail link between the two coasts had been authorized and abundantly assisted by the Federal government as a war project.

Settlement of the internal political problems of the nation and the advances in agricultural and industrial technology growing out of the war combined with the general war-born feeling for adventure and daring to spur the development of the West. Railroads shared and at times led in that development. The decades of the 1870's and 1880's witnessed the greatest increases in rail net expansion. Railway company agents actively promoted migration to the new western lands and, in some cases, roamed parts of Europe with advertisements noting the opportunities available in America and particularly in the American West. The role of the railroads in the settlement of the continent was an active one. The western railroad which did not employ a large staff of agricultural experts, promotional men, and land developers was rare.

More will be said about railroad promotion in Chapter 22. It should be noted here, however, that the land grant policy of the 1850's to 1870's was partly responsible for much of this promotion. Beginning with sizable grants of land by Congress to the Illinois Central in 1850, the pattern of stimulating rail expansion by granting alternate sections of federal land continued until the final large grant was made in 1871 to the Texas and Pacific. More often than not, this land was wholly undeveloped and the building of the railroad made the remaining alternate sections of some value to the government. The general idea, however, was to settle the country, promote private ownership and development, and tame the continent. In this regard the policy was a success.

Additional aid by cities, states, and individuals was also substantial. Nearly every town wanted to be, indeed had to be, on a railroad. Cities offered free land, tax exemptions, guarantee of bonds and public subscription of securities to entice railroads to build through their bounds. Substantial sums were involved. Unfortunately, some unscrupulous promoters took advantage of the desire for railroads to promote spurious ventures.

Even with these substantial aids, huge amounts of private capital were necessary. This led to two interesting aspects of 19th-Century American business: the reliance on foreign capital, and the development of the corporate form of enterprise. Many states borrowed abroad, only to default on their obligations during the periodic financial panics of the era. Large amounts of capital were also raised by private stock and bond sales in Europe. One expert estimates that during the 1880's, more than $2 billion was raised in Europe by the sale of railroad securities. Naturally, this often resulted in large blocks of stock under foreign ownership, in some cases more than fifty per cent of the stock of a single railroad. Failure of promised profits to domestic security owners, foreign ownership and control, and delay of the envisioned economic development were important factors in the move to regulate railroads.

In order to gather the required capital, the corporate form of business organization was mandatory. A railroad was such a gigantic undertaking that the fortune of one man or a small group of men was insufficient for its construction. Hence, the corporate form was used early in railroad development; and as successive issues of securities became necessary, this business form was further developed and refined. Indeed, one of the often overlooked benefits of the expansion of the domestic railway system was the acceptance and development of the modern corporation. While some government-owned railroads were built, the expansion of the American rail net generally was a phenomena of private ownership via the corporate form. It was, after all, the high period of the free enterprise, laissez-faire system. Many state governments had become overinvolved in the canal era; and while they might be willing to aid in railroad construction, they generally avoided public ownership. The Constitutional question of internal improvement remained from the Jackson and early highway era, so the Federal government pursued a policy of promotion but not ownership. Thus the railroads typify the private-ownership, corporate form of business during the 19th Century.

Excesses in railroad promotion and construction were common. Overcapitalization was prevalent. Many personal fortunes of some of the best-known financial names of America came out of abuses in railroad finance. Business ethics were at a low level, and there was little public concern over the excesses. The result often was to leave railroads with grossly overcapitalized corporate structures faced with tremendous pressures to pay bond interest and show profits on securities which frequently did not represent assets. Many of the financial and operating problems of later periods were a direct result of these abuses.

By 1900, the basic rail network had been laid. While expansion continued even into the 1920's, and a few remaining transcontinental connections were built between 1900 and 1910, the age of rail expansion was predominantly a 19th-Century phenomena. The building of branch lines and the filling in of railroad systems formed most of the expansion during the 20th Century. Finally, by 1930, the number of railroad miles began to decline. Uneconomical and unwise expansion could not sustain itself, particularly in the face of new competitive threats which characterized the 20th Century. The total number of railway miles has steadily declined since the 1920's as the railroads have attempted to readjust their plant to the needs of the nation.

Railroads developed in a romantic and significant period. Beginning with a competitive struggle, they proved their supremacy, knit the nation together, and triggered much of the economic development of the American economy. But new 20th-Century modes of transportation with other inherent advantages arose to share the glory of the railroad as the underlying basis of the American transport economy.

REVIVAL OF HIGHWAY TRANSPORTATION

Even while railroads were enjoying their greatest expansion, interest was reviving in highway transportation. Movement over roads had continued, of course, during the rail expansion, but it had been primarily local. During the 1890's, however, the concerted interest of three groups—the railroads, farmers, and bicyclists—led to a renewal of general concern for improved highways.

Railroads felt the need for improved roads primarily to provide local transportation from the point of production to the railroad. Farmers felt the need to get out of the mud, thus improving their mobility and enabling them to reach markets more readily. Cyclists saw the condition of the nation's roads as a positive deterrent to their sport and pleasure, and bicycle manufacturers heartily concurred. Collectively these groups sponsored the good roads movement which led to the first modern attempts to improve our highway system.

With the advent of the internal combustion gasoline engine and its application to transportation via the early automobiles of the 1890's and early 1900's, a fourth group was added to the advocates of improved highways. Automobile owners joined the growing pack and built upon early efforts to promote better roads.

During the 1890's, some states established aid systems in order to spur highway development. New Jersey was first in this area, establishing a state highway department to advise local officials and setting forth a formula by which landowners paid 10 per cent, the county 60 per cent, and the state 30 per cent of the cost of highway improvements. Other states followed with similar plans; and in 1893, Congress created the Office of Public Road Inquiry within the Department of Agriculture. However, massive financial-aid programs to governmental units owning the highways, usually state and county governments, did not come until the automobile became popular.

By 1915, forty-five states had enacted state aid laws, forty had established State Highway Departments, and twenty-four had designated state highway systems. Ownership, maintenance, and administration of highways remained primarily local and development was somewhat chaotic. Few road systems existed, most counties were able to improve but a small portion of their road mileage, and finances were inadequate. It remained for the two developments of Federal aid and the state gasoline tax to launch the modern highway system.

The Federal aid system was originated in 1916 when Congress appropriated $75 million to be expended over five years on highway improvement. The basic pattern of the domestic highway system was established in the 1916 act with (a) state ownership, construction and maintenance of the highways; (b) a formula by which the Federal government allocated funds among states on the basis of population, area, and mileage; and (c) the provision of state highway departments to coordinate, engineer, designate, and contract for highway improvements. This pattern, or variations of it, has been followed since.

Two dimensions of highway improvement came during the 1920's. Congress recognized in the Highway Aid Act of 1921 that funds had to be concentrated upon a relatively few road systems if the enormous task of improving the nation's highways was to be accomplished. Hence, the designation of a system of primary highways not to exceed seven per cent (later changed to eight per cent) of all state mileage was enacted. Although there have been subsequent variations, the principle of concentration has continued. The second factor was the broad adoption of the state gasoline tax, pioneered by Oregon in 1919, which proved to be the principal source of funds for highway improvement. Here the principle of user charges was adopted.

Following World War I, with the improvement of the highway system and the broad acceptance of the automobile, numerous persons went into the business of providing truck and bus transportation. While there had been companies earlier, the system of improved and toll-free highways proved an impetus to individual enterprise. Many of the leading motor transportation companies of today date from this era of expansion. Likewise, the individualistic and competitive characteristic of motor transportation was firmly established by the public provision of the way and the ease of entry into this mode of transportation.

With the Great Depression of the 1930's, highway improvement was accelerated. Highway building was a favorite way of promoting employment and generating income. While the road system expanded somewhat in total mileage, it was primarily the improvement of existing highways that occupied the attention of the nation. In many areas, the first large-scale building of hard-surfaced roads was a depression phenomena. Large sums were expended over a relatively short period, and the highway system was rapidly improved.

With the continued ease of entry into highway transportation, plus the provision of even more improved highways, the individualistic and competitive aspects of motor transportation intensified. Small truck and bus companies abounded, and many individuals attempted to sustain themselves by offering highway transport services for hire in a highly competitive market. These conditions of extreme competition played a prominent role in bringing about regulation of this mode of transportation, as will be shown in Chapter 17.

With the advent of World War II, the situation completely reversed itself. Little or no highway improvement took place, vehicles for commercial use were rarely available, gasoline was rationed, and travel was restricted. Much of the highway system and motor transportation equipment was dissipated with little or no replacement. This led to the need for tremendous postwar expansion in highways and motor transportation plants, ushering in perhaps one of the nation's greatest eras of highway and motor carrier expansion.

The principle of concentration of highway building funds was further refined in 1944 by the authorization of a system of high-speed, top-quality, limited-access highways known as the Interstate System. These plans were not implemented until 1956 when Federal financing was put on a Trust Fund basis with the Federal gas tax and other Federal highway excise taxes, first imposed in 1917, directly linked to the construction of the Interstate System. This system, made up of 41,000 miles of the most densely traveled highways, connects most of the major cities and state capitals of the United States, and also connects with Canada and Mexico. The Interstate System is being constructed over a short period of years and is financed 90 per cent by the Federal government and 10 per cent by state or local governments. It is and will be the backbone of the nation's highway system.

With the improved highway system plus the accelerated business activity of the postwar years, the motor transportation industry expanded tremendously. Railroads are limited by the location of their rails, but motor carriers have almost unlimited flexibility. Streets and roads are everywhere, and motor carriers are equipped to give an extremely flexible and personalized transportation service. These characteristics will be further described in Chapter 4, but it is well to note here that motor transportation expanded very rapidly during the post-World War II period. From a relatively minor role of approximately 6 per cent of the intercity ton-miles hauled during the war years, motor carriers are today the second most important type of transportation from a ton-mile viewpoint. To many cities and shippers, trucks are the sole means of freight transportation available. Certainly motor transportation has taken its place as a basic and integral part of domestic transportation.

AIR TRANSPORTATION

Air transportation is the only truly 20th-Century mode of domestic transport. Beginning with the historic 1903 flight of heavier-than-air craft at Kitty Hawk, North Carolina, by the Wright brothers, this mode has reflected the astounding technological growth of the present century.

Air transportation has been interconnected with two great forces: war and government. It was not until World War I led to the training of numerous persons in the art of flying that travel by air was anything but an oddity. With many surplus war planes readily available, former World War I pilots popularized the airplane by barnstorming all over the nation. The romance of war-born air aces was brought to practically every hamlet of America during the 1920's by these early flying pioneers. The adventurous had an opportunity to experience a new thrill, and the critic an opportunity to scoff.

The role of government in training pilots during World War I and in furnishing surplus "jennys" after the war is evident. However, its more important role of promoting air transportation by way of the U.S. mails is not as apparent. Experimentation with airmail service began in 1918, with the first transcontinental airmail service during 1919. By 1924, technology had developed to the point where continuous day and night service for transcontinental airmail could be established. These pioneering efforts were made by the Federal government. It was not until 1925 that privately owned air transportation companies were given the opportunity to carry the mails.

The Kelly Act of 1925 authorized the Post Office to contract with air transportation companies to carry mails, and by 1927 the government had retired from the field. With the exception of a few months during 1934 when the government again carried airmail, privately owned air transportation has continued as the major form of air transport in this country. This has not been the same in other countries. The United States is somewhat unique in having private air transportation companies promoted, but not owned, by the government.

Air transportation companies not only depended upon mail contracts in the early air age, but they also depended on government-provided airways. Federally maintained airways remain to this day. Locally owned and operated airports, with the exception of military or private fields, have also been provided, with nominal landing fees. The Air Commerce Act of 1926 prohibited the Federal government from constructing or operating airfields and airports, but Federal aid for airport building has been a part of domestic transportation promotion since 1933.

Throughout the 1930's, travel by air remained primarily emergency travel where speed was of utmost importance. Aircraft developed slowly, and air travel was expensive and uncomfortable by today's standards. Most airline companies were highly subsidized by airmail contracts and were more in the mail business than any other. It remained again for war to push air transportation forward.

Because of its outstanding characteristics of speed and flexibility, the airplane was widely used during World War II. Aircraft design was greatly accelerated, and many principles of aircraft construction were perfected under the stimulus of war. Additional thousands of persons were taught to fly, and the basic principles of handling air freight were developed. But perhaps more important was the fact that large numbers of military and civilian personnel were carried as passengers in wartime flights. Widespread knowledge about and popularity of air transportation were established.

Following World War II, a tremendous expansion in air passenger traffic occurred. Flying became a common thing. Airline companies, applying war-developed techniques, offered frequent schedules and reliable equipment. Under competitive pressure from nonscheduled lines which sprang up after the war using surplus equipment and former military pilots, fares were driven down and service was greatly improved. By the late 1950's, air transportation was carrying more passengers than any other form of domestic transportation. The day of air travel had arrived.

With the coming of jet aircraft, air transportation matured into a speedy and reliable passenger transportation medium. By developing both trunk line services between major cities and feeder line services between smaller towns, air transportation routes blanketed the nation. Travel by air has continued to increase, and today it is the leading type of commercial passenger travel.

Air freight and air express have likewise grown, but remain relatively small in the total freight carriage picture. New jet equipment, however, provides unusual potentials for air freight, and this type of movement is gaining popularity in today's accelerated business world activity.

REVIVAL OF WATER TRANSPORTATION

In any given period of time, several modes of transportation exist; and although one may seem to dominate, the others are evolving. The distinguishing feature among various modes is rate of development. For example, transportation by water did not die out with the passing of the canal era or the steamboat's loss of supremacy to the railroad. It merely developed at a much slower pace. Water transportation remained throughout the latter half of the 19th Century, but more recent developments have led to increasing interest in and emphasis on this type of transport.

To anticipate Chapter 5, it should be noted that domestic water transportation may be thought of in three divisions: (1) the Great Lakes, (2) inland rivers and canals, and (3) coastwise and intercoastal shipping. Each has distinctive characteristics and problems.

The Great Lakes, one of the outstanding inland waterways of the world, provided our country with a ready-made transportation route. Canals and locks connecting the various lakes were constructed as early as 1829, but it was not until the locks at Sault Sainte Marie (the Soo) were constructed in 1855 that the great inland water traffic developed on the Lakes. The Soo locks plus the deepening of the river channel connecting Lake Huron and Lake Erie made available a magnificent waterway covering four lakes nearly a thousand miles in length and a natural channel spanning a third of the continent. Further work on the Welland Canal around Niagara Falls in 1916 plus a 14-foot channel down the St. Lawrence River (completed by Canada in 1903) allowed the Great Lakes to be used by some shallow-draft ocean vessels. The completion of the Saint Lawrence Seaway in 1959 and the deepening of various lake channels have now made the Great Lakes, in effect, a part of the Atlantic Ocean and created what is popularly known as America's Fourth Seacoast.

Interest in further development of inland rivers and canals is also a 20th-Century phenomenon. Beginning with the $100 million conversion of the old Erie Canal into the New York Barge Canal by the State of New York during the early 1900's, new interest was stimulated in inland water transportation. The first conservation movement, during the administration of Theodore Roosevelt, also stimulated interest in waterways; and in 1907, Roosevelt appointed the Inland Waterways Commission to prepare plans for improving inland water transportation.

This revival of interest in inland water transportation was considerably more than a part of the conservation movement. A feeling that water transportation was inherently cheap and a vital resource was also involved. Perhaps even more important was the feeling that water transportation could be used as a competitive vehicle to keep railroad rates low. With increases in the general rail rate level after 1910, this became a particularly important argument for improved waterways. Furthermore, waterway improvements have always been looked upon with favor by Congress. Political advantage to Congressional delegations can be gained by securing Federal improvement of the waterways of the home district.

Rivers of the nation have always been owned and controlled by the Federal government in the name of the people. Except for artificial waterways, such as the successful schemes by New York and a few other states, developments in waterway improvements have always been a Federal responsibility. As early as 1789, the Federal government began improving harbors. The first of many Rivers and Harbors Acts was passed in 1823; and since 1866, Congress has made appropriations for waterway improvements almost annually. The question of who should provide the way has, therefore, rarely been a problem in water transportation.

Due to the political implications of waterway improvements, there has been a problem of coordination. Since Congress has favored expending funds as widely as possible in order to gain the greatest political advantage, improvements have rarely been planned to set up specific water transportation systems. Nevertheless, with a century of various aids plus the interest in planning generated during the early 1900's and with a vastly improved technology, the inland waterways of the nation have developed into prime transportation media.

More will be said about the promotional problems of transportation in Chapter 22. It should be noted here, though, that considerable sums have been expended on waterways over the years. One of the Hoover Commissions estimated that $1.6 billion had been spent by the Federal government from 1824 to 1954 on waterways improvement, excluding the Great Lakes and seacoast projects. State and local governments have likewise spent large sums on waterways. The New York Barge Canal was said to have cost $177 million up to the 1930's. Illinois spent $99 million on the Illinois Waterway and the Chicago Sanitary Ship Canal which connects the Illinois River to Lake Michigan. Many hundreds of millions of dollars have been invested in terminal facilities by local and state governments. As a result of these improvements and efforts, the United States has today a very active inland waterway transportation system.

Coastal canals are also important. Protected passage virtually from the Middle Atlantic States to the Mexican border is possible by way of a series of canals connecting bays and inlets. This waterway serves coastal as well as intercoastal traffic. During World War II, this protected passage was of great significance in view of the submarine menace off the Gulf and Atlantic coasts.

Coastal waterways, plus the many miles of inland rivers and canals, and the Great Lakes system, provide the domestic economy with a most significant transportation system. Ton-miles carried have greatly increased in recent years as improvements have allowed wider use of inland waterways. Although the characteristics of this transportation will be discussed in Chapter 5, it is worth noting at this point that inland water transportation has vied with pipelines for the position of the third largest carrier of freight during recent years.

PIPELINES: A MODERN GIANT

Pipeline transportation is not new in the American economy, although its importance in modern times has greatly increased. At present, pipelines are the third largest carriers of freight from a ton-mile viewpoint and constitute a most important part of our domestic transportation system.

The first pipelines were laid shortly after the first oil fields were developed in Pennsylvania. In 1865, a short two-inch line was laid as a means of providing cheaper transportation than by teamsters. Prior to that time, crude oil had moved on large horsedrawn wagons which mounted heavy wooden tanks. The pipeline experiment was a success, and a new type of transportation was born.

Even though the first major pipeline (110 miles in length) was completed in 1879, pipelines were used primarily as local gathering agents and little long-distance transportation by pipeline was attempted for nearly half a century. Part of the reason for this slow development was the strong vested interests of railroads and teamsters. For example, railroads often refused to allow early pipelines to go under their tracks. Since the rail network was quite extensive by the latter part of the 19th Century, this greatly restricted pipelines.

Pipeline transportation basically is a highly specialized type of carriage. The products hauled are limited to but a few types, and the service is one way. The products carried must be able to flow; and because of the substantial amounts of the goods actually in the pipeline at one time and limited storage capacity at either end, there is no reversal of movement.

It is possible to distinguish two types of long-distance pipelines: the more numerous crude oil pipelines and the more recent product pipelines. Each specializes in a given group of commodities. The older crude oil pipelines are by far the most developed.

Pipeline transportation has been closely connected with two other factors: the development of the petroleum industry and the development of technology. It was only after the discovery of substantial petroleum fields following the turn of the century that pipeline transportation became important. Additionally, the market for petroleum products awaited widespread acceptance of the automobile and the widespread use of the internal combustion gasoline engine. Since these were primarily 20th-Century events, there was little real need for pipelines during earlier periods. The product pipeline was an even later development, the first movement of gasoline by pipeline occurring in 1930.

Heavy steel pipe of small size was used in early pipelines. Economy in pipe use awaited development of welded joints which solved earlier problems of leakage and corrosion. The submarine menace of World War II caused new experimentation with lighter weight pipe, and the famous Big Inch (24 inch) pipeline and Little Big Inch lines were constructed. These federally constructed pipelines had a tremendous throughput, and were laid safely inland away from the hazards of wartime water transportation. Experience gained from these projects proved that large-diameter, thin-walled pipe was practical. Since World War II, many miles of large-diameter pipeline have been laid.

Technology in pumping has likewise improved. Older pipelines used steam-driven reciprocal pumps spaced relatively close together. Diesel engines later replaced steam pumpers and allowed a reduction of manpower and energy. Since World War II, remarkable strides have been made in pumping by use of electrically driven centrifugal pumps which can be remotely conrolled from a central dispatching point. The modern pipeline employs but a small fraction of the labor previously used in the many pumping stations on the pipeline. It is highly automated, with electronic controls turning the motors on and off, opening valves, and doing the mechanical tasks of pipeline operation, and it has far fewer pumping stations than were previously necessary. Indeed, pipeline transport is the most highly automated type of domestic transportation.

The pipeline system today is a large network of unseen yet highly important transportation routes. Most states have some pipelines within them, and it is said that no point in the United States today is more than 200 miles from a pipeline. Total throughput has steadily increased, and pipelines have successfully taken more and more crude and product petroleum movement from railroads and water carriers, their principal competitors. Today the invisible though ever-present pipeline is the third largest carrier in our domestic transportation system.

SUMMARY: THE POLITICAL AND ECONOMIC IMPACT OF TRANSPORTATION DEVELOPMENT

The political and economic impact of the development of domestic transportation has been significant. Because of improved means of moving about and getting goods to and from distant points, the whole nation has become less isolated and independent and a more unified body. Political unity has developed. Less need is felt for local governmental units, and some (such as the one-room school districts) have become almost a thing of the past because of transportation developments. Less provincialism prevails since goods and ideas can travel efficiently and rapidly over today's highly developed transportation system.

While the economic, business, and political impact of transportation has been very great, it has not been without its ramifications on the environmental-sociological aspects of our nation. Before studying the domestic transportation system in depth, we should be aware of some of these other effects. The following chapter considers some of the many environmental and sociological aspects of transportation.

ADDITIONAL READINGS

1. Bigham, Truman C., and Merrill J. Roberts, **Transportation: Principles and Problems.** 2nd ed. New York: McGraw-Hill Book Co., Inc., 1952. Chapter 4. "From Indian Trail to Airway," pp. 49–119.
2. Cranmer, H. Jerome, "Canal Investment 1615–1860," **Trends in the American Economy in the Nineteenth Century.** Princeton, N.J.: Princeton University Press, 1960, pp. 547–564.

3. Fair, Marvin L., and Ernest W. Williams, Jr., **Economics of Transportation.** Rev. ed. New York: Harper and Brothers, 1959.
Chapter 4. "Early Highway and Water Transportation in the United States," pp. 46–59.
Chapter 5. "Development of Railroads," pp. 61–88.
Chapter 6. "Motor Transportation," pp. 89–104.
Chapter 7. "Modern Water and Pipeline Transportation," pp. 110–137.
Chapter 8. "Air Transportation," pp. 134–152.

4. Fogel, Robert, "A Quantitative Approach to the Study of Railroads in American Economic Growth," **Journal of Economic History,** June 1962, pp. 163–197.

5. Goodrich, Carter, **Government Promotion of American Canals and Railroads 1800–1890.** New York: Columbia University Press, 1960. "Federal Debate and Decision," pp. 169–207.

6. Levy, Lester S., and Roy J. Sampson, **American Economic Development.** Boston: Allyn & Bacon, Inc., 1962.
Chapter 11. "Establishing the Pattern of American Transportation and Trade," pp. 221–241.
Chapter 12. "America's Place in Twentieth Century Transportation and Trade," pp. 243–262.

7. Locklin, D. Philip, **Economics of Transportation.** 6th ed. Homewood, Ill.: Richard D. Irwin, Inc., 1966.
Chapter 5. "Before Railroads," pp. 67–83.
Chapter 6. "The Era of Railroad Building," pp. 84–116.

8. Morton, Stephen, "The Politics Behind the Route of the First Transcontinental Railroad in the United States," **I.C.C. Practitioners' Journal,** February 1963, pp. 561–568.

9. Pegrum, Dudley F., **Transportation: Economics and Public Policy.** Rev. ed. Homewood, Ill.: Richard D. Irwin, Inc., 1968.
Chapter 3. "Development of Transportation in the United States," pp. 47–76.

10. Ransom, Roger L., "Canals and Development: A Discussion of the Issues," **American Economic Review,** May 1964, pp. 365–376.

11. Segal, Harvey H., "Cycles of Canal Construction," and "Canals and Economic Development," in Goodrich (Editor) **Canals and Economic Development.** New York: Columbia University Press, 1961, pp. 169–249.

12. Troxel, Emery, **Economics of Transport.** New York: Rinehart & Company, Inc., 1955.
Chapter 4. "Historical Change," pp. 67–91.

13. Westmeyer, Russell E., **Economics of Transportation.** Englewood Cliffs, N.J.: Prentice-Hall, Inc., 1952.
Chapter 2. "History of Transportation in the Early United States," pp. 23–40.
Chapter 3. "Development of Railroad Transportation." pp. 43–67.

14. Wicker, E. R., "Railroad Investment Before the Civil War," **Trends in the American Economy in the Nineteenth Century.** Princeton, N.J.: Princeton University Press, 1960, pp. 503–524.

3

Environmental and Sociological
Aspects of Transportation

Transportation has meant "progress" in our growing and developing country. The whistle of the train, the roar of the plane, the noise of the truck, have all been outward signs of progress to past generations and have typified the romance of transportation.

But recently we have begun to look once more at "progress." We have begun to realize that progress, like everything else, has costs. These costs may not always be measurable easily in dollars and cents, and they are not always individual in nature. They may be what the economist calls "social costs." That is, the costs of some undertakings affect so many persons in such indirect ways that, in effect, all of society bears the burden of the activities. Even though widespread and hard to assess, these costs are very real and must be considered.

Before we begin our examination of the operation of our domestic transportation system and its regulatory, economic, and business environment, it is well to consider the environmental and sociological aspects of transportation.

ENVIRONMENTAL ASPECTS

One does not need to understand the details of the operation of our transportation system to see its environmental effects. Transportation is both shaped by, and shapes the physical environment. In this sense, it is closely interrelated to and interacts on the physical environment. Basically, this interaction is from two viewpoints: locational and operational.

Locational Interactions

The location of much of transportation activity has already been established. But the system is not static. New activity and development takes place, old activity diminishes and occasionally ceases. Thus, the environmental aspects of transportation are really twofold, namely, the effects of present location of transport activities on the one hand, and the effects of new transportation activities on the other.

Present Location

The locations where transportation functions are presently performed have environmental effects on the surrounding communities. For example railroad tracks and super highways divide towns and neighborhoods; location of interchanges affects location of manufacturing, retailing, and distribution and give a "character" to a neighborhood or area of a city. Indeed, the existence of transportation facilities gives some cities their unique characters as the "railroad town" of old, the manufacturing or distribution center idea, or the port city. We will examine more completely the effects of transportation on the location of cities in Chapter 15.

There may be both positive and negative aspects of present transport locational effects. The positive aspects are the progress, development, economic growth and activity arising from these historical locations. The negative aspects are the character this locational effect brings with it. Examples are the rowdiness of a port, the transitory nature of the air terminal, the bleakness of a warehouse district, and the dirtiness of a railroad terminal. Some of these will also be considered below under sociological aspects, but the point here is that the location of transportation activities has affected and interacted on surrounding territory.

Location of New Transportation Activity

While little can be done about present historical locations, much can be done about future developments. Transportation is so essential that it cannot be denied. But a community or neighborhood or region can decide if the positive locational effects offset the negative locational effects. Does the community want the "character" transport activity brings? Are the benefits worth the costs?

This is not an easy choice. The mechanics of decision-making are not clear-cut. Political action and regulations are usually the way in which society manifests its choices. Rarely are votes taken or such issues put to rational analysis. But that is the way of democracy. The majority must be convinced that the benefits of a new transportation activity outweigh the social costs, or the contrary. Then action is taken on these convictions.

Operational Interactions

A more important environmental interaction comes from the operation of transportation activities. Here also there are social costs. The beneficial operation of transportation brings with it the social costs associated with pollution congestion and ecological interaction. Each of these will be considered briefly in turn.

ollution

Basically, three types of pollution arise from the operation of transportaion facilities. To a considerable degree these are connected with the movenent of people, particularly via private automobiles; but other means and nodes of transportation contribute to pollution as well. Indeed, all economic ictivity adds to pollution in some way even though we do not always notice it. Transportation, since it is so universally visual as well as universally necessary, s more apparent as a polluter than other activity.

The three types of pollution are air pollution, water pollution, and noise oollution. Each has separate aspects, causes, cures and ramifications. This is aot a text in ecology, thus detailed analysis of each of these phenomena is not n order here. Yet we should be aware of each.

1. Air pollution. There is little doubt that transportation operations add to iir pollution. Almost all of transportation uses the internal combustion engine n one form or another. Internal combustion engines using gasoline produce our pollutants: carbon monoxide, gaseous hydrocarbons and benzene com->ounds, nitrogen oxide compounds, and non-gases or heavier particles, the nost important of which is lead. Additionally, there is a degree of thermal >ollution involved when energy is converted into use by automobiles, trucks, planes, locomotives or ships. While all of the chemical effects of these polluants are not known, their presence in the form of smog and haze cannot be lenied.

From a technological viewpoint, progress is slowly being made in learning .o control this problem. During the late 1960's, automobile manufacturers)egan to introduce emission control devices on vehicles. The federal govern-ment has established emission standards which must be met by 1975. Many ;tate and local governments have passed laws or instituted legal actions against ransportation firms in an effort to abate pollution. A good example of the atter type of action is the numerous lawsuits filed by government against air-ines polluting the air with exhaust emissions at major airports.

Many persons have suggested that the most effective answer to auto-nobile pollution lies in the area of new power systems such as the electric >owered vehicle, steam powered cars, or atomic powered transportation levices. Other persons are working on modifications of the internal com-bustion engine, such as lower compression engines, the use of lead-free gasoline, and the use of LPG or natural gas as a fuel.

Exhaust emissions apparently can be controlled or abated and made less obnoxious. However, this can be done only at a cost. It is an open question as to who should pay the initial price of air pollution control. Ultimately the public will have to pay these social costs in the form of higher prices for auto-mobiles and higher charges by for-hire transportation firms.

2. Water pollution. Transportation activity also adds to water pollution. Ships must flush tanks, sanitary facilities on trains must be cleaned, automobiles

and trucks must be washed, and so forth. It is often a matter of how these activities are done which is important. With proper precautions, water pollution can be controlled.

One of the visual and most publicized types of water pollution is the "oil spill" from ocean-going freighters or from off-shore drilling accidents. While these are not directly connected to the operation of domestic transportation they are very closely related to our subject.

Here again social control takes the form of regulation and legal action Both the federal and the state-local levels of government are involved. Once more there is a cost to these controls, and this cost will be reflected in the price of the product or transportation service involved.

3. Noise pollution. Operation of transportation facilities creates noise The neighborhood near an airport, subway, freight yard, or freeway knows this fact only too well. The din of the city, the jarring incessancy of airport activity the ceaseless traffic of the freeway, all affect the quality of life.

Once more technology is helping slowly. Buildings can be noise-proofed schools may have to be relocated, jets and engines may have to be muffled Abating or ameliorating noise pollution will be costly. Relocation of airports freeways, and railways will be difficult and very costly.

Social action to control noise pollution has been primarily limited to the local government level. The problem of noise from local metropolitan airport has gained much attention. Once more a social cost is involved, and contro versy exists over who will pay the cost of decreasing the noise level caused by the operation of transportation facilities.

Congestion

Basically there are three types of congestion arising from the operational aspects of transportation: street congestion, highway congestion, and airway congestion. If walking is considered a mode of transportation, crowd or people congestion could also be added.

Congestion has many attributes. Perhaps its outstanding characteristic is variability. The degree of congestion varies with the size of the city or town the location of the suburban area relative to the central business district, and the demographic distribution within the urban area.

There is also a time variable to transportation congestion. Traffic, both vehicular and pedestrian, varies by the time of day, the day of the week, and the season of the year. The daily peak traffic in the journey to and from work is easily observed. Weekend congestion on streets and highways leading to recreational attractions such as parks, beaches, and mountains present more evidence of this time variability. Finally, the summer vacation peak presents a third easily observable variable transportation phenomenon.

Congestion costs time and money to all users of transportation facilities The cost in efficiency of the carriers can be measured in terms of extra crew time and operational expenses for planes delayed in "stacks," or for delivery

rucks held up in traffic, or busses delayed in the five o'clock rush. But the time
nd value loss to the passengers of these transportation modes also is a very
eal cost, although difficult to measure. Also unmeasurable is the time value
oss to individuals in their own vehicles as they are held up or delayed. A final
ubjective aspect of congestion is its effect on the quality of life. The frayed
nerves, the indigestion and disrupted routine caused by delay, is a cost to
nillions of users and operators. This is part of the cost of progress. Increasingly
the question is asked: Is the cost worth the benefit?

Without answering that question here, one must note that street, highway
nd airway congestion are facts of life. They exist and every reader has no
doubt witnessed them. Technology can help somewhat by the use of computers to schedule better and thus to reduce delay by better control systems
ver traffic, and by new alternative means of movement. Economics can also
help by varying transportation to provide an incentive not to transport or travel
during peak periods. There are many other possible ways to ameliorate a
portion of this congestion but they are beyond the scope of this book and remain
the task of works on urban transport and urban analysis. Yet the reader should
e familiar with the existence of these problems.

These are some of the many social costs of transport. Whether the benefits
f the system outstrip its costs in terms of congestion must be carefully
weighted. Here, too, the path of action is not precise and the matter evokes
ontroversy. Yet social decisions must be made and will be made. They will
ll affect transportation and are part of the dynamic and changing nature of
the transport system.

cological Interaction

Mention must be made of one final aspect of the operation interactions of
the transportation system. Transportation operation has varying effects on
ther ecological systems in nature. All of nature is a carefully balanced system
f creation, birth, life, and death. Transportation may interrupt or alter
portions of these systems. We do not always comprehend the complexities of
cology or appreciate that one action may affect a far removed ecological sub-
ystem. Examples of this are seen in the reported disastrous effects on the
rowth of Ponderosa Pine trees in San Bernardino National Forest by vehicular
missions some eighty miles away on streets and highways in Los Angeles, the
ffects of oil spills on marine ecological systems in the Gulf coastal area and
lsewhere, and the effects of water pollution from road building projects on
sh downstream, and the like.

Not all of these ecological interactions can be predicted or even known,
et they exist. They, too, became a part of the natural and social cost of transportation. Study is necessary to correctly assess the various causes and effects.
ndeed, sometimes they cannot be found. Yet they do exist, and we must
e aware of them.

SOCIOLOGICAL ASPECTS

The sociological interactions of transportation activities are not as easily seen as are the environmental interactions. Yet they exist, and they provide materials for study by sociologists, cultural anthropologists, and others. It must also be mentioned that it is often transportation aspects in connection with a whole series of other factors which interact to cause sociological effects; rarely is it the transportation factors alone.

We do not intend to compile a complete list of sociological effects and interactions. This is the task of books with goals other than this. But the point of sociological interactions can be emphasized by noting that transportation affects the characters of neighborhoods, cities, and depressed areas, and acts as a status symbol. Other sociological effects also exist, of course.

Character of Neighborhoods

Transportation to some degree helps to establish the distinct character of a neighborhood in an urban region. Some areas are "bedroom communities," others are manufacturing districts, and still others are warehouse districts. Everyone is familiar with "central business districts." The availability and means of transportation are pivotal factors in establishing the "character" of these districts or neighborhoods. Transportation makes the "bedroom community" possible; manufacturing and warehouse areas depend on the means of transportation, and central business districts often exist because transportation allows many people to be concentrated in one place during the day. Other examples, such as regional shopping centers, higher income commuter enclaves, and resort-vacation-amusement districts also depend upon transportation. Sociologists, urbanologists, and others have many ways to classify the character of neighborhoods. For our purposes, it is enough to note that transportation availability, the types of transportation, and the relative costs of transportation affect the character of neighborhoods.

Character of Cities

Whole cities may assume a sociological character. "The "port city," the "distribution center," the "government city," are examples of this sociological fact. The availability, type, and extent of transportation is an important attribute in city character. While many factors typically are involved, transportation is usually a factor of considerable importance.

Depressed Areas

There seems to be some evidence that transportation plays an important role in "depressed areas." When means of moving readily to and from work are denied or are not easily available, an area is likely to have lower than average per capita income. Sometimes depressed areas develop very close to transporation facilities where the location for living is less desirable than other areas. It is apparent that both the existence and the non-existence of different types of transportation—mass transit or heavy freight transportation—have a role to play. However, for our purposes, it is enough to indicate that transportation, both the lack of and the nearness to, have a role to play in depressed area problems.

Status Symbols

Finally, it should be noted that transportation traditionally has provided sociological status symbols. Ownership of a spirited team of horses and a "surrey with a fringe on top" was a status symbol of a by-gone age. Ownership of an automobile was once a status symbol. In modern society multiple ownership of automobiles and ownership of certain brands or types of automobiles provide status symbols. In some parts of society, ownership of a boat is a status symbol, ownership of a private plane means "status" in other communities and so forth. The point is that ownership of some "preferred" means of transportation is the focal point of one important type of status symbol. Many status symbols exist of course, but the ones relating to transportation are among the most common and readily recognizable ones.

ECONOMIC BENEFITS COMPARED TO SOCIAL COSTS

The environmental and sociological aspects of transportation generally involve social costs of some type. To a marked degree these aspects are related to urban developments and to the movement of people. But freight transportation also has environmental and sociological aspects. Recognition of these particular aspects as "problems" of transportation is relatively new. These features always have existed; it is only the recognition which is new. But society is now much more concerned over these aspects of the quality of life than was true during prior ages.

When these aspects of the quality of life become problems, and call forth changes to ameliorate these problems, an evaluation process is involved. Choices must be made. Decisions and actions to change, or not to change, these aspects must depend on a comparison of economic benefits to social costs. Few things are either all "good" or all "bad." Thus, both the good (economic benefits) and the bad (social costs) must be considered.

Two problems arise with any comparison of economic benefits to social costs. One of these is the problem of measurement. It is often most difficult to translate social costs and the environmental-sociological aspects of transportation into dollars and cents. It is nearly impossible to quantify the social costs of pollution, for example. It also may be difficult to measure carefully the economic benefits of transportation. Yet measurements of both costs and benefits must be made somehow.

The second problem is that the social decision-making process is inexact. When the whole of society is involved, and the function in question is as vita as transportation, it is not easy to get a clear decision on what to do or not to do. It is impossible to take a vote with everyone affected voting their preferences. Hence, much of the action, or inaction, takes place through politica processes. The political process probably does not reflect the ideas of everyone in a completely satisfactory manner. Some political action is based more on emotion than on fact or on a careful weighing of economic benefits and socia costs. But even though the decision-making mechanism is inexact, it does exist and it provides virtually the only means for social action.

These problems of measurement and social decision-making exist, or course, whether we are considering the environmental-sociological aspects or the regulatory-economic control aspects of transportation. The history and development of social action in the regulatory-economic control aspects of transportation are discussed in Part Five of this book. Perhaps the lessons al ready learned from economic regulatory experience will provide useful guide lines in dealing with these "newer" environmental-sociological problems.

SUMMARY

There are environmental-sociological aspects of transportation just a there are historical and economic aspects. Sometimes these become socia problems. These aspects are particularly difficult to measure in dollars-and cents terms, yet they must be measured and evaluated in terms of economic benefits versus social costs. Broad social decisions must be made relative to the environmental-sociological impacts of transportation, just as broad socia decisions must be made relative to its regulatory-economic control aspects In both instances, decisions may not always reflect adequate or careful analysi. and will be political in nature. Yet by understanding these environmental sociological aspects, regulatory-economic control aspects, and historical and developmental aspects, hopefully better decisions result.

It is worth emphasizing that our domestic transportation system exist. today as a balanced system. No one mode of transportation is supreme, as was true in the past. All forms have a role to play, and all possess separate economic characteristics and advantages. The next part of this book discusse. these characteristics and advantages in some detail.

ADDITIONAL READINGS

1. Demaree, Allan T., "Cars and Cities on a Collision Course," **Fortune**, February 1970, pp. 124–128, and 187–188.

2. Fabos, Julius, "Highway Design—The Need for Goals and Integrated Environmental Planning," **Transportation Journal,** Winter 1969, pp. 51–59.
3. Haskell, Robert H., "Tranpsortation and the Environment," **Transportation & Distribution Management,** April 1970, pp. 28–33.
4. Pegrum, Dudley F., **Transportation: Economics and Public Policy.** Rev. ed. Homewood, Ill.: Richard D. Irwin, Inc, 1968.
   Chapter 22. "The Urban Transportation Problem," pp. 547–577.
5. Rose, Sanford, "The Economics of Environmental Quality," **Fortune,** February 1970, pp. 120–123 and 184–186.
6. Simpson, John W., "Balancing the Natural and Total Environments," **Public Utilities Fortnightly,** May 7, 1970, pp. 17–20.

Part Two

Economic Characteristics and Performance of Domestic Transportation

The physical transportation plant of the United States is composed of a variety of types of rights of way, terminal facilities, vehicles which provide locomotive power and which contain space for freight or passengers, communications equipment to facilitate centralized operational or managerial supervision or control over far-flung activities, and numerous forms of specialized accessorial equipment designed to make the transportation process more efficient or to cater to the needs of particular types of freight or passenger traffic.

The agencies of domestic transportation may be divided broadly into land carriers, water carriers, and air carriers. Land carriage includes transportation by railroad, highway (truck, bus, automobile), and pipeline. Air carriage today is confined to the airplane or to helicopters. Water carriage may be by oceangoing vessels between the East and West Coasts of the United States (intercoastal) or between ports on a single coast (coastwise). Or it may be by barge and tugboat on inland waters, or by specialized steamers between ports on the Great Lakes. Superimposed upon these basic or primary modes of transport, in addition, are such forms of secondary carriage as freight forwarders, express companies, and parcel post service, which use the facilities of one (or sometimes of more than one) of the basic modes in providing transportation services.

Legally, we may think of carriers as being either for hire or not for hire. The latter category frequently is referred to as private carriage, that is, it is the situation in which a person (or a firm) uses his (or its) own vehicle or vehicles to transport his (or its) own goods or personnel. The for-hire carrier, on the other hand, is in the business of hauling for others.

For-hire carriers, in general, are subject to a considerable amount of Federal or state economic regulation—Federal if the carrier is engaged in interstate carriage, and state if it is operating in intrastate carriage. Private carriage, however, is not subject to this economic regulation, but is regulated only in such matters as public safety, license fees, and taxes. In order to escape economic regulation, persons engaging in actual for-hire carriage, especially itinerant or "gypsy" truckers but sometimes others, often attempt by devious illegal means to disguise their activities by appearing to be engaging in private carriage.

For-hire carriers may be further classified legally as common carriers and contract carriers. A common carrier is one who makes a standing offer to serve the general public. This does not mean that the common carrier necessarily offers to haul anything anywhere at any time. Rather, it means that whatever product or products he offers to carry within his operating territory will be carried for anyone desiring his services. A contract carrier, on the other hand, hauls only for those with whom he has a specific formal contract of service and does not hold himself out to serve all comers. The difference between common and contract carriage, then, is in the general or the limited nature of the carrier's offer to serve—not in terms of what or where the carrier offers to haul, but in terms of whether or not he is offering to haul for everyone or only for a selected clientele. The legal duties, responsibilities, privileges, and regulations applicable to common and to contract carriage are quite different in many respects, as will be shown in Parts Three, Four, and Five. Thus the category into which a carrier is classified is of considerable importance to the carrier as well as to those who use his services.

Sometimes, also, a carrier may be referred to as an exempt carrier, or a carrier may engage in exempt carriage. This means that the particular kind of service performed, or the product hauled, is such that the carrier is not subject to certain kinds of governmental regulations (usually rate or operating rights regulations) which in general apply to other for-hire carrier services. Exempt carriage may be either common or contract in form.

Although they may have some things in common, in general each mode and each legal type of carrier has peculiar service, operating, economic, and legal characteristics and problems. Many of these things affect the quality and quantity of available transportation services and facilities. It is essential, thus, that the users of carrier services, as well as those in responsible carrier management or governmental regulatory positions, understand the differing features of various forms of transport; otherwise, intelligent decisions relating to carriage cannot be made. A primary purpose of the following three chapters, therefore, is to describe, compare, contrast, and evaluate some of the most important features and problems of various forms of domestic carriage and to evaluate specific and overall performances of our transport system. Our approach in doing this will be mainly, but not entirely, from the viewpoint of the users of transportation services.

4

Land Carriers

Intercity freight movements in the United States, excluding ocean-borne coastwise and intercoastal movements, amounted to approximately 1,894 billion ton-miles in 1969 (the ton-mile, one ton moved one mile, is a recognized standard of measurement in freight transportation). Of this total, land carriers accounted for approximately 84 per cent. Railroads led in ton-mileage volume, with about 41 per cent of the total ton mileage, followed by oil pipelines with more than 21 per cent and trucks with more than 21 per cent. Waterways, including Great Lakes carriers but excluding deep-sea coastwise and intercoastal shipping, accounted for almost all the remainder of the total volume handled (that is, almost 16 per cent), while air carriers moved less than two tenths of one per cent of the total. In addition, coastwise and intercoastal ocean movements, a large portion of which consisted of petroleum products, accounted for more than 200 billion ton-miles. It is evident that railroads, as they have been for a century, still are the backbone of our intercity freight movement. Other forms of carriage have been cutting deeply into rail dominance during recent years, however. See Table 5 on page 52.

Intercity passenger mileage (one person for one mile, and excluding strictly local movements) in the United States was in the neighborhood of 1,130 billion passenger-miles during 1969. Of this volume, apparently a little less than 90 per cent moved by automobile and a small amount by private aircraft. The remainder, that is, the for-hire passenger traffic, was divided among airlines, about 72 per cent, railroads 8 per cent, busses 17 per cent, and waterways around 3 per cent.

RAILROADS

The railroad network of the United States consists of a little less than 220,000 route-miles. If double or multiple trackage, sidings, and yard trackage are added to this, the total track-mileage becomes around 340,000. Roll-

51

Table 5

Estimated Approximate Total Intercity Freight Ton-Mileage, and
Per Cent Moved by Each Mode of Transport, Selected Years

Year	Total Ton-Mileage (billions)*	Rail	Highway	Inland Water	Oil Pipelines	Air
1941	811	64.2%	10.0%	17.3%	8.4%	0.002%
1946	944	68.0	8.7	13.1	10.1	0.010
1951	1209	56.8	15.6	15.1	12.6	0.030
1956	1376	49.2	18.1	16.0	16.7	0.040
1961	1305	43.4	22.3	15.9	18.4	0.070
1964	1557	42.8	23.8	16.1	17.2	0.100
1969	1894	41.2	21.3	15.6	21.7	0.170

*Includes Great Lakes, but excludes coastwise and intercoastal deep-sea traffic.
Source: Based upon figures published by the Interstate Commerce Commission.

ing stock used on these tracks is made up of approximately 27,000 locomotives, 1,800,000 freight cars, *not all railroad owned, however,* and around 8,000 passenger-carrying cars. Altogether, the book value of railroad investment in plant and equipment is in the neighborhood of $35 billion. Total railroad operating revenues during recent years have averaged more than $10 billion, with net profits after taxes averaging around $500 million.

Operating this plant and equipment are about 70 Class I railroads (an Interstate Commerce Commission classification which includes railroads with average annual operating revenues of $5 million or more each—increased from $3 million in 1965), some 300 Class II railroads (average annual revenues less than $5 million each), and about 200 terminal and switching companies. Also, there are around 200 "nonoperating" rail companies. A labor force of less than 600,000 employees, with a wage bill of $5.4 billion, was utilized in operating this system in 1970, as compared to a labor force of 1,439,000 and a payroll of $3.9 billion required to operate approximately the same route-mileage in 1946.

Although there are more than 350 line-haul railroad companies, a large part of the railroad operation is confined to a comparatively small number of firms. Class I railroads, about one fifth of the total number of line-haul operating companies, account for approximately 96 per cent of the total mileage operated, for 93 per cent of railroad employment, and handle around 99 per cent of all freight and passenger traffic as measured by ton-miles and passenger-miles. Ten leading companies, for example, operate about 44 per cent of the mileage, 50 per cent of the freight cars, 57 per cent of the passenger cars, 52 per cent of the locomotives, and account for one-half of railroad employment. Less than one per cent of the operating companies control more than 20 per cent of the entire investment in railroad facilities.

Although people sometimes tend to think of railroads as prime examples of big business, the above statistics indicate that there is a considerable variation in the size of firms making up the industry. Actually, there are giants and pygmies even among the Class I lines. For example, among these larger railroads, about a dozen companies operate less than 100 miles of route each, and more than forty companies each operate less than 500 miles. At the opposite extreme, about nine companies operate more than 8,000 miles of route each, and two dozen operate more than 2,000 miles. Thirteen railroads each had assets in excess of $1 billion as of 1969, and six in excess of $2 billion, and one was in the $7 billion class, while several of the smaller Class I lines control less than $10 million each in assets. Class I annual operating revenues during recent years have ranged from around $3 million for the smallest lines up to more than $1 billion for a few of the giants.

Although fast freight trains moving on a main line may go at speeds up to 60 miles an hour, delays on sidings and in terminals reduce the railroad industry's average speed per car between origin and destination to a little more than 20 miles per hour. This is an increase of about 25 per cent over immediate post-World War II speeds, however. Due to fewer terminal and other delays, passenger-train speed averages about twice that of freight trains. The average load moved in a freight car is about 44 tons, while the average freight train hauls about 1,800 tons. The average length of haul per shipment is around 495 miles for the entire railway system, with an average per carrier haul of about 270 miles. Average revenues received per ton-mile are approximately 1.3 cents, while revenues per passenger-mile average about 3.6 cents.

All United States railroad carriers are legally classified as common carriers. This means that the interstate activities of all railroads are regulated by the federal government, and that their intrastate activities are subject to state regulation. As common carriers, members of the country's railway system are not, of course, required or equipped to haul anything anywhere at any time, but they come nearer this than does any other form of carriage.

As indicated above, a small proportion of leading railroads operate a relatively large proportion of our rail facilities and account for a substantial amount of the total freight and passenger traffic. Also, there are sizable geographic areas, and a considerable number of communities, usually the smaller towns, which are served by only one railroad. It is a mistake, however, to think of present-day railroads as monopolies, although for a considerable period during their earlier history railroads did have a virtual monopoly on long-distance transport in this country. Some critics of railroad regulation practices maintain that our regulatory laws and their administration, even today, reflect an earlier antimonopoly bias.

Competition, Costs, and Coverage

Today, railroads have to compete vigorously with airlines and busses if they expect to share in the intercity passenger traffic left over from the inroads of the private automobile. Most of this passenger traffic has been written off as forever lost to the rails, of course, but a few railroad managements still seek passenger business. Late in 1970, Congress established the National Railroad Passenger Corporation to provide a minimum amount of basic intercity rail passenger service through contracts with railroads (see Chapter 23).

In the carriage of freight (the meat and potatoes of the railroad industry) keen competition is encountered from trucks for a large variety of commodities throughout the country. Pipeline and water carriers, although more specialized by product and geography, also have cut deeply into traffic formerly moving by rail and, in some instances, have almost completely taken over certain movements. Present indications are that these three alternate modes of transport will continue to compete effectively with rail carriers. Air movement of freight has not as yet created any significant problem for the railroads.

Railroads also compete keenly among themselves. Most large communities and many smaller ones are served by more than one railroad, often by several. In addition, the interchangeability of· equipment and, thus, of shipments among our various railroads (which is a unique characteristic of our railway system) provides an opportunity for numerous lines to compete for shipments which proceed beyond the line of the originating carrier. Even though a shipper may have only one railroad entering his town, he may have a choice between literally dozens of alternate railroads over which his shipments may move before reaching a cross-country destination. Any industrial traffic manager or other person in a position to control the routing of large volumes of freight can testify to the steady stream of freight solicitors from competing railroads and other forms of carriage who are constantly attempting to sell their transportation services to him.

The cost structure of the railroad industry is such that railroads can be very competitive in their short-term pricing policies and in the pricing of particular services. Because of the very large investment in long-lived facilities—track rights of way, terminals, and rolling stock—a large portion of railroad costs are fixed or "indirect" in nature. That is, during the life of these facilities, expenses of interest, depreciation, property taxation, maintenance to some extent, and similar costs do not vary with the amount of traffic handled. In addition, the usable life of much of the railroad plant is considerably longer in calendar years than is the life of most of the plant used by competing forms of carriage. Also, railroads have a large overhead expense in the form of executive, administrative, clerical, and other salaries which are not directly related to the volume of business handled. As a consequence, many railroad managers believe that perhaps as much as two-thirds of their total costs under usual operating conditions may be classified as fixed rather than variable (meaning varying with volume). This fixed expense, as a per cent of total expense, whatever it may actually be, apparently is higher for railroads than for other forms of transport with the possible exception of pipelines.

All students of elementary economics learn that in the short run ("short run" being defined as the time necessary for a given investment to become fully depreciated or converted to other uses) it is necessary that a business cover only its variable costs to remain in operation. In other words, although it may be desirable that revenues exceed expenses, it is better to remain in operation under conditions which permit the direct or variable expenses to be covered and leave something to apply on fixed costs than to close down completely and be obligated for all the continuing fixed costs. By the same token, in the short run it pays to accept any particular traffic at a price which more than covers the direct costs associated with the particular movement. Railroad managements long ago learned these economic realities. Also, they learned that railroads, due to their heavy fixed, low variable cost structure, usually have a short-run pricing advantage over competitors with relatively higher variable costs and that rate wars with competing modes, in the absence of restraining regulation, usually can be "won" by railroads. In the past, this cost structure has encouraged rate wars among railroads and between rails and other forms of carriage and the development of various kinds of discriminatory pricing policies. These matters will be discussed in more detail in Part Four.

A shipper, of course, is interested in what he gets for his transportation expenditure. In addition to the actual freight rate, he may be concerned with such things as area coverage, frequency of departures, reliability of service, and speed of movement as well as special or accessorial services. Some general comparative statements about these items may be made. It must be recognized, of course, that there usually are exceptions to broad generalizations.

Railroad freight rates between a given origin and destination are published in tariffs and usually are quoted in cents per one hundred pounds. As in most pricing, a distinction is made between large and small quantities, with carload (CL) rates being lower than less-than-carload (LCL) rates. Very few railroads continue to haul LCL traffic. Also, as will be more fully explained in Part Four, rates may be "class" rates, which apply on all items moving from all origins to all destinations. Rates may also be "commodity" rates which apply only to specifically named items moving between specified origins and destinations and usually requiring some designated routing or involving certain other restrictions. Typically, commodity rates are quoted on heavy-volume, bulky, low-value, long-haul goods; while class rates apply on items with opposite transportation characteristics. Actually, although class rates are more generally applicable, most railroad traffic (perhaps 90 per cent or more in terms of ton-miles) moves under commodity rates.

In general, rail freight rates are lower than truck rates on large shipments moving for long distances. Because of lower terminal handling costs and other cost features, however, this may not be true for small shipments or for some kinds of large shipments which move only for short distances. "Long" and "short" distances, of course, will vary by product and by physical conditions of transport such as terrain and traffic congestion. Depending upon the particular circumstances, a "short distance" in this connection might vary from 100 miles or less to 350 miles or more. Rail rates usually are higher than pipeline or water rates, although we must remember that these two forms of transport are specialized by product and geographical limitations.

On a national or regional basis, railroad area coverage is excellent. Not many areas or population centers are without rail transport. Some 3,000 United States counties, containing more than 99 per cent of the country's population, are served by rail. Wide area coverage is made possible by highly developed railroad cooperation which permits rail cars to move with almost perfect freedom from the lines of one rail carrier to the lines of others. So far as the shipper is concerned, in effect, in this respect it is as if we had only one railroad serving the entire country. A shipper in the state of Washington deals with his local railroad, paying one rate (a joint rate) for a shipment perhaps destined to move over several rail lines (a through route) to a consignee in Florida. The details of this interline exchange and division of freight revenue is handled between the various railroads involved in the movement and are of no concern to the shipper. Although other forms of transport quote through routes and joint rates to a limited extent, no form begins to approach the extensive cooperation on a nationwide scale which is characteristic of the railroad industry.

Railroad cars, though, can only go where railroad tracks exist. Trucks on the other hand, can go wherever roads are found and sometimes even where there are no roads. This means that goods destined for communities not served by railroads and individuals without direct access to rail tracks in rail-served communities must be delivered by truck. On the local scene, therefore area coverage by rail is much less complete and less flexible than truck coverage, although railroads provide a more flexible and complete coverage nationally. Recent developments in "piggyback" or trailer-on-flatcar (TOFC) service, where truck trailers are brought to and loaded on rail cars for a line-haul movement and pulled from the destination terminal to the consignee's establishment by a truck tractor, are designed to combine the long-haul and national area coverage advantages of railroads with the local flexibility advantages of trucks.

Pipeline and water-carrier area coverage is more restricted both nationally and locally than is rail carriage. Most shippers and consignees using these modes of carriage, however, ship or receive large volumes and are located and equipped to minimize the amount of necessary supplementary handling and transport.

Trains operate on timetable schedules which, in some respects, may be an advantage to shippers. This means, however, that departures from a given point are less frequent than those of a trucking company. A truck can leave a shipper's door at any time and can schedule its departure to arrive at the consignee's door at any desired time, whereas rail shipments are bound by timetables and sometimes by the necessity for building up a complete train before departure. In situations where a particular hour of arrival or of departure is important, therefore, railroads frequently are at a competitive disadvantage as compared to trucks. Railroad departures, however, are generally more frequent than are water-carrier departures.

Reliability of traffic movements involves the on time and undamaged delivery of the goods shipped, as well as the settlement of claims for damages or unusual delays en route. In areas of severe weather conditions, such as heavy snow or rainfall, trains are more likely to run on schedule or be subject to fewer delays than are trucks. Storms and seasons also may affect water movements, and labor disputes may tie up any form of transportation. The loss or damage (L&D) to railroad carload shipments in general appears to be as favorable, if not more favorable, than for competing modes of transport. Loss and damage appears to be somewhat higher on LCL shipments, but even here the railroad experience seems to be comparable to that of trucks who are their principal competitors for small shipments. Common carriers by land, with certain exceptions, are held to fairly strict accountability for goods entrusted to their care (see Chapter 7) whereas the legal liabilities of water common carriers for lost or damaged goods are much less. Contract and exempt carriage reliability varies considerably, and the owner himself must be responsible for losses incurred in his own private carrier operations.

A shipper, of course, wants his goods to reach his customer. Even though the shipper or the customer may eventually be reimbursed for losses or damages occurring en route, such occurrences may disrupt the orderly flow of production or merchandising and certainly does not win good will or contribute to good shipper-receiver or carrier-customer relations. Also, there is always the possibility that financial responsibility for losses cannot be proven. And small losses which are too insignificant to report and administrative and clerical expenses of claims must be considered. It is possible that a shipper's loss experience with different carriers of the same mode will vary more widely than his experience between the different competitive modes, but, in any case, railroads in general appear to be at least as reliable from the loss and damage viewpoint as are any of the other modes.

With an average en route speed of approximately 20 miles per hour, railroad freight in general moves considerably faster than water-borne freight. On shorter hauls, truck transport usually is much faster than rail movements. On some long-haul runs, however, fast rail schedules have been established to compete effectively with the speed of trucks. Carload shipments, which do not have to remain in terminals for further loading and are not stopped en route for partial unloading, naturally may be expected to move at greater average speeds than less-than-carload shipments.

Financial Conditions and Outlook

The financial problems of railroads have been well publicized during recent years. Despite generally prevailing prosperous economic conditions, the percentage rate of return on investment in the railway industry as a whole has reached as high as 4 per cent only during five years since World War II, with the highest return 4.3 per cent in 1948. The rate of return declined constantly after the mid-1950's, reaching a low of less than 2 per cent during 1961, with more than one fifth of the principal lines operating at a loss during that year. The trend then reversed, and average earnings reached a level of 3.9 per cent on depreciated investment during 1966. Then a decline started, leading to a 2.38 per cent return in 1969. Some railroads have been more prosperous than others, of course, but even the most prosperous railroads do not compare favorably with average or mediocre performances in most other major industries. There is a real question as to how long the railway industry can continue to operate in its present form if these conditions do not improve. The nation's largest railroad went into bankruptcy in 1970.

This unfavorable railroad situation is not only a problem for railroad management, investors, and employees; it is a concern of everyone. Shippers and businessmen are concerned with the availability and quality of services and the levels of rates. Consumers, who ultimately bear the rate burden, are concerned about higher prices. Taxpayers have an interest from the viewpoint of possible subsidies or governmental ownership. Citizens in general also have a stake in the maintenance of adequate rail facilities for national defense purposes.

Simply stated, the current railroad problem is that railroads are not taking in enough total revenues in proportion to their expenses. Many factors contribute to this, however. Much business has been lost to competing forms of transport. Automobiles, airlines, and busses have taken most of the passenger traffic. Freight has been lost both relatively and absolutely (see Table 5), and much of this lost freight traffic has been in high value and high revenue-producing movements.

Because of the long-lived nature of most of its large investment in plant and facilities, the railroad industry, with its decline in traffic, has been left holding excess fixed capacity. In the short-run period, which may actually extend for a long period of calendar time, the industry cannot adjust its capacity to the decreased demand for services and thus is stuck with its high fixed costs. Also, to some extent, federal and state regulations limit whatever flexibility railroads otherwise might have by requiring that portions of this excess capacity be maintained, that is, by forbidding the abandonment of certain services or runs even though they may be unprofitable or by opposing attempts to attain economies by consolidating duplicating facilities. Governmental regulations, too, hamper price flexibility, both upward and downward, so that railroad managements are not free to adjust to rapidly changing traffic conditions by what they think are appropriate price adjustments.

Railroad managements also blame obsolete union labor rules (the basis for which were established more than fifty years ago) for some of their financial difficulties. And railroads allege that their properties are overtaxed through assessments generally higher than assessments on other properties of similar value—for every dollar paid in railroad dividends during recent years, about three dollars have been paid in the form of Federal, state, and local taxes. And railroad managements, maintaining that railroads and pipelines currently are the only forms of nonsubsidized transport, strongly object that railroad tax dollars are used to build rights of way for and to otherwise subsidize their motor-, air-, and water-carrier competitors.

Under present technological conditions and within the foreseeable future, railroads will remain the backbone of our long-distance bulk commodity carriage. It is not possible to operate our economy as we know it without adequate and extensive railroad transport. Despite the unfavorable financial aspects of the railway industry, then, we are not faced with a choice between rail service and no rail service. Rather, the question is whether or not rail services will continue to be performed under our present form of private ownership and control or whether heavy subsidization or even governmental ownership may prevail in the future. The United States is the only major industrial nation with a completely privately owned railway system (one of Canada's two major railroads is privately owned and the other is owned by the government). Very few responsible persons in this country favor government ownership of railroads as such, but more and more persons fear that it is inevitable unless the present trends can be substantially improved.

TRUCKS

The United States highway system is made up of almost 3.5 million miles of roadway and streets more than two thirds of which is surfaced. During the mid-1950's, construction and improvements were started on a 41,000-mile system of interstate and defense "superhighways" designed to link all areas of the country. From World War II to the end of 1970, Federal, state, and local governments spent about $249 billion on improving and maintaining our highway system. About 1.1 million miles of our highways now are classified as having high-type or intermediate-type surfacing. In addition to more than 80 million automobiles and about 350 thousand busses, about 17 million trucks of various kinds, including more than one million for-hire vehicles, operate over this vast highway network. Around 7 million persons are directly employed in various phases of trucking. The wholesale value of trucks and busses produced in the United States from 1961 to 1970 was about $36 billion.

Unlike railroads, the for-hire trucking industry is made up of contract carriers as well as common carriers. Also, there is a sizable amount of exempt (that is, not subject to economic regulation) carriage, as well as private carriage. It is estimated that not more than one third of truck carriage as measured on a ton-mileage basis is subject to economic regulation comparable to that applied to railroads, and this regulation itself is not as strict for contract as for common carriers. The following discussion, unless otherwise indicated, will include only the for-hire segment of the trucking industry.

Interstate truck carriers regulated by the Interstate Commerce Commission are classified by that body as Class I (annual gross operating revenues of more than $1 million per year), Class II ($300,000 to $1 million), and Class III (less than $300,000). Also, trucking firms are classified into about a dozen types, depending upon the nature of the services performed. Of these types, the General Freight Carriers probably are of most importance to most shippers, although other specialized types such as Household Goods Carriers, Automobile Carriers, Refrigerated Haulers, and various other specialized types are of particular importance to special shipping and receiving groups.

The trucking industry basically is made up of a large number of comparatively small firms, although there are notable exceptions. Around 14,000 intercity for-hire companies are subject to Interstate Commerce Commission regulation. Of these, nearly 1,400 are Class I, more than 2,600 Class II, and the remainder Class III carriers. In addition, of course, thousands of firms engage only in intrastate or exempt transportation and around 11 million trucks are registered in the private (not-for-hire) category. Private, intrastate, and other exempt carriers, of course, frequently haul commodities which otherwise would be moved by regulated trucking firms or other forms of carriage.

In an industry with firms ranging in size from the single-vehicle owner-operator up to companies with assets of tens of millions of dollars each, industry averages must be viewed with reservations. Certain kinds of averages, however, do aid in understanding the nature of the trucking industry.

The overall trucking industry (that is, including private and all for-hire categories) essentially is characterized by short hauls. More than half of all truck trips are less than five miles one way and the average trip is about 11 miles. Only a little more than one per cent of trips are more than 100 miles one way. These 100-miles-and-up trips, however, account for almost 25 per cent of all vehicle mileage. Thus, we got a picture of a large number of very short trips at one extreme and a smaller number of much longer trips at the other.

The average length of haul by Class I intercity motor common carriers is around 260 miles and by Class I contract carriers around 155 miles. Some large carriers, of course, have average hauls of several times these lengths. The average load handled by Class I and Class II carriers is about 12 tons per vehicle, the average revenue received per vehicle-mile is approximately 78 cents and per ton-mile approximately 7.4 cents. All of these averages have increased rather steadily since World War II.

In performing its transportation services, our hypothetical "average" Class I or Class II motor carrier utilizes an investment of $580 thousand, including

60 pieces of power equipment plus trailers, real estate, fixtures, and other facilities. It employs 145 persons, and receives gross operating revenues of more than $2.4 million annually.

Costs, Competition, and Coverage

The trucking industry's cost structure differs drastically from that of the railroad industry in that variable or "direct" costs are very high in proportion to fixed or "indirect" costs. This is in large part due to the trucking industry's use of publicly owned rights of way and to its comparatively smaller investment in terminal facilities and vehicles.

The wage bill alone including fringe benefits takes around 60 cents of every revenue dollar received by truck common and contract carriers. Viewed in another way, line-haul expenses typically account for more than one half the revenue dollar; terminal expenses for around 13 cents; administrative, general, taxes, and licenses for another 13 cents; while depreciation and equipment maintenance require another 15 cents. The balance of the revenue dollar is spread over such items as traffic solicitation, insurance and safety, and profits. It is generally considered that a well-managed trucking firm can operate profitably with an operating ratio (percentage of operating income going for operating expenses) of 93; by contrast, railroads usually are in financial difficulties if operating ratios exceed the low or middle 70's.

It is easy to see why trucking costs vary much more directly in relation to the volume of traffic moved than do rail costs. And it follows, therefore, that the rates charged for trucking services even in a short-run period cannot fall very far below total costs. This gives railroads, which have a larger cushion of fixed costs, considerable pricing advantages in many short-run competitive situations. (See Part Four.) Also, it must be remembered that due to the nature of its investment, a short-run period for a railroad may include a much longer calendar time than it does for a trucking firm.

As indicated above, probably two thirds of all intercity truck transportation is not subject to economic regulation by the Interstate Commerce Commission. Some of this, however, is regulated by state agencies. Insofar as economic regulation applies, common carrier truck regulation is generally comparable, with a few exceptions, to the regulations applying on railroad carriage. Contract carriers are subjected to less regulation, while private carriers generally are regulated only by state officials and in matters such as speed, safety, size and weight limits, and similar noneconomic aspects.

Truck carriage competes primarily with rail carriage for relatively high-class (that is, high value in relation to weight and bulk) traffic, particularly on shorter hauls. To a lesser extent, trucks compete with rail and water carriers for lower class traffic and on longer hauls, as well as with air freight carriers. Also, the various segments and firms in the trucking industry compete vigorously with each other. Common carriers compete with contract carriers, and both with exempt and private carriage. Most shippers using for-hire truck services have a variety of carriers to choose from. In addition, many shippers have found it advantageous to operate their own private trucks for all or some of their movements.

Like rail rates, truck rates usually are quoted in cents per 100 pounds. Also, generally there are differences between less-than-truckload (LTL) and truckload (TL) rates, and in addition volume (vol.) or any quantity (AQ) rates frequently are available. In comparing rail and truck rates, however, one must not forget that a shipment so small that it would take a rail LCL rate often may be large enough to qualify for a truck TL rate.

Because of the differing terminal and line-haul handling expense characteristics, truck rates generally are lower than rail rates on small shipments and on short hauls. It is harder to generalize on larger shipments subject to intermediate length or long-haul movements by rail class rates, but the rate differences between rail and truck on a considerable amount of such traffic are not great one way or the other. Truck lines, however, usually cannot quote rates competitive with the long-haul rail commodity rates which apply generally (but not exclusively) or heavy and bulky low-value goods moving in heavy volume.

Shippers may have to consider expenses other than rates, however. For example, packaging used for truck shipments may be less costly and weigh less than rail shipment packaging. Also, trucks usually furnish pickup-and-delivery services for small shipments and provide loading services for truckload movements, while rail carloads are loaded by the shipper and LCL pickup or delivery may not always be free or available.

Up to fairly long distances, trucks (which do not have to become involved with congested terminals or delayed on sidings) usually give much more rapid service than do rails. Even on very long hauls, truck speed generally is as good as fast rail freight. Trucks, too, are able to operate on a flexible time schedule, leaving and arriving according to the customer's wishes.

As pointed out above, local area coverage by trucks is excellent. On the national or even regional scene, however, area coverage is less complete due to the restricted operating territories and scarcity of interchange agreements (through routes and joint rates) in the trucking industry. Where it is available, long-distance service generally is "pinpoint" in nature, that is, from one major center to another, with little or no coverage of intermediate or surrounding smaller communities. These weaknesses in trucking carriage are being improved steadily, however, as the industry becomes more mature.

Adverse weather affects truck schedules more than it does rail movements. As to loss and damage experience, it appears that there may not be any significant differences between rails and regulated truckers in general Statistics on percentage loss and damage ratios are somewhat misleading because of the different inherent natures and values of the goods shipped and the kinds of packaging and protection used by the two modes.

Industry Outlook

Although reliable financial data is very incomplete and despite the apparently increasing amount of private truck carriage, it does not appear that the for-hire trucking industry as a whole is faced with the serious problem confronting railroads. Rather, the industry's basic problems are related to its achieving its proper place in the transportation scheme. Differences between common, contract, exempt, and private carriage, as well as other modes of transport remain to be resolved. The kinds of commodities, the lengths of hauls, and the most efficient sizes of firms under various operating circumstances have not been determined. Much remains to be done in the area of interchange of shipments and equipment, not only between trucking firms but also between other modes of transportation. These and similar problems can never be completely solved for all times and conditions, of course, but better solutions than those now in use can and will be reached.

BUSSES

Although this book is concerned primarily with the movements of things rather than with movements of people, passenger transportation cannot be ignored. Bus carriers, for example, transport persons (some of whom would otherwise move by rail) and thus divert revenues from rail carriers (as well as from air carriers). Also, busses frequently haul mail, newspapers, and express shipments which otherwise would move by other forms of carriage. Around 10 per cent of bus revenues come from nonpassenger services.

Less than 10 per cent of the 350,000 busses in this country are operated in regular-route, intercity service. The remainder are used for hauling school children, in local transit and commuter services, in national parks and resorts, and for similar purposes. The intercity busses, however, provide more than a half-billion paying passengers with 26 billion passenger-miles of service annually. Busses transport many more individuals than do either railroads or airplanes and account for twice as many intercity passenger-miles as do the rails. More than 50,000 bus company employees are engaged in performing these intercity services.

The average bus trip by passengers on Class I interstate carriers (annual gross revenues of $200,000 or more) is about 92 miles. Class II ($50,000 to $200,000) and Class III (less than $50,000) average passenger trips are even shorter. In comparison, rail coach passengers average about 85 miles and air passengers about 651 miles per trip. Bus fares per passenger-mile average around 3.2¢, about the same as average rail coach fares, and about 2¢ per passenger mile lower than air coach fares.

More than 1,300 companies provide intercity bus services, and about 1,200 of these are engaged in interstate transport and thus are subject to Interstate Commerce Commission regulation. In this latter group, about 200 Class I carriers receive approximately 90 per cent of the total interstate bus traffic revenue, leaving 10 per cent for about 1,000 Class II and Class III carriers. Total revenues received by all Class I carriers have averaged well above $500 million annually for the past several years. This is considerably more than twice the value of the property owned by these carriers.

The bus industry has proceeded much further than the truckers in providing through services and interchanges among different firms. This is in part due to the much smaller number of companies and to the dominant position of a few large organizations which provide nationwide or regionwide services.

The various divisions and subsidiaries of Greyhound Corporation, the nation's largest bus organization, for example, operates more than 5,000 busses over 100,000 route miles in almost all parts of the country. Busses of this organization are driven more than one million miles a day. Greyhound receives more than 60 per cent of Class I bus revenues. The more than forty companies associated into the nationwide Trailways System account for one fourth of the country's bus mileage. Transcontinental Bus System (Continental Trailways), second only to Greyhound in size, also provides transcontinental services. Most of the other intercity bus companies of any significant size have interconnections and passenger interchanges with the larger systems, so that a passenger can go from and to almost any place in the country without the necessity for making more than one ticket purchase.

PIPELINES

In American transportation, the term "pipeline industry" refers to oil pipelines only. Although natural gas is transported for long distances by pipeline, gas pipelines generally do not compete directly with other transportation modes, and their interstate operations are regulated by the Federal Power Commission rather than by a transportation regulatory agency.

Oil pipelines have surpassed inland water carriers in ton-mileage volume to become our third major form of carriage. (Actually their ton-mileage slightly exceeded that of trucks in 1969.) These pipelines are made up of more than 100 organizations, representing an investment of more than $4 billion, and owning more than 210,000 miles of pipeline. About three fourths of these organizations are regulated as common carriers by the Interstate Commerce Commission.

The pipeline network consists of gathering, crude, and product lines. Gathering lines collect oil in the field and carry it to a central distribution point. Crude lines then pump this unrefined oil to refineries. Product lines distribute the various refined products from refineries to consuming centers. About one fourth of the pipeline mileage is in the form of product lines. The average length of movement by crude lines (excluding gathering) is about 325 miles, while the average product's move is around 270 miles.

Most states contain some pipelines, but the geographical concentration of oil-producing centers and of consuming centers affect the concentration of pipelines. Texas alone contains one fourth of the nation's pipeline mileage, and the next three leading states—Oklahoma, Kansas, and Illinois—contain another one fourth. One third of the states containing pipelines have less than 500 miles each. A glance at a map of our pipeline system, however, reveals that it consists in considerable part of an interconnected network similar to the railroad pattern.

Oil movements by pipeline have reached the neighborhood of one fourth trillion ton-miles annually. In terms of barrels moved, the figure is around five billion per year. Pipelines handle almost 45 per cent of all oil traffic, with railroads accounting for around 3 per cent, and the remainder split almost equally between water and truck carriage (with water carriage a little in the lead). This tremendous ton-mile movement is handled by less than 20,000 employees.

Oil pipelines range in size from more than 10,000 to less than 10 miles, with one third being less than 500 miles in length. Although some are "independent," most pipelines are affiliated with major oil companies as subsidiaries or pipeline departments, or through at least partial ownership. Several railroads have constructed pipelines during recent years.

Considerable pipeline mileage also is owned jointly by more than one pipeline organization through unique "undivided interest" contracts which are based upon each owner's investment in the project. One company usually builds and operates such an undivided interest line, dealing at arm's length with other participating organizations. It should be noted that such ventures are legally neither corporations, partnerships, nor shippers' associations.

Pipelines are fond of pointing out that their industry is the only form of transport which has never received any form of government subsidy—railroads can deny present but not past subsidization. Pipelines, in general, may also claim to be the most profitable form of transportation. On gross revenues of more than one billion dollars a year (about three fourths of a billion dollars for Interstate Commerce Commission-regulated organizations), they earn an overall return on investment approaching 7 per cent. Maximum earnings are limited by the Interstate Commerce Commission and by a Justice Department "consent decree" signed by many companies as a result of a pre-World War II antitrust prosecution.

As common carriers, oil pipelines are obligated to transport on an equal basis for all customers making offerings ("tenders") under defined conditions. Rates are published in tariffs on a cents-per-barrel (42 gallons) basis from point to point or zone to zone. On a ton-mile basis, rates average about one fourth of one cent. The average revenue per barrel handled is around 14¢, which means that the pipeline transportation cost from oil field through refinery and to the consuming center, an average distance of almost 600 miles, is less than one third of a cent per gallon.

A pipeline represents a comparatively large investment, but its operations are so highly mechanized and automated that very few employees are required for its operation. This means heavy fixed costs as compared to variable costs, and thus a low operating ratio (in the mid-50's, as compared to the low 90's for trucks or the mid-70's for railroads) is common.

Such cost characteristics, of course, require that a large and steady volume of oil be available for a considerable period of time in order that pipelines be feasible. With such conditions, though, pipeline transport is considerably less costly than rail or truck movements.

In general, bulk movements of oil by water transport are even less costly than pipeline movements, but water transport is more limited geographically and usually is much more circuitous. Historically, pipelines have been built mainly in areas not served by water transport or as feeders into or distributors out of ports. Pipeliners today, however, maintain that their "large diameter" or "big inch" pipe, 30 to 36 inches or larger in diameter, is competitive on a cost basis with water movements. It is only under very special conditions, however, that such large diameter pipe is economically sound.

The efficiency of oil pipeline operations, coupled with rising costs for other forms of carriage, has stimulated interest in moving other commodities by pipeline. Coal, crushed and suspended in water, was first moved successfully for more than 100 miles in a commercial operation in 1957. This operation ceased in 1963, but since then serious consideration and some experimentation has been devoted to pipeline transport of such products as coal, ore, wood chips, and grain. The pipeline technique apparently is physically capable of being adapted to many commodities, but such innovations can be expected to come about only under rather unique economic circumstances.

ADDITIONAL READINGS

1. Fair, Marvin L., and Ernest W. Williams, Jr., **Economics of Transportation,** Rev. ed. New York: Harper and Brothers, 1959.
   Chapter 5. "Development of Railroads," pp. 61–88.
   Chapter 6. "Motor Transportation," pp. 89–109.
   "Pipe-Line Transportation," pp. 126–132.
2. Locklin, D. Philip, **Economics of Transportation,** 6th ed. Homewood, Ill.: Richard D. Irwin, Inc., 1966.
   Chapter 7. "The Railroad System of the United States," pp. 117–129.
   Chapter 28. "Pipelines," pp. 601–615.
   Chapter 30. "Highway Transportation," pp. 638–660.

3. Norton, Hugh S., **Modern Transportation Economics.** Columbus, Ohio: Charles E. Merrill Books, Inc., 1963.
Chapter II. "Railroads, Motor Carriers, and Air Carriers," pp. 18–35 ("The Railroad System") and pp. 36–50 ("Motor Carriers").
Chapter III. "Water Carriers, Pipelines, and Indirect Carriers," pp. 72–76 ("Pipelines").
4. Pegrum, Dudley F., **Transportation: Economics and Public Policy.** Rev.ed. Homewood, Ill.: Richard D. Irwin, Inc., 1968.
"Railroads," pp. 28–32.
"Motor Transport," pp. 32–35.
"Pipe-Line Transport," pp. 43–44.
5. Taff, Charles A., **Management of Traffic and Physical Distribution,** 4th ed. Homewood, Ill.: Richard D. Irwin, Inc., 1968.
Chapter 4. "The Transportation System," pp. 72–82 and pp. 90–95.

5

Water, Air, and
Other Forms of Carriage

WATER CARRIAGE

Much of the United States is well blessed with an excellent system of natural waterways. In addition to our Atlantic, Gulf, and Pacific seacoasts and their bays, we have the Great Lakes and a considerable number of important navigable rivers. Although various kinds of improvements and maintenance are necessary to make these waterways usable for modern commercial transportation and large sections of the country are entirely without navigable waterways, our water transport system historically has played, and continues to play, an important role in our economy.

Excluding seacoasts and the Great Lakes routes, the United States contains about 29,000 miles of navigable waterways. More than 20,000 miles of these routes are in commercial use at present. Approximately 15,000 miles of these routes, with a "standard" operating depth of nine feet or more, carries the great bulk of the nation's internal water traffic.

Internal Water Transport

About one third of our internal navigable waterways are in the Mississippi Basin, that is, it is made up of the Mississippi, Missouri, and Ohio Rivers and several principal tributaries such as the Tennessee and Cumberland Rivers. The Illinois River and Illinois Barge Canal connect Chicago and Lake Michigan with the Mississippi above St. Louis (the Lakes-to-the-Gulf system), while the New York State Barge Canal connects Lakes Erie and Ontario with the Hudson River above Albany.

Intracoastal waterways, including connecting rivers, canals, channels, and bays protected from the open seas, are found along most of the Atlantic and Gulf Coasts. Except for a few short stretches, these waterways permit interconnected continuous navigation from New York to the mouth of the Rio Grande on the Texas-Mexican border. Numerous river systems, including the Mississippi and Hudson Rivers, the Alabama-Tombigbee-Black-Warrior system, and other smaller rivers (and canals) all along the Atlantic and Gulf Coasts connect interior points with the *Intracoastal* waterways.

In the far west, internal waterways are limited mainly to the Columbia-Snake River system, San Francisco Bay and Puget Sound and the rivers flowing into these great natural harbors, and a few small bays and their entering rivers on the Washington, Oregon, and California coasts. Other rivers west of the Mississippi Basin generally are unsuitable for commercial navigation under present conditions.

About 1,700 companies with an investment of around $1.7 billion, operate tugboat (or towboat) and barge services on the nation's internal waterways. Of these, about 1,300 perform for-hire services and the remainder are engaged in private transportation. Most of the for-hire operators—more than 1,100—are operating as exempt carriers, that is, they are not subject to Interstate Commerce Commission regulations. More than 100 of these river and canal carriers are certificated as common carriers by the Interstate Commerce Commission, and less than 50 hold contract carriage permits.

For regulatory purposes, the Interstate Commerce Commission classifies domestic water carriers into three groups. Class A carriers are those with annual gross operating revenues of more than $500,000, Class B have revenues between $100,000 and $500,000, and Class C includes those with gross revenues of less than $100,000 per year. Freight revenues of all Class A and Class B carriers subject to Interstate Commerce Commission regulation during the late 1960's amounted to less than $400 million annually. This includes intercoastal and coastwise as well as Great Lakes, river, and canal carriers.

Basically, as compared to railroads, most internal water carrier firms must be classed as small businesses. Altogether, the 1,700 companies involved operate about 4,300 towboats or tugs, 15,000 dry-cargo barges and 3,000 liquid-cargo barges, and employ around 80,000 persons. The largest Mississippi River common carrier does not exceed $25 million in gross operating revenues—about one fiftieth as much as the largest railroads.

The barge and towboat operation has made rapid technological strides during the past 30 years, however, and under suitable circumstances is very efficient. It accounts for around 9 per cent of the country's intercity ton-mileage. During the mid-1930's, the typical towboat perhaps was around the 700-horsepower range. Today, 4,000 to 6,000 horsepower is quite common, and some giant tugs of 8,500 and 9,000 horsepower are in use.

A typical lower-Mississippi barge "tow" (actually a "push," as the tugboat is behind rather than in front of its barges) may be more than one fourth mile in length and 200 feet wide. Such a tow will move at an average line-haul speed of 4 to 5 miles per hour and, under exceptionally favorable conditions, as rapidly as 8 to 10 miles per hour. One barge may carry as much tonnage as 40 railroad cars, that is, 1,800 tons, and a single large towboat may push a string of 40 barges or the cargo-capacity equivalent of 16 100-car freight trains. This cargo moves at an average cost to the shipper of considerably less than a half-cent per ton-mile, or at around one fourth the average cost of railroad shipments.

Barge cargoes mainly consist of heavy, bulky, low-value-per-unit-of-weight mineral, petroleum, and agricultural products which can be rapidly loaded and unloaded by mechanical methods. Coal, petroleum products, and sand and gravel account for more than three fourths of the Mississippi system's traffic. In some areas, especially in the Pacific Northwest, grain and lumber movements are important. Also, a variety of chemicals, iron and steel products, and manufactured items such as automobiles can be moved handily by barge.

Great Lakes Transport

The five Great Lakes, with an area of 95,000 square miles and a coast line of 8,300 miles, in effect form a fourth seacoast for a large portion of the United States. The eight states bordering these lakes contain about 70 commercial harbors, and products move for considerable distances to and from interior points in order to take advantage of cheap water transport. Highly specialized and efficient lake steamers, designed particularly for the mass transport of mineral products and grain, shuttle back and forth continuously during the eight-month ice-free navigation season to make the lakes the world's busiest, as well as largest, inland waterway. In addition to playing a tremendously important role in the early settlement and development of the Midwest, the Great Lakes waterways and their connecting transport arteries continue to support an inland "industrial heartland" without peer.

Many improvements were necessary to adapt the Great Lakes to modern commercial water transport, of course. The Welland Canal, around Niagara Falls, was opened in 1829 to connect Lake Ontario with Lake Erie and to tie the lakes system into the St. Lawrence River and the barge traffic of the Erie Canal-Hudson River system to the port of New York. The Soo Canal, connecting Lakes Superior and Huron around St. Mary's Falls and opened in 1855, today carries more freight tonnage than any other canal in the world, surpassing such noted international waterways as the Panama and Suez Canals. Other improvements include the Detroit River Channel between Lakes Huron and Erie, and a host of smaller channel, canal, and harbor development projects.

Great Lakes eastbound traffic is dominated by iron ore and grain movements supplemented by pulpwood products and other semi-processed or raw materials. Westbound, coal dominates, followed by petroleum products, limestone, and several less important industrial and manufactured items.

The Mesabi Range, west of Lake Superior, has long been the nation's principal source of iron ore. This ore has supplied the giant steel mills of the east lake areas with the raw materials necessary for United States steel leadership. Sufficient supplies are stocked during the busy summer navigation season to permit the mills to continue operations during the months when the lakes are icebound.

The continent's great grain-producing area, the states and Canadian provinces west of the Great Lakes, pours great quantities of wheat and smaller amounts of other grains into the United States ports at Duluth-Superior, Milwaukee, and Chicago, and into Canada's Fort William-Port Arthur area. This grain moves to east lake points for milling, transshipment by other forms of carriage, or for export via the St. Lawrence.

On their westbound return, ore and grain steamers carry coal from Lake Erie ports to the great cities of the western lakes areas such as Detroit, Chicago, Milwaukee, Duluth-Superior, and to smaller cities, as well as for land or barge transshipment to interior west lake areas. Also, petroleum products, automotive vehicles, iron and steel items, and similar manufactured commodities are moved in smaller volumes.

During the 1950's, the long-discussed St. Lawrence Seaway project was undertaken by the governments of the United States and Canada. In 1959, the Great Lakes finally were made accessible to large oceangoing ships via the St. Lawrence River. Although navigation of such vessels through the locks and channels of this project is somewhat tricky and many of the very largest ocean vessels cannot be accommodated at all, it is likely that at least three fourths of the world's ocean merchant marine vessels now can get into the Great Lakes. In no other place in the world does ocean transport penetrate so deeply into an interior industrial and agricultural complex equivalent to this.

Not all important lake ports have the necessary physical and institutional facilities for handling a large volume of ocean-borne commerce, of course, and many areas of the lakes themselves are inaccessible to large ocean ships, but a rash of improvements was touched off along the lakes in expectation of a booming ocean commerce. The most rosy expectations were not realized during the years immediately following the opening of the project's facilities, although ocean trade was greater than some opponents of the project had predicted. Also, it is quite apparent that the Seaway will have a considerable influence upon previously established traffic patterns into and out of Atlantic Coast seaports and upon the rate structures of railroads and other forms of transport. It may be many years, however, before these adjustments are completed and a new stability reached in rate and traffic patterns.

Coastwise and Intercoastal Transport

In addition to river, canal, intracoastal, and lake transport, our domestic water system includes coastwise and intercoastal ocean water transportation. Historically, from our beginning as a separate nation, coastwise and inter-coastal shipping has been restricted to vessels built, owned, and operated by United States citizens. (The current expression of this principle of "cabotage" is in the so-called "Jones Act," or Merchant Marine Act of 1920.) A considerable volume of coastwise water transport is by barge; the remainder, and the intercoastal traffic, is by regular ocean cargo ships. As late as the 1930's, these trades moved large tonnages of commodities such as lumber, canned goods, and iron and steel products.

During World War II, as a result of submarine attacks and government requisition and regulation of oceangoing vessels, coastwise and intercoastal water transport was drastically restricted. This traffic has not been healthy since the end of that war. Rate and service competition from other forms of carriage, especially rail, but also truck and pipeline, has prevented any great resurgence of intercoastal and coastwise ocean shipping of general cargoes. By the early 1960's, for example, intercoastal tonnage accounted for not much more than 2 per cent of the nation's total water tonnage. (In comparison, tonnage in the Mississippi Basin amounted to almost 50 per cent of the total water tonnage, the Great Lakes accounted for almost 20 per cent, while the remainder was fairly evenly divided between the Pacific Coast on the one hand and the Atlantic-Gulf Coasts on the other.) There is little basis for belief that ocean-borne domestic tonnage will regain its former area of importance within the foreseeable future; actually, quite the contrary seems to be indicated.

Costs, Regulation, and Competition

Water carrier ton-mile costs under the best conditions probably are lower than the costs of any other form of carriage. Less power is needed to propel on water than on land. Rights of way and terminal facilities often are provided at no cost or at very little cost to the carrier. Also, as water cargoes typically involve large tonnages, the carrier's overhead costs are spread over many units with a resulting low per-unit cost of movement. The ratio of fixed to variable costs is fairly low. Fixed costs consist mostly of the costs of owning the vessels used, while line-haul costs (as is true in the trucking industry) typically account for a considerable part of the water carrier's total costs.

It is difficult to generalize about operating ratios (see Chapter 4) in the water-carrier industry as a whole due to its many different types of equipment and trades. It appears, however, that a profitable level of operating ratio for most water carriers falls somewhere between what is considered adequate for trucks (93 to 95) and railroads (low 70's), that is, not higher than the low 80's.

There is another side to the water-carrier cost issue, though. Some expenses of providing water transportation are borne by the general taxpayer. Improved rights of way (canals, channels, harbors, and various navigational aids) are costly, and insofar as the expenses of these facilities are not charged to carriers, they have to be supported out of general public funds. Also, substantial portions of terminal facilities and terminal costs often are levied against the public, shippers, or both.

In addition, even though the ton-mile costs of movement by water may be low, the actual ton-mileage involved in moving a given cargo between specified points by water may be much greater than if the cargo were moved by land. Water routes often are long and winding rather than direct. For example, the water route over the lower Mississippi River is twice as long as the direct airline route, while the intercoastal water route is several times as long as the competing land routes. And a ton of freight moved five miles results in five times as much ton-mileage as the same ton moved for only one mile!

The economic regulation of domestic water carriage cannot be considered comparable to that of other major competing forms of carriage. Although water carriers are subject to Interstate Commerce Commission regulation, there are numerous exemptions and exceptions. Two of the most important of these exemptions exclude from regulation the carriage of liquid cargoes in bulk and the bulk carriage of three or less commodities. Many other less important exemptions apply. Private carriage which is very important is, of course, not regulated. The Commission has estimated that not more than 12 per cent of domestic water transportation is subject to its regulation, as contrasted to approximately one third of truck transport and virtually 100 per cent of rail and pipeline carriage.

Water carrier competition is mainly with railroads and with other water carriers. And, actually, competition is not keen among water carriers themselves as usually there are not many carriers offering the same type of water-borne service between any two points. Some competition exists between trucks and water carriers, but this is not of great importance in most situations because of the specialized bulk nature of water carriage.

Competition between oil pipelines and water carriers of petroleum products has increased during recent years as larger pipe and more efficient pumping techniques have been developed (see Chapter 4). This competition is somewhat lessened, however, due to the fact that both pipelines and oil tankers frequently are owned or controlled by major oil producers. This, in general, has led to pipelines designed to supplement rather than to duplicate water capacity. When and if the pipeline techniques becomes more widely used for other bulk products such as coal, however, the competitive picture may be altered.

From the individual shipper's viewpoint, the principal advantage of using water transportation for domestic shipments in preference to land transport is low freight rates. Sometimes, in addition, water carrier facilities are more suitable for handling (loading and unloading) certain kinds of bulk commodities. A principal disadvantage, even for bulk shipments, is the generally slower and less frequently scheduled service available from water carriers. Goods in transit represent funds tied up in inventories—speed is money to the shipper. Also, slowness and less frequent departures and arrivals on the part of water carriers virtually preclude the filling of rush orders and sometimes requires that shippers carefully plan their production and shipping schedules in advance. Then too, water carriage typically gives only "pinpoint" area coverage (see Chapter 4). Where it is available, water carriage generally serves only major points and bypasses many smaller intermediate communities. Also, delays due to adverse weather conditions frequently must be anticipated.

As previously explained, from the viewpoint of the economy as a whole there are costs involved in water carriage which are not completely reflected in the costs of individual carriers. Likewise, from the shipper's individual viewpoint, rates alone do not always tell the complete story. Other costs, in addition to rates, may be of importance to shippers in comparing their total water transportation outlays with outlays for transportation by other modes of carriage.

For example, unless the shipper and the consignee are located directly adjacent to water facilities, goods must be transported to and from water by land carriers. This may involve extra handling expenses. That is, goods must be loaded onto a land carrier, hauled to the water carrier's dock, and reloaded onto the river carrier's vessel. At destination, the goods must be unloaded from the water carrier, hauled to the consignee's place of business, and again unloaded from the land vehicle. In addition to the extra handling charges, terminal fees of various kinds may also be incurred.

Another factor which water shippers must keep in mind is the generally limited liability of water carriers as contrasted with land carriers. Although no carrier is an absolute insurer of safe delivery of merchandise entrusted to its care, the responsibilities of water carriers for loss and damage to shipments are in general much less than the responsibilities of land carriers. (See Chapter 7). For this reason, if a shipper wants cargo protection for his water shipment equivalent to the protection available on land movements, he frequently must purchase insurance.

Despite the above qualifications, however, from an individual shipper's viewpoint, water carriage may be the lowest priced transport available (if it is available at all) under many circumstances, and it sometimes may be better tailored to individual service needs than are the other modes of transport. Water carriage by nature is particularly suited for movements of heavy, bulky, low-value-per-unit commodities which can be loaded and unloaded efficiently by mechanical means in situations where speed is not of primary importance, where the commodities shipped are not particularly susceptible to shipping damage or theft, and where accompanying land movements are unnecessary.

AIR CARRIAGE

United States commercial airlines now operate some 2,100 jet and piston aircraft. These lines have an investment of roughly $4 billion and employ approximately 300,000 persons. Their total operating revenues are in the neighborhood of $6 billion annually and are increasing each year.

Passenger and Mixed Services

Air transportation still is primarily a passenger operation. Well over four fifths of the industry's revenues come from this source. Not much more than six per cent of total airline revenues, on the other hand, come from freight and express services. Other revenues come from carrying mail, direct subsidies ("public service revenues"), excess baggage charges, and miscellaneous other sources. Direct subsidies, although much discussed, account for only about two per cent of the airline industry's total revenues.

Domestic intercity passenger miles handled by airlines at the beginning of World War II amounted to not much more than 2 per cent of the nation's total for-hire carrier passenger mileage. By 1957, airlines had surpassed railroads as the leading common carrier of passengers. Not only has the number of passengers carried by airlines increased to some seventy times the immediate pre-World War II level, but the average length per passenger trip (now around 550 miles for domestic passengers) has increased by about 60 per cent.

During the same period, average scheduled airline passenger fares have increased from a little more than 5 cents to a little more than 6 cents per mile, while railroad average first-class fares have gone from a little more than 2.3 cents to about 3.9 cents, and rail coach fares from 1.8 cents to about 3.2 cents per mile. Lower priced coach, tourist, or economy services have grown rapidly during the past few years and now exceed first-class services in volume. The increased speed, convenience, and popularity of air travel seems to assure a continued growth of this service even if fares should be increased substantially. Obviously, however, air travel cannot be expected to increase as rapidly percentagewise during the next twenty years as during the last twenty.

Although aggregate statistics and trends are useful in an overview of the airline industry, one must realize that the industry is made up of several types of carriers with different operating situations and problems. The Civil Aeronautics Board, the Federal airline regulatory agency, classifies airlines into at least nine different groups. (There is, however, some overlapping between groups, that is, a carrier may be classified in one group for a part of its service and in another group for a different kind of service.)

The most familiar group to most persons probably is the Domestic Trunk Lines which have permanent operating rights between principal population centers in the continental contiguous United States. This group contains eleven carriers. Thirteen Domestic Local Service Lines (sometimes called "feeder lines") operate in and between areas of lesser traffic density and connect smaller population centers with major centers. Two firms make up the Intra-Hawaiian classification. Alaskan carriers are composed of four lines operating between Alaska and the other continental states, plus twelve lines operating wholly within Alaska.

International and Overseas Lines, as indicated by the name of the group, operate between the United States and other countries, or over international waters. Some of these nineteen lines are merely extensions of other domestic carriers. Helicopter carriers provide airport-to-downtown services for passengers as well as for freight, express, and airmail in several of the country's larger cities. All-Cargo Lines, six in number, are authorized to carry only cargo—not passengers—between specified areas of the United States or between the United States and designated foreign countries. About three dozen Supplemental Air Carriers perform mainly charter services and a limited number of individually ticketed flights. The miscellaneous or "Other" category includes air-taxi operators (more than 2,600) and about 75 air-freight forwarders.

All major commercial airlines are common carriers, and their interstate activities are subject to economic regulation by the Civil Aeronautics Board (C.A.B.). In general, this regulation is comparable to that exercised over interstate land carriers by the I.C.C., although it differs in some important respects (see Chapter 18). The C.A.B. also administers the direct-subsidy program related to airmail carriage. (Domestic Trunk Lines have not received the subsidy for a number of years, and All-Cargo Lines never have.) The Federal Aviation Agency (F.A.A.) regulates safety matters and engages in promotional activities such as the development of airports and navigational facilities. Both the C.A.B. and the F.A.A. are concerned with accident investigation.

It is safe to say that historically the government's impact on commercial airlines has been much greater in the areas of safety and promotion, including direct and indirect subsidies such as airports, airways, experimentation and development in connection with new types of aircraft and "public service" payments than in economic regulation as such. This has been justified on the grounds that air transport is a new mode in which the public has a vital peacetime commercial and wartime defense interest and that this newcomer would not be able to develop rapidly without subsidization if forced to compete on an equal basis with already well-established competitors.

Domestic airlines compete with railroads and busses as well as with private automobiles for passengers. They compete with both rails and trucks for freight. And, of course, they compete with each other. During the earlier years of C.A.B. regulation, which began in 1938, intramodal airline competition was limited. During more recent years, however, the C.A.B. appears to have encouraged more airline versus airline competition, especially on the more dense traffic routes. Some persons fear that this competition may have been allowed to become too intense, thus contributing to the financial difficulties of some airlines.

Airline cost structures are more comparable to trucking-industry cost structures than to railroad costs. That is, the industry is one of relatively high variable costs in proportion to fixed costs. As airports and airway navigational aids are provided by the public, the principal fixed airline costs are those associated with aircraft ownership. And even though a fully equipped jet plane may cost several millions of dollars, only 12 or 13 per cent of the industry's total costs are chargeable to such items as interest, depreciation, and amortization. In contrast, wages and salaries, fuel and oil, and various materials, supplies, and services account for around four fifths of total costs. A large part of these expenses and some other less important ones must be considered as variable in nature. It appears that a profitable industry operating ratio for airlines would be considerably higher than for the railroads, somewhat higher than for water carriers, but lower than for the trucking industry—perhaps in the high 80's.

Freight Services

This book is primarily concerned with the transportation of things rather than with the transportation of people. In air carriage particularly, however, the two are difficult to consider in isolation. Only the All-Cargo Lines carry freight exclusively. Other lines carry both passengers and freight, with passenger movements being of much greater relative importance. Freight haulage is increasing rapidly (even though from a small base) among the mixed carriers, however, and these carriers do compete with the All-Cargo group as well as with each other and other forms of freight transport.

Three kinds of freight transport are offered. The most important in terms of volume is "air freight." Except for high minimum charges on small shipments, this service is the most attractive in terms of rates, and it moves at fairly rapid speeds. "Air express," offered in cooperation with the REA Express, is the fastest and generally the most reliable air service. It also is the highest priced except on the smallest shipments. "Air parcel post" is a U.S. Mail service which has the lowest air rates for small shipments generally, but which loses some of the potential air speed advantages because of the lack of pickup and the slowness of delivery services.

For several years, a "Greyhound air express" service has been offered to areas isolated from major airports. Small shipments are carried by bus to connect with airlines. More recently, joint services have been worked out between trucking lines and airlines in some areas which provide for truck pickup and delivery and a line haul by air.

Speed of movement is the primary advantage of air shipments, but terminal delays and congestion and out-of-town terminal location may considerably reduce this advantage unless air express is used. Frequency of departure is very high, and reliability of service (even in the face of adverse weather) is being rapidly improved. Coverage of service generally is limited to movements between major points on a single airline, and "feeder" service has not been notably efficient. Better area coverage is being developed by more interline cooperation, however, and especially by cooperation with REA Express, bus lines, and trucking companies.

A high rate level, of course, is the principal disadvantage of shipment by air. Average rates per ton-mile by air freight still are ten or twelve times as high as average rail ton-mile rates and three or four times as high as truck rates. Such averages must be used with caution, however. Many individual rail and truck rates are much higher and many air rates lower than the average. Also, airline distances typically are somewhat shorter than the routes usually followed by land carriers. In addition, the bulk of rail and even of truck carriage involves quite different products than those making up an air cargo. One would not normally expect to ship coal or lumber by air any more than one would expect to ship live lobsters, cut flowers, or high-style women's clothing long distances by rail.

Some airline managements recently have been attempting to change the frequently conceived picture of air freight as an expensive emergency service suitable only for high-value and highly perishable traffic. The industry spokesmen emphasize the speed advantages which may make it possible for distributors to reduce their overall costs (even though transportation costs may be increased) by carrying smaller inventories and eliminating far-flung warehouse services. Actually the cost (and rate) trend is downward in the still rapidly expanding and improving airline industry, while costs and rates are tending upward among competing forms of carriage. New and more efficient aircraft which are being developed for air-freight services may be expected to reduce service costs significantly.

Although the most optimistic predictions concerning the future of air freight may not be realized for a good many years, if ever, it seems certain that air-freight movements will continue to increase for some time. More of the presently moving commodities will be handled and many items not moving in any appreciable quantity will be added. Even if the ton-mile volume of air freight doubles and redoubles several times, however, it still will not bulk large in the overall ton-mile picture. But it may be extremely important (it is now, in fact) for some types of commodities and over some routes.

Industry Outlook

The widespread adoption of jet services greatly increased the speed, comfort, and convenience of air transport. These services, however, also increased the industry's capacity, caused heavy expenditures for the new aircraft, and forced many of the old craft into obsolesence. These factors, plus duplications of routes in many instances and other temporary cost-revenue relationships brought the industry face to face with a severe financial situation by the early 1960's. Various measures including mergers designed to eliminate duplicating routes, changes in passenger fares and services, more aggressive promotion and salesmanship, and increased subsidies were considered to better the overall profit condition of various troubled airlines. The industry made a quick recovery, however, once the shock of transforming to jets had been absorbed. Business continued to increase; and by 1964, overall industry profits had approached the 10.5 per cent considered to be "fair and reasonable" for the trunk lines by the C.A.B. By the late 1960's, however, airlines were again beginning to encounter financial difficulties.

ꓛTHER FORMS OF CARRIAGE AND RELATED SERVICES

In addition to the five basic agencies or modes of transport discussed in ꓱhis and the preceding chapter, several other organizational forms provide ꞃansport services. These forms, although they may operate equipment of ꓱheir own, especially for pickup and delivery purposes, rely mainly on one ꞁr more of the five basic modes for line-haul services.

ꞁreight Forwarders

Freight forwarders make up an important part of these secondary or inꓱirect modes of transport. They may be classified according to the basic kinds ꞁf line-haul equipment utilized. Surface freight forwarders use the facilities ꞁf rail, motor, or domestic water carriers, while air-freight forwarders use ꓱirline facilities in either (or both) domestic and foreign transport. (Also, ꞁoreign freight forwarders perform services somewhat different from domestic ꞁorwarders in connection with international water shipments, but this is outꓲide the scope of this book.)

Domestic surface freight forwarders are regulated as common carriers ꞃu a way similar to railroads, motor carriers, pipelines, and domestic water ꓲarriers under the Interstate Commerce Act (see Chapter 18). They deal ꓱirectly with and are directly responsible to shippers and receivers (see ꓵhapter 7). More than 80 forwarders are subject to Interstate Commerce ꓵommission regulation. Of these, about 60 are classified as "Class A" forwardꞏrs (gross revenues of more than $100,000 annually), and the remainder as ꓵlass B" (less than $100,000 in annual revenues). The range of assets of inꓱividual forwarder firms varies from more than $11 million down to a few ꓱhousand dollars.

The primary function of these forwarders is the consolidation of small ꓲhipments (LCL or LTL) of several or numerous shippers into large shipꞃnents (CL or TL) which move at lower rates. The forwarder sells his transꞏortation services directly to a shipper. Then, in turn, he buys line-haul ꞏervices from the basic modes (in effect, to use an analogy, he subcontracts a ꞏart of the movement). His operating expenses and profits are covered by the ꞏpread between rates on small shipments and rates on large shipments. The ꓱhipper pays no more (or perhaps less) than he otherwise would have to pay ꞁn a small-lot movement. In addition, he is relieved of the chores of dealing ꓱirectly with the basic or primary carriers and may receive better pickup and ꓱelivery services, a faster line-haul movement, and even other services related ꞁ distribution.

As forwarders do not have equipment for line-haul movements, their inꞏestment is low in relation to revenues compared to the basic modes. During ꓱhe late 1960's, with an investment of around $120 million, surface forwarders ꞏere doing a business bringing in gross revenues of approximately $565 milꞁon. Almost three fourths of these revenues are paid, in turn, to line-haul carriers. In performing their transportation services, these forwarders use about 1,100 motor vehicles for pickup and delivery and employ more than 10,000 persons.

Although the volume of tonnage handled by freight forwarders is relatively small, typically something over 4 million tons annually for surface forwarders, the average length of haul is two to three times the average of all movements by primary surface modes. Also, the number of individual shipments handled is quite large—around 23 million during a recent year. This indicates an average weight per shipment of less than 600 pounds.

Some surface forwarders operate on a national basis, while others are regional. Generally the service is point to point between important commercial centers, but some forwarders do cover outlying areas for many miles with their pickup and delivery services. In many cases where these services are available, small shippers and even large shippers with occasional small shipments find them considerably more convenient, more efficient, and less expensive than regular small-lot shipment by the basic modes of transport. This of course, is not always true.

About 75 air freight forwarders operate under the provisions of the Federal Aviation Act (that is, under the regulatory jurisdiction of the Civil Aeronautics Board). These are about equally divided between domestic and international services, with some firms operating in both fields. Air-freight forwarders are less restricted in some regulatory aspects than are the surface forwarders.

Express Services

REA Express also provides important services for small-lot shippers. This common-carrier agency, regulated by the I.C.C., attaches its cars to fast trains and also makes extensive use of trucks. It also utilizes other forms of line-haul carriage, both domestic and international, wherever appropriate. It is the most completely coordinated of our forms of transport in that it may use any or all of the basic modes (except pipelines). It was jointly owned by a group of railroads (and known as the Railway Express Agency) for many years, but recently became completely independent of the railroads.

REA Express assets are roughly twice that of all surface forwarders and its employees about three times as many, but its gross operating revenues are not as large. As the agency owns a considerable quantity of rail line-haul equipment, however, its payments to other forms of carriage are proportionately smaller. During recent years, REA Express has greatly expanded its equipment and services and has aggressively sought new business by attempting to tailor its services and types of freight rates more closely to the needs of individual shippers or groups of shippers.

REA Express has all of the advantages usually associated with railroad services, plus much greater speed and more individual services for smaller shipments. These extra advantages come from its pickup and delivery services more rapid and better terminal handling, and fast line-haul movements as well as specialized equipment and services and quick loss and damage claim settlement. Because of its special services, express charges usually, but not always, are the highest of any form of land transport.

Several other express companies, as United Parcel Service and a number of firms transporting money and other valuables, offer highly specialized services for particular kinds of movements.

Parcel Post

Parcel post services of the U.S. government (that is, via U.S. mails) are used extensively by mail-order houses and some other types of shippers. Specific size and weight limitations apply on parcel post shipments, but within these limitations parcel post in general offers the widest possible geographical coverage at the lowest available price. Somewhat offsetting these advantages in addition to weight-size limitations, however, are several disadvantages. Parcel post may be relatively slow and inconvenient (for example, shipments generally must be taken to the post office and prepaid, the customer may have to wait in line, etc.). Also, the service does not appear to be too reliable from the loss and damage viewpoint. Although payments for loss and damage is certain if the shipment is properly insured, damaged or non-delivered goods do not improve customer relations. And it is often alleged that parcel post rates are low only because the service is subsidized by first-class mail or by the general taxpayer.

Brokers, Associations, and Private Cars

This survey of transportation agencies would not be complete without mention of transportation brokers, shippers' associations, and private car lines.

Transportation brokers, licensed in domestic surface transportation by the Interstate Commerce Commission, are intermediaries or middlemen who bring shippers and carriers together for a fee. They are not carriers and have no responsibilities in connection with the actual transportation or safe delivery of the goods concerned. (Special types of brokers also operate in international water transportation.)

Shippers' associations are nonprofit organizations, usually employing a small managerial and clerical staff designed to perform services similar to freight forwarder services for their members. They may be concerned with only one type of product (as an agricultural commodity) or with a variety of merchandise (as associations of retailers). They are not carriers, although investigations have sometimes revealed that particular associations are not bona fide cooperative organizations but in actuality have been operating illegally as freight forwarders.

A considerable number of rail cars are not owned by railroads themselves. Such cars, usually specialized in nature (as tank cars or refrigerator cars), may be owned by private shippers or by private car lines which make a business of leasing cars to others. The utilization of these cars and the charges made are determined by the contractual arrangements and by special railroad tariffs. Approximately 180 companies own at least 10 private cars each. The total ownership of this group is in the neighborhood of 325,000 cars. Equipment owned by such organizations as Pacific Fruit Express (refrigerator cars), General American Transportation Corporation (tank cars), and several smaller private car lines are everyday sights in every part of the country.

INTERMODAL CARRIAGE

Although the various basic modes of transport have been considered separately in this and the preceding chapter, one should not suppose that a given shipment may not move over the facilities of more than one mode. Not only do separate carriers within the same mode cooperate in interchange of shipments, but separate modes frequently coordinate on the interchange of through movements. This intermodal coordination is permitted and sometimes required between some forms of carriage under certain circumstances by our transportation regulatory laws.

Coordinated transport of freight is found most often between rail and water, rail and truck, and truck and water. As has been mentioned above, there is some coordination between truck and air carriage, and REA Express uses combinations of land, water, and air transport facilities. Also, there is coordination and cooperation between United States and foreign carriers. In the passenger-transport field, also, a large amount of cooperation and coordination exists.

Although intercarrier coordination (and even intramodal cooperation in some cases) is far from complete, improvements are being made. One of the most successful recent efforts seems to be the trailer-on-a-flatcar (TOFC) or "piggyback" development.

Piggyback, the technique of carrying a loaded truck trailer on a rail flatcar for the line-haul portion of its journey, with pickup and delivery made by attaching a truck tractor, was revived during the early and middle 1950's. Since then it has grown very rapidly. More than 1.3 million piggyback cars moved in 1969, as contrasted with less than 200,000 in 1955. Several piggyback plans are used. The trailers may be owned by shippers, railroad companies, or trucking companies. A few truckers have virtually abandoned line-haul runs, confining their operations to terminal areas. Even freight forwarders began attempting to enter the piggyback field during the 1960's despite vigorous objections from truckers and the Teamsters Union.

Along with its obvious advantages in combining many of the best features of rail and truck transport, piggyback seems to be appreciated by the general public (with the exception, of course, of those who may stand to lose financially by the innovation). Not only does it demonstrate clearly that creative imagination still exists among railroad managements, but it removes many slow-moving trucks from already cluttered highways.

Fishyback (movement of truck trailers or rail cars on "roll-on, roll off" water carriers), and birdyback (truck trailers via air transport) have not developed to any extensive degree as yet, although a number of companies are engaging in this form of coordination and others are considering it.

One of the most discussed technological concepts today is containerization. A great deal of thought and experimentation is being given by both public and private agencies to the development of durable and standardized interchangeable containers. Ideally, a shipper should be able to load a cargo of small items into a container, lock it, take it by truck to a rail terminal, send it by rail to a seaport, by ocean carrier to a foreign port, and on to an inland destination by rail or truck. The development of such freely exchanged containers, of course, involves many problems other than technological ones. It has implications for intercarrier revenue division agreements, rate structures, and customs practices for foreign commerce as well as for loading and unloading methods and the obtaining of back-haul cargoes, among other things.

Several advantages of coordination in its various forms may be of great benefit to shippers. It may bring lower rates and better and more flexible services as well as wider area coverage. And the general consuming public (which includes all of us) stands to benefit by the more efficient use of transportation resources inherent in combining the most desirable features of all forms of transport into a tailored transportation package for each particular shipment or shipper. There is no doubt that the public itself will eventually force a much greater reliance upon coordinated transport even if some carrier managements are reluctant and some shippers are content with the status quo.

ADDITIONAL READINGS

1. Fair, Marvin L., and Ernest W. Williams, Jr., **Economics of Transportation,** Rev. ed. New York: Harper and Brothers, 1959.
   "Water Transportation," pp. 110–126.
   Chapter 8. "Air Transportation," pp. 134–152.
2. Landon, Charles E., "Technological Progress in Transportation on the Mississippi River System," **Journal of Business,** January 1960, pp. 43–62.
3. Locklin, D. Philip, **Economics of Transportation,** 6th ed. Homewood, Ill.: Richard D. Irwin, Inc., 1966.
   Chapter 33. "Water Transportation," pp. 712–737.
   Chapter 35. "Air Transportation," pp. 762–788.
4. Norton, Hugh S., **Modern Transportation Economics.** Columbus, Ohio: Charles E. Merrill Books, Inc., 1963.
   Chapter II. "Railroads, Motor Carriers, and Air Carriers," pp. 50–61 ("The Air Carriers").
   Chapter III. "Water Carriers, Pipelines, and Indirect Carriers," pp. 64–72 ("Water Carriers") and pp. 76–81 ("The Indirect Carriers").

5. Pegrum, Dudley F., **Transportation: Economics and Public Policy.** Rev. ed. Homewood, Ill.: Richard D. Irwin, Inc., 1968.
"The Domestic Waterways Systems," pp. 36–40.
"Air Transport," pp. 40–43.
6. Taff, Charles A., **Management of Traffic and Physical Distribution,** 4th ed. Homewood, Ill.: Richard D. Irwin, Inc., 1968.
Chapter 4. "The Transportation System," pp. 82–90 and 95–102.

6

Transportation Geography:
Routes and Commodity Movements

That wise Scotsman Adam Smith in the first portions of *The Wealth of Nations* set forth three leading propositions which may be summarized as follows:

One: The wealth of a nation is the product of its labor;
Two: The greatest improvements in the product of labor result from the division of labor;
Three: The division of labor is limited by the extent of the market.

With due humility we may add a fourth proposition, namely, "The extent of the market is controlled by the cost of transportation." In other words, transportation is not only a *necessary* factor in any organized economy. It also is a *limiting* factor in overall economic activity and development as well as that of a particular region, industry, or firm. The availability of adequate transportation does not necessarily insure prosperity, but its absence guarantees economic stagnation.

Assuming that adequate physical transportation facilities exist, the pertinent limiting "costs" in for-hire transport are the rates (prices) actually charged users by carriers. These rates may be more or less than the carriers' actual costs of performing services. (This distinction between "carriage rates" and "carriage costs" does not exist in private carriage, of course. Here the two are identical.) It has been said rightly that transportation geography is largely rate geography. This statement is based on the fact that rates (or "costs" from the users' viewpoint) often may be based as much or more upon economic or political considerations as upon geographical factors.

Freight rates will be more fully discussed in Part Four. It is only necessary at this time to point out that geography, inasmuch as it affects the location of transportation routes and the kinds and directions of commodity movements, does have a bearing on carrier transportation costs. To some extent, then, geography affects freight rates and thereby influences patterns of producer location, marketing areas, and routing practices, and sometimes even the availability of adequate transportation vehicles or rolling stock. At least a general knowledge of transportation geography, including available routes, and of the characteristics of commodity flows and their determinants is essential for any well-informed transportation student or practitioner.

THE LOCATION OF TRANSPORTATION ROUTES

Other things being equal, the ideal land transportation route between a fixed producing point and a given consuming center would be a straight line. This would minimize construction, maintenance, and movement costs. Other things are almost never equal, however. Numerous physical obstacles intervene. Often extensive detours are less costly than climbing, tunnelling or removing hills, bridging rivers or canyons, filling valleys, firming unstable soils, or draining swamps.

To detour or not to detour is both an engineering and an economic problem. Engineers can calculate the costs of going over, through, or around a mountain. The ultimate decision must be made on an economic basis, however.

It may be considerably more expensive to construct a route through an obstacle, but operating costs through the years ahead may be much lower over a direct than over a circuitous route. From the long-run viewpoint, it may be preferable to blast rather than to bypass. But builders, even if they recognize the long-run advantages of more expensive construction, may not have the necessary funds to undertake it. A cheaply built route with high operating costs may be chosen over more costly construction which could be utilized more cheaply, or there may be no choice.

Many thousands of miles of this country's highways and railways have been straightened or relocated to correct cheap building which could not have been avoided in their original construction because of lack of funds. But even in our affluent society, it is not economically practical to meet all geographic obstacles to transportation head-on. No one seriously proposes tunnelling completely through the Rocky Mountains or bridging the broadest expanses of Lake Superior. Geography still severely limits the location of our transportation routes and forces up operating costs.

Many of our basic transportation routes were surveyed and laid out millenniums ago by migrating animals. Following the path of least resistance seems to be a basic principle of nature. This is as applicable in transportation as in other natural phenomena. Old-time woodsmen and boy scouts advise us never to go over anything that we can go around. Animals also follow this principle; thus they discovered the best routes while seeking fresh food and water.

Indians followed the animals. Later, white explorers, missionaries, hunters, trappers, and traders followed both. Then pioneer settlers followed the same ancient trails, and highways and railroads followed the pack trains and wagon tracks of settlers. Finally, trading posts, communities, and great cities grew up alongside these transportation routes and at points where routes intersect or change in form (as from water to land, or later from railway to highway). Even airways, physically the most flexible and obstacle-free of all routes, have tended to follow the same ancient paths in order to serve already existing communities located on or at the terminals of these routes. The general location and character of our internal waterways has been described in Chapter 5. Inland waterways are even more limited geographically than are land routes. Vessels can go only where there is enough water to float them. This completely excludes large areas of the country. River traffic must follow the often meandering courses of streams. Coastal, lake, and river navigation often is limited by the existence of promontories, shoals, dangerous rocks, adverse currents, and other natural obstacles as well as by the absence of suitable harbors.

Many natural hindrances to navigation have been overcome, of course, by man-made canals, locks, and breakwaters, or by dredging, lighthouses, and similar aids. But these devices, like tunnels through mountains or bridges over streams, are expensive. As in land transportation route construction, what is possible from an engineering viewpoint often is not economically feasible.

Geographical factors other than natural obstacles also influence the location of all types of transportation routes. Some persons may have a desire for travel as such, but merchandise has no such desire. Long-distance transportation of goods grows principally out of trade between unlike regions, that is, surpluses of one region are exchanged for surpluses of another.

Geographical specialization or division of labor, which exists in every nonprimitive economic society of any significant geographic size, is just as productive and just as essential as is personal specialization. Much of this regional specialization is based directly upon geographical factors such as climate, soils, or the location of particular kinds of natural resources (fuels, ores, timber, water, etc.). Some patterns of specialization, of course, may be attributed to historical accident or to a long evolutionary development from some now-forgotten first cause. Regardless of the original first cause, however, geography does at least set limits or boundaries around the kinds of production in which a given region may engage, that is, geography exercises a veto power.

Without infringing too deeply into the subject matter of economic geography (which is another must for the well-informed transportation man), it is necessary that we point out that a definite pattern of regional specialization exists in the United States. Softwood lumber and other forest products, for example, come from the Pacific Northwest and the Southeast. Coal comes largely from the Appalachian districts; citrus fruits from California, the Southwest, and Florida; iron ore from the Mesabi Range; corn from the Midwest; wheat from the Plains states; and cotton from the Southeast, Southwest, and California. This illustrative list of geographically influenced or determined products could be greatly extended, of course.

Some type of manufacturing activity occurs in every metropolitan area. In this country, however, the region specializing most in manufacturing is the

Northeast—roughly that area east of the Mississippi and north of the Ohio rivers. Geographical factors and historical evolution have given that region comparative advantages in many types of manufacturing which competing regions apparently have not yet been able to overcome. (Factors influencing the location of various kinds of economic activity will be considered in Chapter 14.)

Many cities also serve as distribution centers for their surrounding countrysides, and ocean-borne foreign imports and exports are channelled mainly through several large seaport cities. Like sand moving through the center of an hourglass, commodities converge into and diverge out from these points. Inbound and outbound transportation routes, like spokes in a wheel, run to and from a common center. Such communities, which perform financial, storage, and other transport-accessory services, as well as the transshipment function, have a transportation role relatively much greater than the primary production and consumption roles of their populations. Usually some geographical advantage of location, present or past, accounts for the importance of such centers to transportation. Sometimes, however, artificial economic or political favoritism, such as unusually low freight rates or favorable transit privileges, is responsible.

There is considerable interaction, of course, between existing transportation routes and the development of centers of population and economic activity. Nature apparently abhors a transportation vacuum as much as any other kind. It seems to be a principle of transportation that the creation of new routes, or the development of new types of facilities, or the expansion of existing facilities generally leads to a demand for their use. That is, supply precedes demand, and service demands tend to expand to fill service capacity—a kind of Parkinson's Law of utilization or a Say's Law of markets (which incidentally, if accepted, might have significant implications for so-called underdeveloped countries or regions).

This principle of transport supply-pull development was demonstrated very clearly in the settlement of the American West after the building of western railways. Rail lines wandering across trackless wastes between nonexistent terminals soon attracted people, economic activities, and traffic. Numerous other historical and contemporary examples of this kind might be cited for all forms of transportation in this country and abroad.

After people, economic activity, and traffic agglomerate at various points on a transportation route, the mass tends to grow by its own internal activities and by attracting other people and activities. Eventually, economic activity at these points of agglomeration becomes so important to the route or to the transportation organizations operating over the route that it becomes economically impractical to abandon or substantially relocate the route. Likewise in laying out new routes today, the presence of now-thriving communities on the old routes cannot be ignored—they must be served even if this means costly circuity and higher construction and operating costs. Thus, the dead hand of past mistakes tends to perpetuate its rule over many present-day transportation routes.

Practicing transportation and traffic personnel naturally are more concerned with existing routes than with the location of new routes. A detailed knowledge of what routes are available, what carriers operate over these routes, what time schedules and rates are in effect over various alternate routes, and where interchanges between carriers can be made are among the indispensable tools of the traffic executive. Such knowledge is acquired only by long study and practice. Practical routing of shipments can be an extremely technical and complex affair. Not every existing natural route can be used without penalties of time or money. Obviously, a detailed discussion of these matters is beyond our present scope. It is possible, however, to make some general concluding statements within the framework of our present consideration of routes.

As a generalization, it is correct to say that the main long-distance routes of all our forms of transportation, and especially rail, highway, and air transport, tend to connect the same principal population centers and producing areas over the same major paths. This generalization holds for water transportation where it is available and (perhaps to a slightly lesser extent, because of its one-way movement) for pipeline transport. The routes of other modern carriers tend to follow roughly those laid down by the railroads as the railroads are the oldest of our modern forms of carriage. Remember, however, that the rails themselves generally followed older pathways.

It is generally true, also, that interregional routes east of the Mississippi River tend to run in a north-south direction, while those west of the Mississippi are mainly east-west routes. In addition to numerous strictly local (intraregional) exceptions to this generalization, there are a few major exceptions. These are found mainly on the Pacific Coast and in the Gulf area, and between the Great Lakes and North Atlantic seaboard cities.

Figure 1 pictures the principal long-distance land transportation routes of the United States. (These routes, of course, are general paths of transportation rather than the specific routes of individual carriers or highways.) As indicated above, air, water, and pipeline routes show a considerable tendency to conform to the prevailing basic rail-highway pattern. Comparison of this figure with a relief map of the United States showing mountains and mountain passes, rivers, valleys, and plains will greatly aid one in understanding why these routes are located as they are. Further comparison with a map showing population centers and densities and the kinds of commodities produced in various regions will complete the explanation. Although not consistently or centrally planned by some omnipotent governmental agency, the pattern is a logical one. Generally it has met, and continues to meet, our country's economic needs.

Ten major interregional routes are shown on Figure 1. An Atlantic Seaboard route parallels the East Coast, east of the Appalachians, connecting the Southeast with the North Atlantic area. An Interior Southeastern route, con-

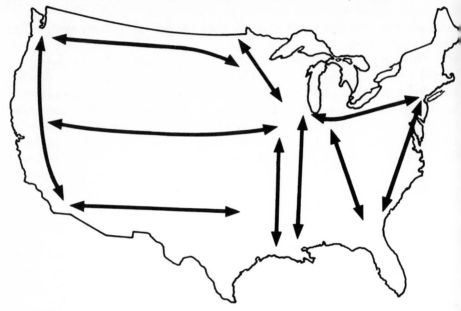

Figure 1: Principal Land Transportation Routes of the United States.

necting the Southeast with the Great Lakes, runs between the western side of the Appalachians and the valley of the Mississippi. A Mississippi Valley route parallels that river on the east, while a South Plains-Gulf route is found on the west. The Northeastern route joins the Great Lakes with the North Atlantic seaboard, while the North Plains-Great Lakes route runs somewhat northwest-southeast to connect those two areas.

Moving west, we find a Northern Transcontinental, a Central Transcontinental, and a Southern Transcontinental route. A substantial branch of the Central Transcontinental route, not shown, also runs into the Pacific Northwest, while an offshoot of the Southern Transcontinental route goes to the Gulf. Finally, we find the north-south Pacific Coast route connecting California and the Pacific Northwest.

We must re-emphasize the fact that Figure 1 shows only a composite skeleton of our system of transportation routes. Figures 2 through 7, covering railways, highways, waterways, airways, and pipelines, put meat on the individual bones. Even these figures, however, cannot show all existing routes in detail.

Even a cursory glance at Figure 1, or at the more detailed maps of our transportation network, shows that most of the important routes run from and to the Northeastern section of our country. This is no coincidence. Why it is so will be explained in the following section.

Figure 2: The Railroad Network of the United States.
Courtesy: Association of American Railroads.

COMMODITY MOVEMENTS

A principal environmental fact in the United States is that most people live in the Northeastern section of the country. Population density per square mile in that section is about two-and-one-half times as great as in the Southeast and some six or seven times as great as in the West. (There are smaller and scattered areas of dense population concentrations in both the latter sections, of course.)

Necessarily, most consumption occurs where most people are. Likewise, since people make up the labor supply, most intensive forms of economic activity (manufacturing) also must take place in areas of concentrated population. Even if they wished to do so, inhabitants of a densely populated area could not engage in extensive forms of activity such as large-scale agriculture, cattle grazing, or timber growing. They do not have the necessary *space* resource, even if terrain, soil, and climatic conditions are otherwise suitable.

Aside from the factors of historic accident and evolution, then, this means that the densely populated Northeastern portion of our country must be a manufacturing center. This region does have, of course, other locational advantages such as the proximity of coal and iron ore, good local transportation facilities, and a favorable location for access to European markets. Also, due to population density, it has a substantial home (intraregional) consumer market for its products.

The Southeast and West, on the other hand, are well suited for extensive forms of production. In addition to the necessary conditions of terrain, soil, and climate, they have space in considerable abundance. And, generally speaking, they do not have the Northeast's favorable conditions of labor supply, built-in home markets, and other desirable locational advantages. Their manufacturing activity is handicapped also by late arrival. Thus, the economic destiny of these two areas has been and is likely to be for some time related to the production of foodstuffs and raw materials.

This economic environment forms the base for our long-distance commodity flow. As noted earlier, long-distance trade and its accompanying transportation is based upon the exchange of surpluses between unlike regions. This means that the predominant long-distance traffic movement in this country is a flow of foodstuffs and raw materials (including crude manufactures or semiprocessed items) from the West and the Southeast to the Northeast, and a backflow of manufactured or highly processed goods from the Northeast to the Southeast and West. In effect, the latter two areas are economic colonies of the Northeast in the same sense that the original American settlements were economic colonies of England, or that pre-Civil War United States was an economic colony of Europe.

There are exceptions to this general picture, of course. Some foodstuffs are shipped out of the Northeast and some manufactured goods out of the West and Southeast. Also, there are significant areas of concentrated population, consumption, and manufacturing (which might be described as a pattern of subcolonization) within the colonial areas themselves. For example, the state of Oregon has been called an economic colony of California and Washington, and both of these Pacific Northwest states have been called economic colonies of California.

The word "colony" has acquired unpleasant moral and political connotations during recent years. It should be emphasized that the economic colonial pattern described above is not intended to carry such connotations. It may be bad or good, depending upon one's individual viewpoint. But actually it is nothing more than a logical geographical division of labor or specialization. Each of the described regions, like separate nations in foreign trade, have comparative or absolute advantages in certain types of production. Under our free-enterprise system, it must be assumed that each region, like each individual, tends to engage in the kind of economic activity most profitable to it. Someone must grow trees, tomatoes, and tulips, just as someone must manufacture automobiles, anvils, and altimeters.

Such a pattern of interregional trade and transportation does create problems, however. Raw materials generally are heavier and bulkier than the manufactured items made from them, and consumed foodstuffs are completely removed from the stream of transportation. As the Northeast exchanges lighter manufactured goods for the heavier raw materials and foodstuffs of the West and Southeast, outbound freight tonnages of the latter regions are considerably in excess of inbound tonnages. Railroad cars and other freight vehicles which go to the Northeast fully loaded must return empty or only partially loaded to the West and Southeast.

An unbalanced freight movement creates problems for the management of transportation firms which naturally wish to operate with as little excess capacity as possible. It costs almost as much to move an empty vehicle, which brings in no revenue, as to move a fully loaded one. Such a situation does not encourage the enlargement of vehicle capacity. It also tends to shift vehicles into geographic areas where they will be more fully utilized both inbound and outbound.

These factors contribute to an almost chronic shortage of vehicle capacity, especially of the most desirable kinds of rail cars, during periods of peak seasonal demand for transportation. Unfortunately, many kinds of products tend to peak at the same time: lumber and plywood, wheat, tree fruits, and various kinds of fresh vegetables, for example. Often, during periods of shortages, rail cars must be allocated between various competing regions by the Association of American Railroads or even by the Interstate Commerce Commission.

In addition, as will be seen in Part Four, unbalanced freight movements tend to become reflected in the overall interregional freight rate structure, and actually may contribute to a continuation of the imbalance.

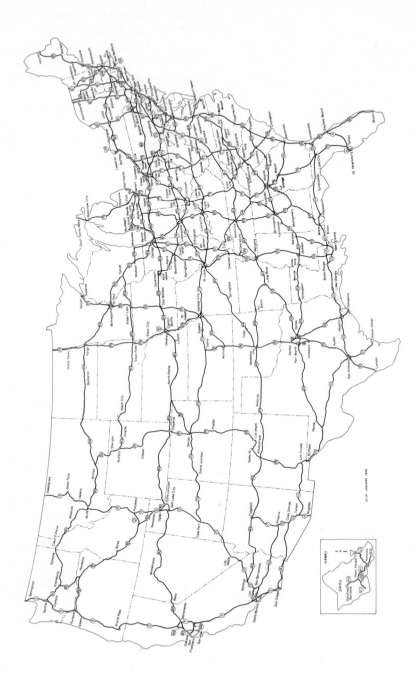

Figure 3: The National System of Interstate and Defense Highways.

Courtesy: United States Bureau of Public Roads.

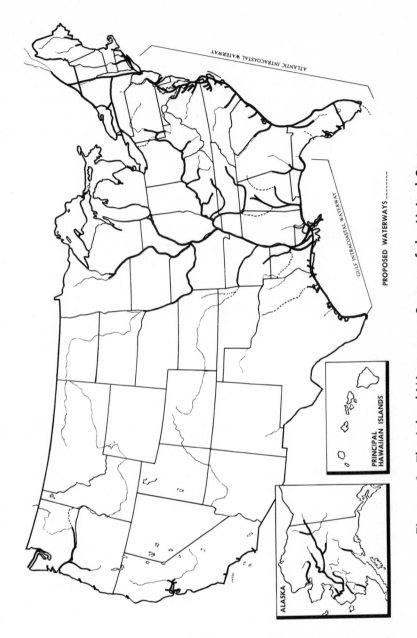

Figure 4: The Inland Waterways System of the United States.
Courtesy: American Waterways Operators, Inc.

Although we do have a definite pattern of broad regional specialization in this country, with direct or interconnecting transportation routes between these large regions, we must not forget that these broad regions themselves are made up of many little regions or subregional groups specializing in various types of production.

For example, different regions in the agricultural Southeast produce cotton, citrus fruits, and tobacco, and different parts of the agricultural West specialize in growing range cattle, apples, and melons. Likewise, various areas of the manufacturing Northeast specialize in automobiles, steel, and electronic devices. Also, as already noted, manufacturing areas do produce raw materials (coal in the Northeast, for example) and agricultural commodities, while raw materials or agricultural areas do engage in manufacturing activities of various kinds.

Actually, most transportation (even excluding that which may be classed as strictly local in nature) occurs as the result of exchanges between the specialized little regions within the larger regions which we have been considering. Commodity-flow statistics for almost any one of our individual states, for example, will show that most of its out-of-state traffic comes from and goes to adjoining or nearby states, and that transportation within the state accounts for considerably more tonnage that its interstate volume. As indicated in Chapter 4, the average length of haul per shipment by railway, our basic form of long-haul transportation, is only around 495 miles. The average haul by Class I intercity truck common carriers, you will also recall, is about 260 miles, and the average of all truck trips is about 11 miles.

The transportation of almost any commodity tends to decrease with distance (or, more accurately, with shipping costs or freight-rate charges which usually are in some way related to the distance moved). High transportation costs or charges cause distant consumers to search for usable substitute products or to engage in perhaps less efficient local production. A domestic freight charge in this respect has an economic effect similar to a protective tariff in international trade. Many essential or highly desired products without close substitutes do move in considerable quantities for long distances, of course. But even these commodities usually are aided in their movement by some kind of favorable freight-rate structure, and they usually are more heavily consumed in and near their producing area than in far-distant markets.

A comparatively small number of commodities account for most of the tonnage (and ton-miles) in long-distance transportation. This is more true for raw than for finished products, as one might imagine, but it is true even for manufactured goods. The annual railroad waybill-statistics publications of the Interstate Commerce Commission (based on a one per cent sample of all railway movements) dramatically illustrate this.

During a recent year, out of the 260 classifications into which the I.C.C. groups all commodities moving by rail, 17 classifications (a little more than six per cent of the total) accounted for about 70 per cent of all railroad tonnage originated.

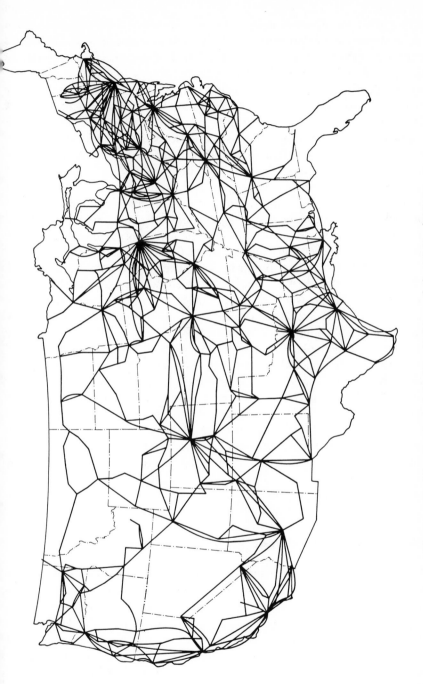

Figure 5: The Regional Airline Routes of the United States.
Courtesy: Air Transport Association of America.

During that particular year, out of 54 agricultural product classifications, the leading five (wheat, corn, flour, soybeans, and sugar beets) accounted for more than 57 per cent of all originating railroad agricultural tonnage. Three mines products (coal and coke; sand, gravel, and stone; and iron ore) out of 24 classifications contributed 93 per cent of the mines tonnage. Among ten forest-products classification, three items (pulpwood; lumber, shingles, and lath; and logs, butts and bolts) were responsible for 83 per cent of the total volume. Fresh meats and cattle and calves made up 44 per cent of the tonnage of 24 animal and animal-product classifications. Manufactured and miscellaneous products were represented by 147 classifications out of which four (manufactured iron and steel; cement; scrap iron and scrap steel; and animal and poultry feed) accounted for 28 per cent of the tonnage.

In the same year, incidentally, the total rail tonnage contributions of each of the five major commodity groups mentioned above was divided approximately as follows: products of mines, 54 per cent; manufactured and miscellaneous, 28 per cent; agricultural products, 9 per cent; forest products, 6 per cent; animals and animal products, 1 per cent. (The total does not add up to 100 per cent due to rounding.) The ten leading products shipped in order of tonnage volume were: coal and coke; sand, gravel, and stone; iron ore; manufactured iron and steel; cement; pulpwood; wheat; scrap iron and scrap steel; lumber, shingles, and lath; and corn.

As indicated in Chapter 5, a high degree of product concentration exists in water carriage. Coal, petroleum products, and sand and gravel account for more than three fourths of the tonnage moved by water in the Mississippi River system, while Great Lakes steamers specialize heavily in the carriage of mines products and grain. Pipeline traffic, of course, is the most specialized of all forms. Available statistics indicate that commodity concentration is not as pronounced in truck transportation as among these other major forms, but information on the actual composition of truck tonnage is somewhat scarce and unreliable. Air cargo, as you know, is only a statistically minute portion of the nation's overall freight tonnage.

CHANGES IN INTERREGIONAL RELATIONSHIPS

The output-mix, or specialization, of all regions and subregions varies constantly over time, of course. This variation usually is gradual in nature; but over a period of several years, it may have considerable cumulative effects upon interregional and intraregional commodity-flow patterns and upon the utilization of competing modes of carriage.

It is "common knowledge" that the Northeastern portion of the United States has been declining in relative importance as a manufacturing center as industrialization has increased in the outlying colonial-type areas, for example. Table 6 shows how this trend affected the comparative railroad origi-

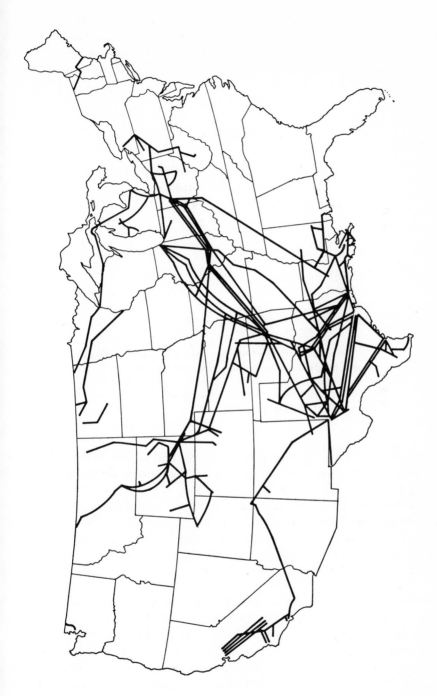

Figure 6: The Crude Oil Pipeline System of the United States.

nation of manufactured goods in various sections of the country over a 24-year period. (It is possible, of course, that other factors, such as a relatively greater increase in the use of nonrail forms of carriage for Northeastern manufactured products, may have been partly responsible for the percentage changes shown in this table.)

Table 6

Approximate Percentage of Railroad Freight Tonnage of Manufactured and Miscellaneous Products Originated in Various Regions, 1940 and 1964

Region	1940	1964
Northeast	65	39
Southeast	9	15
Plains	18	24
Rocky Mountain-Pacific Coast	8	22

Source: Calculated from Interstate Commerce Commission, *Tons of Revenue Freight Originated and Tons Terminated in Carloads by Classes of Commodities and by Geographic Areas, 1940;* and *Carload Waybill Statistics: Tons of Revenue Freight Originated and Tons Terminated by States and by Commodity Class, 1964.*

As industrialization develops in an agricultural or raw-materials-producing region, at least during the earlier stages of the process, the region's relative demand for long-haul transport is likely to decrease. The initial stages of industrialization will be based largely upon the manufacture or processing of locally produced raw materials. This has a double-barreled effect upon long-haul transportation. Not as much tonnage is sent to distant regions for manufacture, and not as much manufactured-goods tonnage is required from distant regions for local consumption. In other words, intraregional or short-haul transportation (for which trucks are well fitted) increases at the expense of interregional or long-haul transportation (in which railroads dominate).

It is not likely that all of the new manufactured goods resulting from a region's developing industrialization will be consumed locally, however. Thus, such a region's demand for long-haul outbound transportation will not decline in direct proportion to its increased industrialization. Also, increased manufacturing activity, even though based primarily upon the utilization of locally produced raw materials, may require various kinds of subsidiary raw materials from outside areas.

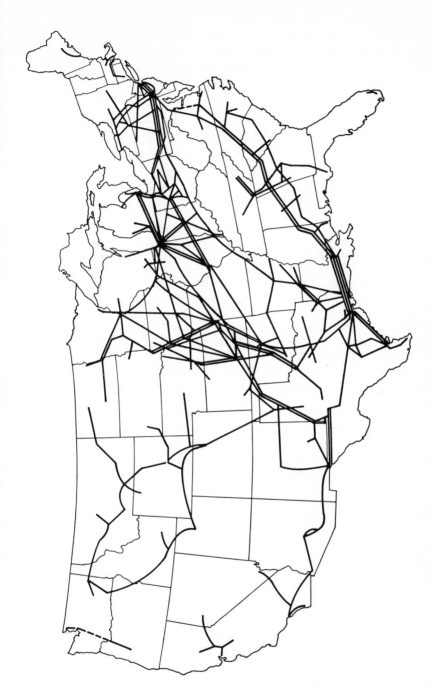

Figure 7: The Product Oil Pipeline System of the United States.

After a region reaches a high level of industrialization, of course, its local raw materials may no longer be sufficient to support its manufacturing activity, and its foodstuff production may be inadequate for the needs of its population. Then its dependence upon long-haul interregional transportation again increases. As will be explained in Part Four, these various stages in regional industrial development, from the economic viewpoint of the individual region, may be greatly facilitated or hampered by the kind of interregional freight-rate structures in effect and may lead to regional producer pressures for modifications of existing rate structures.

ADDITIONAL READINGS

1. Becht, J. Edwin, **A Geography of Transportation and Business Logistics.** Dubuque, Iowa: Wm. C. Brown Company, 1970.
   Chapter 1. "Introduction to Transportation Patterns," pp. 1–5.
   Chapter 2. "The Relative Decline in the Importance of Terrain and Climate in Shaping Transportation Patterns," pp. 6–16.
2. Dagget, Stuart, **Principles of Inland Transportation,** 4th ed. New York: Harper and Brothers, 1955.
   Part III. "Transportation Geography," pp. 127–226.
3. Gilmore, Harlan W., **Transportation and the Growth of Cities.** Glencoe, Ill.: Free Press of Glencoe, Inc., 1953.
   Chapter V. "Transportation Systems and Types of Communities," pp. 86–102.
4. Hay, William W., **Introduction to Transportation Engineering.** New York: John Wiley & Sons Inc., 1961.
   Chapter 15. "Route Design and Location," pp. 432–454.
5. Pegrum, Dudley F., **Transportation: Economics and Public Policy.** Rev. ed. Homewood, Ill.: Richard D. Irwin, Inc., 1968.
   Chapter 4. "Transport Geography." pp. 77–103.
6. Sampson, Roy J., "Another View of Comparative Regional Development," **Land Economics,** May 1960, pp. 216–220.
7. Sampson, Roy J., **Railroad Shipments and Rates From the Pacific Northwest.** Eugene, Oregon: Bureau of Business Research, University of Oregon, 1961.
   Part Two. "Principal Rail Export Commodities and Their Destinations," pp. 5–32.
8. Sampson, Roy J., **Railroad Shipments and Rates Into the Pacific Northwest.** Eugene, Oregon: Bureau of Business Research, University of Oregon, 1963.
   Part Two. "Principal Inbound Movements," pp. 6–19.
   Part Three. "Sources and Rates for Inbound Shipments," pp. 20–37.
9. Ullman, Edward L., **American Commodity Flow.** Seattle, Wash.: Washington University Press, 1957.
   Chapter I. "American Internal Commodity Flow: Rail and Water Traffic," pp. 1–12.
   Chapter IV. "State-to-State Rail Freight Movements," pp. 28–169.

Part Three

Carrier Services in Domestic Transportation

In addition to the line-haul services, which are discussed in various parts of this book, there are other elements in the transportation bundle of services. This part is concerned with these services.

Some transportation services are legally required of the carrier and must be fulfilled under the law. Thus, the common carrier has four required duties: to serve, to deliver, to charge reasonable rates, and to avoid discrimination. Some services, on the other hand, are voluntary on the part of the carrier. While the carrier is not obligated by law to offer or to perform these voluntary services, once they are offered the carrier becomes subject to rule-making and various regulatory requirements. Numerous terminal and accessorial transportation services are found in this group.

Line-haul services, terminal services, and optional or accessorial services offered by carriers involve a single shipper and carrier. A third group of carrier services involves the shipper and more than one carrier cooperating or coordinating with other carriers. Cooperative and coordinated carrier services present many combinations of carriers to shippers; some of these services may be legally required, while others are not. Some, such as joint routes and through rates, may be legally required of one type of carrier (particularly railroads) and not of other carriers. Many cooperative and coordinated services, such as piggyback, are completely voluntary. However, just as with terminal and optional or accessorial services, once offered these voluntary services become subject to rule-making and other requirements of regulatory authorities.

In this part we will discuss the legal framework and basis within which carrier services are offered, thus making the reader better acquainted with carrier services in general. It is not our object to provide a complete description of all carrier services, but to discuss the type of service carriers are engaged in supplying to their customers.

Finally, it should be noted that this part is concerned almost wholly with for-hire transportation, and that it places emphasis on common-carrier service. Private transportation is a very important ingredient of the domestic transportation system; but as it is administered by shippers, it will be considered in Part Seven.

7

Legal Service
Obligations

The provision of carrier transportation services has always been highly important to the social and economic welfare of every nation. Because of its pivotal nature in economic growth and development, transportation is carried on under special circumstances or rules. While more will be said about the regulation of domestic transportation in Parts Five and Six, the object here is to discuss the basic legal framework under which carrier transportation services are rendered. In subsequent chapters of this part, we will discuss other elements of the framework of carrier services.

OBLIGATIONS IN COMMON CARRIAGE

The common carrier is a special type of business undertaking found in transportation and a few other areas of business in our economy. Special legal obligations have been placed upon these businesses by society because of the extraordinary dependence of society and its need for their services. These special obligations may be considered as both duties and rights. Basically, a common carrier has four duties which it must fulfill: the duty to serve, the duty to deliver, the duty to charge reasonable rates, and the duty to avoid discrimination.

To assure that these obligations are met, society may impose regulations or restrictions on those undertaking this necessary service. Society also imposes duties or obligations on the users of the service; in this case, the shippers. Hence, the duty to pay for the movement in a prompt and complete fashion is imposed upon the shipper. (Shippers may be relieved of their basic obligation to pay if (1) they sign the "without recourse" clause of a Bill of Lading or (2) carriers deliver without collecting charges due or contrary to the shipper's order.)

Likewise, society in its regulation of these special types of businesses imposes a duty upon itself to see that the common carrier is not legally prevented from earning enough revenue to carry on its business. This is the very knotty problem of rate-level regulation and the reasonable rate of return allowed so as to obey the fifth and fourteenth amendments of our Constitution, commonly called the "due process" provisions. This problem of social regulation of earnings will be discussed in some detail in Parts Four and Five. Here we are concerned principally with the duties imposed upon the common carrier.

ORIGIN OF CARRIER OBLIGATIONS

The duties or obligations of common carriers come out of common-law doctrine handed down through the ages, although most of them now have been embodied in statutory law.

Our common-law tradition comes directly from our English heritage. This type of social rule-making apparently originated in northern European or Germanic tribes. Basically, it was tribal law evolved by groups or councils who determined what was acceptable social behavior. This contrasts with the Mediterranean or codified law of southern Europe, where the lawgiver, the sovereign, a great scholar, or deity set down a code or written law, a rule of behavior. Examples of codified law are the Ten Commandments, the Code of Hammurabi, the Code of Justinian, or the Napoleonic Code.

Common law is passed on by tradition and by the law of precedents. Courts (using a jury of peers, again out of the tribal council idea) interpret the law in its application to the particular question at issue. One does not consult a statute book to read common law. Rather, one looks at past decisions to see if the present situation is analogous enough to apply a previously used remedy. Obviously, changing conditions and ideas gradually introduce new concepts and interpretations in common law. Thus common law developed as time passed and as problems arose for consideration by courts.

As already noted, many common-law concepts were in time written into statutes or law codes by legislative bodies. Hence, many of the obligations or duties of transportation firms are embodied in the laws of the various states, the basis of sovereign power under our governmental system. This is, however, a fairly recent phenomenon.

Since by its very nature common law is an evolving thing, the exact genesis of the obligations of common carriers is not known. We do know, however, that during the late 1300's courts in England were imposing obligations on carriers similar to the four common-law duties discussed here. Liability obligations commonly found written in contracts are even older, and evidence exists that common carriers were liable for the goods they carried in the ancient world.

The word "common" can be literally translated to mean "public" in the sense of being available to all. By 1670, the noted jurist Lord Hale discussed the distinguishing feature between "public" or "common callings" and private business affairs. At that time he declared that "common callings" had customarily been regulated by the sovereign since "time immemorial." Businesses "affected with the public interest," therefore, had to expect regulation. This doctrine was later used to justify statutory regulation of business by the States (*Munn v. Illinois*, 94 US 113, 1877). The place of the common law in regulation of transportation, its shortcomings, and its application in statute law will be discussed in Chapter 16. For our present purposes, it is sufficient to note that the common law imposes the four duties of service, delivery, reasonableness, and nondiscrimination on common carriers.

THE DUTY OF SERVICE

One of the oldest of the common-carrier obligations is the duty to serve all comers. It is on the basis of this obligation that the carrier is "common" or "public." One making a general offer to the public as being willing to perform certain kinds of carrier services must actually perform these services upon reasonable demand.

Qualifications of the Duty to Serve

Ordinarily a carrier desires to serve all customers, since it is in the business of transportation. However, extraordinary circumstances may arise when its duty to serve must be qualified. It does have the right, within limits, to refuse service.

A carrier, for example, is obligated to serve only its own public. This qualification extends to kinds of goods and kinds of persons. A motor common carrier of sand cannot be forced to haul petroleum. A court has held that a railroad may refuse to take dogs as baggage. In another case, a court held that a railroad need not install scales which would serve the public in weighing goods but which are not essential to the railroad business. Likewise, a carrier of passengers holds itself out to serve only the traveling public and cannot be forced to carry newsboys or similar vendors on its trains. In the absence of published tariffs including a particular commodity, a carrier cannot be made to install special equipment to handle a specific type of goods. Also, a carrier of freight does not have to carry passengers.

The offer of the shipper must be reasonable as to time and condition. Shipments may be picked up only during ordinary business hours. The duty to serve does not force carriers to accept shipments at all hours. Likewise, a shipper must present his goods at the proper place and cannot expect the carrier to extend his published pickup-and-delivery area to unusual distances or for unusual weights. Of course, if the carrier's pickup-and-delivery tariff provides for special areas or weights, the carrier has included this in its public offering and must serve accordingly. Also, a carrier may not be forced to accept a shipment it cannot deliver either because of unusual conditions or because it does not or cannot serve the delivery point. The "public" of a motor carrier cannot extend, for example, to points which the carrier is not certificated to serve. Additionally, a carrier is allowed to require reasonable notice of intended shipment.

Finally, obligation to serve is qualified by certain circumstances. A carrier may refuse to haul dangerous commodities or objectionable persons. Poorly packed dynamite need not be carried nor deceased persons if the carrier wishes to refuse. Indeed, a carrier may always refuse to service poorly packed shipments since it is liable for loss or damage of freight during shipment. Offensive or objectionable persons may be refused, as may goods which might impregnate or contaminate other goods. Nor can a carrier be forced to carry items of extreme value, such as diamonds, money, or valuable papers, which expose it to unusually large liabilities for loss.

Adequacy of Service

In addition to the duty to serve all comers within its ability, a common carrier must supply adequate facilities and services. Adequacy has been interpreted to mean that facilities must be available for normal or usual demands; facilities must be in reasonably good condition for the type of traffic; and the service must be performed with reasonable dispatch.

As to normal demands, a carrier cannot be forced to provide for infrequent peak shipments. Wherever such conditions prevail, as in seasonal shipments of some agricultural goods, the carrier must distribute its facilities fairly among its customers. Reasonably good condition means that vehicles, ways, and equipment must be adequate for the type of service offered. For instance, vehicles used to haul livestock are not adequate to haul food in the absence of thorough cleaning or modification. Cars to haul grain are not adequate if their state of repair is such that they leak. The matter of reasonable dispatch will be considered below under the duty to deliver.

A carrier may be forced to do whatever is necessary to fulfill the need for adequate service, yet it cannot be forced into a new line of business or into a new geographic area not previously served. The carrier's duties are limited by its established routes and its certificate to serve. However, once the carrier has entered into an area or line of business voluntarily, it may not abandon or withdraw its service without permission from the appropriate regulatory authorities.

Withdrawal of Service

Common law holds that a rail carrier has accepted a franchise or charter from the sovereign and enjoyed the privileges thereof. Hence, withdrawal of services can come only on permission of the sovereign or his representative. Statutory law has placed control over interstate rail abandonments or withdrawal of service generally in the hands of the Interstate Commerce Commission. In the case of motor carriers, however, federal regulatory authorities have no control over abandonment or withdrawal of service.

A rail carrier cannot withdraw from a segment or part of its service solely because it is unprofitable to serve that segment. If profit is made on a part or on the service as a whole even though a portion is unprofitable, the unprofitable portion may not be abandoned. Regulatory authorities may impose various conditions during a trial period and force the carrier to prove not only that the service is unprofitable, but that it has no chance of ever being profitable.

The carrier may, of course, withdraw all its service if the total is unprofitable. It cannot be made to serve indefinitely at a loss due to the fifth and fourteenth amendments of the U.S. Constitution. But even here regulatory authorities will require that it is clearly established that the whole service is unprofitable, and the permission of the representative of the sovereign is required. Reference to the statistics on the total rail network in Chapter 2 shows that withdrawal and abandonment has been permitted.

These limitations on abandonment or withdrawal have been highly important in recent times in the rail passenger-transportation business. Until the Transportation Act of 1958, many abandonments were controlled by state regulatory authorities who tended to be very reluctant to permit withdrawals. Subsequent to allowing Interstate Commerce Commission control under specified conditions in the 1958 act, abandonments of rail passenger service greatly accelerated.

THE DUTY OF DELIVERY

It is the duty of a common carrier to deliver the goods entrusted to its care. This duty is a common-law obligation, although it also appears in various forms in statute law. It is commonly referred to as "carrier liability" and is perhaps the oldest of all carrier obligations.

Because of the shipper's absolute dependence upon the carrier to protect his goods, plus the ease with which carriers could consort with robbers or pirates, the common law of carrier liability was very strict. In 1703, Lord Holt, in the famous English case of *Coggs v. Bernard* (2 Ld. Raymond 919), stated the common-law liability of carriers as ". . . he is bound to answer for the goods in all events." The Justice further stated that

> The law charges this person thus intrusted to carry goods, against all events, but Acts of God, and of the enemies of the King. For though the force be ever so great, as if an irresistible multitude of people should rob him, nevertheless he is chargeable. And this is a politic establishment, contrived by the policy of the law, for the safety of all persons, the necessity of whose affairs oblige them to trust these sorts of persons, that they may be safe in their ways of dealing; for else these carriers might have an opportunity of undoing all persons that

had any dealings with them, by combining with thieves, etc., and yet doing it in such clandestine manner as would not be possible to be discovered. And this is the reason the law is founded upon in that point.

The general obligation of the land common carrier, then, is to deliver goods in the same condition as they were received, with reasonable dispatch, and to the right party. Different liabilities apply to ocean carriers, which are excluded from the scope of this discussion. Air-carrier liability still is evolving, with some similarities and some differences from that of land carriers.

Limitations of Liability

As noted above, the common law originally held the carrier absolutely responsible except in the case of Acts of God or Acts of the enemies of the King. Statutory law over time has added four other limitations, namely, Acts of Public Authority, Acts of the Shipper, Inherent nature or Vice of the Goods, and a highly qualified Acts of Riots or Strikes.

Acts of God refer to some extraordinary and unavoidable events, such as flooding, lightning, tornado, or extreme ice and snow. Bad weather which might reasonably be expected to occur from time to time is not an Act of God. Acts of the King's enemy (or the public enemy) refer to organized foreign or public enemies and is important principally in wartime. Acts of Public Authority concern seizure of goods by legal process or by quarantines laid by public officials. The carrier's liability is limited by Acts of the Shipper when goods are not properly marked or are not packed or loaded according to accepted regulations or standards. Shipper acts which mislead the carrier, such as failure to declare extraordinary values of the goods, cannot be used to force liability onto a carrier.

Inherent nature or Vice of the Goods refers to such things as livestock injuring one another, molasses fermenting while in transit, or goods which damage other goods, assuming the carrier is not negligent. The uniform bill of lading exempts the carrier from liability for loss, damage, or delay due to riots or strikes unless the carrier is negligent. The meaning of negligence, particularly when labor disputes are involved, is hard to define. It should be obvious that the exact definition and application of all these legal terms is a study in itself and far beyond the scope of an introductory textbook. Everyone concerned with transportation, though, should have some familiarity with these matters.

None of the above limitations of liability apply if the carrier is guilty of contributory negligence or lack of due diligence. The burden of proof is on the carrier. It must show that it was not negligent and that due diligence was exercised. The carrier cannot contract out of negligence.

A carrier is expected to deliver with reasonable promptness. What is reasonably prompt varies with circumstances, but a carrier cannot be charged with loss due to delay unless the delay is unusually long and unreasonable. Carriers may voluntarily bind themselves to meet a time limit and pay special damages in case of default of that part of their contract. This is done for a consideration, of course, but some shippers feel that delivery under a time limit is worth the extra charges, particularly where highly perishable goods are involved.

A carrier may, on occasion, attempt to overcome some of the statute limitations of liability by special contract and considerations. Thus, a released value agreement and rate may be in effect. Here the carrier agrees to carry the goods at a lower rate if the shipper agrees to release it from liability above a stated value. Such rates are in effect generally on household goods and baggage. The shipper may, of course, pay the regular rate and force the carrier to assume full liability. However, it is often worthwhile for the shipper to use the released value rate and buy insurance to cover losses for which the carrier is not responsible.

Generally, the amount a shipper can recover in case of loss or damage is the value of the goods to the owner at destination at the time the shipment should have arrived. There are many variations of this, of course, and many ways of determining this value. Again this indicates the specialized legal nature of the subject of liability.

Duration of Carrier Liability

The carrier's liability commences upon delivery of the goods to it, that is, when the shipper has nothing more to do with the shipment. Many problems arise concerning when the carrier becomes liable and assumes the obligation to deliver. In carload and truckload shipments, this generally is when the motive power is attached. In LCL and LTL shipments, liability is assumed when the shipment is loaded on the vehicle. The presence or lack of presence of an agent of the carrier may be of importance here.

Carrier liability ends upon delivery to the correct consignee. However, there are various rules or regulations on this. Generally, the liability to deliver as a common carrier ceases when reasonable notice has been given to the consignee of the arrival of the shipment. (Reasonable notice usually is interpreted to mean 48 hours in rail transportation and seven days in motor transportation.) After these times, the carrier's liability as a common carrier ceases and his liability becomes that of a warehouseman only. Liability as a warehouseman is limited to acts of negligence, which means the responsibility for ordinary care only.

It should be stressed that the duty to deliver is not a matter of commission regulation; but it is a matter of common and statutory law, and statutes may vary somewhat between states. Liability matters are settled according to court decisions and not before regulatory bodies.

THE DUTY OF REASONABLE RATES

A common carrier must charge reasonable rates. Originally this duty or obligation arose because the carrier was in the position of being able to exploit he use of his service. Common callings, under English common law, included various types of persons and business undertakings such as wharfingers, ferrymen, innkeepers and victualers, millers, blacksmiths, tailors, bakers, brewers, and of course, draymen, teamsters and common carriers. Because entry into these undertakings was limited and controlled either by guilds or the government, customers often had very limited choice and the possibility of exploitation existed. Therefore, the sovereign and the courts imposed the duty of charging only "reasonable" prices for these services. In effect, this meant maximum rate control, although the definition of what was reasonable probably was as difficult hen as it is now.

Recently the idea of reasonable rates has taken on a new connotation. The dea has developed that rates or charges can be too low, thus the problem becomes one of controlling minimum as well as maximum rates and charges. A ate or a price that is unreasonably low basically is one which does not permit he carrier to earn enough revenue to fulfill its obligations to serve. Recognition of this point is included in the shipper's obligation or duty to pay. But the matter is not that simple. A rate on one particular commodity may be unreasonably ow if it causes unduly high rates to be charged on another commodity. Here a matter of comparative rates and discrimination is involved. Again, a rate may be unreasonably low if it is designed to drive competing carriers of the same or different modes out of business. This involves intramodal and intermodal competition.

Federal and state regulatory commissions have been given the authority o determine reasonableness, subject to court review. The evolution and application of this concept and some of its problems will be discussed in greater detail in Parts Four and Five.

THE DUTY OF NONDISCRIMINATION

Another common-law duty of common carriers is the obligation to avoid discrimination. This duty is related to the other three, but it has become more defined and defined in statutory law than have the other duties.

Our society opposes discrimination on at least two grounds: the philosophical-political and the economic. Our philosophy of democracy is based on the ideal of fair play and equal treatment for all. Discrimination implies unequal treatment and, hence, is objectionable from a philosophical viewpoint.

Economically our society is based on the idea of competition and relative price stability. Discrimination may involve capricious pricing and perhaps even changing prices from day to day, as the firm practicing discrimination may prefer a favored few while prejudicing other customers. This is a move away from stable price relationships necessary for competitive economic growth and development as well as away from our ideal of equal opportunity for all.

Discrimination implies a degree of monopoly power. If all firms were perfectly competitive, none could discriminate. Hence, as our society generally disapproves of monopoly, it naturally disapproves of this manifestation of its power.

Definition of Discrimination

Discrimination, defined in simplest terms, is different treatment under similar circumstances or similar treatment under different circumstances. In transportation, discrimination usually takes two forms, service discrimination or rate (price) discrimination. Thus our preliminary definition could be amended to read: "Discrimination is different service or rates under similar circumstances, or similar service or rates under different circumstances."

The common-law definition of discrimination is quite vague and is stated in general terms only. It is necessary, then, as a practical matter, to look to statutory law for an explicit prohibition against various types of discrimination. In these prohibitions, discrimination in transportation is well defined. For example, Section 2 of the 1887 Act to Regulate Commerce (Interstate Commerce Act) states in part:

> . . . if any common carrier . . . shall, directly or indirectly, by any special rate, rebate, or drawback, or other device, charge, demand, collect or receive from any person or persons a greater or less compensation for any service rendered . . . in the transportation of persons or property . . . than it charges, demands, collects or receives from any other person or persons for doing for him or them a like and contemporaneous service in the transportation of a like kind of traffic under substantially similar circumstances and conditions, such common carrier shall be deemed guilty of unjust discrimination, which is hereby prohibited and declared to be unlawful.

Section 3 of the same act notes various types of discrimination by stating

> . . . it shall be unlawful for any common carrier . . . to make or give any undue or unreasonable preference or advantage to any particular person, company, firm, corporation, association, locality, port, port district, gateway, transit point, region, district, territory, or any particular description of traffic, in any respect whatsoever, or subject any particular persons . . . (list again repeated) . . . to any undue prejudice or disadvantage in any respect whatsoever.

Types of Discrimination

It is obvious from the above that there are at least four types of discrimination and many subtypes or applications. These are discrimination of persons, organizations, places, and types of traffic. Both service and rate (price) discrimination could exist either in favor of or to the detriment of each.

Persons with similar transportation circumstances and conditions must be treated alike. A carrier cannot provide more service to a particular shipper than it provides to a substantially similar shipper, or vice versa. Organiza tions, whether corporations, associations, or firms, must receive equal service and rates if the transportation situation is similar. One town, district, region, or locality cannot be treated differently from a service or rate viewpoint than a similar locality. And all types of traffic and commodities which are similar from a transportation viewpoint must be given similar treatment as to service and price.

It is simple to state the principles involved, but it is most difficult to define "similar circumstances and conditions" or to give meaning to the terms "advantage," "disadvantage," "preference," and "prejudice." The difficult task of defining these terms and giving meaning to these statutory prohibitions is a never-ending problem of transportation regulatory commissions and the courts. Some of the implications of commission and court interpretations will be considered in the portions of this book dealing with rates and regulations.

Permissible Forms of Discrimination

Discrimination is common in our economy, particularly price discrimination. For an equal service, doctors charge unequal prices; magazine subscriptions are persistently advertised at special rates for new subscribers; price discounts for quantity purchases, whether it is the large economy size or large industrial purchases, are common; electric utilities lower the price per unit of use as more units are used; theater tickets for the same performance typically vary as to location or as to time; in short, different prices for substantially the same thing is a very common phenomenon in our society and, in most cases, this discrimination is widely accepted.

It is apparent, then, that there are two categories of discrimination: that which is legal and acceptable, and that which is not. This is particularly true for price discrimination. What is objectionable and illegal is not price discrimination as such, but "undue" price discrimination. But this raises another problem. Just what is "undue price discrimination"?

In a competitive economy, prices are based substantially on cost. Economists, recognizing this fact, long ago defined undue price discrimination to mean differences in prices not reflecting differences in costs. Hence, if savings can be made and costs reduced by packaging items in the large economy size, the price should be less per unit; if large users of electric power allow the producing company to gain economies of scale and lower its costs, the large user should gain part of these economies in lowered prices, and so forth.

Under this cost-oriented definition, price discrimination takes on a different dimension. Now the matter becomes one of the cost of producing the service. Differential pricing, or charging customers different prices, is not objectionable if the different prices actually reflect differences in costs. A major problem in transportation discrimination, then, is one of tracing or ascertaining the cost of producing the service in question. It should be noted, though, that the determination of exact per unit costs in transportation is very difficult and is thought by some to be impossible. Thus, following the economist's definition, a great deal of price discrimination exists in transportation because costs are unknown, and much of this discrimination is not definable.

It should also be clearly understood that the duty to avoid discrimination does not necessarily prohibit charging different prices or rates for different types of traffic. A ton of gravel is not transported at the same rate as a ton of automobiles. Some consideration is given to the value of the service involved. Transporting the ton of automobiles usually creates more place utility than transporting the ton of gravel, hence the rate on automobiles can be and is higher without violating the statutes.

The problem of similar items or circumstances also is quite complex. Various types of freight have different transportation characteristics and no two types are completely alike. The same may be said for localities, persons, and organizations. This was recognized in regulatory law by making "*undue* preference and prejudice", unlawful. Thus, it becomes a matter of the degree of discrimination or what is "undue." Again, the final responsibility of deciding what is permissible and what is "undue" has been placed in the hands of the regulatory commissions and the courts.

Finally, it should be noted that some discrimination in transportation is permitted on the grounds of public policy. For example, persons employed by religious or charitable organizations may be allowed to travel at special low rates; Federal government traffic was given special low rates on railroads until the 1940's and still qualifies for special rates under Section 22 of the Interstate Commerce Act. The Hoch-Smith Resolution of 1925 provided for special rates on certain classes of agricultural goods as a matter of public policy. Proponents of these and similar forms of discrimination feel that their advantages outweigh their disadvantages.

In addition, the obligation to avoid discrimination does not mean that certain types of quantity discounts are not allowed. Rates based on carload or truckload quantities are substantially lower than LCL or LTL rates. Presumably there is a cost differential between the two types of traffic, but there may be some question whether the degree of price differential reflects the actual amount of cost differential. There are some examples of trainload rates which are lower than carload rates. However, these quantity discounts generally are noncumulative. Cumulative-discount-type rates generally have been considered to be discriminatory in this country on the grounds that they tend to favor large shippers over small shippers, although such rates are widely used in several other countries. It should be further noted that some practices which are illegal domestically are permissible in ·international ocean transportation. In this area, price discrimination and price differentials are widespread.

In summarizing the duty to avoid discrimination, then, it can be said that the common carrier is under the obligation of avoiding undue discrimination. However, discrimination is sometimes difficult to define, and the application of this obligation by way of commission regulation is one of the most challenging and most complicated areas of domestic transportation.

CONTRACT CARRIER OBLIGATIONS

Most of the common carrier obligations discussed above are covered in the individual contracts between contract carriers and their shippers. There are no common-law obligations of the contract carrier as such outside of the contract for its services. However, when the individual contract does not cover an obligation such as liability, the laws of the state of jurisdiction will apply. Since a contract carrier provides a highly specialized and limited type of service, it does not offer to serve the general public in the same manner as a common carrier. Its public is very limited. Indeed, if it does offer to serve all comers and enter into a substantial number of contracts, it risks being declared a common carrier and being brought under the duties and obligations of a common carrier or of incurring the penalties of engaging in unauthorized common carriage.

CONCLUSION

In this chapter, we have considered the basic legal framework under which for-hire transportation services are rendered. These duties of service, delivery, reasonableness, and avoidance of discrimination will be referred to again in other contexts throughout this book. Our object here was merely to introduce the concepts and give a basic understanding of what is involved in each of these duties. Our next step will be to consider further the framework of carrier services, so that a more complete understanding of the supply side of domestic transportation is attained.

ADDITIONAL READINGS

1. Bugan, Thomas G., **When Does Title Pass?** 2nd ed. Dubuque, Iowa: Wm. C. Brown Co., 1951.
   Chapter XV. "Time and Place of Shipment or Delivery," pp. 222–259.
2. Conant, Michael, **Railroad Mergers and Abandonments.** Berkeley, Calif.: University of California Press, 1964.
   Chapter VI. "Regulation of Abandonments, 1946–1962," pp. 113–131.
   Chapter VII. "Railroad Service Discontinuances," pp. 132–165.
3. Daggett, Stuart, **Principles of Inland Transportation,** 4th ed. New York: Harper and Brothers, 1955.
   Chapter 12. "The Duty of Service," pp. 229–243.
   Chapter 13. "Common Carrier Liability," pp. 244–262.
   Chapter 14. "Equality of Charges," pp. 263–281.
4. Dewey, Ralph L., **The Long and Short Haul Principle of Rate Regulation.** Columbus, Ohio: Ohio State University Press, 1935.
5. Fair, Marvin L., and John Guandolo, **Tedrow's Regulation of Transportation,** 6th ed. Dubuque, Iowa: Wm. C. Brown Co., 1964.

Chapter 2. "Local Basis for Regulating Transportation," pp. 7–14.

Chapter 3. "Carriers: Kinds of, and Legal Status," pp. 15–21.

6. Fair, Marvin L., and Ernest W. Williams, Jr., **Economics of Transportation,** Rev. ed. New York: Harper and Brothers., 1959.

Chapter 10. "Service Obligations and Liability of Carriers," pp. 178–189.

Chapter 26. "Control of Discrimination," pp. 533–558.

7. Locklin, D. Philip, **Economics of Transportation,** 6th ed. Homewood, Ill.: Richard D. Irwin, Inc., 1966.

Chapter 21. "Personal Discrimination," pp. 449–467.

Chapter 22. "Long-and-Short-Haul Discrimination," pp. 468–489.

Chapter 23. "Discrimination Between Places and Commodities," pp. 490–517.

8. McElhiney, Paul T., and Gerald T. Boyle, "Inconsistencies in the Domestic Air Freight Contract," **Transportation Journal,** Summer 1962, pp. 7–14.

9. Miller, John M., and Fritz R. Kahn, **Law of Freight Loss and Damage Claims,** 2nd ed. Dubuque, Iowa: Wm. C. Brown Co., 1961.

Chapter I. "Source of Carrier Liability for Loss and Damage," pp. 1–11.

Chapter II. "The Transportation Contract," pp. 12–85.

Chapter III. "Common Carrier Liability Generally," pp. 86–114.

Chapter IV. "Specific Phases of Carrier Liability," pp. 115–521.

10. Morton, Newton, "Transportation of Goods of Extraordinary Value by Common Carriers," **I.C.C. Practitioners' Journal,** Feb. 1965, pp. 393–420.

11. Pegrum, Dudley F., **Transportation: Economics and Public Policy.** Rev. ed. Homewood, Ill.: Richard D. Irwin, Inc., 1968.

Chapter 5. "Transport Services," pp. 104–124.

12. Shinn, Glenn L., "Freight Rate Prejudice and Preference," **I.C.C. Practitioners' Journal,** Feb. 1964, pp. 531–547.

13. Taff, Charles A., **Management of Traffic and Physical Distribution.** 4th ed. Homewood, Ill.: Richard D. Irwin, Inc., 1968.

Chapter 16. "Carrier Liability," pp. 391–416.

8

Terminal and Special
Line-Haul Services

The previous chapter discussed the legal framework within which carriers operate in domestic transportation. This chapter will discuss additional parts of the transportation package of services. Some of these are required as part of the obligation to serve already discussed. Others may be offered voluntarily by the carriers, but once offered may be subject to regulation and rule-making by regulatory authorities. Generally, when these services are regulated, it is on the basis of reasonableness of charges, nondiscrimination among users, and adequacy of service.

TERMINAL SERVICES

Terminals are of major importance in domestic transportation. A terminal is more than a place where the line-haul for freight and passengers stops and starts. It is a place where various necessary carrier operations take place, where changes in the shipment occur, and where various special services are performed for shippers, sometimes as a part of the line-haul charge and sometimes at extra charges. Finally, a terminal is a place where carrier co-operation and coordination take place, as will be discussed in the next chapter.

Terminals vary in physical size from relatively small installations used by busses or trucks to the very large airports in metropolitan areas or rail marshaling yards in or adjacent to key shipping points. Many acres of land are necessary for rail terminals, airports, and seaports, while only small amounts of land are necessary for motor operations. Of course, the flexible motor vehicle depends upon the many miles of public streets and highways for part of the same terminal function which the railroad uses its yards to perform.

Because of the need for space for terminal operations, there is a definite relationship between transportation terminals and the problems of urbanization. In the case of the motor carrier, it is often traffic congestion on the public streets; in the case of the rail carrier, the problem is sometimes urban blight and deterioration near its yards and shops; and in the case of the air carrier, noise and safety factors cause urban problems. Since terminals are a focal point of movement, they markedly affect the flow of traffic and people in an urban system. Hence, terminals are a very important factor in urban systems' analysis and planning as well as an integral and essential part of intercity domestic transportation. Our concern here is primarily with the transportation role of terminals.

Functions of Terminals

There are five basic functions of terminals: providing a place for concentration, dispersion, shipment service, vehicle service, and interchange.

Concentration

A terminal provides a point of consolidation. This function is performed for the transportation of both freight and people. People are consolidated or concentrated into groups in the terminal according to the size of the transportation vehicle. People load themselves into planes, trains, and busses, thereby simplifying the problem of getting the concentration to be shipped onto the vehicle.

With goods, the concentration is similar. Freight moves to a terminal point, either by carrier-provided pickup vehicles or by the shipper's own actions, and is consolidated or concentrated into vehicle lots. The terminal provides the point for this concentration. Once the concentration is complete, the shipment can start on its journey. But in order to gain economies of lower costs and use of vehicles, each shipment is concentrated to some degree and does not move separately. This is true whether the function of concentration is applied to packages or carloads. With packages and individual items, the concentration into larger units to fit the vehicles is obvious. But the same function is involved when rail cars are made into trains in terminals or barges are assembled into tows.

To facilitate the function of concentration, goods are handled in terminals. This may involve the physical movement of many items in LCL or LTL concentration, or it may involve the handling of vehicles such as making up railroad trains. This handling is expensive and makes up a major part of the terminal costs. It also subjects the shipment to the possibility of loss or damage. The expense and hazards of this concentration are two of the great problems of domestic tranportation.

Allied to concentration are the tasks of dispatching vehicles and crews. The terminal furnishes a point where this function is carried on.

Dispersion

The function of dispersion is the opposite of concentration. This is also an important function of terminals which is performed for both people and goods. In intercity transportation, the terminal is the point of destination. From the terminal people disperse to their homes, offices, jobs, and so forth; goods disperse to their ultimate destination. Again, the fact that people unload themselves and generally provide their own dispersion makes this function fairly simple in passenger transportation. However, in the movement of freight, the delivery aspect of the dispersion function is expensive and time-consuming. The function remains the same whether the goods are in LCL, LTL, or in vehicle or carload lots. Freight cars have to be dispersed upon arrival at a terminal, full-load trucks have to be delivered or dispatched locally. And the task of dispatching vehicles and crews in delivery is carried on at the terminal.

The two functions of concentration and dispersion are often carried on simultaneously, of course. When freight cars are picked up for concentration into trains, other cars may at the same time be dispersed. When LTL shipments are picked up for concentration into over-the-road units, other shipments may be delivered. Both functions can often be performed by the same vehicle or crew.

Shipment Service

Terminals provide a place where shipments are serviced in various ways. In passenger transportation, the provision of waiting rooms and ticketing are the prime shipment-service functions of terminals. In the transportation of goods, the same functions take place but in a somewhat more complicated manner. Thus terminals provide storage and elevation for goods being shipped, and protection for goods against the elements, theft, and damage. This is, essentially, the same service as a passenger waiting room provides. Terminals likewise provide a point at which routing and billing of shipments take place. This is the same documentation service as the ticketing of passengers. These shipment service functions of storage and documentation are provided for shippers or passengers as part of the line-haul charge.

Vehicle Service

Carriers, too, use terminals for their own function of vehicle service. The terminal is a place to store vehicles until they are needed in the concentration or the dispersion function. It also provides a space to maneuver vehicles where needed. Cleaning, repairing, and servicing vehicles is generally undertaken at terminals. Repair shops often are maintained, and vehicles are made ready for departure.

Sometimes the terminal provides the carrier with his principal place of doing business. While this is not a vehicle service aspect, it is a related terminal function. The terminal may be the site of carrier executive offices, sales offices and administrative offices, although some of these carrier functions may be carried on at locations other than terminals.

Finally, terminals provide the place for interchange of passengers and freight. This interchange may involve moving people from plane to plane, rail car to rail car, or bus to bus. Goods, too, are interchanged. Interchange may be between vehicles of the same line or between different lines. It may even involve interchange of shipments between different modes of transportation.

Summary

These five terminal functions of concentration, dispersion, shipment service, vehicle service and interchange are essential to the movement of all goods and people in intercity transportation. They are generally included in the line-haul charge of carriers and must be provided in a nondiscriminatory and adequate manner. There are, however, other terminal services which are accessorial or optional in some cases.

Accessorial Terminal Services

The terminal functions already discussed are essential to shipment of all goods and passengers. Accessorial terminal services are not essential to all shipments but are offered by carriers, in many cases voluntarily, but often at an extra charge. These include the following five services: pickup and delivery, loading and unloading, weighing and reweighing, industrial switching, and storage and elevation.

Pickup and Delivery

While motor carriers generally have provided pickup and delivery as part of their regular line-haul freight service, it is incorrect to say that free pickup and delivery is universal. Prior to the 1930's, this service was not provided as part of the line-haul freight service by railroads. There often is a pickup and delivery charge on air cargo and air freight. Passengers are rarely picked up or delivered; carriers usually rely on public transportation or special limousine companies to provide this service at an extra charge. Additionally, there are size, weight, and geographic limits to free pickup and delivery even where it is part of the line-haul service.

If a shipper performs this service in his own vehicles, an allowance may be offered by rail carriers. In some cases, the shipper must specifically request pickup and delivery, otherwise it will not be offered. In some territories, rail pickup and delivery of LCL shipments is only at an extra charge. Naturally, when pickup and delivery is at a point quite distant from the terminal, additional charges are to be expected. The same may be said for unusually bulky or heavy goods. The rules establishing the boundaries of free pickup and delivery districts and the weight and size limitations before extra charges are assessed, along with the various pickup and delivery charges, are found in Pickup and Delivery tariffs. (Tariffs will be discussed in Chapter 11.)

Pickup and delivery is performed by special pickup and delivery vehicles. In the case of motor carriers, these are smaller vehicles which are more maneuverable on the city streets. In LCL rail shipments, this service is performed by rail-owned motor vehicles or by special rail cars. These special rail vehicles are called trap or ferry cars for pickup, and peddler cars for delivery. A trap or ferry car is left on public tracks or on an industrial siding and several shippers load LCL shipments into it. The car may later be switched to the terminal for rehandling or proceed to destination after it is loaded. When delivery to several consignees is involved, peddler cars may be used. Here numerous LCL shipments, sometimes for several points along the rail route, are placed in a single car and delivered as the car moves along. In large destination points, peddler cars within a rail terminal may also be used.

Loading and Unloading

In carload and truckload shipment, it is the obligation of the shipper or the consignee to load or unload the shipment. Generally the shipper does this for himself, but upon request the railroad will load and unload cars for a shipper or consignee at a charge. This service also provides for checking, sorting, coopering, and other tasks allied to the loading and unloading function. In motor transportation, loading and unloading is usually provided as part of the line-haul service as long as it can be done by one man and does not involve unusual tasks. There are various exceptions to this general rule, of course.

Weighing and Reweighing

Since freight charges are based on weight, the weighing of shipments is part of the line-haul service. The weight of a shipment must be accurately determined in order to protect both the shipper and the carrier, and to avoid discrimination. Most of the weighing is done on the carrier's scales or by carrier-supported independent Weighing and Inspection Bureaus. There are five rail and sixteen motor Weighing and Inspection Bureaus which carry on this function.

Reweighing is also done by these bureaus. If the shipper questions the weight assigned by the carrier, the shipment will be reweighed. The charge for this service is assumed by the carrier if reweighing determines that the initial weight and charge was in error by more than a recognized tolerance. Otherwise, the shipper pays for this reweighing service.

In order to avoid repeated weighings on standardized shipments, an average weight agreement is often arranged between shippers and carriers. This device helps both parties by cutting the carrier's cost and by expediting the shipment. Where shipments are of standard size such as cartons of canned goods, citrus cartons, fruit boxes, barrels of liquid, etc., a test over time can determine the average weight of such containers and the weight of a shipment can be readily ascertained without physically weighing each shipment each time. Weighing and Inspection Bureaus administer weight agreements and supervise transit-privilege administration and various other functions.

Industrial Switching

The movement of rail cars within a terminal, as distinguished from movement between terminals or stations of a carrier, is called "switching." There are several types of switching services, some of which are performed as part of the line-haul charges and some of which are performed at extra charges. Where an industry owns rail sidings or tracks within a plant, industrial switching is involved at an additional charge.

Just as motor carriers use pickup and delivery as a competitive device, railroads sometimes use switching in the same manner. Line-haul charges usually include the switching and spotting of cars on industrial tracks; but in large terminal areas, a shipper may not be located on the tracks of all carriers. Here he may have to pay an extra charge (unless it is absorbed by the carrier) to send or receive his cars on a certain rail carrier. Sometimes the carriers have a reciprocal switching agreement where the parties to the agreement reciprocate and do not charge for switching cars among themselves. In large terminal areas, special belt-line or switching railroads may exist which do nothing but switch cars from carrier to carrier or shipper to shipper. These belt-line companies may be owned by all the carriers jointly as a Union or Terminal railroad, or they may be separately owned. These companies' charges for their services may or may not be absorbed by the carriers.

Switching often is carried on over a wide area. The municipal boundaries of a city are not necessarily the switching district or switching limit. The Chicago Switching District, for instance, covers 400 square miles and is 40 miles in length from north to south and 7 to 15 miles wide from east to west, with 5,000 miles of track. This district is served by 30 railroads, 20 of which are line-haul carriers.

Floatage and Lighterage services in harbors are another form of switching, using barges instead of tracks. These special services, which are particularly important in port areas, may or may not be offered at an extra charge.

Storage and Elevation

Storage of freight on the premises of the carrier and elevation service for grain at terminals and ports are other optional services. Sometimes storage will be provided free of charge at the owner's risk, but more often a warehousing or storage charge is made. Elevation for weighing, inspection, or transfer from car to car is part of the line-haul service, but elevation for storage is an accessorial service provided by many carriers at an extra charge.

Ownership and Management of Terminals

Ownership and management of terminals may be either public or private. In railroads, it is generally private, either by a single carrier or by several carriers cooperating in a Union Terminal arrangement. Terminals are typically privately owned and managed in motor transportation as well. There are some union terminals or cooperative undertakings in motor transportation, but this is not as extensive as in rail transport. It must be remembered, of course, that motor carriers use public streets to perform part of the same terminal services that rail carriers perform with their tracks. Pipeline terminals are privately or cooperatively owned and managed.

Water terminals and air terminals usually are publicly owned and managed. Port Authorities are often used for water terminals, and sometimes for air terminals. These are publicly financed and are sometimes self-supporting. Even though public terminals do charge for their services and use, few of them are profitable organizations and various degrees of subsidy prevail.

Importance of Terminal Services

Terminal services are important from at least four points of view: space, cost, time, and hazard. We have already mentioned the connection between terminals and urban problems. Not only do terminals affect the area adjacent to themselves, but they require large amounts of geographical space. This land is usually expensive prime industrial land. Much of the fixed cost of railroads is involved with expensive terminals in prime locations.

The cost of terminal services is high. As noted in Chapter 4, around 13 cents out of every dollar of motor-carrier revenue goes for terminal expense. In rail transportation the cost is even higher. Goods often are lost, damaged, or go astray in terminals, and a considerable part of the elapsed time between origin and destination is attributable to terminal delays.

Regulation of Terminals

While the regulation of transportation will be discussed in Part Five, it is proper to note here that because of the terminal problem and monopoly, partial regulation of rail terminals was given to the Interstate Commerce Commission by the Transportation Act of 1920. Terminals, being users of space, are necessarily limited in number in any city. But since terminals are private property, no rail carriers could be forced to accommodate competitive rail carriers by opening its terminals to use by competitors. However, once a railroad allowed another railroad to use its terminal, it was obligated to avoid any discrimination among users.

One of the functions of terminals is as a place of interchange of traffic. If all the best-located terminals were closed to joint use, interchange of rail cars would be most difficult and the shipping public might suffer. The regulations of 1920 allowed the I.C.C. to open terminals by requiring joint use if (1) the grant was in the public interest, (2) adequate and reasonable compensation was paid, and (3) the business of the carrier owning the terminal was not impaired. This subsequently led to more joint use of rail terminals and helped promote railroad cooperation, a matter more fully discussed in the following chapter.

ACCESSORIAL LINE-HAUL SERVICES

In addition to line-haul terminal services and the various optional or accessorial terminal services, carriers also voluntarily offer a group of services which are accessorial to the line-haul. There may or may not be an extra charge for these supplemental or accessorial services. The following six of these important services connected with the line-haul are discussed here: reconsignment and diversion service, stopping-in-transit service, pool-car service, protective services, tracing and expedition, and transit privileges.

Reconsignment and Diversion Service

While the terms "reconsignment" and "diversion" are often used interchangeably, there is a technical difference in the two services. "Diversion" means to change the destination of a shipment while it is enroute; while "reconsignment" means to change the destination or consignee of a shipment after it has arrived at its initial destination, but before delivery. These services are found most frequently in rail transportation, although some motor carriers also offer reconsignment and diversion.

Uses of Reconsignment and Diversion

A shipper or owner may wish to change the destination of a shipment or change the consignee on a shipment for several reasons. In at least eight conditions, this privilege proves valuable to the shipper. 1. The shipper may wish to start the shipment on its way prior to sale in order to avoid spoilage. If goods are perishable, they must move to market in as short a time as possible. The shipper consigns the car to himself; and after he has sold its contents, he reconsigns the shipment to the buyer. 2. The shipper may wish to avoid demurrage or detention charges. Only a limited number of hours or days are allowed for loading. Thus, in order to avoid penalty, the shipment may leave only to be reconsigned or diverted after it is sold. 3. The shipper may wish to send the shipment on its way to facilitate the flow of work in his plant. Limited loading facilities exist at most production points. Rail cars or trucks must be started away from the plant in order to accommodate more vehicles even though sale has not been made. 4. The shipper may wish to reconsign or divert a shipment on its way to market for price or service reasons. With a constantly changing price for goods, diversion allows the owner to change the destination of the shipment en route in order to get the highest price. Competition often calls for quick delivery, and many sales are made on the service aspect of ability to deliver in the shortest possible time. When a producer is some distance from the market, the shipment may be billed to the shipper himself and sent on its way. By diverting or reconsigning after it is sold, the distant producer often can offer as quick a delivery as the producer closer to the market. 5. The reconsignment and diversion privilege may be used to slow down a shipment until it is sold or until it is needed. In this manner, the service provides a means of delay which may be as valuable as speed in some circumstances. 6. The buyer of the goods may resell the shipment to another buyer and use the reconsignment and diversion privilege. Some shipments may be sold several times while they are en route. 7. The buyer may cancel his order after the shipment has left the production point. By reconsignment and diversion, the seller may be able to dispose of the goods without loss due to cancellation. 8. The shipper may wish to avoid financial loss due to bankruptcy of the buyer.

While there are no doubt other conditions under which this service is used, it is apparent that this valuable privilege is one of the important services of a carrier. This privilege is granted under certain uniform rules and charges, and shippers should know the circumstances under which it may be used.

From the conditions stated, it is obvious that the reconsignment and diversion privilege is more important for some commodities than for others. Where goods are perishable, where the market price fluctuates daily, and where delivery time is a prime factor in selling goods in competition with producers closer to the market, the reconsignment and diversion service is highly valuable. Where these conditions do not exist, the service is not so important. It is logical, then, to find this service being offered and used most frequently in the shipment of lumber, citrus, fresh fruit and vegetables, and dairy products. In these shipments, the rail carriers are particularly liberal in granting such privileges, often allowing reconsignment or diversion as many as three times before a charge is made for the service, and only nominal charges thereafter. It is estimated that over half the rail traffic out of California and Florida is reconsigned at least once.

Reconsignment and diversion is important to the general public as well as to the individual shipper. It allows more producers to compete in a market and extends the economic supply to a wider area. Additionally, the effect of reconsignment and diversion of shipments on price can be considerable. Any marked variation in price in a given market can soon be brought into line by having shipments diverted to it.

Stopping in Transit

Another important accessorial line-haul service offered by the carriers is the right to stop shipments in transit for loading or unloading. This benefits the shipper or the consignee because he can apply the cheaper carload rate even though a part of the journey is made with only a part of the vehicle filled. If the shipment had to proceed on LCL rates for both parts of the journey, the overall rate might be much higher.

Under this service, a producer may sell goods at two or more points or to several customers, ship the goods in a single car at the lower carload rates, and stop the car to partially unload at the point of each sale. Of course, the carload rate to the most distant point is charged. Also, a manufacturer may have two or more plants and use the privilege of stopping in transit to complete loading to ship at lower carload rates from both points without having a full carload at either point. For commission merchants and persons who buy and sell, the advantage is obvious.

This service was developed by railroads as a competitive device. However, many motor carriers also offer similar services. Stopping in transit to complete loading or unloading should not be confused with transloading. In transloading, the carrier may combine several loads of different shipments in a single vehicle for his own convenience.

Pool-Car Service

Another accessorial line-haul service offered by carriers, both rail and truck, is that of the pool car. This is a type of shipper operation which is much like the concentration function carried on by the carriers themselves. The carrier allows several shippers from one point of origin with the same type of commodity or a single shipper with several small shipments to pool shipments for the same destination. In this manner, shipments are moved at lower carload or truckload rates and at more frequent intervals than would be possible for LCL or LTL movements. Distribution or concentration of pool-car shipments is typically not handled by the carrier. Warehousemen or local cartage firms often offer this service at a small charge.

The advantage of pool-car service is not only that the smaller shipper can get lower rates, but also that inventories can be kept under more careful control, thus reducing costs.

Protective Services

In the shipment of perishable goods, protection of the shipment can be of vital importance. Protection here refers to protection against the elements and not protection against theft or pilferage.

A charge is made by the carrier for icing, refrigeration, ventilating, or heating cars. These services are made available to assist the shipper to bring his goods to market in good condition. The feeding and watering of livestock is another type of protective service offered by the carriers at an additional charge.

Tracing and Expediting

The shipper often needs to know the progress of his shipments. Many carriers provide a tracing service for carload or truckload movements. No charge is made for this service even though rather elaborate means are often employed to keep track of shipments. In fact, some carriers use their complex tracing service as a competitive aid in selling their transportation service.

Expediting, or speeding up a shipment, uses tracing procedures. When assembly lines are threatened with shutdown or repair parts are necessary for production to resume, the shipper and the consignee both want to know not only how the shipment has progressed, but also if the shipment can be speeded to destination. In some firms, one particular person in the Traffic Department is assigned to this task. These functions will be further discussed in Chapter 26.

During World Wars I and II and the Korean conflict, expediting was used extensively to speed shipments of high priority. Various techniques have been developed, and carriers cooperate in this service in order to retain the good will of important shippers.

Transit Privilege

The final accessorial line-haul service discussed here is the transit privilege. This privilege or service has a long history in rail transportation and is found in modern motor transportation as well.

With transit privileges, a shipment may be stopped while in transit from origin to destination and be physically changed in form before proceeding to destination. The advantage is that the carrier considers the whole movement, even with a stop to change form, as a single movement and charges the long-haul rate rather than two short-haul rates. Thus, the economies of long-haul rates are made available to the goods.

There are many types of transit privileges. The most common are milling in transit on grain, storing in transit, fabrication in transit, refining in transit, and treating or processing lumber in transit. In the common milling-in-transit privilege, grains move to the point of milling, are unloaded and milled into flour, and proceed to market as flour all under the long-haul or through rate. The effect of this is to allow more milling points to compete in a given market, thus neutralizing the location advantages of being near the market. Transit privileges are administered by Weighing and Inspection Bureaus. A more detailed discussion of various transit rates and their effect on marketing and the location of industry is included in Part Four.

CONCLUSION

This chapter has considered the importance of and functions of terminals in domestic transportation, accessorial terminal services, and the setting in which these carrier services are performed. Additionally, we have noted some of the optional or accessorial line-haul services which are offered by carriers. The next chapter will consider cooperative and coordinated services.

ADDITIONAL READINGS

1. Bryan, Leslie A., **Traffic Management in Industry.** New York: The Dryden Press, 1953.
   Chapter 13. "Expediting and Tracing," pp. 232–249.
2. Daggett, Stuart, **Principles of Inland Transportation,** 4th ed. New York: Harper and Brothers, 1955.
   Chapter 24. "Terminals," pp. 487–522.
3. Flood, Kenneth U., **Traffic Management,** 2nd ed. Dubuque, Iowa: Wm. C. Brown Co., 1963.
   Chapter 8. "Weights and Weighing," pp. 203–221.
   Chapter 11. "In-Transit Arrangements," pp. 256–279.
   Chapter 12. "Reconsignment and Diversion," pp. 280–292.
   Chapter 13. "Switching," pp. 293–309.
4. Hay, William W., **An Introduction to Transportation Engineering.** New York: John Wiley & Sons, Inc., 1961.
   Chapter 9. "Terminals," pp. 290–313.
5. Hudson, William J., and James A. Constantin, **Motor Transportation.** New York: Ronald Press Company, 1958.
   Chapter 15. "Motor Freight Terminals and Material Handling," pp. 331–358.
6. Locklin, D. Philip, **Economics of Transportation,** 6th ed. Homewood, Ill.: Richard D. Irwin, Inc., 1966.
   Chapter 26. "Railroad Service and Service Regulation," pp. 559–585.
7. Morton, Newton, and Frank Mossman, **Industrial Traffic Management.** New York: Ronald Press Company, 1954.
   Chapter 15. "Switching," pp. 278–295.
   Chapter 16. "Diversion and Reconsignment: Transit and Stopoff Privileges," pp. 296–317.
8. Pegrum, Dudley F., **Transportation: Economics and Public Policy.** Rev. ed. Homewood, Ill.: Richard D. Irwin, Inc. 1968.
   Chapter 23. "Transport Terminals," pp. 578–600.
9. Taff, Charles A., **Commercial Motor Transportation,** 4th ed. Homewood, Ill.: Richard D. Irwin, Inc., 1969.
   Chapter 11. "Terminal Operations," pp. 250–274.
10. Taff, Charles A., **Management of Traffic and Physical Distribution.** 4th ed. Homewood, Ill.: Richard D. Irwin, Inc., 1968.
    Chapter 14. "Special Transport Services," pp. 342–363.
    Chapter 15. "Terminal Services, Demurrage, and Detention," pp. 364–387.
11. Van Metre, Thurman W., **Industrial Traffic Management.** New York: McGraw-Hill Book Co., 1953.
    Chapter XVII. "Terminal Services: Switching and Lighterage," pp. 335–370.
    Chapter XVIII. "Terminal Services: Pickup and Delivery, Storage, Weighing, Elevation," pp. 371–389.
    Chapter XIX. "Reconsignment and Diversion: Transit Privileges," pp. 390–409.
12. Wilson, G. Lloyd, **Traffic Management.** Englewood Cliffs, N.J.: Prentice-Hall, Inc., 1956.
    Chapter 14. "The Tracing Function," pp. 214–232.

9

Cooperative and Coordinated Service

The two previous chapters have been concerned with the legal service obligations and the optional or accessorial services of carriers. However, in both cases we have been discussing single-carrier service. In this chapter, we are concerned with services offered by more than one carrier in cooperation or coordination with other carriers. With the growing complexity and interdependence of the U.S. economy, cooperation and coordination in transportation becomes more important. Additionally, with the emerging of newer modes of transportation during the last forty years, coordination of transportation services becomes more feasible and cooperative transportation services gain a new dimension.

It is well at the outset to note that the terms "cooperation" and "coordination" are not the same even though they are often used synonymously. Also we should note that there is sometimes confusion between the terms "unification" and "integration," and "cooperation" and "coordination." Unification and integration in transportation will be discussed in detail in Chapter 20, but for now it should be noted that these terms are primarily concerned with common ownership. Hence, when a transportation firm integrates with another transportation firm of a different mode, it has a common ownership. An example of this would be when a railroad integrates by buying a truck line. When a transportation firm enters into unification with another transportation firm, common ownership is again involved. Merger or consolidation is the most common type of unification today. An example of unification, then, would be two railroads or two airlines merging. On the other hand, cooperation and coordination does not involve common ownership. Indeed, it implies separately owned firms cooperating together in some action or coordinating their services in some way. The distinction between the two sets of terms is principally in ownership patterns.

But cooperation and coordination are themselves distinct and separate things. Here the distinction is in terms of the mode of transportation. Cooperative service refers to firms in the same mode of transportation working together in some way. Interchange of railroad equipment is a good example. Coordinated service refers to firms in different modes of transportation working together. The popular T.O.F.C. or "piggyback" service is a good example of a coordination.

The distinction, then, between unification and integration on the one hand and cooperation and coordination on the other is ownership. The distinction between cooperation and coordination is in the mode of transportation. With these distinctions clear, we can proceed to discuss types of cooperative and coordinated service and the framework under which such service is offered.

COOPERATIVE CARRIER SERVICE

Carriers of the same mode have entered into cooperative agreements of various types for many years. Typically these arrangements are voluntary, although in some circumstances regulatory bodies may have the authority to prescribe them and in other circumstances regulatory bodies may supervise these undertakings.

There are various purposes or aims of cooperation. Without question, some of the very earliest cooperative efforts among railroads were aimed at lessening competition between carriers. Here the pool was a familiar device whereby railroads agreed to divide business of a particular kind among themselves on a predetermined basis. These were generally of two types, tonnage pools and revenue pools. In the tonnage pool, competitive traffic was divided up among the carriers on a predetermined percentage of all tonnage. If a carrier had already reached his share or percentage of tonnage, he was to discourage a shipper from using his line or turn the shipment over to his competitor to handle. This type of pool was most difficult to enforce and administer.

The revenue pool was more common and more easily enforced. Choice of carrier by the shipper remained uncontrolled, but revenue was divided among competitors on a predetermined formula by various transfers of funds. These arrangements were popular with railroads in the 1870's and 1880's, and were usually set up after drastic rate wars among carriers had ensued. However, the existence of these pools hastened federal regulation, as we shall discuss in Chapter 16, and they were in violation of the Sherman Antitrust Act after 1890.

The vast majority of cooperative carrier services are not aimed at lessening competition and are not illegal. Basically, most of the cooperative activities have two purposes: to facilitate physical interline operation and to facilitate legal joint-carrier action.

Cooperation to Facilitate Physical Interline Operation

In general, most of the cooperative action in transportation is aimed at facilitating physical interline operation. With cooperative carrier service, much of the domestic transportation system can be operated as a single unit. Such cooperative carrier action benefits the carrier by allowing it to share more easily in all traffic, benefits the shipper by simplifying his task, and ultimately benefits the general public by allowing a more efficient and economical transportation system to operate.

Although there are various kinds of possible cooperative action, the most common types which promote physical interline operation are equipment interchange, ancillary physical cooperation, through rates and routes, through billing, advisory board activities, and interline agreements.

Equipment Interchange

Perhaps the most important cooperative carrier action of all is the free exchange of equipment. In rail transportation, freight cars circulate freely from one railroad to another with little regard to ownership. These cars may be owned by any one of a number of railroads, private car companies, or the shippers themselves. Equipment interchange, most highly developed in the rail mode, has existed for many years. It allows freight to move literally to any spot in North America served by rail in the same vehicle. If equipment interchange were not possible, the whole transportation system would be much less efficient and much more expensive.

This free interchange of equipment depends, of course, on several things. Of greatest importance is standardization of the equipment, the way upon which the equipment travels, and the rules under which equipment operates. Standardization of rail cars, whether railroad-owned, car-company-owned, or shipper-owned has been achieved. While some changes in height and length have appeared from time to time, couplings, braking systems, width, type of wheel, and so forth are standardized. The way, too, has been standard among rail carriers for decades, and the standard gauge of the United States has been adopted in Canada and Mexico, further facilitating physical equipment interchange.

Standardization of the rules of interchange is highly important although not as apparent as physical standardization. In rail cars, maintenance and repair rules are standardized under the Master Car Builder Rules of the Association of American Railroads (AAR). These rules define conditions under which a railroad may refuse to receive a car in interchange, assign responsibility for various types of repairs between owning and using railroads, and contain a detailed list of prices to be charged for repair of cars.

The distribution of rail cars is also standardized. Here the AAR has its Code of Car Service Rules which prescribe when and in what manner cars will be sent to their home owners. The accounting and payment problem is also governed by AAR rules. The Code of Per Diem Rules specifies the charges which must be paid for cars by the using line to the owning railroad. This accounting is on a time basis, although other accounting and payment devices have been tried from time to time. Recently these rules have been changed under the supervision of the Interstate Commerce Commission in an attempt to make it less profitable for a railroad to use the cars of another railroad than to buy its own.

Physical equipment interchange is more highly developed in rail transportation. The reasons for this are technological, the age of the industry, and the economic characteristic of a relatively few large firms who could easily cooperate. In motor transportation, equipment interchange is less highly developed. Not only are there technological problems in standardization of equipment, but the relative youth of the industry, plus the fact that motor transportation is made up of many small and competitive firms, has made cooperative action more difficult. Additionally, state laws on size and weight have not been uniform, and different local traffic conditions on the highways have made uniformity difficult. Even so, great progress in motor-carrier trailer interchange has been made in recent years. Rules and regulations have been established and rental charges determined for trailer interchange. When the vehicle itself is interchanged (not just the trailer) a lease arrangement may sometimes be used.

Physical interchange in air transportation is in its infancy. The standardization of equipment and the way is present; but except for a relatively few instances, physical interchange of airline equipment has not been permitted by regulatory authorities. There has been very minor interchange in inland water transportation and, of course, none in pipeline transportation due to its technology. Perhaps the future will see considerably more physical interchange of equipment in motor, air, and water transportation to the mutual benefit of the shipping public and the carriers.

Ancillary Physical Cooperation

Auxiliary to equipment interchange are a group of cooperative actions such as interline switching, interline drayage, and joint use of terminals. Standardization of procedure and charges can again be found here. In rail transportation, the switching of rail cars in large terminal points such as Chicago is so important that separate switching railroads and so-called belt-line railroads have developed. In motor transportation, interline drayage is an important factor in offering cooperative service. Joint use of terminals, particularly in rail transportation, is such an important cooperative device that the Interstate Commerce Commission has been given the power to prescribe it.

These cooperative services, usually done in connection with terminals, were discussed in Chapter 8. We need only remind ourselves here that they are excellent illustrations of carrier cooperation and that they are auxiliary to physical interchange or interline movement.

Through Routes and Rates

Being able to interchange equipment physically is not enough to facilitate interline transportation. Additionally, through routes and rates are necessary. A through route has been defined by the U.S. Supreme Court as "an arrangement, expressed or implied, between connecting railroads for the continuous carriage of goods from the originating point on the line of one carrier to destination on the line of another" (*St. Louis-Southwestern Ry. Co. v. U.S.*, 245 U.S. 136, 1917). These arrangements are set up by carriers; and even though two carriers serve a common point, this does not mean that a through route over that point exists. Routing guides are published to assist shippers in their choice of combinations of carriers offering through routes.

If a through route is agreed upon, a through rate is also necessary. Again, unless the whole movement is under a single rate, much of the benefit of physical interchange is lost. It is common for carrier transportation personnel to refer to joint rates in the same breath with through routes. However, some through routes take combination rates or the sum of local rates, while joint rates are usually lower than combination rates. Both combination rates and joint rates in this instance are through rates. Rate terminology and distinctions will be discussed in detail in Chapter 12.

It should be noted that the Interstate Commerce Commission has the power under law to prescribe through routes and joint rates for railroads.

Through Billing

An additional cooperative device is necessary to supplement physical equipment interchange and through routes and rates. The accounting problem of billing for the whole movement and the division of revenues received also must be standardized. In rail transportation, through billing has long been standardized to cover movements originating on one line with destinations on another. The division of the revenues from cooperative movement is also standardized. Various methods of prorating revenues have been used, and the Interstate Commerce Commission may regulate this division of revenues regardless of the mode of transportation. Recently, a change in some of the division of revenues in rail transportation has been prescribed after a great deal of study. This is an example of cooperative carrier action which has been standardized and controlled by regulatory authorities.

Although through routes and rates and through billing are not themselves physical, they facilitate physical interchange of equipment and greatly assist in making the transportation system operate as a single unit.

Advisory Board Activities

Another cooperative undertaking, primarily in the rail field, is the shippers' advisory boards. Organized in 1923 by the Association of American Railroads, these groups bring together carriers and shippers for a discussion of mutual problems. In 1936, a cooperating agency for the thirteen regional boards was set up and called the National Association of Shipper Advisory Boards. Although originally designed to deal primarily with the problem of railroad car distribution, the boards provide common ground for carrier representatives and shippers to discuss mutual problems. These boards greatly facilitate cooperative carrier activities and physical interline operation. They have been especially successful in dealing with car distribution to meet seasonal production patterns. In some areas, motor carriers are likewise involved with shipper-carrier boards of a similar nature.

Interline Agreements

Even though the equipment may not interchange in some instances, interline agreements using through routes and rates, through billing, and interline switching, drayage or joint use of terminals often exists. While the economies are not always as great as when equipment interchanges, these interline agreements do assist passengers and help to move freight in a smooth flow.

Motor carriers enter into numerous cooperative interline agreements; and while the freight usually must be unloaded from one vehicle and loaded upon another, these agreements speed the shipment. Typically, these agreements are between noncompeting carriers that meet end to end. Likewise, some airlines have similar agreements (particularly on journeys involving overseas transportation) with through routes and rates, through billing, joint use of terminals and so forth.

A unique type of interline agreement is found in pipeline transportation. Here the freight flows while the vehicle is stationary. Equipment interchange is obviously impossible. However, by connections, switching devices, through routes and rates, and through billing, crude petroleum and petroleum products can move almost across the nation without being removed from the pipeline. Here interline agreements and other cooperative devices allow the refinery or the purchaser of petroleum products a wide choice of suppliers, and, conversely, allow the owner of crude oil or refined petroleum a wider market for his product.

Cooperation to Facilitate Legal Joint Carrier Actions

In addition to the cooperative undertakings which facilitate physical interline operations, there are a group of arrangements in which carriers cooperatively enter into other joint action. These include cooperative rate-making, joint or collective ownership patterns, and interfirm public relations.

Cooperative Rate-Making

Cooperative action on rates has been common in all modes of transportation for some time. That is, carriers meet periodically or maintain boards of representatives to consider changes in rates and other matters affecting the price of transportation.

Originally, each carrier established its own rates. However, as a result of pools in rail transportation as well as the need for standardization and uniformity, cooperative rate-making was undertaken. This action is particularly important relative to uniformity in classification of items, which will be discussed in detail in Chapter 11. Standardization and uniformity greatly facilitate through movement and the equitable solution to the many problems involved therein.

Cooperative undertakings involving pricing are commonly referred to as conference rate-making and are carried on by Rate Bureaus. The techniques used by these bureaus also will be discussed in Chapter 11. For a period of time, there was some question about the legality of rate bureaus under the antitrust laws even though it was an accepted practice in transportation and the bureaus functioned openly. With the passage of the Reed-Bulwinkle amendment to Section 5 of the Interstate Commerce Act in 1948, though, the legality of these cooperative undertakings was firmly established.

Joint and Collective Ownership

A somewhat unique type of cooperative undertaking is found in pipeline transportation. Joint or collective ownership of pipelines is common. Because of capital requirements and the close connection of pipelines to the parent petroleum industry, a new pipeline venture is often financed under an "undivided interest" concept of collective ownership. Various petroleum companies or other pipeline companies finance the new venture, each owning a percentage share of the whole, but none owning a specific portion of the pipeline. Thus a new pipeline might be owned collectively by any number of existing pipeline or petroleum companies, but operate as a completely separate and independent entity. This type of collective and joint action is sometimes the only way to raise the massive capital necessary to construct a pipeline, and it prevents uneconomical duplication by competitors.

Interfirm Public Relations

Another type of cooperative action is that to facilitate interfirm or industry public relations. These are the familiar trade associations, many of which exist in the transportation field. While their activities vary considerably, their main task is to improve the public relations of their branch of transportation by lobbying and protecting the interests of their members in various ways. They also provide a common arena for discussing mutual problems, offer advisory service on trade practices, and often carry on research and development for the mode as a whole. Some, like the Association of American Railroads, are very active in standardization and rule-making which greatly facilitates interline movement. Besides the AAR, major groups include the American Trucking Associations, the American Waterways Operators Association, the Air Transportation Association of America, the Association of Petroleum Pipelines, and the Private Truck Council of America. Additionally, some of these have regional and state organizatons.

Summary of Carrier Cooperation

Transportation provides an interesting case study of industry cooperating on a voluntary basis. Rarely has this cooperation been forced by government edict, although it has often been encouraged by regulatory authorities. While questions of legality under the antitrust laws have arisen in connection with some of these cooperative undertakings, cooperative action in transportation has generally proved to be legal.

Often, cooperation between firms in the economy benefits only the cooperating firms. However, cooperation between transportation firms benefits not only the transportation firms, but also the general public. This type of cooperative action has much to recommend it, and undoubtedly the fact that the public is benefited by this cooperation has led regulatory authorities to encourage it and has probably helped establish its legality.

COORDINATED CARRIER SERVICES

Coordinated carrier service involves firms in separate and different modes of transportation coordinating their services and working together in some way. Separate ownership of the modes is implied, otherwise the joint action would be what we have defined as integration. The distinction is an important one as integration is somewhat controversial, whereas coordination is usually not. While many groups, including regulatory authorities, are concerned if a railroad attempts to buy and to integrate a truck line into its operations, these same groups are not alarmed if a railroad and an independently owned truck line enter into an agreement to coordinate their service. This cooperation between modes is considered beneficial and indeed, in some instances, may be required. In all instances coordination is permitted.

Required Coordination

For joint movements by rail and water, coordination may be required by law. In 1912, the Interstate Commerce Commission was given the power to require physical interconnection between rail carriers and water carriers. Later, rail carriers were forced into publishing through routes and joint rates with water carriers on the Mississippi River. A large volume of tonnage moves by rail from inland points to ports on the Great Lakes, down the Lakes, and then inland by rail. This movement is an example of rail-water coordination. Some rail-water movement on other inland waterways occurs as well. By forcing the establishment of through routes and joint rates as well as physical interconnections, this coordination of services was developed.

Permitted Coordination

While the power to force coordination does not exist in other than rail-water areas, coordination between modes has always been permitted and encouraged by regulatory authorities. Rail-truck coordination in piggyback service has been permitted, and recently the Interstate Commerce Commission has been concerned with the rules, conditions, and rates under which this type of coordinated service takes place.

Water-truck, air-truck, air-rail, water-pipeline, rail-pipeline, and truck-pipeline coordination are all permitted and encouraged. Water-air coordination and air-pipeline coordination are technologically almost impossible at present.

Types of Coordinated Service

A glance at both the required and permitted coordination noted above illustrates that ten types of intermodal coordinated service using two modes each could exist. (These are rail-truck, rail-water, rail-air, rail-pipeline, truck-air, truck-water, truck-pipeline, water-pipeline, water-air, and air-pipeline.) Many exist in experimental form or are technologically possible, but are not widely practiced. In addition to these ten possible combinations, coordination by way of containerization and express service is also possible.

The flexibility of the motor truck causes it to be combined most readily with other modes. In many cases, after the versatile truck has picked up the freight at the door of the shipper and hauled it to a terminal, the trailer itself moves by some other mode to a distant terminal where again the flexibility of the truck and the streets and highways allows delivery to the receiver's door. The most common "truck-other" combination is the familiar piggyback service. Here the economy and efficiency of long-haul rail service is combined with the convenience of the flexible truck. This service started many years ago on an experimental basis and began to be adopted widely and grow rapidly in the 1950's. It has now firmly established itself as an integral part of domestic transportation.

It should be noted that a good deal of T.O.F.C. service involves railroads hauling the trailers of their truck subsidiaries or their own pickup and delivery vehicles. This type of service was called "Plan II" service for many years. While this type of service is both piggyback and intermodal, it is not "coordination" as we use the term here to mean a joint service of separately owned modes of transportation.

Other truck-related coordination services also exist. Fishyback service is used where trailers are moved by barge in coastwise or intercoastal traffic or on inland waterways. It should be noted also that a rail-ship service, where rail cars are driven onto ships, has been in limited operation between a few points for some time. A water-rail combination, even with piggyback trailers on rail cars, is possible.

We have seen little birdybacking of trailers by planes as yet, even though the armed services have developed the techniques and have used this type of service with their own vehicles. Rail-air coordinated service was common in the days when airlines did not fly at night. Indeed, the first transcontinental air passenger service involved flying during the day and riding in Pullman cars at night. Both trucks and railroad cars have been used in connection with pipeline transportation, and water-pipeline coordination has been used.

By use of containers, which have great flexibility, it is possible to coordinate several modes. After all, a truck trailer is really only a container on wheels. Service whereby specially designed truck trailers or vans are detached from their wheels and loaded on specially built rail cars is common. Sometimes these "vans" are further loaded on ships for overseas points, making another type of coordinated service. Actually, there is little to prevent flexible containers from using several modes of transportation.

The whole field of containerization affects transportation and may be considered an integral part of the subject. In reality, any shipment packed in a box is containerized. Thus, containerization is really a matter of degree. The whole point of containerization is to minimize expensive handling of freight. Great strides have been made in the use of larger containers, but lack of standardization of sizes has held back complete development of this area. Further standardization would promote further coordinated services using joint routes, rates, and billing between several modes. Many feel that containerization, when more highly developed, will bring great changes in transportation.

Express service, using several modes of transportation, through the REA Express Company and others, is also a type of coordinated service. Here an independent agency handles the movement and deals with other carriers. In this same sense, freight forwarders could be considered as offering coordinated service.

Beneficial Results of Coordinated Service

The rationale of these various combinations of line hauls as well as other coordinating devices is that the results are highly beneficial to all concerned —carriers, shippers, and the public. This is the major reason, of course, why these services are permitted and encouraged.

Carriers benefit in several ways. Usually coordinated service allows them to share in traffic they might not otherwise handle. In the popular piggyback service, for example, railroads have been recapturing traffic which they had lost because of the flexibility of the truck. At the same time, trucks often have been able to offer long-distance transportation more cheaply by piggyback. Less labor is involved, equipment can often be better utilized since fewer expensive power units are necessary, and less wear and tear on equipment results. Railroads, too, make better use of their capital and find that piggyback rail cars have a high degree of utilization. This means that rail investment is recovered from piggyback equipment faster than from some other types of equipment. In this case, both carriers benefit by sharing traffic and having lower costs and increased efficiency.

Shippers benefit in several ways also. Coordinated service is usually better service. Through routes from door to door, through billing by one mode, and fewer arrangements to negotiate are all a convenience. Sometimes the charges are lower and generally the service is faster by coordinated service than by one mode. Less damage may occur, too, since freight is not handled as often.

The public also benefits from coordination. While it may be hard to see on the surface, poor usage of the resources devoted to transportation is detrimental to the public in general. If each mode can undertake the task that it performs best in coordination with other modes, better allocation of resources results. From the broad viewpoint, the better the use of resources, the more the public benefits.

Obstacles to Coordinated Carrier Service

If coordination is both beneficial and noncontroversial, why is there not more of it in domestic transportation? Cooperation between carriers of the same mode is highly developed and very beneficial, as we have seen. Coordination also is beneficial to carriers, the shipper, and the public, but perhaps not in the same degree. The fact that the various modes naturally compete in at least a portion of their service hampers coordination. Each mode wishes to give the most complete service possible and have for itself the greatest possible amount of tonnage. This is natural and expected in a competitively structured system of transportation. This tendency to wish to hold all possible freight to the detriment of competitive modes is one reason why regulatory authorities were given the power to enforce rail-water coordination. Here it was necessary for the public, acting through legislation, to change the attitude of the carriers concerned and make them coordinate.

The matter of attitude is highly important. More coordination of transportation is technologically possible, legally possible, and highly desirable. No new laws need to be passed, no new public attitudes need to be cultivated. A great deal more coordinated carrier service may be employed in the future with each mode doing that part of the transportation movement which it does best. (Later in this book, we shall call this "inherent advantage.") Coordinated service is an excellent device to bring out the inherent advantage of each mode. Nothing stands in the way of the use of this service except the attitudes of the various carrier managements.

SUMMARY OF PART THREE

In this part, we have considered the supply side of for-hire transportation, with considerable emphasis on line-haul service. We have looked into the legal framework within which this service is rendered, the optional and accessorial services which carriers perform and which thus become a part of the transportation bundle, and the framework of cooperative and coordinated carrier services.

Now that some basic knowledge of carrier services and practices has been outlined, we will next consider the costs of transportation and the rates and prices under which domestic transportation operates, plus some of their economic effects.

ADDITIONAL READINGS

1. Bigham, Truman C., and Merrill J. Roberts, **Transportation,** 2nd ed. New York: McGraw-Hill Book Co., 1952.
   Chapter 18. "Regulation and Coordination of Service," pp. 498–535.
2. Daggett, Stuart, **Principles of Inland Transportation,** 4th ed. New York: Harper and Brothers, 1955.
   Chapter 23. "Cooperation Between Railroad Companies," pp. 459–485.
   Chapter 26. "Coordination," pp. 551–564.
3. Fair, Marvin L., and Ernest W. Williams, Jr., **Economics of Transportation,** Rev. ed. New York: Harper and Brothers, 1959.
   Chapter 30. "Coordination of Transportation," pp. 636–660.
4. Grossman, William L., **Fundamentals of Transportation.** New York: Simmons-Boardman Publishing Corp., 1959.
   Chapter 6. "Vehicles," pp. 108–138.
5. Hudson, William J., and James A. Constantin, **Motor Transportation.** New York: Ronald Press Company, 1958.
   Chapter 9. "Coordinated Transportation Service," pp. 203–221.
6. Locklin, D. Philip, **Economics of Transportation,** 6th ed. Homewood, Ill.: Richard D. Irwin, Inc., 1966.
   Chapter 38. "Transportation Coordination and Interagency Competition," pp. 854–873.
7. Mossman, Frank H., and Newton Morton, **Principles of Transportation.** New York: Ronald Press Company, 1957.
   Chapter 21. "Piggy-Back Operations," pp. 383–399.
8. Troxel, Emery, **Economics of Transport.** New York: Rinehart & Company, Inc., 1955.
   Chapter 14. "An Allocative Question: Transport Coordination," pp. 325–348.
9. Van Metre, Thurman W., **Industrial Traffic Management.** New York: McGraw-Hill Book Co., 1953.
   Chapter 16. "Car Service and Demurrage," pp. 306–334.
10. Wilson, G. Lloyd, **Traffic Management.** Englewood Cliffs, N.J.: Prentice-Hall, Inc., 1956.
    Chapter 22. "Associations in Traffic Management," pp. 374–386.

Part Four

The Role of Costs
and Rates in
Domestic Transportation

Expenditures for moving freight, with which we are concerned in this part, have hovered around or slightly below 9 per cent of GNP for a good many years. A substantial part of GNP, however, clearly well over 40 per cent, is composed of expenditures for personal, business, and governmental services rather than the purchases of tangible goods. Freight charges are not paid on services. If we exclude the services portion of GNP, then, and apply the expenditures for freight movement only to the goods we buy, the average increases from around 9 per cent to around 15 per cent.

More than 40 per cent of these freight-movement expenditures are for the services of common or contract carriers whose rates are subject to federal regulation. In addition, a sizable portion of the nonfederally regulated amount is for the services of carriers, mainly trucks, whose rates are regulated by state authorities. Clearly, well over one half of the total expenditures are for payments to regulated for-hire carriers. The remainder is for private or exempt carriage, or for expenses directly associated with for-hire or private transport.

As the costs of moving goods must be reflected in prices paid for goods, even these average figures indicate how directly transport costs and for-hire freight rates affect all of us. These charges, of course, are much less than the 15 per cent average for some products, but on others they range up to one half or more of the prices paid by consumers. Cost and price elements of this magnitude affect sellers as well as buyers. Higher prices mean fewer sales; and in a competitive situation, those sellers with higher transport costs may find themselves relatively handicapped or even excluded from some markets because of the lower transport costs or freight rates of their competitors.

Literally, a freight-rate level or a rate structure may economically make or break an individual business, an industry, a community, or a large geographic region. Both the level of rates and the comparative rates paid by competitors are important to sellers of products. Freight rates may determine whether or not a business will be successful and whether its employees will continue to have jobs. Likewise, from the carriers' viewpoint, comparative rate levels may determine which mode or which carrier gets the bulk of the traffic and which goes into bankruptcy.

With the vital economic interests of consumers, producers and sellers, employees, carrier modes and individual carriers, and even entire industries, communities, or large sections of the country involved, it is easy to see why proposed freight rates or rate changes often lead to bitter controversy. Also, it is understandable why such controversy often results in the creation of more heat than light.

Unfortunately, the typical individual (even including the businessman whose transportation costs are quite important in his operations) is woefully lacking in knowledge concerning freight rates. He does not understand their economic and legal characteristics, their regulation, how they are made and changed, their application, their terminology, their structures, or their economic effects. Even if he realizes their importance as a cost factor, he is inclined to regard this as a necessary evil about which he can do little except complain and leave the details to that rather odd character surrounded by mountains of incomprehensible freight-rate tariffs in a corner of the shipping department.

This lack of general knowledge of freight rates and their effects is both unnecessary and undesirable. In this part, therefore, the authors propose to dissipate some of the clouds surrounding this subject.

The Economic and
Legal Basis of Rates

Transportation rates are simply prices charged by carriers for performing their services. It is a mistake to think that the subject of rates and rate-making is a simple one, however. All major price systems are complex and none more so than that used in transportation. Problems of supply and demand, or of costs and value of service, regulation and legal obligations, competition and capacity, and the forces of tradition are intricately interwoven into a pattern of chaos and confusion not unlike the Gordian Knot. Those who would unravel this pattern, like Alexander, must cut directly into its heart.

One transportation man, speaking to a nontransportation audience, compared freight rates to prices of bags of potatoes. This is a great oversimplification. To a consumer, any bag of potatoes (of a given weight and grade) is like every other bag. Almost every freight-rate bag, however, differs from every other bag in its volume of content, grade, cost of production, and desirability in the consumer's eye. Every offer by every transportation company to every consumer for every specific piece of transportation is a different bag.

To become an expert on rates, even for one form of carriage, requires lengthy study and practice (as well, perhaps, as a certain amount of talent along such lines). Despite their complexities, though, the principles of rates and rate structures, and their formation and effects, are not beyond the understanding of anyone with average intelligence and a basic grasp of the economics of pricing. The first step in this understanding is to comprehend what it is that rates are designed to do.

ECONOMIC FUNCTIONS OF RATES

Economically speaking, freight rates have two primary functions, one for the user and one for the carrier. These are (1) to permit freight to move, and (2) to compensate the carrier.

Whether or not a shipper uses a rate depends upon its level. If the rate is too high, that is, if it is higher than the value of the service to the shipper, goods will not move. Rates sometimes may be set at unusably high levels for several reasons. The carrier's cost of performing the service may be higher than the value of the service to the shipper; the carrier may *believe* his costs are this high, which amounts to the same thing; or the carrier may overestimate the worth of the movement to the shipper.

Also, for some reason a carrier may not wish to handle particular traffic and thus may deliberately set out to price itself out of a specific market. (In view of the common carrier's obligation to serve, discussed in Chapter 7, such a policy *if proven* might have legal repercussions. Proof of intent is difficult to obtain, however.) It has been alleged that some railroads during recent years have deliberately attempted to discourage business by overpricing. Trucking firms and airlines have also been accused of consciously setting rates at levels which discourage the movement of less profitable forms of traffic, thus leaving such traffic for the railroads.

Finally, individual carriers or particular modes of carriage may sometimes be forced by government regulation to keep some rates at a higher level than they wish.

There is considerable debate about what is a compensatory rate or rate level. In any case, rates in the aggregate must be high enough to pay carriers for their costs of performing such services as the public demands, including whatever profits are necessary to attract or retain sufficient capital investment for this purpose. The alternative ultimately is bankruptcy and cessation of service or some form of public subsidy which reduces the carriers' costs or increases their revenues. It should be remembered, however, that it is not necessary that any particular rate be high enough to cover all costs or even the direct costs associated with it, nor that rates in the aggregate do this at all times. It is only necessary that *aggregate rates in the long run* cover all costs if services are to be continued. (See Chapters 4 and 5 for a discussion of fixed and variable costs, long-run and short-run periods, and operating ratios of the various forms of carriage.)

In the regulated public utility industries (which includes transportation), there has been a traditional belief usually supported by law that rate levels which yield a net return (accounting profit) of from six to eight per cent annually on investment in a well-managed company or group of companies are "reasonable" rates. If the yield, therefore, is higher, there is a suspicion that the rates are too high and that the company or industry is enjoying monopoly profits. If, on the other hand, the yield is lower, assuming competent management and a normal level of demand for services, it may be suspected that rates are too low and that the company or companies concerned are entitled to rate increases on the grounds of inadequate compensation.

Such an absolute earnings yardstick, of course, brings on problems of interpretation. What is a well-managed company? What is a normal level of demand? And, in particular, what is the investment base against which the yield is measured? Should investment be calculated at original cost of the assets used less accrued depreciation, at current replacement costs of assets, or by some other method? Should the allowable yield be measured against all assets, or should a distinction be made between firms with widely differing ratios of equity and debt financing? Many court cases have dealt with these and similar questions, but answers satisfactory to all parties involved have not been found.

Economists in particular have criticized absolute formulas of reasonableness. In the Hope Natural Gas Case (*Federal Power Commission v. Hope Natural Gas Company*, 320 U.S. 591, 1944), the United States Supreme Court finally gave recognition to what economists had been saying for a long time. The decision of that case held, in effect, that a specific percentage rate of return on a specific evaluation of investment is not the most crucial test of reasonableness. Rather, the pertinent rate level is one which yields a rate of return sufficient to permit the firm to maintain its financial integrity, that is, a yield which will permit a company to retain or attract whatever capital investment is necessary to provide the services expected from it by the public.

Certainly the Hope Case formula more adequately meets the economic criterion of what constitutes a compensatory level of rates than does the more rigid fixed percentage of a fixed amount of investment. Even with the Hope formula, however, there are serious and unsolved problems. How are we to know whether or not a particular level of rates will permit a carrier or mode of carriage to maintain financial integrity? Market-place testing over a period of time provides the only sure answer, but this may be devastating to carriers with consequent disruption of desired transportation services if rates are set too low. If rates are established at unnecessarily high levels, on the other hand, the result may be higher charges for the users of transport services (the entire public) and a misallocation of economic resources. Clearly the Hope formula is no panacea, but it does shift the approach from a narrow legalistic path into the economic arena where it belongs.

Measured even against such a flexible yardstick as the Hope formula, it is obvious that the rate of return of many carriers falls considerably short of reasonable. This is especially true among railroads (see Chapter 4). Apparently pipelines as a group are not experiencing financial difficulties, and current airline problems may soon work themselves out. (Many airlines are also aided by direct subsidies.) The picture is more cloudy in the inland water- and truck-transport industries, with specific financial data not as readily available. It seems, however, that these two modes of carriage are doing better than the railroads as a group, even though they are not doing as well as they would like.

In summary, one of the pressing transportation problems of our era is to devise a system of rates which in practice will allow traffic to move while adequately compensating carriers performing the desired services. Like most such problems, this one can never be solved for all time. Today's solution will be tomorrow's problem. In a dynamic world and an ever-changing economy, con-

stant attention to major problems is essential to assure even reasonably satisfactory results.

REGULATION AND REASONABLE RATES

English Common Law, which has been carried over into our statutory law,
requires that common carrier rates must be reasonable. As seen in Chapter 7,
this is one of the historic duties of a common carrier. Part I, Section 1 (5) of
the Interstate Commerce Act, for example, states that "All charges made for any
service . . . shall be just and reasonable, and every unjust and unreasonable
charge . . . is prohibited and declared to be unlawful." Other sections of the
Interstate Commerce Act and other Federal and state transportation regulatory
statutes contain wording to the same effect.

The obligation to charge reasonable rates originally was designed to prevent carrier exploitation of the public. That is, it was aimed at unreasonably
high rates in monopolistic situations. Today, however, it is interpreted to apply
with equal force against unreasonably low rates. Also, the standards of reasonableness are as binding upon governmental regulatory agencies which approve,
disapprove, or set rates as they are upon carriers.

Many thousands of pages have been written in attempts to define or describe just what is meant by an unreasonable rate. For our present purposes,
however, it is sufficient to define an unreasonably high rate as one which allows
a carrier to collect considerably more than is necessary under the circumstances
to provide its service, in other words, to take advantage of some ability to exploit its public. An unreasonably low rate, on the other hand, is one which does
not adequately compensate the carrier for its services. Obviously, both of these
kinds of unreasonableness are in some way related to carrier costs, although
other factors (such as demand, competition, and even public policy or public
welfare) may enter into the picture.

The general prohibition of unreasonably high rates requires little discussion
or justification at this point. Such rates are contrary to our long-established
Anglo-American laws and ideas of economic justice and efficiency, just as are
monopolistically exploiting prices in other areas of economic endeavor. The
concept itself is not seriously questioned by many, although heated discussions
may develop as to whether a particular rate or price does fall into the "unreasonably high" category.

The prohibition of unreasonably low rates, on the other hand, may require
a little more discussion. Here, too, ideas of equity, efficiency, and allocation of
economic resources are involved. If a particular rate does not adequately compensate a carrier for performing its services, one of two things must follow.
Either the low-rate traffic is being subsidized by higher-than-necessary rates
paid by shippers of other traffic, or the carrier itself (that is, those who have

invested in the transportation business) is subsidizing the low-rate movement by receiving lower profits (or taking greater losses) than it otherwise would. If the aggregate rate level (that is, rates in general) is unreasonably low, it follows that the capital value of the carrier or carriers concerned is being eroded; in other words, transportation investors as a group are subsidizing shippers and the general public as a group. Only those who are not opposed to one or some of the above results can support unreasonably low rates as such. But, of course, there may be a difference of opinion as to whether or not a particular rate or rate level is unreasonably low.

For some reason, a carrier may deliberately choose to charge an unusually low rate—one which it or others may believe to be less than adequate. This may, and very likely will, bring protests from other carriers or from producers of commodities competing with the low-rate traffic on the grounds that the carrier concerned or its shippers are thereby engaging in unfair or destructive competition. Shippers of noncompeting products may protest likewise on the grounds that unduly low rates to some mean unduly high rates to others. Even the general public, which has an interest in the maintenance of adequate facilities for desired transportation services, may be concerned about unduly low rates. Actually, for a good many years there have been many more protests before Federal and state transportation regulatory agencies about proposed rate decreases than about proposed increases.

In the absence of convincing objections of this kind, however, many people would say that a carrier's decision to put even extremely low rates into effect on portions of its traffic is its own concern. If stockholders do not like to subsidize users or do not trust the decisions of their management, they can remove the managers.

It is quite a different matter, however, if a regulatory agency attempts to force carriers to put into effect or maintain particular rates or aggregate rate levels which are noncompensatory (however that may be defined). All courts have long held that such action by regulators constitutes "taking property without due process of law," which is a violation of the United States Constitution (the Fifth Amendment if done by Federal action, and the Fourteenth Amendment if done by state regulatory agencies).

Constitutional protection then, coupled with poor carrier earnings, may effectively tie the hands of regulatory authorities in rate-increase cases. The years following World War II saw several successive rounds of railroad rate increases, many of which were accompanied by similar increases by other modes of carriage. There may be some grounds for questioning the economic judgment of carriers in instituting many of these increases, but there is little ground for questioning their legal rights to put them into effect. Legal reasonableness, based largely upon a cost-revenue concept, may be quite different from economic reasonableness which is governed in considerable part by demand considerations.

DEFINITIONS OF DEMAND AND SUPPLY

Demand is based on the purchaser's estimate of the value of a good or service to him, while supply is based upon the seller's estimate of his cost of making the good or service available. It is a commonly accepted truism that demand reacts with supply to determine prices, that demand establishes upper limits for prices, and that producers' costs (with a given demand situation) establish limits to the quantity which will be supplied. Since freight rates or passenger fares are prices for transportation services, these generalizations are as valid in transportation as in other forms of economic activity.

Like most truisms, however, those dealing with demand and supply describe only surface effects. To understand the workings of the described phenomena, it is necessary to probe into the depths. This and the following section will consider some deeper aspects of demand, while the final section of this chapter will more fully explore costs (supply) as related to the provision of transportation services.

First, it is necessary to have several definitions firmly in mind. The term "demand" as used by economists refers to the quantities of a good or service which would be purchased *at all possible prices* (just as "supply" means the quantities that would be offered for sale at all possible prices). An *increase* in demand, then, means that buyers are willing to purchase more than formerly at a given price or at all possible prices. Conversely, a *decrease* in demand means that buyers are no longer willing to purchase as much as before at any given price or prices.

Sometimes one hears that "a decrease in price increases the demand, and vice versa." This is not correct, according to the above definitions. Actually, the correct statement should be that "a decrease (or increase) in price increases (or decreases) the *quantity* that people are willing to buy." Price changes as such *do not* increase or decrease *demand*.

Study of Figure 8 may further clarify these definitions and relationships. In that figure, the line SS is a supply curve or schedule showing how much sellers will be willing to provide at various prices, for example, one unit at $2 and 10 units at $4. The quantities that purchasers will buy at various prices is shown by the demand curve or schedule, line DD, ranging from two units at $7 to eight units at $2. The price which will just "clear the market," that is, where the quantity offered will equal the quantity purchasers are willing to buy, is at about $3.25. At this price, between six and seven units will be offered and bought. At lower prices, purchasers will be willing to buy more; but unless supply conditions change, sellers will not be willing to furnish more. Or at higher prices, sellers will make more available, but purchasers will not buy more.

Line D^1D^1 shows an increase in demand. Now, as can be seen, purchasers are willing to pay higher prices for the same quantities or to buy more at the

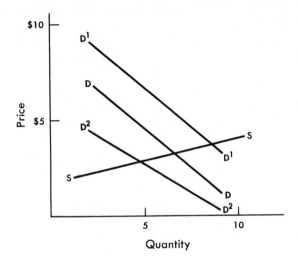

Figure 8: Demand and Supply Schedules
and Changes in Demand.

original prices. A decrease in demand, which means that less can be sold at
the original prices or that the original quantities can only be sold at lower
prices, is shown by line D^2D^2. Changes in demand, increases or decreases, are
caused basically either by changes in income levels (purchasing power) or by
changes in consumer tastes or preferences. These basic causes, of course, may
be influenced by any number of factors.

The incorrect statement to the effect that "demand varies with price" really
recognizes, in a loose way, the important concepts which economists label as
elasticity or *inelasticity* of demand. In normal pricing situations, it is almost
always true (assuming that "other things are equal," or unchanged) that a
price decrease encourages people to buy more and a price increase causes
them to buy less.

Sellers usually are more interested in the effects of price changes on their
revenues (and profits) than in the effects upon quantities sold as such. Sometimes a relatively small price decrease will generate so many additional sales
that revenues will be substantially increased above their original level. Conversely, even a small price increase may reduce sales so much that revenues are
significantly lowered. In these situations, it is said that demand is *elastic*. On
the other hand, *inelasticity* of demand exists when a price increase results in
increased total revenues or when a price decrease causes decreased revenues.
Stated concisely, *total revenues vary inversely with price changes if demand is
elastic, and directly with price changes if demand is inelastic.* Elasticity, unlike

changes in demand itself, is purely a price phenomenon. Obviously, those who contemplate price changes should have some knowledge of the elasticity or inelasticity of demand for their product even if they are not acquainted with the economists' terminology.

Economists usually draw demand and supply curves as narrow lines, such as are shown in Figure 8. This is convenient for exposition. In many situations, however, it may be more realistic to think of demand and supply "curves" as encompassing "bands" rather than narrow lines, as in Figure 9. That is, within some "zone of indeterminateness," where the DD and SS schedules overlap in that figure, variations in price, production cost, or quantity have little or no effect on the other variables. The size of such a zone, if one exists, will, of course, vary with products and marketing and cost conditions at any given time.

Before proceeding with a discussion of the nature of the demand for transportation, three other terms must be defined. *Aggregate demand* for transportation refers to the demand for services in general, that is, to the total of all of the individual demands for all services of all carriers. *Modal* demand means all demands for the services of a particular mode or form of carriage. *Particular demand* is used in referring to demands for the services of an individual carrier.

THE DEMAND FOR TRANSPORTATION SERVICES

As already indicated, demand is related to value of service. But we might well ask, "value of service to whom?" There may be a social or community aggregate demand for transportation which is greater than the sum of the conscious individual demands. That is, all of us as a group may want more transportation facilities and services to be available than we are willing to pay for through our use of these services on an individual basis.

Demands of Society

The citizens of regions A and B may wish to have a highway or railway between their communities. For national defense or other reasons, a country may wish to maintain extensive commercial airline or merchant marine facilities. Or an underdeveloped nation, as our own country was a century ago, may desire expanded transport facilities to exploit latent natural resources or economic opportunities. But it may be that revenues from the actual or potential use of these facilities by private shippers or travelers is not sufficient to pay their costs. Still, society as a whole "demands" that these facilities and services be available, making the social demand higher than the sum of the individual user's demands.

If this social demand is to be met, the gap between what users are willing to pay for individual services and the revenues necessary to build, maintain, and operate the desired facilities must come from public subsidy. This may lead to at least a temporary excess of available services, or we might say that

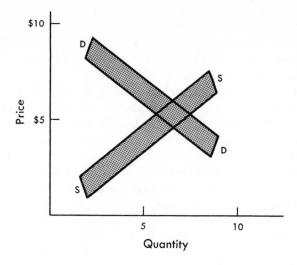

Figure 9: A "Zone" Concept of Demand and Supply.

"supply has outrun demand." Such a situation, in addition to creating a different allocation of resources than would exist in the absence of subsidy, may have a depressing effect on rates and revenues of unsubsidized forms of competing carriage. These effects are inevitable in meeting a social demand for excess capacity.

Demands of Individuals

Even from an individual user's viewpoint, it is not easy to determine the value of a transportation service. As indicated in Chapter 6, long-distance transportation of goods is based primarily upon either inherent regional differences or upon regional specialization (which may or may not be attributable to transportation factors). One might think, therefore, that the individual shipper's value of transportation service could be measured by the price difference between his product at its point of origin and at some other point. This is not necessarily so.

Interregional price differences are as likely to be determined by freight rates as are freight rates to be determined by price differences. As an economist might say, "Freight rates are both price determined and price determining." Many products sell at a standard price throughout the country even though freight rates from their points of origin to their numerous destinations may vary considerably. Much interregional cross-haulage of similar or identical products occurs, often with little or no interregional price differences.

Strictly speaking, a shipper's value of service insofar as the transportation of a particular shipment is concerned is measured by the additional net revenue that he will receive if he makes the shipment, that is, by the difference between a "do ship" and "don't ship" decision. Freight charges must be viewed alongside this revenue. If the freight charge is lower than the additional revenue, it will pay him to make the shipment; if higher, it will not pay; if the two are identical, it becomes a matter of indifference.

Additional net revenue (or what economists sometimes call "marginal revenue product" or "marginal value product") obviously is not the same as "price times quantity," nor can it be precisely measured by calculations based upon interregional price differences (if any). Price is only a starting point. Additional net revenue from a shipment may be influenced by a shipper's (producer's) fixed versus variable cost situation, his existing inventory coupled with anticipated future market conditions, alternative opportunities for employing his resources, long-run considerations of customer good will and market development, and numerous other factors, all of which vary from shipper to shipper and from time to time. Even the shipper himself is not likely to know exactly how his additional net revenue will be affected by a given shipment. But as long as he *thinks* he knows and acts accordingly, his demand for transportation is determined.

In view of the foregoing, it must be clear that a carrier, a group of carriers, or a regulatory agency cannot easily determine what freight rate or level of rates will maximize transportation revenues or attain any other objective. Factors determining the level and nature of the demand for transportation are complex and ever-changing. At best, only a reasonable approximation of an ideal rate structure can be expected. Nevertheless, it is possible to make some useful generalizations concerning the nature of transportation demand.

Determinants of the Degree of Elasticity

First, we must remember that the demand for freight transportation (and even for a considerable part of passenger transportation) is a *derived* demand, that is, it is dependent upon or originates from the demand for the *product* being transported. No freight (and probably very few people) moves from place to place merely for the sake of movement. Thus, for products which are available or *may be* produced locally as well as brought in from more distant sources (which may include many more items than we might at first imagine), it follows that the demand for transportation will be *more elastic* than the demand for the product itself. If the price of transporting a particular product is unduly high, or if its transportation rate is significantly increased, local sources of supply may be utilized even though production costs locally may be higher than in outside areas. Conversely, low or lowered rates may encourage outside shipments and discourage higher-cost local producers.

The aggregate demand for transportation, which grows out of the demands for all products, is closely related to the general level of economic activity. Thus it is relatively inelastic. Prosperity with high production, incomes, and purchasing power necessarily requires a great amount of transportation. Needs and demands for transport are not as great during depressed periods. Changes in general economic conditions, therefore, rather than changes in transportation prices as such, are of most importance in determining changes in the total quantity of transportation services used.

This does not mean that rate changes do not have some effects on aggregate transportation demand, both during periods of prosperity and of depression. As mentioned above, local production, which requires less transportation, may be stimulated by higher or discouraged by lower rates. But unless such rate changes are widespread and extreme in size, their impact on aggregate demand is likely to be minor.

The elasticity or inelasticity of modal demand is significantly affected by the availability, or the lack of availability, of other forms of carriage (in addition, of course, to the above-mentioned factors which affect aggregate demand). If only one form of carriage is available to or suitable for the transportation needs of a shipper, region, or type of traffic, we would expect to find a much greater degree of modal inelasticity than if alternate suitable modes of transport are available. Suitableness, of course, is made up of many things, including type of equipment, routes, departure times and running time, reliability, pickup- and-delivery services, and other components of the transportation bundle.

The type and extent of intermodal competition faced may be quite important in shaping the rate structure of a given mode. For example, suppose that railroads are competing more keenly with trucks for short-haul than for long-haul traffic. Then if the railroads need additional revenues, it may be more practical from a demand viewpoint to make proportionately greater rate increases on long-haul than on short-haul movements. On the other hand, if transcontinental railroads are competing primarily with intercoastal water carriers, more of the additional revenues may have to be derived from short-haul or intermediate-haul traffic. This creates obvious problems for the railroads concerned if both kinds of competition exist!

The inelasticity or elasticity of a particular demand for transportation is, of course, influenced by the same factors that influence aggregate and modal demand. In addition, various kinds of business ties and arrangements and existing physical facilities of the shipper or his customer may be important. Such things may include purchasing reciprocity, particular kinds of loading and unloading docks and equipment, spur tracks, and similar items. Also, noncost or nonrational factors, such as family ties, personal friendship, and even ignorance of alternate transportation facilities or shipper inertia often are important.

In review, it appears that of the three types of transportation demand which we have considered, aggregate demand is least elastic (or more inelastic). Modal demand generally is next in order of elasticity, followed by particular demand which is most elastic (or least inelastic) of the three. No doubt an informed observer can find exceptions to this generalization, as is true of all generalizations, but basically this seems to be the existing situation.

Several other general factors which contribute to the elasticity or inelasticity of all three types of demand should be mentioned. Demand is likely to be more *inelastic* if (1) the burden of increased rates (prices) can be passed on to an intermediate purchaser or final consumer, that is, if the demand for the product itself is extremely inelastic; (2) the burden can be passed back to earlier production stages, as labor, or the owners of land, or natural resources; (3) the shipper's or receiver's profit situation is such that higher rates can be absorbed easily; or (4) when freight charges are only a small part of the total delivered cost (this condition may be found often with goods that are highly valuable in proportion to their bulk or weight); or (5) when freight rates are very low (demand usually is more elastic at higher than at lower price levels).

It is possible, also, because of "tapering" rate structures (see Chapter 13) which make the per-mile price of transportation significantly lower as the distance moved increases, that the demand for much long-haul transportation tends to be more inelastic than that for short-haul transport (again, because of a generally greater inelasticity at lower price levels). The evidence and logic is not quite as conclusive on this point as on the other five above-described situations, however. It may depend upon whether buyers think of transportation price increases or decreases in absolute dollars-and-cents terms or in terms of percentage increases or decreases in the total delivered price. It may be, too, that this thinking varies among buyers and with the products concerned.

We have now looked at several factors which may contribute to inelasticity. Situations opposite those which have been mentioned, of course, contribute to elasticity of demand.

It is difficult to develop empirical evidence of elasticity or inelasticity, and even more difficult to measure accurately the degree to which this condition exists in transportation. In the dynamic world of business and economics, a researcher cannot exclude alien elements as easily as can a chemist in his test tubes. The demand schedule itself may be shifting while rates are changing. There is a tendency for freight rates to increase during periods of high or rising levels of economic activity, thus aggregate traffic losses from price increases may be more than offset by a higher level of demand growing out of higher incomes and greater production. Also, rates of competing modes are likely to change in the same direction at about the same time, thereby minimizing the shift of traffic between modes as a result of rate changes.

Elasticity and inelasticity are more than matters of faith, however, although difficult to measure accurately. The nature of demand creates real problems for those involved with pricing carrier services, but its understanding also creates real opportunities. Demand stands on an equal footing with costs in determining what price level is economically sound.

TRANSPORTATION COSTS AND RATE-MAKING

Everyone would agree that the costs of providing services determine an economically sound floor for rates. Costs are the underlying basis of the supply schedule already described. There is considerable disagreement, however, concerning just what costs are pertinent. Although at first glance it might seem that costs are more tangible and less controversial than demand, this is not always so.

Fixed and Variable Costs

You will recall that a distinction between fixed or constant costs (those not varying with volume of output) and variable costs (which do vary with the quantity produced) was made in Chapter 4. This is a "short-run" distinction only as all costs are variable in the long run. Chapters 4 and 5 discussed what is meant by short run and long run, as well as the differing fixed-variable cost situations and operating ratios faced by each basic mode of transport.

You know, too, that a firm which can cover its variable costs and have sufficient additional revenues to apply something toward its fixed costs will prefer to operate in this manner during the short run rather than to cease operations entirely. In a competitive situation, then, this gives a short-run pricing advantage to firms which have relatively high fixed costs as compared to high variable-cost firms, assuming total costs are approximately the same.

Figure 10 graphically illustrates the short-run pricing situations of two firms each of which has *total costs* (fixed plus variable) of $8 for producing ten units of output, but one of which has a fixed cost (FC^1) of $6 and the other a fixed cost (FC^2) of only $2. Variable costs are represented by the areas between the total-cost (TC^1 and TC^2 respectively) and the fixed-cost lines. Firm A, thus, can "afford" to operate in the short run at a price of anything more than $2 for ten units (even though it obviously will *prefer* at least $8, and will *require* this in the long run if it remains in operation). Firm B, on the other hand, cannot afford to price its ten units lower than $6 even in the short run.

Although accounting techniques often do not permit clear-cut distinctions between, or measures of, fixed and variable costs, there is little doubt that railroads (and pipelines) generally are characterized by high fixed costs as compared to motor, water, and air carriers. Also, as indicated in Chapter 4, railroad assets are long-lived, giving that mode a long run of more calendar years than is found in other forms of carriage (again, with the *possible* exception of pipelines). As many, perhaps most, competitive-pricing decisions are made on a short-run basis, the implications are obvious.

Further, since a long run is made up of a series of short runs, it is equally obvious that price policies which are economically logical from a short-run viewpoint may never cover total costs, leading ultimately to bankruptcy or

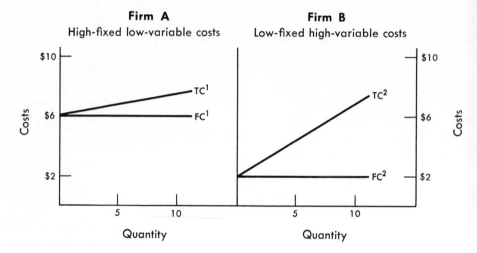

Figure 10: A Short-run Competitive Pricing Situation.

some form of subsidy. This is why regulatory agencies in establishing minimum rates sometimes say they are acting in the public's interest by protecting a carrier or mode of carriage from its own follies as well as protecting other carriers.

Out-of-Pocket Costs

Out-of-pocket cost is a term widely used in transportation circles in referring to the added costs incurred in performing an additional service. For example, this might be the cost added by increasing a 100-car freight train to a length of 101 cars, or of transporting another 100 pounds on a partially loaded truck. Economists would call this a "marginal cost"; but as generally used in the transportation industry, out-of-pocket cost is not as clearly defined as is the economists' term. Its meaning varies with the speaker. It may actually mean marginal cost, average variable cost at some particular level of output, or one of these plus some additional arbitrary overhead amount to cover a portion of fixed costs.

Regardless of which meaning is used, the analyses and the arguments for and against out-of-pocket cost pricing are about the same as for variable cost pricing discussed above. In the short run and with excess capacity, it does make sense to handle any additional traffic which does not contribute as much to direct costs as it does to revenues. In the long run, however, it does not make sense to replace capacity unless all costs associated with it and its employment can be recovered.

Unallocable Costs

Common costs and joint costs arise out of situations in which two or more kinds of production or units of output are so interrelated that some costs cannot be allocated to either one on any rational economic basis. (As used by economists, common and joint costs are slightly different concepts—joint costs referring to a fixed proportion of by-product output—but their effects on pricing decisions are the same.) Examples of unallocable costs might be portions of the fixed and variable costs of hauling more than one type of product in a vehicle or of hauling a return load. How much of the expense involved cannot be attributed to any one product or movement?

Unallocable costs are very prevalent in transportation, as in other types of production. If all costs of moving a particular shipment or type of traffic cannot be determined, however, it is not possible to base a price for this particular movement on its specific cost alone. The best that the rate-maker can do is to attempt to see that the total revenues generated by such common movements cover the total costs involved. At worst, he must hope to cover the specific allocable costs.

Terminal and Line-Haul Costs

A carrier's operating costs are made up of terminal costs and line-haul costs, with elements of both fixed and variable costs in each. Terminal costs of a particular shipment, in addition to fixed costs, may include expenses of such operations as pickup, billing, and loading into a vehicle. Normally terminal costs will be the same for a given shipment whether it moves for a long or a short distance. Line-haul costs, however, made up in considerable part of such variable items as wages and fuel costs, will be more or less proportionate to the distance hauled.

Terminal costs must be recovered quickly on short hauls, but they can be spread over many more miles on longer movements. This difference between long and short hauls frequently is reflected in tapering rate structures (see Chapter 13), that is, in higher per-mile rates on short than on long hauls. (Also, of course, even though line-haul costs do increase with distance, they may not increase in direct proportion to mileage.) Further, even if line-haul costs are approximately the same, a carrier with high terminal costs will likely have higher rates on short hauls or a higher absolute minimum rate than a carrier with lower terminal costs.

Figure 11 illustrates the cost (and probable rate) structures of two firms, one with high and the other with low terminal costs. Firm A is perhaps fairly typical of railroads which generally have relatively high terminal costs, at least on small shipments, while Firm B is more representative of lower terminal-cost motor carriers. This aids in explaining why trucks often have a significant pricing advantage over rail carriers in moving small shipments for short distances.

Cost of Service versus Value of Service

From the foregoing, it can be seen that costs are of equal importance with demand in establishing freight rates (or passenger fares), and that both are more complex than they at first appear. During recent years, there has

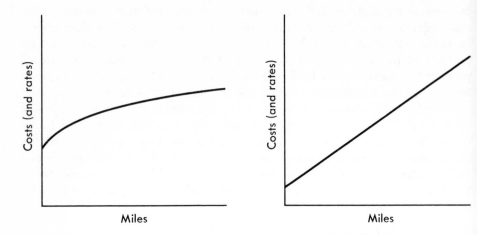

Figure 11: Effects of Differing Terminal Costs.

been considerable controversy over the cost-of-service principle versus the value-of-service principle (sometimes called "charging what the traffic will bear") in rate-making. During an earlier and less competitive era, value-of-service pricing was heavily favored by railroads. Losses on low-demand traffic could easily be offset by higher rates on high-demand movements. Today, though, when other forms of carriage are actively competing for the more valuable shipments leaving commodities with a lower value of service for the rails, the value-of-service rate-making concept is being questioned more and more.

The Interstate Commerce Commission has allowed competitive value-of-service rates, based on out-of-pocket or "incremental" costs, throughout most of its history. Sometimes this has resulted in traffic moving by rail (where out-of-pocket costs are relatively low) rather than by competing modes with lower *total* costs (including fixed costs) but higher out-of-pocket costs. The Commission took a different stand, though, in the celebrated *Ingot Molds Case* (Ingot Molds, Pennsylvania to Steelton, Kentucky, 323 I.C.C. 758 and 326 I.C.C. 77).

In that case, it was found that the total cost ("fully distributed cost," as defined by the Commission) of the rail movement involved was higher than a combination water-truck movement cost, but that the rail out-of-pocket cost was lower. The full Commission finally decided that the rail rate could not be lower than the total cost of the water-truck movement. This decision was upheld by the U.S. Supreme Court in 1968 (392 U.S. 571). If this case becomes a widely-followed precedent, as many believe that it may, considerable changes are likely to occur in future competitive rate-making. Whatever happens, it certainly seems to be true that the Commission now is much more cost-conscious than it was during earlier years.

Actually, neither value of service nor cost of service can be safely ignored, nor is it economically sound to overemphasize one at the expense of the other. As stated earlier in this chapter, an economically practical freight rate is one which allows traffic to move (based on value of service), while at the same time covering the carrier's costs of movement (cost of service). If either of these criteria are not met, the carrier or the public, or both, may have a problem. But there still is considerable dispute over what kind of "cost" is most appropriate for rate-making.

ADDITIONAL READINGS

1. Baumol, William J., et al., "The Role of Cost in the Minimum Pricing of Railroad Services," **The Journal of Business,** October 1962, pp. 1–10.
2. Calmus, Thomas W., "Full Cost Versus Incremental Cost: Again," **Transportation Journal,** Winter 1969, pp. 31–36.
3. Daggett, Stuart, **Principles of Inland Transportation,** 4th ed. New York: Harper and Brothers, 1955.
   Chapter 16. "Rates on Particular Hauls—The Theory of Pricing," pp. 299–315.
4. Dean, Joel, "Competitive Pricing in Railroad Freight Rates," **Journal of Marketing,** April 1961, pp. 22–27.
5. Fair, Marvin L., and Ernest W. Williams, Jr., **Economics of Transportation,** Rev. ed. New York: Harper and Brothers, 1959.
   Chapter 18. "Principles of Rate Making," pp. 350–367.
6. Jones, Eliot, **Principles of Railway Transportation.** New York: The Macmillan Co., 1931.
   Chapter IV. "The Theory of Railroad Rates," pp. 71–90.
7. Locklin, D. Philip, **Economics of Transportation,** 6th ed. Homewood, Ill.: Richard D. Irwin, Inc., 1966.
   Chapter 8. "The Theory of Railroad Rates," pp. 130–157.
8. Meyer, John R., Merton J. Peck, John Stenason and Charles Zwick, **The Economics of Competition in the Transportation Industries.** Cambridge, Mass.: Harvard University Press, 1959.
   Chapter III. "Railroad Cost Characteristics," pp. 33–63.
   Chapter IV. "The Cost Structure of Highway Transportation," pp. 64–110.
   Chapter V. "Cost Characteristics of Other Modes of Domestic Transportation." pp. 111–144.
9. Mossman, Frank H., and Newton Morton, **Logistics of Distribution Systems.** Boston: Allyn & Bacon, Inc., 1965.
   Appendix A. "Carrier Pricing Theory and Policy," pp. 349–366.
10. Mossman, Frank H., and Newton Morton, **Principles of Transportation.** New York: Ronald Press Company, 1957.
    Chapter 9. "Theory of Rate-Making," pp. 211–218.
11. Nelson, James C., **Railroad Transportation and Public Policy.** Washington, D.C.: The Brookings Institution, 1959.
    Chapter 10. "Pricing Policies for the Railroads," pp. 327–373.
12. Norton, Hugh S., **Modern Transportation Economics.** Columbus, Ohio: Charles E. Merrill Books Inc., 1963.

Chapter VI. "The Demand for Transport Services," pp. 123–133.
Chapter VII. "Pricing the Service," pp. 134–148.

13. Pegrum, Dudley F., **Transportation: Economics and Public Policy.** Rev. ed. Homewood, Ill.: Richard D. Irwin, Inc., 1968.
Chapter 8. "Theory of Pricing for Transport," pp. 174–197.

14. Roberts, Merrill J., "Some Aspects of Motor Carrier Costs: Firm Size, Efficiency and Financial Health," **Land Economics,** August 1956, pp. 228–238.

15. Roberts, Merrill J., "Transport Pricing and Distribution Efficiency," **Land Economics,** May 1970, pp. 181–190.

16. Rose, Joseph R., "Limits on Marginal Cost Pricing," **Transportation Journal,** Vol. 4, No. 2, Winter 1964, pp. 5–11.

17. Ruppenthal, Karl M. (ed.), **Issues in Transportation Economics.** Columbus, Ohio: Charles E. Merrill Books Inc., 1965.
Section Six. "Transportation Pricing Theory," pp. 137–158.
Section Seven. "Some Competitive Aspects of Transportation Pricing," pp. 159–194.

18. Sampson, Roy J., "Discussion of 'Pricing and Resource Allocation in Transportation and Public Utilities'," **Papers and Proceedings of the 75th Annual Meeting of the American Economic Association,** Vol. LIII, No. 2, May 1963, pp. 487–489.

19. Sampson, Roy J., "The Case for Full Cost Ratemaking," **I.C.C. Practitioners' Journal,** March 1966, pp. 490–495.

20. Smykay, Edward W., "An Appraisal of the Economies of Scale in the Motor Carrier Industry," **Land Economics,** May 1958, pp. 143–148.

21. Troxel, Emery, **Economics of Transport.** New York: Rinehart & Company, Inc., 1955.
Chapter 8. "Demands for Movements of Goods," pp. 169–193.

11

Freight Classifications and Tariffs: Their Preparation and Use

Despite their foreboding appearance, the transportation publications known as "classifications" and "tariffs" actually are simplifications. There may be as many as two million different kinds of commodities subject to transportation in the United States, and every one of these items conceivably is subject to transportation between any two of thousands of origin and destination points. Further, in moving from origin to destination, an exceedingly large number of alternate routes may be used. For example, the House Committee on Interstate and Foreign Commerce in a 1956 publication (*Transportation Policy*, 84th Congress, 2nd Session) reported that there are more than 4,700,000 possible rail routes between Dallas, Texas, and Detroit, Michigan.

In selling their services, transportation companies must establish prices on all the items they carry between any of the points and by any of the routes served. If you will attempt to calculate the astronomical number of individual prices required to do this and compare your findings with the relatively small number of items (at most, a few thousand) contained in the thickest classifications and tariffs, you will appreciate the tremendous simplification involved.

Even so, however, the amount of effort devoted to preparing, changing, and using classifications and tariffs is staggering. A survey by a leading transportation journal (*Traffic World*, September 15, 1962) found that 205,275 active tariffs were on file with the Interstate Commerce Commission. These tariffs covering existing prices of rail, motor, and water carriers, pipelines, freight forwarders, and express companies, contained from one to 1,500 rates each. They occupied 4,480 cubic feet or 5,366 linear feet of shelf space. Further, about 800,000 pages of tariffs are filed annually with the I.C.C., and this volume is increasing. The same survey found that a printing cost of $12 per page is not unusual for tariffs. The price of simplification is high, but the alternative is unthinkable.

THE PREPARATION AND USE OF CLASSIFICATIONS

The first step in pricing a shipment is to determine what it is that is to be shipped. This is the purpose of a classification. That is, each of the hundreds of thousands of shippable commodities, ranging from aardvarks to zymometers, is placed (classed or classified) in some one of a relatively small number of "classes." Then instead of shipping a commodity, in effect one ships a certain quantity of a certain "class." In the basic railroad classification, all goods are reduced to about 31 classes. This might be compared to sorting potatoes. Every potato falling into a certain grade (that is, with similar characteristics) is placed in a bag with other like potatoes (the classification), and all in a particular bag are priced alike.

Development and Present Status of Classifications

Classifications originally were developed by railroads, and rail classifications still are more extensive and comprehensive than are those used by other modes of carriage. The following discussion, therefore, will emphasize railroad classifications, with the necessary differences between railway and other carrier practices being pointed out.

Originally there were many railroad classifications in use, usually one for each major railroad. This was confusing. As rail transportation grew, however, these eventually were combined into one of three major classifications (Official, or Eastern; Southern; and Western) based on the territories primarily served by the participating railroads, plus a few minor or special classifications. The Illinois Classification was one of the best known of the minor group. The same commodity often was classed differently, had different minimum weights distinguishing between CL (carload) and LCL (less-than-carload) shipments, and had differing rules for packaging in each of the several classifications.

Government operation of railroads during World War I clearly showed the need for and the benefits of more rail cooperation. The three major classifications were published together in one volume—the *Consolidated Freight Classification*—in 1919, and the Illinois Classification was added a few years later. This was a major step forward, and yet each of the separate classifications retained its own identity. Opposite the description of each commodity, the classification applicable in each of the respective classification territories was shown in separate columns.

Finally, in 1952, after considerable pressure from the I.C.C., all railroads went over to the present *Uniform Freight Classification,* which applies the same classification to a commodity regardless of territory. (There was one fairly important exception. The old *Consolidated Freight Classification* continued to be used for shipments in "Mountain-Pacific Territory," roughly west of the Rocky Mountains, due to special competitive conditions. Some, but not all, traffic in this region shifted to the new classification in 1956.) The Uniform Classification Committee, with headquarters in Chicago, replaced the regional Official, Southern, and Western classification committees in 1964.

The present uniform railroad classification is made up of 31 numbered classes, with the old "First Class" of the *Consolidated* classification now being "Class 100." Other classes are based on multiples or fractions of Class 100, expressed in percentage terms, ranging from Class 400 to Class 13.

The format of the published classification consists of rules and regulations for its use and of the classes themselves. Commodities are listed alphabetically and described, and the pertinent CL and LCL Class is shown with minimum CL weights (normally LCL shipments are at least one class higher than CL movements). Class rates based on these classifications are higher or lower as the classifications go up or down numerically. (In the *Consolidated* classification, however, lower numbers mean higher rates.)

The format and arrangement of motor-carrier classifications is similar to that used by the rails. There is less uniformity in truck practices, however, as not all trucking companies use the National Motor Freight Classification. New England truckers, for example, still use a separate five-class classification based on a density (weight-space) formula. Ocean-water carriage rates usually are quoted on a "weight or space, whichever gives the highest charge" basis, while domestic water carriers often use the rail- or motor-carrier classifications. REA Express uses three basic classes, while pipelines which carry only one "commodity" have no classification problems. Classification practice is in its infancy in the air-freight business, with no generally used uniform national classifications. Freight forwarders use motor or rail classifications as appropriate to their mode of line-haul movement.

Figures 12 and 13, respectively, are reproductions of railroad and motor-carrier classifications. Comparison of these reveals their similarities. Actually, the motor-carrier classification was adopted in large part from the rail classification, with charges based upon the differing characteristics of the two modes (for example, lower TL or volume minimum weights than for rail CL or simpler packaging rules).

Classification-Committee Procedures

Procedures employed by rail and motor-carrier classification committees are approximately the same. Typically, a shipper (or a carrier) will propose that an existing commodity be reclassified or that a new product be brought into the classification. This proposal must be in the form specified by the rules of the committee. If it appears to be in order, it is docketed (that is, scheduled for discussion). After adequate notice to the industry by publication in specified traffic journals and distribution of dockets to interested parties, a public hearing is held. Proponents and opponents of the proposal are heard, then the committee votes. After a specified waiting period for objec-

Item	ARTICLES	Less Carload Ratings	Carload Minimum (Pounds)	Carload Ratings
2000	**ABRASIVES:**			
2010	Abrasive cloth or paper, including emery or sand paper, in packages...........................	55	36,000	37½
2020	Corundum, emery or other natural or synthetic abrasive material consisting chiefly of aluminum oxide or silicon carbide:			
2030	Crude or lump, LCL, in bags, barrels or boxes; CL, in bulk or in packages.................	55	50,000	27½
2040	Flour or grain, in packages..	55	36,000	35
2050	Refuse, including broken wheels, wheel stubs or wheel grindings, loose, see Note, Item 2051, or in packages...........	55	50,000	20
2051	Note.—LCL shipments may be loose only in lots of 10,000 lbs., subject to minimum charge as for 10,000 lbs.; shipments to be loaded by shipper and unloaded by consignee; shipper to furnish and install all dunnage and packing material; freight charges to be assessed on basis of gross weight of article and all dunnage or packing material.			
2060	Wheels, other than pulp grinding, in barrels, boxes or crates, or on skids if weighing each 300 lbs. or over; also CL, loose packed in packing material...........................	55	30,000	40
2070	Wheels, pulp grinding, in boxes or crates, or on skids..................................	55	30,000	40
2085	**ACIDS (see also Item 33800):**			
2090	Abietic, in barrels or in Package 84......................................	55	40,000	22½
2100	Acetic, glacial or liquid:			
	In carboys, other than Package 800.........................	100	30,000	45
	In glass in barrels or boxes or in Packages 514 or 800.........	77½	30,000	40
	In bulk in barrels or in Package 595; also CL, in tank cars, Rule 35...........	70	30,000	30
2110	Acetylsalicylic, in barrels, boxes or Package 1157...........	85	30,000	45
2120	Acids, noibn, dry:			
	In glass or in cans or cartons in barrels or boxes.........	92½	30,000	55
	In bulk in barrels, boxes, steel pails or 5-ply paper bags, or Benzoic acid or Fumaric acid in Package 1380.........	85	30,000	50
2130	Acids, noibn, liquid:			
	In carboys................	100	30,000	60
	In glass in barrels, boxes or Package 514.	92½	30,000	55
	In bulk in barrels; also CL, in tank cars, Rule 35.	85	36,000	50
2135	Adipic, in bulk in barrels, boxes, steel pails or 5-ply multiple-wall paper bags, or Packages 1171, 1217 or 1380; also CL, in bulk in covered hopper cars, Rule 37, see Note, Item 2136.........	65	30,000	30
2136	Note.—Minimum weight on shipments in covered hopper cars will be marked capacity of the car, except when shipper certifies on bill of lading that car has been loaded to 90% of full visible capacity freight charges will be assessed on basis of actual weight.			
2140	Arsenic, fused, in barrels or boxes, or in bars wrapped in paraffined paper in wooden boxes only..	70	36,000	37½
2150	Arsenic, other than fused:			
	In carboys................	100	30,000	45
	In barrels; also CL, in tank cars, Rule 35	70	36,000	37½
2160	Azelaic, from animal or vegetable fats, in bags, barrels or boxes...............	65	30,000	30
2170	Boric (boracic):			
	In glass in barrels or boxes...........	85	30,000	45
	In cans or cartons in barrels or boxes, or in bulk in bags, barrels, boxes or steel pails; also CL, in double-wall paper bags or in bulk.	70	36,000	35
2180	Carbolic (phenol):			
	In carboys................	100	30,000	55
	In glass or in metal cans in barrels or boxes.........	77½	30,000	40
	In bulk in barrels, or in metal drums in barrels or boxes, or in Package 598; also CL, in tank cars, Rule 35.	70	36,000	37½
2190	Chlorosulfonic, in bulk in barrels; also CL, in tank cars, Rule 35.........	60	36,000	35
2200	Chromic:			
	In glass or in metal cans in barrels or boxes, or in Package 800.........	85	30,000	45
	In bulk in steel barrels.........	70	36,000	37½
2205	Citric, dry:			
	In inner containers in barrels or boxes.........	85	30,000	45
	In bulk in barrels, in 5-ply multiple-wall paper bags or in Package 1388.........	70	30,000	40
2210	Cresylic (cresol):			
	In glass or in metal cans in barrels or boxes.........	77½	30,000	40
	In bulk in barrels; also CL, in tank cars, Rule 35.........	70	36,000	37½
2215	Decanedioic, in barrels, boxes, pails, or 5-ply multiple-wall paper bags.........	65	30,000	30
2220	Electrolyte, containing not to exceed 47% sulphuric acid:			
	In carboys, other than Package 800.........	100	30,000	45
	In inner containers in barrels or boxes, or in Package 800.........	70	30,000	40
	In lined barrels or rubber drums.........	60	36,000	35
2230	Fluophosphoric, in bulk in barrels; also CL, in tank cars, Rule 35.........	70	36,000	37½
2240	Formic:			
	In carboys, other than Package 800.........	100	30,000	35
	In glass in barrels or boxes or in Package 800.........	85	30,000	35
	In bulk in barrels; also CL, in tank cars, Rule 35.........	70	30,000	35
2250	Gluconic, liquid:			
	In carboys.........	100	30,000	60
	In bulk in barrels; also CL, in tank cars, Rule 35.........	85	36,000	50
2260	Hydrocyanic, in glass or metal cans in barrels or boxes, or in steel cylinders; also CL, in tank cars, Rule 35.........	85	30,000	45
2270	Hydrofluoric:			
	In containers in barrels or boxes, in steel jacketed lead carboys, or in Package 800.........	85	36,000	45
	In bulk in barrels or rubber drums, or in steel cylinders; also CL, in tank cars, Rule 35.....	70	36,000	37½
2280	Hydrofluoric and sulphuric, mixed, in bulk, in metal barrels; also CL, in tank cars, Rule 35....	70	36,000	35
2290	Hydrofluosilicic:			
	In carboys.........	100	36,000	45
	In containers in barrels or boxes.........	85	36,000	45
	In bulk in barrels or rubber drums; also, CL, in tank cars, Rule 35.........	70	36,000	37½

For explanation of abbreviations, numbers and reference marks, see page 474 and last page of this Classification; for packages, see pages 778 to 886.

Figure 12: Page from the Uniform Freight Classification.

Courtesy: Uniform Classification Committee

tions to or appeals from the decision, the docket is closed. If the action taken results in a change in or an addition to the classification, the committee's publishing agent is notified and the revision is made.

Sometimes, for special competitive reasons or other peculiar circumstances, some carrier or group of carriers serving a particular area will request permission to deviate from the established classification rate for some commodity or commodities. If approved, these deviations are published as "exceptions" to the classification for the carriers or areas.

What do the committees consider in establishing a classification for a particular commodity? Extensive lists of considerations have been developed, but, basically, perhaps four things are of most importance. *First,* the costs of transporting the good must be considered. This involves such characteristics as density (weight and size), shape, ease of handling, and susceptibility to loss or damage. *Second,* value of the service to the shipper, or "what the traffic will bear." *Third,* the potential volume of the movement, including whether it will be CL or LCL (or TL or LTL), as well as the direction and the origin and destination of the principal flow of traffic. *Fourth,* the competitive situation between carriers, modes of carriage, and intraregional and interregional producer and market competition. Or, perhaps, we could simply say that these factors and other considerations can be reduced down to cost of service and value of service.

Many commodities, of course, are classified by comparison with commodities possessing similar transportation characteristics, that is, by analogy. In fact, pending the establishment of a specific classification, shippers may use the "analogy rule" for movements, that is, an unclassed article will be shipped at the class and rate applicable to some similar item.

Needless to say, classification is a never-ending process, and classification committees and their publishing agents are quite busy. Shippers constantly demand lower classifications for their products in order to benefit from lower freight rates. Carriers want higher classifications for increased revenues (if they feel that demand is inelastic) or lower classifications to meet competition from other modes. And numerous new commodities are being developed each day, all of which eventually may require classification.

As stated above, however, classification is merely the first step in establishing or determining the price for transporting a commodity. The classification only tells *what is being shipped.* In order to determine the price for moving it "from here to there," one must resort to a *tariff.*

KINDS OF TARIFFS AND THEIR USE

Simply speaking, a tariff is a price list. The word "tariff" was derived from an Arabic word meaning "explanation" or "information." It explains or gives information on shipping prices (freight rates).

Item	ARTICLES	CLASSES (Ratings) LTL	TL	(MW)
1010	**ABRASIVES GROUP:**			
1030	**Abrasive Cloth or Paper, including Emery or Sand Paper,** in packages........................	55	37½	36.1
1050	**Alundum, Corundum, Emery or other Natural or Synthetic Abrasive Material** consisting chiefly of aluminum oxide or silicon carbide:			
1070	Crude or lump, LTL, in bags, barrels or boxes; TL, loose or in packages..................	55	35	50.1
1090	Flour or grain, in packages...	55	35	36.2
2010	Refuse, including broken wheels, wheel stubs or wheel grindings, see Note, item 2052, LTL, loose, subject to a minimum charge as for 10,000 pounds, see Note, item 2012, or in packages; TL, loose or in packages...	55	35	40.1
2012	**Note**—Shipments must be loaded and securely braced by shipper and unloaded by consignee. Freight charges to be assessed on gross weight of freight and dunnage or packing material.			
2030	**Wheels,** pulp grinding, see Note, item 2052, on skids or in boxes or crates..................	55	40	30.2
2050	**Wheels,** other than pulp grinding, see Note, item 2052, in barrels, boxes or crates, or on skids if weighing each 300 pounds or over; also TL, loose, packed in packing material..........	55	40	30.2
2052	**Note**—Such articles may be composed in part of materials other than abrasives.			
2080	**ACIDS:**			
2082	**Note**—For ratings dependent upon agreed or released value applicable in connection with items making reference to this note, see item 60000.			
3000	**Abietic,** in barrels, see Note, item 2082..	55	35	40.2
3020	**Acetic,** glacial or liquid, see Note, item 2082:			
Sub 1	In carboys other than specification 1D carboys. see Rule 55...........................	100	45	30.2
Sub 2	In glass in barrels or boxes, in Package 1190, or in specification 1D carboys, see Rule 55......	77½	40	30.2
Sub 3	In bulk in barrels, or Package 691: also TL in tank trucks, see Rule 23..................	70	35	30.2
3040	**Acids,** NOI, dry, see Note, item 2082:			
Sub 1	In cans or cartons or in glass in barrels or boxes.....................................	92½	55	30.2
Sub 2	In bulk in barrels, boxes, steel pails, 5-ply paper bags or Packages 1380 or 1388; also TL in Package 916...	85	50	30.2
3050	**Acids,** NOI, liquid, see Note, item 2082:			
Sub 1	In glass in barrels or boxes, or Package 1190..	92½	55	30.2
Sub 2	In carboys..	100	60	30.2
Sub 3	In bulk in barrels, or Packages 691 or 1014...	85	50	30.2
3070	**Arsenic,** fused, see Note, item 2082, in barrels or boxes, or in bars wrapped in paraffined paper in wooden boxes only..	70	37½	36.2
3080	**Arsenic,** other than fused, see Note, item 2082:			
Sub 1	In carboys...	100	45	30.2
Sub 2	In barrels, also TL in tank trucks, see Rule 23.......................................	70	37½	36.2
4000	**Azelaic,** from animal or vegetable fats, in bags, barrels or boxes......................	65	35	30.2
4020	**Boric (Boracic),** see Note, item 2082:			
Sub 1	In glass in barrels or boxes...	85	45	30.2
Sub 2	In cans or cartons in barrels or boxes, or in bulk in bags, barrels, boxes or steel pails; also TL, in double-wall paper bags or in bulk..	70	37½	36.2
4040	**Carbolic (Phenol),** see Note, item 2082:			
Sub 1	In carboys...	100	55	30.2
Sub 2	In glass or in metal cans in boxes...	77½	40	30.2
Sub 3	In bulk in barrels, or in metal drums in barrels or boxes; also TL, in tank trucks, see Rule 23.	70	37½	36.2
4060	**Chlorosulfonic,** in bulk in barrels; also TL, in tank trucks, see Rule 23, see Note, item 2082....	60	35	36.2
4080	**Chromic,** see Note, item 2082:			
Sub 1	In glass or in metal cans in barrels or boxes..	85	45	30.2
Sub 2	In bulk in steel barrels...	70	37½	36.2
4100	**Cresylic (Cresol),** see Note, item 2082:			
Sub 1	In glass or in metal cans in barrels or boxes..	77½	40	30.2
Sub 2	In bulk in barrels; also TL, in tank trucks, see Rule 23...............................	70	37½	36.2
4120	**Electrolyte,** containing not to exceed 47 percent sulphuric acid, see Note, item 2082:			
Sub 1	In inner containers in barrels or boxes, or in plastic carboys, or Package 278............	70	40	30.2
Sub 2	In carboys other than plastic carboys..	100	45	30.2
Sub 3	In lined barrels or rubber drums, or Package 691......................................	60	35	36.2
4140	**Formic,** see Note, item 2082:			
Sub 1	In glass in barrels or boxes, or in specification 1D carboys, see Rule 55..................	85	35	30.2
Sub 2	In carboys other than specification 1D carboys, see Rule 55............................	100	35	30.2
Sub 3	In bulk in barrels...	70	35	30.2
4160	**Hydrocyanic,** see Note, item 2082, in glass in barrels or boxes, in metal cans in barrels or boxes, or in steel cylinders...	85	45	30.2
4180	**Hydrofluoric,** see Note, item 2082:			
Sub 1	In containers in barrels or boxes, in lead carboys in steel jackets, or in plastic carboys.......	85	45	36.2
Sub 2	In bulk in barrels or rubber drums or in steel cylinders; also TL, in tank trucks, see Rule 23..	70	37½	36.2
4200	**Hydrofluoric and Sulphuric, mixed,** see Note, item 2082, in bulk in metal barrels; also TL, in tank trucks, see Rule 23...	70	35	36.2
4220	**Hydrofluosilicic,** see Note, item 2082:			
Sub 1	In carboys...	100	45	36.2
Sub 2	In containers in barrels or boxes...	85	45	36.2
Sub 3	In bulk in barrels or rubber drums; also TL, in tank trucks, see Rule 23................	70	37½	36.2
4240	**Hydroxy Acetic,** in bulk in barrels; also TL, in tank trucks, see Rule 23.................	70	35	30.2
4260	**Lactic,** see Note, item 2082:			
Sub 1	In glass in barrels or boxes..	77½	40	30.2
Sub 2	In glass bottles, each packed in rattan or willow basket or hamper......................	200	85	30.2
Sub 3	In carboys...	100	55	30.2
Sub 4	In barrels; also TL, in tank trucks, see Rule 23.......................................	70	35	30.2

For explanation of abbreviations and reference marks, see last page of this tariff.   257

Figure 13: Page from the National Motor Freight Classification.

Courtesy: American Trucking Associations, Inc.

In the strict sense, any type of carrier publication having to do with prices or charges may properly be called a tariff. This would include classifications, passenger-fare tables, routing guides, and similar publications. As commonly used, however, and as used in this book, the term "tariff" refers to publications quoting freight rates.

Basically, there are three kinds of freight tariffs: (1) *class* tariffs (and modifications of these, called *exceptions* tariffs), (2) *commodity* tariffs, and (3) *services* tariffs. These will be discussed in this order. Then the general format and use of tariffs will be briefly described.

Class Tariffs

The class tariff is the most basic type of freight-rate tariff in that it supposedly includes the price of shipping everything from and to everywhere (subject, of course, to the limitations of the geographical areas served by the carriers participating in the tariff and the kinds of commodities they offer to haul). It can only be used in conjunction with a classification. That is, one must first look up an item in the classification to determine its class. Then one must use the class tariff (which shows only the prices of moving *classes, not named commodities*) to determine the rate (usually given in cents per one hundred pounds) for transporting items in this particular class from one point to another.

Since class tariffs typically cover shipments from and to a large number of specific points, some further simplification is necessary. Usually the points of origin and destination themselves are assembled into several "groups" which are identified by numerical or alphabetical symbols. Thus, instead of shipping widgets from the city of Mohawk to the city of Marcola, in effect one ships "Class 40" from "Group C-1" to "Group A-2." This grouping of points obviously greatly decreases the number of entries in a tariff, but makes its use somewhat more complex. It should be noted that this type of "group," made for tariff simplification, differs from the blanket, zone, or group-rate territories described in Chapter 13.

Class rates may properly be called distance-scale rates. Although they generally do not increase in direct proportion to the distance hauled, there is certainly a demonstrable relationship between rate level and distance. This tendency has become more pronounced during the past several decades. Figure 14 is a reproduction of portions of two pages from a railroad class tariff.

Exceptions tariffs, as indicated above, are modified class tariffs. That is, although the classification still is used, certain specified items between specified points or in specifically named areas move at rates different from those shown in the basic class tariff. These modifications or exceptions usually are made for competitive reasons or for peculiar regional or local operating conditions.

SECTION 1—PART A—APPLICATION OF RATE BASES

Item	BETWEEN (See Item 110) AND Points on pages 123 to 203 in following Groups (See Item 110)	NORTH COAST TERRITORY (See Item 215)				SOUTH COAST TERRITORY (See Item 220)				
		Points shown on pages 13 to 130 as taking the following bases								
		NORTH COAST	CASCADE	PRAIRIE OR VALLEY	SPOKANE	SOUTH COAST	KELSO	SIERRA	NIPTON	LAS VEGAS OR RENO
		RATE BASES APPLICABLE (For rates, see Section 2)								
675	A.................	905	956	915	878	905	956	936	915	878
	B.................	912	875	840	805	912	875	858	840	805
	C, C-1...........	870	836	801	768	870	836	819	801	768
	D.................	829	796	763	731	829	796	780	763	731
	E.................	787	756	725	695	787	756	741	725	695
	E-1...............	787	756	725	695					
	F.................	746	717	686	658	746	717	702	686	658
	G.................	705	677	649	622	705	677	663	649	622
	H.................	829	796	763	731	705	677	663	649	622
	I.................	663	636	611	585	③663	③636	624	③611	②585
	J.................	639	613	588	563	③639	③613	601	③588	②563
	J-1...............	①639 / ②705	613	588	563					
	J-E...............	①590 / ②673	561	533	505					
	K, K-1...........	995	956	915	878	995	956	936	915	878
	L.................	912	875	840	805	912	875	858	840	805
	M.................	870	836	801	768	870	836	819	801	768
	N.................	779	748	718	686					

①Applies only from or to points in North Coast Territory in Washington and British Columbia; also points in Oregon named in National Rate Basis Tariff 1-A as taking Bonneville, Condon, Dike, Heppner, Kent, Portland, Rainier and The Dalles basis for rates.

②Applies from or to points in California and Oregon other than those included in "①" above.

③(a) Not applicable BETWEEN California and Nevada on the one hand AND New Mexico and Texas points on the other included in key groups shown in Items 700 to 979.

(b) Arbitraries referred to opposite the California points, pages 17 to 72 of this tariff, in Column headed "Basis Applicable" are NOT to be added to Items 700 to 979.

SECTION 2
CLASS RATES IN CENTS PER 100 POUNDS

RATE BASES NUMBERS	CLASSES															
	400	300	250	200	175	150	125	110	100	92½	85	77½	70	65	60	55
693.........	3172	2379	1983	1586	1388	1190	991	872	793	734	674	615	555	515	476	436
694.........	3176	2382	1985	1588	1390	1191	993	873	794	734	675	615	556	516	476	437
695.........	3180	2385	1988	1590	1391	1193	994	875	795	735	676	616	557	517	477	437
696.........	3188	2391	1993	1594	1395	1196	996	877	797	737	677	618	558	518	478	438
697.........	3192	2394	1995	1596	1397	1197	998	878	798	738	678	618	559	519	479	439
698.........	3196	2397	1998	1598	1398	1199	999	879	799	739	679	619	559	519	479	439
699.........	3200	2400	2000	1600	1400	1200	1000	880	800	740	680	620	560	520	480	440
700.........	3204	2403	2003	1602	1402	1202	1001	881	801	741	681	621	561	521	481	441
701.........	3208	2406	2005	1604	1404	1203	1003	882	802	742	682	622	561	521	481	441
702.........	3212	2409	2008	1606	1405	1205	1004	883	803	743	683	622	562	522	482	442
703.........	3216	2412	2010	1608	1407	1206	1005	884	804	744	683	623	563	523	482	442
704.........	3220	2415	2013	1610	1409	1208	1006	886	805	745	684	624	564	523	483	443
705.........	3228	2421	2018	1614	1412	1211	1009	888	807	746	686	625	565	525	484	444
706.........	3232	2424	2020	1616	1414	1212	1010	889	808	747	687	626	566	525	485	444
707.........	3236	2427	2023	1618	1416	1214	1011	890	809	748	688	627	566	526	485	445
708.........	3240	2430	2025	1620	1418	1215	1013	891	810	749	689	628	567	527	486	446
709.........	3244	2433	2028	1622	1419	1217	1014	892	811	750	689	629	568	527	487	446
710.........	3248	2436	2030	1624	1421	1218	1015	893	812	751	690	629	568	528	487	447
711.........	3252	2439	2033	1626	1423	1220	1016	894	813	752	691	630	569	528	488	447
712.........	3256	2442	2035	1628	1425	1221	1018	895	814	753	692	631	570	529	488	448
713.........	3264	2448	2040	1632	1428	1224	1020	898	816	755	694	632	571	530	490	449
714.........	3268	2451	2043	1634	1430	1226	1021	899	817	756	694	633	572	531	490	449
715.........	3272	2454	2045	1636	1432	1227	1023	900	818	757	695	634	573	532	491	450
716.........	3276	2457	2048	1638	1433	1229	1024	901	819	758	696	635	573	532	491	450
717.........	3280	2460	2050	1640	1435	1230	1025	902	820	759	697	636	574	533	492	451

Figure 14: Portions of a Railroad Class Tariff.

Courtesy: Trans-Continental Freight Bureau.

Commodity Tariffs

Figure 15 is a reproduction of a page from a railroad commodity tariff. Commodity tariffs differ from class tariffs in that they cover only the specific items and the specific movements *named* in the tariff. As items are listed by name and described in the commodity tariff, it is not necessary to use the classification in looking up a rate.

Commodity rates generally are established on products which move in large quantities between specific points. They do not necessarily apply in both directions, that is, a commodity rate on widgets may exist from Mohawk to Marcola but not from Marcola to Mohawk. Also, specific named routings may be required. Like class tariffs, commodity tariffs often make extensive use of groupings of points of origin and destination, and even of similar commodities. Sometimes the two forms of tariff are published together in a single volume as a class and commodity tariff, but usually commodity tariffs are separate publications. Often a separate commodity tariff will be published for a specific product such as coal or lumber, for example. Sometimes, though, commodity tariffs will include several types of products. These rates generally are less related to distance moved than are class rates.

Since commodity rates are established for special movements, they usually are lower than and take precedence over class rates. (A shipper normally is legally entitled to use the lowest published rate for his movement regardless of where it is published.) In reality, however, it is somewhat misleading to think of commodity rates as special deviations from class rates. Actually, the great bulk of freight tonnage and ton-mileage both by rail and truck moves under commodity rates. (Perhaps more than four fifths of rail tonnage in the country as a whole, and more than 90 per cent in some areas, is commodity tonnage.) The commodity-rate tail wags the class-rate dog.

Services Tariffs

A considerable number of carrier services other than line-haul movement may be included in the transportation bundle (see Chapter 8). Some or all of these services may be included in the carrier's line-haul rate. On the other hand, additional charges may be made for various kinds of additional services, such as switching, storage, icing, or diversion in transit. As all charges collected by a carrier must be based on published tariff rates, a variety of services tariffs are used for this purpose. As compared to rate tariffs, these services tariffs are fairly straightforward and easy to understand.

General Tariff Format and Use

The general format of interstate tariffs (except those of air carriers, which come under C.A.B. jurisdiction) is subject to I.C.C. prescription or approval. Although this format varies in detail and complexity from tariff to tariff, in

---

SECTION 1—MISCELLANEOUS COMMODITY RATES

ITEM	ARTICLES	FROM	TO	RATES In Cents per 100 lbs (Except as noted)	WESTERN GATEWAYS (See Item 9805)
962	Aluminum can stock, for can manufacture, not further processed than degreased, relubricated, coated, trimmed and sheared, not thinner than U. S. Standard Gauge 38 or thicker than U. S. Standard Gauge 24, in straight lengths not less than 20 inches, nor more than 40 inches in length or width, or in coils, commercially known as "Aluminum Can Stock", in packages or on platforms. ㉑Min CL wt 65,000 lbs. ㉒Min CL wt 80,000 lbs. ㉓Min CL wt 100,000 lbs.	Torrance......Cal. Trentwood....Wash.	Points taking following Group Rates (See Item 555): C (In Ky.), C-3,L, L-1,M,M-1...... D,D-1,D-3,D-4,E, E-1,E-2,E-3,E-4, E-5,E-6,F,G,H,I, J,N............. K,K-2............. K-1.............	㉒149 ㉑120 ㉒187 { ㉒202 ㉓187	Via Gateways shown opposite point of origin in TCFB Territorial Directory. (See Item 490)
963	Aluminum sheet, lengths of, semi-finished, in coils, requiring further rolling. **Min CL wt 100,000 lbs.** ㉑Rates in cents per 2,000 lbs. ㉒The provisions of Rule 24 of Uniform Classification or Exceptions thereto and Paragraph 2 of Part 1 of Item 545 do not apply. ㉖Subject to Item 9835.	Riverside......Cal. Torrance........Cal. Trentwood....Wash.	Points taking the following Group rates (See Item 555): B,B-1,C............. C-1,C-2,C-3,C-4,D, D-1,D-3,D-4, E,E-1,E-2,E-3, E-4,E-5,E-6,F, G,H,I,J,N.......	㉑㉖3412 ㉑㉒3412	Via Gateways shown opposite point of origin in TCFB Territorial Directory. (See Item 490)
		Points taking Rate Basis 1 or 4 rates (See Item 560).....	A,A-1............. K,K-2.............	㉑㉒3859 ㉑3859	
965	(See Note 2) Aluminum or Aluminum Articles, viz.: Angles, Bars, Beams, Channels, Molding or Tees, Blanks, Stampings or Unfinished Shapes, flat, in packages, Extrusions, noibn, loose or in packages, Fittings, pipe, in crates, Forms, structural, noibn, fabricated from bars, plate or shapes ⅜ inch or thicker (See Note 4), Pipe (Subject to Note 1), Rods, in packages, Tubing (Subject to Note 1), Window and Window Frame Sections, unfinished. In straight or mixed carloads. **Min CL wt 30,000 lbs.** Note 1.—Shipments from Phoenix, Ariz., are entitled to storage-in-transit privileges as authorized in tariffs of individual lines, parties hereto and lawfully on file with the Interstate Commerce Commission. Note 2.—Shipments are entitled to partial unloading in transit privileges as authorized in tariffs of individual lines, parties hereto, and lawfully on file with the Interstate Commerce Commission.	Phoenix........Ariz. Spokane......Wash. Trentwood....Wash.	Points taking following Group rates (See Item 555): A................. A-1,㉓K,㉓K-2...... B,C,M-1............ B-1,L,L-1,M........ C-1,C-4............. C-2,C-3............. D,D-1,D-3,D-4,E-1, E-2,N............. E,E-3,E-4,E-5,E-6... F,G,I,J............ H................. K-1.................	289 281 257 ㊸251 236 230 223 213 201 { ㉒223 ㉓201 303	Via Gateways shown opposite point of origin in TCFB Territorial Directory. (See Item 490)
		Riverside......Cal. Torrance........Cal.	A................. A-1,㉓K,㉓K-2...... B,C,M-1............ B-1,L,L-1,M........ C-1,C-4............. C-2,C-3............. D,D-1,D-3,D-4...... E,E-3,E-4,E-5,E-6... F,G,H,I,J.......... K-1.................	311 303 279 ㊸273 258 252 245 235 223 325	Via Gateways shown opposite point of origin in TCFB Territorial Directory. (See Item 490)

Note 4.—Aluminum structural forms may be made partly from iron or steel not to exceed thirty percent by weight and not in excess of ten percent of the total weight may consist of bronze or brass bushings or shims.

㉒Applies from Spokane and Trentwood, Wash.

㉓Applies from Phoenix, Ariz.

㊸Subject to Note 53, Item 9815.

226

Figure 15: Page from a Railroad Commodity Tariff.

Courtesy: Trans-Continental Freight Bureau.

general all show in fairly uniform order such things as who issued the tariff; what tariff, if any, is replaced by it; what kinds of commodities and what geographical areas are included in its coverage; a table of contents; a list of the participating carriers; indexes of the specific commodities and points included; explanations of the abbreviations and symbols used; rules for using the tariff; routing instructions and restrictions, if any; the actual charges applicable.

As it is expensive and time-consuming to publish a large tariff, but since rate changes occur frequently, some provision must be made to keep tariffs up-to-date. This is handled by the publication of supplements as minor changes take place. These supplements must be checked by the tariff user in order to make certain that he is using the latest legal rate. Eventually, when an existing tariff is republished under a new number, all changes to date are incorporated in it.

One can understand what a tariff is, why it is necessary, and a little of how to use it by reading about the subject. For those actually using tariffs, however, there is no substitute for experience, and there are few if any short cuts. You know that in order to find the applicable rate on a particular movement it may be necessary to consult a commodity tariff, a classification, a class tariff, an exception tariff, and all current supplements. All of these may appear to be formidable documents.

The novice tariff user should not become discouraged too easily, however. Anyone with a basic understanding of tariffs and average intelligence and reading ability can look up a rate. (It will takes years to become an expert, however, and even the experts sometimes make mistakes.) For the beginner, a law of increasing returns seems to apply; that is, as one uses a tariff more and more, it becomes increasingly easy to find new rates. Also one who has developed some proficiency in using one reasonably complex tariff can very quickly learn to use an entirely different one.

Fortunately, most shippers are concerned with a relatively small number of products, and these may move from one origin to only a few destinations. If this is so, the shipper can very easily reduce his rate work to a routine by preparing a system of rate cards, rate sheets, or rate maps from the pertinent tariffs. Sometimes this is done by trade associations for their members or for branch plants by a headquarters traffic office.

One can always ask the carrier for rate information, of course. This is the procedure usually followed by those who ship infrequently. Large and frequent shippers like to have rate information at their finger tips, however, to aid in quoting customer prices quickly, to expedite paperwork connected with their shipments, and to eliminate the delays and inconveniences of continual calls to carrier rate clerks. Also, carriers, like shippers, sometimes make mistakes.

Carrier and shipper rate errors sometimes can amount to significant sums over a period of time. For this reason, many large companies maintain an internal staff of freight-rate auditors to look for overpayments and apply to carriers for refunds. Small shippers (and some large ones) often use the services of independent freight-rate audit bureaus or firms, which usually operate on a percentage of the recovery basis, for the same purpose.

HOW RATES ARE MADE OR CHANGED

The Interstate Commerce Commission divides the United States into several major rate territories for railroad rate-making and various kinds of reporting and statistical purposes. Eastern (Official), Southern, and Western classification territories were mentioned above. These form the basis for rate territories, but are further subdivided.

The five most commonly considered rate territories are Eastern, Southern, Mountain-Pacific, Western Trunk Line, and Southwestern territories. The first two named are equivalent to the Eastern and Southern classification territories, while the last three are subdivisions of Western classification territory. These five areas making up the major rail-rate territories are shown in Figure 16.

Eastern territory, however, for some purposes is further divided into New England, Trunk Line, and Central Freight Association territories, or zones A, B, and C. Both Mountain-Pacific territory and Southwestern territory are further subdivided into zones 1, 2, and 3. In addition, the coal-mining area of the central Appalachians is sometimes referred to as the Pocahontas district.

Similar but not identical rate territories exist within the motor-carrier industry. Its major divisions east of the Mississippi River are New England, Middle Atlantic, Central States, and Southern territories. West of the Mississippi are the Middle West, Southwestern, Rocky Mountain, Pacific Northwest and Pacific Southwest areas.

The types of economic activity and traffic conditions vary among the different rate territories. Consequently, carriers primarily based in different territories may have differing revenue and rate problems. Carriers as a group may be prospering in one region, while conditions are bad in another. This leads to a natural association of interest among intraregional carriers of a given mode and may result in differing rate levels and carrier practices as well as different I.C.C. treatment of proposed rate changes in the different territories.

The mechanics of rate-making usually are handled for carriers by their rate bureaus (or traffic associations). These are carrier-maintained organizations for joint action in establishing prices. Such a joint activity is illegal for businesses in general under the antitrust laws. Carriers subject to Interstate Commerce Commission regulation, however, under conditions prescribed by the Commission may be exempted from these laws.

Railroads discovered the practicality (some would say the necessity) of joint action in rate-making well before the turn of the century. Despite anti-

Figure 16: Major Railroad Rate Territories.

trust laws, traffic associations continued to exist, however shaky their legal status, without legal challenge for many years. During World War II, though, the State of Georgia and the Department of Justice filed suits against conference (association) rate-making which led to a Supreme Court decision adverse to the practice (*Georgia versus Pennsylvania Railroad,* 324 U.S. 439, 1945). Congress, therefore, in 1948 enacted the Reed-Bulwinkle Act, now Section 5a of the Interstate Commerce Act, permitting joint carrier rate-making activity through bureaus approved by the I.C.C.

Five major rate bureaus now operate east of the Mississippi and four in Western territory. In addition, a Transcontinental bureau (with its main office in Chicago) handles rates on transcontinental traffic (that is, between the West Coast and areas east of the Rockies). Also, several smaller bureaus handle rate matters for carriers in more localized situations. These rate bureaus are further organized into four Associations (Eastern, Illinois, Southern, and Western) to deal with matters common to more than one bureau in the respective territories.

The internal organization of rate bureaus varies according to their charters and bylaws, but generally there are three levels of organization: (1) A Standing Rate Committee of permanent staff employees of the bureau, headed by a permanent chairman, does the necessary research and leg work on rate proposals, but has no vote; (2) a Rate Committee composed of the traffic managers, or someone designated by them, of each of the participating carriers, which actually votes on rate proposals; and (3) an Executive Committee, usually made up of carrier vice-presidents in charge of traffic, to whom appeals may be made by those dissatisfied by the results of Rate Committee votes. In some instances, appeals can be carried still higher, to a President's Conference of the member carriers.

Any carrier in a given geographical area is entitled to participate in that area's rate bureau, and any participating carrier has the right of independent action either before or after a vote on a rate proposal. Votes generally are taken in closed session with no public announcement as to how individual carriers voted. Matters affecting more than one bureau, after being passed on by the originating bureau, must be concurred in by the others affected. Actions of the Transcontinental bureau, which usually affect bureaus in several other regions, must have the concurrence of the Eastern and Southern Associations. Carriers sometimes publish their own tariffs, but most are issued by the rate bureaus through their publishing agents.

The organization pattern of motor-carrier and water-carrier rate bureaus is similar to that of the rails, although concurrence between different bureaus usually is not necessary or required. Motor-carrier bureaus are more numerous and generally are limited to smaller territorial coverage than are those in rail carriage. Only five or six domestic water-carrier bureaus can be classed as having major status.

At this point, one might well ask what are the specific steps or procedures involved in establishing a new rate or in changing an existing rate. Basically, of course, rates are made by carriers through their bureaus, but several formal steps are involved. Let us suppose that you, a shipper, want to get a specific rate reduced.

The first step is to make your proposal to the appropriate rate bureau or, better yet, to persuade a carrier serving you (who is agreeable to your suggested lower rate) to make the proposal for you. The proposal should be supported by clear and concise evidence as to why the rate should be changed.

The rate bureau will study your proposal and docket it for a public hearing, probably after 30 or 60 days' notice to its member carriers and all other interested parties. At the hearing, your proposal should be supported as forcefully as possible with documentary evidence and verbal testimony from you, your supporting carrier, and anyone else with an interest in the matter whom you can persuade to appear. After considering all pro and con factors, the bureau's Rate Committee will vote on your proposal.

Let us assume that you have been successful in persuading the bureau to adopt your proposal. It will then file the new rate with the I.C.C. (or with the appropriate state regulatory agency if the rate is strictly intrastate). The rate will be considered by the I.C.C. or the state regulatory body, and if there are no serious objections to it from any source or if the matter is not considered to be of major transportation importance, it will probably be more or less automatically approved (that is, approved by the absence of formal disapproval or suspension) and will become effective in about 30 days after filing by the bureau.

This is a history of a typical routine rate change to which no one objects. The new rate may become effective within 60 to 90 days after your application. By far the largest percentage of rate changes (perhaps 90 per cent) will come within this category.

Let us suppose, however, that your rate proposal is contested by one of your competitors. (During recent years, about 90 per cent of protests against rate changes have been protests against *decreased* rates rather than against rate increases.) This protest, due to the necessity for considering further evidence and possible appeals, will delay your proposal's processing through the rate bureau. Then, if it is approved by the bureau, it likely will be suspended by the I.C.C. or state regulatory body.

The regulatory body, in turn, will docket the proposal and hold public hearings on it after adequate notice to interested parties. The evidence for and against will again be considered. After a lapse of several months, your rate may finally be approved by the regulatory agency to go into effect after 30 days (or it may be disapproved, or approved only in part).

This does not necessarily end the process. Protestants may appeal to the regulatory agency for reconsideration; and, if they lose again, the matter may be appealed to the courts. Eventually the case may even reach the U.S. Supreme Court for settlement. The court may uphold the commission's decision, or it may be remanded to that body for further action in line with the court's views of its legality. In the meantime, many months or even years may have passed.

From this very brief summary of procedures, it can be seen that major rate changes are not easily made. Carriers and shippers often feel, with some justification, that the process is too cumbersome and time-consuming. On the other hand, regulatory agencies operate within a framework of law established by Federal or state legislation, and must constantly bear in mind that their every action may be subjected to court review. Although some lags might be eliminated from the regulatory procedures within the existing pattern of laws, any substantial changes must come from legislators rather than regulators.

It has been alleged, probably correctly, that rate changes sometimes are opposed simply as a delaying tactic. That is, those carriers or producers who might be placed at a competitive disadvantage by the proposed new rates may choose to fight changes and thus enjoy the advantages of existing rates for a considerable period of time, even though they may anticipate losing in the end. Again, this seems to be inherent in our existing legal framework. It is one of the prices we pay for protecting the public against unreasonable and arbitrary rates and rate changes.

ADDITIONAL READINGS

1. Cushman, Frank M., **Transportation for Management.** Englewood Cliffs, N.J.: Prentice-Hall, Inc., 1953.
   Chapter 9. "The Rate-Making Process," pp. 371–399.
2. Daggett, Stuart, **Principles of Inland Transportation,** 4th ed. New York: Harper and Brothers, 1955.
   Chapter 17. "Classification Practice," pp. 316–338.
3. Fair, Marvin L., and Ernest W. Williams, Jr., **Economics of Transportation,** Rev. ed. New York: Harper and Brothers, 1959. "Freight Classification and Commodity Rates," pp. 368–377.
4. Flood, Kenneth U., **Traffic Management,** 2nd ed. Dubuque, Iowa: Wm. C. Brown Co., 1963.
   Chapter 4. "Freight Tariffs and Their Interpretation," pp. 65–94.
   Chapter 5. "Freight Classification," pp. 95–135.
5. Mossman, Frank H., and Newton Morton, **Principles of Transportation.** New York: Ronald Press Company, 1957.
   Chapter 11. "Formulation and Publication of Rates," pp. 238–259.
6. Pegrum, Dudley F., **Transportation: Economics and Public Policy.** Rev. ed. Homewood, Ill.: Richard D. Irwin, Inc., 1968.
   Chapter 10. "Rate Making in Practice," pp. 227–251.
7. Starr, Edward A., **The Interpretation of Freight Tariffs.** Fort Worth, Texas: The Transportation Press, 1961.
   Chapter One. "Freight Tariffs—Their Purpose and Status," pp. 1–13.
   Chapter Two. "Freight Tariffs—Their Format and Mechanics," pp. 14–26.
8. Taff, Charles A., **Management of Traffic and Physical Distribution,** 4th ed. Homewood, Ill.: Richard D. Irwin, Inc., 1968.
   Chapter 9. "Classification," pp. 192–218.
   Chapter 11. "Tariffs and Rate Formulation," pp. 262–285.

12

Kinds of Freight Rates

It is essential that anyone actively concerned with buying or selling transportation services understand the language of freight rates. Like other areas of buying and selling, this one has a professional jargon which is likely to be confusing or incomprehensible to outsiders. It is also highly desirable, both from the general information and the professional viewpoints, that business people have some knowledge of how carriers quote prices for their transport services and how the different kinds of prices quoted relate to each other, that is, the freight-rate structure.

This chapter will explain some of the basic terminology of freight rates and describe some of the more common types of rate structures. Emphasis will be placed primarily upon the rates of railroads and common-carrier trucking as these rate systems are more comprehensive as well as most important for most persons. Rates of other forms of carriage, which generally are closely related to rail and common-carrier truck rates, will be noted as appropriate.

The following discussion obviously does not purport to tell everything about the kinds of freight rates and their structures. To do this would require many volumes. Instead, it is the authors' intent to mention briefly the most important things about this topic that beginners in transportation ought to know. The next chapter will discuss in more detail some of the economic effects of various kinds of rates.

THE TERMINOLOGY OF FREIGHT RATES

To better understand the terminology identifying particular kinds of rates, it is sometimes convenient to group these descriptive expressions together according to some similar characteristics. For example, Chapter 11 distinguished between class tariffs and their exceptions and commodity tariffs. We can say, then, that *class rates,* or *exceptions rates,* and *commodity rates* are rates based on the *kinds of things shipped.* Other rates falling into this descriptive category are *all-commodity* or *all-freight* rates, that is, the rate quoted is applicable to any kind of product.

In addition to the above category, we may group rates into categories based upon the quantities shipped; route or routing characteristics; previous or future shipments of the product; agreements between carriers and shippers; and miscellaneous, that is, rates which do not clearly fall into either of these categories. The principal kinds of rates falling into each of these groups will be discussed in order.

Rates Based on Quantities Shipped

The most familiar of quantity rates are rail *carload* (CL) and *less-than-carload* (LCL) and corresponding *truckload* (TL) and *less-than-truckload* (LTL) rates. As indicated in Chapter 4, CL and TL rates usually are considerably lower in cents per 100 pounds than are LCL or LTL rates on the same product.

A carload is generally understood to mean a single shipment from one consignor at one origin to one consignee at one destination, moving under a single Bill of Lading, at least meeting a minimum weight specified for the product, and loaded and unloaded by the consignor and consignee. Various tariff modifications, however, *may* permit stoppage en route for partial loading or unloading, deliveries to more than one party at destination (split deliveries), and carrier loading or unloading, or similar deviations. A carload may contain only one product or it may be a mixed car (two or more products). The same general specifications apply to truckload. Shipments not meeting the authorized tariff specifications cannot legally move at CL or TL rates.

In addition, truck carriers often quote *volume* (Vol.) rates or *any-quantity* (AQ) rates. Volume rates when used customarily but not always are applied to shipments larger than truckload quantities and are lower than TL rates; they frequently are used to meet rail CL competition. Any-quantity rates may be applied to shipments either larger or smaller than truckload quantities.

In a limited number of instances, also, railroads quote *trainload* rates or *multiple-car* rates which may be considerably lower than CL rates. This kind of price quotation usually is defended by railroads on the grounds that it is necessary to meet competition from other forms of carriage and is justifiable on the basis of lower carrier costs incurred in handling large volumes regularly as contrasted with the costs of handling carload traffic. Such rates are not illegal as such, although they often have been discouraged by regulatory authorities and frowned upon by the general public because of their alleged discrimination against small shippers who do not ship enough to take advantage of them. The Anglo-American tradition tends to favor the small business over the large business, instead of the opposite.

During recent years, many railroads have been making extensive applications of *incentive* rates for some commodities. These are carload rates lower than the normal CL quotations and given to shippers who load considerably more into a car than the minimum quantity required for a CL rate. Railroads and shippers using these rates justify them on the grounds of lower shipper rates, lower costs (and, consequently, higher revenues per car and per unit of weight) for carriers, and better utilization of limited railroad resources. This last justification is particularly pertinent during the periods of rail-car shortage which have been almost chronic in some areas during recent years. Shippers who are not able to use incentive rates because of their own output characteristics or the quantity desires of their customers, however, as well as some competing carriers understandably oppose special incentive rates just as they oppose trainload or multiple-car rates.

Both railroad and truck carriers commonly impose *minimum* rates or charge for a minimum weight even though the actual shipment may weigh less than the minimum, or both. This type of rate is based upon the supposition that certain costs, especially those related to billing and other paper work, do not differ greatly if at all in proportion to the weight handled or the distance moved. That is, the direct clerical expenses and various fixed-expense items may be as large for a 50-pound shipment moving only 50 miles as for a 5,000-pound shipment moving 500 miles.

Rates Based on Route or Routing Characteristics

A *local* rate is one covering a haul over the lines of only one carrier, while a *joint* rate is one involving a movement by two or more carriers. A *through* rate means one published rate from origin to destination in one tariff; these may be either local or joint in nature.

Combination rates are made up simply by adding one rate to another. For example, if the rate from A to B is 30¢ and the rate from B to C is 40¢, the combination rate from A to C would be 70¢. A combination rate differs from a *proportional* rate in that in the latter form only a part of one rate is added to another rate to get the total applicable rate. Using the above illustration, the proportional rate from A to C might be 30¢ (A to B) plus 60 per cent of the rate from B to C (24¢), or 54¢. Combination or proportional rates may be either local or joint as well as through.

A *differential* rate is one in which some sum, a differential, is added to or subtracted from a standard rate. Differentials may be used over unusually circuitous or inferior routes, in connection with export and import shipments (see following), or for various other reasons. An *arbitrary* rate adds an arbitrary to a standard rate. Arbitraries may be added to rates applying to major destination points for shipments which move beyond these points to outlying minor destinations, or they may be used on small shipments or on shipments with undesirable handling characteristics.

As one can imagine, there often are instances in which more than one rate may be found between given origins and destinations. Frequently this is not intended by or even known to the carriers concerned. As an illustration, a carrier may quote a rate of 90¢ per 100 pounds on some item from A to D in its tariff. An astute shipper's rate clerk, however, may find that the tariff provides for shipment of the same product from A to B for 30¢, from B to C for 40¢, and from C to D for 15¢. In such cases, as shippers are legally entitled to use the lowest published rates, the shipper usually could use a rate of 85¢ rather than 90¢. This is called the "aggregate of intermediates rule," that is, the aggregate rate cannot exceed the sum of the published intermediate rates and is regulated under Section 4 of the Interstate Commerce Act.

Rates Based on Previous or Future Shipments of the Product

Rates based on previous or future shipments of a product are quoted in cases where a shipment stops in transit for some reason. This stoppage may be for processing, fabrication, or manufacture (as wheat into flour, logs into lumber into furniture, ore into metal, etc.), or for temporary storage. Such rates often are called *transit* rates (transit rate as used in this sense should not be confused with the privilege of diversion or reconsignment discussed in Chapter 8, which also is sometimes loosely referred to as transit or transit marketing).

The fiction or rationale back of such rates is that there is only one movement of the product involved from a first origin to a final destination despite its stopover and perhaps even a change in form. Thus, since rates in cents per 100 pounds or per ton-mile typically are lower proportionately on long hauls than on short hauls, it is maintained by advocates of this type of rate-making that shippers should not be forced to pay as much as the sum of two short-haul rates in getting their product to its final destination. Usually if there is a rate difference between the inbound and the outbound form of the product, the higher of the two rates is considered the appropriate rate for the entire movement. An additional charge may or may not be made for the stopover privilege. Certainly the carriers' expenses are increased as a result of extra handling, paper work, and necessary policing, but carriers sometimes prefer to absorb these extras in order to obtain or maintain business.

Transit rates are an important competitive device among carriers, shippers, and localities. As such, they are subject to abuse and require a considerable amount of policing. Carriers are not supposed to use them to discriminate between shippers or localities, a supposition that probably has not always been borne out by the facts. A carrier is not obligated to quote such rates; but once it does, they supposedly must be given to all who wish them under similar circumstances. But what are similar circumstances? And what if competing shippers are on the lines of another carrier which does not wish to quote such rates?

Shippers must also be policed by carriers or their agents to make sure that the transit-rate privilege is not violated. Careful records of incoming and outgoing tonnages must be kept and allowances made for wastage or accretion. Assume that a ton of corn can be milled into 1,200 pounds of edible corn meal and 800 pounds of cattle feed (a 60-40 ratio). A miller who consistently brought in 1,000 tons of corn per month and shipped out 400 tons of cattle feed, but wanted to ship out 800 tons of corn meal at reduced transit rates, would be suspect. Aside from the policing aspect, transit rates may involve a considerable amount of shipper and carrier bookkeeping.

The lower reshipping or transit rate benefits may be applied either before or after stoppage depending upon the pertinent carrier tariff. That is, a lower-than-standard inbound charge (floating in rate) may be applied on products which are to be reshipped later, or a lower-than-standard outbound charge (cutback rate) may be applied on shipments out of the transit point. Sometimes, too, the shipper pays a standard rate inbound and outbound and presents a claim to the carrier for a refund of the amount due under a particular transit rate arrangement.

This discussion has only touched upon the essential elements of transit rates. This is an extremely complicated topic, involving at least several hundred commodities in many areas of the country and under a wide variety of operating arrangements and tariff rules. Transit rates, both in operation and in practical economic effect, are among the least understood of rates. Much additional research and analysis is needed in this area, but that task is beyond the scope of this book. Some additional comments will be made regarding the probable locational effects of transit rates in the following chapter, however.

Export rates and *import* rates are versions of reshipping rates in which the stoppage in transit is to permit loading onto an ocean carrier bound for a foreign destination or in which foreign-originated goods are transferred onto domestic carriers. These rates, although sometimes considerably lower than equivalent regular domestic rates for similar commodities moving over the same routes and by the same carriers to or from the same seaports, are usually not included in discussions of domestic transit rates.

Very few laymen are even aware of the existence of export-import rates, and only a comparatively small number of shippers have occasion to use them. Further, it appears that most contemporary academic students of domestic transport consider these rates to be a proper subject for students of ocean transportation, while ocean-transportation students apparently relegate them to the realm of domestic transport. The next chapter, dealing with rate structures, will further describe the structure of export and import rates as compared to other domestic rate structures.

Rates Based upon Shipper-Carrier Agreements

Under *agreed* rates, sometimes referred to as loyalty-incentive rates, a shipper enters into a formal agreement with a carrier or a group of carriers of the same mode to ship a certain volume, or in some cases a specified percentage of his total volume, by the particular carrier or group of carriers. In return, the shipper pays less than the standard published rate or receives a refund from the carrier for the difference between the standard rate and the agreed rate at the end of a named period of time. Under such agreements, the shipper normally is not under an absolute obligation to use the services of a given carrier or group of carriers; but if he fails to live up to the agreed volume, he must pay the standard rate on all his shipments.

Contract carrier rates, of course, are always agreed upon by the shipper and carrier by negotiation. These rates, however, are not generally included as agreed rates in the sense that the term is used here. Actually, in the United States, agreed rates between shippers and common carriers in domestic transportation generally have been considered unlawful. Such rates are widely used in Canada, Britain, and some other areas, however. Also, agreed rates are an integral part of ocean steamship conference rates, even for United States ocean carriers in foreign trade; if the steamship conference cannot supply needed vessel capacity, of course, the shipper is allowed to use other lines without penalty.

Agreed rates have been frowned upon in this country's domestic transportation on several grounds. It is felt that this may be a form of discrimination between shippers, particularly between larger shippers who may be able to negotiate favorable agreements and smaller shippers who do not have as much bargaining power. This argument certainly may be valid if the agreement is based upon an absolute amount of tonnage. On the other hand, it is less sound if similar agreements are offered to all shippers on a percentage-of-total-tonnage basis.

Carriers (particularly rail carriers who have been advocates of agreed rates) point out that such agreements, in addition to reducing shipper costs, allow carriers to do better planning for utilization of their equipment and enable better service to be given at lower carrier cost. Competing forms of carriage, though, which are not in as good a position to offer agreed rates, oppose them on the grounds that agreements tend to reduce competition by tying shippers to particular carriers or modes. This, of course, is true, but shippers are not obligated to utilize the services of the contracting carriers. Thus if a shipper could get better or lower-priced services from other carriers, he would be free to do so by paying standard rates on shipments moved by agreed rate carriers.

Governmental agencies are permitted by Section 22 of the Interstate Commerce Act to negotiate with carriers for lower-than-standard rates. These *Section 22* rates are used extensively by the Federal government due to its bargaining power resulting from a tremendous tonnage of shipments. Carriers are not particularly fond of this situation as it permits government to play one carrier against another in bargaining and results in considerably lower carrier revenue on government freight. Many private shippers also oppose Section 22 rates as they feel that the resulting lower carrier revenues require higher rates from private shippers which means, in effect, that private shippers are subsidizing government shipments. Various proposals have been made during recent years to amend the Interstate Commerce Act by eliminating this practice, with both railroad and shipper support.

Released value rates may be considered as still another version of rates based upon agreements. Under these rates, the shipper, in return for considerably lower rates than otherwise would be applicable, agrees that in case of loss or damage to his goods, only an agreed-upon maximum loss or damage claim will be paid by the carrier. This kind of agreement is customarily used for passenger baggage and is widely used in shipping household furniture and personal effects by truck. Some other types of goods also usually move under released-value rates. The carriers' liability may be limited to a maximum absolute amount, as in baggage or ordinary livestock, or to a maximum amount per unit of weight, as in household furniture. The shipper, of course, can acquire the protection of full carrier liability by paying higher rates, but full-liability rates on such goods often are considerably higher than full-coverage transportation insurance purchased from an insurance company; the carrier itself may sell this insurance as an agent.

Miscellaneous Rates

Several kinds of rates do not fall clearly into either of the categories discussed above. For exposition purposes, therefore, the authors have grouped a number of these rates under the "miscellaneous" heading rather than enlarge the basic grouping of categories.

Piggyback rates, or trailer-on-flatcar (TOFC) rates, are rapidly increasing in importance as the piggyback movement continues to expand (see Chapter 5). Several versions or plans of piggyback services are offered, each with different rate-quotation methods.

Plan I— Railroads haul trailers, with or without wheels, for common carrier truckers. The trucking company charges shippers rates from applicable motor-carrier tariffs.

Plan II— Railroads offer a door-to-door service with their own trailers under their own rates.

Plan III— Railroads haul trailers owned or leased by shippers or freight forwarders. This is a line-haul service without rail pickup or delivery, a flat charge regardless of the trailer's contents.

Plan IV— Railroads make a flat charge for moving flatcars and trailers, owned or controlled by forwarders or shippers, whether loaded or empty; that is, railroads supply only the right of way and motive power.

Plan V— Railroads and trucks publish joint through rates, with the carriers agreeing between themselves on such matters as trailer ownership, freight solicitation, revenue division, and similar matters.

Fourth section rates, sometimes called long-and-shorthaul rates, take their name from the famous Section 4 of the Interstate Commerce Act. This section, which has a checkered history of interpretation and administration, generally prohibits railroads (and domestic water carriers, but not trucks and freight forwarders) from charging more for a ". . . like kind of property, for a shorter than for a longer distance over the same line or route in the same direction, the shorter being included within the longer distance. . . ." Under some circumstances, however, exceptions or deviations are permitted from this rule, thus giving rise to long-and-short-haul rate-making. The structure and economic effects of these rates will be further considered in Chapter 13.

Sometimes shippers are in no particular hurry to get shipments to their destinations and thus are willing to ship under lower *space available* rates. This implies that the goods may not move promptly; rather, the movement will be made when higher priority freight is not available to utilize the carrier's full capacity. Shippers usually are promised that the goods will move not later than a specified date, however. This device is used most often in air and water carriage.

Some marketing businesses, especially in the marketing of fresh fruits and vegetables, lumber, and a few other items, specialize in selling or reselling carloads of commodities while they are en route to a general destination area. These brokers, wholesalers, or commission men, as they are variously called, make extensive use of diversion and reconsignment privileges (see Chapter 8). Even these devices sometimes do not give enough time for selling the commodity, however. Thus, a need for slow transit or delay en route, especially on the part of Pacific Coast lumber wholesalers, has given rise to various proposals for *delayed* rates. Under these proposals, due to deliberate stoppages or delays en route, considerably more than the usual amount of time would be required for a given movement, thus giving the seller more time to make his sale. These proposals have not been sympathetically received by the Interstate Commerce Commission and have been opposed by many shippers and carriers primarily on the grounds that such delays would unduly tie up rail cars and contribute to car shortages, and perhaps decrease participating carrier revenues without corresponding benefits to the public in general.

Cube rates, that is, rates based primarily upon the amount of cubic space occupied rather than upon weight have been proposed recently. This concept has not been generally accepted, although it does not differ greatly in principle from piggyback Plans III and IV, some steamship rates, oil pipeline rates, some kinds of movements handled by REA Express, and even some air freight situaations.

Opponents of a cube-rate system maintain that in addition to cubic volume, some attention must be given to weight (as feathers versus lead, for example), susceptibility to loss and damage, value (at least insofar as this might affect loss and damage claims), handling characteristics, the product's need for special or accessory services, and various other so-called classification factors. It is not likely that pure cube rates will be widely used by many carriers within the near future, but it is possible that cubic volume may become relatively more important in classification and rate-making than it has been heretofore.

A somewhat related form of rate quotation, *weight or space at carrier's option,* in which carriers equate 40 (or 50, depending on trade practices) cubic feet to one ton (short ton or long ton, again depending on the trade), with metric equivalents used in nations under the metric system, is widely used in ocean-steamship carriage. Under this system, the carrier collects the highest of the measurement or weight charges. Even steamships, however, make use of class, commodity, and all-cargo rates as well as pricing many items in terms of customary units such as barrels, bales, cases, or board feet. Also, various special accessory, handling, penalty, and other charges may be added to basic steamship rates.

It should be re-emphasized at this point that all of the above-mentioned common-carrier rates, as well as various kinds not mentioned, are legally required to be published in tariffs and thus fall into the categories of class, exception, and commodity rates. For example, one might have a class or a commodity CL rate which is joint, through, proportional, transit, released value, incentive, and includes an arbitrary. Various other linkings of terminology may be encountered or imagined.

As indicated near the beginning of this chapter, most of the foregoing discussion, except where otherwise specified, has been in terms of rail rates or of common-carrier truck rates which originally were (and still are largely) patterned after the already-established rail rates. Some brief comment on the rates of other forms of carriage now is necessary.

Contract motor-carrier rates are individually negotiated between the carrier and the shipper, but the level and structure of these rates obviously are influenced by other existing transport alternatives, which include both common carriage and private carriage. The actual rates charged by interstate contract truckers must be filed with the I.C.C.

Freight forwarders often quote the line-haul rates of the common carriers used in their services or closely pattern their rates after those of the common carriers. Domestic water carriers, as they are in direct competition with rail and truck carriers, often use the same tariffs as their competition or base their rates on them (usually somewhat lower, of course). Rates of ocean carriers have already been described.

Air-carrier rates involve no particularly new terminology; these carriers do, however, make extensive use of released value and considerable use of space-available rates. Air-freight classification is not unduly complex.

Basic REA Express rate-making uses a simple system of classification with rates based to a considerable extent upon the distance moved. These rates, again, involve no special new terminology. A version of cube rates has been used for some types of shipments during the past few years. Air-express shipments also are handled by REA Express.

The other major form of domestic carriage—oil pipelines—uses a standard barrel as its pricing unit. This barrel is precisely defined not only in terms of cubic volume (a form of cube rate), but with attention to such variables as specific gravity and temperature which affect volume.

In addition to the above line-haul rates, any carrier may levy additional surcharges or accessorial charges for the performance of special or nonstandard services in connection with a movement. Among others, such services might include refrigeration or heating, transit, diversion or reconsignment, drayage, livestock feeding, special switching, and similar items. Any such additional charges made by common carriers must be duly authorized and published in tariffs.

ADDITIONAL READINGS

1. Flood, Kenneth U., **Traffic Management,** 2nd ed. Dubuque, Iowa: Wm. C. Brown Co., 1963.
   Chapter 6. "Freight Rates," pp. 136–177.
2. Hoffman, Joseph V., "Motor Carrier Research in Rates and Tariffs," **Transportation Journal,** Vol. 4, No. 1, Fall 1964, pp. 5–13.
3. Lundy, Robert F., **The Economics of Loyalty-Incentive Rates in the Railroad Industry of the United States.** Pullman, Wash.: Washington State University Press, 1963.
   Chapter 3. "Loyalty-Incentive Rate Experiments by the American Railroads," pp. 36–66.
4. Starr, Edward A., **The Interpretation of Freight Tariffs.** Fort Worth, Texas: The Transportation Press, 1961.
   Chapter Three. "Various Kinds of Freight Rates and Their Significance," pp. 27–33.
5. Taff, Charles A., **Management of Traffic and Physical Distribution,** 4th ed. Homewood, Ill.: Richard D. Irwin, Inc., 1968.
   Chapter 10. "The Effect of Rates on Physical Distribution," pp. 219–261.

13

Freight Rate Structures

Now that much of the basic terminology of rates has been introduced, it is appropriate to consider the structures of freight rates. (Structures, as used here, refers to the relationship of line-haul transport charges to the distance moved and the comparative interrelationships of different kinds of rates and of rates in different geographical areas.)

In this discussion, some of the rates identified in the preceding section will be further described, while some new rate terminology will be introduced. Also, as in the preceding chapter, rail rates will form the basic reference point for discussion as an understanding of this most comprehensive rate system will lead concurrently to an understanding of the usually less complex rate structures of other modes.

At the extreme opposite ends of the rate-structure spectrum, one might imagine, on the one hand, a rate which for a given unit or weight of a particular product does not vary at all with the distance moved—a *postage-stamp* rate. The other extreme would be a rate which increases directly proportionate to the distance moved—a pure distance or *straight mileage* rate. Actually, most freight moves under rates falling somewhere between these two extremes, under modified mileage rates, under rates which may not vary at all over considerable distances (a modified mileage and postage-stamp combination known as *blanket,* group, or zone rates), or even under rates which may vary inversely with distance (as Fourth Section rates, or movements to intermediate points under the formerly popular *basing point* rate structure). Each of these rate structures has its advantages and disadvantages, its supporters and opponents.

THE POSTAGE-STAMP RATE STRUCTURE

The postage-stamp rate, as its name implies, is chiefly used as a government-determined price for the movement of mail (a form of freight transportation, although often not treated as such in transport textbooks). This method of rate quotation is used for the movement of small parcels, either on a nation-wide basis or within defined geographic zones, with charges increasing as zones are crossed in many countries. Also, limited application of the postage-stamp concept is made in almost all actual mileage freight-rate structures as well as in blanket rates (see following).

Postage-stamp pricing is not only confined to the movement of mail and freight. The same device is commonly used in transporting passengers by streetcar, bus, and subway within cities, and often in commuter services. To some extent, too, it appears in intercity passenger transportation. But it extends even beyond these areas into marketing and pricing areas not usually thought of as being directly connected with transportation. The department store which charges the same price for a piece of merchandise whether it is carried from the premises by the buyer or delivered six blocks or six miles by the store is engaging in postage-stamp pricing. So is the large manufacturer in the Northeast who sells his toothpaste at the same price in New York as in San Francisco. Numerous other examples of the use of this pricing concept could be cited.

Proposals

It has even been seriously proposed in earlier years that all United States railroads should base their rates mainly upon a postage-stamp system. In 1898, for example, the so-called Cowles Plan proposed U.S. Post Office Department control of railroads, with passenger fares set at a specified charge per trip regardless of the distance traveled and the only fare differences dependent upon the kind of accommodations used. Under this plan, the use of freight cars would also have been paid for at a fixed rate, varying only with type of car, regardless of distance, contents, or weight of the shipment, in effect, a combination of the postage-stamp and cube-rate concepts.

As late as 1935, the Hastings Plan calling for three railroad fares based upon short distance (up to around 50 miles), regular train service other than short distance, and express train service was submitted to the Senate Committee on Interstate Commerce. A later modification of this plan proposed that fares would be based on the number of 250-mile concentric circular zones traversed. The Hastings Plan dealt only with passenger fares, but apparently it was intended that if adopted it later would be extended to freight service. As the proposed level of fares was fairly low, the plan involved railroad subsidies by the Federal government, at least during an initial transitory period. The House Committee on Interstate and Foreign Commerce voted in 1940 to postpone indefinitely an investigation of the proposal.

Effects

Advocates of postage-stamp rates maintain that such rates remove all personal and local discrimination by placing all persons and places upon an equal basis; that rate-quotation problems and tariffs are reduced to the ultimate in simplicity, thus greatly benefiting both shippers and carriers; and that tickets, or stamps, could be sold in numerous places besides ticket offices in the same ways that postage stamps are now sold. Further, both the Cowles Plan and the Hastings Plan, because of their unusually low level of proposed fares and rates, envisioned a great increase in carrier patronage based upon the assumed elasticity of demand for transport services. Proponents of these plans felt that the resulting full use of carrier capacity would eventually lower carrier per-unit traffic costs to a point where very low rates or fares could be profitably maintained.

Opponents of postage-stamp pricing, on the other hand, point out that inevitably under a non-distance-related rate structure, some users must subsidize other users or some users must pay considerably more than is justified by the carrier's cost of providing the service. If a person (or ton of freight) moves for 500 miles at the same price as another moves for 50 miles, for example, the carrier's costs must be somewhat higher on the former movement. Then if the carrier must recover all of its costs from all movements (as it must in the long run to remain in business unless it is subsidized by the general taxpayer), a portion of the charge paid for the short movement may be used to offset the higher costs involved in the long movement. Or if the price is set at a level sufficient to cover long-movement costs, the carrier will be making unduly high charges for short movements.

Under such a pricing system, one might expect that demand elasticities or inelasticities would considerably increase the patronage of those benefiting most from the prevailing established price, while those benefiting least or disadvantaged by the price would decrease their use of transport services or turn to alternate sources of supply. Such an effect, of course, could be construed as either personal or regional discrimination, and it would obviously have effects on established location and distribution patterns. It would, probably, also result in significant shifts in the balance of the carriers' utilization of their capacities and might have an adverse effect on carrier net revenues.

At first glance, it might appear that this discussion of postage-stamp rates is unduly lengthy in proportion to their importance. The concept, even if not the pure form, however, is so widespread among other existing and important rate structures that its implications must be clearly appreciated before one can understand and analyze these other structures.

MILEAGE RATE STRUCTURES

The straight mileage rate, wherein the charge increases in direct proportion to the distance moved, is the most simple of distance-rate concepts. If the charge for moving one ton for one mile is five cents, then the charge for moving one ton for 100 miles is five dollars. The simplicity, orderliness, and apparent equity of such a rate structure is appealing at first glance. It is seldom used in practice, however, and for good reasons.

Terminal Cost Effects

As explained in Chapter 10, carrier costs are made up of both terminal and line-haul costs. A considerable portion of terminal costs are fixed costs insofar as the distance moved is concerned. That is, a particular shipment may cost the carrier $10 for direct handling and billing whether it moves one mile or 1,000 miles. Thus if the carrier's charges are to recover even the direct costs of the movement (excluding, for simplicity, any elements of unallocable costs), it must charge at least $10 plus the direct line-haul costs incurred for the one-mile movement or a rate equivalent to something more than $10 per ton-mile. But if the shipment moves for 1,000 miles, the carrier must recover only one cent per mile or one one-thousandth as much in terminal costs. The farther the shipment moves, the lower the terminal costs per weight-mile unit. Figure 11 in Chapter 10 illustrates this situation.

If one should assume that line-haul costs are directly proportionate to the distance moved, one might devise a cost-based rate structure which would include a flat charge, determined by the carrier's terminal expenses in connection with a given shipment, plus a straight distance line-haul rate, in other words, a terminal charge plus straight mileage rate. Actually, terminal charges and line-haul charges are made separately in some countries, but United States carriers have found it to be less confusing and more convenient to quote a single rate or charge which includes both the terminal and the line-haul elements.

There is no reason other than convenience in rate quotation and custom why line-haul and terminal charges should be amalgamated, but most carriers and shippers in this country seem to prefer it this way. Conversely, of course, there is no strong logical argument for separating the two—supposedly, the total amount charged and paid will be the same in either case. Carriers can and do at least partially handle the terminal-cost problem, particularly for very small shipments or shipments which move only short distances, by minimum charges (either absolute fixed minimums or by charging for a specified weight even though the actual weight may be less), and by higher rates per unit of weight-distance on small shipments and short hauls.

Tapering Rates

One cannot safely assume that all line-haul costs are directly proportionate to distance, however. The amount of proportionality may be debatable (and obviously it varies between modes and even between carriers of the same mode), but most transport students and practitioners agree that line-haul-per-unit costs generally decrease as distance increases. Even if this were not so, or if the rate-makers should overemphasize the amount of the decrease, the effect on rate structures would be the same. Insofar as rates are influenced by costs, it is the imagined cost rather than the actual cost (if the two are different) which is pertinent at least in the short run. (In the long run, the wrong misconception might lead to bankruptcy.)

Actually, then, distance rates or, more precisely, distance-related rates, are generally influenced by the spreading of some or all of the terminal costs over the entire distance of the movement, by the rate-makers' image of the behavior of line-haul costs over distance, and by the carriers' estimation of the value of the service to the shippers. Further, this latter estimation includes estimates of the strength of competition from other carriers and from producers located on the lines of other carriers as well as ideas concerning the relative sizes of fixed and variable costs, unallocable costs, and out-of-pocket costs.

The result is that in practice, distance rates are commonly tapering mileage rates; that is, they increase with the distance moved, but not as rapidly as distance increases. For example, total charges for moving a particular shipment 100 miles might be $6, but it might move 200 miles for $10, 300 miles for $13, and 400 miles for $15. Such rates, of course, normally start with a minimum charge.

Graphic comparisons of the various types of mileage rates and the postage-stamp rate are shown in Figure 17. It should be understood, of course, that successive distance-rate quotations are not infinitely divisible, as indicated by the smooth lines shown for distance-rate profiles in this figure. In reality, a magnified distance-rate profile would show a series of stair steps representing rates to and between successive stations along the carrier's route. The smooth lines shown for distance rates in Figure 17 may be considered as intersecting the midpoints of these numerous small steps.

All rate structures, with the exception of pure postage-stamp rates, are in some way related to distance. The directness of this relationship varies greatly, however. Railroad class rates in general tend to show a more direct relationship to distance than do commodity rates, but even class rates are not straight distance rates and commodity rates do not ignore the distance factor.

Logically, insofar as rates are influenced by costs, one would expect to find rates more closely approaching the straight mileage structure among carrier modes where (1) variable costs are high relative to fixed costs, (2) allocable costs are high relative to unallocable costs, (3) line-haul costs are high relative to terminal costs, and (4) line-haul costs are most directly proportional to distance. As these conditions generally are more closely approximated in motor and air carriage than in water, rail, and pipeline transport, it should not be surprising that rates of the first two modes tend to be more closely related to distance than is true of the latter modes. Rates of secondary carriers, with the exception of the United States mail, naturally tend to follow the rates of the primary line-haul carriers used.

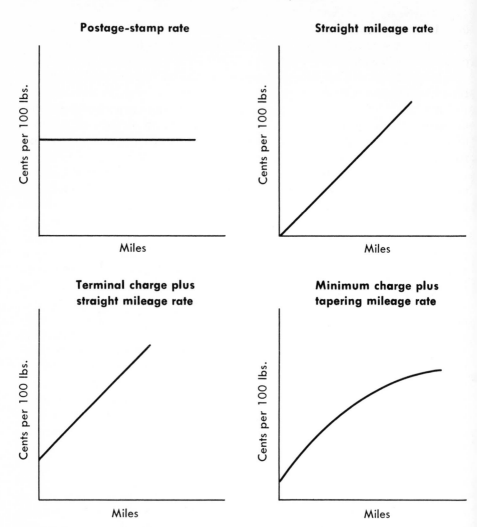

Figure 17: Illustrative Rate Profiles.

Export and Import Rates

Export and import rail rates are similar to other class and commodity distance-related rates in their overall patterns. Differences between the rates on domestically originated and destined products and products going to or coming from foreign sources by ocean carriage, however, are worthy of some brief comment. These differences have persisted for around a century. The two principal differences are that these rates may be considerably lower in some instances than applicable rates on domestic movements of similar traffic, and they may be structured in such a way as to equalize port or seacoast advantages. Note the word *may*. These permissible differences are not required or found on all products.

A vague but recognizable geographic pattern of export-import rates can be distinguished. At least five principal directional flows of traffic are involved: Between the North Atlantic Coast and the Midwest, between the South Atlantic Coast and the Midwest, between the Gulf Coast and the Midwest, between Gulf and Atlantic Coast points and interior Southeastern areas, and between the Pacific Coast and the Midwest, East, and South.

Lower export rates are designed to aid United States producers competing with foreign producers in foreign markets. This obviously benefits domestic producers. It also creates or stimulates business for the seaport cities and the carriers involved, without disadvantaging United States producers. Not much controversy exists about lower export rates.

Justification for lower import rates on products which are or might be produced in this country, however, is not as clear. Their effect may be to create additional business for some carriers and port cities, while decreasing the traffic of non-port carriers and the output of domestic producers. Each such case would seem to require an analysis of its individual merits before any general conclusions are reached.

Export-import seaboard and port equalization rate schemes are more controversial. The rates being equalized are not for the domestic portion of the movement, but rather for the total movement, domestic plus ocean. Due to geographical location or other factors, ocean rates between some United States ports or coasts and given foreign areas are higher or lower than from other ports or coasts. In a competitive situation, if domestic export or import rates to or from two ports (or coasts) were equal, the one with the lower ocean rate would be favored. Domestic carriers serving the port or coast with the higher ocean rate would not participate in the movement.

Competition between railroads serving different Atlantic Coast ports led to several severe railroad-rate wars during the 1870's. Finally, in 1877, a compromise agreement was reached which established differentials between the ports concerned. Those ports favored with lower ocean rates received higher rail rates, and vice versa. Although the specific rates and relationships have been altered over the years and some differentials have been eliminated recently, this still is the basic pattern of seaboard and port equalization.

North Atlantic Coast port differentials continued to exist for many years after the ocean-rate differences which brought them about had been removed. Ports receiving lower rail rates were upheld by the I.C.C. in their contention that the loss of business resulting from a removal of these differentials would have an adverse effect upon economic conditions and investment already made in the low-rate ports. It was not until 1963 that the United States Supreme Court, in a rate action started by New York and New England railroads, overruled the I.C.C. and struck down differentials between "northern tier" ports (Portland, Maine; Boston; Albany; New York City) and the "southern tier" group (Philadelphia, Baltimore, Hampton Roads) on export-import traffic moving from and to the Midwest.

Export-import rates were in existence prior to the establishment of the I.C.C. Whether or not the Commission would permit the establishment of such a system under its present procedures is questionable. Faced with an accomplished fact, however, the Commission has not been inclined to readjust established patterns of economic activity by undue tampering with these rates. The Commission, though, has more or less developed some guideposts concerning the minimum level below which export-import rates cannot fall. These rules of thumb are used when considering potential ton-mile and car-mile earnings under proposed rates, as well as the percentage relationship between export-import rates and other domestic rates.

BASING POINT AND FOURTH SECTION RATE STRUCTURES

In order to eliminate any possible terminological confusion, it is desirable to distinguish between basing point *pricing* and basing point *rates*, particularly as both do involve the performance of transportation and both are highly controversial.

Basing Point Pricing

The simplest form of basing point pricing, the single basing point system, involves the quotation of a delivered price consisting of the mill or factory price of the seller (wherever located) plus transportation charges from the basing point. That is, regardless of whether or not the buyer orders from the basing point mill or city, he in effect pays transportation charges from that point. If he orders from a nearer seller, from where actual freight rates are lower than from the basing point, he still pays the seller a price which includes an amount equivalent to the rate from the basing point; that is, his price includes phantom freight. On the other hand, if the purchase is made from a mill where the freight rate is higher than the rate from the basing point, his delivered price is still based on the lower rate from the basing point; the seller, in this case, is engaged in freight absorption.

Perhaps the most discussed single basing point system is that formerly used for many years in the steel industry—the so-called Pittsburgh-plus system—in which quoted delivered prices from all mills, wherever located, included an equivalent of the freight rate from Pittsburgh. Other industries have used similar systems, and some industries have used a multiple basing point system in which instead of one nationally controlling basing point, several regional basing points were established around the country. In this latter system, the price quoted a buyer includes an equivalent for the freight rate from the nearest basing point mill in his region.

Such a system of freight equalization is designed to neutralize the advantages or disadvantages of geographical location by putting all competing sellers on a par insofar as freight rates are concerned, in effect (from the sellers' and buyers' viewpoints), the equivalent of a postage-stamp rate. Defenders of such practices maintain that equalization of freight charges puts seller competition on a mill-cost-only basis, thus giving an edge to the most efficient plant and that it gives buyers a greater choice of sellers with whom they may do business. In other words, it leads to keener competition.

Opponents, however, argue that such pricing practices are conspiracies designed to prorate business, maintain the status quo among present producers, and lessen competition. From a transportation viewpoint, the transportation equivalent paid by the buyer may have little relationship to the actual transportation costs (or rates) of the hauling carriers, and the system also may lead to a misallocation of limited resources due to extensive cross-hauling of identical or similar goods. Generally, basing point pricing systems have been severely frowned upon by regulatory authorities and courts under the provisions of the Anti-Trust Acts, although the practice of freight absorption as such is not illegal if engaged in as a part of valid competition (whatever that may mean).

It should be clearly understood that basing point pricing is a device used by sellers of products and does not involve carrier participation. The carrier is paid the authorized rate for any movement regardless of whether the buyer is charged for phantom freight or the seller absorbs freight. There is no reason for a carrier to be interested in or even to know about seller-buyer arrangements.

Basing Point Rates

Basing point *rates*, however, are a carrier invention which grew out of carrier competition or out of the desire of particular carriers, for reasons of their own, to build up particular localities as centers of distribution or other economic activity at the relative expense of other communities. Although the latter could not be easily defended as a legitimate carrier activity, basing point rates established as a method of meeting competition are perhaps as defensible as many other kinds of legitimate competition. Individuals or localities favored by a particular form of competition generally defend it staunchly, while those harmed by it can usually convince themselves that it is bad. Or, as someone has said, "Everyone believes competition is a good thing for the other fellow."

A basing point rate structure, of course, is a distance-related structure. Its peculiar characteristic is that the total rate is made up of a rate from origin to the specified basing point or terminal plus an arbitrary from the basing point to destination.

In classic examples, such as the so-called Old Southern Basing Point System and many early westbound transcontinental and Pacific Coast north-south rail rates, the arbitrary used was relatively high in weight-mileage charges as compared to the longer haul between origin and the basing point. Often the arbitrary added from the basing point to nearby destinations was the full amount of the local or short-haul rate between the basing point and destination. Further, the arbitrary was added even to shipments destined to points *between* the origin and the basing point on the same line and which, therefore, were never actually transported to the basing point (an example of long-and-short-haul rate-making now regulated under Section 4 of the Interstate Commerce Act).

Upon what competitive grounds might such a rate structure be based? Let us imagine a railroad operating from point A to B to C to D. Water carrier competition, or some other competition, exists between points A and C, but not to points B and D. Further, this competition is from a low-cost carrier who can and does quote lower rates from A to C than would normally be charged by the railroad.

In this competitive pricing situation, if the railroad wishes to participate in the traffic from A to C, it will have to meet or beat its competition by charging a lower rate than it otherwise would. For illustration, let us suppose that the low-cost water carrier charges 60¢ per 100 pounds for a particular commodity between A and C and that the railroad feels that it must charge this same rate. Note that the water carrier does not serve B or D, however, and assume that shipments destined for those points must either go all the way by rail or go by water to C and thence by rail on to D or back to B.

The railroad rate-makers, then, might well reason that since the lowest alternative rate from A to either B or D is the 60¢ water rate to C plus its own short-haul rate from C to those points (which we will assume is 30¢ in both cases), an appropriate charge from A to B (a shorter haul than to C) is 90¢, the only possible charge from A to C is 60¢, and it is also possible to charge 90¢ from A to D, which is farther than C. This situation is diagrammed in Figure 18.

Citizens at B might vigorously protest such rates. They would allege discrimination, saying that shipments to C are not paying their proportionate or fair share of the rail carrier's transportation costs. Someone else then, namely the citizens of B, must make up this deficit by paying more than their fair share since the carrier must cover all its costs (including whatever profits are necessary to retain and attract its required capital) if it is to remain in business and provide the desired services.

An even more practical argument from B would be that the use of C as a basing point builds up the economy of C at the expense of B. For example, a wholesale distributor at C, buying merchandise from a manufacturer at A at the same price paid by a B wholesaler, would have a 30¢-per-100-pounds price advantage over his competitor at B. This would mean that he could underprice the B wholesaler at any point between C and B and could even deliver his goods into B at the same price as the local B wholesaler!

The railroad would reply that rates to B and to C are based on entirely different competitive situations and that even though its rates to C are neces-

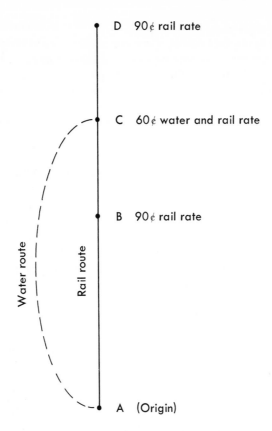

Figure 18: A Basing Point Rate Situation,
Showing a Fourth Section Deviation.

See Text for Explanation.

sarily depressed, rates to B are no higher as a result of this. In fact, the railroad might point out that if its rates to C were higher, it would lose a substantial part of its traffic to that point and the effect might cause even higher rates to B. That is, it would argue that even if the rates to C are not covering the total cost of movements to that point, they are at least covering out-of-pocket costs plus an additional amount that can be applied to overhead costs. The loss of this contribution to overhead, then, would mean that rates to B, D, and other noncompetitive points would have to be increased in order to cover the carrier's total costs!

Citizens of C would maintain that they have a natural advantage due to their favorable geographic location which enables them to benefit from carrier competition. Artificial removal of this natural advantage, they would say, would be discriminatory against C. Citizens of D might or might not enter the controversy. If they did, they would use arguments similar to those of B.

This somewhat simplified sketch describes the essential elements and arguments for and against a classic basing point rate structure, which might have come about either by rail-versus-water or rail-versus-rail competition. The economic causes and effects of such a situation can be analyzed, but there is no general agreement on its absolute rightness or wrongness. Rather, a neutral analyst would be likely to decide for or against a basing point rate structure according to his views on cost-based versus competitive carrier pricing.

Even though the classic basing point rate structures have to a considerable extent broken down or evolved into other forms, important vestiges of them remain in existing rail rate structures. To some extent, also, although to a much lesser degree due to differing cost characteristics, basing point influence has affected truck rates which are competitive with and patterned after rail structures. Some knowledge of the historical causes, effects, and arguments for and against classic basing point rate structures, therefore, is essential in understanding important present rate patterns. Contemporary Fourth Section rates, for example, can only be understood in the context of the rates from A to B and to C.

BLANKET RATE STRUCTURES

A blanket rate structure, sometimes referred to as group or zone rating, applies the same rate from a given origin (or destination if it is an originating area blanket) to all points within a specified geographical area. In effect, within the area in which this common rate prevails, it is a postage-stamp rate. Blanket rate structures, however, do make use of the distance rate technique in that the typical product moving for a considerable distance may move through a series of blanket zones each with a higher rate than the preceding one. Often, also, blanket rate zones are separated by intermediate buffer zone areas in which rates are quoted on some type of distance-rate basis. Because of rail cost characteristics and the wide area coverage by this mode, blanket rates are most widespread in rail transport. This discussion, therefore, is centered around rail blankets. Other modes, however, do make some limited use of blanket rates.

Blanket rates are quoted both in class and commodity tariffs and on short or intermediate hauls, as well as on long movements. They are most typically used and most highly developed in transcontinental or long-haul movements under rail commodity rate tariffs, however. Blankets on other types of movements usually are fewer and smaller. Either origin or destination points, or both, may be grouped together under a common rate blanket. For purposes of simplicity of exposition in the following discussion unless otherwise indicated, the authors will discuss only destination blankets. The same principles and arguments can easily be applied to origin blankets.

Blanket Forms

In respect to their size and shape, rate blankets are found in at least four distinct forms.

The form of blanket which most readily comes to mind is the very large one which may cover several states or even several different regions of the country. Extreme versions of this type of blanket were pictured and described by Stuart Daggett and John P. Carter in *The Structure of Transcontinental Railroad Rates* (Berkeley and Los Angeles: University of California Press, 1947). One of these involved rates on eastbound California wine which were blanketed for all destinations roughly east of the Rocky Mountains (more specifically, beyond the eastern boundary of Arizona and beyond Salt Lake City). Another similar blanket shown by these authors, with only a few minor differences, applied to eastbound California dried fruits and vegetables.

As noted, these two examples must be considered as unusually large blankets which apply a postage-stamp system over by far the larger portion of the country's territory and inhabitants. Fairly large blankets covering both origin and destination points, however, are not at all uncommon in both eastbound and westbound rail-commodity movements. In fact, this is the typical rate pattern of such traffic. Figures 19 and 20 show a profile and a map illustrating eastbound rail rates for one important product, lumber, originating in the Pacific Northwest.

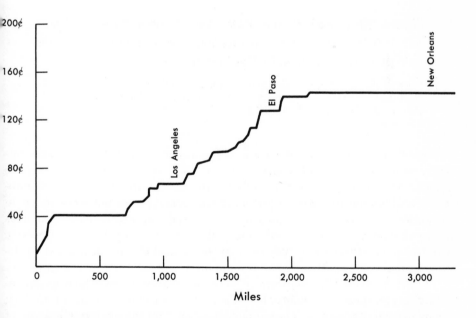

Figure 19: A Rail Blanket Rate Profile: Lumber Rates in Cents per 100 lbs., to Various Points from Portland, Oregon, to the Gulf Coast, Via the Southern Route.

Source: Roy J. Sampson, **Railroad Shipments and Rates From the Pacific Northwest** (Eugene: University of Oregon, Bureau of Business Research, 1961).

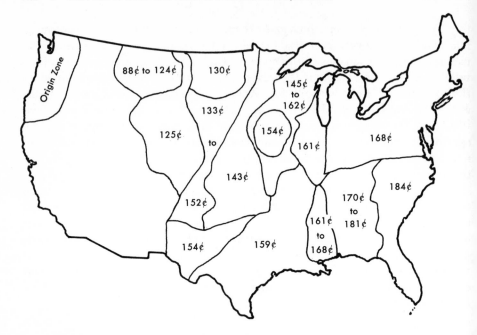

Figure 20: A Rail Blanket Rate Map: Lumber Rates, in Cents per 100 lbs., from Western Oregon and Washington Origins to Various Transcontinental Destinations.

Source: Roy J. Sampson, **Railroad Shipments and Rates From the Pacific Northwest** (Eugene: University of Oregon, Bureau of Business Research, 1961). Revised to June 9, 1970, courtesy Western Wood Products Association.

Another and much smaller form of blanket often includes the small outlying communities around a larger or key point city under a common rate blanket with the larger city. This relieves the carrier from the burden of publishing and administering many small arbitraries and places buyers or sellers in the entire given metropolitan area upon an equal competitive basis insofar as transport charges are concerned. One effect of this may be that economic activity which otherwise would occur in the central city is encouraged to develop in some of the outlying small communities.

Other blankets take the form of long and narrow strips which group together several successive points along the route of a particular railroad or along somewhat parallel routes. These blankets usually are found through areas of scant population and low traffic density. They are primarily a method of lessening the work of publishing and quoting rates and have little effect on either local economic activity or carrier revenues.

A fourth definite form of rate blanket is one which also is long and narrow, but usually not as narrow as the type just described. This form runs crosswise to the prevailing flow of traffic, which means that it is commonly found running north and south near or east of the Mississippi Valley where the great east-west rail traffic arteries are intersected by north-south rail lines or by north-south water carrier routes. Also, rivers have influenced blanket zone boundaries through the historical use of river crossings as rate break points where rates increase sharply.

These transverse blankets permit carriers connecting with transcontinental or long-haul carriers to participate in traffic movements originated or terminated by the latter carriers without any increase in rates. This benefits the transverse carriers, of course, allows greater routing flexibility, and permits shippers and receivers a greater choice among the long-haul carriers.

Blanketing practices extend well back into the Nineteenth Century before the establishment of the I.C.C. The Commission, however, has not discouraged blanketing as such, and numerous important blankets have been established during the present century.

In some instances, the coming of motor-carrier competition has disturbed existing rail blanket patterns. One can imagine two adjacent blankets with a sizable rate difference between them. In such a case, a shipper desiring to send goods to a point just inside the nearer boundary of the farther and higher rated blanket might ship by rail to a point just at the farther edge of the nearer and lower rated zone. Then, conceivably, he could have his shipment transferred onto a truck and hauled to its ultimate destination at a truck rate lower than the difference in the rail rates between the two zones.

Such maneuvering involving the transfer of lading, however, may be both expensive and impractical. Often the rate differences between two adjacent blanket zones are not sufficient to justify it even in those instances where it might be geographically feasible. Many of the blanket boundaries are located in areas where available truck transportation is not abundant, and many of the commodities moving under blanket rates are of the type least suited to truck transport. Finally, buffer zones with rapidly increasing distance rates may be inserted between blanket zones with large rate differences if railroads fear such behavior (see Figure 20). In general, truck competition between adjacent zones has disturbed blanket rate patterns much less than some earlier transport students and motor-carrier enthusiasts thought probable.

The Rationale of Blanketing

Rate blankets have been established for various reasons. By grouping a considerable number of points together, they greatly simplify rate publication, quotation, and administration, which benefits both carriers and their customers. Particularly, they may facilitate shipper use of simplified rate maps, cards, circulars, or books based upon the applicable tariffs in lieu of continual resort to the more complex tariffs themselves. Carrier and shipper savings from this feature alone at least partially offset carrier revenue losses on longer hauls or shipper additional payments on shorter hauls within a given large blanket.

Other reasons have probably been of even greater importance, however. Blanket rates provide a compromise method by which carriers may meet their competition without resorting to long-and-short-haul rates. That is, instead of charging a lower rate to a competitive point than to an intermediate noncompetitive point, the carrier may choose to charge the same lower rates to both points.

For example, in the situation pictured in Figure 18, already described, the carrier might choose to establish a 60¢ blanket covering shipments from A to both B and C. This still would allow the rail carrier to meet its water competition at C and prevent or control the movement of goods from A to C by water for eventual back-haul to B. The carrier no doubt would receive less revenue on a given volume of traffic from A to B, but the lower rate might generate additional traffic to B, and this intermediate point might be much less important than C as a revenue producer in any case. Even if the carrier should receive somewhat less revenue as a result of its rate blanket, this action would not be a Fourth Section deviation and normally would be unquestionably legal. Community B's arguments alleging local discrimination would be considerably weakened, and the carrier might not have to incur hearing and litigation expenses in fighting B's protests.

Pressures from producers or purchasers in a given area, many of whom wish to have rate equality with other area sellers or buyers, or who may wish to have a larger geographic area in which to sell or buy without rate penalties, also have contributed to blanket rates. The arguments used by such groups, and the counter arguments used by their opponents, are similar to the arguments for and against the basing point pricing system discussed above. But whereas basing point pricing is in ill repute legally, blanket rate-making as such does not suffer from legal handicaps.

Producers in one region who are competing in a common outside market with producers of similar items in other regions (which may be nearer the common markets) clearly have applied considerable pressures for large destination blanket rates in common marketing areas. By this device, sellers located in the first-named producing region may be able to expand their marketing territory into areas formerly dominated by their competitors. As different railroads may serve the different producing regions, railroad interest in the expansion of markets usually is similar to producer interest. If the producer customers of a particular railroad or group of railroads serving a given region increase their sales, rail traffic of the serving rail line or lines increases correspondingly.

Many sellers and buyers also like the flexible routing arrangements available within a blanket zone without additional rates. This is particularly important to shippers who make use of diversion and reconsignment in their marketing operations (see above). Cars may be freely diverted or reconsigned in a given zone without any increase in the freight rate itself, subject, of course, to any applicable tariff restrictions or additional service charges. In addition, a series of diversions or routing over known slow routes provides additional time for completing sales of moving cars. In effect, the shipper is receiving benefits similar to those which would be available under the delayed rate proposals, while the carrier's vehicle is being used as a storage place for the goods (and the carrier has a considerably greater responsibility than that of an ordinary warehouseman for loss or damage of goods). Again, carriers eager for traffic which might otherwise be lost to them because of interregional producer competition may be willing to make considerable concessions to allow producers in their own region to expand or remain in business.

Shippers and receivers almost always like to be in a position to use, or to threaten to use, alternate competing carriers. Potential loss of traffic to a rival carrier is a powerful stimulus in inducing top-quality service and favorable consideration of customer problems from an individual carrier. Blanket rates, which may allow shippers to choose from among several originating or connecting carriers, give these customers a powerful bargaining tool in dealing with individual carriers and thus may create pressures for such rates.

Pressures of intermediate or terminating carriers on originating carriers also have influenced the formation, size, and shape of blanket zones. Obviously, a geographically large blanket usually requires the participation of many railroads, each of which wants an opportunity to participate in important traffic movements. This influence is especially noticeable in the location and shape of those relatively narrow transverse blankets previously described which run crosswise to the prevailing traffic flow and begin the process of dividing the large originating eastbound traffic streams into a number of smaller streams, or the reverse. But the influence of intermediate and terminating carriers on originators is not limited to this situation.

Carriers which are originators of the products of one region also are terminators or intermediate carriers of products of other regions. This means that rate structures on long-haul traffic, as well as rate revenue divisions among the participating carriers, must be established on some mutually agreeable basis. In other words, long-haul rates are influenced to some extent by the preferences and relative bargaining positions of carriers other than the originating line or lines. These various reasons for the creation of rate blankets outline the principal advantages of or arguments for such structures. In summary, although rate simplification and the desire both among customers and carriers for widespread and unhampered carrier participation are important, perhaps competition is the most important cause as well as the most important advantage of blanketing practices. Although at first glance a map picturing a blanket rate structure may appear to be completely chaotic or arbitrary, study of the location of carrier routes and of the competitive conditions existing at the time of its formation usually will reveal a surprisingly logical pattern.

The competition leading to blanketing may be intermodal or intramodal carrier competition. Or it may be interregional or intraregional producer or consumer competition, involving both a desire for uniform rates in a given area and a desire for flexible routing. Often, of course, a structure which is brought into being to deal with a particular competitive problem tends to remain in being long after the peculiar competitive situation has ceased to exist. Although they do change, rate structures have an inherent stability. Typically they change only gradually. Many vested interests, shipper, consumer, and carrier, local and regional, usually are built up around any major rate structure which exists for any length of time, and such interests can be expected to fight vigorously any proposed changes adverse to their own economic welfare.

The Effects of Blanketing

It is clear that an effect of blanket rates is to give sellers a wider choice of territory and buyers in marketing their products and to give buyers correspondingly wider choices. Also, users are given a wider choice of carriers, at least of the mode quoting such rates (although other modes may be excluded). These effects no doubt increase competition, although producer delivered-price differentials may be decreased. This wider participation of buyers and sellers as well as carriers may even lead to lower consumer prices through lower seller and carrier profit margins and to better qualities and services. Many sellers and buyers, however, especially those who are economically harmed by blanket rates and even many neutral students of transportation economics and management oppose blanketing practices.

The arguments used or the disadvantages cited by opponents of blanket rates are similar to the arguments against and the disadvantages of basing point pricing, postage-stamp, basing point and Fourth Section rates, and similar freight equalization or non-mileage rate devices.

To summarize, opponents of blanket rate structures point out that to a considerable extent they ignore distance and resulting cost-of-service differences and lead to cost-increasing circuitous routing and cross-hauling. Some pay higher freight charges than would be exacted under a structure more closely related to distance and the carriers' costs of providing particular services, while others pay less.

It is said, too, that such structures offset natural locational advantages of some shippers or buyers (as a shipper of eastbound products who is located near the eastern boundary of an origin zone, or the buyer of western-produced goods who is located near the western edge of a destination group). Also, opponents say that locational advantages of producing regions located nearer consuming regions are offset by large destination blankets which allow more distant producing regions to penetrate the natural market of the nearer group.

Parenthetically, it should be noted that those who use the expressions "natural market" or "natural locational advantage" in this sense are equating these expressions primarily to distance from market. It has been counter-argued that a natural locational advantage is the effect of any circumstances which enable producers or regions to obtain lower rates (and thus quote lower delivered prices) than their competitors or rates lower than they would have to pay under other circumstances. Likewise, a natural market is one in which a seller or a producing region can sell at a lower price than rival sellers or regions. Under such concepts, locational advantage or natural markets might be determined by the relative distances of competitors from the markets in question. On the other hand, nearness in distance might be offset by various other equally natural competitive advantages which result in lower rates and possibly lower prices in common markets for the more distant sellers.

Since good arguments can be made both for and against blanket rate structures, it is likely that those sellers, consumers, modes of carriage, and individual carriers who benefit from them will find grounds for their continuance. Likewise, their counterparts who feel themselves harmed will complain. As in many freight-rate and other economic controversies, there is no absolutely good or bad solution. Insofar as neutral observers or scholars are concerned (if such exist), their judgments on blanket-rate structures as well as on other types of rates are likely to be based upon their personal values concerning such matters as cost of service versus value of service and the relative merits of different varieties of competition. And finally, regardless of arguments, this type of rate-making is well established, almost as old as the railroad industry itself, and is surrounded by strongly entrenched economic interests. Such rates are likely, therefore, to continue to play their significant role in our transportation economy through the foreseeable future.

ADDITIONAL READINGS

1. Bigham, Truman C., and Merrill J. Roberts, **Citrus Fruit Rates.** Gainesville, Fla.: University of Florida Press, 1950.
   Chapter III. "Development of the Rate Structure," pp. 49–83.
   Chapter IV. "Comparison of Rates," pp. 84–92.
   Chapter V. "Appraisal of the Rate Structure," pp. 93–115.
2. Daggett, Stuart, **Principles of Inland Transportation,** 4th ed. New York: Harper and Brothers, 1955.
   Chapter 18. "Freight Tariffs—Mileage Scales," pp. 339–362.
   Chapter 20. "Group and Basing Point Rates," pp. 381–405.
3. Daggett, Stuart, and John P. Carter, **The Structure of Transcontinental Railroad Rates.** Berkeley, Calif.: University of California Press, 1947. Pp. viii, 165.
4. Fair, Marvin L., and Ernest W. Williams, Jr., **Economics of Transportation,** Rev. ed. New York: Harper and Brothers, 1959.
   "Freight Tariffs, Rate Scales, and Structures," pp. 377–400.

5. Locklin, D. Philip, **Economics of Transportation,** 6th ed. Homewood, Ill.: Richard D. Irwin, Inc., 1966.
   Chapter 9. "Railroad Rate Structures," pp. 158–196.

6. Sampson, Roy J., **Railroad Shipments and Rates From the Pacific Northwest.** Eugene, Oregon: Bureau of Business Research, University of Oregon, 1961.
   Part Three. "Outbound Rail Rates," pp. 33–60.

7. Troxel, Emery, **Economics of Transport.** New York: Rinehart & Company, Inc., 1955.
   Chapter 25. "Structures of Freight Rates," pp. 587–614.

8. Westmeyer, Russell E., **Economics of Transportation.** Englewood Cliffs, N.J.: Prentice-Hall, Inc., 1952.
   Chapter 12. "Principles of Rate Making," pp. 246–265.

14

Transportation Costs
and Spacial Economic Activities

In the three preceding chapters, the authors have attempted to blaze a trail for the tenderfoot lost in the wilderness of proliferating freight rates. This chapter will continue by considering some of the effects of freight rates or transportation costs upon the levels and the types of economic activities carried on in particular localities, regions, or areas. (For simplicity of exposition, "freight rate" will be used in this discussion as a synonym for "shipper transportation cost." The economic effects described below are similar whether the shipper pays a carrier or pays the costs of private transportation.) After a brief review of some further relationships between competition and rate structures, we will discuss three questions insofar as they are affected by freight rates. 1. Where does economic activity locate? 2. Once located, where is the product marketed? 3. What are the relationships between freight rates and area (local, regional, national, etc.) economic development? These questions deal with what might be called "spacial economics."

In this connection it is well to remember that by its very nature, no freight rate can be neutral as an influencer of economic activity, not even if the rate is set at a zero level, that is, free transport. Any existing rate or rate structure in a competitive producing or consuming situation and any change in existing rate relationships necessarily benefits some and harms others. Many of the most bitter controversies regarding rates are about the rate relationships between competing points or products rather than the absolute level of charges. Thus, as transport exists in a highly competitive world, it is desirable that those involved with transportation understand something of the nature of the varieties of competition which directly affect their livelihoods.

COMPETITION, TRANSPORT COSTS, AND SPACIAL ACTIVITY

On the demand side of the demand-supply determinants of prices, there are very close and circular-type interrelationships between competition, freight rates, and spacial economic activity. As has been developed to some extent in the preceding chapter, the presence or the absence of competition affects both the level and the structure of freight rates. The level and structure of rates, as will be discussed later, affect both the types and the volumes of economic activity carried on in particular localities. Existing rates, often competitively determined, help to determine an area's stage of economic development. The area's stage of development (or its type and level of production and consumption) further affects competition and rates. The circular interrelationship is never-ending. Thus, it is not too farfetched to maintain that the whole body of the theory and practice of economic development, past, present, and future, is intimately tied to transportation costs (or freight rates).

The pertinent varieties of competition affecting freight rates, and thereby spacial economic development, include competition between carriers, producing centers, consuming centers, and commodities. Each of these is worthy of additional attention at this point.

Carrier Competition

Carrier competition may be intermodal, intramodal, or both, and it may be over parallel (approximately equidistant) or extremely circuitous routes. The preceding chapter discussed some examples of carrier rate competition. Like other sellers, however, carriers engage in spirited service or quality competition such as greater speed, lesser damage, pick up and delivery, transit, and a host of others. Also, like many other sellers they may spend considerable effort in promotional competition, including direct-sales solicitation, advertising designed to convince buyers that a particular service is better or cheaper than that of competing carriers (whether it is or not), and the like.

These various forms of carrier competition bring lower rates to some points than would otherwise be forthcoming, and perhaps as an offset to carrier revenue losses may bring higher rates to some noncompetitive points. For example, as noted in Chapter 13, competition is in considerable part responsible for blanket rates, Fourth Section rates, and similar deviations from distance structures.

Producing Center Competition

The freight-rate effects of competition between producers or groups of regional producers served by different carriers also were considered in Chapter 13. Such producing center competition is especially keen when products of the different centers are identical or reasonably close substitutes. Examples coming readily to mind are Western and Southern softwood lumber or California and Florida oranges marketed in the Northeast.

The more nearly identical competing products are, either physically or in the buyer's mind, the less can be the price difference between them. Prices charged consumers, of course, must include the costs of transportation (freight rates) plus all other costs of production and distribution (including profits).

Given producers or regional groups of producers may feel, at least in the short run, that their nontransport costs cannot be substantially lowered. Presumably in a highly competitive situation, these other costs would already be as low as the producers' controls could bring them. But competitively squeezed producers may be able to get lower freight rates if the carriers serving them can be convinced that the alternative is producer closure and consequent carrier loss of traffic. It may thus be considerably easier in many instances for producers to lower their transportation costs than their other costs. Such action, in addition to "harming" competitors in other areas and leading to protests of rate discrimination and demands for readjustments, may significantly affect the economies and the development of the regions concerned.

Producer competition may result in the primary effect just described in which freight rates to a common marketing center are lowered for one regional producing group. A secondary effect also may result, however, in which rates on inbound raw materials are lowered for a particular group in order that lower costs may enable it to quote a lower price on its finished product. For example, a primary effect would be the establishment of lower rates on Oregon lumber to the Northeast, thus aiding Oregon mills in competition with Southern lumbermen. A secondary competitive effect might be the granting of lower freight rates on logs bound to Oregon sawmills, thus reducing Oregon costs to the point where its product can compete even without lower rates on the finished product. The end result is the same in either case, but the secondary form provides much less ammunition for attacking producers in other regions.

Consuming Center Competition

Competition between consuming centers, or directional competition, also may have considerable impact on the economic activities of given areas. A profit-minded and well-informed producer naturally wishes to sell in the market where his net return above all costs, including both transportation and other costs, is greater.

The most profitable market is determined, of course, both by the relative local prices prevailing in the alternative markets and by the producer's costs of transporting his goods to those markets. His other costs of production and distribution should be about the same, regardless of where the product is sold. If market prices are the same, he will sell to the area with the lowest freight rate. If freight rates are the same, he will sell in the market with the highest price. If, as is likely, both prices and freight rates vary between the different markets, he will choose that combination (not necessarily either the highest price or the lowest rate) which will maximize his net return.

To a pure theorist, or from an overall long-run view, the situation just described might appear to be an aberration. Under purely competitive textbook conditions, the producer's net would tend to be the same in all markets. But even though we do live in a competitive world, it is not purely competitive. Producers more often than not do have choices between more profitable and less profitable alternatives if they are well informed about ever-changing market conditions.

Also, freight rates may be price-determined as well as price-determining. It is often difficult to tell whether differences in local prices are caused by freight rates or whether differences in freight rates are responses to differences in local prices This, however, poses no particular problem to a producer with goods to sell. To him a given price and rate pattern exists at a given time, offering him an opportunity to increase profits by selling in the appropriate market. And actually, due to various factors (market imperfections, as an economist might describe them), such a situation may exist for a considerable period of time.

We might use a simple example to illustrate some of the possible spacial economic effects of directional competition. Let us suppose that Illinois widget producers can sell either in New York or California markets which are served by different rail carriers and, further, that the market price and freight rate combination is such that it is most profitable for them to sell in New York. But the rail carriers connecting Illinois and California, desiring to participate in hauling this lucrative traffic, decide to lower their rate on widgets to a level which makes it more profitable for producers to shift their sales from New York to California.

A probable reaction of the Illinois to New York carriers is a similar rate cut. Eventually, it is likely that rate adjustments will be reached which will permit both groups of carriers to participate in this traffic. As a result, consumers both in California and New York will be buying widgets at lower prices than previously. Then with these lower prices, the elasticity of demand will permit considerably more widgets to be sold in the two markets than were formerly sold in New York alone. To satisfy this demand, producers must increase their outputs, or new producers must enter the field, or both. Thus the Illinois widget industry grows.

It may be, however, that widgets are also produced in Texas for the New York and California markets. If so, Texas producers will correctly allege that the rate cuts have placed them at a competitive delivered-price disadvantage relative to their Illinois competitors. If this results in serious sales losses for the Texans, they will have no difficulty in convincing the different carriers operating between Texas and the California and New York markets that rate reductions will mutually benefit both these carriers and Texas producers. Such reductions, designed to restore previous competitive relationships, may further reduce prices in the consuming areas, lead to still more widget consumption, and alter the widget industry in both producing areas.

Although the illustration used is simple, further reflection on consuming center competition could lead one into many possible complex effects. In addition to directly affecting the economies of the consuming centers involved and a single producing area, the competition of directions may also bring in elements of both carrier competition and producing center competition.

Commodity Competition

Competition between commodities exists when raw materials or components of finished goods may be processed, manufactured, or assembled either at the point of origin, the point of consumption, or perhaps somewhere between. For example, mills near wheat-producing areas may grind grain into flour which is then shipped to consuming centers, or the grain itself may be shipped to consuming centers or intermediate points for manufacture. Cattle may be slaughtered in cattle-growing areas and sent to consuming areas as dressed meat or they may be shipped on the hoof to packing houses in consuming centers.

The problem of where processing or manufacture shall occur is one of the classic topics of industrial location theory which will be further considered. It is also an extremely practical problem, often a matter of economic survival, for individual processors or manufacturers, their employees, and the communities or regions in which they are located.

The establishment, failure, or survival of this type of production in a given locality may be largely dependent upon the comparative levels of the freight rates applicable to the raw material and the finished product. If rates on wheat and flour are such that it is less costly for a miller to ship wheat in its original form than in the form of flour after taking into account the weight losses involved in manufacturing, for example, milling normally will occur near consuming centers. A different rate pattern, making it less costly to ship flour than wheat, would influence the location of mills in or near wheat-growing areas. The same principle is applicable to numerous commodities at various stages of production. (Such simplified generalizations, of course, assume that other things affecting production costs at the different possible locations are equal or are not unequal enough to offset freight rate differences. This may not be true. On the other hand, inequalities among other things may reinforce rate differences. We are concerned here only with freight-rate effects, not with the host of other things which might influence production costs and help determine location.)

In addition to comparative rate levels between raw and finished products, rate structures which permit stoppage in transit for various kinds of finishing operations may be powerful determinants of plant location. Many communities, intermediate between raw materials producing areas and heavy consuming areas, owe their important position in some processing, fabricating, or assembling industry to a long-established favorable transit privilege granted it by some railroad. It may have been the whim of a long-dead railroad official who was influenced by his stock ownership in a local plant, by ownership of real estate in the favored community, or by some more worthy or less tangible reason.

During the more than a century in which railroad freight rates and rate structures have played an important role in determining "how much of what shall be done where," many delicate balances between raw materials rates and finished goods rates have grown up and become more or less accepted by all concerned in numerous industries and communities (as is the case, also, for many rates from rival producing centers to common markets). Rates of other forms of carriage have sometimes modified these production and distribution patterns, but not significantly in most instances. Other modes, rather, have tended to adapt to existing patterns of economic activity and existing rail rates.

Sometimes rate structures or other factors have concentrated finishing operations at the raw materials producing center, sometimes in consuming areas, and sometimes in between. Often, too, the balance between rates and other factors is such that some finishing occurs both at raw materials and consuming centers as well as between the two.

In a multi-finishing-point locational pattern, output may be fairly evenly divided among the various points or it may be heavily concentrated in one area with relatively small outputs occurring elsewhere. Regardless of the proportionate shares, however, and regardless of the original causes of the existing division of output, the competitive relationships often are so delicately adjusted that even a slight change in freight-rate relationships will throw the entire mechanism out of balance. As changes in the delivered-price possibilities of the different producing areas vary, output will be shifted toward or away from raw materials areas, consuming areas, or transit points. Production and employment will increase at the favored locations, while mill and factory doors are closing and merchandising and service incomes are diminishing in those areas adversely affected by the rate change.

Those who propose rate changes which are likely to affect well-established cost, price, and productive balances, then, usually encounter a hornet's nest of entrenched resistance from those individuals, businesses, communities, or regions which fear a loss of their investments, jobs, and incomes. Some of the most controversial rate hearings have grown out of such situations. Carriers, understandably, are somewhat reluctant to touch off such controversies unless the potential rewards are great, and the I.C.C. in general has been rather sympathetic to the arguments of those likely to be severely hurt by changing rate patterns. As a result, some flexibility in rate-making is lost and perhaps some economically inefficient production is protected in exchange for more local economic stability. Again, the effects of such actions may be subjected to economic analysis, often with fairly convincing answers, but whether or not one agrees or disagrees with such policies is largely a matter of personal values.

TRANSPORT COSTS AS LOCATION DETERMINANTS

Freight rates (or producers' transport costs) are generally considered to be only one factor, but often a very important factor, in determining where a particular plant will or should locate, or how much of what kind of economic activity will occur in particular areas.

Economic Rationality

In a competitive situation, a producer naturally will prefer a location which, all cost factors taken into account, will enable him to lay down his goods in his potential market at a price lower than, or at least as low as, the prices of his competitors. He must meet or beat his competition if he is to prosper. Even if competition is not keen, the producer will prefer the lowest-cost location as this will increase his profits. This lowest-cost location principle is as valid for a neighborhood grocery store as for a giant manufacturing concern with national or worldwide markets, and it underlies all location and market-area theory and rational practice.

Many businesses have located and thrived in economically irrational locations, of course, due to combinations of circumstances which may or may not be explainable. Also, many barely literate persons have become multimillionaires. These numerous exceptions do not negate the value of a choice business location or of education, however. It is possible, although not subject to proof, that many of these exceptional successes would have been even more successful with the benefits of a good location or a good education. (This assumes, of course, that other things in the personal make-up of the individuals concerned which contributed to their successes would not have been changed by preferred business locations or better educations.) As a generalization, no one would seriously dispute the proposition that those with the greatest competitive advantages, whether in location or education, are most likely to be successful, while those operating under the greatest competitive handicaps are most likely to fail.

In the remainder of this chapter, as this book is on transportation rather than on the whole gamut of location, marketing, and development, we will be primarily concerned with the transportation cost or freight-rate aspects of location, market areas, and regional economic development. This emphasis does not imply that other cost or even noncost factors should be ignored. Location and marketing, as already stated, are not always economically rational. Neither is it true that economically rational action always dictates that producers locate at the point where their total transportation costs (inbound plus outbound) will be lowest, any more than it is always economically rational to sell in markets accessible by the lowest freight rates. An economically rational producer, as usually defined, tries to maximize his profits. This involves minimizing his total costs of production and distribution, of which transportation is only one, and selling in the markets where prices yield the largest return over costs (or if forced to sell at a loss, in markets where prices most nearly cover costs).

The following discussion, then, will assume that producers are economically rational and well-informed, and that other things (nontransport factors) are equal. Starting from this base and with an understanding of the principles involved, a reader or a decision-maker can relax these analytical assumptions as he chooses to fit particular circumstances.

Because of space limitations, our discussion will also be mainly concerned with theory. In practice, almost every decision must be based on numerous factors that differ in detail. It would be difficult even to list all these factors and impossible to properly weight them to cover all potential situations. But the practitioners with a working knowledge of theory can reach workable answers in a variety of situations. It is possible to have good theory and bad practice, but it is virtually impossible to have good practice without good theory (even though the practitioner may not consciously realize that he is applying good theory or any kind of theory and may not admit it even if he does realize it).

Actually, if we conceive the term "transportation cost" in a broad sense, we can convincingly argue that *all* regional or spacial production and distribution cost differences (except a few kinds of extractive production such as mining, fishing, and certain kinds of agriculture requiring particular localized resource endowments of nature) can be reduced to transportation cost differences. In other words, the economically rational location of all forms of refining, processing, manufacturing, fabricating, assembling, and distribution, as well as some extractive operations, is in the final analysis based upon transportation considerations alone.

Production and Distribution Requirements

Production or distribution basically requires a site (land), people, tools (including physical plant), raw materials (the raw materials of distribution may be finished goods), and perhaps power (from fuels or electricity). People, tools, raw materials, and power certainly are mobile. They can be transported to any location at a cost.

Land usable as a site also is available anywhere on our planet, and the value of any site is dependent upon its best alternative use. Real estate prices, thus, are governed by comparative site advantages to buyers or renters who calculate that they will receive more benefits from a particular site than do other potential users, and thus are willing to pay more for it. These benefits or advantages of a site, of course, are derived from its accessibility to something—markets, scenery, climate, cultural attractions, and so forth. Accessibility is a matter of transportation involving costs in resources (including time en route). A location most accessible to the desired attraction entails lower transportation costs to reach it and thus has a higher market value, while less accessible locations require higher transport costs and result in lower land values. A producer always has the choice of paying more for land and less for transportation or paying less for land and more for transportation. Even land required for sites of production or distribution activities, therefore, can be viewed as mobile or transportable at a cost, just as are the other basic requirements.

Artificial Locational Offsets

A practical individual, even though agreeing with the above conclusions, might raise questions concerning the locational effects of tariffs (in the "import" sense, not freight-rate tariffs), local taxation, and subsidies. But even the artificial politically imposed costs of import tariffs and local business taxes and the negative costs of subsidies to business can be related to transport costs in an inverse way and ultimately can be reduced to transport costs.

Tariffs and local taxes paid by producers increase their costs of getting their products to buyers. This offsets the market and materials accessibility (transport cost) advantages of producer site locations by decreasing site values. The effect is the same as removing a producer whose transport costs are related to distance farther away from his markets or materials. This, of course, benefits competing producers not subject to the tariffs or taxes, as relative costs (and delivered prices, or profit margins, or both) are changed in favor of the nonpayers. The effect is the same as making the nonpaying sites more accessible from the transport-cost viewpoint, or of moving them closer to their markets or materials in the distance-rate sense. Economically, their site values are increased.

The same type of analysis can be applied in determining the effects of producer subsidies or tax forgiveness. Those sites favored by such devices are made more accessible, or moved closer to markets or materials in the distance-rate context. Again, relative costs are changed in favor of subsidized as opposed to nonsubsidized producers, with accompanying site-value increases for the former and decreases for the latter.

Most direct and indirect business subsidies (excluding, perhaps, some designed to maintain income, preserve a way of life, or conserve natural and human resources such as our United States agricultural subsidies) are consciously designed primarily to make site locations more valuable for particular kinds of production by offsetting or reducing the relative competitive disadvantages of the subsidized sites as compared to other potential producing sites. Likewise, many import tariffs are levied primarily to offset domestic production disadvantages. Even though such actions are clothed with threadbare parochial phrases such as "Promote community development," "Encourage regional growth," "Protect infant industry," or "Save American jobs," they may be completely rational economically from the viewpoints of the areas taking these actions and their political representatives even if not contributing to national or world economic efficiency. A particular area under some circumstances may gain more than it loses by action which brings the same results as would come from moving its own producers closer to markets or pushing competitors in other areas farther from markets.

Business taxes which increase production costs, however, cannot be altogether economically rational in a spacially competitive situation. The only rational element involved is to keep such taxes in one's own area lower than those of competing areas, or at least so low that overall production and distribution costs, including taxes, in one's own area are lower than in competing areas. Such a policy, if followed in all areas, probably would tend to eliminate all or most of such taxes, which would be the only economically rational procedure in cases of spacial competition. Any increase in production costs decreases the ability to compete.

To review, then, local taxes and import tariffs which increase production and distribution costs as well as subsidies which decrease costs have the identical competitive effects of increases or decreases in transportation costs of the paying or receiving producers. These same effects occur whether or not the programs adopted by the appropriate political bodies are economically rational or irrational either from the narrow regional or the overall viewpoints.

Further, since everything used in production can be transported at a cost except the production site itself, and even the effect of site mobility can be obtained at a transportation cost, it follows that economic activity is not bound to areas in which it suffers tax or tariff handicaps or is denied the benefits of the subsidies received by its competitors. These things, too, are reducible to transportation costs. If, after considering all comparative pertinent costs and prices, a producer finds that it would be more profitable for him to incur the costs of transporting his establishment from a high-tax, high-tariff area to a subsidized site or to locate a business there and pay whatever higher transport costs on his raw materials and finished goods may be necessary, he is usually free to make such a move. And if he acts in an economically rational manner, as that term is defined, he will do so.

In summary, then, one can logically defend the proposition that alternative producer transportation costs determine the rational location of economic activity, except for a few resource-tied extractive operations. And perhaps these exceptions are not as common as one would suppose at first thought.

Use of Transport Cost Data in Locational Decisions

The authors hasten to point out, however, that the above type of approach, which reduces rational location to transport costs alone, has been presented primarily to emphasize the role of transport in location. It is not the analytical approach generally followed either in traditional location theory or in actual decision-making practice. Generally in such analyses, transportation costs (sometimes divided into inbound and outbound categories) are included at a fixed or given level for each of the various possible locations under consideration. Other fixed location factors for each location may include such cost items as labor, taxes, power, site costs, financing charges, and similar factors. In practice, also, decision-makers may consider such noneconomic or nonmeasurable factors as climate, living conditions, schools, political attitude toward business, and other things which are reflected in the costs of other more measurable location factors.

The authors have no criticism of analytic schemes using any number of location factors or variables. Analysis is undertaken to develop answers, and if ten factors or one hundred can be more conveniently used than one or a few variables to reach satisfactory solutions, so much the better.

Earlier location theorists and even practitioners were necessarily constrained to the use of very few variables in their analyses. The human mind, even when aided by two-dimensional or three-dimensional diagrams, blackboards, or reams of paper covered with hand-computed calculations, can handle only a few variables, and these comparatively slowly. The speed of modern electronic computers, however, now makes it possible for an analyst to work with large numbers of variables and have calculations performed in minutes which a few years ago would have required several lifetimes.

A large corporation today can determine alternative costs for as many factors as it considers pertinent at any number of possible locations, program this data for its computer, and be assured of the best location for a branch plant (assuming the data and program are correct) during the time the president is having his coffee break. Location in a relatively few years has advanced from an exotic and unreliable art, or the plaything of a small group of theorists whose writings were read by few and understood by fewer, to something approaching the stage of an "exact" science.

This does not mean that all the problems are solved and that location no longer offers a challenge. A monster computer is only a fast-calculating idiot. It does not make one's decisions, and the answers it cranks out are only as good as the material fed into it. Someone must know which data are pertinent, see that these data are properly collected and programmed, interpret the results, and make a decision. Even in a large operation, such as we are describing, this calls for several skilled specialists, including the theorist. And in smaller operations, where it is not possible or feasible to call upon the speed of a computer, more simple methods relying largely upon basic theory must be used.

TRANSPORT COSTS AND REGIONAL ECONOMIC DEVELOPMENT

The topic of regional economic growth or development has received considerable attention from economists as well as from numerous "practical" individuals and groups during recent years. ("Region" as used in this sense may include any defined geographical area from a local community to several nations, such as the European Common Market.) In the United States alone, several thousand agencies, including Chambers of Commerce, state and local development boards, and similar organizations, are actually attempting to promote economic growth in their own areas.

Most of such promotion is devoted to the industrial sector of the economy. That is, it involves efforts to get new manufacturing or processing plants established in the region or to encourage the expansion of existing plants. This emphasis on industrialization, which has almost made industrialization synonymous with growth or development, apparently is based on two assumptions. One, relative demand factors or terms of trade are such that more value is added by manufacturing than by agricultural or extractive enterprises, thus more manufacturing means more regional income. Two, more economic diversification means more regional stability or less susceptibility to cyclical economic fluctuations or the impacts of particular declining industries. Whether or not these assumptions are always valid is immaterial for our discussion as long as they are believed in and acted upon.

Many economic and noneconomic factors allegedly preventing, causing, controlling, or influencing regional economic growth have been suggested and discussed at length. In addition to considering such obvious factors as physical location, resources, and environment, the population's size, social, cultural, and educational characteristics, regional history, and prevailing institutional patterns, some analysts have attempted to quantify such concepts as "critical masses" or combinations of the factors of production and consequent "take off" points in growth. Discussions range from the extremely qualitative to the highly quantitative, and some even verge on the metaphysical (at least it seems so to the nonspecialist).

In essence, however, the new "science" of regional development continues to draw heavily upon traditional location and market-area theory and practice. New combinations, approaches, and assumptions are used, but it is doubtful if much new substantial theory has been developed.

Transportation (and its rates or costs) is generally recognized as an important factor in regional development as in earlier location theory. Often, however, theorists concerned with regional growth tend to take transportation for granted or to assume that the existing patterns of facilities and rates are virtually fixed. Many regional promotional groups tend to do likewise or, even worse, work at cross-purposes through failure to understand the nature of transportation effects.

A "Transportation Effect" Development Hypothesis

Few would disagree that adequate transport facilities, routes, and rates (however "adequate" may be defined) are a necessity for the development and maintenance of a complex economic society. Freight rates by themselves certainly cannot cause or force economic development, but they just as certainly can and do either aid or limit it. In the following paragraphs, therefore, the authors will point out some relationships between freight rates and regional economic development. In doing this, we will isolate the freight-rate effect by the common analytic device of assuming that all other things are equal except the freight-rate variable.

First, it is convenient and realistic to think of a freight-rate charge as having the same economic impact as an import tariff in international trade. Both increase sellers' laid-down costs or buyers' prices, and thus limit markets geographically and in volume of sales. Both protect or result in a relative shift of advantage toward the sellers not subject to the charges or who pay lower charges than their competitors. This, of course, expands the sales and market areas of the lower-charge sellers, with consequent restrictions on the higher-charge group.

With this concept in mind, we will now consider a relatively simple and understandable theory or hypothesis of the relationship between freight rates and regional economic activity. Note that this does not purport to be a complete theory of growth or a substitute for other growth theories which have been propounded; rather it is concerned only with the freight-rate aspect.

Our model assumes that a region, like a living organism, may grow economically into or through various stages. During its first or beginning state, which we will call a *colonial* economy, the region relies mainly upon extraction and export of materials from its basic natural resources, for example, agricultural products, livestock, forest products, minerals, or fish. Surpluses of these products are marketed outside the region in crude or semi-processed forms, while most highly processed and manufactured goods are imported from outside sources.

At a higher level of industrialization, which can be called an *intermediate* stage, regional plants process or manufacture export products from the area's own natural resource base into highly finished goods ready, or almost ready, for consumption use. Most of the region's finished-goods requirements, other than those goods derived from its local natural resources, however, are still brought in from outside regions.

At a third or *mature* level of industrialization, the region becomes primarily an importer of foodstuffs and of raw materials which it processes or manufactures into finished goods for resale in other areas as well as for its own consumption.

Possibly, and involuntarily, a region may reach a fourth or *senile* stage in which its own natural resources have been largely exhausted and the outside markets for its manufactures have been taken over by more efficient or more aggressive sellers located in younger or more favored industrial regions. Temporarily the region may remain relatively prosperous from returns on previous investments, through providing financial, governmental, or other services, or from some other kinds of outside remittances. Eventually, however, it is likely to become a stagnant or depressed area if it does not develop some rejuvenating type of economic activity which enables it, in effect, to move back into a younger stage.

History contains many examples of economic evolution of nations as well as of specific areas within nations which seem to conform to this model of change or growth. These examples are so numerous that particular citation appears unnecessary.

Although we have been discussing regional economies as a whole, it should be noted that particular industries or even particular firms in a given area may evolve along similar lines. In the context of our model, industries or firms at all four stages of development may be found in any given region at any time. This complicates the model's details and policy applications, even if not its principles, in situations of diversified regional economies. It makes no particular difference, however, if all or most of a region's dominant industries are at a similar stage of development.

It is not necessary to assume any inevitable pattern of growth or any growth at all in this hypothesis. A region may remain in any one stage indefinitely, or it might even skip a stage. Our model is concerned only with what kind of freight rates are most conducive to attaining regional goals, whether these goals be the enjoyment of prosperity at a lower level of industrialization or the moving up to a higher stage of development.

A colonial region wishing to remain in that stage obviously would be benefited by low inbound and outbound freight rates. This would keep its employment and income high by encouraging heavy and widespread use of its raw materials. At the same time, consumption costs would be held down by low prices resulting from low freight rates on imported finished goods.

If a colonial region wishes to move into the intermediate stage and perhaps eventually reach the mature level, though, different freight rates would best serve its purpose. Higher inbound rates on manufactured goods, leading to higher regional prices, would encourage more local manufacturing activity while at the same time protecting the region's new and small manufacturers from better-established outside competitors. Likewise, higher outbound rates on raw materials would depress regional raw-materials prices and encourage more local manufacture of these materials at the same time as it increased prices and made manufacturing more costly for outside competitors.

Once the mature stage is attained, low inbound and outbound rates again are most useful. This enables the region to import its necessary foodstuffs and raw materials as well as to export its finished products at a low price. At this stage, the region is dominant in its manufacturing and exporting activities and has little fear of an invasion of its local markets by outside manufacturing competitors.

Finally, in the senile stage, a region would be best served by low inbound rates on its foodstuffs and raw materials which cannot be produced locally in sufficient quantities for its local needs. High inbound rates on manufactured goods will aid in preserving at least the local regional markets for the old and inefficient regional manufacturers who have lost most of their outside markets to more efficient competitors. As the region no longer exports foodstuffs and raw materials, outbound rates on these items are unimportant. Low outbound manufactured-goods rates, however, might aid the region's more efficient manufacturers in hanging onto portions of their outside markets, at least for a time.

It appears that from the viewpoint of attaining regional goals, there is no one best freight-rate level or structure fitting all situations (the same thing can be said of tariffs in international trade). What is best can be determined only when we know where the region is now and where (if anywhere) it wishes to go. Further, what is best economically for a given defined geographical area is not necessarily best when considered in a larger economic or geographical perspective.

Application of "Transportation Effect" Hypothesis

It is not surprising, then, that freight-rate policy recommendations and actions of regional promotional groups often appear to be inconsistent with such groups' primary purpose of encouraging regional industrial growth. Even assuming that these agencies are fully aware of the probable effects of various freight-rate patterns on their specific regions and goals, which is indeed a heroic assumption, various regional cross-currents and pressures must be considered (again, similar to a nation's consideration of free trade as opposed to protective tariffs in the international sphere).

Those who pay most of the necessary immediate costs of increasing industrialization are not necessarily those who reap most of its immediate benefits. Or even if they are, they are more likely to be aware of the easily recognizable costs than of the more nebulous rewards. Consumer interests may differ from producer and employee interests even though the individual is a member of both groups. Also, producers' interests may differ according to their various stages of development. For example, raw materials and food-stuffs producers might differ sharply from finished-goods manufacturers on freight-rate adjustments.

The authors are not necessarily advocating the manipulation of freight rates to direct regional growth into particular channels. We have merely pointed out the influence of various rate patterns upon various types of regional economic activity and aspirations. Rate manipulation, however, could be consciously used as a very effective tool in attaining regional objectives and in improving the consistency of agencies concerned with regional planning.

We know of no instance in this country where attempts have been made on a broad scale to apply such conscious and consistent rate policy to channel the overall pattern of regional economic activity. Some other countries, however, have made conscious use of this device, at least on a limited scale, as a part of their overall national economic planning. Even in the United States, somewhat the same end results have often been achieved through pressures from dominant regional industries concerned with preserving or improving their own positions, but probably not as a part of a conscious overall regional economic plan. The import tariff (or export subsidy), however, which is an international trade counterpart of domestic trade's freight rate, has been long and widely accepted as a legitimate tool for achieving national economic aims.

The overall application of deliberate, broadly conceived, and effective interregional freight-rate controls designed to stimulate certain kinds of economic activity in particular regions probably would be politically difficult, if not impossible, in the United States. Vigorous protests would come from those regions, producers, and consumers fearing adverse economic effects as well as from those who disagree with the ideology of such planning.

Even if ideological opponents could be convinced that no freight-rate structure can have a neutral effect, and thus that any policy or even no conscious policy benefits some and adversely affects others, their opposition might continue. They might argue that due to human imperfections, any consciously planned policy of this type is likely to produce worse economic results than would come from the lack of a conscious plan. In any case, arguments involving either ideology or conflicting economic interests seldom are settled by logic.

This does not mean, though, that an understanding of the freight-rate effects described in our above model can have no practical application in this country. Regional developmental groups, producers and potential entrants, and buyers can use this framework in realistically assessing their positions and prospects. This may contribute to more consistent and effective policies, more rational decisions, and to a better adaptation to economic circumstances which in all likelihood cannot be significantly changed. Those responsible for proposing or initiating new or changed rates, as well as rate regulatory authorities, obviously should understand the effects of various alternatives actions. Further, as most major interregional or interindustry freight-rate-adjustment disputes usually result in a compromise under our regulatory system, those bargainers best armed with an understanding of the effects of various possible actions are likely to come out of the bargain with better results than if they had negotiated blindly.

Any theory may have practical usefulness to someone, but the gap between theory and practice is greater (or greater modifications in the assumptions must be made) in some cases than in others. The authors are convinced that this particular simple regional freight-rate-effect theory is one which can be used to achieve major practical results with a minimum modification of assumptions.

ADDITIONAL READINGS

1. Bowersox, Donald J., Edward W. Smykay, and Bernard J. LaLonde, **Physical Distribution Management.** Rev. ed. New York: The Macmillan Company, 1968. Chapter 4. "Geomarket and Georeference Patterns," pp. 66–100.
2. Campbell, Thomas C., "Transportation and Regional Economic Development," **Transportation Journal,** Vol. 3, No. 1, Fall 1963, pp. 7–13.
3. Daggett, Stuart, **Principles of Inland Transportation,** 4th ed. New York: Harper and Brothers, 1955. Chapter 19. "Varieties of Competition," pp. 365–380.
4. Fair, Marvin L., and Ernest W. Williams, Jr., **Economics of Transportation,** Rev. ed. New York: Harper and Brothers, 1959. Chapter 20. "Rate Structures and the Effects of Competition," pp. 401–423.

5. Locklin, D. Philip, **Economics of Transportation,** 6th ed. Homewood, Ill.: Richard D. Irwin, Inc., 1966.
   Chapter 4. "Freight Rates and the Location of Industries and Market Centers," pp. 44–66.
6. Moses, Leon F., "A General Equilibrium Model of Production, Interregional Trade, and Location of Industry," **Review of Economics and Statistics,** November 1960, pp. 393–397.
7. Mossman, Frank H., and Newton Morton, **Logistics of Distribution Systems.** Boston: Allyn & Bacon, Inc., 1965.
   Chapter Three. "Processing Centers and the Spatial Extent of Distribution Systems," pp. 70–104.
8. Peters, William S., "Measures of Regional Interchange," **Papers and Proceedings of the Regional Science Association,** Vol. 11, 1963, pp. 285–294.
9. Yaseen, Leonard C., **Plant Location,** Rev. ed. New York: American Research Council, 1960.
   Chapter 2. "The Transportation Factor," pp. 14–44.

15

Location Theory
and Transportation

Traditional location theory has been concerned with two principal types of problems. 1. Where does economic activity (a firm or an industry) locate in order to maximize its profits assuming that markets are fixed, or, stated another way, why do particular patterns of location develop? 2. Where is it most profitable for the firm or industry to market its product assuming a given or existing locational pattern? This version is often called market-area theory. Both of these problems have been approached from a least-cost viewpoint, and transportation costs have been considered an important location factor.

Some theorists, principally geographers or historians, also have been interested in the factors determining the location of cities. And more recently, considerable theoretical and practical attention has been given to what is variously called regional economics, regional development, or even regional science. City location and regional economic development also, as will be shown, are closely related to transportation and its costs.

The spadework of J. H. von Thunen (for agriculture) and Alfred Weber (for industrial operations) is considered classical in the "fixed market" approach to location. Frank A. Fetter and August Losch have done almost equally classical work in the "fixed production points" area. Other theorists have elaborated upon, refined, or empirically tested much of the work of these pioneers and perhaps have even developed some new theory. Location literature is large and growing, encompassing so much that even a brief mention of all its notable contributors exceeds our space limitations.

Those interested in any aspect of transportation, therefore, might find it interesting and rewarding to delve more deeply into this literature and especially into the relationships between transport costs and location, marketing areas, and regional or community economic development. In order to acquaint readers with the bare skeletons of some of this theory and to stimulate further interest in it, the authors outline what they feel are the most pertinent portions of von Thunen's and Weber's theories and of city location in the following three sections of this chapter. The fourth section treats market-area theory in the same way.

AGRICULTURAL LOCATION: J. H. VON THUNEN

The theoretical work of von Thunen, one of the earliest efforts systematically relating transport costs to specific locational patterns, was based upon some forty years of his experience in managing a large Nineteenth-Century German agricultural estate. He was primarily interested in finding what kind of crops and methods of cultivation were most profitable under certain marketing conditions.

Although his voluminous study was empirical in that it was based mainly upon a careful study of his own records and accounts beginning in 1810 and extending until his death in 1850, von Thunen expressed the theory for which he is famous in a very formalized way. The principal criticism of his published study is not the theory itself. His logic is virtually unassailable within the framework of its assumptions, and his empirical data were monumental. Rather, it has been his highly simplified assumptions that have been questioned by some.

In setting forth his theory, von Thunen assumed an "isolated state" made up of one central city located in the center of a large plain. The plain was of equal fertility, climate, and terrain throughout its extent and was used for agriculture. The city received all its agricultural products from its surrounding plain or "hinterland" and was the only market available to the farmers on the plain. The farmers were conscious profits-maximizers and were perfectly free to engage in whatever type of agriculture they chose. But prices for agricultural products were set by the city market, that is, prices were not subject to farmer control. Finally, there was one form of transportation, equally available to all farmers on the plain and moving from all points in a direct line to the city, with freight rates set on a straight ton-mileage basis regardless of the kind of product hauled. The problem to which von Thunen addressed himself, then, was what kind of agricultural production would occur in what parts of the plain.

By his assumptions, making most of the variables equal, von Thunen kept his variables and unknowns to a manageable number even for the precomputer era. Transportation costs, the key variable, could be computed from any point simply by weight times miles times whatever rate the analyst chose. Costs associated with the two unknowns—types of crops and methods of cultivation— also could be set at any chosen level. Actually, von Thunen's extensive records provided a basis for establishing transportation, crop, and method costs, and city prices.

The problem was attacked by a model or equation as follows: Profits equals Market Price minus Production Costs and Transport Costs. Market Price was given and was the same for any product grown by any method at any point in the plain. Production Costs also were given and were the same for any crop and method at any point. Transport Costs varied directly with distance from the city. Now it was only necessary for von Thunen to feed his numbers into the model to determine which crops and methods were most profitable at various distances from the market.

Note that all points at an equal distance from the city paid the same transportation costs for the same product. This means that whatever crop and method is most profitable at any given point is also most profitable at all other points the same distance from the market; and if all these equal-distance points are connected, a circle is formed around the city. Thus crops and methods are grouped into a series of concentric circular zones, with only one crop and method prevailing in any one zone.

The absolute outward boundary for any crop or method, of course, would be where profits (as shown by the model) equals zero. In case of overlaps, that is, where two or more crops or methods at the same points would yield profits greater than zero, the most profitable alternative naturally would be chosen. Outward and inward boundaries of the various concentric circular zones of differing production, therefore, were precisely determined by the model.

As one might guess, within the limits of early Nineteenth-Century transport technology and assuming a straight ton-mileage rate, von Thunen proved that perishable products and products heavy in relation to their value will be produced near the market, while items which are less perishable and are more valuable per unit of weight will be produced farther away.

Specifically, he found that items such as milk and vegetables would be produced in the first zone surrounding the city (remember, neither fast nor refrigerated transport was available). Zone Two would grow timber for lumber and fuel (high weight, low value). Zones Three, Four, and Five would grow grain with the intensity of cultivation decreasing as one moved from Zone Three to Four to Five. Zone Six, the outermost area of the plain, would produce livestock for slaughtering and cheese. Figure 21 diagrams this situation.

The decreasing intensity of cultivation with increasing distance from the market was explained by von Thunen's observation that net farm prices were gross city prices minus transport costs. Thus, the farther a given farm is from the city, the lower its net price for a given quantity of product. A given quantity of land near the city, yielding high net prices per unit of product, can be made much more profitable with intensive applications of labor and capital which increase its per-acre output. But land farther away with lower net prices cannot profit proportionately as much by such intensive use of labor and capital and, consequently, its owners cannot afford to spend as much for these services as can landowners nearer the market. Thus extensive agriculture, relying more on land and less on labor and capital for its inputs, becomes more profitable as distance from the market increases.

A theory of rent or of land value based upon site location also was developed by von Thunen's analysis. As net farm prices per unit of output decrease with increased distance from the market, land nearer the market yields its owners greater returns per acre than more distant land. Thus, as economic values are

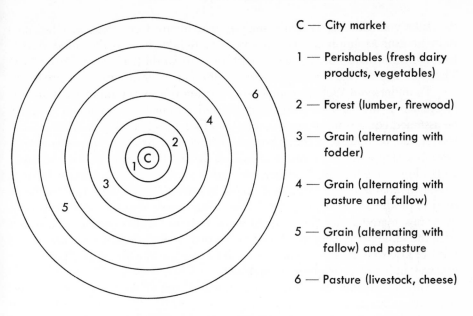

C — City market

1 — Perishables (fresh dairy products, vegetables)

2 — Forest (lumber, firewood)

3 — Grain (alternating with fodder)

4 — Grain (alternating with pasture and fallow)

5 — Grain (alternating with fallow) and pasture

6 — Pasture (livestock, cheese)

Figure 21: Thunen's Zones.

based on economic yields, those sites nearest the market are most valuable and can command the highest sale or rental prices. Given specific price and cost data such as used by von Thunen, the relative values of different sites can be easily calculated.

Although von Thunen's analysis was very formalized and his assumptions necessarily highly restrictive, his work must be classed as a notable contribution to location theory and its relationship to transportation as well as to some other areas of economic theory. It was a pioneering effort which still is much discussed more than a century later for its conclusions as well as for its methodology. By modifying von Thunen's assumptions to fit today's very different transport technology and real world facts, today's students or analysts can obtain valuable insights into the theory of location not only as it concerns agriculture, but also in the fields of industrial location, distribution, and regional development.

INDUSTRIAL LOCATION: ALFRED WEBER

Alfred Weber, also a German economist, published his "Theory of the Location of Industries" in 1909. Although much of his work was original, some of it drew upon work done by Wilhelm Launhardt, a German mathematician, during the 1880's. Also, in a different context, it built upon von Thunen. Weber was concerned with manufacturing and processing operations.

Like von Thunen, Weber's analysis was highly formalized and hemmed in by limiting assumptions. His assumptions, though, were perhaps less restrictive and somewhat more in accord with the real world than were those of von Thunen. Also, Weber dealt with several different types of locational situations.

To understand Weber's conclusions relating transportation to location, one must clearly understand his assumptions and terminology. Like von Thunen, he assumed equal transport accessibility and straight ton-mileage rates regardless of the product carried. Also, his market was fixed in a specific place. Several assumptions were made regarding the work force, its skills, and labor costs. For our purposes, however, we can assume that the necessary labor is equally available at the same costs in all locations. Some of the raw materials used in production are "ubiquities" (available everywhere at the same price); other raw materials are "localized" (found only in specific fixed locations, but with the same price wherever found). Further, some raw materials are "pure" (do not lose weight in processing or manufacture), while others are "gross" (do lose weight in processing or manufacture).

Although Weber used much more involved terminology and assumptions, these are sufficient for the portions of his work to be discussed here. Basically we will consider two cases, one dealing with a single market and a single raw material, and the other dealing with single market and two raw materials. Several different locational situations and their solutions will be presented under each of these cases, however. Once the solutions to these relatively simple situations are understood, readers will be well on their way toward understanding Weber's concept of the role of transport in location and better fitted to apply his type of analysis in solving much more complex problems.

Three different situations may be imagined under Weber's "one market, one raw material" case. *First,* the raw material may be ubiquitous (equally available everywhere). If so, production obviously will occur at the market. It would not be rational to pay freight charges on a raw material which can be obtained without transportation cost at the consuming point of the finished product. *Second,* the raw material may be a pure (nonweight-losing) material localized at a point away from the market. Then production can take place either at the raw-material source or at the market. Or if we ignore extra handling costs, production could occur at any point on a direct line between the raw-material source and the market. *Finally,* the raw material may be gross (weight-losing) and localized away from the market. In this situation, production occurs at the source of the raw material as it is less expensive to ship a smaller tonnage of finished product than a greater tonnage of raw materials.

In the "one market, two raw materials" case, four different situations may exist. *One,* both raw materials may be ubiquities, which will lead to production at the market. *Two,* both raw materials may be pure but localized at different points away from the market. If so, each will be transported directly to the market for production as this minimizes ton-mileage by eliminating the extra movement which would be necessitated in bringing one raw material to the source of the other. The only exception would be a situation where one raw material must pass directly through the source of the other on its way to the market. *Three,* both raw materials may be pure, with one being ubiquitous and the other localized away from the market. Again, production will occur at the market as this involves only the payment of transport costs in moving the localized material to the consumption point which is the minimum necessary payment. *Four,* both raw materials may be gross and localized at different sources away from the market.

This last situation is the most complex and most comparable to the majority of real-world, industrial-location problems. Both raw materials lose weight, thus costs cannot be minimized by market-point production unless the market is located on a straight line directly between the two materials and unless the combination of weight-losing characteristics of the two materials or the pro-portionate representation of each in the finished product, or both, fall within certain percentage limits. Readers can demonstrate this for their own satisfaction by a few simple calculations using varying weight-loss and combination patterns. Likewise, ton-mileage can be kept to a minimum by moving one raw material to the other's source for production only if the two material sources are on a straight line with the market and only if the weight-losing and combination characteristics of the materials fall into limited percentage relationships (again, this can be demonstrated by a few calculations using varying assumptions).

It is in the less restricted situation of two localized gross materials located away from the market and not located such that a straight line will connect them and the market that the Weberian solution becomes less obvious but of more general practical importance. In picturing this situation, imagine three straight lines one of which connects the two raw-materials sources, with the other two connecting each source with the market; that is, a triangle with the market at one corner and a raw-materials source at each of the other two corners. Obviously production will not occur at any point outside the triangle as this would mean more transportation than is necessary. It must occur, then, on one of the legs of the triangle (including the corners) or at some point within the area of the triangle. But where?

Simple calculations using any assumed weights and weight-losing char-acteristics on a scale model of such a locational triangle or even simple inspec-tion should show that ton-mileage cannot be minimized by producing at any corner or on any leg of the figure. Production, therefore, occurs at some point within the triangle, that point being the one where the two raw materials can be brought together and the finished product shipped from there to the market with the least ton-mileage expenditure. A Weberian locational triangle is pictured in Figure 22.

Just where within a triangle a specific least-cost point will fall will be determined by a combination of the relative quantities of each of the materials used and by their relative weight-losing characteristics. If equal quantities of the two materials are required, but one loses more of its weight when combined

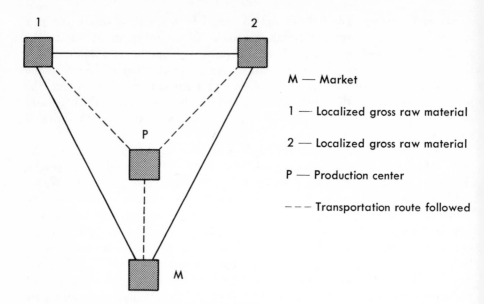

Figure 22: Weber's Locational Triangle.

into the finished product, for example, the production point will be located nearer the greater weight loser. Or, if absolute weight losses are equal but one material is used in greater quantities than the other, the two will be brought together for production nearer the material used in greatest quantity.

To borrow physical science terminology, the center of gravity, where total ton-mileage of raw materials and finished product is minimized, is a balance or equilibrium resulting from the relative weight pulls. Greater weights pull harder than lesser weights, and larger weight losses pull harder than smaller weight losses. The computations involved in finding the exact center of gravity can become involved for the ordinary arithmetic-and-pencil mathematician, but the principle is easy to understand and the calculations can easily be done by a slightly higher level of mathematics or a computer. Some students have demonstrated the relative strengths of the various pulls by simple physical model consisting of a triangular frame over the corners of which run interconnecting lengths of string with weights attached.

Weber's contribution, like von Thunen's, called attention to the influence of transportation costs upon the spacial location of specific kinds of economic activity. Also, it further explained why some types of production are said to be market oriented (ubiquitous or low weight-losing materials), some raw materials oriented (high weight-losing materials), and why a great many are most profitably located at a specific determinable point in an area intermediate between raw-materials sources and the market. (The so-called foot-loose industry, that is, one which can locate equally well in any spot or in a wide variety of locations, in terms of the discussion presented in this chapter must be a misnomer or at least so rare as to be a great curiosity.) Not the least of Weber's contributions was the presentation of a methodology which can be expanded far beyond his basic use of it in dealing with a variety of details and more complicated situations.

Like von Thunen, Weber has been criticized for his unrealistic assumptions. His variables were few. (His work preceded the electronic computer by a half-century.) Most producers use several raw materials and sell in several markets. Blanket, tapering, Fourth Section, and similar deviations from distance structures were not brought into his basic analysis, nor were transit privileges, existing carrier route patterns, and many other transport and nontransport factors which often affect or are thought to affect location in the real world.

Such criticisms at best are invalid as they are based on a misconception of the nature and purpose of theory. A theory is a model, perhaps based to some extent upon an abstraction from the real world (and sometimes not), making use of a limited number of variables chosen by the theorist according to his judgment of their relevance for his particular explanatory or predictive purpose. As such, Weber's theory was well constructed and answered his questions. It seems doubtful if his questions could have been better answered, and it is certain that his analysis would have been much more lengthy and complicated had he used a computer to grind out solutions from a great mass of complicated empirical real-world data. Those interested simply in understanding fundamental location principles as related to transport can be thankful for Weber's unrealistic assumptions.

Those interested in the practice of location, however, can and do modify and build upon the Weberian framework in many ways. Especially since the advent of high-speed computers, it is possible to expand his simple models to include almost any number of markets, numerous raw materials (in any desired quantities, ubiquitous, or localized at many sources, pure or gross in any degree) as well as various freight-rate structures and levels, and even such so-called nontransport factors as differing labor costs, tax rates, land values, and raw-materials and finished-goods prices in different areas. As stated earlier, simple location theory has blossomed into complex practice. But the fundamentals remain unchanged.

THE LOCATION OF CITIES

Except in those resort and retirement areas where cities grow up because of such attractions as unusual scenery, climate, or similar manifestations of nature, or legalized gambling or quickie divorces, cities have been founded, have grown up and exist primarily to serve the needs of commerce. This is their principal if not only reason for being.

Incidentally, of course, cities may make it possible for one to enjoy cultural advantages not readily brought into the hinterlands. (This could be considered a necessary fringe benefit or an offset to other conditions which encourages persons to live in cities.) Another incidental result of cities is that they concentrate many people in small areas thus perhaps making it easier to house, feed, clothe, amuse, police, and otherwise cater to the needs and demands of large populations.

Cities serve commerce by bringing together in one place the necessary quantity and kind of labor and facilities needed to perform large-scale manufacturing, storage, and distribution functions including concentration and dispersion of goods, break-bulk operations and transshipments, and their associated financing and numerous other business services. Secondarily, they provide large markets in concentrated areas for almost every kind of product. Thus, as most cities exist to serve commerce (which depends upon transportation) and also are large consumers of the output of commerce, it is reasonable to expect that there is a relationship between transport and the location of cities.

Actually, if one looks carefully at a detailed map of the world or any large section of it, showing major transportation routes as well as population concentrations, a striking fact is discernible. Almost all great cities, and even most of the not-so-great, are located either where transportation routes intersect or where goods change from one mode of transport to another. The principal exceptions are the resort cities mentioned and those communities based upon the exploitation of some fixed natural resource.

This situation is hardly coincidental. Since long before the dawn of written history, men met and exchanged products where trails or trade routes crossed or where navigable waters ended and land routes began.

It was only natural as time passed that some persons would take up permanent residence at the most important of these trading places to make their living by providing food, housing, and other necessities for the traders and by aiding in the performance of the labor involved in transferring goods from one mode of carriage or from one person to another. It was natural, also, that some of these permanent residents would see profitable opportunities in supplying storage space for traders and eventually go into the merchandising business and even into manufacturing and financing operations. The success of these residents attracted others to do likewise or to serve the needs of the now growing community. Thus the crossroads, the harbor, the fall line, or the end of the rail line developed into a trading post and eventually into a great redistribution, merchandising, manufacturing, financial, cultural, and consuming center.

It is unnecessary to go further into this aspect of history which is amply documented in our own country's development as well as elsewhere. It is clear that transportation factors have been and are major determinants in city location and development. Chambers of Commerce and other civic groups are well aware of this and leave no stones unturned in their quest for more favorable freight rates and more and better carrier services and transport facilities.

Not all transport-induced city growth has come from the existence of natural or even man-made transport routes, however. Transit privileges and rates and basing point and Fourth Section rate structures, discussed in Chap-

ter 13, have given advantages in manufacturing and distribution to cities otherwise without significant natural advantages. Some large communities have
grown up and still are very dependent upon such artificial rate benefits.

Other cities once favored by natural or artificial transport advantages have
become diversified with size and age and have managed to remain important
or could remain important even with the loss of the advantages which led to
their founding and earlier growth. As a city develops a broader economic base
and devotes relatively more of its efforts to producing goods and services for its
own inhabitants, it naturally develops more resistance to particular transportation shocks. No large city, however, is self-sufficient enough to survive for any
lengthy period of time without adequate transport facilities and rates.

In summary, then, city location and growth is related to transport in more
than one way. As servers of the commerce of wider areas, they are initially
located at points where the most and best services can be supplied, and they
grow and prosper as the commerce served grows and prospers. As their size
and importance increases, their employment opportunities attract additional
people. Additional industry is attracted because people are available as employees and consumers and because of the convenience of the available services
as well as the existing transport routes. This development, in turn, leads to
pressures for the development of even better transport services and often for the
creation of new routes or the extension or deviation of existing routes in other
areas to serve the city. Transportation and the city feed upon each other for
their mutual benefit.

TRANSPORT COSTS AND NATURAL MARKETING AREAS: FETTER, LOSCH, ET AL.

The "fixed production points and variable markets" question (as contrasted
with the "fixed market and variable production points" approach illustrated by
von Thunen and Weber) is the second major topic of traditional location
theory. As several aspects of this problem have already been commented upon
in this and the two preceding chapters, discussion will be brief and mainly confined to theoretical features. Frank Fetter, an American economist, and the
German economist August Losch, among others, have made notable contributions to this theory.

Unless otherwise indicated, the discussion assumes rational and informed
sellers and buyers and a natural market area as a space in which a seller has a
laid-down cost or price advantage over his competitors if both transportation
costs and all other costs of production and distribution are considered. (A seller,
of course, as the term is used here, may also be engaged in industrial, agricultural, or extractive operations rather than in distribution alone. This makes no
difference in the cases which we will consider.) There are many reasons why a
seller might find it desirable or profitable to sell in areas in which he does not

have such an advantage and even to sell in some markets at less than his total laid-down costs. Such reasons are beyond the scope of our discussion, however. To illustrate transportation-cost effects, we can limit our consideration to transport costs and their changes by assuming that other factors remain constant.

For simplicity, we can imagine that our marketing operations occur in a von Thunen-type plain where transport is equally accessible on a direct line between any given selling center and all of its potential buyers, and freight rates are on a straight ton-mileage basis for the particular product concerned. In addition, assume that all buyers in the plain have an equal demand (willingness and ability to pay) for the product, but as prices increase, less will be bought until at some level of prices, no sales at all will be made. The basic principles illustrated by this device can be applied in real-world problems involving a variety of freight-rate structures and levels as well as varying other production and distribution costs.

One Seller

First, assume one seller located in the center of our plain. What will determine the extent and shape of his marketing area? Obviously the extent of his operations, that is, the distance from his base at which he will be able to sell, will be determined or limited by his given other costs plus his transport costs which vary directly with distance. At some point, an equal distance in all directions from the selling point, high prices will cause sales to cease, thus defining the marketing area. As all sales stop at an equal distance from the selling point, clearly the shape of the marketing area, or its boundaries, are a perfect circle centered on the selling point (see Figure 23 (a)).

Two Sellers

Second, assume the same conditions, except that two sellers of the same product with equal other (nontransport) costs are now located on our plain. What will determine the sizes and shapes of their respective natural marketing areas? Each seller will have an advantage at all buying points closer to his than to his competitor's base, thus no buying points except those on an imaginary line intersecting the plain at an equal distance from each seller can have the same laid-down costs or prices. It is fairly obvious, therefore, that the boundary between the two natural marketing areas would be a straight line midway between the sellers which intersects at right angles another straight line drawn directly connecting the sellers (Figure 23 (b)). Each seller would dominate in the territory on his own side of the boundary, and the other seller would be excluded.

Third, assume these exact conditions, except that freight rates from Seller X to all points are increased across the board by some specified percentage or amount, while rates from Seller Y remain unchanged. What happens to the sizes and the boundary between the two marketing areas? Clearly, as Seller X's costs to all points now have increased, his natural marketing area will be

(**a**) One seller, straight
mileage rates

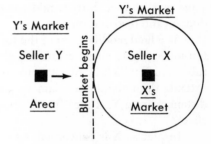

(**b**) Two sellers, equal straight
mileage rates and "other" costs

(**c**) Two sellers, straight mileage
rates higher from X than from
Y, equal "other" costs (broken
line at equi-distance points
sellers)

(**d**) Two sellers, straight mileage
rates from X, straight mileage
from Y modified by blanket
beginning at equi-distance points,
"other" costs equal

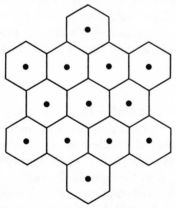

(**e**) Many sellers (center
points), equal straight
mileage rates and "other"
costs

Figure 23: Natural Market Areas Under Various Transport
Rates.

reduced as Seller Y's area increases. The equal-cost point on the direct line between the two will be pushed closer to Seller X. But the market area dividing boundary will no longer take the form of a straight line. Instead, as insertion of hypothetical cost figures for the two sellers on a scale diagram easily show, the boundary line will bend backwards around Seller X in a hyperbolic curve (not a segment of a perfect circle) whose ends will not come together even if extended to the ends of our plain (Figure 23 (c)). The specific location of this dividing line will be determined by the amount of X's rate handicap.

Incidentally, note that the same kind of market-area-boundary shift would occur if instead of an increase in X's freight rates: (1) Y's rates are decreased; (2) rates from both selling points are decreased, but with greater decreases from Y; or (3) rates from both are increased, but with greater increases from X. Also, with transportation costs remaining identical for the two sellers, the same market-area shifts would come from relative changes in their other production and distribution costs.

As a final modification of the two-seller case, let us assume that the straight ton-mileage rate structure from Seller Y's base is modified by adding a blanket rate from Y which begins at some point on a direct line between Y and X and extends throughout the plain to points at this particular distance or greater distances from Y. Rates from X remain unchanged. What is the market-area effect?

Insofar as X is concerned, he will be placed in a similar condition to that of the single seller first described above. That is, his market will be limited to those buyers whom he can reach at a laid-down price lower than his competitor's. Then, as Y's costs do not change once the blanket zone is reached, but X's transportation costs increase on a straight ton-mileage basis, all points on the outermost limits of X's area will be at an equal distance from his base. Seller X's natural market area, therefore, will take the form of a perfect circle with its boundary running through the points where his outbound transport costs equal the level of Y's blanket rate. Seller Y will dominate the remainder of the plain; and if his blanket rate is low enough in comparison to X's mileage rate, he can dominate the area beyond X even though he may ship directly through X to reach some of his buyers (Figure 23 (d)).

Many Sellers

As our final case, we will consider a multi-seller situation. Imagine again our von Thunen plain with its peculiar transport and demand conditions. Instead of one or two sellers, assume that a considerable number of sellers of the same product, all with equal nontransport costs (and with straight ton-mileage transport costs), are located at various points throughout the plain. What determines the size and shape of the natural marketing area of each seller?

Market-area size, of course, is fixed by laid-down, delivered costs; and as we have assumed other costs equal, this reduces to transport costs. The area in which each seller will have an advantage, therefore, is determined by his geographical location in relationship to immediately surrounding competing sellers and his distance from them. With given specific transport-cost figures, this can easily be computed.

At first glance, though, it may not be obvious what shape the marketing areas (or the imaginary lines bounding them) of the various sellers will take. Marketing areas cannot take the form of circles as this either would mean that some parts of the plain would not fit into any seller's area or that natural marketing areas would overlap. Both these solutions are excluded by our assumptions and definitions.

To completely cover the plain without overlap, then, requires that all market areas must take the shape of some regular polygonal figure. Squares or regular triangles with a marketing point located at the center of each would satisfy our requirements that the entire plain be covered without overlap, but distances (and thus transport costs and prices) would be considerably higher from centers to buyers located in or near "corners" than to other buyers. As one of our basic assumptions is that higher prices result in fewer sales, it follows that sales in the plain as a whole as well as of individual sellers can be increased by reducing the price differentials applicable to these "corner" buyers if this can be done without offsetting transport-cost and price increases elsewhere. What shape of figure can do this?

It can be demonstrated rigorously by mathematics, or perhaps to a non-mathematician's satisfaction by doodling on a sheet of regular graph paper, that a group of regular hexagons—figures with six equal sides and angles—not only completely covers the plain without overlap, but best meets the requirements of reducing transport costs and consequent price differentials to outlying buyers. That is, this form of market area both enables each seller to maximize his profits over a given geographic area by selling more at lower transport costs, and allows a larger volume of total sales by all sellers in the plain as a whole. Under our assumed conditions, then, the entire plain would be divided into a honeycomb-like arrangement of natural marketing areas, each with a seller at its center. As a physical analogy, we might imagine a group of tangent circles being pressed together from without (by rational desires for maximum profits) until they assume the form of a group of hexagons. Figure 23 (e) shows such a situation.

The above few simple examples illustrate the principal workings of transportation-cost effects in market-area determination. Insofar as the real-world conditions surrounding competitive marketing differ substantially from the rigid assumptions of our models, as they do, real-world marketers necessarily must analyze their problems by appropriate modifications of the models. But we repeat, a good grasp of fundamentals greatly aids one in dealing with problems involving numerous complex details.

Gravitational or Interaction Models

The models discussed above are most often used in nonlocal or long-distance marketing-area analysis, but they might easily be modified to fit strictly local situations. In addition to these, various models have been especially designed for analyzing or predicting local trade patterns, or for measuring or predicting the interactions between areas. These latter models also might be adapted to long-distance situations.

In general, this latter group of models postulates that size of an area or city exerts a demand "pull" and that distance brings a supply "drag." Trade or other interaction between two communities varies positively according to their sizes and negatively according to distance. In the simple size-distance formulation of such models, there is an implicit assumption that other factors are equal. On the demand side, this means similar cultural, social, and physical environments, and income levels; for supply, it means that distance, usually under a straight-distance formula, is the only pertinent cost difference to be overcome. For completeness and because overcoming distance involves transport costs, some of these so-called gravitational or gravity models will be briefly described.

One of the most celebrated of these models in retailing circles is W. J. Reilly's so-called "Law of Retail Gravitation." One version of this "law" purports to show, strictly and directly based upon population and distance, how the volume of retail-trade patronage of an intermediate city, Z, is divided between two other cities, X and Y. Reilly's conclusion, expressed in proportional terms for X and Y, is derived from the following equation:

Z's trade with X divided by Z's trade with Y *equals* (the population of X *divided by* the population by Y) *times* (the distance between Z and Y *divided by* the distance between Z and X) *squared*.

A derivation from Reilly's Law, sometimes called the "breaking point" model, is designed to determine the boundary between the retail marketing areas of a small city, X, and a competing large city, Y. The equation for this may be expressed as:

The distance of X's boundary from X *equals* the distance between X and Y *divided by* [one plus the square root of (the population of Y *divided by* the population of X)].

Another "interaction" theory, which has been developed (among other uses) to compare the relative transport significance of different areas, gives its results in the form of a so-called "transportation index." This index or measure of the interaction between two communities, X and Y, may be computed as follows:

Transportation Index *equals* (the population of X *times* the population of Y) *divided by* the distance between X and Y.

Various other similar models, some of which include sociological and other noneconomic factors, have been developed for specific purposes. If viewed simply as first-approximation explanatory devices, these models may be useful. Despite the sometimes extravagant claims of some of their builders and users who view these formulae as realistic substitutes for expensive field research, however, their success in actual prediction has not been spectacular.

It seems reasonably certain that distance, or transportation costs related to distance, exerts a considerable drag on long-distance flows, and that this retarding effect tends to become relatively greater in comparison to pull factors as distance increases. In local marketing, however, the distance factor may be such an insignificant portion of other cost and demand elements that it becomes submerged and of little effect.

In addition, no one has conclusively demonstrated that population size alone generally determines the attraction between different communities in a Newtonian sense. Gravity models which exclude by assumption numerous physical, social, cultural, and income factors, and institutional ties, are likely to exclude thereby the major forces of gravitational attraction. When these models are constructed to include some of these additional pertinent variables, they may be more useful real-world working tools. If this is not done, their usefulness in actual decision-making is limited.

In closing, it should be noted that a considerable amount of work has been done and is continuing in the building and testing of gravity models intended for practical prediction.

SUMMARY

Transportation costs and location theory are inseparable. Traditional location analysis assumes either fixed markets and undetermined producing centers or fixed producing centers and undetermined marketing areas. Both industrial (or agricultural) location theory and market-area theory assume given transportation facilities, however. Analysis involving the determination of transport routes and facilities themselves under varying production and marketing assumptions and the relationships between such routes and city location is not so well developed. Both the "fixed (or given) transport" and the "variable (or undetermined) transport" type of analysis, however, lead directly into the analysis of the types and levels of regional or spacial economic activity. The interrelationships of these various threads of theory and assumption are pictured in Figure 24.

ADDITIONAL READINGS

1. Daggett, Stuart, **Principles of Inland Transportation**, 4th ed. New York: Harper and Brothers, 1955.
   Chapter 22. "Theories of Location," pp. 426–455.
2. Greenhut, Melvin L., **Plant Location in Theory and Practice.** Chapel Hill, No. Car.: University of North Carolina Press, 1956.

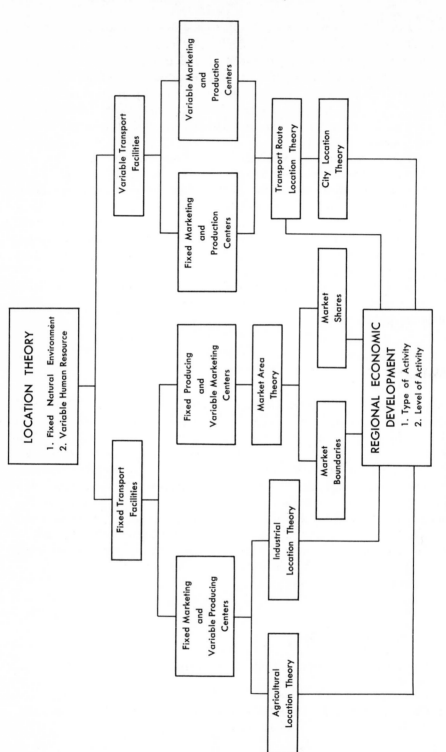

Figure 24: Transportation and Location Theory.

Part One. "Review of Location Theory," pp. 3–100.
Part Four. "A General Theory of Plant Location," pp. 251–291.

3. Greenhut, Melvin L., "Size of Markets Versus Transport Costs in Industrial Location Surveys and Theory," **The Journal of Industrial Economics**, March 1960, pp. 172–184.

4. Heskett, J. L., Robert M. Ivie, and Nicholas A. Glaskowsky, Jr., **Business Logistics.** New York: Ronald Press Company, 1964.
Chapter 6. "Theory of Location and Area Development," pp. 120–151.

5. Hoover, Edgar M., **The Location of Economic Activity.** New York: McGraw-Hill Book Co., Inc. 1948.
Part One. "Locational Preferences and Patterns," pp. 15–141.

6. Isard, Walter, **Location and Space-Economy.** Cambridge, Mass. The M.I.T. Press, 1956.
Chapter 2. "Some General Theories of Location and Space-Economy," pp. 24–54.
Chapter 7. "Market and Supply Area Analysis and Competitive Locational Equilibrium," pp. 143–171.
Chapter 8. "Agglomeration Analysis and Agricultural Location Theory," pp. 172–199.

7. Losch, August, **The Economics of Location.** New Haven, Conn.: Yale University Press, 1954.
Chapter 6. "Site and Reasons for Town Settlement," pp. 68–84.
Part Two. "Economic Regions," pp. 101–220.

8. Mossman, Frank H., and Newton Morton, **Logistics of Distribution Systems.** Boston: Allyn & Bacon, Inc., 1965.
Chapter Three, Appendix. "Summary of Plant Location Theory," pp. 105–112.

9. Nicholls, J. A. F., "Transportation Development and Loschian Market Areas: An Historical Perspective," **Land Economics**, February 1970, pp. 22–31.

10. Richards, Hoy C., "Transportation Costs and Plant Location: A Review of Principal Theories," **Transportation Journal**, Winter 1962, pp. 19–24.

11. Troxel, Emery, **Economics of Transport.** New York: Rinehart & Company, Inc., 1955.
Chapter 13. "Transport Costs and Production Locations," pp. 301–324.

Part Five

Regulation of
Domestic Transportation

Neither carriers nor their rates operate and develop in a laissez-faire environment. Public regulation is extremely important. Only by understanding the regulatory framework within which transportation operates can one fully appreciate the complexities of transportation.

Transportation has always been regulated to some degree. In Part Three we noted some of the common-law obligations of carriers which have existed for centuries. Comprehensive regulation of transportation by statute is built upon that common-law base and is of relatively recent origin. This part of the text will trace the growth and development of this comprehensive regulatory structure and will give an introduction to the regulatory institutions responsible for that structure.

Since the regulation of transportation is an evolutionary thing, continuing to develop as conditions change and as society's ideas change, the first three chapters of this part have a chronological organization. The basic problems of transportation regulation, however, are emphasized by organizing one chapter around the regulation of transportation monopoly and two chapters around the regulation of transportation competition. The final chapter on regulatory institutions is descriptive.

16

The Regulation of
Transportation Monopoly

The economic market for transportation has many facets. In some places and at some times it is extremely monopolistic. At other places and in other times it is quite competitive. Sometimes transportation operates simultaneously both as a monopolistic venture and as a competitive enterprise. An example of this would be competition at terminal points served by several carriers or modes, with monopoly at in-between locations served by only one carrier or mode.

Historically, transportation has tended toward monopoly. Where only one carrier serves a given location, monopolistic abuse is possible. This abuse may take many forms; and over time, society has become alert to many of these abusive actions. When a monopolistic firm charges extremely high rates or practices discrimination, it is quite likely that some sort of social control or regulation will be exercised. This chapter will discuss the steps taken by society to regulate transportation monopolistic markets which have developed in our economy.

THE EVOLUTIONARY NATURE OF TRANSPORT REGULATION

Society provides the ground rules under which business enterprise operates. These ground rules are never static. They may seem to be changing but slightly in any one period; but if viewed over long expanses of time, changes are apparent. The structure of regulation grows as a slow process, not by revolution. In transportation regulation, the change may be considered "evolutionary." Our present regulatory structure evolved or developed out of the past and was modified as conditions changed over time.

The evolutionary nature of transportation regulation is most easily appreciated by tracing the building up of our regulatory structure. This structure reflects economic conditions and characteristics of the particular time period under question to a very marked degree. As conditions change because of technological advances or other new circumstances, regulations likewise change.

Change in transportation regulation was not always immediate or concurrent with changed conditions. A considerable lapse of time sometimes occurred between the two. Society needs strong evidence that a social structure is outdated and no longer provides satisfactory solutions before change takes place. This is known to social scientists as "social lag."

Regulation During the Promotional Era

Early in the development of our nation, the necessity for adequate transportation was so great that society did little in the way of transportation regulation. Most transportation efforts were directed toward developing and promoting an adequate system. While excesses did take place, as they inevitably do during the promotion of any undertaking, society was largely concerned with conquering the continent, having transportation facilities, and providing the basis for economic growth. With such prodigious tasks, there was little concern for the niceties of protection against the abuses of monopoly.

There probably was little need to regulate during the pre-Civil War period. This was a period of struggle for supremacy between various modes of transportation. Infant railroads struggled against canals, teamsters and wagoners against river boats, and they all competed against each other. Intermodal competition was the order of the day. There was little need to supplement the natural forces of the market place with regulatory laws and procedures.

This is not to say that regulation did not exist during the promotional period prior to the Civil War. The older areas were faced with problems of social control while promotion was continuing farther west. Thus, the promotional era was not always the same span of time for all regions. Indeed, as Chapter 2 points out, railroads continued to expand in mileage well into the Twentieth Century even though the second half of the Nineteenth Century is generally thought of as the time of greatest railroad competition.

Additionally, the promotional period prior to the Civil War may be thought of as a period of experimentation with various types of social control. In those regions where problems arose, various types of solutions were attempted. These early attempts at transportation regulation took three forms: common law and judicial control, regulation by charter, and investigatory commissions.

Common Law and Judicial Control

Common law, which continues to exist today, is a body of rules and obligations based mainly on custom. Our common-law foundation came from England and serves as the basis for our whole legal system. It is largely based on precedent. If one wishes to consult the common law, he refers to past court decisions and jurists' opinions rather than a statute book or legislative enactment.

Common-law regulation of transportation has often been called "regulation by lawsuit." Basically, rights and obligations under common law apply to individuals. Thus, the right of the customer to reasonable service, at reasonable rates, and without unreasonable discrimination was the basis of some early lawsuits. The obligation of the common calling of certain industries was the basis of some rule-making also. This obligation of common calling served as the legal basis for later statute law regulations of transportation.

Common law failed as an adequate method of regulating monopolistic abuses for several reasons. First, it was subject to judicial interpretation, and rarely did two jurists find the same precedent for or make the same interpretation of a similar situation. Secondly, the common law is inherently unsuited for regulation of a modern-day business monopoly. Under medieval conditions of individual redress for past wrongs, it was adequate. Under complex modern-day capitalistic business arrangements where a business enterprise deals with another business enterprise, it is inadequate. Specifically, common law lacks the ability to prevent abuses (it considers only abuses committed), to promote beneficial activity (it punishes but cannot promote), to have continuous regulation (each matter must be dealt with individually as the need arises), to control in the social interest (the common law is based on individual rights and cannot protect the rights of society as a whole), to expediently address itself to business abuses (lawsuits are very time-consuming and expensive), and to deal with the specialized nature of commerce cases (judges often are not trained in the intricacies of business relationships and have to consider business cases melded with personal injury, murder, fraud, etc.). Modern-day circumstances called for social controls which were preventive, promotional, continuous, socially oriented, expedient, and specialized. The common law did not provide these.

Charter Regulation

Another device used during the promotional period was regulation by charter. As previously noted, popularity of turnpikes led to the development of joint stock companies. These early corporation-type organizations were also used to promote some canals and most early railroads. They were created as artificial persons by a special act of the legislature of the state. Obviously as the state granted this special privilege, the opportunity to specify rules and regulations arose. Early charters at times specified maximum rates which could be charged, sometimes maximum earnings on capital, and sometimes details of operations. Additionally, the right of eminent domain (right to take private property for public use) was often granted. Here again an opportunity to control was evident. Some early grants specified routes, and controlled construction and extensions.

Often charters were without a term or had almost unlimited life (such as ninety-nine years). Uniformity was difficult since it was necessary to secure a charter in each state where the transportation firm operated and each charter was a special act of the legislature. Sometimes charters provided for tax exemptions or tax limitations as well as other valuable privileges such as the right to operate banks. As such, they were much sought after, and scandal arose over the methods by which some transportation firms secured their charters.

Charter regulation did not prove effective as a device of social control. Maximum rate control proved ineffective since conditions and costs changed. Maximum earnings control, usually in terms of returns on stock, could easily be subverted by issuing more stock. With a long or unlimited life on these charters, it was almost impossible to specify operating details or to foresee the need for future routes or extensions. Finally, after the Supreme Court ruled that a charter was a contract which could not be later changed by a subsequent legislature in the famous *Dartmouth College Case* (4 Wheaton 518, 1819), the difficulty of regulation by charter was apparent. In spite of these difficulties, attempts were undertaken to regulate the various modes of transportation by charter.

Investigatory Commissions

Another type of regulation experiment was that of the commission with power to investigate only. In the latter part of the 1830's and the 1840's, such agencies were created, principally in New England, to investigate railroads. Typically, these commissions had no control over rates, but were given power to investigate and report upon the operation of the railroads and, often, to appraise the value of land when eminent-domain proceedings were involved. Occasionally they were given power to specify accounting systems and require statistical information. This type of regulation failed because it was powerless to protect the public, but the concept of a body of experts (called a "commission") meeting in continuous session was established.

State Regulation and the Emergence of Monopoly Controls

It was not until after the Civil War that positive control over monopoly abuses was instituted. Indeed, the immediate post-Civil War period was one in which much of the foundation of the present system of social control over all types of business was established. These controls were developed to deal principally with transportation and more specifically with railroad transportation.

Economic Conditions

Economic circumstances were such that the whole problem of social control came to a head during this period. Many social and economic changes had been caused by the war. Families had been broken up, the South was in devastation, many were restless, and the great surge of settlers into the open spaces of the West was about to begin. President Lincoln had signed the Homestead Act in 1863 opening up vast areas of the public domain to the stouthearted. Land grants had promoted railways in advance of settlement, and railroads were interested in settling people upon their land. Technological advances in agriculture had led to great increases in production, particularly in grain crops. Immigration only added to the large numbers of people opening new lands in the West. The result was an increasing agricultural surplus with plummeting agricultural prices.

New technology born of the urgency of the war was leading to rapid industrialization. Monetary problems from the war-born inflation added to the unrest. Business ethics were at a low ebb, and great fortunes were being made from the industrial revolution. Some investors felt they were being short-changed in the resultant excesses of stock promotion and corporate manipulation. This was particularly true of railroad investors, many of whom were farmers or small businessmen who had invested personally or had urged cities, counties, and state governments to invest in order to construct transportation facilities.

The situation was particularly acute in the Midwest, the states of the old Northwest Territory. This area, one of the principal agricultural producers of the nation, found itself in dire competition with new areas of agricultural production to the West. Many agrarians of the region had invested in railroad promotions only to find that once the transportation system was operating, the rates were high, the service poor, discrimination rampant, and return on investment nil. These farmers were in a mood for action. Something akin to an agrarian revolution was in the making.

The agriculturalist of Illinois, Iowa, Wisconsin, and Minnesota (the major states involved) did not understand the facts of supply and demand. Agricultural prices continued to decrease as excess production was generated on new Western lands and as war-promoted demand ceased. Railroad and elevator rates went up as these businesses were able to exploit their new monopolistic positions. Farmers banded together in semi-fraternal organizations called "Granges" (more properly known as Patrons of Husbandry) and struck out at their apparent enemies—the railroads and elevators. The tool of the agrarian revolt was the ballot box, and agricultural representatives to state legislatures were repeatedly elected in the latter 1860's and early 1870's.

The Granger Acts

The reaction was the famous Granger Legislation or, as it is sometimes called, "The Granger Movement." In the 1870's, legislatures of Granger states passed stringent laws broadly regulating railroads and grain elevators. Typically, these laws had four parts: (1) establishment of maximum rates, (2) prohibition of local discrimination, (3) attempts to force competition by forbidding railroad mergers, and (4) prohibition of free passes to public officials.

In some states, the legislature itself specified maximum rates. But the matter of rate construction is complicated and requires trained personnel plus a great deal of information about costs and movement. Since the composition of the legislatures changed with each election and most legislators lacked the necessary knowledge to attack such a complicated task, this method of rate-making was a failure. In some states, however, railroad commissions were established. Persons appointed to these bodies either had knowledge of the task or were able to learn its intricacies and stay in office over a span of time.

Local discrimination was regulated by "pro-rate" clauses which were much more stringent than the later long-haul-short-haul clauses. Basically, these regulations provided that a railroad could not charge the same or more for movement of a commodity over a short distance than it charged for movement of a similar commodity over a longer distance anywhere on its line. Although this was the basis of the long-and-short-haul regulation of today, it was found necessary to modify pro-rate clauses so that branch lines had separate rate schedules and the hauls involved were over the same route and in the same direction.

Railroad mergers were common. One of the means of securing a transportation monopoly was by consolidations and mergers. In prohibiting mergers, these early laws were merely reflecting the prevailing opinion of the day that competition was the most effective regulator. The impropriety of granting free passes to public officials, particularly judges, legislators, and others in authority, is obvious. Such actions were considered a form of bribery.

The reaction of the railroads was vigorous. A widespread educational campaign akin to modern-day public-relation programs was undertaken. This campaign pointed out the injustices of the laws as well as their impracticability and their hasty passage. Railroads claimed they could not do business under such regulation. This claim was further backed up by the problems arising out of the Panic of 1873. The economy of the expanding nation experienced another of the brief, periodic, severe and sudden depressions which characterized the Nineteenth Century. Some railroads did go bankrupt, railroad construction did decrease, and many railroads suspended dividend and interest payments. Railroads claimed that many of their problems during this crisis were due to regulation. Faced with this "proof," plus the obviously unsound nature of some of the regulations, most states repealed or modified their Granger laws in the middle and late 1870's. Illinois with its railroad commission remained the exception.

The Legal Basis of Regulation

Even though the Granger laws were short-lived, they were of great significance in the evolution of transportation regulation. This was the first time our society had regulated a whole industry and had set up a structure of ground rules outside of the courts and the common law. The idea of regulation had been firmly implanted. Second, the Granger laws served as the basis for later regulation of transportation. The similarity between the Granger Acts and the Federal government's Act to Regulate Commerce of 1887 is not a coincidence. Finally, the Granger laws provided a legal precedent for subsequent regulation of many other types of business.

In addition to the educational campaign and the results of the Panic of 1873, railroads challenged the legal right of states to regulate or control business. Court cases concerning constitutionality were instituted. While the question was being argued through the Courts, many of the Granger laws were repealed or modified. By 1877, however, the U.S. Supreme Court ruled that the states had indeed acted legally when they had regulated railroads and elevators.

Some six separate major cases were involved, but the most important (and only case which was not a railroad-case) decision was in *Munn v. Illinois* (94 U.S. 113, 1877). All the other so-called Granger cases rested upon the opinion in this case, as does much of the legal foundation of regulation of other kinds of business.

Railroads and grain elevators claimed that they were private businesses and that setting their charges and rates by public enactment violated the Fourteenth Amendment of the U.S. Constitution which provides that a state cannot deprive one of his property without due process of law. The Fourteenth Amendment was new (1868) and somewhat untested. These cases, therefore, were also important as tests of this part of the Constitution.

The Court drew upon an opinion of Lord Chief Justice Hale in the 1600's which noted that common carriers had always been regulated in early societies. It noted that some businesses become "affected with the public interest" and are no longer private, but may be regulated in the public interest without ncessarily violating the Constitution. Specifically, the Court stated in part, that:

> When . . . one devotes his property to a use in which the public has an interest, he . . . grants to the public an interest in that use, and must submit to be controlled by the public for the common good, to the extent of the interest he has thus created.

Struggle for Federal Control

The Granger movement had not gone unheeded in Washington. Monopolistic abuses of railroads were nationwide. In 1872, President Grant sent a recommendation to Congress that an investigation of transportation be undertaken. The Senate set up a special committee, the Windom Committee, to investigate the possibility of cheaper transportation between the interior and the seaboard. This committee's report in 1874 began a long struggle which finally culminated in Federal control in 1887.

The Windom Report, the first of many investigations and reports by Congressional committees on transportation monopolies, concluded that the defects and abuses of the railroads were insufficient facilities, unfair discrimination, and extortionate charges. The report recognized that competition was the best regulator, but noted that private competition "invariably ends in combination." The solution recommended by the Windom Report was public competition by way of state or Federally owned and operated railroads.

Partially as a result of the Windom Report, the House of Representatives passed a bill to regulate railroads in 1874. The Senate took no action and the bill died. Again in 1878 the House passed a regulatory bill. The Senate likewise acted and passed its own version of public regulation of railroads. The two approaches differed greatly, however, and the Senate and House became deadlocked over the matter. Then a special committee, the Cullom Committee, was appointed to make a thorough investigation of railroad monopoly abuses.

The Cullom Committee filed its report in 1886. It placed great emphasis upon the abuses of monopoly power by railroads. Many discriminatory practices of the railroads were investigated and highlighted. Discrimination between persons, places, and commodities was common. Stated rates were only a place for bargaining to begin for the large shipper, whereas the small shipper without bargaining power was forced to pay the quoted price. Rebates were common. The investigation disclosed that not only did the railroad monopoly exploit small shippers and noncompetitive points, but industrial monopolists in turn exploited railroads by demanding rebates. For instance, in 1885 the Marietta and Cincinnati Road (later part of the Baltimore and Ohio) charged the Standard Oil Company a rate of 10 cents per barrel for moving crude oil from Macksburg, Ohio, to Marietta while at the same time charging smaller shippers 35 cents. Then the railroad additionally rebated to Standard 25 cents a barrel for each barrel shipped by the small producers. The Cullom Report did much to hasten Federal regulation of railroads.

The final action leading to Federal regulation was the decision in the *Wabash Case* (118 U.S. 557), also in 1886. In the earlier Munn Case, the U.S. Supreme Court had upheld state regulation of matters that obviously were interstate in nature, apparently on the grounds that Congress had taken no regulatory action. In the Wabash Case, the Court decreed that the Federal government alone had power to regulate interstate commerce.

The Wabash Case grew out of the Granger period and the Illinois regulatory law. The Wabash, St. Louis and Pacific Railway charged $39 for the carriage of goods from Peoria, Illinois (near the center of the state) to New York, while it charged $65 for the carriage of a like quantity from Gilman, Illinois (some 87 miles to the east) to New York. The reason for charging more for the shorter than the long haul was the existence of competition at Peoria. This was a clear violation of the Illinois Act, but the Supreme Court took careful note of the fact that the U.S. Constitution provided that Congress had the power to regulate interstate commerce. It held, thus, that a state could only regulate commerce within its borders (intrastate commerce). Since the destination here was New York, Illinois could not apply its law. Unless and until the Federal government acted to regulate commerce, interstate movements could not be regulated. The Wabash Case, coupled with the Cullom Report, forced a solution. A compromise was worked out between the House version of regulation and the Senate views. The result was the Act to Regulate Commerce of 1887. It should be noted that many provisions of this law were supported by railroads which often had been forced by economic circumstances and pressures to grant preferences which decreased their revenues. Now they could fall back on the law as a protection against requests for such preferences.

The Act to Regulate Commerce

The Act to Regulate Commerce, now known as the Interstate Commerce Act, became effective on April 5, 1887. This statute has been amended many times since. It presently contains separate parts covering all types of public transportation except air.

Basically the Act was aimed at monopoly abuses. Control of discrimination was stressed in almost every section. (See Chapter 7 for a discussion of various types of discrimination and the meaning of reasonableness.) Each of six principal sections of the Act dealt with a different phase or abuse of monopoly power.

Section One required that all rates must be "just and reasonable" and that all "unjust and unreasonable rates" are unlawful. This provision applied both to rates for freight and for passengers. It was left up to the Commission to determine what was "just and reasonable." Basically, the idea of justness and reasonableness was merely a formalization of the common-law rule on charges of common carriers.

Section Two dealt with personal discrimination. This section orders the carriers to give equal treatment to shippers where transportation service is performed under similar circumstances and conditions. Specifically, the law stated that it was unlawful for any carriers:

> . . . directly or indirectly, by special rate, rebate, drawback, or other device, to charge, demand, collect, or receive from any person . . . greater or less compensation . . . than it receives from any other person . . . for doing . . . a like and contemporaneous service in transportation of a like kind of traffic under similar circumstances and conditions . . .

Exceptions were later allowed for freight and passengers of Federal, state, and municipal governments, for charitable purposes, and for rail employees entitled to free passes.

The third section was a general discrimination clause. It contained a blanket prohibition of all "undue preference or prejudice" to any person, locality, or traffic either in rates or services. This clause appears to be broad enough to cover both personal discrimination (Section 2) and long-and-short-haul discrimination (Section 4), but these types of discrimination were so prevalent that Congress decided to give them special treatment. It is well to note that all discrimination was not prohibited by Section 3, but only "undue" preference and prejudice. Again, the determination of "undue" was left up to the Commission.

Section Four contains the famous long-and-short-haul clause. This provided that it was unlawful for any common carrier:

> . . . to charge or receive any greater compensation . . . for the transportation of passengers or . . . property, under substantially similar circumstances and conditions, for a shorter than for a longer distance over the same line, in the same direction, the shorter being included within the longer distance.

The Commission was authorized to make exceptions in special cases upon application by carriers. Further, it should be noted that the inclusion of the phrase "over the same line, in the same direction, the shorter being included in the longer" made this section considerably less stringent than corresponding earlier clauses of the Granger Laws. Nevertheless, Congress felt strongly enough about this type of monopoly abuse to give it special treatment even though Section 3 probably would have been applicable.

The fifth section prohibited pooling agreements of various types, reflecting the popular opinion that enforced competition would protect the public. This provision is also directly related to the earlier prohibition of any consolidations or mergers by the Granger Laws.

Section Six required that all rates and fares should be published and strictly observed. Because of the popular practice of suddenly changing rates after giving advance notice to but a few favored shippers (often called "midnight tariffs"), the act also ordered that specific public notice be posted of any rate change.

Finally, the Act set up the Interstate Commerce Commission, originally consisting of five members appointed by the President with the consent of the Senate, and enumerated the powers and duties of this new type of governmental agency. The Commission was patterned to a considerable degree on the investigatory-type commission of the promotional era and the strong Granger commissions.

The Commission was charged with administration of the act. It could hear complaints, take testimony, subpoena documents and generally inquire into the business of common carriers. Upon adequate finding, it could issue cease and desist orders, and determine awards of damages suffered because of violations. Penalties were to be imposed by courts of law, however. The Commission had to go to court if carriers did not obey its orders. Finally, the Commission was to report to Congress annually and recommend legislation which it considered necessary.

Weaknesses and Early Regulatory Experience

It must be remembered that regulation by an administrative commission was a precedent-breaking step. The Granger experience had been relatively short and limited. Earlier commissions in New England and the East had generally little power to enforce. All previous regulations had been on the basis of state jurisdiction. Now a whole industry across the entire nation was to be regulated by a quasi-judicial body of five men. Obviously, such a procedure was a step away from the laissez-faire philosophy of capitalism; and, just as obviously, the Commission had to proceed slowly and lay the foundation for regulation as it progressed.

As the Commission began its work, certain weaknesses in the Act became evident. Basically, these were four in number: (1) testimony, (2) enforcing orders and review, (3) rate power, and (4) discrimination interpretations. All of these involved court decisions and arose within the first ten years of the Act's life. Perhaps the courts were jealous of this new body which had all the trappings of a court without all the formalities. Certainly the carriers were testing the Act. Likewise, economic conditions played a role in that the carriers did not feel entirely free to exercise monopolistic abuses during the depressed period up to the mid-1890's. With increased prosperity after 1895, violations became more numerous.

The matter of testimony came to a head early. In 1890 a shipper refused to divulge whether he had received a rebate on the grounds that he might incriminate himself. When the Supreme Court held in favor of the shipper in 1892, Congress began a long series of remedial laws by passing the Compulsory Testimony Act in 1893. This act gave witnesses immunity with respect to their testimony and closed one of the basic weaknesses of the law.

The matter of enforcing orders was not so simple. Orders of the Commission had to be enforced by a court order. Carriers automatically appealed Commission orders to the court of jurisdiction (the lowest Federal court). While the court considered the case, the carrier did not have to obey the Commission's orders. Much time elapsed as the carrier pursued its appeal through successive levels of courts. Commission cases had no preference in crowded court dockets. Some cases dragged on as long as nine years after the Commission had issued cease and desist orders.

In a series of cases in 1896 and 1897, the Commission was shorn of all power to prescribe rates. The original act was quite clear that the Commission could declare a rate to be unreasonable and unjust, but it did not specifically allow the Commission to prescribe what was a just and reasonable rate. Up to 1896, the Commission assumed this power, and in 68 out of 135 formal cases it had set maximum just and reasonable rates once it had found existing rates to be unjust and unreasonable. But in the *Social Circle Case* (162 U.S. 184, 1896), the Supreme Court noted that no explicit power to set rates seemed to exist; and in the *Maximum Freight Rate Case* (167 U.S. 497, 1897), the Court held that the Commission was without power to set rates. These decisions were of great importance as they left the Commission with little power. Once a finding of reasonableness was made and orders issued to cease and desist, the carriers would appeal to a court. After a long lapse of time (while the carrier continued to charge the unjust rate), the court might uphold the Commission. But since the Commission could not specify the new rate, a very small change in the charge would necessitate the Commission's going through the whole long and costly process again.

Another weakness was in the court interpretation of Section 4. The phrase "under substantially similar circumstances and conditions" came under question. In the *Alabama Midlands Case* (168 U.S. 144, 1897), the Supreme Court held that it was up to the carrier to determine whether or not conditions were similar and that competition at an end point and not at intermediate points created dissimilarity of conditions. This decision effectively destroyed the prohibition against local discrimination since it could nearly always be shown that differences in competition existed. Railroads rarely charged less for the longer hauls unless they were forced to do so by competition.

The effect of these court decisions and statutory weaknesses was to convert the Interstate Commerce Commission into little more than a fact-finding and reporting agency.

Strengthening Monopoly Regulation

Each of the weaknesses which had hampered the commission was dealt with between 1897 and 1910 in a series of separate statutes designed to strengthen the regulation over monopoly.

Congressional action to enforce testimony has already been noted. The matter of court review was partially dealt with when Congress passed the Expediting Act of 1903. This act allowed commission cases to be given priority over other cases upon certification by the Attorney General that the matter was of public importance. This shortened the long lapse of time between commission deliberation and judicial review.

The Elkins Act, also in 1903, is often called the "Anti-Rebate Act." Pressure on carriers to give rebates where competition existed was extreme. The railroads themselves recognized that the effect of rebates was cumulative and that shippers with competitive means of transportation were able to play one carrier off against another. Therefore, they sponsored the Elkins Act which (1) made the receiving of a rebate unlawful, (2) made departure from the published rate a misdemeanor and adherence to published tariffs enforceable by court injunction, (3) eliminated the imprisonment penalty for rebates while increasing the fine to $20,000, and (4) made the railroad corporation liable for violations as well as the personnel of the carrier.

After the turn of the century, another reform movement somewhat similar to the Granger movement swept the country. Under President Theodore Roosevelt, attention was called to trusts and various other monopolistic abuses. Certainly the railroads, operating under extremely weak controls, were still guilty of abuses. Roosevelt called for new monopoly regulation over railroads in his messages of 1904, 1905, and 1906. The so-called "Progressive movement" was underway, and many new ground rules for the control of business were being born.

One result was the Hepburn Act of 1906 which has commonly been called the "rehabilitation of the I.C.C." This act, sponsored by Senator Hepburn of Iowa, erased two of the previous weaknesses of the original Act to Regulate Commerce and strengthened monopoly control in several areas. Commission orders became binding on carriers and had to be observed while appeal was being pursued in the courts. A fine was provided ($5,000 a day) for failure to comply with commission orders after not less than thirty days from the date of issue, and the order had to be observed for up to two years. The Commission was given power to seek enforcement in court.

The second weakness erased was the matter of rate power. The Commission was given authority to prescribe *maximum* rates once it had determined that a rate was unjust and unreasonable. The carrier could charge less than the maximum, but at least the Commission had the power to establish how high a just and reasonable rate would be. It should be emphasized that the Commission could exercise this power only after it had investigated and formally declared a rate to be unjust and unreasonable.

Regulatory powers were stengthened in several other ways. Jurisdiction of the Commission was extended to include related and accessorial services such as express companies, sleeping-car companies, terminal services and storage services. Privately owned rail cars came under Commission jurisdiction. Oil pipelines were controlled. The domination of petroleum companies in the ownership of pipelines seems to have been the predominant reason for extending regulation into this area. This extension is extremely significant as it was the first step in the application of transportation regulation to non-rail carriage.

Additionally, the Commission's control over accounts and reports was strengthened. The original act had given the Commission no power to enforce uniform accounting rules or to inspect the books of carriers or require reports. Many carriers had simply ignored this part of the law. Without adequate and correct information, effective regulation was impossible. The Commission, therefore, was given power to inspect accounts, prescribe uniform accounting systems, and require reports.

Further, discrimination control was strengthened. Regulations were authorized concerning the issuance of passes, the "Commodities Clause" was established, and the Commission was given power to establish through routes and joint rates among participating carriers.

Under the Commodities Clause, Congress forced railroads to divest themselves of their noncarrier interests. Prior to this time, railroads had been producing many goods in competition with their shippers. This was particularly true of coal. By charging shippers high rates and charging themselves low or no rates, railroads were gaining a competitive advantage. Henceforth, rail carriers were prohibited from transporting articles in commerce which they produced or had an interest in with the exception of lumber. They could produce commodities for their own use, but they could not transport them in commerce.

Additional strengthening took place with the passage of the Mann-Elkins Act (1910). This statute removed the phrase "under substantially similar circumstances and conditions" in Section Four, thereby restoring the long-and-short-haul clause which interpretation by the Supreme Court had virtually killed in 1896–97. Control over local discrimination was thereby re-established.

The Mann-Elkins Act strengthened further Commission control by allowing the I.C.C. to suspend a proposed rate change for 120 days while it investigated the reasonableness of the proposal. An additional 120 days were allowable if necessary to complete the investigation. Previously, a carrier might prepare a rate change and begin charging the new rate after 30 days. The Commission might later find the new rate unreasonable and award reparations to the shipper. But this procedure was unsatisfactory as the shipper had usually already passed on the rate change to his customer. Moreover, the act shifted the burden of proof of reasonableness to the carrier, whereas formerly the shipper had to contest and show that the changed rate was unreasonable.

Additionally, the Commission was given power to control railroad classification procedures, its jurisdiction was extended to telegraph, telephone and cable companies (this control was later shifted to the Federal Communications Commission), the President was given the power to set up a special commission to investigate railroad securities, and shippers were given the right to designate the route over which they preferred their shipments to move.

Certainly, in the period from 1903 to 1910, transportation regulation was strengthened and many previous weaknesses overcome. By the time of World War I, transportation regulation of monopoly seemed to be almost complete.

The Refinement of Monopoly Regulation

The basic structure of the control of monopoly in transportation seemed complete by 1910. However, the economy is never static and neither is transportation. Conditions change and under new circumstances, transportation regulation also needs changing. The outstanding refinements of monopoly regulation came out of the World-War-I years.

The basic philosophy of monopoly regulation had been to force railroads to compete vigorously with each other and, where competition was impossible, to substitute controls of the Interstate Commerce Commission. All carriers were forced to bid for the shipper's favor. Where there was but one carrier to a given destination, Section Four was rigorously applied. The provisions of Section Three (undue preference and prejudice) attempted to insure that all areas, shippers, and types of traffic were treated on a parity. In case these controls failed, the Commission had power to specify maximum rates where unreasonableness existed. From all points of view, regulation should have been most successful in protecting the public.

Unfortunately, regulation was not effective. A fundamental weakness was that it failed to provide for an adequate and healthy transportation system. This lack of positive control was pointed up by wartime transportation experiences where railroads were unable to provide adequate and coordinated service for the nation's needs.

Railroad credit was poor due to overcapitalization. No financial controls had existed and many carriers were overburdened with excessive capitalization from an earlier period. Also, no control over the extension of rail lines existed; and in line with the idea of greater competition for the existing transportation demand, unwise and unneeded expansion of railroad plant had occurred. Little control over service standards existed since it was assumed that competition would naturally bring better service. Yet with rates and earnings restricted, the reaction of the carriers was to decrease the service level. Car shortages appeared, delays were common, and cooperation and coordination were very poor.

All of these weaknesses became apparent under the strain of wartime transportation conditions. Although the United States did not enter the European conflict immediately, tremendous amounts of war materiel were produced in this country. Traffic increased greatly, placing a severe burden upon railroad plant which had not kept up due to restrictive earnings and excessive competition. In 1917, the Federal government, finding the railroads completely unable to offer the efficient service needed to pursue the war, seized the railroads. The carriers were so accustomed to competition, poor service, and individual action that they would not or could not offer a cooperative, efficient and adequate transportation service in this time of need.

During the period of Federal control, cooperation was forced upon the carriers. In an attempt to stem the inflationary pressures of a wartime situation, the government did not allow rate increases. Instead, railroad companies were guaranteed a profit while the government poured vast sums into updating and operating the railroad plant. Additionally, labor costs increased as the Federal authorities granted railroad labor an eight-hour day in the Adamson Act. The result was a deficit, met out of the Federal treasury, of more than $1.5 billion during the Federal governments operation of the carriers. It should be noted, though, that this deficit was a deliberate governmental policy decision.

The Transportation Act of 1920 and the Recognition of Adequacy

After hostilities had ceased and against this background of inadequate service, Congress contemplated returning the carriers to private ownership. Extended debate as to what should be done about the railroads ensued. Out of all this deliberation emerged a new philosophy sometimes characterized as "positive control."

It became apparent that controls based solely upon fostering competition and a commission charged with restrictive control where competition was impossible were not the answer. Instead, regulations aimed at increasing the financial health and adequacy of transportation became the key philosophy. In this sense, then, the Transportation Act of 1920 (the Esch-Cummins Act) marks the departure from reliance upon enforced competition and the substitution of increased emphasis on adequacy of transportation through positive controls.

The Act of 1920 had many provisions aimed at positive controls. Basically, however, the changes in attitude are seen in the five areas of rates regulation, service regulation, regulations on combinations, security regulation, and labor regulation. Each will be considered in turn.

The new attitude of positive control was emphasized in the changes in rate control. Congress included the famous Rule of Rate Making in Section 15a which mirrored these new goals. Basically, this section instructed the Commission, in exercising its power to prescribe just and reasonable rates, to see to it that the railroads *as a whole or in groups* should earn a "fair return on a fair value." This phrase was taken from the pivotal 1898 case of *Smyth v. Ames* (169 U.S. 466) wherein the United States Supreme Court had prescribed a general level of compensation for regulated enterprises. The

Commission was authorized to determine what would be considered a fair return and was to ascertain aggregate fair value from time to time. But Congress set 5½ per cent as a fair return for the first two years of the application of the Rule of Rate Making and allowed the Commission to add another one half of one per cent for improvement and betterments. Thus the fair return became generally accepted at 6 per cent.

It should be emphasized that the Rule of Rate Making did not constitute a guarantee of a certain return. It was more of an aim or a goal upon which rate control was to be based. Since the return was to be based on the value of all assets in the industry or in a geographic segment of it, it was possible for some carriers to earn much less than the "fair rate" while others were earning more. The important thing was that Congress recognized the carriers' needs for adequate revenues and set a goal with this in mind.

The problem of some carriers earning more than 6 per cent and some less was covered in the "Recapture Clause." Since carriers competed with each other, it was necessary that they all charge a like rate. But all were not equally efficient or similarly capitalized. Congress, therefore, provided that one half of all earnings in excess of 6 per cent would be paid to the Interstate Commerce Commission and placed in a fund from which loans (at 6 per cent interest) could be made to carriers earning less than the ideal. These loans were to assist weak carriers in updating their plant and increasing efficiency. The one half of the excess not paid into the fund was to remain with the carrier as a type of incentive to be efficient. This carrier half, however, was to be placed in a reserve fund to be used by the carrier to offset possible low earnings in some years. When the reserve fund made up of the carrier's one half exceeded 5 per cent of the valuation of the particular carrier, it could be used for any purpose the carrier wished.

Besides the Rule of Rate Making and the Recapture Clause, Congress gave the Commission power to prescribe minimum rates. Maximum rate power had been exercised since the Hepburn Act; but prior to 1920, the Commission had little control over how deeply rates might be cut in a competing situation. This new minimum rate power was very much in accord with the new philosophy of positive control in that Congress recognized the need for carriers to obtain adequate revenues.

The minimum-rate control power was coupled with new jurisdiction over the division of joint rates. The Commission already had the power to prescribe the exact division of rates between carriers when they could not agree among themselves on the share of revenue each should receive from a joint haul. However, Congress directed the Commission to consider the *revenue needs* of the carriers in future division. Again, the recognition of financial adequacy is apparent.

Finally, the Commission was granted broader powers over the level of intrastate rates in order to remove discrimination against interstate rates. Several examples of state regulatory authorities forcing unusually low rates for the movement of goods within individual states had come before the courts. In effect, this type of discrimination caused the carrier to force interstate traffic to subsidize intrastate traffic by charging unduly low rates on intrastate movements. The Supreme Court had dealt with this problem in the *Shreveport Case* (234 U.S. 342) in 1914. Congress now specifically allowed the Commission to end intrastate discrimination against interstate rates by turning this court decision into statute law. Again Congress was concerned with adequate revenues.

Car shortages and poor service in time of seasonal movement had characterized rail operations under the philosophy of enforced competition. Powers over car service had been granted in the Esch Car Service Act of 1917, but the wartime seizure had intervened. Now Congress redefined service regulation powers and forced carriers to file their own regulations concerning service with the Commission. The Commission could change these rules so that better coordination and service could be offered to the shipping public. In case of emergencies, the Commission was granted strong powers over the use of equipment.

Likewise, the Commission was given the power to order the joint use of terminal facilities, with adequate compensation to owners. Previous to this, carriers with superior terminal facilities refused to allow carriers with terminals located less advantageously to use their facilities. Upon finding that the public was better served and that joint use would not impair the owner's ability to handle its own business, the Commission could now order joint use.

Finally, the Commission was given powers over carrier extensions and abandonments. This belated control was designed to prevent uneconomic expansion of trackage. The carrier now had to convince the Commission of public need by securing a certificate of public convenience and necessity before extending its tracks. Abandonment control, which has been of more importance recently, was aimed at maintaining service on lines already established.

The new philosophy of positive control and the need for adequacy is again seen in the change of policy on carrier cooperation and combination. The Act of 1920 allowed pooling agreements when they could be shown to be in the public interest. The Act of 1887 had prohibited all types of pooling.

More important, however, was the new policy of allowing railroad consolidations and acquisitions of control. Regulations, almost from their beginnings, had forbidden carrier consolidation. During the Granger period, it was considered proper to force the carriers apart and make them compete. The Act of 1920, however, allowed consolidations and recognized that the public might be better served by financially healthy, larger railroad systems than by more numerous competing, near-bankrupt carriers.

While this aspect of regulation will be further developed in Chapter 20, it is well to note here that Congress ordered the Commission to draw up a master plan for a limited number of railroad systems which as fully as possible would preserve competition, maintain existing routes of commerce, and provide equal earning power for the consolidated systems. Consolidation was to be voluntary. Although the Commission could approve those consolidations conforming to the master plan, it had no power to compel them.

Somewhat belatedly, Congress recognized that if the carriers were to serve the public adequately, they could not be allowed to issue securities indiscriminately. Much of the problem of inadequate earnings arose because of the gross overcapitalization of railroads in their earlier days. Pressure to pay interest and dividends often resulted in poor service and high rates. After 1920, railroads had to get approval of the I.C.C. before issuing new securities or changing their financial structure.

Finally Congress recognized that special treatment was necessary in the railroad labor field if the public was to be assured of consistent and adequate transportation. The problem of adequate labor legislation in the area of public service enterprises such as railroads has a long history. (More will be noted on this in Chapter 21 as well as in the next section of this chapter.) The Transportation Act of 1920 established the Railroad Labor Board, composed of nine members divided equally between carriers, labor unions, and the public. This Board was to hear disputes which could not be settled by other means and recommend a solution, although its decisions were not binding. No anti-strike provision was included. The significant aspect of the labor provision of the Transportation Act of 1920 is that it was a part of the pattern of recognition of the need for adequate service.

Results of the Act of 1920

The results of the Transportation Act of 1920 were disappointing. While railroad credit was improved, great difficulties were encountered in administering the Act. Carriers had been in a competitive struggle for so long that coordination and cooperation were quite alien to them. Likewise, resentment over increased regulation led to a series of court tests. By the time the Supreme Court had finished considering the provisions of the Act, economic conditions had changed and the Great Depression was upon the nation. In a subsequent period and under changed economic conditions, many of the provisions of the Transportation Act of 1920 were modified or discontinued. The important thing about this Act was not any specific provision, but the new philosophy of positive regulation and the recognition of the need for adequacy.

Labor and Bankruptcy Problems

The final phases of the regulation of transportation monopoly came in 1926 with the Railway Labor Act and in 1933 with amendments to the Bankruptcy Act. In these two pieces of social legislation, the Congress recognized the essential nature of rail transportation and the necessity for having a somewhat different set of values for an essential monopoly operating in a predominantly competitive economy.

The labor provisions of the Transportation Act of 1920 did not prevent a nationwide work stoppage on the railway system in 1922. It was obvious that the machinery of settlement of labor disputes without strike was inadequate, and it was also obvious that work stoppages in the essential railway industry were intolerable. While the Railway Labor Act of 1926 did not prohibit work stoppages, its philosophy was that of making every effort to settle industrial disputes by every possible means short of compulsory arbitration. Many of the devices pioneered in this Act were later adopted for labor disputes in general.

Disputes were to be settled, when possible, by conference between carriers and labor representatives. If this failed, a set of procedures involving the National Railroad Adjustment Board or the National Mediation Board were to be evoked. The composition and task of these Boards, the procedures to be followed, and the alternative outcomes will be discussed in more detail in Chapter 21.

Amendments to the Bankruptcy Act in 1933 were designed with the same idea in mind, although in a different problem area. It had long been established that railroads could not be permitted to fail in the usual sense of businesses failing and going out of operation. The public depended upon their services too much to allow this to happen. But when a railroad was reorganized, it was handled under the common-law provisions on bankruptcy. Under these proceedings, several courts could be involved and all creditors had to agree to the reorganization, while the receivers operating the railroad might issue new securities or borrow money.

The new procedures attempted to simplify railroad reorganization by allowing but one court of jurisdiction and giving the Interstate Commerce Commission the right to approve reorganization plans as well as to approve court-appointed trustees. Additionally, only two-thirds of any creditor class needed to agree to a proposed plan. Trustees were generally disinterested third parties rather than creditor representatives. With but one court to satisfy, time in receivership was shortened; and by requiring I.C.C. approval of reorganization plans, increased capitalization during bankruptcy became rare (whereas it had previously been common). The whole idea was to try to get the carrier back on its feet with a better, rather than a worse, financial position. Again, recognition of the need for financially stable and adequate transportation is evident.

THE ESSENCE OF MONOPOLY REGULATION

Although numerous other statutes were enacted during the period up to the 1930's, the major philosophy was that of regulating a monopoly. From the post-Civil War period, society had increasingly regulated and set up ground rules against transport monopoly. While the emphasis had changed from time to time and various problems had been attacked as they occurred, the public was primarily concerned with the fact that the railroads as the transportation monopoly of the era would abuse their economic power. By 1930, nearly all aspects of transportation monopoly had been controlled. The following summary illustrates this point and presents the essence of the regulation of transportation monopoly.

Elements of Transportation Monopoly Control

Rates and Discrimination Elements

1. All rates must be just and reasonable; all unjust and unreasonable rates are illegal. The I.C.C. has power to determine reasonableness and prescribe maximum and minimum rates.
2. All shippers must be treated equally if they have similar transportation circumstances and conditions (no personal discrimination).
3. All undue preference and prejudice to any person, locality, or type of traffic is illegal (broad discrimination prohibition).
4. A carrier may not charge more for a short haul than for a long haul where the short is included in the long haul over the same line and in the same direction. Exceptions allowed by petition.
5. Rates must be published and available to all. No deviation from the published rate is allowed under penalty of law. Rebates and passes illegal (except for certain exceptions relative to passes).
6. The general level of rates for carriers as a group are to be so established as to allow the carrier to earn a fair rate of return on a fair value. Excessive individual carrier earnings are to be recaptured in part and made available as loans to carriers earning less than the determined fair level.
7. Rates may be suspended for a limited time while they are being investigated.
8. A carrier may not carry its own products in competition with other shippers (except lumber).
9. Commodity classification procedures may be controlled by the I.C.C.
10. Intrastate rates may be raised so as not to discriminate against interstate commerce.

Service Elements

1. Car service rules must be formulated, filed, and approved by the I.C.C. The Commission may control car movement in emergencies.
2. The I.C.C. may establish through routes and joint rates.
3. The Commission may order joint use of terminals.
4. All abandonments and extensions must be approved by the I.C.C.
5. All pooling or combination must be approved by the I.C.C. (after both were illegal *per se* for some time).

6. Labor disputes must progress through a complicated series of time-consuming administrative procedures in an effort to effect settlement of industrial conflict without work stoppage.

Security and Financial Elements

1. All accounts must be uniform and open for inspection.
2. Periodic and detailed financial reports must be rendered.
3. The I.C.C. may divide revenues from joint rates with the needs of carriers as a standard.
4. All changes in capital structure and the issuance of securities must be approved by the Commission.
5. All reorganization and bankruptcy must be approved by the I.C.C. A special procedure is established to facilitate restoration of the carrier to sound financial health.
6. All consolidations and mergers must fit a master plan and have I.C.C. sanction (after being absolutely illegal for a period of time).

ADDITIONAL READINGS

1. Bigham, Truman C. and Merrill J. Roberts, **Transportation: Principles and Problems,** 2nd ed. New York: McGraw-Hill Book Co., Inc., 1952.
   Chapter 7. "Beginning and Constitutional Basis of Regulation," pp. 189–210.
   Chapter 8. "Establishment of Federal Regulation of Railroads," pp. 211–232.
   Chapter 9. "Positive Regulation of Railroads," pp. 233–256.
2. Daggett, Stuart, **Principles of Inland Transportation,** 4th ed. New York: Harper and Brothers, 1955.
   Chapter 30. "Railroad Regulation," pp. 639–654.
3. Fair, Marvin L. and Ernest W. Williams, Jr., **Economics of Transportation,** Rev. ed. New York: Harper and Brothers, 1959.
   Chapter 21. "Early Railroad Regulation," pp. 427–451.
   Chapter 22. "Railroad Regulation Since 1920," pp. 452–470.
4. Koontz, Harold and Richard W. Gable, **Public Control of Economic Enterprise.** New York: McGraw-Hill Book Co. Inc., 1956.
   Chapter 4. "Transport Regulation: Evolution of a Pattern," pp. 75–96.
5. Locklin, D. Philip, **Economics of Transportation,** 6th ed. Homewood, Ill.: Richard D. Irwin, Inc., 1966.
   Chapter 10. "Beginning of Railroad Regulation," pp. 197–207.
   Chapter 11. "Federal Legislation 1887–1920," pp. 208–225.
   Chapter 12. "The Transportation Act of 1920," pp. 226–239.
6. Norton, Hugh S., **Modern Transportation Economics.** Columbus, Ohio: Charles E. Merrill Books, Inc., 1963.
   Chapter X. "Development of Regulation: 1887–1920," pp. 179–192.
   Chapter XIII. "Regulation of Railroads," pp. 239–257.
7. Pegrum, Dudley F., **Transportation: Economics and Public Policy.** Rev. ed. Homewood, Ill.: Richard D. Irwin, Inc., 1968.
   Chapter 12. "The Foundations of Transport Regulation," pp. 287–311.

8. Roberts, Merrill J., "Maximum Freight Rate Regulation and Railroad Earning Control," **Land Economics** (May 1959), pp. 125–138.

9. Troxel, Emery, **Economics of Transport.** New York: Rinehart & Company, Inc., 1955.
   Chapter 15. "Public Utility Controls: The Beginnings for Transporters," pp. 349–369.
   Chapter 16. "More Public Controls," pp. 370–393.

10. Westmeyer, Russell E., **Economics of Transportation.** Englewood Cliffs, N.J.: Prentice-Hall, Inc., 1952.
    Chapter 5. "Regulation of Railroad Transportation to 1887," pp. 92–108.
    Chapter 6. "Federal Regulation of Railroad Transportation (I)," pp. 109–130.
    Chapter 7. "Federal Regulation of Railroad Transportation (II)," pp. 131–155.

17

Regulation of Transportation
Competition: Beginnings

As we noted at the beginning of the previous chapter, the economic market for transportation has many facets. Transportation can operate both as a monopolistic venture and a competitive enterprise at the same time. While the previous chapter was concerned with the regulation of transportation monopolistic abuses, the present chapter will be concerned with the regulation of transportation competition.

THE NATURE OF TRANSPORTATION COMPETITION

The term transportation competition can have three meanings. It can mean the competition between firms of the same mode, as when railroads compete with each other for shippers' rail traffic. This is called intramodal competition. A second meaning for the term transportation competition is when firms of different modes compete, such as the motor carriers competing with the rail carriers for a given type of traffic. This is generally referred to as intermodal competition. A third meaning is private versus for-hire competition. In this chapter, transportation competition will be discussed in all three senses, although primary stress will be placed on intermodal competition.

This is not to say that intramodal competition is unimportant or does not exist. Indeed, competition between the firms in each of the five modes of transportation not only exists but is of major importance, particularly to the shipper. Competition for the consumers' business is and has always been one of the finest natural market regulators available to society. As a general rule, society depends upon it in most economic undertakings. However, there are some areas, transportation among them, where natural competition does not always work to the benefit of society.

Private versus for-hire likewise is an important type of transportation competition and appears to be increasing. With highways, waterways, and airways furnished by the public, shippers often operate their own vehicles to carry their own freight. This type of competition and its consequences will be considered in more detail in Part Seven.

As noted in the previous chapter, where competition between carriers (intramodal) leads to a deterioration of service and an unstable financial situation, society's goals of an adequate transportation system go unfulfilled. Unnecessary and unwise duplication of plant may also be the result of uncontrolled intramodal competition. Where the resources used are small, the duplication and waste of competition may be tolerated and considered a price for a market which better serves society's desires. But where investment is very large and where service is inferior because none of the competitors are strong, duplication and waste of resources may be too high a price to pay for an end result which is not satisfactory.

These remarks concerning the dangers of intramodal competition seem especially appropriate to rail transportation. We have already seen that this was finally recognized by society with changes in the regulatory philosophy in 1920. Extension and abandonment of the rail network was controlled in order to avoid duplication and assure adequate service. While the regulation involved here came too late to be effective, it was recognition that the price of wasted resources and poor service was too great. Likewise, concern for adequate rail earnings in order to secure an adequate rail transportation system for the needs of defense and commerce was the very heart of the 1920 Act. Again, this is recognition of the need to limit intramodal competition. Finally, acceptance of the idea of railroad mergers where they fit a preconceived plan of consolidation was further proof of belief in the necessity to limit competition among railroads. That all these controls were either too late or were not well designed and hence worked imperfectly does not detract from the recognition of the necessity of limiting intramodal competition in rail transportation.

Intramodal competition may also lead to unreliable service. Not only is duplication socially wasteful in some cases, but the spur of competition may bite too deeply and lead to unreliable service. The search for the cheapest method may lead to a poorer service level. The shipping public demands and expects a high level of performance from a transportation operation. This service should be available at all times when it is needed. Transportation agencies handle the goods of others and must have the highest degree of trustworthiness. Many times a search for the cheapest way brought on by competition between firms is not conducive to reliability, availability, and trustworthiness. To achieve high service standards, society has found it necessary to mitigate intramodal competition from time to time.

Where public safety is involved, intramodal competition does not always lead to a desirable goal. The desire to achieve the cheapest service in a competitive struggle may lead to lower standards of maintenance, unusual hours of work for operators with resultant accident hazards, and unsafe operation of transportation vehicles which endanger either the users of the service or the innocent co-user of the facilities. These matters are of particular importance in air and motor transportation, and society has seen fit to regulate these agencies with the safety of the public at least partially in mind.

Intramodal competition, then, has both its desirable and undesirable aspects. Choice among the various firms providing a given type of transportation is highly desirable, but only to the extent that choice does not lead to unusual duplication and unusual waste of resources, inadequate service from the point of view of reliability, availability, and trustworthiness, and service which is unsafe for the public and the operator.

REGULATION OF INTRAMODAL RAIL COMPETITION

The fact that some of the provisions of the Transportation Act of 1920 were too late and were ill-conceived has already been mentioned. Merely changing the regulatory philosophy does not change management techniques nor methods of operation. Railroads continued to compete much as they had always done. While minimum rate control helped to limit this intramodal competition, many of the other provisions of the Act of 1920 did not work well.

While the 1920's are generally thought of as a time of national prosperity, all sectors of the economy did not share equally. The agricultural sector particularly was experiencing difficult readjustments from its wartime highs and was in great difficulty. Our first significant Federal intervention in the agricultural market came in the 1920's. Additionally, the whole economy experienced a series of fluctuations with some years (notably 1921–1922) witnessing depression conditions.

General economic conditions always affect transportation since it is a service industry. If industrial or agricultural production is low, little is shipped and transportation suffers. Periodic declines in activity, therefore, aggravated the painful problem of adjustment of the transportation plant downward from its overexpanded condition. We saw in Chapter 2 that the 1920's was the peak decade for rail mileage and the beginning of the railroad plant's downward readjustment.

Merely saying that railroads should earn a "fair return on a fair value" did not produce increased rail earnings. While some rail systems prospered, others had poor earnings. The recapture clause did not work well, and provisions for carrying over losses made in one year to apply to gains made in another year (common in our modern income-tax structure) were missing. Additionally, the legality of this provision of the Act of 1920 was strenuously challenged in the courts.

Further problems developed as the carriers were unable to agree upon plans for consolidation into a limited number of systems. The Interstate Commerce Commission made a special study of this matter in 1921; but when it was presented to the carriers, a period of endless bickering ensued. Indeed, the so-called "master plan" of merger and consolidation was long delayed and was not finally devised until 1931. Even after the plan was finalized, the mergers were to be voluntary. No power of compulsion by the I.C.C. existed. This matter will be further developed in Chapter 20.

Finally, in the 1925 Hoch-Smith Resolution, Congress became concerned with problems of the agricultural sector of the economy and ordered the I.C.C. to consider "the conditions which . . . at any time prevail in . . . industries . . ." (43 Stat., 801) when determining minimum rates. The Commission was directed to establish the "lowest possible lawful rates" for the products of agriculture, including livestock, in view of the depressed condition of agricultural markets. It is hard to see how railroads were to earn a "fair return" while at the same time laboring under the "lowest possible lawful rates" for a substantial share of their traffic!

With the start of the general depression late in the decade, the situation deteriorated rapidly. Rail systems suffered greatly, and bankruptcy and receiverships were accelerated. By 1933, it was obvious that some change was necessary in order to preserve the transportation system from complete collapse. The results of these conditions were the amendments to the Bankruptcy Act, noted in the preceding chapter, and the Emergency Transportation Act of 1933.

The Emergency Act created the Office of Federal Coordinator of Transportation (its head to be appointed by the President) and specified that it perform two functions. 1. The coordinator was to bring about economies in railroad operation by promoting cooperative efforts among carriers. In other words, the coordinator was to try to mitigate intramodal competition. Any plans approved by the coordinator along these lines were to be exempt from the antitrust laws. 2. The coordinator was to investigate new means of coordination and make recommendations to Congress and the Commission for action leading to these ends. Additionally, the Recapture Clause was repealed, the Rule of Rate Making was amended, and consolidation provisions were strengthened.

Unfortunately, the Act limited the action of the coordinator by providing that no employee could be deprived of employment or placed in a lower position than he held in May, 1933, because of any action authorized under the Act. This inability to reduce labor costs stymied most of the coordinator's potential plans. The Office expired in 1936 with few concrete results.

The importance of this attempt to help the carriers lies primarily in the recognition of the undesirable effects of intramodal competition. Although its attempts were fruitless, Congress had acted to limit intramodal competition with the explicit recognition that the economy needed a healthy rail transportation system rather than one racked with financial ills and locked in a competitive struggle which prevented adequate service.

THE CHANGING CHARACTER OF THE
TRANSPORTATION MARKET

Returning now to intermodal competition and to our historical or evolutionary approach to the subject of transportation regulation, the character of the transportation market in the 1930's must be noted. Although it may seem static at any given time, the transportation market is always changing and developing. The decade of the 1930's was perhaps the period of greatest change for transportation during the Twentieth Century. This period saw the emergence of keen intermodal competition in domestic transportation and the establishment of ready means for private versus for-hire competition.

As noted in Chapter 2, the domestic highway system dates its accelerated development to the Federal Aid Act of 1916 and the coming of the state gas (user) tax in 1919. The Highway Act of 1921 completed the institutional framework of matching Federal and state funds, that is, concentration of expenditures on a limited number of miles, allocation of matching funds to states by formula, and coordination of planning and development by approved state Highway Departments. A great deal of money was spent on improving the nation's highways all through the 1920's. With the depression of the 1930's, greatly accelerated spending on highways took place in an effort to combat unemployment. Public works, and especially highway improvement, were prime depression-fighting weapons and Congress was liberal in its appropriations. The matching concept was temporarily abandoned and a new system (the Federal Aid Secondary System) of farm-to-market roads was authorized.

All of this activity in the 1920's and particularly the 1930's provided better toll-free roads for the use of everyone. This naturally stimulated the development of motor carriage for hire. Highways were there to be used, capital requirements to enter the trucking business were small, legal barriers to entry were low, and the necessary level of skill or managerial ability was generally not high. Almost anyone could start a truck operation, and many did. With the extremely depressed conditions in the 1930's, this trend was greatly accelerated. Men without work and with little to lose could purchase vehicles with a very small (if any) equity from sales-hungry truck equipment firms. The number of small for-hire truck operators increased markedly. Intramodal competition was extreme and intermodal competition was prevalent as shippers, also seeking to reduce costs, were only too happy to shift their business to the numerous and battling truckers from the monopolistic and often haughty railroads. Intermodal competition was intense, and railroads found their traffic beginning to erode away.

Much the same story applies to water carriers. Following the renewal of interest in water transportation at the beginning of the Twentieth Century, increasing sums were spent by Congress on waterway improvement and development. Rivers and harbors appropriations have always had political importance. During a depressed period such as the 1930's, it became almost politically mandatory that each Congressman get a rivers and harbors appropriation for his district. The waterways also were available. No user charges were levied, not even gasoline taxes, to recover a portion of the cost of waterways improvement. Capital requirements were relatively low, and entry was easy. In areas served by waterways, therefore, barge competition also arose during the 1930's, although its impact was somewhat restricted due to geographical factors.

To a lesser degree, the depression period brought accelerated intermodal competition between air and rail transportation. One phase of depression spending concerned airports. Prior to 1933, airports were almost wholly financed by local governments, indeed the Air Commerce Act of 1926 had explicitly barred the Federal government from airport construction and operation. But during the depression, substantial sums were spent by the Civil Works Administration and Public Works Administration on airport improvements. It was not until after World War II, however, that a matching plan for airport construction was established.

In addition to relief expenditures on airports, the Federal government began a program of improving airways in the 1930's. This program has continued.

Finally, contracts to carry the mails stimulated the origination and growth of air carriers. The Air Mail Act of 1925 (Kelly Act) authorized the Post Office Department to award such contracts on the basis of competitive bids. There were no provisions that the bids must correspond to the cost of providing the service. Passenger fares, therefore, could be at a promotional level as long as a carrier retained its airmail contracts as a source of steady income. These contracts permitted intermodal competition between air and rail transportation on both passengers and freight.

One notable characteristic of the transportation market in the 1930's was the degree of social lag between regulation and transportation development. While intermodal competition was growing and a new era of transportation was developing, social regulation continued in its monopoly-oriented cast. Only belatedly did regulation begin to catch up to the times, and even then it failed to appreciate fully that the whole structure of the transportation market had changed. Thus, transportation regulation when it came merely extended the rail pattern of monopolistic regulation to the newer competitive modes. This extension will be our next topic.

REGULATION OF MOTOR CARRIERS

Regulation of motor carriage exists basically on two levels: state control over intrastate commerce and Federal control over interstate commerce.

The same is true of all domestic transportation; but due to the characteristics of the motor carrier industry (see Chapter 4), the state level of control is more important in highway transportation than in other modes.

State Regulatory Attempts

Generally, control of highway transportation takes two forms. One is regulation of the use of the highways and the safety controls imposed upon operators. The other is economic regulation over the method of operation, the level of service, and the charges made.

State governments have always exercised their police power to regulate in the general welfare. Almost from the time that automobiles were introduced, speed limits were imposed and minimum levels of skills required of the vehicle operator were established. In the case of larger vehicles, regulations designed to protect, the public as well as the operator extend to such matters as width and height limitations, length of vehicle or combinations of vehicle, brakes and lights, and the existence and operation of various other safety devices. The public has every right to impose these types of controls, and the transportation agency must expect to conform. However, commerce may be impeded or restricted when such controls are so lacking in uniformity as to unduly restrict vehicles operating in one state from moving into or through another state.

In regulating the use of highways, state governments again are fully within their rights. This may be thought of as primarily protecting their investment in highways. Typically, such regulations prescribe maximum weights of motor vehicles and the licensing of truck rigs. Weight limitations take many forms varying from simple overall gross-weight limitations to complicated axle-weight limitations—weight per inch of tire width, spacing of wheels beneath a load, and the like. Registration and licensing rules also take several forms. These various regulations are established according to the conditions and desires of each state. Unfortunately, the variety and lack of uniformity among the various states has often impeded the free flow of commerce across state lines. Sometimes competitive modes of transportation, particularly railroads, have viewed state weight limitations or safety controls as a means of limiting intermodal competition.

Economic regulation by states has been even more comprehensive in scope and has been partially designed to assure adequate service to the public. These controls predate Federal economic regulations. In fact, some of the early state experimentation with economic controls established a pattern which was used when Federal regulation was enacted in 1935.

Passenger service by bus was regulated shortly after World War I and existed in practically all states prior to 1930. This regulation apparently was designed to protect street and urban railroads. Regulation of truck lines was less widespread and had a varied history of experimentation at the state level. Basically, this state regulation imposed the obligations of common carriers upon all for-hire motor-carrier operators. Typically, this required an operator to secure a certificate of public convenience and necessity by proving that his service was not only in the public interest, but also that he was fit, willing, and able to provide such service. Rates had to be published and adhered to, and discrimination was regulated to some degree. Insurance provisions to protect the public were sometimes included as well. While these regulations did much to assure adequate service, it is interesting that railroads were very active both in proposing economic regulation of motor carriers on the state level and often in opposing the issuance of specific certificates of public convenience and necessity on the basis that they (the railroads) already adequately served the public. Without doubt one of the primary motives for regulation of motor carriage was the control of intermodal competition.

The legality of controlling all motor carriers as common carriers came under question during this period. That a state could regulate common carriers was not questioned, as the common law doctrine of "common callings" applied. But in the 1925 *Duke Case* (266 U.S. 570), the Supreme Court declared that a state could not make a contract carrier into a common carrier for purposes of regulation by simply passing a law. Texas got around this decision by requiring contract carriers to secure "permits" to operate. These permits had slightly less stringent requirements than the common-carrier certificates of public convenience and necessity. In the 1932 *Stephenson Case* (287 U.S. 251), the Texas law was upheld by the Supreme Court. Hence not only was the legality of state regulation firmly maintained, but the precedent of having several classes of carriers with different regulatory treatment was established. Even though all railroads were regulated as common carriers, Federal regulatory law a few years later followed the Stephenson pattern. Most states changed their existing regulatory laws to conform to this pattern as well.

The matter of state control over interstate commerce proved more difficult. A state certainly has a constitutional right to regulate commerce within its own borders, but what about interstate commerce and the operators crossing state borders? In the *Duke Case* previously noted, the Supreme Court held that a state could not deny a permit to an interstate operator. In the same year (1925), the court held that the State of Washington could not deny an interstate bus operator a certificate of public convenience and necessity on the grounds that adequate service by rail and other bus lines already existed (*Buck vs. Kuykendall,* 267 U.S. 307). The effect was the same as the earlier *Wabash Case* in which a state attempted to control railroad interstate commerce. Only the Federal government could regulate economic aspects of interstate commerce regardless of the mode of transportation.

State regulation of motor carriage possessed the obvious weakness of being nonuniform. Indeed, it did not exist at all in some states. The additional limitation that state controls did not apply to interstate commerce only strengthened the demand for Federal regulation.

Federal Regulation of Motor Carriers

After the Duke and Buck cases, there was a period of controversy over the desirability and the form of Federal control over motor carriers. In 1925, the National Association of Railroad and Utilities Commissioners called for Federal regulation. In 1928, the Interstate Commerce Commission recommended Federal regulation of buses and extended its recommendations to trucks in 1932. In 1934, the Federal Coordinator of Transportation (established under the Emergency Act of 1933) urged Federal regulation of motor carriers.

Support for Federal regulation came from both railroads and the larger existing motor carriers. Railroads felt that regulation would limit their competition and made the plea that since they were regulated, equity demanded that their competition also be regulated. The already existing motor carriers desired regulation to protect them from the less firmly established newcomers. Their case was one of mitigating a disorderly and unstable market and the promotion of reliable, safe, and responsible service. Most regulatory agencies supported regulation on the grounds of consistency. In all cases, support came not because of transportation monopoly and monopolistic abuses such as discrimination, as it had in rail transportation, but rather because of transportation competition, both intramodal and intermodal, and the excesses of a competitive transportation market.

Opposition to regulation was firmly expressed by agricultural groups who feared transportation monopoly and by some of the existing motor carriers, particularly contract carriers. However, with the continuation of the intense competition in trucking brought on by the depression, Federal regulation was established by Congress in 1935.

The Motor Carrier Act of 1935 was enacted as Part II of the Interstate Commerce Act. It brought control of motor carriers under the Interstate Commerce Commission, and in no small way it was an extension of the existing rail-monopoly type of regulation. The major provisions of the Act may be summarized under the six headings of carrier classification, entry controls, rate controls, consolidation and merger regulation, securities and accounts supervision, and regulatory innovations. Each of these will be considered in order.

Carrier Classification

Previous state regulatory experience had shown that it was necessary to establish several classes of carriers. The number of firms is much larger in the motor-carrier industry than in the rail industry, and the character of the firms varies considerably as shown in Chapter 4. While all railroads could be regulated as common carriers, the law had to recognize that only a portion of the motor carriers operated in this fashion. Therefore, five classes or groups of operators were defined in the law. These were:

1. Common carriers which hold themselves out to serve the general public;
2. Contract carriers which operate for hire under specific contract and special arrangements with a limited number of shippers;
3. Private carriers who own the goods that they transport and do not directly serve the public;
4. Brokers who sell and arrange transportation but do not actually perform transportation services;
5. Exempt carriers not subject to the economic provisions of the law but still controlled as to safety, hours of work by employees, and standards of equipment.

The very fact that several classes of carriers were established makes the regulation of motor carriers somewhat more complicated than the regulation of railroads.

Entry Controls

Common carriers in bona fide operation on June 1, 1935 and contract carriers in bona fide operation on July 1, 1935 were automatically granted the right to continue to operate in the same manner. No proof of public convenience and necessity or consistency with the public interest was necessary for these carriers. (This is known as the "grandfather clause.") All new carriers entering the industry after that date had to secure certificates or permits from the Commission.

In order to secure a certificate of public convenience and necessity, a common carrier must convince the Commission that it is "fit, willing, and able" to perform the proposed service and that its service is required by present and future public convenience and necessity. Common carriers wishing to extend their right to serve additional territories or traffic must also meet these requirements. Certificates must specify the route served and the type of service to be rendered, including a commodity description.

A contract carrier must secure a permit. To do so, it too must show that it is fit, willing, and able to perform the service and that its proposed operation is consistent with the public interest and national transportation policy. Presumably, "consistent with the public interest" is a less rigorous requirement than showing "public convenience and necessity." Since the service of a contract carrier is more specialized and for a limited number of shippers who are presumed to be able to protect themselves, regulations over contract carriers are mainly designed to control their competition with common carriers.

Since the requirement of being "fit, willing, and able" generally means that a carrier wishing a certificate must demonstrate fitness by presenting a record of good operations and since operation is not possible without a certificate or permit, it is quite difficult to secure the right to operate. Additionally, it is necessary to show positively that the public convenience will be served or that the service is necessary by presenting evidence of lack of service on the part of existing carriers and the need for more competition. This, too, is not an easy task. Even extensions of service of existing carriers must meet these same requirements. It seems obvious that the regulations in this regard are aimed at control of entry of new firms and the control of carrier competition.

Rate Controls

The Motor Carrier Act provided that all rates and fares must be just and reasonable, rates must be published and strictly observed, and adequate notice must be given of proposed rate changes. The Interstate Commerce Commission is empowered to determine the reasonableness and lawfulness of rates. Undue and unreasonable prejudice or preference in rates towards persons, places, and commodities is prohibited also, and the Commission may suspend a proposed rate in order to carry on an investigation. All these provisions are the same as those found in Part I pertaining to rail transportation and clearly illustrate the application of the rail pattern of control to motor carriers.

The Commission has the power to prescribe the maximum, minimum, or actual rate to be charged by common carriers if an existing rate is found unreasonable or unlawful. This also follows the rail pattern. The act originally provided that contract carriers file only minimum rate schedules with the Commission and gave the Commission authority to control only minimum rates. In 1957, this filing provision was changed to require filing of the actual rates charged rather than the minimum schedule. This was largely due to common-carrier complaints that contract carriers had an unfair competitive advantage by knowing common-carrier rates although common carriers did nok know the actual contract rates. These provisions further illustrate that the Act was aimed at controlling transportation competition.

Consolidation and Merger Regulation

Use of the rail pattern of regulation is particularly evident in consolidation and merger regulation. The provisions of Part I (rail) of the Interstate Commerce Act were made applicable to motor carriers with but small change. Consolidations, mergers, or unifications must be approved by the Commission and be shown to be consistent with the public interest. An exception was made, however, because of the large number of small firms in the motor-carrier industry. Any consolidation or merger involving less than twenty vehicles did not have to be approved (except that a railroad seeking control of a motor carrier had to obtain approval regardless of the number of vehicles). This 20-vehicle exemption was changed in September, 1965, to permit exempt mergers of motor carriers with aggregate annual gross revenues of not more than $300,000.

Securities and Accounts Provisions

The issuance of securities by common carriers in the motor-carrier industry were also brought under the same controls as applied to railroads. Again an exception was made for small motor carriers. If the total par value of the securities outstanding and to be issued did not exceed $1,000,000 or notes and debentures with a term of less than two years did not exceed $200,000, Commission approval was unnecessary. The Commission was given the same power to require, prescribe, and inspect the books and accounts of motor carriers as it had for rail carriers.

Regulatory Innovations

One cannot say that there were no new or different regulations imposed by the Motor Carrier Act. Basically, Part II contained four areas of innovation by giving recognition to:

1. the competitive market structure of the motor-carrier industry;
2. the complexities of the industry;
3. the existence of a well-developed state regulatory structure;
4. the need to protect the safety of the traveling and shipping public.

The Motor Carrier Act took cognizance of the more competitive market in motor transportation in three ways. Because of the existence of so many carriers, no provisions for the prescription of through routes and joint rates by the Commission were included. It was assumed that the choice of the shipper would be so wide that such control was unnecessary. Likewise, no Section 4 or long-and-short haul provisions existed. This type of discrimination by railroads is almost completely dependent on a monopoly structure and cannot exist when several firms operate in competition in a given locality. Finally, the ease of entry of new firms made control of abandonments unnecessary.

The complexities of motor carriers were also recognized in three ways. First, the very classification of carriers into five groups recognized that motor carriers differed and could not all be treated alike. Second, because of the possibilities of discrimination in favor of large shippers in a highly competitive market, dual operation as both a common carrier and contract carrier by a single firm over the same route or in the same territory was prohibited. Finally and most important, eleven classes of carriers were exempted from economic regulation, although not from safety regulations. Basically, these fall into approximately the three categories of special groups, terminal operations, and local and contiguous groups.

For a variety of reasons, no doubt partially political, the Act exempted from regulation the transportation of agricultural commodities and newspapers. The agricultural commodity exemption applies to vehicles owned and operated by farmers carrying products of farms and supplies to farms, vehicles operated and controlled by agricultural marketing cooperatives, and all vehicles carrying livestock, fish (including shellfish), horticultural (added in 1952) or agricultural commodities, not including manufactured products thereof. This exemption, plus the exemption of vehicles carrying newspapers, was designed to allay the fears of some of the groups opposing motor-carrier regulation. Additionally, in the case of agricultural commodities there was concern with the seasonal nature of the movement. This also simplified regulation since a tremendous number of vehicles are involved in these groups.

Vehicles owned and operated by railroads, water carriers, and freight forwarders in pickup-and-delivery service were exempted from economic regulation. Vehicles used exclusively in the transportation of persons and property when incidental to transportation by aircraft were added to this exemption in 1938. Service in most of these cases is part of a movement already controlled, and therefore regulation of this portion was felt unnecessary. This also decreased the number of vehicles covered and simplified regulation.

Carriers essentially local in character, such as school busses, taxis, hotel vehicles, trolley busses, and vehicles under the control of the Secretary of the Interior and operated principally in national parks and monuments, were exempted. Additonally, vehicles transporting passengers and property wholly within a municipality, between contiguous municipalities, or within a zone adjacent to and commercially contiguous to a municipality were exempt. Again this cut down the scope of regulation and gave recognition to the fact that state regulatory procedure was quite highly developed.

The act gave recognition to the state regulatory structure in two ways. First, the Interstate Commerce Commission is explicitly denied jurisdiction over intrastate motor-carrier rates providing that the carrier is operating legally under the jurisdiction of a state regulatory agency. (In rail regulation, the I.C.C. was given power to order changes in intrastate rates under the Act of 1920 under the so-called Shreveport Rule.) Additionally, the Act allowed the use of Joint Boards. Where a problem involves no more than three states, a joint board consisting of representatives of the regulatory agencies in the states involved may hear the matter and act in place of the Interstate Commerce Commission. Appeal to the I.C.C. is possible, of course, but this innovation considerably simplified the work of the Commission. It also recognized that since so many more firms are involved in motor transportation than in rail transportation and so many of the problems are regional rather than national in scope, a new approach is possible.

The final group of innovations concerns the regulation of safety standards and the necessity to protect the public by assuring adequate financial responsibility on the part of the carriers. First, it was recognized that motor carriers in using public highways should operate within a uniform set of safety standards. Rules governing the maximum hours of operator service, equipment safety standards, and other matters of safe operation are permitted under the Act. These rules apply to all classes of carriers. Periodic inspection attempts to enforce these rules. Second, the Commission may require carriers to purchase surety bonds and insurance to protect shippers and the general public or to show financial responsibility. No such rule was needed for railroads because they do not use public ways and because fewer financially irresponsible operators existed. Both of these provisions recognized the different character of motor transportation.

Problems in Federal Motor-Carrier Regulation

A number of problems of interpretation, definition, and administration of the Motor Carrier Act have arisen. Over the years the definition of the agricultural commodity exemption clause has been particularly troublesome. The problem of distinguishing between private and for-hire transportation has likewise been difficult. Both of these difficulties will be considered further in Chapter 24.

Problems of definition of contract carriage in distinction from common carriage, problems of the scope of the rights issued under the grandfather clause, problems of applying consolidation and merger provisions (particularly where railroads apply to purchase motor carriers), problems of control over the rate level, problems of determining reasonableness and discrimination, and problems of control of entry of new firms and extensions of existing firms are all involved in the administration of the Act. Wherever an industry as diverse and with as many separate firms as motor transportation is involved in regulation, administrative difficulties are bound to arise. Consideration of these interesting matters, however, is beyond the scope of a general book of this nature and properly belongs in a special treatise on motor transportation.

In conclusion, we can say that the changing character of the transportation market had forced society to look once more at its regulatory objectives. The structure of the regulation of transportation competition was established in the regulation of motor transportation. Our next chapter will discuss how this regulatory structure evolved.

ADDITIONAL READINGS

1. Alexander, David and Leon N. Moses, "Competition Under Uneven Regulation," **American Economic Review,** May 1963, pp. 466–473.
2. Daggett, Stuart, **Principles of Inland Transportation.** 4th ed. New York: Harper and Brothers, 1955.
   Chapter 31. "Motor Vehicle Regulation," pp. 655–687.
3. Fair, Marvin A. and Ernest W. Williams, Jr., **Economics of Transportation.** Rev. ed. New York: Harper and Brothers, 1959.
   Chapter 24. "Regulation of Motor Highway Carriers," pp. 487–508.

4. Harper, Donald V., **Economic Regulation of the Motor Trucking Industry by States.** Urbana, Illinois: University of Illinois Press, 1959.
5. Harper, Donald V., "The Shipper Views Economic Regulation of For-Hire Trucking," **I.C.C. Practitioners' Journal,** December 1963, pp. 299–316.
6. Hudson, William J. and James A. Constantin, **Motor Transportation.** New York: Ronald Press Company, 1955.
   Chapter 19. "Development of State and Federal Regulation," pp. 461–482.
7. Kahn, Fritz R., **Principles of Motor Carrier Regulation.** Dubuque, Iowa: Wm. C. Brown Co., 1958.
   Chapter 2. "Transportation Exempt from Regulation," pp. 14–28.
8. Koontz, Harold and Richard W. Gable, **Public Control of Economic Enterprise.** New York: McGraw-Hill Book Co., Inc., 1956.
   Chapter 4. "Transport Regulation: Evolution of a Pattern," pp. 75–96.
9. Locklin, D. Philip, **Economics of Transportation.** 6th ed. Homewood, Illinois: Richard D. Irwin, Inc., 1966.
   Chapter 13. "Railroad Legislation Since 1920," pp. 240–262.
   Chapter 31. "Development of Motor-Carrier Regulation," pp. 661–679.
10. Maxwell, W. David, "The Regulation of Motor-Carrier Rates by the Interstate Commerce Commission," **Land Economics,** February 1960, pp. 79–91.
11. Norton, Hugh S., **Modern Transportation Economics.** Columbus, Ohio: Charles E. Merrill Books, Inc., 1963.
    Chapter XI. "Evolution of Regulation 1920–1958," pp. 193–203.
    Chapter XIV. "Regulation of Motor Carriers," pp. 258–267.
12. Norton, Hugh S., **National Transportation Policy: Formation and Implementation.** Berkeley, California: McCutchan Publishing Corporation, 1966.
    Chapter 1. "Historical Background," pp. 3–13.
    Chapter 2. "Technology, Change, and Competition," pp. 14–35.
    Chapter 3. "The New Era, Public Control, and the Body of Regulation," pp. 50–73.
13. Pegrum, Dudley F., **Transportation: Economics and Public Policy.** Rev. ed. Homewood, Illinois: Richard D. Irwin, Inc., 1968.
    Chapter 13. "Railroad Regulation Since World War I," pp. 312–333.
    Chapter 14. "The Regulation of Motor Transport," pp. 334–360.
14. Phillips, Charles F. Jr., **The Economics of Regulation.** Rev. ed. Homewood, Illinois: Richard D. Irwin, Inc., 1969.
    Chapter 13. "Regulation of the Transportation Industries," pp. 441–482.
15. Taff, Charles A., **Commercial Motor Transportation.** 4th ed. Homewood, Illinois: Richard D. Irwin, Inc., 1969.
    Chapter 17. "Regulation of Motor Carriers," pp. 377–401.
16. Troxel, Emery, **Economics of Transport.** New York: Rinehart & Company, Inc., 1955.
    Chapter 16. "More Public Controls," pp. 370–393.
    Chapter 17. "Public Control of Entries," pp. 394–417.
17. Westmeyer, Russell E., **Economics of Transportation.** Englewood Cliffs, N.J.: Prentice-Hall, Inc., 1952.
    Chapter 19. "Regulation of Highway Transportation," pp. 389–410.

18

Regulation of Transportation Competition: Evolution

Once transportation competition had been recognized as an emerging characteristic of the transportation market and the foundations of regulation of transportation competition had been established by the regulation of motor carriage, it was only a matter of time before the concepts were applied to other modes of transportation. This chapter will show how the regulation of transportation competition has evolved over time.

AIR TRANSPORTATION

The second extension of regulation during the 1930's, the decade of transportation competition, came in 1938 with the regulation of air transportation. To a somewhat lesser degree than in motor carriage, the regulation of this developing mode of transportation reflected the changed character of the market into a more competitive one. Added to this were the national defense aspects of air transportation and the need to promote and develop this new mode.

This mixture of promotional and economic aspects of the regulation of air transportation is illustrated by the "Declaration of Policy" contained in the Civil Aeronautics Act. Congress directed that the regulatory body should consider the following as being in the public interest and in accordance with the public convenience and necessity:

1. the encouragement and development of an air transportation system properly adapted to the present and future needs of the foreign and domestic commerce of the United States, of the Postal Service, and of the national defense;
2. the regulation of air transportation in such a manner as to recognize and preserve the inherent advantages of, assure the highest degree of safety in, and foster sound economic conditions in such transportation . . . ;

3. the promotion of adequate, economical, and efficient service by air carriers at reasonable charges, without unjust discrimination, undue preferences or advantages, or unfair or destructive competitive practices;
4. competition to the extent necessary to assure the sound development of an air transportation system properly adapted to the needs of the foreign and domestic commerce of the United States, of the Postal Service, and the national defense;
5. the regulation of air commerce in such a manner as to best promote its development and safety;
6. the encouragement and development of civil aeronautics.

It is readily apparent that the regulation of air transportation was to be both remedial and promotional. The promotional and safety aspects were somewhat of a departure from the general scheme of regulation to protect the public from the excesses of competition as was the case in motor transportation.

Emergence of Air Transport Regulation

The regulatory structure in air transportation was developed during the mid-1920's and early 1930's. The background of regulation was principally on the Federal level, in distinction to the emergence of the Motor Carrier Act out of state regulation. Also, air regulation developed faster in point of time, as distinguished from the long history of attempts to regulate rail transportation. Basically, comprehensive promotional and economic regulation of air transportation emerged out of four Federal statutes, all dealing with airmail and airways. These four were the Kelly Act of 1925, the Air Commerce Act of 1926, the McNary-Watres Act of 1930, and the Air Mail Act of 1934.

The pivotal matter of the way in air transportation first involved the Federal government when the Air Commerce Act of 1926 created the Bureau of Air Commerce (in the Department of Commerce) and directed it to establish, operate, and maintain all necessary air nagivation facilities except airports. Air safety regulations were also allowed, and the Bureau began to inspect and register aircraft and pilots, establish air traffic rules, and require minimum safety standards for airlines using Federal airways. Subsequent depression spending in the 1930's and the removal of limitations on Federal participation in airport development in 1938 brought the Federal government into airport improvement on a Federal-aid matching program.

As noted in Chapter 2, the Kelly Act of 1925 authorized the Post Office Department to contract with private companies for carriage of the mails. These contracts were let on competitive bids on a weight basis and thus provided an assured income base upon which investment and private development could proceed. The McNary-Watres Act of 1930 changed airmail payment provisions from weight to a space-mile concept. This formula was designed to stimulate the development of passenger carriage. With the government paying for the basic costs of operating the aircraft, any passenger fares collected were by-product income produced without additional costs to the operator. The Post Office Department was given power to certificate routes, control consolidations and extensions, and prescribe a system of accounts.

Because of alleged airmail scandals in 1934, Congress attempted to impose the control of an independent regulatory group and to break up the close relationships between air operators and the Postmaster General. This was done by giving the Interstate Commerce Commission authority to review the rates of airmail pay, to fix fair and reasonable rates for each route, and to prevent mergers and holding-company control. The overlapping and confused situation relative to airmail contracts, subsidies, and regulation under the Air Mail Act of 1934 hastened more comprehensive regulation in 1938.

Civil Aeronautics Act of 1938 and Revisions

With the passage of the Civil Aeronautics Act in June, 1938, a new pattern of regulation was established. Prior to that time, all regulation over both transportation monopoly and transportation competition came under the Interstate Commerce Commission. Now a new regulatory authority was created, and while its organization, powers, and procedures were patterned after the existing regulatory authority, it had different goals and was given a somewhat different mission. After long legislative debate and discussion, some of which finally overcame President Roosevelt's initial desire to regulate air transportation under the I.C.C., a separate regulatory structure was established with both remedial and promotional roles. These dual roles are illustrated in the Declaration of Policy previously noted. The structure and organization of the Civil Aeronautics Board will be discussed in the next chapter.

Basically, the regulation of air transportation has three main elements: control of entry and service competition, control of rates and earnings, and safety and miscellaneous controls. While these elements parallel the controls over motor transportation to a great degree, the dual-role mission gives them a distinctive setting.

Air carriers in bona fide operation on May 14, 1938, were automatically granted the right to continue to operate in the same manner under the familiar grandfather-clause type of regulation used in motor transportation. No proof of public convenience and necessity was required of these existing carriers, but new carriers or extensions of operating rights of existing carriers had to show the C.A.B. that the applicant was fit, willing, and able to serve and that a public need existed. Since the Postmaster General had previously certified carriers to carry the mails, this provision merely validated these permits and utilized the already existing pattern of routes. It is well to note, however, that due to the pioneering state of aircraft technology as well as the substantial capital requirements necessary to provide airmail service, the number of carriers certified by the Postmaster General and under the grandfather provisions was quite small. This is a contrast to the grandfather rights problem in motor transportation where the number of initial firms granted rights was considerably larger.

Since new entrants and extensions of the operating authority of existing firms required certificates from the C.A.B., effective control over service competition was possible. By withholding certificates on a given route, competition could be restricted. By issuing certificates to new entrants or extending the rights of existing firms on given routes or between given points, competition could be increased. While much has been written as to the actual policy followed by the C.A.B. on certificates, the Board has generally tried to avoid the wasteful duplication, overexpansion, and poor service which could easily arise from transportation competition.

The ability to regulate closely competition in air transportation is a very real one. Since Federal regulation appeared at a very early stage in the development of the mode, effective regulation was possible. The problems of measuring demand and potential growth of given air transportation markets, choosing among the several carriers which might apply to extend their service, and establishing the type of service to be offered have not been easy. Additionally, C.A.B. route decisions affect other agencies of the government (by way of airmail contracts, subsidy payments, and the necessity for providing more control over air safety and the airways, for example).

Following the intent of Congress to build up an adequate and well-rounded national air transportation system, the C.A.B. had to establish a pattern of route competition and a number of operating criteria. The evolution of the so-called "one carrier principle" of through service, the local or feeder system of regional carriers complementing through service, the concept of direct competition where demand warranted, the problem of balancing carrier systems to equalize competition, and the postwar struggle to resolve the nonscheduled carrier and supplemental carrier problem are all involved in administering the Act. Discussion of these interesting administrative problems properly belongs in a more specialized treatise on air transportation. The point, for our purposes, is that the C.A.B. has had and continues to have the ability to control transportation competition in the air.

An integral part of the control of competition in air transportation is the control of rates and, thereby, the earnings of air carriers. It is impossible to have adequate service without adequate earnings. Promotional elements and safety factors are also involved for financially weak carriers who can rarely promote, use, and afford the degree of safety demanded by the public.

Recognition of the important role of rates and earnings control was shown by a Rule of Rate Making similar in philosophy to that laid down in the Transportation Act of 1920 and in the Motor Carrier Act of 1935. Specifically, the air-carrier rule requires that the regulatory body in setting rates consider:

1. the effect of such rates upon the movement of traffic;
2. the need in the public interest of adequate and efficient transportation of persons and property by air carriers at the lowest cost consistent with the furnishing of such service;
3. such standards respecting the character and quality of service to be rendered by air carriers as may be prescribed by or pursuant to law;
4. the inherent advantages of transportation by aircraft;
5. the need of each air carrier for revenue sufficient to enable such air carrier, under honest, economical and efficient management, to provide adequate and efficient air carrier service.

This policy statement was implemented by granting approximately the same degree of rate control to the C.A.B. which the I.C.C. possessed. Rates and fares had to be published and observed. Changes in rates required notice, and the C.A.B. had power to suspend rate changes while it investigated. All must be just and reasonable; and upon finding a rate to be unreasonable, the C.A.B. had power to determine minimum, maximum, or exact rates. Undue discrimination was prohibited, but no long-and-short-haul provision was included nor was the Shreveport principle incorporated since intrastate air service was minor. The main problems of rates has centered about the adequacy of earnings and the promotion of air transportation.

The final element of control involved public safety and various miscellaneous controls. First, the miscellaneous group of controls involves power over consolidations and mergers, accounts (but not securities), authority to issue permits for foreign and domestic carriers to engage in overseas air commerce where the continental limits of the United States are involved (although the executive department has the ultimate authority in overseas air commerce), and power to exempt carriers not engaged in scheduled air transportation from economic regulations.

Second, the control of safety is such an important part of air transportation that a new approach was used and a separate regulatory board was established to oversee this aspect of the industry. It will be recalled that control over air safety actually predates the economic regulation of the 1938 Act as it was included as a part of the Air Commerce Act of 1926. Under the 1926 Act, the Bureau of Air Commerce was established in the Department of Commerce to inspect and certify aircraft, pilots, air schools and equipment as well as to set up traffic rules and establish and operate airways.

Initially, the safety function in the 1938 Act was split between the Civil Aeronautics Administrator in the Department of Commerce and the Air Safety Board, an investigatory group concerned with aircraft accidents and recommendations concerning accident prevention. In 1940, a reorganization was effected which centralized safety and airways regulation and operation under the Civil Aeronautics Administrator. The total effect of the reorganization was to place air safety regulation in the Department of Commerce under the C.A.A. while maintaining economic regulation under the independent C.A.B. The matter was further clarified and refined in the Federal Aviation Act of 1958 when the Federal Aviation Agency was created and given comprehensive authority over air safety and the control of air space. While safety regulation certainly has economic significance and is integrally connected to adequacy of earnings, its importance causes it to be controlled by a separate agency and to be considered apart from economic regulations.

In summary then, the regulation of competition in air transportation rests upon the twin factors of control of entry and control of rates. Minor regulation comes from various miscellaneous controls. The control of safety is emphasized both by being effectively separated from economic control and by the use of an entirely different agency established in the executive branch of the government. Economic control is administered by an independent regulatory body patterned upon but separated from the traditional regulatory group, the Interstate Commerce Commission. Finally, the C.A.B. has a unique dual mission of both regulation and promotion of air transportation.

WATER TRANSPORTATION

During the decade of the 1930's, regulation had been extended to two major modes of transportation: motor and air. Coupled with prior regulation of railroads and pipelines, regulation of almost all modes of for-hire transportation and their competitive relationships was complete. Only water carriers and freight forwarders remained unregulated after 1938. Freight forwarders will be considered shortly. This section will discuss the regulation of water transportation.

The Act of 1887 allowed the I.C.C. to exercise partial control over water transportation if the movement was a joint rail-water move. Additionally, under the Panama Canal Act of 1912, the I.C.C. was given control over rail-owned water operations. Regulation of other aspects of domestic water transportation (if it existed at all), however, was under the United States Shipping Board and its successor, the United States Maritime Commission. Until 1940, there was no separation of matters of ocean transportation from domestic water transportation.

The regulation of domestic water transportation is an excellent example of the regulation of transportation competition. There were few shipper complaints of abusive practices by water carriers. Almost all the interest in regulation stemmed from railroads, who were interested in bringing their competitors under control and placing some limits on intermodal competition. The regulation of water transportation as finally evolved illustrates this concern.

Transportation Act of 1940

The Transportation Act of 1940 covered several areas of transportation. For our present purposes, its importance is that it established I.C.C. control over domestic water transportation.

This regulation was very much in the rail pattern which had been developed earlier, with certain modifications to fit water transportation. Actually, the regulation of water transportation is contained in Part III of the Interstate Commerce Act (Part II being the Motor Carrier Act) and provides that some sections of Part I (Rail-Pipeline and general provisions) are applicable to water transportation. Section 4 (long-and-short haul) from Part I was extended to water transportation; pooling agreements (Section 5) were prohibited; mergers and consolidations were subject to I.C.C. approval under Part I; and free passes and the Elkins Act provisions were extended to water carriers. Basically, the regulation of domestic water transportation has three main elements: rates and certificates, exemptions, and miscellaneous provisions.

The 1920 provisions requiring rail carriers to obtain certificates of public convenience and necessity had been used as a pivotal element in the control of motor and air transportation. The same principle was used in 1940 in the control of domestic water transportation. Existing carriers were protected by grandfather-clause provisions if they were in bona fide operation on January 1, 1940. New carriers had to secure certificates by showing that the public convenience would be served and that they were fit, willing, and able to perform the proposed service. The same provisions applied to the extension of existing common-carrier certificates, just as in motor and air regulation. Contract carriers were required to secure permits upon showing that their proposed service was consistent with the public interest, as in motor transportation. In effect, this gave the I.C.C. control over route competition and the number of firms entering the industry, thereby facilitating a major objective of the Act—the control of intermodal competition.

Rates were controlled in the usual fashion. All charges had to be published and observed. A change in rates could be made only after due notice. Rates were to be just and reasonable. Upon finding of unreasonableness, the Commission could establish maximums, minimums, or exact rates. Undue discrimination or preference among persons, ports, localities, regions, or types of traffic was prohibited. Carriers had to establish through routes and joint rates, and the Commission could establish these joint relationships and divide revenues among carriers if it desired. No Shreveport principle existed since intrastate water transportation was of little importance, although Section 4 did apply as noted previously. Contract carriers had to publish minimum rates only, and a Rule of Rate Making similar to the rail Section 15a was included.

As in motor transportation, several exemptions from economic regulation in addition to private transport were allowed. Commodities shipped in bulk were exempt where no more than three commodities make up the cargo, as were liquid cargoes in bulk in tank vessels. Due to the economic characteristics of water transportation, as noted in Chapter 5, this effectively freed the greater part of domestic water transportation from regulation. Also, miscellaneous water transportation, such as ferries, vessels used in a single harbor, small craft of less than 100 tons capacity, vessels used incidental to movement by rail, motor, or express companies or for lighterage, towage, floatage, or car ferries, was exempt.

A unique feature of the exemptions under Part III illustrates the goal of control of intermodal competition. Congress provided for the exclusion of ". . . transportation by contract carriers by water which, by reason of the inherent nature of the commodities transported, their requirement of special equipment, or their shipment in bulk, *is not actually and substantially competitive with transportation by any common carrier . . .*" (54 Stat. 948, emphasis added). Contract carriers must apply for this exemption and show that the service is noncompetitive, however.

Dual operations as both a common and contract carrier were prohibited, although the I.C.C. could grant exceptions to this rule. Abandonment of service was not controlled, nor were water carriers subject to financial regulations under the Act.

In summary, it seems quite clear that control over domestic water transportation was primarily aimed at the intermodal competition which existed between rail and water transportation. Maximum rate cases have never been important under the Act, few charges of discrimination have been lodged by shippers, and the public has rarely charged that water carriers have abused their privileges. Clearly, water transportation was controlled because of its competitive effect on other transportation.

NATIONAL TRANSPORTATION POLICY AND "INHERENT ADVANTAGE"

Perhaps nothing conceptualized the idea of transportation competition better than the "Declaration of National Transportation Policy" which was added as a preamble to the Interstate Commerce Act by the Transportation Act of 1940. For the first time, Congress attempted to set down in one general statement the transportation policy of the nation. This policy statement is as follows:

It is hereby declared to be the national transportation policy of the Congress to provide for fair and impartial regulation of all modes of transportation subject to the provisions of the Act, so administered as to recognize and preserve the inherent advantage of each; to promote safe, adequate, economical and efficient service and foster sound economic conditions in transportation and among the several carriers; to encourage the establishment and maintenance of reasonable charges for transportation services, without unjust discriminations, undue preferences, or advantages, or unfair or destructive competitive practices; to cooperate with the several States, and the duly authorized officials thereof; and to encourage fair wages and equitable working conditions—all to the end of *developing, coordinating,* and *preserving a national transportation system* by water, highway, and rail as well as other means, adequate to meet the needs of the commerce of the United States, of the Postal Service, and of the national defense. All of the provisions of this Act shall be administered and enforced with a view to carrying out the above declaration of policy. (54 Stat. 899, emphasis added.)

It should be noted that the language of this declaration of policy encompassed all modes of transportation subject to the Act. With the addition of water transportation, nearly all modes were regulated at this point. The terms "safe, adequate, economical, and efficient service" and "sound economic conditions" are recognition of the need for adequate earnings and regulation of competition which might lead to unsafe or inadequate service. Additionally, the Declaration not only repeats the policy of avoiding discrimination and preference, but also calls for the avoidance of "unfair or destructive competitive practices." Without doubt, the Declaration of National Transportation Policy was a recognition of the changed market in transportation and it clearly is aimed at transportation competition, not transportation monopoly.

This recognition of transportation competition is based primarily on the new idea that each mode is part of a "system" of transportation and has certain peculiar and "inherent" advantages. Each mode does certain tasks better than the other modes. Each mode has a place in a transportation system of several modes. While all modes should compete where they are competitive, the national policy should also be to preserve the "inherent advantage" possessed by each. The policy Congress was aiming at, therefore, was one of an *integrated transportation system* based upon *inherent advantage* of each mode with *controlled competition.* The implementation of these policy objectives was not as easy as stating the policy. Translating policy aims and declarations into direct action—interpretation and controls—is a complicated task.

The Transportation Act of 1940 contained several specific provisions aimed at implementing the Declaration of National Transportation Policy and at correcting or updating regulatory procedure and approach. Those intended to implement the Declaration of Policy were the creation of a Board of Investigation and Research, changes in the burden of proof, and changes in the Rule of Rate Making. Two provisions apparently aimed at updating regulation were the discontinuance of land-grant railroad rate provisions and modification of the consolidation and merger provisions.

Although the Board of Investigation and Research was temporary and ceased to exist in 1944, it was tangible recognition by Congress that the central regulatory problem was the regulation of transportation competition and the determination of "inherent advantage." This three-man Board was to investigate in depth and report upon three matters: the "relative economy and fitness" of rail, motor, and water carriers; the "subsidy question"; and the extent to which taxes were imposed on rail, motor, and water transport. If transportation was to be treated as a "system" with intermodal competition between its parts, some idea of the relative fitness and economy of each part obviously was necessary. Additionally, if each part has peculiar inherent advantages which should be preserved, the degree to which one part was subsidized or taxed in preference or in prejudice to another was necessary. This was the task of the B.I.R.

Prior to 1940, the burden of proof in hearings involving rate increases was on the carriers, while the burden of proof involving rate decreases was on the Commission. Hereafter, the carriers had to prove that rate decreases were "just and reasonable" or not "unduly preferential or prejudicial" when proposed. Since intermodal competition most typically takes the form of rate decreases, this procedural change both recognized that the central problem was intermodal competition and strengthened the Commission's powers to control it. A final change giving recognition to intermodal competition was the amendment to Section 15a (Rule of Rate Making) which directed the Commission to give due consideration to the "effect of rates on the movement of traffic by the carriers for which the rates are prescribed." The purpose here was to prevent the Commission from prescribing rates designed to protect the traffic of another mode of transportation, i.e., keeping rail rates high to protect water traffic.

The abandonment of land-grant rates was long overdue. Rail carriers had been forced to carry government freight and passengers at reduced rates for nearly a hundred years and had thereby more than adequately repaid the Federal government for its grants of land. These obligations, which were contained in the land grants made between 1850 and 1871, were lifted for all nonmilitary traffic in 1940. In 1945 they were abandoned for military traffic as well.

Merger and consolidation provisions were modified in recognition of the actual pressures of intermodal competition. These changes will be further discussed in Chapter 20.

Without question, the major accomplishment of the provisions of the Transportation Act of 1940 was formal recognition that the problem facing transportation was one of intermodal competition, not monopoly. The recognition and attempted response to the changed transportation market was contained not only in the regulation of water transportation, but in the Declaration of National Transportation Policy and the modification of specific regulatory provisions.

While the Transportation Act of 1940 established the general tone of the regulation of transportation competition, various later refinements and adjustments were necessary with the passage of time. Although a number of adjustments have been made over the years since 1940, three refinements seem important enough to warrant mention here. These are the regulation of freight forwarders in 1942, the Reed-Bulwinkle Act of 1948, and the Transportation Act of 1958.

FREIGHT FORWARDERS

Freight forwarders were the final mode of for-hire transportation to be regulated. As explained in Chapter 5, forwarders are important secondary or indirect carriers which consolidate or combine many small shipments (LCL or LTL) into larger lots (TL or CL) and use the services of line-haul carriers. The forwarder deals directly with both shippers and carriers and provides a necessary service to the small shipper.

In May, 1942, this part of the transportation system was regulated by the addition of Part IV of the Interstate Commerce Act. The rail pattern was applied to forwarders in virtually the same manner as to the other modes. That is, the usual entry, rate, and service controls were applied. Forwarders had to secure permits to operate and had to file rates which were open to inspection, just and reasonable, and not unduly discriminatory. A Rule of Rate Making similar to that contained in Parts I, II, and III of the Act was also included.

One unique feature of the Freight Forwarder Act was that forwarders could not own or control any carriers regulated under Parts I, II, or III of the Interstate Commerce Act, but those carriers might own and control freight forwarders. Additionally, forwarders had to utilize common carriers in their line-haul operations and could not set up or utilize contract carriers. Forwarders themselves were specifically declared to be common carriers under a 1950 amendment to the Act even though they are, in effect, also "shippers."

THE REED-BULWINKLE ACT

Reference was made in Chapter 11 to the earlier questionable legality of joint action in rate-making. As a result of a Supreme Court decision in 1945 (*Georgia v. Pennsylvania Railroad,* 324 U.S. 439), Congress enacted the Reed-Bulwinkle amendment to the Interstate Commerce Act in 1948. Basically, this amendment legalizes conference or bureau rate-making in which the carriers decide among themselves what rate changes they will propose. The Commission was given power to control the procedures, rules, and regulations of rate bureaus, to require periodic reports, and to inspect records, accounts, files, and memoranda.

The Reed-Bulwinkle Act also provided that the right of "independent action" on the part of any carrier or group of carriers must be allowed. Thus, while rate bureaus do serve a most useful purpose, they cannot impose their will upon all carriers. A carrier may publish its own rates if it desires. Hence, one of the more objectionable aspects of joint action is eliminated.

The Reed-Bulwinkle Act (now Section 5a of the basic Act) is an important refinement of the regulation of transportation competition. It allows the Commission to supervise the rate-making function and thus to have a degree of control over intramodal competition. At the same time, it recognizes the competitive nature of transportation and preserves the right of an individual carrier to pursue a course of independent action.

THE TRANSPORTATION ACT OF 1958

Another refinement of the regulation of transportation competition is contained in the Transportation Act of 1958. This act basically affects rail transportation and the relative position of the railroads in the intermodal struggle, even though two of the six major provisions of the Act deal with motor-carrier regulatory problems. The six major provisions of the Act of 1958 were: (1) temporary loan guarantees to railroads, (2) amendment and liberalization of the Shreveport rule of control over intrastate rail rates, (3) amendment of the discontinuation of service provisions, (4) amendment of Section 15a (the Rule of Rate Making), (5) interpretation of the agricultural commodities exemption clause in motor-carrier regulation, and (6) clarification of the distinction between private and for-hire motor carriers.

A major concern of tthe 1958 Act, designated as Part V of the Interstate Commerce Act, was a provision for the federal guarantee of loans to railroads. The aggregate amount which could be committed in loan guarantees by the Commission was $500 million. The Commission had to find that the carrier could not obtain loans from ordinary sources without a guarantee, that the interest charges proposed were reasonable, and that the railroad could repay the loan. No guarantee could apply on more than a 15-year loan. The Commission was allowed to charge for these guarantees, and provisions were made for recovery in case of default. Restriction on the payment of dividends if the loan guarantees applied to funds borrowed for maintenance purposes was allowed. Although originally for a limited time only (until March 1961), this provision was extended several times, but subsequently has expired.

The major significance of this provision of the Act was the recognition that a problem of railroad credit exists and that all modes of transportation have not been equally treated as far as public assistance is concerned. In attempting to help rail carriers with their financial problems, Congress recognized that it must play a more active role in intermodal transportation competition.

Commission control over intrastate rates was liberalized so that less proof was necessary to find an intrastate rate burdensome on interstate commerce. It was no longer necessary to make a separation of revenues and expenses into interstate and intrastate commerce to show that intrastate rates were unduly burdensome. Further, the procedure of applying for relief was streamlined to avoid long delays while state authorities considered the matter.

Traditionally, states have controlled passenger service within their boundaries and have been extremely reluctant to allow railroads to discontinue unprofitable train service. A new procedure in the Act of 1958 allows the Commission more control and allows the railroads to bypass state authorities in certain instances. The effect again is to relieve the financial ills of railroads and to extend I.C.C. control into new areas.

Perhaps the most significant part of the Transportation Act of 1958 was its attempt to insure more intermodal competition in rates by further amending the Rule of Rate Making by adding the phrase "Rates of a carrier shall not be held up to a particular level to protect the traffic of any other mode." Even though Section 15a had directed in 1940 that the Commission "give due consideration to the effect of rates on the movement of traffic by the carrier or carriers for which the rates are prescribed," it was believed that the Commission had often prevented railroad rate decreases to meet intermodal competition and "preserve the inherent advantages" of the competitors. The addition of the new phrase was designed to prevent this from occurring. Clearly Congress was calling for more intermodal competition.

Clarification of the distinction between private and for-hire carriers and further interpretation of the agricultural exemption both were refinements of the Motor Carrier Act (Part II of the Interstate Commerce Act). In effect these were attempts to plug loopholes which had developed out of interpretations (particularly Court interpretations) of the original Act. Conflicts growing out of interpretation of these provisions will be considered in more detail in Chapter 24.

In summary, virtually all provisions of the Transportation Act of 1958 were aimed at promoting or clarifying the control of intermodal transportation.

During the years since this last major regulatory act several related events have occurred. The railroad guaranteed loan program has ceased after committing only a portion of the possible $500 million guarantees; passenger train discontinuances have vastly accelerated; several court actions have been necessary to clarify Commission control over intrastate rates; additions to the "Rule of Rate Making" have been clarified further in the *Ingot Molds Case* (see Chapter 10); some previously exempt carriers of frozen food products have been certificated under a new "Grandfather clause"; and the "primary business test" definition of private motor carriers has been clarified by court and Commission actions. This is not to say, however, that all these questions have been settled. Indeed, some observers claim that the Act of 1958 not only has failed in its role of promoting and clarifying intermodal competition, but that it has created a series of new problems. Final judgment on the effects of this Act must await further developments and perhaps future Congressional action to further amend the basic regulatory structure.

An Era of National Planning

A new emphasis has been added to transportation regulation since 1958. In that year, Congress passed the Federal Aviation Act (72 Stat. 731) which established the Federal Aviation Agency as an independent board with comprehensive authority over air safety and control of air space. At the same time, the status of the Civil Aeronautics Board as a regulatory agency concerned with the economic aspects of air transportation was further clarified. The C.A.B. was given the task of regulating rates, routes, and services, while the F.A.A. was given the task of regulating safety and controlling air space. Additionally, the F.A.A. was given broad planning and research functions in connection with the development of the nation's airways and airports. In effect, considerable national transportation planning was undertaken.

Dissatisfaction with the operation of intermodal competition led to special Presidential messages by both Presidents Kennedy and Johnson, both of which will be discussed in Chapter 24. Although the philosophy of the Act of 1940 was stated as recognition of a system of transportation, regulatory action had continued to be modally oriented. Congress chose to recognize the "transportation system" idea by approving a major administrative reorganization recommendation from President Johnson, and established a Cabinet-level Department of Transportation as a coordinating, planning, and operating agency.

Details of the organization and tasks of the Department of Transportation are discussed in the following chapter. It is worth noting here, though, that the creation of this agency gave recognition to (a) the extreme importance of transportation to the nation, (b) the need for coordination of the many governmental agencies involved with transportation, (c) the need for national planning in transportation, and (d) the fact that transportation is a system with many competing parts and not just five separate carrier modes of transport.

THE ESSENCE OF COMPETITION REGULATION

Changing conditions of the transportation market caused a changed emphasis on regulation of transportation after 1930. Realization of the new market condition came slowly. Nevertheless, by the decade of the 1940's, Congress had recognized that intermodal competition and not monopoly by a single mode was the prevailing market condition. Since that time, most regulatory efforts have been in adjusting to these new conditions and using the established rail pattern of regulation under different circumstances. This adjustment process continues and is far from complete.

Even though the rail pattern is utilized in the regulation of transportation competition, several facets of monopoly regulation are not used in the control of competition. Specifically excluded are the long-and-short-haul clause, the Shreveport principle, the commodity clause, and the service elements except extensions. Most of these controls came about because of monopolistic control of the transportation market. On the other hand, the elements stressed in the control of transportation competition are entry, minimum rate control, inherent advantage, exemptions, carrier classification, safety, and liability. It should not be assumed, of course, that all these elements are necessarily consistent with one another.

In order to more clearly see the differences between monopoly regulation and regulation of transport competition, readers should compare and contrast the following summary with that at the end of Chapter 16.

Elements of Transportation Competition Control

Entry Controls

1. Entry is controlled to preserve competitive relationships, insure safe operation, and guarantee adequate financial health of carriers.
2. Established firms at the date of regulation are preserved by grandfather clauses.
3. New firms must secure certificates of public convenience and necessity, or permits.
4. New carriers, or those desiring to extend their services, must prove they are "fit, willing, and able" to serve and that the public interest will be served by their entry.
5. Carriers may operate only over specified routes and carry specified commodities.

Minimum Rate Control and Inherent Advantage

1. Minimum rates are controlled with the goal of limiting intramodal competition.
2. Minimum rates are controlled with the goal of limiting intermodal competition and preserving the inherent advantage of each mode.
3. Minimum rates of one carrier cannot be held up to a particular level to protect the traffic of any other mode.

Exemptions and Carrier Classification

1. For-hire carriers are classified in numerous ways according to operating characteristics, as common, contract, supplementary, or non-scheduled.
2. Numerous carriers are exempt according to type of commodity hauled, as agricultural commodities, bulk movement by water, newspaper haulers.
3. Numerous carriers are exempt according to geographic operating characteristics, as carriers wholly within one or contiguous municipalities, movement incidental to other transportation, carriers operating in national parks and monuments.
4. Private carriers moving their own goods where the primary business is other than transportation are exempt.

Safety and Liability Controls

1. Control over motor vehicle condition, hours of labor of drivers, and safety devices is allowed.
2. Control over aircraft, pilot training and pilot qualifications is provided.
3. Mandatory insurance provisions to protect shippers and the public are included.

Rates and Discrimination Controls

1. All rates must be just and reasonable. Regulatory bodies may suspend rates, determine reasonableness, and prescribe maximum and minimum rates.
2. Shippers must be treated equally if they have similar transportation circumstances and conditions. Undue preference and prejudice is prohibited.
3. Rates must be published and available to all. Public notice of rate changes is required. No deviation from published rates is allowed and rebates are illegal.

Security and Financial Controls

1. All accounts must be uniform and open for inspection.
2. Periodic and detailed financial reports must be rendered (although some classes of carriers are exempt from this requirement).
3. Changes in capital structure and the issuance of securities must be approved by regulatory authorities (with some exemptions).
4. Consolidations and mergers must be approved by regulatory authorities.

ADDITIONAL READINGS

1. Bigham, Truman C. and Merrill J. Roberts, **Transportation: Principles and Problems.** 2nd ed. New York: McGraw-Hill Book Co., Inc., 1952.
   Chapter 10. "Extension and Administration of Regulation," pp. 257–287.
2. Caves, Richard E., **Air Transport and Its Regulators.** Cambridge, Mass.: Harvard University Press, 1962.
   Part II. "Public Regulation," pp. 123–302.
3. Cherington, Paul W., **Airline Price Policy.** Boston: Graduate School of Business Administration, Harvard University, 1958.
   Chapter III. "The Regulatory Environment," pp. 74–135.
4. Daggett, Stuart, **Principles of Inland Transportation.** 4th ed. New York: Harper and Brothers, 1955.
   Chapter 32. "Inland Water Regulation," pp. 686–712.
   Chapter 33. "Air Regulation," pp. 713–738.
5. Fair, Marvin L. and Ernest W. Williams, Jr., **Economics of Transportation.** Rev. ed. New York: Harper and Brothers, 1959.
   Chapter 23. "Regulation of Domestic Water and Pipe-line Carriers," pp. 471–486.
   Chapter 25. "Regulation of Air Transportation," pp. 509–532.
6. Frederick, John H., **Commercial Air Transportation.** 5th ed. Homewood, Ill.: Richard D. Irwin, Inc., 1961.
   Chapter 4. "Regulatory Legislation," pp. 107–125.
   Chapter 6. "Civil Aeronautics Board Policy—Competition," pp. 142–162.
   Chapter 7. "Civil Aeronautics Board Policy—Competition, (continued)," pp. 163–197.
7. Friedlaender, Ann F., **The Dilemma of Freight Transportation Regulation.** Washington, D.C.: The Brookings Institution, 1969, 216 pp.
8. Harbeson, Robert W., "The Transportation Act of 1958," **Land Economics,** May 1959, pp. 156–171.

9. Hilton, George W., **The Transportation Act of 1958: A Decade of Experience.** Bloomington, Indiana: Indiana University Press, 1969, 262 pp.

10. Keyes, Lucile Sheppard, **Federal Control of Entry into Air Transportation.** Cambridge, Mass.: Harvard University Press, 1951.
Part II. "Regulatory Policy," pp. 59–306.

11. Koontz, Harold and Richard W. Gable, **Public Control of Economic Enterprise.** New York: McGraw-Hill Book Co., Inc., 1956.
Chapter 4. "Transport Regulation: Evolution of a Pattern," pp. 75–96.

12. Locklin, D. Philip, **Economics of Transportation.** 6th ed. Homewood, Ill.: Richard D. Irwin, Inc., 1966.
Chapter 34. "Regulation of Water Transportation," pp. 738–761.
Chapter 36. "Regulation of Air Transportation," pp. 789–829.

13. Norton, Hugh S., **Modern Transportation Economics.** Columbus, Ohio: Charles E. Merrill Books, Inc., 1963.
Chapter XI. "Evolution of Regulation, 1920–1958," pp. 193–203.
Chapter XV. "Regulation of Air Carriers," pp. 268–279.
Chapter XVI. "Regulation of Water Carriers, Pipeline and Indirect Carriers," pp. 280–288.

14. Pegrum, Dudley F., **Transportation: Economics and Public Policy.** Rev. ed. Homewood, Ill.: Richard D. Irwin, Inc., 1968.
Chapter 13. "Railroad Regulation Since World War I," pp. 312–333.
Chapter 15. "Regulation of Air, Water, and Pipe-line Transportation," pp. 361–392.

15. Richmond, Samuel B., **Regulation and Competition in Air Transportation.** New York: Columbia University Press, 1961, 309 pp.

16. Rose, Warren, "The Air Coach Policies of the Civil Aeronautics Board," **Transportation Journal,** Spring 1963, pp. 12–19.

17. Spychalski, John C., "On the Nonutility of Domestic Water Transport Regulation," **I.C.C. Practitioners' Journal,** November-December 1969, pp. 7–20.

18. Straszheim, Mahlon R., "Airline Profitability, Financing, and Public Regulation," **Transportation Journal,** Summer 1969, pp. 16–33.

19. Troxel, Emery, **Economics of Transport.** New York: Rinehart & Company, Inc., 1955.
Chapter 16. "More Public Controls," pp. 370– 393.
Chapter 17. "Public Control of Entries," pp. 394–417.

20. Westmeyer, Russell E., **Economics of Transportation.** Englewood Cliffs, N.J.: Prentice Hall, Inc., 1952.
Chapter 23. "Regulation of Domestic Water Transportation," pp. 481–497.
Chapter 27. "Regulation of Air Transportation," pp. 565–586.

19

Regulatory Institutions

Understanding how society has regulated transportation monopoly and competition does not end by simply learning how the regulations are implemented. This involves the study of regulatory institutions and their structure, jurisdiction, and procedure.

The term "institution" may be used in various ways. When one uses it in conjunction with "economic" or "social," it is usually taken to mean the rules of society. These rules include customs, laws, techniques, practices, and all sorts of ways in which the group or society organizes to gain its common goals. The last two chapters have been involved in explaining the development of such transportation rules or institutions for transportation.

When one speaks of a university, a court of law, or a governmental agency as an "institution," however, he is using the term to mean a specific thing, body, or device. Often this "thing" implements various economic or social rules or institutions. In this chapter, we shall be using the term "institution" principally in this second sense of a specific thing used to implement or put into practice the social or economic rules or regulation.

In domestic transportation there are four main regulatory institutions: Commissions and Boards, Courts, the Legislative process, and the Executive. Each will be considered in turn.

COMMISSIONS AND BOARDS

While there is a great deal of overlapping and confusion between regulatory institutions, the most important and unique of the group is the administrative commission. This particular institution has antecedents in the early attempts of society to regulate by way of investigation prior to the Civil War. These early commissions, mentioned in Chapter 2, were important particularly in New England. The investigatory commission was followed by Granger Commissions, sometimes called "western commissions" or "strong commissions," which were established in the post-Civil War era of state regulation. These direct ancestors of the present-day regulatory commissions had great power under the law not only to investigate, but also to enforce. Within the broad scope of jurisdiction set down by the legislature, these boards and commissions became a law in themselves. Much of the organization, jurisdiction, approach, and procedure of these state Granger Commissions carried over into the Federal regulatory commissions of modern times.

A commission or board as a regulatory institution is unique. If society wishes to lay down rules in other economies, it does so either by passing specific laws which directly govern the behavior of private enterprise or, more frequently, by instituting public enterprise and ownership. In the American economy, we have a tradition of maintaining private enterprise but regulating it through the medium of commissions or boards created by the people through their legislature or assembly. While the legislative process will be discussed more fully later, it should be noted that commissions are generally creations of legislatures and are granted broad policy limits within which they independently develop specific regulations and procedures.

In considering the various commissions and boards involved in implementing transportation regulation, it should be clear that there are two levels of control, Federal and state. This comes from our political structure as well as from the differentiation between interstate and intrastate commerce. Both levels have commissions and boards, although with different jurisdictions. To a surprising degree, the procedures and approaches at each level are quite similar. Conflict between these levels, however, is not only possible, but provides one of the ever-present difficulties of transportation regulation.

The Federal Level

Domestic transportation regulatory institutions at the Federal level are two in number: the Interstate Commerce Commission, and the Civil Aeronautics Board. The first is the oldest of all Federal commissions and regulates a number of modes of transportation. The second is relatively new and is principally concerned with economic regulation of air transportation.

The Interstate Commerce Commission

As described in Chapter 16, the Interstate Commerce Commission was created by the initial Act to Regulate Commerce in 1887. As the first regulatory institution at the Federal level, the I.C.C. pioneered the development of regulation. Much of its procedure and approach has been used by subsequent boards and commissions. Likewise, the structure, functions, and role of the I.C.C. have served as a pattern for subsequent regulatory institutions at both the Federal and state levels. Therefore, by examining the Interstate Commerce Commission in some detail, one can learn the basic elements of all similar regulatory institutions.

The I.C.C. illustrates a usually preferred structure of a commission. It has an odd number of commissioners serving long-term staggered appointments, and with a division of political affiliation. The eleven commissioners are appointed by the President with the consent and approval of the Senate for terms of seven years. No more than two commissioners fulfill their term of office in any one year unless a commissioner resigns. The seven-year term makes it almost impossible for one President to appoint a majority of the Commission. Further, the law provides that no more than six of the eleven commissioners may be from the same political party. Since 1970, the President designates the Chairman of the Commission.

The function of a commission is to be an independent body of experts providing administration of the regulatory statutes. Independence comes from the fact that commissions generally are created and directed in a broad policy sense by the legislature, but appointed by the executive. The I.C.C. reports to Congress and is not considered a part of the "administration," even though the President has an opportunity to appoint its members. Removal of a commissioner is difficult during his term. He is protected much as judges are protected. The I.C.C. has a fine reputation for expert and highly qualified commissioners well acquainted with their tasks.

Legislatures and courts are ill-equipped to carry on continuous regulation of an expedient nature to promote the public welfare and prevent abuses. The legislature, meeting only periodically and made up of constantly changing personnel, is unable to act in an administrative fashion even if it should contain the desired degree of expertise. Courts cannot administer laws directly since they can act only on the issues brought before them. Further, they are extremely busy with many other matters and do not have the opportunity to become specialized in regulation. Commissions can act upon their own motion and do have the attributes of continuity, expediency, promotion, preventativeness, specialization, and concern with broad public welfare.

The role of the Interstate Commerce Commission basically is to administer the law. However, it has a judicial and a legislative function as well. Indeed, students of administrative law have often pointed out that a commission exercises some of all the three roles of administrator, judge, and legislator.

By applying the general policy and enforcing the rules of the game as established by Congress, the Commission acts in an executive capacity. The making of rules, the extension of operating authority, and the establishment of rates are examples of the Commission's legislative function. The hearing of evidence, the determination of what is "just and reasonable" or "unduly preferential or prejudicial" are examples of its judicial function.

In order to accomplish its task, the Interstate Commerce Commission is divided into three divisions, each division having three members. The Chairman and Vice Chairman do not serve on any particular division. Division One, the Operating Rights Division, is concerned with the issuance of certificates and permits to motor carriers, brokers, water carriers and freight forwarders. Division Two, the Rates, Tariffs and Valuation Division, handles all rates and charges, the valuation of rail and pipeline property for rate-setting purposes, and tariffs. Division Three, the Finance and Service Division, has jurisdiction over carrier securities, consolidations and mergers, purchases and acquisitions of control of carriers, discontinuation of service and other service matters. It should be stressed that the divisions handle matters of general transportation interest. The divisions often act as appeal boards, the initial decision having been made by one of the several "employee boards" of the Commission. (Divisions are made up of commissioners, while boards are staffed by certain categories of high-ranking Civil Service employees of the Commission.) Decisions of these boards may be appealed to the appropriate division. Matters assigned to the boards do not involve taking testimony at public hearings. Matters which the Commission considers to be of "general transportation importance" are handled by the Commission itself.

Proceedings before the Commission can be either formal or informal. The informal complaint is usually handled entirely by mail and does not involve an appearance before the body. The formal complaint, on the other hand, is a carefully drawn document which is usually supported by evidence in a public hearing. Typically, formal complaints are heard by an examiner who holds the hearing, collects evidence, "makes the record" on the matter, and renders his finding. If the finding is acceptable, the order recommended by the hearing examiner becomes a commission order. However, appeal to a division of the Commission, and even to the full Commission in cases of general transportation importance, is possible. Finally, orders of the Commission may be appealed on certain grounds to a court of law.

The Commission maintains its own "bar." That is, it specifies who may appear or practice before it. Persons desiring to take cases before the Commission must have various educational and technical qualifications in order to be admitted to the Commission bar. A total of 33,896 persons were admitted to practice before the Commission from 1929 to 1970. Thirty per cent were non-lawyers who qualified by educational and technical grounds and passed a competitive national examination given by the Commission twice a year.

The case load of the I.C.C. is large. During a recent year, 7,436 formal proceedings were received by the Commission and final action was taken on 8,122 cases. Many cases pending before the Commission are carried over into following years. During the year noted above, 4,704 cases were pending at the end of the year. This large formal case load is in addition to numerous informal complaints.

The Commission has gone through an extensive reorganization during recent years in an attempt to streamline procedures and modernize its organization. Additionally, the formation of the Department of Transportation caused a shift of some of the work of the I.C.C. to the new Department. Internally, the Commission is organized into four staff offices (Office of Proceedings, Office of

Managing Director, Office of the General Counsel, and Office of the Secretary),
along with the offices of the Chairman and Vice-Chairman, and five bureaus
(Bureau of Accounts, Bureau of Enforcement, Bureau of Operations, Bureau of
Traffic, and Bureau of Economics), and six Regional Managers.

Figure 25 shows the internal structure of the Commission. These offices
and bureaus carry on the huge task of administering transportation regulation
on a day-to-day basis, developing reports on transportation, and assisting both
the public and the carriers with their transportation regulatory problems. The
Commission maintains field offices in 79 cities, and during a recent year had
more than 1,800 employees and received operating appropriations of $27.6 mil-
lion.

The scope of the authority of the I.C.C. has been summarized in a government report as follows:

(1) to issue certificates of public convenience and necessity for the construction, extension and abandonment of lines of railroads; certificates of public
convenience and necessity for the establishment or extension of motor common
carriers and water common carrier operations; the issuance of permits for the
institution and extension of motor contract carrier operations, water contract
carrier operations, and freight forwarder operations; (2) to require that rates
and practices of all common carriers, including freight forwarders, subject to
the act be just, reasonable, and nondiscriminatory, and that such rates be published, filed with the Commission and observed; and to require that motor contract carriers and water contract carriers establish and observe just and reasonable minimum rates; (3) to regulate railroads and motor carriers, including
private carriers by motor vehicles, with respect to safety of operations, standards of equipment, and hours of service of personnel whose activities affect
safety of operations; (4) to require personal injury, death, and property damage insurance of motor carriers and freight forwarders for the protection of
the public and cargo insurance for the protection of shippers; (5) to pass upon
the unification, mergers, and common control of two or more railroads, motor
carriers, water carriers, express companies or sleeping car companies, and to
approve or disapprove the pooling or division of traffic, service or earnings by
two or more such carriers; (6) to regulate the issuance of securities by railroads and motor carriers, the financial reorganization of railroads, and the
guarantee of loans to railroads; (7) to prescribe regulations governing the packaging, marking and handling of explosives and other dangerous articles which
are binding upon all carriers subject to the Interstate Commerce Act and shippers, and which regulations as to marking and packing are adopted by the
Coast Guard for application to water carriers; and (8) to investigate alleged
violations, prosecute in court and assist the Department of Justice in prosecut-
ing civil and criminal proceedings arising under all parts of the act and related
acts such as the Elkins Act, the Clayton Antitrust Act, and the Transportation
of Explosives Act. (*Independent Regulatory Commissions*, Special Subcommittee on Legislative Oversight of Committee on Interstate and Foreign Commerce, Subcommittee Print, 86th Congress, 2nd Session, Dec. 1960).

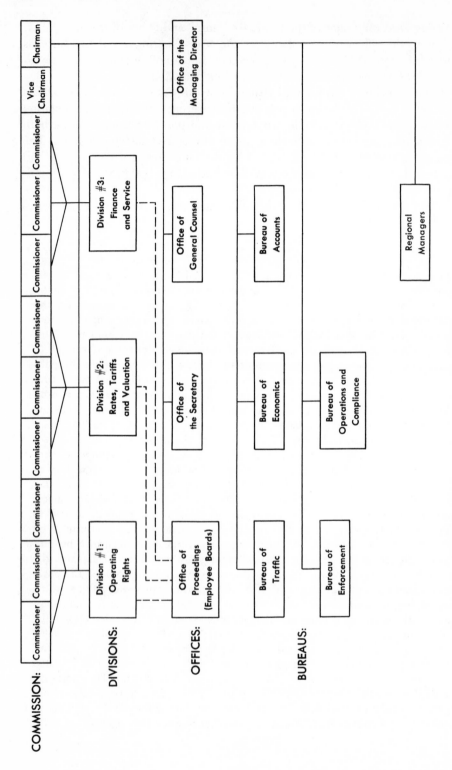

Figure 25: Organization of the Interstate Commerce Commission.

In addition, the I.C.C. prescribes time zones under the Standard Time Act, determines reasonableness of parcel post rates, and performs several miscellaneous other duties in connection with surface transportation.

By noting these very diverse and complicated duties, one can readily appreciate not only the great power and influence of the I.C.C. on surface transportation, but also the immense responsibility of the Commission to the public and the carriers. Undoubtedly the Interstate Commerce Commission is the most important regulatory institution in domestic transportation.

The Civil Aeronautics Board

The Civil Aeronautics Board is a second major regulatory institution at the Federal level. This Board was created in 1938 with the passage of the Civil Aeronautics Act, as discussed in Chapter 18. While a number of organizational changes have taken place during its life, basically the C.A.B. is a specialized institution concerned with the economic regulation of air transportation only in contrast to the I.C.C. which is a general regulatory institution concerned with all surface transportation.

It should be emphasized that the Civil Aeronautics Board is an economic regulatory institution in the same sense as the Interstate Commerce Commission in that it regulates the economic climate in which carriers operate. The Federal Aviation Agency, to be discussed below, has a more specialized role than the C.A.B. as it affects transportation mainly by making rules which affect the operations of the carriers and their personnel, and by operating the airways.

The Civil Aeronautics Board has a structure similar to the I.C.C. It is made up of five members appointed by the President with the consent and approval of the Senate. Members of the Board serve six years with their terms staggered so that rarely can one President appoint the full Board. No more than three of the five members may be from the same political party. The President designates the Chairman and Vice Chairman of the C.A.B. each year. Because of its structure, the C.A.B. is considered an independent regulatory institution just as the I.C.C., and it carries on many of the same judicial, legislative, and administrative roles.

To accomplish its tasks, the Civil Aeronautics Board is organized into eight offices (Office of the Secretary, Office of Community and Congressional Relations, Office of Information, Office of the General Counsel, Office of Administrative Services, Office of the Comptroller, Office of Personnel and Security, and Office of Management and Programs) and six bureaus (Bureau of Hearing Examiners, Bureau of Accounts and Statistics, Bureau of Economics, Bureau of Enforcement, Bureau of International Affairs, and Bureau of Operating Rights). The reader can note the similarity to the I.C.C. pattern (see Figure 26).

However, in one important aspect the Civil Aeronautics Board differs from the Interstate Commerce Commission. While the I.C.C. is principally remedial in character, the C.A.B. is both remedial and promotional. As developed in Chapter 18, the C.A.B. was charged with the development and promotion of

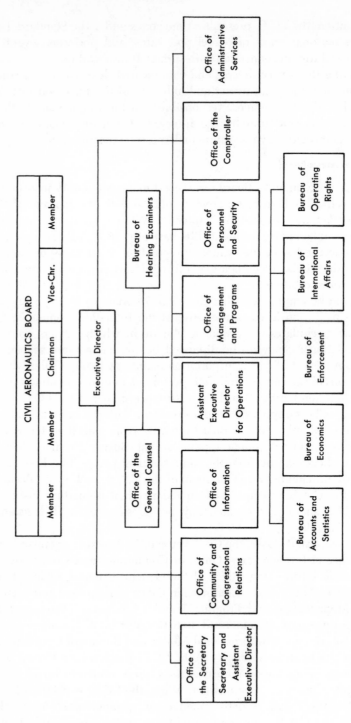

Figure 26: Organization of the Civil Aeronautics Board.

air transportation as well as its regulation. This dual role can be seen in the internal structure of the Board.

The procedure for cases before the Civil Aeronautics Board is quite similar to that of the Interstate Commerce Commission with two exceptions. One, much more use is made of the informal procedure and complaint. More than eighty per cent of the matters appearing before the Board use the informal method. For example, during a recent year, informal procedures accounted for more than 3,600 of the 3,900 matters brought before the Board. Two, the C.A.B. does not use "employee boards" to handle the mass of detail necessary for regulation and for matters "not of general transportation importance." Since a considerably smaller number of carriers are involved in air transportation than in surface transportation; the case load is less and the amount of detail is less. Even so, during a recent year 3,902 matters were brought to the Board and final action was taken on 4,043 cases (with 1,041 cases carried over as pending). The C.A.B. staff is made up of more than 650 persons, and the Board has an annual appropriation of more than $11 million.

Regulatory responsibilities of the C.A.B. are similar to those of the I.C.C. Briefly, it approves rates and fares, controls mergers and intercarrier agreements and relationships, and regulates accounting and tariff practices. A very important task of the C.A.B. is to award routes to domestic air carriers and to watch out for the interests of the United States in IATA (the International Air Transport Association). In this activity, the Board has a voice in determining overseas air fares and practices. It also has a role in the awarding of permission to foreign airlines to serve the United States. In addition, it determines subsidies and public service revenues, and is concerned with certain kinds of loan guarantees for carriers. While these major activities stress the remedial role of the agency, it is apparent that the promotional role is also important.

The dual role of the Civil Aeronautics Board is not an easy one. Much criticism has been leveled at it because of its activities protecting the public, its lack of action to protect the public, actions to promote carriers, and lack of action to promote carriers. Indeed, there is real question whether both remedial and promotional roles can be carried out by the same Board at the same time. Nevertheless, the C.A.B. has played and continues to play a most significant and important part in domestic transportation.

The State Level

As noted previously, regulation at the state level actually antedated Federal regulation, and much of the state regulatory experience served as a testing ground for subsequent Federal regulation.

Every state and the District of Columbia has a state regulatory commission or board. Because there are so many of these commissions, only broad general statements can be made about their jurisdiction, organization, membership, and procedure. Each state commission is a study in itself. However, since the state level of control is quite important to some portions of domestic transportation, a general understanding of this regulation is essential. It should be noted at the outset, though, that transportation regulation is only a part of the control functions of state commissions. They also regulate various other businesses "affected with the public interest" (that is, public utilities). In fact, in many state commissions, transport regulation plays a relatively minor role as compared to the regulation of these other industries.

Of the fifty-one state commissions, the typical size is a three-man group. Thirty-eight state commissions are made up of three persons, eight states have five-man commissions, two use seven-man commissions, two use one-man commissions, and one state has an eight-man commission. Typically, commissioners serve for six years (in staggered terms), although a tenure of four years is also popular. Some serve as long as ten years, a few serve seven years, and on one commission the term is three years. In thirty-five states commissioners are appointed, usually by the Governor with the approval or consent of the State Senate (the House or Assembly approves in some states rather than the Senate). Fourteen states elect their commissioners by popular vote, and two states allow the legislature to elect the commission.

State regulatory commissions are especially important in the motor-transportation field in two ways. First, it will be recalled that when the Motor Carrier Act was passed in 1935, Congress specifically denied the Interstate Commerce Commission jurisdiction over intrastate motor carriers operating legally under the jurisdiction of a state regulatory agency. It was also pointed out in Chapter 17 that the Federal act to regulate motor carriers evolved out of a long struggle to control these carriers effectively at the state level. Thus it is obvious that state control was quite well developed in this area prior to Federal control.

Most states require motor carriers of persons or property to secure certificates of public convenience and necessity if they are common carriers and permits if they are contract carriers. The procedure for showing that the carrier is fit, willing, and able is similar to Federal procedures. Intrastate rates are likewise controlled, and various reports, accounting, and financial controls are often exercised. Additionally, insurance provisions are common. It should be emphasized that state commissions control only the intrastate portion of carrier operations, although the line between interstate and intrastate is sometimes hard to draw.

Second, state regulatory commissions are important in the motor-carrier field because of joint boards. In recognition of the state regulatory structure, as well as to simplify the Federal regulatory task, the Motor Carrier Act of 1935 allowed these boards. It will be recalled from Chapter 17 that where a matter involves three states or less, a joint board composed of representatives of the state regulatory agencies in the states involved may act for the I.C.C. Appeal to the Federal commission is allowed, of course, but in many matters the joint boards are quite important.

State regulatory commissions were very important in the past in the area of rail transportation and are still important where the movement is primarily intrastate in character. Since many bulky raw materials move primarily in intrastate commerce, many shippers and carriers find that they must appear before state commissions. In the railroad-passenger field, and especially its abandonments, state commissions until recently have been most important. They exercised principal jurisdiction over this aspect of service until the Transportation Act of 1958.

Since there is little intrastate commerce in air, water, or pipeline transportation, most state regulatory commissions have had but a minor role in the regulation of these modes. Occasionally, in large states such as California or Texas, intrastate air operations are important. Typically, however, state control of transportation has been in the motor and rail modes, with motor by far the most important.

COURTS

A second major regulatory institution is the courts or the judicial process. Again there are two levels of control, Federal and state. However, the distinction between the Federal and state court levels is not as sharp as it is in terms of commissions. It is feasible, therefore, to consider both Federal and state courts as a single regulatory institution.

Role of the Courts

In a very real sense, courts may be considered partners of commissions in transportation regulation. Typically, a commission has no power to enforce its own orders and must rely on the courts for this. In this the two institutions are partners. On the other hand, courts can and do review commission decisions (on certain grounds). Here the two institutions may be at variance with each other. Thus, in general the role of the courts is an independent one which may or may not be in harmony with the commissions.

Basically, the role of courts may be summarized under four main headings: Constitutional interpretation, Congressional interpretation, an enforcement role, and an adjudicative role.

Constitutional Interpretation

A primary role of the judicial process in our country is that of interpreting the Constitution. This is the principal function of the United States Supreme Court for all economic activity. The separation of powers between the executive and the legislative branches is one area in which the role of constitutional interpretation comes into play. Where conflict exists between the two branches, the courts are the final arbitrators of what the Constitution means. Administrative commissions, existing somewhere between (yet somewhat independent of) both administrative and legislative branches, are particularly involved here.

Provisions of the Fifth and Fourteenth Amendments protecting property are prime areas of constitutional interpretation. An individual may not be deprived of his property without due process of law under these amendments, and the courts decide when these amendments have been violated. The courts, therefore, are constantly called upon to interpret the Constitution and its application to the ever-changing social and economic scene. This is of particular importance when a commission is dealing with prices, such as transportation rates.

Further, our governmental system is a dual one based on both Federal and state levels. Congress has been given the power to regulate "commerce among the several states" under the Constitution (Article I, Section 8 (3)). Power to control commerce not included in that phrase normally resides with the states. The actual determination of what is to be considered interstate commerce (under Federal control) and what is to be considered intrastate commerce (under state control) is a matter for judicial interpretation.

Congressional Interpretation

Even when Congress is quite explicit in its statutes, disagreement often arises when a law is applied. More often than not, this disagreement is over the exact meaning or interpretation of the law. Here again the courts have an important role to play. Basically it is the courts who determine the intent of Congress and settle disputes as to the meaning and application of laws. As far as transportation is concerned, it has been the courts over the years who have been the final arbitrators of the meaning of the Act to Regulate Commerce. The same may be said for the state courts in interpreting the meaning of state regulatory statutes.

At the Federal level, for example, it was the courts who interpreted what was meant by an "agricultural commodity" under the exemption in the 1935 Motor Carrier Act. This interpretation defined the law and in this particular case, Congress found it advisable to return to this question in the Transportation Act of 1958. This is an example of Congress becoming dissatisfied with the court's interpretation of Congressional intent and basically redefining its terms. Nevertheless, the task of interpreting the law is a basic one for the courts.

Enforcement Role

As mentioned above, the Interstate Commerce Commission has no power to enforce its own orders. It must go before the courts and solicit a writ of injunction or writ of mandamus for enforcement. Likewise, the I.C.C. cannot impose penalties for violations of the law. The Interstate Commerce Act specifically authorizes the courts to issue injunctions to prevent violations of

Commission orders. Similarly, the Elkins Act authorizes the courts to enforce observance of published tariffs. Fines for not heeding commission orders or for violating various acts are provided in the law. However, it is the courts who impose the prescribed penalties and enforce the law.

Adjudicative Role

Finally, the courts have a primary role in dealing with litigation arising out of the application of regulatory statutes. Hearing cases on violations of the acts is a part of this role. However, it is well to remember that certain common-law obligations of carriers also exist. Here again, the courts act as adjudicator. Likewise, damages and reparations, both those awarded by the I.C.C. and those granted under the common law concept of liability, are matters for the courts to enforce and award.

Review of Commission Decisions

The role of the courts in reviewing commission decisions is a combination of interpretation and adjudication. As noted in Chapter 16, review of commission decisions shortly after the original Act to Regulate Commerce was passed made the law meaningless for a period of time. A major rationale of court review is to place a limit upon commissions. An administrative commission has very broad powers and could act in an arbitrary and unreasonable fashion. The courts protect against this possibility.

Originally there was some concern over the delegation of the powers of Congress to control commerce to an administrative body. The Constitution specifically prohibits Congress from delegating its powers to others. However, where adequate standards to guide the administrative commission have been set forth by the legislature, such a delegation of power has been held to be constitutional. These standards may be broad ones such as "rates must be just and reasonable" in the Interstate Commerce Act. But without "limitations of a prescribed standard," Congress cannot delegate its powers (*United States v. Milwaukee Railroad,* 282 U.S. 311, 1931).

Within these broad standards, though, the commission determines matters of fact. That is, the Interstate Commerce Commission has primary jurisdiction to determine what is "just and reasonable" or what is "unduly prejudicial or preferential." Over time the I.C.C. has set up careful procedures and definitions of these terms. The courts on matters of review have generally accepted the commission determination of "facts" and have restricted themselves, at least in recent times, to "matters of law."

But this does not mean that judicial review of commission findings is not possible. It merely means that the courts ordinarily will review a commission's decision only on certain limited grounds, primarily "matters of law." These grounds for judicial interference can be summarized under the five headings of constitutionality, jurisdiction, procedure, evidence, and capricious and arbitrary actions.

The constitutionality of regulatory statutes is always a matter for judicial review. This ground for judicial interference, while it is often cited, has not been a generally successful one. The plea that a commission has exceeded its jurisdiction or has misinterpreted the law is more often used. Again, the exact meaning of a statute (a common ground for appeal) is a matter for the courts to decide.

Review because of incorrect procedure is also important. Basically, this involves such matters as proper notice, knowledge of alleged violations, right of counsel and a fair hearing, and other constitutional guarantees of individual rights. Likewise, a commission decision must be made upon substantial evidence and cannot be contrary to the finding of fact involved in the particular case. That is, a regulatory agency cannot act in an arbitrary or capricious fashion and must be able to sustain by fact the reason for its actions. Again, the limitation upon commission action is self-evident.

In summary, it may be said that the courts play a very important role as regulators of transportation. Not only do they act as a limitation upon commission action, but they also act as enforcers and give commission action its basic strength. In their interpretative role, they actually regulate carriers and shippers; while in their role of review, they attempt to set bounds beyond which the commission may not go. In general, they try to protect the rights of all parties. They are indeed a most important regulatory institution in domestic transportation.

THE LEGISLATIVE PROCESS

A third regulatory institution in domestic transportation is the legislature and the legislative process. It is essentially Congressional action with which we are concerned here, but the same concepts of the legislature as a regulatory institution apply equally at the state level.

Congress, or any legislature, acts as a regulatory institution in three ways. It is a promulgator of general transportation policy by way of statute enactment, a creator of commissions (and a delegator of authority to them) and an appropriator of funds to implement regulation. By its actions or lack of actions in each of these three general functions, the legislature acts as a regulator.

General Policy

The transportation policy of the nation is promulgated initially by Congressional action. What is and is not included in these regulatory acts sets the stage for commissions and the climate within which transportation operates. The development of transportation regulation described in the three previous chapters is an illustration of this legislative function.

Delegation of Authority

Congress creates the various commissions and boards which implement its regulatory laws. How these commissions are established, their jurisdiction and powers, their organization and make-up all are part of the legislative process acting as a regulatory institution. The matter of delegation of authority has been mentioned above. Here again the standards or guidelines established in creating a commission are of primary importance. Commissions are creatures of the legislature, and it is from them that commission jurisdiction and authority are derived.

Appropriation of Funds

Once established, commissions must look to the legislature for financial support. Appropriations to operate commissions come principally from the legislature. While fees may be charged (and may be an important source of financial support, particularly for some state commissions), the major source of commission income is the annual legislative appropriations. Some appropriations for the Federal commissions have already been noted.

Procedures

Typically, legislatures act through committees. In the United States Congress, the Senate and House Interstate and Foreign Commerce committees are the most important for regulatory purposes. New legislative proposals are referred to these committees, hearings are held to ascertain opinion on changes in the regulatory climate, and compromises are worked out. Committee members, especially where long service on the committee is involved, become very expert on transportation matters, and new regulatory laws often carry the name of the Chairman of the Senate or House Committee.

On some occasions, the Congressional committees have sponsored special studies of transportation problems. Here the committee staff becomes important. The much-quoted so-called "Doyle report" (*National Transportation Policy*, Report of the Commerce Committee of the U.S. Senate, Report No. 445, 87th Congress, 1961) is an example of a Congressional Committee study of the whole transportation system.

The process of writing regulatory statutes, creating commissions, granting them authority, appropriating funds to implement their operations, hearing proposals for new laws, and working out compromise solutions to current transportation problems is all an integral part of transportation regulation.

THE EXECUTIVE

The final regulatory institution is the executive. Basically he recommends legislation and administers or carries out the statutes set down by the legislature. In our economy, the executive branch of government has become more and more powerful as society has become more complex and interrelated.

As a regulatory institution, the executive exercises four important powers which affect transportation. These are the power of appointment, the power of enforcement, the power of investigation, and the power of recommendation.

Power of Appointment

The executive appoints members of the regulatory commissions. On the Federal level, this gives the President the power to influence transportation regulation. (On the state level, this power does not exist in all states as we have already seen. However, in most of the states it does exist, and governors have the ability to influence state transportation regulation.) This power is not without limitation, however. Because of the organization of commissions, no one executive ordinarily can appoint a majority of a commission. Even so, this power is a real and important one.

Whom the President appoints to the I.C.C., or C.A.B. can be quite important. Commissioners' background, knowledge, and qualifications affect regulation. Many appointees, particularly to the I.C.C., have been excellently qualified and have served long terms by way of reappointment. Unfortunately, politics has a role in commission appointments, and sometimes persons have been appointed not so much for what they could contribute to effective regulation as because of political debts or pressures. This unfortunate situation seems to have existed more at the state than at the Federal level.

The power of appointment is further limited at the Federal level by the provision that only a bare majority of the I.C.C. or C.A.B. can be from one political party. However, this is not too often an effective actual limitation since members of the opposite political party can usually be found who agree with a President.

Power of Enforcement

As noted above, the orders of a commission must be enforced by a court. It is the Department of Justice who represents the I.C.C. or C.A.B. before the court to secure this enforcement. Likewise, it is the Attorney General who must defend the Commission in any legal action. Hence, the executive branch has the power to initiate enforcement, and how it proceeds can be very important to effective transportation regulation.

Power of Investigation

The executive's power of investigation has become of increasing importance during recent times. A whole series of studies and investigations by various departments or appointive groups of the executive branch have been made since World War II. The Sawyer Report, the Weeks Report, and the Mueller Report, all named for the Secretaries of Commerce who supervised their preparation, are examples of this power of investigation. The Landis Report and the Hoover Commission Reports are examples of the work of appointive groups from the executive branch who have investigated transportation regulation. Finally, the rather extensive investigations of both air and surface safety, experiments in urban transportation and high speed rail sytems, and the like, undertaken by the Department of Transportation, are prime examples of the power of investigation.

Power of Recommendation

Another power exercised by the executive is that of recommendation to Congress. Basically, this takes two forms: budgetary and policy. Although Congress appropriates the funds to operate regulatory commissions, it is the executive branch which draws up the budget and recommends the appropriations. All of the commissions are included within the Federal budget and must submit their requests to the Bureau of the Budget. By action or lack of action within the general budgetary framework as laid down by the President, regulatory commissions may be affected.

The power of executive recommendation on the policy level has been of primary importance. One need only recall that it was President Grant whose recommendations caused Congress to establish the Windom Committee and President Theodore Roosevelt who called for the Hepburn Act. In more recent times, President Kennedy's historic "transportation message" of April 1962 is an excellent example of the power of recommendation. In this instance, a special message was sent to Congress recommending rather substantial revisions in transportation regulation. Not only was this the first time that a President had singled out transportation regulation for a special message (not embodied in his general message), but most of the proposed changes in transportation regulation in recent times have been derived from that message. Finally, President Johnson's transportation message in 1966, which recommended the establishment of the Department of Transportation, probably is one of the best examples of how the power of recommendation under certain circumstances can have a major impact on transportation.

The Department of Transportation

Unlike the Kennedy message, the Johnson "transportation message" of March 1966 did not propose sweeping changes in economic regulation. Instead, it dealt mainly with safety, technological research, and internal federal reorganization and regrouping of existing agencies dealing with these matters and with promotional activities. Its most significant recommendation was for the creation of a new cabinet-level Department of Transportation. This was not a new proposal. Similar suggestions were made at least as early as the 1870's, and at least nine serious similar recommendations had been made during the previous thirty years. This time, however, Congress acted and created the twelfth cabinet department.

Basically, the creation of the Department of Transportation (D.O.T.) did two things. First, it initially brought together under one cabinet official all or parts of eleven major agencies or functions, and about twenty less important ones, primarily concerned with research, promotional, safety, or administrative aspects of transportation. Subsequent action has added other operating agencies, such as the Urban Mass Transit Administration in 1968, but it should be noted that the vast majority of the parts of D.O.T. came from already existing agencies (see Figure 27). Hence, the first major task of the new Department was to coordinate the executive functions of these many agencies of the government dealing with transportation and related matters.

The second major task of D.O.T. is a planning, research, and recommendation function. Section 2 of the Department of Transportation Act of 1966 set forth several objectives in this connection. The Department is charged not only to "assure the coordinated, effective administration of the transportation programs of the Federal government," but also "to facilitate the development and improvement of coordinated, effective transportation service, to be provided by private enterprise to the maximum extent feasible," "to encourage cooperation of Federal, State and local governments, carriers, labor, and other interested parties toward the achievement of national transportation objectives," "to stimulate technological advances in transportation," "to provide general leadership in the identification and solution of transportation problems," and "to develop and recommend to the President and the Congress for approval national transportation policies and programs to accomplish these objectives with full and appropriate consideration of the needs of the public, users, carriers, industry, labor and the national defense." (See Public Law 89–670, October 15, 1966.) The planning, research and recommendation functions of D.O.T. are quite obvious.

In order to facilitate its goals, the Department is organized into seven operating divisions and six administrative divisions. The law provided for assistant secretaries for Administration, Research and Technology, Urban Systems and Environment, Policy and International Affairs, and Public Affairs, as well as a General Counsel. The operating divisions are the United States Coast Guard, Federal Highway Administration, Federal Aviation Administration, Federal Railroad Administration, Urban Mass Transportation Administration, St. Lawrence Seaway Development Corporation, and the National Highway Safety Bureau. (See Figure 28.)

Actually, very few new powers were given to D.O.T. Rather, its formation brought many existing scattered powers and programs together into one organization, under a single head, where hopefully better coordination and more effective results can be obtained. To a considerable extent, the actual effectiveness of the Department will depend upon its head—that is, upon his ability to bring about coordination among diverse interest groups of federal and state officials, carriers, and shippers, as well as his ability to obtain firm backing from the President and to "sell" his Department's (the administration's) transportation proposals to Congress. It may be expected, of course, that additional powers, either new or presently existing in other agencies, will be given the Department by legislation or reorganization from time to time.

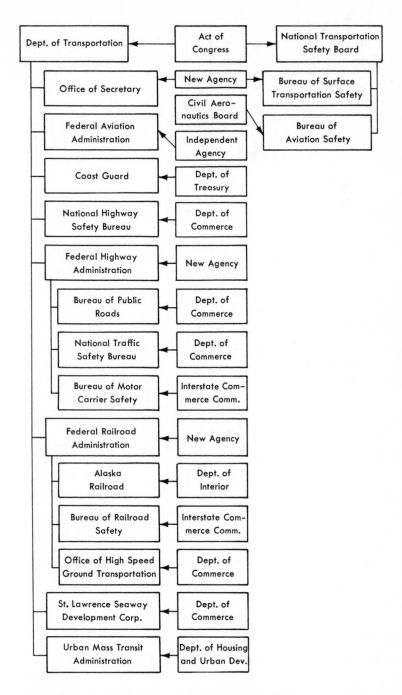

Figure 27: Origin Chart, Department of Transportation.

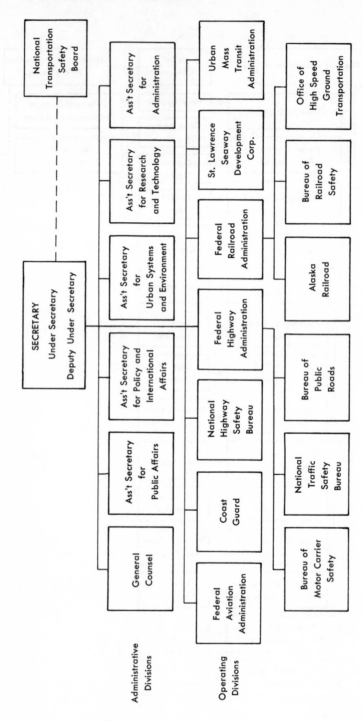

Figure 28: Organization of the Department of Transportation.

Although the Department of Transportation is new, it is the fifth largest in size among our cabinet departments. It has almost 100,000 employees, with 3,000 field offices in the United States and 40 offices abroad. Its annual budget during its first years was around $6 billion, but as emphasis on transportation research, experimentation and planning increases, considerably larger budgets no doubt will become common.

Some idea of the extent of the operational aspects of the various operating divisions of D.O.T. can be obtained by considering the budget allocations for each of these divisions for the 1970 fiscal year. These were:

Federal Aviation Administration	$1,139 million
U.S. Coast Guard	571 million
Urban Mass Transportation Administration	222 million
Federal Highway Administration	37 million
Office of the Secretary	24 million
Federal Railroad Administration	15 million
Other miscellaneous agencies	310 million

The remainder of the year's $6.6 billion budget was in highway aid funds.

Since national transportation safety has become such an important public issue, the Act establishing the Department of Transportation also established an autonomous agency called the National Transportation Safety Board. This five-man independent board, appointed by the President, each member with a five-year term, reports directly to Congress. The National Transportation Safety Board has the authority to investigate and issue reports and to review continually safety in all transport modes. The Board works closely with the Department of Transportation on safety matters, and uses D.O.T. personnel in some of its investigations. Its budget is around $4.5 million annually, and it has about 260 employees. It should be emphasized, though, that the Board is separate from the Department of Transportation even though it was created by the same Congressional Act which created D.O.T.

ADDITIONAL READINGS

1. Bigham, Truman C. and Merrill J. Roberts, **Transportation: Principles and Problems.** 2nd ed. New York: McGraw-Hill Book Co., Inc., 1952.
   Chapter 10. "Extension and Administration of Regulation," pp. 257–287.
2. Bunke, Harvey C., "A Critical Analysis of Some Aspects of Interstate Commerce Commission Policy," **Land Economics**, May 1956, pp. 134–143.
3. Daggett, Stuart, **Principles of Inland Transportation.** 4th ed. New York: Harper and Brothers, 1955.
   Chapter 27. "The Legal Basis for Regulatory Control," pp. 569–586.
   Chapter 28. "State Regulation," pp. 587–611.
   Chapter 29. "Federal Regulation—Interstate Commerce Commission: Expenditures and Organization," pp. 612–638.

4. Davis, Grant M., **The Department of Transportation.** Lexington, Mass.: D.C. Heath, 1970.
5. Locklin, D. Philip, **Economics of Transportation.** 6th ed. Homewood, Ill.: Richard D. Irwin, Inc., 1966.
   Chapter 14. "Agencies of Control," pp. 263–290.
6. Norton, Hugh S., **Modern Transportation Economics.** Columbus, Ohio: Charles E. Merrill Books, Inc., 1963.
   Chapter XII. "The Administrative Agencies of Control and Their Policy Making Role," pp. 204–234.
   Chapter XXIII. "Regulation in the Modern Economy, Problems and Policy Issues," pp. 406–426.
7. Norton, Hugh S., "National Transportation Policy and Regulation," **Public Utilities Fortnightly,** April 9, 1964, pp. 25–35.
8. Norton, Hugh S., **National Transportation Policy: Formation and Implementation.** Berkeley, California: McCutchan Publishing Corporation, 1966.
   Part III. "The Policy Making Institutions," pp. 123–205.
9. Pegrum, Dudley F., **Transportation: Economics and Public Policy.** Rev. ed. Homewood, Ill.: Richard D. Irwin, Inc., 1968.
   Chapter 11. "The Agencies of Regulation," pp. 255–286.
   Chapter 21. "Regulation and Administration in Transport Policy," pp. 522–543.
10. Sampson, Roy J., "The Economic and Legal Environment of Domestic Transportation in the United States," **European Transport Law,** Vol. III, No. 2, 1968, pp. 294–317.
11. Taff, Charles A., **Management of Traffic and Physical Distribution.** 4th ed. Homewood, Ill.: Richard D. Irwin, Inc., 1968.
    Chapter 16. "Federal Transport Policy and Programs," pp. 438–465.
12. Van Metre, Thurman, **Industrial Traffic Management.** New York: McGraw-Hill Book Co., Inc., 1953.
    Chapter XXVI. "Administrative Procedures," pp. 508–526.
13. Westmeyer, Russell E., **Economics of Transportation.** Englewood Cliffs, N.J.; Prentice-Hall, Inc., 1952.
    Chapter 9. "State vs. Federal Regulation," pp. 180–197.

Part Six

Goals in Domestic Transportation Policy

Now that the development and current state of transportation regulation has been established, we will look at some of the problems and some of the goals of our transportation policy in the next five chapters. "Policy," as we use the term here, means the policy established by Congress, interpreted by the courts, often proposed by the Executive, and administered by Commissions or Boards.

Even though we will be discussing primarily public policy and goals, it should be clear that there are many groups in our transportation economy with many different goals. Sometimes these goals conflict and sometimes not. When there is conflict between the goals of various groups, problems of policy arise. Congress, as any elective body, is responsive to these conflicts of goals.

It is possible to generalize on conflicting goals by looking at the groups which originate goals. For our purposes, we can delineate four groups whose goals affect transportation policy in varying degrees and are sometimes in conflict. These are carriers, transportation labor, shippers, and the general public. By noting in a general way the goals of each of these four groups, conflicts in policy become much clearer.

The maximization of profit is the general goal of carriers. Methods of increasing profit include the elimination of excess capacity and the best possible use of capital, the elimination of excess labor and the best possible use of manpower, and the elimination of any element of service not absolutely necessary to satisfy customers. Carriers wish to accomplish these cost-saving goals without reducing rates or decreasing revenues. Indeed, a complementary goal is to charge the highest possible price (rate) that regulation, competition, and the shippers will allow.

The goals of labor, on the other hand, are higher wages for the same or less work, job security for a steady income, and better working conditions. Obviously these goals conflict in varying degrees with carrier goals. The shippers' goal is more service at less cost to themselves, and they desire more choice among firms and between modes. Again, conflicts are evident.

The general public may or may not have the same goals as carriers, transportation labor, or shippers. Public goals are more general and sometimes are not easy to define. In general, the public is interested in a "sound" transportation system which is available as needed and is able to take care of all ordinary and most extraordinary demands (such as defense) placed upon it. Since performance of the transportation system is the test used by the general public, it desires the best possible service at the least possible price and with a high degree of protection for itself. Finally, within the general framework or structure of our economy, the general public is concerned with the structure of the transportation industry and apparently wishes to avoid monopoly exploitation and stimulate competition for its own sake.

The next five chapters will consider these various conflicts and goals and their implementation in some detail.

Unification, Integration, and Diversification

It is appropriate to begin our discussion of transportation policy by considering transportation unification and integration. While there is a great deal of current interest in this subject, it is at the same time a timeless matter. Unification and integration of transportation firms has been going on since transportation firms were first created. Indeed, there is hardly a transportation firm or transportation system in existence today which did not come about by way of unification or integration.

The previous discussion of regulation has shown that the public has long been concerned about the effects of unification and integration. Various regulations have been used from time to time to attempt to control or mitigate the effects of these actions. We will consider some of the public policy questions posed by unification and integration in the latter part of this chapter. At this point it is sufficient to say that public policy has changed over time just as the whole structure of transportation regulation and the transportation market has changed.

CARRIER GOALS LEADING TO CONFLICT

Since transportation is of such great importance to the whole economy, any change in the structure of the transportation industry has a wide impact. Conflict in goals is almost inevitable under such circumstances. As carriers attempt to adjust the transportation plant by unification or integration, conflicts arise with the goals of transportation labor, shippers, and the general public.

A main goal of carriers is to maximize profit. They are no different in this regard than any other business firm. Fundamentally, two avenues of approach are available for a firm wishing to maximize its profit. It may reduce its costs in some way or increase its demand and quantity of services sold. (If regulation permits, of course, rate changes provide another alternative if consistent with demand conditions. We are not concerned with that alternative here, however.)

Actually, increased volume and cost reduction are not exclusive approaches to profit maximization. Both may be used simultaneously. A well-managed firm always wishes to control its costs. It can do this by carefully allocating the amount of labor and supplies used in its services and by economizing on its use of capital. However, if two firms combine in some way, additional economies may be possible. When two equal-sized firms merge and the new firm does twice the business of either of the previous firms, it does not follow that twice the labor, capital equipment, or supplies will be required. Economies and cost savings may be readily effected.

When transportation firms attempt unification or integration to gain the various economies, conflicts in goals may be sharp. Unification often means that some labor will no longer be needed. This conflicts with the goals of transportation labor. Unification often means that duplicating services are eliminated. Shippers have less choice and communities get less service, again creating conflicts. If excess labor is not utilized elsewhere in the economy, the public goal of full employment may be affected. Antitrust goals may also come into conflict with unification and integration of transportation firms. All of these conflicts and others are triggered by carriers rationally seeking goals of profit maximization.

Unification and integration of carrier firms may also lead to gains, of course. Gains to the carrier are obvious. There may also be gains to shippers, to transportation labor, and to the general public. This will depend to a great extent upon the methods and the effects of unification and integration.

METHODS AND PURPOSES OF UNIFICATION AND INTEGRATION

Before proceeding with a discussion of the methods and purposes of unification and integration in transportation, it may be desirable to review our meaning of these terms. As indicated in Chapter 9, both unification and integration involve common ownership (as contrasted with "cooperation" and "coordination"). But unification is intramodal, while integration is intermodal.

A "transportation company" is an example of integration. This would be a single firm owning operating entities in all modes of transportation—rail, motor, water, air, and pipeline. Such a firm theoretically would allocate its traffic to the particular mode which could do the job in the cheapest or most profitable manner. If the movement produced the most profit when carried by truck, trucks would be used. If rail movement were more profitable, rails would get the traffic. Profitability to the firm would be the sole criterion for allocation. Some persons see this as an effective free-market answer to the problems of intermodal competition and the regulatory problems which arise from a competitive transportation market.

A partially integrated transportation firm would be one owning operating entities in two or more (but not all) modes of transportation. Currently many railroads have motor-carrier subsidiaries, and a few railroads own pipelines.

Several motor carriers own international freight forwarders. There are no fully integrated transport firms in this country.

Unification occurs when two firms of the same mode merge or consolidate. Railroad, truck line, and airline mergers or consolidations are current examples of transportation unification. (Legally there is a difference between "merger" and "consolidation," but the economic effects are similar.)

The carrier's purpose in unification or integration is to increase profit, as previously noted. These actions may affect profits in a number of specific ways, but these can be summarized under the categories of cost savings or increased volumes.

Cost Savings

At a given level of rates (prices), any lowering of costs will obviously result in greater profits to the firm. Two approaches to cost savings are possible. These are adjusting to gain economies of scale or utilization and adjusting the scale of operations itself.

Economies of Scale or Utilization

Given the scale of operations or plant of a firm, economies are possible by better use of the inputs into the productive process. Hence, attempts to gain the best or optimum use of labor and supplies without varying the scale of operations is always a challenge to management. Firms vary considerably in their ability to meet this challenge.

In transportation, as noted earlier, there are many fixed and common costs. Many of these are associated with plant size. Once a railroad is constructed, for example, it is difficult to change its scale of operations. About all that can be done is to adjust labor and material inputs in such a way as to gain the best efficiency. The same is true of other large pieces of equipment or terminal facilities. In air transportation, once a fleet of planes is purchased, the main job of management is to adjust labor, materials, and service facilities so as to best utilize the plant. One cannot fly half a plane or operate with half an air crew merely because only half the seats are filled.

Additionally, operation of a transportation plant requires many specialists and persons with a high degree of training. Rate specialists, equipment specialists, and administrative specialists are examples. These positions are very necessary, but sometimes the scale of operations does not justify having large groups of these specialists. In such cases, a firm may decide to use a particular specialist on two or more unrelated jobs and hope he can continue to do an effective job. Or instead of employing a large number of specialists, the transportation system may have but a few and either try to move the specialist about as needed or send the work to a centralized location. The "traveling mechanic" of bygone railroad days is an example of moving the specialist to the job, and the central repair-shop facility is an example of moving the work to the specialist. In both cases, however, some losses are incurred in the movement of either the specialist or the work and in scheduling of work.

When firms consolidate or merge, the combined or surviving firm is often large enough to make more effective use of specialists. Centralization of work or the full-time application of specialties is feasible. Better use of capital equipment may also be possible. When airlines merge, better scheduling of all equipment may result. Small planes can serve light traffic-density routes and larger planes heavy traffic-density routes. The previous firms may not have been able to afford equipment to efficiently serve various traffic-density routes, but the combined firm now has enough planes to do so. Here service is probably improved while cost savings are made.

The same result is possible in administrative expenses. When two motor carriers merge, better use of existing office personnel may result. Each person can now specialize and be more efficient. An example is traffic solicitation. When the firm is small, salesmen must call on all kinds and types of customers, giving little attention to each. If consolidation makes a larger firm, sales tasks can be divided and better solicitation may result from specialization.

To some degree, the same statements may be made about integration. Again using sales effort as an example, a partially integrated firm can sometimes offer a service that a nonintegrated firm cannot. Also, salesmen may easily shift from mode to mode. Hence, specialization of solicitation and promotion is possible where previously it was not. The area of maintenance provides another example of the economies possible under integration. Railroad repair shops can do some of the tasks truck repair shops do. Both use some labor in common.

In summary, both unification and integration can lead to economies in the use of administrative personnel, maintenance personnel, labor of all kinds, equipment, and capital facilities. Many of these lead to better service through specialization of labor or capital and, at the same time, lead to greater profit for the firm.

Adjusting the Scale of Operations

Perhaps better known and somewhat more obvious are the cost savings which arise from adjusting the scale of operations. Every firm is interested in adjusting its scale of operations to most efficiently fit its demand. Here capital costs are probably the most important factor. If size can be increased, specialized pieces of capital equipment which do the job more efficiently can sometimes be employed. Firms which grow to a larger scale of operation can often do tasks which they previously had to have others do for them. Specialists can be hired that were not previously used. More efficient types of management and organization may likewise be possible. Unification often allows for such cost savings.

However, in this day of increased automation, efficiency, and shifting market shares, it is most often the costs which can be saved by reducing excess capacity which are the most important. As we saw in Chapter 2, railroads in our domestic transportation system are still reducing the size of their trackage. Physical duplication of plant and personnel is common in railroad transportation. Many rail merger proposals stress the existing duplication of tracks, stations, terminals and yards, administrative facilities and specialized employees, and the savings which will be accomplished by reducing duplication. This is especially so where the proposed merger is the "side-by-side" variety in which two firms are duplicating services in the same territory or area.

Air mergers likewise propose savings by the reduction of duplication. When route patterns can be consolidated or merged, better use of equipment is often possible. Excess capacity in administrative personnel, in ticketing, or in repair facilities is avoided. Sometimes these savings can be accomplished at little or no reduction in service, although this is not always so.

Mergers and consolidations almost always mean savings in the use of labor. Rarely are all the clerks, salesmen, supervisors, or administrators of two firms necessary in a merged firm. Excess capacity in operating and maintenance crews can often be reduced as well. With better scheduling of vehicles possible because more are available, wasted time and inefficiencies are reduced.

Almost any side-by-side merger, regardless of mode, can make savings of this type. The amount of savings may depend upon the degree of divisibility of the units of input. Motor carriers often have small savings from side-by-side mergers because a truck is a small and readily divisible unit of input. Terminal and overhead savings in truck mergers are possible, of course. Rail and air carriers potentially can have greater savings in side-by-side mergers because they use less divisible units of input and, consequently, the reduction of excess equipment capacity is far greater.

Increased Volume

The second method of increasing profit by unification and integration is to increase the volume of movement. If traffic can be increased, better use of capital is often possible and service can be increased (which may in turn lead to more traffic and more profit). Many of the economies of specialization and scale noted above are equally possible when volume of movement increases.

Increased volume arising from unification may come from "end-to-end" mergers of rail, truck, air, or water transportation lines. Here two routes are connected to make a bigger and longer system. While end-to-end mergers may result in some savings by eliminating some duplication of terminal facilities, these mergers are usually rationalized on the basis of better service. The merged system usually gives through service to shippers, should mean fewer claims and damages because of less handling, and often makes a faster service. Traffic may well increase as through service is offered, and sometimes latent demand may be stimulated by bringing new industries or undertakings into the transportation system with fast, economical through service not previously possible.

In passenger transportation, end-to-end consolidations definitely are an advantage to the public. The need for transferring passengers from car to car or plane to plane is decreased. While the interchange of rail passenger cars has become highly developed, interchange of air equipment between firms is still rare.

Motor carriers, too, have used end-to-end unifications to improve demand and profits. The "tacking" of operating rights into a system with broader geographical coverage is a common way of growth in motor transportation. Here again profits can be increased by allowing the firm to participate in more long-haul traffic and by the substantial economies available when a reduction in the handling or transfer of lading is possible. Sometimes, too, rolling equipment can be more efficiently scheduled and used when two firms merge or consolidate on an end-to-end basis, and very often overhead and administrative expenses can be reduced or labor can be better utilized.

Increased volume may arise from integration because a more complete service can be offered by the integrated firm than by its competitors. An integrated firm can combine the best of several modes and perhaps lower its rates while improving services and increasing its profits.

If these various devices merely result in a shifting of traffic from one firm to another, society may be no better off than before. But if the integrated firm or the firm gaining economies through unification is able to provide service at a lower rate than before the traffic shift, the public may gain. While the purpose of these devices is to increase carrier profits, their effects remain to be considered.

EFFECTS OF UNIFICATION AND INTEGRATION

The effects of unification and integration may vary, depending upon the time period used in analyzing effects and the type or method used for unification and integration. We have already differentiated between methods used. Now we will consider time periods in terms of immediate effects and long-run effects.

Immediate Effects

An immediate effect of unification and integration is conflict. As noted previously, the goals of the various groups concerned differ. The degree of conflict varies somewhat according to the method used. Unification proposals based on increased volume and better service (such as end-to-end mergers) cause conflict only where cost reductions are involved. Proposals of the cost-savings type, however, often bring definite conflicts between carriers and transportation labor, shippers, and the general public. This is particularly true where adjustments in the scale of operations or economies of scale are sought by decreasing labor usage or decreasing services.

Labor Decreases

Decreases in the use of all types of labor are common immediate effects of unifications. These decreases involve not only operating personnel, but also administrative staff and clerical help, and are especially found in the side-by-side mergers where duplication exists. If integration involves savings in labor costs, the effect is the same, of course. While such decreases in labor costs may make the carrier more profitable, they often adversely involve individual workers, the community, and the general public.

The immediate effect on the worker is loss of employment, income, and job security. Much of the labor strife in transportation in recent times has centered around carrier-labor conflicts over job security. Organized worker groups generally have opposed mergers and consolidations. Congress has become enough concerned about these immediate effects on transportation labor to enact various labor-protective provisions in our public policy on transportation.

The community served by the firms involved in unification and integration may likewise be adversely affected by labor decreases. Loss of payrolls is often a very serious community problem, particularly in small towns where carriers are a large factor in the economic existence of the community. Smaller payrolls mean less business, more unemployment, and all the social costs which accompany idleness. Communities have been known to oppose quite vehemently carrier unification, particularly where railroads and large payrolls are involved.

The general public may be adversely affected in the immediate period by labor decreases insofar as the general goal of full employment is undermined. Assuming no immediate shifting of labor made excess by mergers or consolidation, the attainment of full employment is postponed. This immediate effect, as well as some of the effects on individuals and communities, may be entirely different after a period of readjustment has taken place. But these immediate effects do help explain some of the opposition to unification and integration proposals.

Service Decreases

Another immediate effect of many unifications is a decrease in service to someone. This is particularly true of cost-saving types of unifications such as side-by-side mergers which eliminate duplication. To some degree, service decreases are also involved in integration as well. In end-to-end mergers designed to increase volume, some local service decreases may be involved, but they are often offset by increasing through service. Again, service decreases may make the carrier more profitable and better adjust his plant to demand, but they cause conflicts with the same three groups: individuals, the community, and the general public. These conflicts are of a somewhat different nature, however, than those considered before.

The immediate effect of service decreases is upon the shipper. When side-by-side mergers take place or when integration limits the number of competitors, shipper choice is restricted. This is true for passenger service as well. Shippers and passengers desire a wide choice, therefore they look upon service decreases as adversely affecting them.

No community wants less service from the carriers serving it. No city wants to have "second class" status on any rail, motor, or air system. Every town desires "mainline" service of the highest and best type, if only to placate its civic pride. Unifications designed to end duplication obviously mean that all cities cannot be served as they were before. The immediate effect is conflict.

The general public as conceptualized by public policy may find a conflict in service decreases. In a general way, the economy supports competition between many firms as a laudable economic goal. Service decreases eliminate competition and the duplication caused by competition. Many times the Antitrust Division of the Department of Justice has been at odds with the actions of the Interstate Commerce Commission over mergers and consolidations. The desire for competition between many firms and the goal of a more efficient transportation system are not always in harmony.

Besides the conflict over antitrust goals and the elimination of carrier duplication, a national defense conflict sometimes arises. Transportation is absolutely necessary for defense, thus any decrease in service or reduction in plant and equipment may have the immediate effect of decreasing the nation's defense potential. Many have noted the need for excess capacity in domestic transportation to provide for rapid traffic expansion in case of emergency. Some have even suggested that defense needs justify public expenditures to maintain duplication of transportation facilities. One program of action carried on for several years involved the buying and stockpiling of excess rail passenger equipment near military bases.

End-to-end mergers and unifications designed to attain greater volume or to give through service do not involve the degree of conflict with shippers and communities that cost-saving mergers involve. While these types may have great conflict with antitrust policy, they are not generally in conflict with defense needs.

Long-Run Effects

The long-run effects of unification and integration are rarely the same as the immediate effects. Conflicts may or may not continue after adjustment. Some of the effects undoubtedly are beneficial in the long run from several points of view, but again the effects will vary somewhat according to the type or method used.

Given time, unification or integration which increases volume seems to be beneficial to all. End-to-end mergers or consolidations which broaden service areas, allow more through traffic, and make for more financially healthy carriers are especially beneficial. The chance for stimulating new demand seems greater here than in the cost-saving type as service decreases are smaller and better services often result. Of course, the end-to-end merger may prosper because it causes a traffic shift from one carrier or one mode to another. Under such circumstances, long-run benefits will accrue only if the shift is to a less costly and more efficient carrier. Some cost savings are usually involved in end-to-end mergers, however, although to a smaller degree than in the side-by-side type. After adjustments, the long-run effect of unification or integration leading to increased volume and better service leaves only the antitrust problem unsolved.

The long-run effect of cost-savings unification and integration proposals are basically two: increased carrier earnings and more efficient resource allocation. These long-run effects may eventually overcome some of the immediate conflicts noted above, or they may not.

Increased Carrier Earnings

If cost-savings unification or integration has been properly planned, it should result in greater long-run carrier earnings. This can be beneficial to almost all parties concerned if increased earnings lead to lower rates, if they lead to better service at the same rate, or if they lead to financially adequate carriers.

Lower rates for the same level of service obviously benefit the shipper and reduce his costs. Depending upon the conditions of competition and demand in the various products shipped, this may be either translated into lower prices to the consumer or a postponement of price increases. Too many assumptions concerning competition, the pattern of growth of firms, general economic conditions of inflation or deflation, and the elasticities of demand of thousands of individual products in numerous markets are involved for any detailed analysis of the effects of lower rates. However, it is proper to generalize that lower transportation rates are a stimulus to economic growth and development and are considered beneficial to the whole economy.

Better service at the same rate has the same economic effect. Carriers and commissions may prefer to translate greater earnings not into lower rates, but into increased service levels. Here again the higher level of service is beneficial to shippers and ultimately to the general public. Better service levels may even be beneficial to transportation labor by providing more jobs. Again, the long-run effect on any one individual or industry is hard to ascertain without multiple assumptions about economic conditions and particular markets. However, better service is generally considered beneficial to economic growth and development.

Finally, greater earnings may lead to a more financially adequate transportation system. Remember that Congress assumed adequacy of transportation as a public policy goal several years ago. If the financial woes of carriers are such that question exists about their ability to continue to fulfill their role in the future, increased earnings from unification or integration could be most important. Long-run cost savings may be the only hope for some carriers. In such instances, the long-run effect may be a continuation of shipper choice, service, employment and a degree of competition, none of which might be possible without mergers and consolidations to rescue financially weak carriers.

Allocation of Resources

A second long-run effect brought about by unification or integration of the cost-saving type is a change in resource allocation. In the previous discussion of financial adequacy, a tacit assumption is made that we need various types of carriers. This may not be the case. Every industry is constantly changing, all parts of the economy are constantly in a state of shift. We fail to recognize this merely because the degree of change or shift may be small or take long periods to complete. Yet, the proper balance of resources to needs is perhaps the greatest problem affecting the entire economy.

Unification and integration of the cost-saving type may act as a vehicle by which the economy attains a better balance in its use of resources. Perhaps service decreases and labor decreases (immediate effects) are needed because of basic permanent changes in technology or shifts of traffic shares. Perhaps excess capacity needs to be removed and the capital and materials employed elsewhere in the economy. With decreases in some modes and increases in others, society may attain a better balance in resource use. If a shift of resources, including capital and labor, means more productive employment outside transportation, perhaps all parties are better off. In the long run, all will benefit—labor, shipper, communities, and general public—from an economy which uses its resources in such a way that only the amount actually needed is allocated to transportation. Insofar as unification and integration act to assist in attaining a proper balance of resources, society will benefit in the long run even though short-run problems may be acute.

The antitrust problem remains even here, for there is no guarantee that an optimum resource allocation will necessarily be consistent with antitrust goals. Likewise, if no shifting takes place and the resources remain unemployed, a major problem presents itself.

OBSTACLES TO UNIFICATION AND INTEGRATION

Enough of the kinds of conflicts have been noted to make it obvious that many obstacles stand in the way of unification and integration in domestic transportation. Unification and integration do not automatically take place. Sometimes obstacles are insurmountable, at other times they merely delay the ultimate adjustment process. For our purposes, we can note three types of obstacles. These are regulatory obstacles, obstacles inherent in unification itself, and environmental obstacles.

Regulatory Obstacles

Unification and integration cannot take place without permission of the regulatory commissions (except in certain limited cases) and, as previously noted, conflicts arise from various groups when it is proposed. Regulatory procedure allows all interested parties to be heard and takes into consideration their various positions. This in itself slows the process.

Public policy on unification and integration has been established by Congress. Much of this public policy is frankly protective, designed to protect groups such as transportation labor as well as the general public. Even so, some of this public policy is but partially in harmony with other general goals such as the maintenance of competition and antitrust policy. Additionally, it is hard to define what action protects the general public. Policy is not altogether clear on such matters. These goal conflicts, protective provisions, and uncertain criteria are obstacles to unification and integration.

Inherent Obstacles

Unification or integration involves a degree of voluntary action on the part of the participants. Agreement among the firms being merged or being integrated is not always easy. Since many are corporations, many investors with diverse goals and objectives must be satisfied. This involves both debt and equity owners. Management itself may disagree. It is not easy to merge oneself out of a job, and a merged firm can have but one president and set of administrative officers. As we have seen, adjustments in the immediate period are almost inevitable when unification or integration takes place. Adjustment means change and uncertainty. The tendency to avoid adjustment and change is great in all business, and in some of the older transportation firms this inertia itself is a major obstacle. Therefore, there are obstacles inherent in the very idea of unification or integration.

Environmental Obstacles

Transportation does not operate in a vacuum. Unification and integration take place in a political and economic environment. The economic environment of the nation is quite oriented toward individual firms and competition. Unification and integration involve group action on the part of firms and often a decrease in competition. This may present an obstacle.

From another point of view, the political climate may be a very real environmental obstacle. Transportation systems serve many towns, counties, and states. Each is a political unit with its representatives elected to promote the welfare of each particular governmental unit. Laws are passed and pressures arise from the conflicts previously noted. Some politicians may even exploit these conflicts for personal political gain and oppose unification not because it is economically unsound, but because it is politically expedient to do so. The political climate, then, may impose a very real obstacle to unification and integration.

In summary, because of regulatory provisions and conflicts, inertia and inherent difficulties, or the economic and political environment, unification and integration may be delayed or even prevented irrespective of their economic and business goals.

PUBLIC POLICY ON UNIFICATION AND INTEGRATION

Public policy on unification and integration is a part of our general transportation policy. Just as our general public policy on transportation has evolved, developed, and changed over time, so has policy in this area. Basically, the policy has been restrictive. That is, both unification and integration have been controlled. The degree of control varies both over time and by mode. Additionally, public policy is not the same for unification as it is for integration.

Control of Integration

Regulatory controls have prevented fully integrated transportation firms in this country. While the "transportation company" idea has been much discussed, it is necessary to look to our neighbor to the north for the best example of such an operation. The Canadian Pacific Railway Company owns railroads, trucklines, an airline, maritime water carriers, and numerous other subsidiaries. No such example can be found in this country.

Actually, regulations affecting integration apply principally to the railroads. A number of partially integrated rail systems do exist in the United States. Many railroads own truck subsidiaries and a few own pipelines. The reverse, however, is not true. Few truck lines or pipelines own railroads, although there is no prohibition against such ownership. (You will recall, however, that freight forwarders are not allowed to own line-haul carriers.)

The reason for this difference in regulatory treatment relative to integration is fairly obvious. It revolves around historical and economic conditions. Historically, railroads grew into large corporate giants before trucklines, pipelines, and airlines. The dominant position of the railroads caused various controls to be placed on their ownership of the other emerging modes. No such problem was envisioned with the newer modes.

Economically, there are also several reasons for this difference in regulatory treatment. Most of the newer and competitive transportation firms did not possess the financial resources to be able to consider ownership of other modes. Also, because of the economic structure of the newer and competitive modes of transportation, there was less chance of economies of scale through ownership of several modes. Railroads have large fixed expenses and common costs. Some of these could be spread to the other modes and economies easily gained in the use of people and capital. While the opportunity to offer a more complete service might be appealing to motor carriers or air carriers, for example, there was less direct economic justification for such integration in the newer modes than in rail.

Finally, our general economic philosophy in this country has been to idealize competition. Railroads already were monopolistic, and public policy was designed to prevent them from spreading their monopolistic powers to other modes of transportation. The new firms were generally competitive both with railroads and with themselves. Hence there was less concern about the spread of monopoly and the upholding of competition among the newer modes. Naturally, regulation of the possible acquisition of other modes did not come about when competitive conditions prevailed.

Regulation is concerned mainly with rail ownership of motor carriers. Many railroads own truck subsidiaries (many acquired prior to the regulation of motor carriers in 1935), but in all cases the operating rights of rail-owned trucklines are restricted. The railroad-owned motor carrier is not allowed to compete with its parent. Various restrictions are placed on the type of service which may be offered and the routes which may be served. These restrictions in general are designed to assure that railroad-owned motor carriers operate in an ancillary, auxiliary, or supplementary capacity to their rail parents.

Control of Unification

The matter of public regulation of unification is more complicated than the control of integration. Controls vary considerably by mode, thus it is appropriate to survey this topic on a modal basis.

Railroads

The history of unification in railroads is most interesting. Practically all modern railroads grew up in this manner. The history of public policy on railroad merger and consolidation is likewise interesting. Merely the sketchiest account will be given here. (Some of the background of this problem was previously considered in Chapters 16 and 17.)

General fear of railroad consolidation and attempts at public control pre-date Federal regulation. It will be recalled that an integral part of the early Granger laws prohibited consolidation and merger of railroads. Being primarily intrastate in nature, these prohibitions had little effect. Additionally, such acts were generally not in existence for a long period of time.

The initial Act to Regulate Commerce prohibited pooling and other con-certed action by rail carriers. It did not deal with consolidations and mergers as such. However, in a series of legal actions just after the turn of the century, the antitrust laws were applied to railroad consolidations. These actions were found to violate the Sherman Act in the famous *Northern Securities Case* (193 U.S. 197, 1904). Rail consolidation and merger, which had previously been widespread, ceased almost entirely.

In the Transportation Act of 1920, Congress took a more permissive atti-tude toward rail mergers and consolidations. The Interstate Commerce Com-mission was given control over unification and had to apply certain criteria to each proposal before allowing railroads to merge or consolidate. Additionally, the I.C.C. was directed to draw up a nationwide plan of a limited number of railroads. Such a plan, based largely upon a study and recommendation made by Professor William Z. Ripley of Harvard University, was eventually adopted. All mergers had to fit into this preconceived plan. Little merger activity took place under this scheme, although stock ownership and the holding company device was used to achieve some of the financial benefits of mergers.

By 1940, it was apparent that the nationwide plan had failed. Hence, the plan was abandoned and new criteria were drawn up. The Transportation Act of 1940 provided that the I.C.C. must find a rail merger proposal "to be in the public interest," labor protective provisions were added so that workers could not be placed in a worse position due to a merger or consolidation for a period of four years, the I.C.C. had to consider the effect of a merger proposal on other railroads in the territory, and the total fixed charges coming out of a merger proposal could not be burdensome.

No basic change has been made in public policy toward rail mergers and consolidations since 1940. For a period of time few mergers were attempted. However, starting in the late 1950's, a whole series of merger proposals for railroads erupted. Much time must elapse for hearings and for all interested parties to be heard in these proposals. However, during the 1960's and early 1970's, the I.C.C. slowly processed more merger applications and generally looked with favor on rail mergers. A number of lines were merged or consolidated. This movement was not without conflict, and considerable public debate over rail mergers has ensued. But generally, though, the Commission has permitted rail mergers after extended hearings and proceedings.

Motor Carriers

Because there are more motor-carrier firms, unification proposals do not attract as much attention as they do in rail and air transportation. Nevertheless, a large number of mergers and consolidations are taking place. Motor carriers are creating transportation systems by these devices, and public policy questions arise from time to time. Periodically the I.C.C. issues reports on motor-carrier concentration, and some Congressmen have evidenced concern over the antitrust aspects of truck mergers.

Mergers and consolidations of small trucklines are not controlled (the $300,000 rule), but all others must have I.C.C. permission. The typical problem here is the matter of operating certificates or "rights" which are "tacked" together to make a large service system. The I.C.C. must find that proposed mergers or consolidations are "in the public interest" and all interested parties must be heard. Since motor transportation is already highly competitive and has many firms, it is natural that objections to any proposal will arise.

Monopoly considerations are not important in motor-carrier merger proposals, but questions of the degree and type of competition which should be allowed are highly important. Typically, conflicts arise between carrier firms when truck mergers are proposed, while conflicts arise among the rail carriers and individuals (workers and shippers) and communities in rail merger proposals.

Air Carriers

Since there are only a small number of firms involved in air transportation, any unification proposal creates much public interest. Many of the existing airlines have grown by merger and consolidation, although such actions have been infrequent. Public policy in this area is similar to that in other modes in that all unifications must be approved by the Civil Aeronautics Board and must be found to be "in the public interest." Specifically, the board may not approve any unification which would "result in creating a monopoly or monopolies and thereby restrain competition or jeopardize another air carrier." The effect on competition, then, becomes the main criterion of approval.

C.A.B. policy has tended to follow a "two-carrier-system" approach on mergers and consolidations. Mergers have been approved in the past among feeder carriers and, in some instances, among the trunk-line carriers. Typically, however, a trunk-line carrier has not been allowed to grow by absorbing feeder lines. While some merger proposals have been put forth among the trunk-line carriers, only the United-Capital merger has been approved in recent times. Here the C.A.B. was faced with a carrier threatened with bankruptcy unless merged, and here a conscious attempt to balance competition was apparently made.

Water and Other Carriers

Water-carrier unifications are subject to the same regulations as railroads under the same provisions of the Interstate Commerce Act. Little problem with merger or consolidation of water carriers has arisen. Consolidations in pipelines are not controlled.

DIVERSIFICATION AND CONGLOMERATES

Diversification and conglomerate movements in transportation are two corporate activities somewhat allied to unification and integration. Although some of these activities have existed for a long time, it is only recently that the high degree of diversification and the involvement of transportation firms in the conglomerate movement have been issues of considerable concern.

Any corporation which owns operating units in several lines of production may be considered as "diversified." The idea is somewhat akin to the old adage "Don't put all your eggs in one basket." By being part of several industries, a large firm theoretically can spread the risks of economic uncertainty so that a change in demand in one type of business or industry can be offset by increased activity in another industry of which the firm is a part.

Transportation firms often have invested in other firms. Typically, these have been undertakings closely allied to transportation activities. For example, overseas airlines have invested in resort hotels and in-flight and terminal catering firms, motor carriers have invested in truck manufacturing, bus companies have owned restaurant chains, and railroads have owned lumber mills and oil exploration firms. Additionally, railroads have been among the larger owners of real estate and land resources. In almost all of these cases, the ownership pattern has been either in allied supplier-type industries or has been the result of historical events such as railroad land grants. Also, some transportation firms have owned stocks and bonds as investments, but have not actually controlled other firms.

Regulatory laws generally have provided a degree of control over such investments or the ownership of transport-allied industries. The I.C.C. and the C.A.B. both have the authority to control the ownership and investment of transportation firms in non-transportation activities. Generally, it must be shown that the public interest is served by such ownership.

During recent years, two things have taken place which have called attention once more to these regulations and to the problems connected with these complex intercorporate relationships. These are the move by some transportation firms, principally railroads, to diversify by an "industries" approach, and the ownership of transportation firms by highly diversified industrial conglomerates.

Industries Approach

Being large and capital intensive firms, railroads often have substantial funds available from depreciation accounts. Returns on railroad investment have been quite low during the post-World War II period, thus the reinvestment of the cash flow from depreciation and profits into transportation has not always been considered good financial practice on the part of railroads. Additionally, many railroads would like to diversify into non-transportation undertakings, but have not always found the I.C.C. sympathetic to this idea.

Faced with this situation, a number of rail firms have organized holding companies, using their railroad name with the term "industries" added on. Existing owners of railroad stocks have been offered the stocks of the new "industries" company, and often the railroad involved has become an operating subsidiary of the holding company. In this fashion, regulatory prohibitions have been by-passed, and the funds derived from transportation activities have provided the means for investment in firms not even remotely connected to transportation. Diversification is accomplished, and in some instances the former railroad firms have become deeply involved in non-transportation activities.

Conglomerates

The late 1960's witnessed the rapid rise of the conglomerate enterprise, wherein a dynamic management group purchased or obtained control of widely different types of firms in many industries. Much of this growth was accomplished by the issuance of stocks which were traded to existing stockholders of the firms merged into the new enterprise. Very wide diversification was accomplished, and by astute bargaining the conglomerate enterprise, as it came to be called, established a good initial growth of sales, revenues, earnings, and increases in stock prices.

Many transportation firms were purchased by conglomerates during the late 1960's, particularly airlines, truck lines, and freight forwarders. These became operating subsidiaries of much larger firms, and helped provide some of the desired diversification. Additionally, a few transportation firms themselves have become conglomerates. One bus company has evolved into a conglomerate, using its transportation activities as a base. In another instance, a railroad company provided the initial basis for the formation of a conglomerate which later sold the railroad itself but retained a portion of its name.

Control of Diversification and Conglomerates

Use of the holding company device avoids the necessity of getting regulatory commission permission for such diversification. The transportation firm does not have to make the investment; instead, its non-regulated parent holding company invests. If the owners of a transportation firm choose to exchange their stocks for part ownership of another larger conglomerate company, this is beyond the scope of authority of the transportation regulatory agencies. Basically, only the antitrust laws apply to the non-regulated sectors of the economy and provide the ,only present basis for control of these activities. Even here, it is not clear what is our national policy on conglomerates and to what degree the antitrust laws really apply.

At this point it is not clear whether the industries approach and the conglomerate movement are detrimental or favorable to transportation services. Some observers deplore the use of transportation revenues for non-transportation activities, while others argue that being a part of a diversified firm may actually strengthen transportation undertakings during times of economic stress. Some point to the use of transportation assets as providing greater borrowing power to finance non-transportation activities, while others note that these financial developments can take place only if the owners are convinced that it is in their own economic self-interest to exchange their stocks. Finally, some see the danger that a carrier which becomes an operating subsidiary may discriminate in favor of its parent company, while others maintain that the laws regulating discrimination in transportation are clear and make no ownership distinction.

In any case, diversification and the conglomerate movement in transportation have given rise to a great deal of concern and interest, and these developments will be debated extensively during the next several years. If these events do adversely affect transport services, new regulatory legislation no doubt will be forthcoming.

GENERAL SUMMARY

Unification and integration illustrate the conflicting goals which affect public policy in domestic transportation. These conflicts are triggered by carrier goals of maximizing profit. Two approaches to maximizing have concerned us here: unification which is intramodal and integration which is intermodal. The methods of unification and integration are basically to effect cost savings through greater economies of utilization or scale, by adjusting the scale of operations itself, or by increasing volume or demand. The effect of these methods varies considerably. The immediate effect is conflict when cost-saving methods are used. Increased volume methods evoke less conflict. The long-run effect is more difficult to ascertain, but it seems to resolve many of the conflicts over immediate effects. Nevertheless, these conflicts lead to definite obstacles to unification and integration, many of which prevent or limit use of these techniques. Finally, because of these conflicts, public policy has been evolved in an attempt to control unification and integration. That policy has changed over time, has treated the various modes in different ways, and has treated integration differently than unification. Basically, public policy is restrictive and protective. Almost all proposals for unification or integration must be approved by the I.C.C. or C.A.B.

Recent movements toward diversification through holding companies and conglomerate enterprises owning transportation firms have caused interest in an area allied to traditional unification and integration. The potential effects of these developments are not entirely clear at the present time, and public policy concerning them is still evolving. This area is likely to remain controversial for some time, and may lead to new restrictive regulation.

ADDITIONAL READINGS

1. Adams, Walter, and J. G. Hendry, **Trucking Mergers, Concentration and Small Business; An Analysis of Interstate Commerce Commission Policy, 1950–56,** Report for the Senate Select Committee on Small Business, 85th Congress, 1st Session (1957).
2. Barrett, Colin, "Diversification or Scatteration," **I.C.C. Practitioners' Journal,** January–February 1970, pp. 198–208.
3. Barriger, John W., "The Effect of Mergers on Competition," **Transportation Journal,** Spring 1968, pp. 5–17.
4. Conant, Michael, **Railroad Mergers and Abandonments.** Berkeley, Calif.: University of California Press, 1964.
   Chapter II. "The Myth of Interrailroad Competition," pp. 25–41.
   Chapter V. "Functional Mergers: Pooling and Trackage Agreements," pp. 91–112.
   Chapter VIII. "Administrative Regulation of Resource Allocation," pp. 166–186.
5. Farris, Martin T., "Rail Mergers: New Interest in an Old Approach," **Transportation Journal,** Summer 1962, pp. 30–37.
6. Harbeson, Robert W., "New Patterns in Railway Consolidation," **The Quarterly Review of Economics and Business,** Feb. 1962, pp. 7–10.
7. Healy, Kent T., **The Effects of Scale in the Railroad Industry.** New Haven, Conn.: Committee on Transportation, Yale University, 1961.
8. Healy, Kent T., "The Merger Movement in Transportation," **American Economic Review,** May 1962, pp. 436–444.

9. Hudson, William J., and James A. Constantin, **Motor Transportation: Principles and Practices.** New York: Ronald Press Company, 1958.
"Regulation of Railroad Motor Carrier Operations," pp. 509–517.
"Regulation of Services and Business Practices," pp. 575–584.

10. Leonard, W. N., "Issues in Competition and Monopoly in Railroad Mergers," **Transportation Journal,** Summer 1964, pp. 5–15.

11. Leonard, W. N., **Railroad Consolidation under the Transportation Act of 1920.** New York: Columbia University Press, 1946.

12. Morton, Newton, "Carrier Consolidation," **I.C.C. Practitioners' Journal,** Jan. 1963, pp. 425–448.

13. Norton, Hugh S., **Modern Transportation Economics.** Columbus, Ohio: Charles E. Merrill Books, Inc., 1963.
Chapter 21. "Transportation Consolidation and Integration," pp. 364–380.

14. Pegrum, Dudley F., **Transportation: Economics and Public Policy.** Rev. ed. Homewood, Ill.: Richard D. Irwin, Inc., 1968.
Chapter 17. "Consolidation and Integration," pp. 446–466.

15. **The Railroad Merger Problem.** Committee on the Judiciary, Committee Print, 88th Congress, 1st Session (1963).

16. Sampson, Roy J., **Obstacles to Railroad Unification.** Eugene, Oregon: Bureau of Business Research, University of Oregon, 1960.

21

Society's Interest in
Labor-Management Relations

The preceding chapter considered conflicting goals relative to the structure of carrier organizations. This chapter concerns itself with another area of goal conflict. Again several groups are involved, each with conflicting or partially conflicting goals. To some degree, the conflicts here are triggered by transportation labor, while the conflicts described in the previous chapter are carrier-triggered. Irrespective of which group sets off the problem, however, it is the types of goal conflict and the attempts to resolve them which concerns us here.

CONFLICTING GOALS: CARRIER, EMPLOYEE, AND PUBLIC

As noted previously, the goal of the carrier is profit maximization. This may be attempted through unification and integration. More commonly, however, the carrier will achieve this goal by adjusting the inputs of labor, capital, and materials into its productive plant. Labor, being one of the major inputs, is always susceptible to adjustment. This is particularly true where capital can be substituted for labor.

Transportation labor, on the other hand, has an entirely different set of goals. Basically, labor is interested in wages or compensation, conditions under which work takes place, and job security or job continuity. The intensity of transportation labor's goals is equally as great as the intensity of the carrier's goals. A laborer depends primarily upon his job for his economic existence. His job is his life, just as profit is the lifeblood of carrier existence. Transportation labor wants the best labor bargain possible and looks with little sympathy on the carrier problem of minimizing costs at labor's expense in order to be competitive and to maximize profit.

Job security is especially important to transportation labor. Wages traditionally have not been low in transportation. The conditions of employment are shaped to a great degree by the type of operation involved. Hence, continuity of employment and "job rights" have particular importance to transportation labor. Any downward adjustment of the amount of labor affects these goals.

The general public, including shippers, has varying interests in labor-management relations. In the short run or immediate period, the primary and overwhelming goal of the general public is continued service. It is literally true that in the immediate period of a potential transportation shutdown, the public is indifferent as to who wins the labor-management struggle just so long as the service continues.

In the long run, however, the general public has conflicting or split goals. On the one hand, it wants the best, most efficient transportation possible at the lowest possible cost. This may mean the use of less labor and more capital. The problem of resource allocation is again involved. On the other hand, the public is also very interested in full employment of people as well as other resources. National policy explicitly favors the goal of full employment, and much concern is evidenced over rates of employment and unemployment and their effect on the economy. Additionally, society has become very interested in the social problems brought about by labor adjustment. The human and social costs of unemployment have become a real concern as the multitude of social legislation in the employment-unemployment area testifies. Internal conflict between society's desire for the cheapest, most efficient transportation and full employment and minimum social costs of adjustment is self-evident.

One might properly ask if this conflict of goals is not a general problem of all business enterprise in a highly industrialized economy. To some degree this is true. However, because of some of the special conditions in transportation, these goal conflicts and problems are considerably sharpened and brought into public focus.

Service Continuity

The overwhelming special nature of the problem in transportation is the absolute necessity for service to continue. In most other industries, production can cease at least temporarily without great general loss when labor-management strife erupts. But because of the essentiality of transportation services to the economy, society cannot allow these services to cease even on a temporary basis. At the risk of repetition, it is well to reiterate that without transportation, stagnation of the whole agricultural and industrial economy is quick and certain. Interdependency exists in practically all present-day economic activity. When transportation stops, production stops. Continuous service is a must.

There are further reasons why the general conflict of goals comes into sharper focus in transportation than in other areas. These may be classified as historic reasons, and as economic and technological reasons. Each category is worth exploring.

Historic Nature of the Problem

The union movement among workers in the transportation industries is one of the oldest in the country. Early railroad unions facing a strong management in a monopolistic type of industry attained strength much earlier than most labor organizations. The so-called Big Five—the railroad Operating Brotherhoods—were formed long before most unions were effective. The Engineers Brotherhood was founded in 1863, the Conductors in 1868, the Firemen in 1873, the Trainmen in 1883, and the Switchmen in 1894. All but the last of these Brotherhoods predates Federal regulation of transportation, and two were started even before the early state Granger regulation.

The operating labor of railroads, then, was almost completely unionized at an early date. Railroad labor strife provided some of the bloodiest and hardest fought struggles of the latter half of the Nineteenth Century. It involved not only the Brotherhoods, but also the general labor unions of the time (such as the Knights of Labor). These strong transportation unions facing equally strong transportation management gave our country its first real taste of labor-management strife.

Additionally, there has been a tendency to pioneer public policy in the transportation labor field. Some of our society's first attempts at social legislation originated in transportation. The right to bargain collectively, the eight-hour day, social security, outlawing of the "yellow-dog" contract, the cooling-off period, and other now generally accepted labor rights and policies were first introduced in the rail transportation area. It is almost as if new ideas of society's role in labor-management relations were tried and tested on the railroads before being applied to the whole economy. This historic tendency to "try things out" in the transportation labor-management arena is in itself a major reason why goal conflicts are brought into sharper focus in this area.

Economic and Technological Nature of the Problem

The special nature of the problem of transportation labor-management relations is further illustrated by four economic and technological conditions: employment characteristics, carrier costs, process characteristics, and substitutability.

The employment characteristics of transportation labor typically are the requirement of a relatively high level of skill, considerable responsibility by the worker, minimum supervision, with usually higher-than-average pay levels. Equipment operators in all modes of transportation are highly skilled. They must exercise considerable judgment while operating without an immediate supervisor close at hand. Airline pilots are perhaps the outstanding example of this need for skill and judgment, the carrying of great responsibility, the lack of direct supervision, and high pay levels. Most other types of workers in transportation are similarly situated at least to some degree. Rate clerks must make careful judgments which affect the costs of the firm. Maintenance personnel must be especially responsible to protect life and property. Freight handlers must be particularly careful and, above all, trustworthy in their work. All transportation workers are part of an undertaking of "public trust." The economic goods and the personal well-being of the public is entrusted to their skill, care, and responsibility. Generally wages higher than those received by the average worker have reflected this responsibility and skill. Society has a justifiable interest in safe, reliable, and trustworthy service as well as in continuity of service. Certainly this gives a special nature to labor-management relations in transportation.

As pointed out in Chapters 4 and 5, labor costs make up a major portion of the costs of providing service in several modes of transportation. While it is not true for pipelines and water carriers, labor is the largest single cost item for rail-, air-, and motor-carrier service. Labor costs exceed 50 per cent of total costs in all three of these modes, and small changes in labor costs or fringe benefits are reflected in the profitability of the carriers. Hence, the intensity of the labor-management bargain is heightened.

The transportation process is a continuous one. Transportation does not start at 8:00 A.M. and the end at 5:00 P.M. The 40-hour week is a pay week only and not an operating period. Trains, trucks, planes, boats, and pipelines do not stop running between Friday afternoon and Monday morning. Because of this continuous process, the labor-management bargain has many more dimensions than the 8:00 to 5:00, 40-hour-a-week factory work bargain. The technological setting is such that both the economics of compensation and the conditions of labor are infinitely more complex in transportation than in the economy as a whole.

Finally, in recent times it has been increasingly possible to substitute capital for labor in transportation. The use of capital in the place of labor varies by mode, of course, but it has been extremely widespread in pipelines and railroads. With automatic pumping-station devices, remote controls, and electric pumps, pipelines have successively decreased their use of labor while rapidly increasing their through-put. In railroads, employment has declined by more than one half since World War II, as dieselization, Centralized Traffic Control, and other capital innovations have increased. This substitution effect which has been especially strong in transportation serves to intensify the labor-management bargain.

It is understandable, then, why the social necessity for continued service, the historical fact of early unionization and social innovation, and the economic-technological factors of employment characteristics, carrier costs, process characteristics, and substitutability all combine to make labor-management relations in transportation a unique problem.

INSTITUTIONAL ENVIRONMENT

Because it is a unique problem, the labor-management bargain in transportation occurs in an institutional environment of its own. This environment differs from other labor-management relations both from the economic and the legal viewpoints.

Economic Environment

The two factors of an economic type tending to make a different institutional environment in transportation are industrywide bargaining and the necessity for service continuity.

In general, the labor-management bargain is negotiated on an industrywide basis within a particular mode. The only significant exception to this has been the Teamsters' contract which until recently was negotiated on a regionwide intramodal basis, although with but five regions. In 1964, the Teamsters' contract also became industrywide. In this type of negotiation, one bargain generally covers all firms and all workers in the particular union either over the entire country or in a given region.

Under regionwide bargaining there are few differentials, and under industrywide bargaining there are none. That is, a given type of labor is paid the same and works under the same conditions all over the country (or region). Carrier costs tend to be equalized and "low cost labor" areas are prevented.

Unions have often upheld industrywide bargaining as an "ideal." They have felt that each type of labor should be paid the same regardless of where it is performed. In general, unions have looked upon industrywide bargaining as an opportunity for their best negotiators to get the best bargain and thereby erase any effect of weak local unions. Industrywide bargaining has been a sign of labor solidarity, a united front, and equality for all across the country. Finally, it has been an "ideal" because the maximum sanction of complete work stoppage can be applied if a strike becomes necessary.

But when the "ideal" of industrywide bargaining has been attained, the second economic institutional factor—the necessity for service—intervenes. The goal of solidarity, no differentials, maximum sanctions, and equalization conflicts with society's goal of continued service. If negotiations break down, the ultimate weapon is the strike. But a strike means discontinuance of an essential service. Society cannot tolerate this. Hence, once the long-sought economic institutional environment is attained by labor, its effect is blunted by another and more dominant goal of society as a whole. This leads to legal restraints.

Legal Environment

Special legal institutions have been devised within which some labor-management negotiations in transportation must operate. These apply to railway and airline labor negotiations, although not to teamster contracts. This fairly complicated set of legal machinery has been substituted for the usual procedure of settling labor-management differences with the intent of preventing work stoppages and the use of the ultimate weapon, the strike. Basically, the idea is to delay. Both sides must go through time-consuming procedures. With delay, issues are often more refined, tempers cooled, and time for careful reconsideration is allowed. Society hopes to avoid the consequences of work stoppages by the device of legalized delay.

MECHANICS OF LABOR-MANAGEMENT CONFLICT SETTLEMENT

The complicated legal mechanics of the settlement of labor-management disputes assumes that a normal collective bargaining attempt will be made by carriers and their employees. The mechanics are an addition to traditional methods of collective bargaining and are designed to come into play only if and when traditional methods of settlement fail. Unfortunately, the existence of these legal procedures and mechanics sometimes may tend to hasten the breakdown of the traditional methods of bargaining.

Background

The set of complicated legal procedures and mechanics surrounding the transportation labor-management relationship has an interesting background. These procedures, devised by society in an attempt to avoid service stoppages, evolved in the area of railway labor relations. This is not surprising as railroad labor was organized at an early date and the carriers had an even earlier history of acting in concert on other matters of mutual concern.

Basically, five laws serve as background to the Railway Labor Act of 1926 which, as amended, is the present applicable procedure. In 1888, labor unrest on the railroads led to the Arbitration Act which provided for voluntary arbitration and investigation of disputes. This act was used but once and was unsuccessful in dealing with the Pullman strike of 1894 and the American Railway Union led by Eugene Debs. In 1898, the Erdman Act allowed either party to a dispute to request the Chairman of the Interstate Commerce Commission and the Commissioner of Labor to act as mediators. If this mediation failed, these officials were to attempt to get voluntary agreement to arbitration with a decision to be binding on both parties for one year. This procedure was amended by the Newlands Act of 1913 which provided for a permanent Commissioner of Mediation and Conciliation and two other persons, all appointed by the President, who would act as the United States Board of Mediation and Conciliation. This Board could act without waiting for a request for its services and was obligated to hand down a nonbinding arbitration award within thirty days. A number of disputes were handled by this procedure.

During the Federal operation of railways from 1917 to 1920, the Federal government dealt directly with unions and set up several advisory boards to assist the Director General of the Railroads. Also during this wartime period, the Adamson Act providing for the eight-hour day for railroad workers, with no reduction in pay, was applied. This act had been passed in 1916, but was under legal challenge before the courts as well as under investigation by a special commission at the time.

When the rail carriers were returned to private control by the Transportation Act of 1920, two labor-management procedures which had grown out of wartime experiences were provided. One, regional Railroad Boards of Labor Adjustment with both labor and management members could be set up to handle minor disputes arising from grievances, working conditions, and rules interpretations. Two, a permanent Railroad Labor Board of nine members, three representing labor, three representing management, and three representing the public, was established. This group was to settle wage disputes and to act as an appeal board from Adjustment Board decisions. This solution was not successful.

Railway Labor Act of 1926

To some degree, the Railway Labor Act of 1926 drew upon the experiences of previous attempts to solve labor-management problems in transportation. The Act was amended in 1934 and was extended to cover the employees of interstate air carriers in 1936. This discussion is of the Act as amended. It should be emphasized that only rail and air transportation labor-management relations are involved.

Although each step under the Railway Labor Act is not clearly defined or provided under the law, there are five steps in the mechanics of labor-management conflict settlement. These are conference and collective bargaining, Boards of Adjustment or Mediation, voluntary arbitration, Emergency Boards, and Presidential action.

Conference and Collective Bargaining

The mechanics of settlement, as noted above, assume that normally contracts will be reached by use of the traditional methods of free collective bargaining. Disputes over contracts, interpretations, and grievances, it is assumed, will usually be settled by conferences between carriers and employees. These two devices, it is hoped, will handle the majority of the problems occurring and no other procedure will be necessary. Unfortunately, sometimes the mere existence of additional procedures seems to jeopardize the effectiveness of earlier steps, and neither side makes any great effort to settle issues at the lower levels.

Boards of Adjustment or Mediation

Drawing upon previous experience, the Railway Labor Act set up two boards with jurisdiction to act in two broad areas. These are the National Railroad Adjustment Board and the National Board of Mediation.

The Adjustment Board has jurisdiction over grievances and interpretation of agreements on pay, working conditions, and rules. Basically, this is the area of the "conference" noted above. If the employer-employee conference method fails, the Board (composed of thirty-six members, eighteen from each side), makes an interpretation which is binding on both parties. In operation, the Board is divided into four divisions each with jurisdiction over a separate class of labor. If a deadlock occurs in a consideration before a division, a neutral third party is selected to serve until a decision is reached. If there is no agreement upon the selection of the neutral third party, the National Mediation Board appoints him.

The Mediation Board has jurisdiction over disputes that cannot be settled by collective bargaining. Basically this involves contract changes in wages, working conditions, and rules (whereas the Adjustment Board is concerned with interpretation and application). The Mediation Board is made up of three members serving for three years appointed by the President with the advice and consent of the Senate. The primary task of this Board is to institute mediation and attempt to help both parties find a common ground for contract agreement. The Board does not decide issues or make awards. Either party may invoke the services of the Board or it may act on its own motion. Unlike the Adjustment Board, the Mediation Board is made up of impartial public officials not connected with either management or labor.

Voluntary Arbitration

If the National Mediation Board fails in its efforts to bring the parties together on common ground, the law orders it to work for voluntary arbitration. Both sides must agree to abide by the results of arbitration before a temporary arbitration board is established to hear the particular dispute. One third of the arbitrators are chosen by the carriers, one third by the labor organizations, and the other one third by the carrier-labor arbitrators. In case of disagreement concerning the choice of the "neutral" arbitrators, the Mediation Board chooses them. Although arbitration itself is voluntary, once the parties agree to it the arbitration decision is legally binding on both parties.

Emergency Boards

Arbitration may, of course, be refused. In such a case, if the National Mediation Board believes that the dispute threatens to interrupt interstate commerce, it must notify the President. At his discretion, then, the President may create a special Emergency Board charged with investigating the dispute. This Emergency Board has thirty days in which to investigate and report, and during that time no change may take place in the conditions which led to the dispute unless by agreement.

Actually, Emergency Boards make recommended awards or settlements in their reports, but this action is not binding. It is hoped, however, that the power of public opinion will induce acceptance of the findings of the Emergency Board. If the recommendation of the Emergency Board is refused, another thirty days must elapse before any change or action can commence. Hence, it is often said that the appointment of an emergency board postpones any work stoppage for a 60-day, cooling-off period.

If all the foregoing efforts fail and the power of public opinion does not induce a settlement, the President himself may act to avoid disruption of commerce. This "step" is not included in the Railway Labor Act but, in effect, it is a real possibility. On several occasions the President has "seized" the railroads, and on at least one recent occasion his action was to recommend immediate Congressional action to avoid a nationwide rail strike.

In the so-called "featherbedding" issue, President Kennedy during the summer of 1963 requested that Congress pass a special law prohibiting a threatened strike and setting up compulsory arbitration. Congress responded, and an issue which had been in active bargaining for more than five years and which had gone through all the preliminary steps described above plus a special "Presidential Railroad Commission" investigation was solved only by Presidential and Congressional action. In the spring of 1964, President Johnson averted a nationwide rail strike by personally mediating and negotiating a settlement. The President used his considerable personal and official prestige and persuasive powers to force a settlement and avoid a nationwide work stoppage. Again, only the last step of "Presidential Action," this time by bringing the negotiators to the White House itself, saved the nation from a crippling disruption of commerce.

ALTERNATIVE SOLUTIONS

In recent times, the step of "Presidential Action" has caused many persons to ask what alternatives exist. It is obvious that neither the President nor Congress can settle every labor-management dispute in transportation. Indeed there is real question whether or not they should be called upon to settle any specific labor-management dispute. Many have suggested that the mechanics of conflict settlement in this area have broken down and that the institutional structure of transportation labor-management relations must be reconstituted. This was one of the conclusions of the special "Presidential Railroad Commission" in its report on the "featherbedding" issue in 1962 and was one of the several suggestions made by President Kennedy in his precedent-making "Transportation Message" in April, 1962.

There are at least five alternative solutions to this problem: work stoppage, reconstitution of the labor market, compulsory arbitration, government ownership, and private transportation.

Work Stoppage

One approach is to allow labor-management disputes to run their full course, including work stoppages, as they may do in other parts of the economy. This is hardly a possible alternative, however. General work stoppages on our railroads or airlines is unthinkable. Our economy is so dependent upon transportation that a work stoppage of even a few days, especially on the railroads, would paralyze all economic activity. No responsible government would or could permit this. A nationwide transportation strike, at least one involving a major mode, has become an "industrial hydrogen bomb," a weapon too destructive to use.

Reconstitution of the Labor Market

Another approach would be to abandon industrywide bargaining in favor of bargaining between local unions and single companies or between national unions and single companies. While this would avoid a nationwide strike, it would not settle the problem. At best, it only segments it. The effect upon commerce would still be severe, even if only on one geographic segment at a time, and our geographic regions are closely interconnected and highly interdependent.

There is some indication that the railroad Brotherhoods have decided to pursue this alternative. They now seem to wish to bargain as national unions with a single railroad at a time. They do not, as yet, wish to have local unions bargaining with single companies. Their strength would be greatly dissipated by such a move.

In spite of this apparent recent change in tactics by the Brotherhoods, there are real disadvantages to such an approach. Differentials in wages and conditions may easily arise under such segmentation. Solidarity is lost, and the chance of having to settle at less than the "national pattern" with some carriers is a real one. It is also noteworthy that the Teamsters have recently gone from regional to industrywide bargaining. It is not easy to give up the "ideal" of unionism and turn back the pages of time.

There is some question as to whether or not carrier management desires a segmented labor market. By bargaining as individual carriers, they lay themselves open to "whipsaw" tactics, that is, the union can play one carrier off against another. The airlines have recognized this possibility and as a result, in 1958 six of the trunklines entered into a "mutual-aid pact." Under this agreement, all members pledge to pay to an airline suffering a service stoppage because of a strike an amount equal to the increased revenue, minus expenses, resulting from the increased business going to the nonstruck lines. This allows the carriers at least partial protection from successive work stoppages designed to force settlement on successive lines by the whipsaw device.

Finally, it is highly questionable whether Congress could or would pass a statute forbidding industrywide bargaining even if both labor and management agreed to such an approach.

Compulsory Arbitration

In 1963, Congress used the compulsory arbitration approach in the so-called "featherbedding" issue. Various other schemes using this approach have been attempted, primarily at the state level and primarily involving public utilities whose services are considered equally essential. Special boards of arbitrators, special courts of industrial relations, or special awards of public officials have all been suggested or tried. None has worked satisfactorily. Certainly neither party was satisfied with the solution imposed in the 1963 experience. The major advantage of this approach is, of course, that service stoppages are avoided.

There are at least four disadvantages to this alternative. First, no workable plan has been set forth. In the utilities, all efforts to sustain service by forcing arbitration have proved either unworkable or have been declared illegal. People cannot be forced to work against their will. Second, the whole process of compulsory arbitration subverts collective bargaining. There is little incentive to do more than go through the motions of bargaining if both sides know that if they are dissatisfied they can force a board or an official to settle the issue. Bargaining is looked upon as wasted effort since the positions will finally have to be stated to the arbitrators, thus no effort is made to find a settlement without resorting to this ultimate decision. To some degree this is now true with "Presidential Action" as a step.

Third, labor feels that compulsory arbitration imposes "second-class citizenship" upon them. The ultimate weapon of the strike is denied, and a group of arbitrators determine their fate. Intelligent labor leaders wish to avoid compulsory arbitration if for no other reason than because it replaces the need for bargainers or even unions.

Fourth, compulsion goes against our traditional ideas of what is "right." Democracy is based on the idea of free men persuading others in open debate. Compulsory arbitration not only tends toward "involuntary servitude" by labor, but smacks of authoritarianism. The alternative of compulsory arbitrators is not at all a realistic alternative.

Government Ownership

Some have proposed that the government should own the carriers and that thus work stoppages would be prevented. The whole question of government ownership has been debated for many years and involves other aspects than labor-management relations. There is real doubt that government ownership would solve the labor-management issue, however, and this alternative seems like a rather harsh and probably unworkable solution. Public employees do strike on occasion, and there is little reason to suspect that making transportation labor into public employees would make them any less interested in wages, working rules, and conditions of labor. Besides, most observers would agree that other problems brought on by government ownership would be too great a price to pay for labor-management peace even if public ownership would bring such peace.

Private Transportation

The final alternative approach might be to change the structure of the transportation industry itself. Where private transportation is possible, mainly in motor and water carriage, work stoppages have sometimes been avoided by producers providing their own transportation on a nonunion basis. At the very best this is but a partial solution. It assumes no unions, a condition which would be most difficult to impose, and it assumes no common carriers, an equally unrealistic assumption. Extensive private transportation by rail, air, or pipeline would be virtually impossible. Who can own their own railroad or how many air travelers can afford their own plane? Even if such a move were possible, it would call for major traffic shifts and a complete technological, economic, and legal reorganization of the transportation industry. Although some large producers owning their own trucks and barges are partially insulated from national labor-management disputes, this certainly is not a practical solution.

CONCLUSION

None of the alternatives discussed apply or are completely workable in resolving conflicting goals in transportation labor-management relations under our present institutional structure of unionized labor and profit-seeking carriers. The changes necessary to make any of these alternatives workable impose too great a price in other ways. In the authors' opinion, no satisfactory workable alternatives have been suggested to date. Nor do we have any.

Without doubt this serious problem needs additional and continual study and thought. However, as of now, the conflicts in goals between labor, management, and the public, the special nature of the transportation labor-management problem, the institutional environment, the present state of the mechanics of settlement, and the alternative solutions all lead to the essentially negative and pessimistic conclusion that no real solution exists. Perhaps we and our grandchildren will have to "muddle through" from crisis to crisis just as did our grandfathers. Not every problem has a solution.

ADDITIONAL READINGS

1. Bigham, Truman C., and Merrill J. Roberts, **Transportation: Principles and Problems,** 2nd ed. New York: McGraw-Hill Book Co., Inc., 1952. Chapter 21. "Labor Relations," pp. 595–616.
2. Flood, Kenneth U., "Common Carrier's Duty to Service Strike-Bound Plants," **I.C.C. Practitioners' Journal,** Jan. 1956, p. 30.
3. Henzey, William V., "Labor Problems in the Airline Industry," **Law and Contemporary Problems,** Winter 1960, pp. 43–57.
4. Hudson, William J., and James A. Constantin, **Motor Transportation.** New York: Ronald Press Company, 1958. Chapter 11. "Labor Relations in the Trucking Industry," pp. 235–265.
5. Jakubauskas, Edward B., "Technological Change and Recent Trends in the Composition of Railroads Employment," **The Quarterly Review of Economics and Business,** Nov. 1962, pp. 81–90.

6. Marshall, Arthur M., "Carrier Service and the Picket Line," **Transportation Journal,** Spring 1962, pp. 14–21.
7. Norton, Hugh S., **Modern Transportation Economics.** Columbus, Ohio: Charles E. Merrill Books, Inc., 1963.
   Chapter IV. "Transportation Labor," pp. 90–103.
8. Oliver, Eli L., "Labor Problems of the Transportation Industry," **Law and Contemporary Problems,** Winter 1960, pp. 3–21.
9. Pegrum, Dudley F., **Transportation: Economics and Public Policy.** Rev. ed. Homewood, Ill.: Richard D. Irwin, Inc., 1968.
   Chapter 20. "The Special Problems of Labor," pp. 501–521.
10. Simler, Norman J., "The Economics of Featherbedding," **Industrial and Labor Relations Review,** Oct. 1962, p. 100.
11. Taff, Charles A., **Commercial Motor Transportation,** 4th ed. Homewood, Ill.: Richard D. Irwin, Inc., 1969.
    Chapter 10. "Labor Relations," pp. 237–249.
12. Troxel, Emery, **Economics of Transport.** New York: Rinehart & Company, Inc., 1955.
    Chapter 24. "Labor Unions in Transportation," pp. 561–586.
13. Weinstein, Paul A., "The Featherbedding Problem," **American Economic Review,** May 1964, pp. 145–152.
14. Westmeyer, Russell E., **Economics of Transportation.** Englewood Cliffs, N.J.: Prentice-Hall, Inc., 1952.
    Chapter 17. "Railroad Labor and Labor Problems," pp. 343–364.
15. Wisehart, Arthur M., "The Airlines' Recent Experience under the Railway Labor Act," **Law and Contemporary Problems,** Winter 1960, pp. 22–43.

22

Public Aids and Promotions
of Transportation

NATURE OF THE PROBLEM

One of the special problems of domestic transportation is the matter of public aids and promotions. This affects the regulation of transportation. As noted earlier, Congress established as a goal in the "Declaration of National Transportation Policy" in 1940 the ". . . fair and impartial regulation of all modes of transportation . . . so administered as to recognize and preserve the inherent advantages of each . . ." Inequality of public aid, investment, and promotion clouds the determination of the inherent advantage of each mode. The regulation of intermodal competition and minimum rate levels is particularly difficult when all modes do not need to meet their respective total costs of service.

Public aids and promotions are also a problem from the point of view of social policy. At any time, society can afford to invest only a portion of its resources in any one economic undertaking whether that investment be private or public. How much development of a particular type of transportation is needed in our economic system at any one time is a most challenging problem. Not only is the matter of timing involved, but also the amount of investment.

If a free market existed, that is, if competition and the private profit motive were allowed to operate fully in this field, the allocation problem would be much simpler. The particular allocation of resources to transportation would be the one which showed the greatest dollar return after cost. This would be true both between transportation and nontransportation undertakings and between the various modes of transportation. As long as the acquisitive spirit existed and was allowed to operate freely, we could expect men to allocate resources of all types to the most profitable undertaking.

But the free market does not exist. The acquisitive spirit operating freely has not been used as an allocator in transportation for several reasons. These may be summarized as historical, technological, economic, and social.

Historical

From the very first, transportation has been aided and promoted by various governmental levels in our society. An improved domestic transportation system was so important to the economic, political, and social development of our nation that internal improvement schemes were some of the first Congressional problems after our independence. Even though our country was firmly committed to private enterprise, it was recognized that government had an obligation to assist in the creation of an environment conducive to economic development. A transportation system is akin to law and order, coinage, inviolability of contract, and other "essentials" of commercial enterprise.

Additionally, there is real question whether a privately owned transportation system would have been possible. Not only was the necessary investment overwhelming, but by its very nature, transportation uses public resources such as rivers and harbors, roadways and streets, and the air above the earth. It would be unthinkable to have a system of privately owned highways, waterways, or airways even if such a thing were legally possible. Transportation agencies have no choice but to use public facilities in many cases.

Finally, our society did not arise full-grown. There existed a long history in Europe, particularly England, of the common carrier operating by sanction of the sovereign. This service, which was to be provided to all comers under common-law regulation, was transplanted to this continent by the early colonizers. No "free market" existed in the common-carrier tradition. A common carrier could not pick among his customers and serve only the most profitable. No free entry or exit of firms was allowed. The common carrier was never allowed to charge whatever he desired, raising his fee to certain customers or at certain times and lowering it at other times or for other customers. In other words, the free market and competitive nature mandatory for a market type of allocation did not exist in the society which was the historical background of our domestic transportation system.

Technological

The various modes of transportation developed at different periods of time. Technologically it was not possible to have some of the newer modes of transportation until quite recently. The invention of the internal combustion engine and man's conquering of vertical space by flight of heavier-than-air craft are but two illustrations of technological developments which were the genesis of competing transportation modes. Competition and the existence of choice among several modes has simply not been a technological possibility until very recently. Hence, the use of individual choice to allocate among modes was not feasible.

Technology has played a role in transportation aids and promotions in another way. It is often a drawn out and expensive matter to develop technological breakthroughs. Even after the means are technologically available, periods of testing and gaining of public confidence are long and expensive. Oftentimes a portion if not all of the expense of testing, acceptance, development and research has been carried on with public aid. Americans have always been fascinated by new developments. It is not surprising, then, that society has been willing to sponsor research, development, and technology which ultimately leads to transportation choice. As will be noted shortly, a great deal of the research and development of air transportation is the direct result of governmental aid. This is but one example which could be cited to show that a part of the costs of some modes of transportation are paid for by society.

Economic

Another reason why the free market and competitive structure has not existed in transportation, making allocation based on competition possible, is the economic structure of transportation itself. By nature, some types of transportation are monopolistic. In order for a rail system to exist, it had to be a monopoly. The power of eminent domain, itself a type of governmental aid, was necessary in order to acquire right of way. The huge amounts of capital necessary could not be attracted unless there was assurance that the service had a monopolistic element. During the developmental period of rail building, cities and towns were eager to grant monopoly privileges in order to get the desired rail service. The same was true of early canals and, to some degree, of pipelines.

The large capital investment necessary for a rail or pipeline system gives rise to a high degree of fixed costs. When a high degree of fixed costs exists, competition may lower prices drastically. Under such circumstances, it is not unusual for price to fall below total costs, almost to the level of variable costs. Competing means of transportation without similar cost structures found they were unable to continue in the face of drastic price-cutting. In order for them to exist at all in the face of such competition, it was necessary to have public aids or promotions of various types. An example of this situation is the popular justification of expenditures on waterways as a "way to keep rail rates low."

Social Policy

Various social policies of the United States have provided a part of the cost of some modes of transportation and not of others. The provision of the "way" for motor carriers, air carriers, and water carriers are examples. In many cases, carriers were the fortuitous gainers of public aids whose goal was quite divorced from for-hire transportation and the inequality of transportation competition.

For example, interest in conservation has led to stream development for purposes of flood control, bank-erosion elimination, irrigation, and water conservation. All of these laudable goals also provide waterways upon which

inland water carriers may operate. Likewise, our society believes in an educated and informed populace. One of the justifications for Federal expenditures on highways is to provide for rural free delivery of mail in order to bring
educational and informational materials to rural America. However, improved
roads used for mail delivery are equally available to commercial vehicles.
Additionally, the country's defense calls forth public expenditures for airports
and airways. Trained aviation personnel need to be available in case of wartime emergency. Equipment used on commercial airline operations can and
do play a vital role in the defense plans of our society. Here again is a rationali-
zation for an aid to transportation which is quite divorced from competitive
considerations. Finally, it has been our social policy to encourage mobility of
our population. Through mobility, it is assumed that each individual can seek
his own fortune where he pleases or take his pleasure in his own fashion.
There was also an educational aspect in encouraging travel in our society. The
slogan "See America First" illustrates this point. Again, much of the rationali-
zation for highway expenditures has been in terms of other-than-transportation
competition.

In all of these cases, the means of transportation have been provided
publicly or have been publicly aided because of a social policy quite unrelated to transportation competition. Regardless of the social objectives involved, the facilities have been made available to various modes of transportation. Part of the cost of transportation has been absorbed by the public for
some modes and not for others. Even though the carriers may pay a portion
of the cost of the facilities through user charges (taxes), their burden of immediate investment in the "way" has been lifted. Additionally, the users are
not asked to pay taxes on the public investment nor interest on the funds committed as under a privately owned way. True competition, with each competitor paying all of his costs and the traffic going to the low-cost bidder, is
simply not possible under such an arrangement. The same reasoning holds
for types of public aid other than provision of the way.

It is necessary to conclude, then, that a free market and competitive relationship has never existed in transportation. A market allocation of resources
has been impossible because of historical, technological, economic, and social
policy impediments. Allocation of transportation resources has always been
affected by public aids of various types. Given the fact that transportation is
but a part of the whole society which has many diverse goals, the chance that
public aids and promotions will exist in the future also seems reliably certain.

The problem, then, becomes a matter of evaluating the goals of public
aid, the methods of carrying them out, and their effects on transportation.
Only by understanding and carefully evaluating these points can intelligent
choices be made by society. In evaluating goals, methods, and effects of public
aid to transportation, as in other social decisions, readers should keep clearly
in mind that conclusions concerning desirability or undesirability must be based
in considerable part upon subjective value judgments. Rational economic

analysis may tell us what happens under various conditions, but whether a result is "good" or "bad" usually depends upon an individual's or a society's philosophy, and philosophies may change from time to time.

GOALS OF PUBLIC AID

The goals of public aids and promotions in transportation are not always easy to ascertain. This is necessarily true because they are so interwoven with broad social objectives as noted above. Basically, these goals represent a consensus of opinion at any one time. As a consensus, they represent the desires of various groups in our economy, and these desires are not always the same over time. Public policy on transportation aid and promotions is not only hard to define, but has changed as transportation has developed. However, it seems possible to generalize that the broad goals of society in this matter are developmental and competitive.

Developmental Goals

During its first one hundred years as a separate nation, America faced the major problem of developing its resources and physically settling the continent. Much domestic transportation policy was affected by this task. The problem certainly existed prior to the establishment of the nation as an independent country, and it continues to exist at present insofar as all areas of the nation are not equally developed. The developmental goal of public aids and promotions in transportation, therefore, is not only important historically, but currently, and may be a future policy goal as well.

From the historical viewpoint, a great many of the internal improvement schemes of Congress and the states were aimed at settling the country. The rationale behind the railroad land-grant movement, a type of public aid, was that railroads would open up the country. Promotion of canals by states and the building of the National Pike by the Federal government are other historical examples of public aids and promotions with a developmental goal. While it may seem that most of our country now has an adequate transportation system, the plea is still heard for improved transportation to develop the country. A rather substantial amount of the economic and social development program for Appalachia is for road building. In the mountainous areas of the nation, the need for forest roads is often justified as a method of economic development.

Pleas for improvement of transportation systems as an aid to commerce and industry are still heard, even though the initial development has been completed in many areas. Technology moves ahead and old facilities are obsolete. Wider and more direct highways are needed, better waterways are called for, and safer airways become a necessity as development progresses. The rationale of helping commerce and industry develop applies to all levels of government aid. It is argued that with highly developed industry or commerce, more income is generated, more people are employed, and more taxes are collected. While the actual productivity of public investment in transportation facilities is very difficult if not impossible to measure, the feeling is quite general that such expenditures lead to a worthwhile development of industry and commerce.

The matter of timing is implicit in this developmental goal. It is sometimes said that the facilities would be built without special programs and aids if only society would wait. Perhaps this is true and over time the profit potential would have caused railroads to expand and state and local governments to recognize the productivity of public investment in roads and airports and inland harbors. But the point is that the American people in the past did not want to wait, nor do they want to wait now or in the future. Thus the main goal of these programs has not just been to develop facilities, but to develop them faster than they would have come if they had not been promoted. Hence, it is said that the land grants caused the West to be settled sooner, the highway program opened up the off-rail points faster, and the airways program hastened the development of air transportation.

Competitive Goals

In addition to the idea of providing a means of developing the country, there has been a broad competitive goal to much of our aid and promotion activity in transportation. Being constantly interested in improving ourselves and our society, the goal of our aids and promotions has sometimes been to provide new means of transportation. Certainly much of our program in air transportation has been related to this goal. It is really a competitive goal as new means of transportation compete with the established means. Aid to helicopters and local-service airlines is an example of the desire of society to have new means of transportation.

Improvement in one area of transport ought to force improvement in competitive modes. Aid programs to induce waterways to compete with railroads illustrates this thought. Additionally, the desire to supplement and replace regulation with transportation competition has also been a goal. There has always been concern, sometimes not always defined as such, that regulation is not working. Suspicion that the regulated and the regulators were somehow in collusion is often heard, hence the desire to have competition as the "natural regulator." Even when regulation is trusted as a protector of the public interest, promotion of competitive transportation is justified as a supplement to regulation. Competition is relied upon in most parts of the economy, and the change in thinking to a regulated structure is not easy. Competition provided by public aid as a backstop to regulation, or "just in case," has sometimes been sought.

Finally, recognition of the differences in economic structure of the different modes has led to the sponsoring of competitive means of transportation in an attempt to equalize competition. Proposals have sometimes been made for aid programs based solely on the differences in cost of the various modes. Subsidies to help the economically weak compete with the financially strong are sometimes proposed. The evening-up process is also seen in proposals that user charges be utilized to equalize competitive advantage, although this is the opposite of subsidies and aids. In all these proposals the rationale, whether recognized or not, is that competition and choice are the most desirable social policy regardless of the cost involved.

Basically, then, the goals of public aids have been developmental and competitive. While they overlap considerably and are sometimes hard to distinguish among other social goals, they exist nevertheless.

METHODS OF PUBLIC AIDS

Public aids and promotions in transportation have taken many forms. Each program had its own distinguishing features, thus the tendency to discuss programs according to the transportation mode to which they apply is widespread. However, it may be even more meaningful to consider the methods or means of aids to transportation according to the tasks which they are designed to accomplish rather than by mode. Briefly, four methods are used in public-aid programs. These are: financing the way, operating the way, financing operating costs, and providing research and development.

Financing the Way

Perhaps the predominant method of public aid is by financing the way upon which carriers operate. This has not only been historically the most important aid program, but it remains today the best example of promoting transportation. The public has been and is called upon to invest in the way or part of the way of nearly all modes of transportation. Among the for-hire modes of transportation, pipelines alone are the only ones that have not received some public aid through public investment in the way.

Railroad Land Grants and Aids

There were many programs to assist in the financing of the railway during the developmental period of the railroads. Some of these have been mentioned in Chapter 2. All levels of government participated in these programs, and the major purpose of all was the building of the way.

The exact measurement of the amount and type of these aids during the construction period is quite difficult. Some of the aid was in the form of loans, part of which was repaid and part of which was not. Disputes as to the dollar value of such loans is understandable. Records are inadequate and some of the aid was in the form of apparent donations and gifts about which poor records exist. Another form of aid was the guaranteeing of railroad bonds, which thereby permitted them to be sold at lower rates of interest than if they were solely based on railroad credit. Some outright gifts of securities by cities and counties were made to entice railroads to build. Again the problem of measurement is evident. Considerable amounts of land were also involved in land grants and gifts. Here the dispute centers around the value of the land not immediately sold.

One study by the Federal Coordinator of Transportation concluded that Federal aid to railroads amounted to $1.4 billion up to 1938. This included depression loans during the 1930's, expenses of Federal railway surveys, remission of import duties on railway iron, a figure for banking privileges granted by the states, guarantees of bonds, a value for streets vacated and occupied by railroads, a figure for railroad bonds subscribed to by cities and counties, and many other figures. An equally authoritative source, the Board of Investigation and Research which was set up under the Transportation Act of 1940, calculated the amount of aid at $627 million. The B.I.R. study concentrated on land grants, direct loans, street vacations, and expenses of surveys, and calculated values in a somewhat different fashion. About the only thing the two studies agreed upon was that the railroads had net proceeds of between $434 and $440 million from the sale of land grants.

State and local assistance to early railroads involved substantial stock and bond subscriptions, some loan guarantees and land grants, and many millions of dollars in outright gifts of cash or negotiable securities.

Perhaps the best-known aid program was the land grants. While states granted large blocks of land to a few railroads, it was principally the Federal government which gave land to western railroads to aid in their construction. The total acreage involved approaches ten per cent of the country's area. Starting in 1850 with a grant to the Illinois Central, the program, which closed in 1871, included some seventy-five grants of land. The B.I.R. study notes that the aggregate acreage was 179 million of which more than 48 million acres were state grants. It also notes that ninety-five per cent of this land was granted to the predecessors of only fourteen of the present-day railroad companies.

In return for these land grants, railroads agreed to haul government passengers and freight at reduced rates. Practically all railroads extended these reduced rates (even though many received no land grants) in order to share in governmental traffic. The value of these reduced rates, which were not completely removed until 1945, has been estimated by the Board of Investigation and Research at $580 million up to 1943. The sharp increase in movement of troops and government property during World War II increased the value of these concessions immensely. Since the railroads realized somewhat less than this figure from the sale of the land it is generally held that the land-grant rate concessions more than compensated the Federal government for its grants.

In any event, the amount of public aid in providing the way for the rail carriers was substantial. Some contend that since the programs were instituted more than a century ago and that a good part of the state aid was in the South and subsequently destroyed by the Civil War, railroad aid should not be a factor in current policy. Certainly the money is long spent, and current policy should concern itself with current programs. Nevertheless, the aid programs assisting the development of rail carriers are no different in their goals than the current programs of aid to other carriers. The method may vary, but the goal is the same. The experience of rate concessions is worth noting for current policy.

The Highway Program

The highway program is perhaps the most expensive and comprehensive program of public investment in the way. Public investment in the highway system is also one of the oldest types of transportation aid. As noted earlier, the Federal government entered into highway building with the authorization of the "National Pike" or Cumberland Road in 1806. Total cost of this project, including maintenance, was $6.8 million. Other expenditures for roads were made by Federal, state, and local governments.

It was not until 1917, however, that large Federal expenditures for highways began again, although local units of government had continued to spend money on roads between the early period of highway improvement and the revival of highway promotion in the twentieth century. Various types of state-aid programs were in existence beginning in the 1890's as well, as noted in Chapter 2. It is because all units of government have been involved and the expenditures have been continuous that measurement is difficult. Many scholars, therefore, measure highway expenditures from 1921 when the Federal government entered the highway-aid program on a large scale.

While the Highway Act of 1916 set the pattern of Federal aid, it was not until 1921 that the Federal-Aid Primary system was established. This system, originally limited to seven per cent of the total road mileage, is made up of approximately 240,000 miles of roads and has been supported on a 50–50 Federal-state basis. Originally only rural mileage was included, but in 1944 urban extensions of the primary system were brought under the Federal-aid program. Approximately 21,000 of the miles in the Federal-Aid Primary system are city streets.

The Federal-Aid Secondary system, originated during the depression of the 1930's, is concerned with less heavily traveled roads. Approximately 580,000 miles, designated as secondary-aid roads, also receive matching aid from the Federal government. These secondary roads along with the primary and urban systems are known as the ABC aid program. Federal aid is limited to 50 per cent of the expenditures on the ABC system generally.

The most important road system from the point of view of both commerce and aid is the "National System of Interstate and Defense Highways." This system, authorized in 1944, is made up of 41,000 miles of the most heavily traveled highways contained in the primary system. Financing of this system was not undertaken until 1956 when the name was officially changed to "Interstate System." After extended debate, Congress decided that expenditures for this system should be on a pay-as-we-go basis. Consequently, revenues from the Federal gasoline tax and other Federal transportation excises are put into a Highway Trust Fund used to finance these roads. The basic aid formula on the Interstate System is 90 per cent Federal and 10 percent state, with a Federal maximum of 95 per cent under some circumstances. The 1956 act authorized the Federal government to spend $46.2 billion over thirteen years to build this system to the very highest highway standards. In a real sense, this has been a crash program of providing high-speed, limited-access highways for commerce and defense. However, construction has been slower than anticipated and costs have been larger than planned.

Over $3 billion each year has been expended on highways by the Federal government since 1959, most of it on the Interstate System. The ABC system continues to receive aid, and the share of states and cities in both that system and the Interstate System remains large. Additionally, remaining roads and streets are supported by state and local expenditures.

It should be pointed out, of course, that much of this expenditure has a defense goal and a general policy goal of mobility and safety of our population as well as of assisting commerce and industry with an improved transportation system. Very little of the public investment in highways has been explicitly justified on the basis of providing the way for motor carriers, although this certainly is a result.

This tremendous investment in highways carries with it responsibility for repayment by the users to some degree just as land grants were repaid by rate concessions. As noted above, Federal expenditures on the Interstate System come wholly from user or excise taxes on gasolines, tires, rubber, vehicles, and other items. Much of the state revenues for highways also comes from user taxes in the form of gasoline taxes. Most local highway expenditures, however, come from property taxes. Distribution of the tax burden among classes of payers, then, becomes important as a policy matter. Likewise, distribution of the user-tax portion of the burden among various classes of vehicles is of equal importance. These two policy matters, both basically concerning the allocation of the burden of public investment, will be considered later. At this point, our purpose primarily is to point out that public investment in highways has been large, continuous, and comprehensive.

Airways

Airways, like highways and waterways, are publicly owned and operated. Programs of public investment in this area, though relatively new, are not small. During a recent year, the Federal Aviation Agency had jurisdiction over 157,911 miles of low-altitude airways (under 14,000 feet), 102,414 miles of intermediate-altitude airways (14,500 to 24,000 feet), and 72,513 miles of jet routes (over 24,000 feet).

Airways are not as expensive as highways, of course. Marking and navigational aids are the most important items. (Airports, to be discussed, are another matter.) Expenditures for airways have continued since the middle 1920's; and while measurement is difficult, it has been estimated that around $389 million was expended on the establishment of airways between 1925 and 1958. The cost of their maintenance and operation has been several times larger.

Prior to 1933, airports were financed almost wholly by local funds. During the 1930's depression, however, airport construction was included in various public works programs. Upon passage of the Civil Aeronautics Act of 1938, the Civil Aeronautics Authority was ordered to draw up a plan of airport development and make recommendations on the desirability of Federal aid for airport construction. The agency reported in 1939, and Congress made appropriations for this purpose in the early 1940's. In 1946, Congress passed the Federal Airport Act which authorized the expenditure of $520 million over seven years in the form of Federal aid to local governments for airport construction. The time limit on this Act was later extended.

Federal aid to airports depends upon the size and classification of the airport. On smaller airports, Federal aid is generally 50 per cent of the cost. On some of the larger airports, it may be less than 50 per cent. Funds are allocated among states on a formula based on relative populations and areas.

The total amount spent on airports by all levels of government is not easy to measure. The Federal share has not been small. One estimate places the amount at $1.4 billion from 1947 to 1970.

While landing fees and certain other charges are made by cities, airports generally do not have enough income to cover their costs. Some airports do not even cover their operating expenses, let alone repay the capital costs involved. No charge is made by the Federal government for the airway, although some repayment is made by way of the eight per cent excise tax on airline tickets and taxes on aviation fuel.

As far as public investment in airways and airports is concerned, it is possible to say that it has been large, that it involves several levels of government, and that in all likelihood it will increase in the future.

Waterways

One of the oldest types of public investment is that in waterways. Again, all levels of government have been involved and the amount of public investment has been sizable. The history of public aid in this area is most interesting. The Board of Investigation and Research, studying public aids during the early 1940's, notes that Boston erected a "town wharf" in the 1630's, colonial governments built at least twelve lighthouses, and the State of Virginia began a short canal in 1785.

Some of our very first transportation policy regulation is related to waterways. The Treaty of Paris in 1763 guaranteed that the Mississippi River would be free and open to use from its source to the seas without discrimination as to nationality. The peace treaty at the end of the American Revolution contained the significant provision that the Mississippi would be "forever free." Article

Four of the Northwest Ordinance of 1787 declared the navigable waters leading into the Mississippi and St. Lawrence rivers to be "common highways, and forever free" of "any tax, impost, or duty" to citizens of the United States. There is some question, of course, as to whether or not this "freedom" of use should be extended to cover expensive man-made improvements to natural waterways. It is well established that Congress has complete power over navigable waterways of the nation (*U.S. v. Appalachian Electric Co.*, 311 U.S. 377, 1940).

Experiences of the states during the canal era have been noted in Chapter 2. The exact amount of this state aid is hard to measure, but Professor Locklin states that between 1820 and 1840 nearly $200 million in state indebtedness was incurred, presumably mostly for canals. The provision of terminals and other facilities by local governments in modern times has also been substantial.

On the Federal level, the B.I.R. study notes that $2.7 billion was expended on rivers and harbors from 1791 to 1940. In the modern period, the Doyle Report shows that $2.991 billion was expended by the Corps of Engineers for navigational improvements during the period 1917 to 1960. It is obvious that public investment in waterways has accelerated in recent times.

Provision of the way for water carriers has been almost entirely either to assist commerce and industry or for competitive purposes. Until very recently, the amount of use of waterways by pleasure craft has been negligible. Non-transportation policy has come into the picture insofar as some of the cost of multiple-purpose resource projects have been assigned to navigation. It should be emphasized that no tolls are charged on any of the improved waterways of the United States except the St. Lawrence Seaway. Inland waterway policy is a clear case of the public making the entire investment in the way for one means of transportation, while other modes provide their own ways or at least pay a portion of their costs by way of user charges (tolls or user taxes).

Operating the Way

Another method of public aids or promotion of transportation is operating the way. Actual public investment in the way is the major aid, to be sure, but physicial operation and maintenance of the way is often a substantial program. Again inequality exists insofar as one mode must operate and keep up its own way while its competitor has its way operated for it.

Perhaps the most substantial example of the public operating a way and, hence, absorbing a portion of the cost of transportation is the airways. As noted in Chapter 19, the F.A.A. employs a considerable number of highly trained personnel to operate the Federal airways, and spent almost one-half-billion dollars for these operations during a recent year. The cost of operating the airways is many times the investment in airway facilities. While a portion of these funds are spent for general aviation, it is obvious that the majority of the expenditures assist commercial aviation.

Waterways are also operated and maintained with government aid. This is likewise expensive. It has been reported that more than $3 billion was expended by the Corps of Engineers in operation, maintenance, and administration of inland waterways under their jurisdiction between 1917 and 1960 and that the Tennessee Valley Authority has spent more than $1 million a year since 1946 on operation, maintenance, and administration of the navigation improvements on the Tennessee River (Doyle Report).

A final type of this kind of aid relates to highways. Under the highway policy of our nation, the states own, operate, and maintain highways. Each state has a highway department which both lets contracts for the construction of highways in the state and operates and maintains these highways. As indicated in Chapter 1, highway expenditures amount to billions annually. A substantial amount of this is for maintenance and operation which benefits highway carriers as well as motorists.

In all these instances, the operation of the way is another method of public aid.

Financing Operating Costs

A third method used in public aid is a direct operating subsidy or the financing of operating costs in some way. While this method has not been widely used, it is a good illustration of the developmental goal of assisting the early growth of new means of transportation.

A well-known example of this type of aid is the Federal government's direct payments to certain air carriers. Generally these substantial aids have been in the form of mail payments. The Doyle Report estimates that $723.7 million was expended on "airmail subsidies" from 1929 to 1960.

The actual amount of airline subsidy, again, is not easy to determine. Prior to 1951, the C.A.B. established mail rates on the basis of carrier revenue needs. Since 1951, there has been a "separation" of airmail payments and "public service revenues" (subsidies). In this way, the Post Office Department is not burdened with the entire task of financing the development of air transportation. As far as domestic trunk-line air carriers are concerned, "public service revenues" to all but one of these ceased in 1956 and stopped entirely in 1960. While none of the trunk-line carriers now receive this type of support, many of the local service or feeder lines do, along with the helicopter airlines. During a recent year, thirteen local service airlines received $68 million in public service revenues (out of an aggregate revenue of $206 million). During the same year, three helicopter lines received $5.5 million public service revenues (out of $8.6 total revenues). Planned 1970 expenditures for airline public service revenues was in the neighborhood of $41 million.

It will be recalled that under the Transportation Act of 1958, the I.C.C. was allowed to guarantee loans made by private lenders to railroads. Guarantees, it was hoped, would help rail carriers in borrowing money and updating their plants. But guarantees were also possible for loans for operating capital, although with considerably greater restrictions. Insofar as operating capital has been obtained in this manner, an indirect type of subsidization of operating costs is involved.

Payments of considerable size and under various aid programs are made to that part of our merchant marine fleet engaged in foreign commerce. Some of these payments are used to finance steamship operations. Since our subject is primarily domestic transportation, however, these subsidies will not be discussed here.

Research and Development

A fourth method of public aid is the provision of research and development benefiting carriers. When governmental agencies do research and development for some modes of transportation and not for others, another type of inequality is involved. It should be emphasized, also, that much development of a military or defense nature often applies to domestic transportation. Many advances in the designs of bomber planes have subsequently been adopted in commercial planes. Indeed, some types of commercial jet liners were originally developed as military aircraft. In these cases, the carriers benefit although the goal is most certainly a nontransportation one.

Measurement of research and development aids is extremely difficult. Carry-over of military aircraft-design advances to civil aircraft is an example of this difficulty. However, insofar as research and development funds are separately listed, some type of measurement is possible. The Doyle Report notes that $137.8 million was spent by the F.A.A. and C.A.A. in research and development from 1939 to 1960. It should be noted that the majority of this was in recent years. Currently, considerable governmental attention is being devoted to the development of a supersonic commercial aircraft, perhaps to cost one billion dollars.

Air transportation has not been alone in receiving such assistance. For many years the Federal government owned and operated an inland waterway barge line. From 1920 to 1953, when it was sold, this barge line was operated "to demonstrate the practicability of barge operations." In a sense, this is research and development. Professor Locklin notes that this line operated at a profit during only twelve years of its twenty-nine-year corporate existence. Likewise, a great amount of research and development funds is spent by state governments on highway design. Again these are almost impossible to measure.

Summary of Methods of Public Aid

From the above discussion, it is obvious that the four methods of aid programs are not used equally nor are they of equal importance. The provision of the way is by far the most important method we have used to obtain our public-aid goals. While operating the way, financing carrier operating costs, and financing research and development are secondary methods, a substantial amount is involved in each of these lesser programs and they serve the same goals.

It appears that the Federal government alone spent more than $30 billion on various types of direct transportation aid programs from 1917 to 1960 (from figures given in the Doyle Report). The Association of American Railroads estimates all governmental expenditures for highway, water, and air transport development at almost $281 billion from World War II to 1970. While various estimates of this kind can be debated, the totals at least give some idea of the magnitude of aid programs. Taxes paid by transportation ($37.9 billion in 1968) might be considered as offsets to aids. But benefits received by the various modes are not necessarily proportionate to tax payments.

EFFECTS OF PUBLIC AIDS

Now that the goals and methods of public aids to transportation have been discussed, we can consider their effects. Two levels of approach to this may be used: the "macro" and the "micro." By "macro" we mean the broad, overall, or general approach. "Micro" means the individualistic, singular, or specific view.

Macro-Considerations

If transportation in total is considered, analysis of the effect of a public-aid program is simple. It merely means that the general public assumes a portion of the cost of transportation rather than the user of the facilities paying the complete cost. When the goal of the program is a general one, such as developing the country or settling the West, for example, such a program may be easily justified. The rationale of broad aid to transportation is that everyone benefits from improved transportation and everyone should share its costs.

But even if transportation is considered as a whole, an artificial distinction to be sure, the matter of economic allocation again arises. Since unlimited public funds are not available, economic rationale indicates that these moneys should be spent where they make the greatest return to the whole of society. However, as has been pointed out above, it is almost impossible to measure the productivity of public investment, whether it is in transportation facilities, post offices, government power plants, schools, or armaments. About all that can be said on the macro level is that transportation is a necessary prerequisite for economic, social, and cultural development and that our society has decided that spending its public funds in partial support of transportation is a worthwhile undertaking. Sometimes this has been a political decision, sometimes an emotional decision, sometimes a military decision, and sometimes it has been an economic decision. But regardless of motivations, decisions to aid transportation have been made in the past and probably will continue to be made in the future.

Micro-Considerations

Probably a more practical approach is to consider public aids from an individualistic viewpoint. It might be argued that there is no such thing as "transportation" in the broad sense. Individual transportation modes and firms are too diverse, play too many separate as well as complementary and competitive roles, have too many startlingly different economic structures, and otherwise are too dissimilar for realistic consideration as a single entity. Certainly our discussion of public aids, as well as Part Two of this book, have amply illustrated this.

Additionally, the matter of timing is involved. As noted above, society has seen fit to aid and promote some modes at one time and other modes at other times. Aids have helped certain modes to develop, therefore, while penalizing other modes by sponsoring competition. To be sure, transportation as a whole has grown larger by such action, but at the same time, some modes have played a relatively smaller role in that growth due, partially at least, to public aids to their competitors.

It seems evident that the major effect of public aids, considered from an individualistic viewpoint, has been an inequality of treatment. All modes have not been treated alike at any given time. To some degree, as noted at the beginning of this chapter, equality of treatment would have been an impossibility due solely to the vagaries of technology. That is, society obviously could not treat all modes equally when some modes did not exist because they were not then technologically feasible. Additionally, we have noted that equality of treatment is also virtually impossible since some modes by their very nature must make use of public facilities while others can be privately owned. Likewise, the intermingling of aids to transportation with nontransportation programs such as defense, water resource policy, general policy toward mobility, and other social programs has been noted.

To note the reasons for inequalities and how they have arisen, however, does not excuse their existence nor mitigate their effects. Understanding the rationale, the goals, and the methods of public aids is but a first step. Establishing the effects of public aids and promotions is the second step. Finally, social policy to ameliorate the inequality which results is the last step.

Society has from time to time tried to mitigate the effects of public aids by the devices of user charges and rate concessions. These devices also may be used to recoup a part of public investment. Both of these techniques deserve serious consideration. They have two principal objectives: first, to place the cost of public investment on the user of the facility who benefits from it and, second, to recoup as much of the public investment as seems reasonable and fair in view of national or social objectives.

User charges and rate concessions, however, have many inherent problems. Additional inequality is easily possible if rate concessions continue long past the point of recouping investment or if user charges are ill-conceived and poorly planned. User charges are especially prone to abuse. For highways, as an example, how much benefit is properly chargeable to land owners who gain access and increased property values and incomes because of the highways and how much to the actual highway user? Or between classes of users, how much of the cost of an improved highway should be charged to a heavy vehicle using the highway for profit and how much to a motorist using the highway for pleasure? Logic might hold that the heavy vehicle pay at least the additional cost of building the highway to standards suitable to serve his peculiar needs. Various approaches and formulas of cost allocation and benefit measurement are possible, however. There is little unanimity on how these costs should be allocated. The analysis of these and similar problems are beyond the scope of this book, but they do illustrate the point that user charges have many problems inherent within them and are subject to possible abuse. Of course it should be pointed out that user charges are not applied to all modes of transportation. This is another source of inequality.

Insofar as one mode is given more advantages in public aid than another, overcapacity may arise. The favored mode may expand farther than it would have if all costs had been charged to users. Additionally, if one mode is promoted while another is not, the mode without aid eventually may "develop" overcapacity due to a greater decrease in its traffic than in its plant. This is especially possible when the two modes develop at different times. Some scholars feel that our railroads are "overdeveloped" in this sense. Certainly rail overcapacity seems to exist.

Finally, one of the major effects of public aids and promotions is to prevent regulation of the various modes from playing its complete role. Minimum-rates regulation and control of intermodal competition is difficult if all modes are not equally responsible for their respective costs. The finding and application of "inherent advantage" is difficult and insofar as this is a national policy objective, society's wishes are subverted. With inequality of treatment among modes under public-aid programs, regulation is not allowed to be as effective as it is intended to be.

Summary of Effects of Aids

In summary, the effect of public aids and promotions in transportation is to confuse allocation and create inequality. Much of this inequality is unavoidable due to timing, technology, and the necessity for using public facilities. Some of the effects of inequality can be offset and some of the public investment can be recouped through the judicious use of rate concessions and user charges. However, many pitfalls exist in both of these programs, and the chance of additional inequality is possible. The effect of inequality is twofold: It stimulates or causes overcapacity which in reality is a problem in allocation, and it prevents regulation from playing the complete role set for it by the public.

ADDITIONAL READINGS

1. Bigham, Truman C., and Merrill J. Roberts, **Transportation: Principles and Problems.** 2nd ed. New York: McGraw-Hill Book Co., Inc., 1952. Chapter 22. "Public Aids to Transportation," pp. 617–645.

2. Conant, Michael, **Railroad Mergers and Abandonments.** Berkeley, Calif.: University of California Press, 1964.
Chapter 1. "Route Capacity, Excess Capacity and Overinvestment," pp. 1–24.

3. Daggett, Stuart, **Principles of Inland Transportation.** 4th ed. New York: Harper and Brothers, 1955.
Chapter 34. "Public Aid," pp. 739–763.

4. Frederick, John H. **Commercial Air Transportation,** 5th ed. Homewood, Ill.: Richard D. Irwin, Inc., 1961.
Chapter 8. "Civil Aeronautics Board Policy—Mail Rates," pp. 198–235.
Chapter 12. "Financing Airlines," pp. 331–350.

5. Nelson, James C., "Policy Issues and Economic Effects of Public Aids to Domestic Transport," **Law and Contemporary Problems,** Autumn 1959, pp. 531–556.

6. Nelson, James C., **Railroad Transportation and Public Policy.** Washington, D.C.: The Brookings Institute, 1959.
Chapter 4. "Public Promotion of Transport Facilities," pp. 67–110.

7. Nelson, James C., "The Pricing of Highway, Waterway and Airway Facilities," **American Economic Review,** May 1962, pp. 426–435.

8. Pegrum, Dudley F., **Transportation: Economics and Public Policy.** Rev. ed. Homewood, Ill.: Richard D. Irwin, Inc., 1968.
Chapter 19. "Financing Transportation," pp. 467–500.

9. Troxel, Emery, **Economics of Transport.** New York: Rinehart & Company, Inc., 1955.
Chapter 10. "Public Allocations in Transport Organization," pp. 219–245.
Chapter 11. "Public Transport Costs and User Charges," pp. 246–274.

10. Whitehurst, Clinton H. Jr., "Transportation Subsidies: A Plea for Moderation in a War of Words," **Transportation Journal,** Spring 1964, pp. 21–25.

23

Passenger Transportation
Policy Problems

Freight and passenger transportation services are closely interrelated. Often the two services are performed by the same for-hire firm, using the same ways and sometimes even the same vehicles, terminals, and personnel. Profits or losses made by such firms in one service may to some extent offset losses or profits in the other service. Also, public aids in constructing, maintaining, or operating ways, or other kinds of subsidies, or taxes, affect both freight and passenger services. Finally, both private and for-hire transport of both goods and people are intermingled on public ways. Clearly, what happens in passenger transportation may have significant effects on the costs and prices of freight services, as well as upon their quantities and qualities.

The transportation of people is a common element in many seemingly diverse problems such as urban redevelopment, pollution, congestion, safety, budget priorities, bankruptcy, and diplomacy. The purpose of this chapter is not to specify solutions to the problems of passenger transportation, nor even to present a complete list of all its problems. Rather, the purpose is to point out a few of the ramifications of passenger transportation and introduce the very frustrating but pervasive fact that passenger transportation is both a great economic benefit to society and, at the same time, the creator of a multitude of social ills and problems.

THE NATURE OF PASSENGER TRANSPORTATION

There are several distinctive aspects of passenger transportation which lead to problems in this area. These distinctive characteristics include the predominance of private carriage, the supremacy of air transportation for long-distance movements, a by-product effect, the variability factor, and the complexity of markets.

Predominance of Private Carriage

The private automobile provides far more passenger transportation than any other mode. The transportation of people is measured in passenger-miles, and automobiles currently produce almost 90 per cent of all intercity passenger-miles.

Moreover, private automobiles account for by far the largest expenditure of funds for passenger transportation. The purchase of an automobile is a major expenditure for most people. The operating costs of fuel, repairs, depreciation, and the like are a major share of individual budgets. Some idea of the importance of this item can be gained by looking again at the nation's estimated passenger bill in Chapter 1. Most of this huge annual expenditure is for the purchase of new or used automobiles, tires, repairs, gasoline and oil, insurance, tolls, registration fees, and similar items by automobile owners. While for-hire passenger transportation is important, and provides a most valuable communications and cultural link between various areas, private carriage is the predominant form of passenger transportation. This characteristic leads to interesting problems.

First, very little public control exists for private carriage. Safety regulations and controls are well known, and regularly violated or abused. There is practically no price control for vehicles or operating costs. Each individual is on his own as to safety and price. Recently society has begun to impose environmental controls in this area, but even here it is difficult to place restrictions on millions of car owners even though society as a whole might gain by environmental controls.

Second, automobile owners tend to be ignorant of capital costs. The whole area of purchasing and financing private automobiles is one of bargaining and inexactness. Finance charges may be hidden, and equipment options on automobiles are such that no standard price or cost really exists. The "trade-in" situation is chaotic. Each purchase is an individual bargaining transaction.

Third, automobile owners tend to overlook operating costs. Purchases of gasoline and oil are frequent but small expenditures. Most drivers rarely calculate their operating costs per mile. Depreciation is a major operating expense which typically is overlooked by most. Fuel taxes, and support of streets and highways, usually are hidden in the price of gasoline or repairs.

The result of this lack of knowledge of capital and operating costs is that most automobile owners have little idea of what it costs them to operate their cars. Without knowledge of costs, it is imposible to make a rational choice between alternate means of travel. We know or can be quoted the bus, air, or rail fares between two points, but we have little idea of the "auto fare" using our own car between the same two points. Because of the private automobile's convenience, plus the fact that we already have purchased it, we often decide to move by car. If we actually knew our costs, we might find that driving our car is two to three times as expensive as using for-hire transportation. Studies have shown that the average cost of operating a private automobile is 11¢ to 12¢ per passenger-mile, with the average load of slightly more than one passenger per car. The average fare per passenger-mile by train or bus is 3¢ to 4¢, and by plane about 6¢. Even so, travel by private automobile continues to increase markedly, while passenger transportation by for-hire modes grows slowly or not at all.

Finally, a substantial portion of the transportation-related problems of society are directly connected to private automobiles. The environmental effects of transportation, such as congestion and pollution, noted in Chapter 3, are caused predominately by motor vehicles. The difficulty of supporting and maintaining a healthy for-hire passenger transportation industry, whether publicly or privately owned, is directly related to the wide use of private automobiles. The sociological effects of transportation on neighborhoods, urban redevelopment, urban sprawl, and the like are also uniquely related to the private automobile.

The Supremacy of Air Transportation

Air transport has been the most important for-hire intercity passenger mode since the early 1950's. Air transportation carries well over 60 per cent of all for-hire passenger-miles in the nation. If one considers solely the number of passengers, however, the situation changes. Busses carry almost one-half of all the people traveling, with air and rail each carrying about one-fourth. Since air travel typically is for long distances, air passenger-miles are greater.

Air travel is the most expensive type of for-hire passenger movement. Economies of scale are not so readily obtainable by air as by the other modes of for-hire passenger transportation. Additionally, capital costs and operating costs are extremely high by air transport. Nevertheless, travel by air is only about one-half as expensive as travel by private automobile.

If one considers commuter travel and movements within urban places, the picture changes once more. Air transportation is predominantly an intercity or intercontinental mode of transportation. This has some implications, pointed out below, for market complications.

Many of the transportation problems of our society are related to air transportation. Congestion of airways, the condition of highways leading to airports, both air and noise pollution, the locational problems of airports, and controversies over the role of the public in support of air transportation are but a few of the policy problems in this area. Additionally, since air transportation is the only mode of domestic transportation which is deeply involved in international transportation, it creates a variety of political and diplomatic problems.

By-Product Effects

Under certain circumstances, passenger transportation is a by-product of freight transportation. Under other circumstances the transportation of goods is a by-product of the movement of people. Either way, a definite "by-product effect" is at work and causes policy problems.

In rail transportation, passenger business now is a by-product of the much larger and more profitable freight transportation business. Historically, it often was the other way around, with railroads being built into specific areas primarily as carriers of people into new territories. The development of freight transportation came only after settlement. In this sense, it is sometimes said that passenger transportation pioneers for freight transportation.

In motor transportation, the carriage of mail and passengers certainly was the pioneer. Freight transportation came later. The same situation exists in air transportation, where passenger movement still is by far most important, and is thought by many to be pioneering for a future heavy freight movement.

Regardless of which comes first, there is a by-product effect which leads to problems. First, since much of the early development of transportation has been accomplished with public aid, the question arises as to whether it is the transportation of people or of freight which is being subsidized. Given the fact that the various modes of transport have grown up during different historical periods, it is likely that the developed or older mode will find itself in competition with a currently subsidized new mode.

Rail passenger transportation illustrates this problem. Much of our highway system development is "justified" on the basis of providing for easy and better travel for the general public, or for improved mail service. That is, passenger transportation provides a strong rationale for better roads. But improved highways are equally available for truck movements. Railroads pay property taxes, a portion of which go into improved highways, justified as necessary to move passengers, only to find that they are helping their competitors improve their capacities to move freight. Similarly, public aid to air transportation is "justified" on the basis of moving people and improving communications. Yet the capability to move freight is a by-product of better air transportation.

A second problem exists in cost allocation and subsequent pricing. When two services, passenger movement and freight movement, are produced by the same capital and the same operators, what portion of the costs should be allocated to each service? In rail transportation, for example, it is difficult to ascertain completely how much of the total costs should be allocated to passengers and how much to freight. To be sure, some costs are incurred for one specific service. Yet a large portion of common costs remain which are incurred for both services. What is a "fair" allocation?

This question takes on added significance when we remember that rates and fares are at least partially based on costs. Therefore, if the allocation of costs is incorrect, the fare structure probably is incorrect as well, and one service is "subsidizing" another service. Once more, rail transportation illustrates the point.

The allocation of common costs between rail passenger and freight services was specified by the I.C.C. many years ago. Conditions have changed since. Passenger service is no longer as important to railroads as it once was. The upshot is that rail passenger deficits probably have been often overstated. Statistics on losses in passenger service have been used for rate and fare adjustment proceedings. The proper cost allocation is a continuing problem in rail passenger service.

A third problem of service discontinuance and service adequacy, also related to cost allocations, stems from the by-product effect. If a service is not used by the public, it should not be provided. Deficits in operation are prime evidence of non-use or low demand. But, as noted above, reported deficits may not reflect the true cost of the service. In rail service, there is a continuing problem of which rail passenger services should be retained and which services should be abandoned.

To some degree, these same problems of subsidy, cost allocation and pricing, and cost allocation and service are found also in air and motor transportation. Here, however, the passenger services by planes or busses tend to be the dominant services, and the movement of freight, mail or express, the by-product. But once more the question of cost allocation, rates, and which service is subsidized arises.

The Variability Factor

Passenger transportation is characterized by extreme variability during the hours of the day, the days of the week, and the months of the year. While freight tends to move continuously and at all hours, automobile traffic, passenger trains, busses and planes do not. People move to and from work in a definite pattern. The weekend traffic jam is evidence of this variability factor, and the Christmas holiday congestion on planes, busses and trains illustrates the seasonal factor.

Facilities and labor in passenger transportation service tend to be used very intensively during the peak movement periods. Indeed, to some travelers, the capital and labor committed seems inadequate at these times. Yet due to the variability factor, this same labor and capital often remains idle for extended periods of low use or non-use. The rates or fares for the services provided, though, must recoup the costs of this idleness as well as the costs of use.

This factor is particularly acute in urban passenger transportation. Commuter trains and busses are intensively used from 6 a.m. to 8 a.m. and from 5 p.m. to 7 p.m. Much of the rest of the day the crews, equipment and capital facilities are idle or under-used. In the case of labor, it should be noted that these peak periods of use fall in two eight-hour periods. It is not uncommon for one crew of operators to work the morning rush hours, while another crew must be hired for the evening rush hours.

The variability factor also is reflected in streets, highways, bridges, tunnels, and terminals. These facilities should be constructed with peak periods in mind. Sometimes they are not. It is extremely expensive to provide a traffic lane on a street which is used only two or three hours out of the whole day. Resources for transportation are not unlimited. Hence allocations must be made, and the result often is inadequate facilities during peak periods. Many of the problems of urban transportation relate directly to this variability factor.

The variability factor also affects air transportation. Certain hours of departure and arrival are most popular with the traveling public. All airlines would prefer to make profits by serving the public at the most popular hours.

The result has been a jamming of scheduled departures and arrivals at these hours. Recently, the resultant air congestion has increased to the point where the F.A.A. has been forced to impose limits on the number of take-offs and landings at certain hours at a number of the country's busier airports.

Price discounts may help partially in offsetting the variability factor. For some time some airlines have offered lower fares during certain days of the week, during nighttime hours, and during certain seasons of the year. Rail passenger service has made some small use of the same device, and busses have attempted on occasion to shift passenger demand by use of price discounts. It is rare to find price discounts related to time of departure or arrival in freight transportation (with the exception of some differential rates, usually where circuitous routing is involved), but it is common in passenger transportation. The variability factor accounts for this peculiarity.

Market Complexity

The market for all transportation is complex and has many diverse interrelationships. This is particularly so for the market for passenger transportation. Actually, there are at least three distinct general types of markets for passenger transportation—urban, intercity, and international or intercontinental. Different competitive relationships exist and different forces of supply and demand are at work in each.

The urban market is the most complex market for passenger transportation. More social and policy problems exist here, and more transportation modes are involved than in the other two types of markets. People can move within urban areas by private automobile, city bus, streetcars, commuter trains, taxicabs, subways, motorbikes, bicycles, or by walking. No one market encompasses all these modes, but it is common to have at least four or five ways of moving in an urban area.

Space for urban vehicular movement and for parking or temporary storage of vehicles when not in use is at a premium. Congestion and interference on one mode of movement with another is a further problem. Regulation and control of safety, prices and fares, service frequency, and service adequacy are still other problems found in urban transportation.

Ecological and sociological problems become acute in the urban market. Pollution, congestion, urban redevelopment, city planning, traffic engineering, effects on trips to work, effects on the characters of neighborhoods, and the like are examples of the social and ecological problems involved. Some of these effects are discussed below.

The intercity market for passenger movement basically involves air, private automobile, rail, and bus services. Distances traveled are much longer and motivation for travel differs from the urban market. The journey to work is of much less importance, while business and pleasure travel are of primary importance. Sometimes it is useful to separate business travel from pleasure travel in the intercity passenger transportation market. Certainly different motivations for each exist, and the matter of economy, speed, luxury, and mobility for each class of travelers varies.

Since freight movement also tends to be intercity in nature, it is in this market that the question of one service subsidizing another becomes most important. The degree of public support of highways, railways and airways is an important "subsidy question." Variability factors cause problems here, but of a somewhat different type than in urban transportation. Regulatory problems are of a different nature in intercity travel than in the urban market.

The intercontinental passenger transportation market is somewhat different from the intercity market and vastly different from the urban market. The modes involved here mainly are air and steamship. The motivations for travel are quite complex, involving vacations, educational travel, tours, business travel, diplomatic travel, and a variety of other reasons. This market responds differently from other markets to price variations and to the availability of facilities related to transportation, such as hotels, restaurants, guided tours, and recreational facilities.

In addition to the complexities of the three distinctive passenger markets, the marketing institutions and approaches in passenger transportation differ from those in freight transportation. Basically, passenger transportation is retail-oriented, whereas freight transportation is wholesale or producer-oriented. In selling passenger services, many customers are involved and the service usually is sold quite frequently. In freight movements, relatively fewer customers are involved and the sales contact may not be as frequent. Certainly in freight transportation most of the units are large (carload, truckload, large air shipment), whereas in passenger transportation the units are small (a seat or reservation). The buyers of freight transportation tend to be more knowledgeable and specialized, whereas the buyers of passenger transportation are more casual and less informed, and the movement itself is more incidental to other occupations.

Sometimes these different institutions and approaches are not recognized clearly by for-hire carriers. The sales effort differs for each group, and what may appeal to an industrial traffic manager may not appeal to a vacation traveler. More intermediaries, such as travel agents, are involved in passenger transportation, and the matter of how the customer is served often becomes more important than price or other considerations. By and large, buyers of both freight and passenger transportation are concerned with both prices and service. But service to a shipper is quite a different matter than service to a traveler. Service for the latter is considerably more complex.

In summary, the five distinctive characteristics of the predominance of private carriage, the for-hire supremacy of air transportation, the by-product effects, the variability effects, and market complexities cause numerous problems in the area of passenger transportation, thus differentiating it from freight transportation.

SOCIAL AND ECONOMIC PROBLEMS

A number of problems arise from these five distinctive characteristics of passenger transportation, combined with the obvious economic benefits of an inexpensive, fast, and efficient system for moving people. Although not of equal importance, these problems fall into four groups: ecological, sociological, international, and economic.

Ecological Problems

The natural environment in which we live is a carefully balanced system of creation, life and death. Ecology is that branch of biology which studies mutual interrelationships between organisms and their environments. In recent years, the term has come to have a more specific popular meaning, however; it is currently used to refer to the study of the effects of the actions of man on the environmental balance and systems of nature. Passenger transportation is the cause of considerable ecological effects in this popular sense of the term.

As noted in Chapter 3, all transportation has ecological effects. However, because of the predominance of the private automobile and the supremacy of air transportation, the ecological effects of the movement of people are greater and more observable than the effects of transportation in general. These passenger transportation ecological effects are found principally in air and noise pollution and in the disturbing results associated with the construction of transportation facilities such as highways and airports.

There is little doubt that the gasoline-burning internal combustion engine emits a major part of the air pollutants found hovering over the urban places of our nation. In the process of converting gasoline into energy, four classes of pollutants are manufactured. These are carbon monoxide, gaseous hydrocarbons and benzene compounds, nitrogen oxide compounds, and non-gases or heavy particles such as lead. Through chemical reactions with sunlight and dirt and dust particles in the atmosphere, these compounds turn into the distressingly familiar smog which has come to be a sign of man's concentrated presence. To a very marked degree, this type of pollution originates with the private automobile, and to a smaller degree from airplanes.

Devices to control industrial pollutants are available and are slowly being introduced and used. For a time there was a tendency to blame air pollution almost solely upon industry and its rather visible pollution arising from the smokestacks of plants and industrial complexes. Slowly, though, the public learned that some pollutants are not easily visible to the naked eye, and that the major offender is the private automobile. While any one vehicle produces but a small amount of air pollution, in the aggregate automobiles produce up to 90 per cent of the air pollution in some locations. The knowledge that the total of many units, each producing but a little amount of pollution, actually is a serious problem was many years in coming.

During the late 1960's, the "environmental revolution" led to great concern with the ecological effects of passenger transportation. Standards of allowable emissions from private automobiles were established, and goals for the 1970's were set. Various control devices were attempted with varying degrees of success. By and large, the establishment and enforcement of standards of allowable emissions is a governmental problem. Since each vehicle produces such a small increment to the total problem of air pollution, it is difficult to depend on individual action to solve the problem. Similarly, since air pollution does not respect the artificial boundaries of local governmental jurisdictions, an authority with very broad control is needed. Hence, federal standards were established for the 1970's.

One approach to the problem of air pollution from passenger transportation may be in developing new types of engines and fuels. Electric motors, steam-powered vehicles, internal combustion engines burning LPG or natural gas, and gasoline turbine engines are examples of attacking the problem by way of the propulsion system. All these systems have their advantages and disadvantages. But in all cases, these devices must compare favorably economically and in performance with the conventional internal combustion gasoline engine before they will have wide adoption.

The easiest and most direct way to handle the air pollution problem is at the manufacturing level. Equipping all new vehicles with pollution retarding devices at the time they are manufactured will go a long way toward solving the problem. Although devices are available for older vehicles, they must depend upon the individual actions of millions of car owners. Experience has shown that it is difficult to persuade large groups of individuals to act in concert on any social problem. Thus, the solution to automobile air pollution will take a long time to work itself out.

Air pollution from airplanes is being solved in a more direct manner. After a series of lawsuits by local authorities during the late 1960's, airlines began to install pollution abatement devices on planes. Control was somewhat easier here, because local jurisdiction at airports is clear and the problem is localized to airports and to the landing and take-off process. Air pollution arising during intercity flights is not as easily solved.

Noise pollution caused by transportation also is a problem. Transportation by nature is noisy, and with the frequency of the movement of vehicles with small loads of passengers, passenger transportation is particularly noisy. The same problem of the aggregate as compared to the individual vehicle is found here. While no one plane, bus, or car is very annoying, the total noise produced is a social problem. This problem can be very acute at areas located near airports and freeways.

Various devices and plans for muffling noise have been devised. Landscaping of airports and freeways can help. So can the redesign of engines. But perhaps the most hopeful approach is in the design of freeways and airports when they are originally built. Now that the problem of noise pollution is recognized, abatement often can be incorporated as part of the original design concept. Once again, though, the long-run situation seems brighter than that of the short-run.

Control of noise pollution at existing locations is expensive and not entirely successful. It is necessary at times to move schools or places of residence and work away from the sources of noise. Sound-conditioning is an expensive alternative which has been used in some instances. However, noise pollution from passenger transportation is an ever-present problem, and no quick solution appears possible.

Finally, the ecological effects of the construction of passenger transportation facilities is a serious problem. When highways and streets are constructed, atmospheric and water pollution occurs. Since airports require substantial land areas, they often are located outside of cities. As man-created features imposed upon nature, these large complexes upset the ecological cycle in their new countryside locations. The solution to this problem can only come in the twin areas of careful design with an eye to pollution causes and control of the construction processes.

Sociological Problems

Two broad sets of sociological problems arise out of transportation. These are the multiple effects of congestion and the effects on the "quality of life." Passenger transportation with its variability factor, supremacy of air transportation, and reliance on the private automobile is a particular contributor to both of these problems.

There are three generally recognized types of congestion arising from passenger transportation—street congestion, highway congestion, and air congestion. While congestion sometimes is absolute and related to the totality of the facilities available, the most common type of congestion arises out of the variability of passenger transportation. The "rush hour" crowd of vehicles and people is an excellent example of this type of congestion.

A portion of this congestion is caused by work habits and organizational structures. The "habit" of starting work at around 8 a.m. and quitting at around 5 p.m. is involved. Staggered shifts and variations of the 8-to-5 pattern have proved helpful in some experiments. Too little has been attempted on a mass basis, however, and we remain creatures of habit causing our own twice-daily rush periods. In many employments, there is very little reason why the hours of work need be tied to an 8-to-5 pattern. Before the advent of electricity, and when most jobs were outdoors, there was a real need to utilize the daylight hours in meaningful work. Today there is less need to continue this daylight pattern. Society has it well within its means to at least minimize part of the congestion of streets and highways.

The same remarks apply to the weekly and seasonal congestion of passenger transportation facilities. The Monday to Friday work week again is a product of a past era which evolved out of the rural work week of six days.

Part of this problem, of course, is based on religious institutions, but these may not be as dominant as they once were. Why should not some firms be closed on Wednesday and Thursday, or some other two days, rather than on Saturday and Sunday?

So too with seasonal congestion caused by summer vacations. It once was thought necessary to close schools and employ the young in farm work during summer months. This tradition has persisted into modern times. Yet there is very little reason why schools could not operate on different schedules, with vacations during different and varying months.

Seasonal, weekly, and daily congestion factors can be affected by price devices as well as by different institutional arrangements. Not enough "off peak" pricing has been attempted in for-hire passenger transportation, although some modes, such as air transportation, have been active in this area. People respond to some degree to price incentives, thus middle of the week fares, off-season vacation rates, and off-peak daily discounts could be used more effectively.

Efficiency is another approach to congestion problems. This means moving masses of people with the use of fewer vehicles and less space. The private automobile carries, on the average, less than two persons per trip. Various vehicles such as busses, subway trains, and mass transit cars carry far more people per vehicle and use far less space. The use of private automobiles may have to be banned in at least some areas in some of our larger cities within the near future. The problems of congestion and the social costs of providing adequate streets and parking simply may become so expensive that the adoption of a more efficient means of passenger transportation will become necessary. The technology and know-how to reduce a large part of the present street congestion are available. All that is lacking is the desire to use our technology and knowledge.

Airway congestion can be partially solved by better scheduling and more efficient methods of airway control. During the late 1960's the congestion of airways and the matter of airway control became widely recognized problems. Congressional action to establish an airways and airports trust fund, tied to a variety of user taxes, was an attempt to solve this problem. Also, the actions of the F.A.A. in restricting departures and arrivals at several major airports during certain hours, was a late 1960's attempt to deal with this problem.

Street and highway congestion related to airport access is still another matter. Here the answer involves control of times of use of airports and more efficient means of access to and from airports. Plans to connect airports with downtown origination and destination areas by mass transit may have a pronounced effect on this problem.

The effects of passenger transportation on the "quality of life" are complex, and the many suggested solutions are beyond the scope of this discussion. It is sufficient to note here that both the presence of and the lack of efficient and economical means of mass transit have effects on the sociological character of a city or part of a city. Neighborhoods take on a "character" which relates to their passenger transportation availability. The existence of a subway, bus system, or freeway affects the sociological and economic structure of a community. The lack of mass transportation may lead to an economically depressed area. The journey to work is so important that when means for it are not readily available work alternatives may be severely restricted.

Central business districts depend on low-priced and efficient passenger transportation, as do "bedroom" enclaves and suburbs. The automobile has helped bring urban sprawl to America, and the political and economic unity of our urban communities are affected by the existence or lack of passenger transport. Analysis of all these sociological phenomena, and the many others which are related to passenger transportation, is not within the purposes of this book. The authors simply want to emphasize here the point that passenger transportation or its lack creates unique sociological effects and problems.

International Aspects

Although this book is concerned with domestic transportation, international matters are directly interrelated to some aspects of passenger transportation. Domestic airlines often have international operations, and even many that are solely domestic in route structure depend on international interchange of passengers for portions of their business. Although the various modes of land transportation also may interconnect with maritime service (or with Canadian or Mexican land carriers), the interconnection in air transportation is more direct.

Most of the world's airlines are governmentally owned and operated. As such, they are agencies or arms of their own governments. United States airlines are privately owned and operated. This distinctive difference contributes to problems of fare determination, route awards, and international diplomacy.

As agencies of their respective governments, foreign airlines can be operated at a loss if the owning nations feel this is desirable policy. A foreign airline can penetrate a market in competition with a privately owned American airline with little thought of profit or loss. Problems of competitive relationships are obvious.

Some U.S. airlines feel that they should be designated as "flag carriers" and become an instrument of U.S. foreign policy. In some instances, this almost has been the case in the past. Landing rights are negotiated between nations as bilateral agreements. The right of an airline to enter and serve a country is part of the overall international relations between the two nations involved. A "landing right" may come about because of some other type of concession, such as a lower tariff, a changed import quota, or monetary or labor exchanges. Obviously, the privately owned airlines of the United States often find themselves at a bargaining disadvantage since they have no control over tariffs, quotas, labor exchanges, international loans, and the like.

It should be noted, however, that some of these potential international disadvantages have not been too severe. The United States provides such a desirable market as an originator of travelers to foreign points and as a destination for foreign travelers that the mutual exchange of landing rights generally has been accomplished with a minimum of friction. Most foreign governments are only too glad to allow U.S. carriers to land in their countries, if they can land their own carriers in this country.

Some problems have arisen because of the technical efficiency of U.S. carriers. With the coming of "jumbo" jets, some nations attempted to restrict U.S. carriers on the number of serving flights. Their concern was that U.S. carriers would provide a superior service which would dominate air travel to the disadvantage of foreign governmentally-owned carriers. Such restrictions are difficult to handle diplomatically.

International air fares are established at biannual meetings of the International Air Transport Association (I.A.T.A.). Through this vehicle, all concerned airlines meet and bargain out changes in international air fares and procedures. There is no international regulatory agency, such as the domestic C.A.B. or F.A.A. As privately-owned profit-seeking firms, U.S. airlines sometimes find themselves in unusual positions in working with their competitors who are, in effect, governmental agencies.

Finally, because the international air transportation market depends partly upon accommodations such as hotels, restaurants, tours, and recreational activities, air carriers often have constructed or acquired their own hotels and similar facilities. Several major U.S. air carriers have substantial investments in hotels and facilities abroad. This has both advantages and disadvantages. It is good business for the carriers, and often stimulates travel and economic development in the country where the hotel is built. On the other hand, such activities provide competition for local hotels and facilities, and sometimes do not improve the image of Americans abroad.

Economic Considerations

The distinctive characteristics and the ecological-sociological-international aspects of passenger transportation give rise to at least six major economic questions. Other economic considerations exist, but the following six illustrate some of the complexities of passenger transportation.

1. What is the most desirable form of urban passenger transportation? Assuming that a national urban passenger transportation goal of a low-priced, fast, and efficient system of movement is desirable, what physical form should this system take?

Because the steel rail can move more people rapidly and at a low expenditure of energy, some favor a variation of this system. Because existing streets already provide busways, others favor a bus-related system. Still others look to new and as yet experimental systems, such as monorails, tubes, and air-cushion vehicles.

All these systems have advantages and disadvantages. The choice between the various forms must be made as a result of a series of trade-offs between cost, convenience, expediency, mobility, safety, and similar factors. But the initial step involves choosing whatever type of system or systems seems most desirable under the given circumstances at the time of the choice.

2. What pattern of ownership and what degree of public support is desirable for urban passenger transportation? The federal government sponsored a number of experiments during the 1960's, and has passed several acts designed to aid cities in developing better passenger transportation systems. In the Department of Transportation, the Urban Mass Transit Administration and the Office of High Speed Ground Transportation are involved with various aspects of this problem. Numerous bills have been proposed in Congress to sponsor various schemes of urban mass passenger transportation. Some of these proposals involve Mass Transit Trust Funds, shifting of financial resources, and multi-state transit authorities.

3. What is a desirable pattern of control and support for airways? Given the dominance of air transportation in intercity and intercontinental travel, plus the importance of safety, this question must be answered. The federal government owns and operates the airways, while local governments own and operate airports. For many years air travel has increased faster than airports have been improved and than airway control has been developed. The result has been increased airway and airport congestion, and dangerous safety situations. Indeed, delays in airports and on the airways threaten to take away much of the natural advantage of speed possessed by air transportation.

During 1970 Congress passed the Airport-Airways Modernization Act. This set up a trust fund financed by new and increased user taxes. The trust fund, during a ten-year period, is to be used to improve airways and help finance airport improvements. Billions of dollars will be spent for these purposes during the next several years. Whether this will prove adequate for needed improvements remains to be seen.

4. What is a desirable highway policy for the nation? The Highway Trust Fund was established in 1956, and the country embarked on a "crash" program of highway improvement. The major feature of this program was the Interstate System of freeways (about 42,500 miles) which was to be completed by 1972. Because of inflation, design changes, fund hold-backs, and numerous other delays, this system probably will not be completed before the late 1970's. The original cost estimate of $27 billion has long since been proven too low. It appears now that closer to $75 billion will have been spent on this program by the time of its completion.

As this highway construction program draws to a close, the question of "what next" naturally arises. Some propose that the trust fund continue, and that another similar massive highway improvement program be undertaken on secondary roads. Others suggest that the trust fund be used for urban freeways or for other urban transit purposes. Still others propose that the present Interstate System be further extended. There are several other proposals, as well. Clearly, no comprehensive highway policy exists, and passenger transportation is affected by this lack.

5. What is a desirable policy on rail passenger transportation for the nation? Railroad service is important in the commuter and intercity area of passenger transportation. The "Northeast Corridor" or megalopolis, a 400-mile strip from Boston to Washington, contains 30 per cent of our nation's manufacturing and 21 per cent of our retailing establishments, and has almost 50 million people—all this on some 1.4 per cent of the nation's land area. The degree of urbanization in this megalopolis, exceeded in only a few places in the world, points out the problem of mass transportation. Urban and intercity rail passenger services exist here, but have had a long history of financial difficulty. Should the rail passenger system be revitalized? If so, who should support the system, and how?

The unexpected bankruptcy of the Penn Central Transportation Company during 1970 led to considerable concern about rail passenger transportation policy. This railroad carried about 20 per cent of all rail passengers in the United States. Its inability to operate passenger trains at a profit may have contributed to its financial failure. Certainly the unfortunate problems of this rail giant have caused a reexamination of the nation's passenger transportation problems. Even before this failure, there were several proposed plans for government subsidy or even government ownership of at least a minimum amount of "essential" rail passenger transport facilities.

Federal support of experimentation through the Office of High Speed Ground Transportation during the 1960's was a pioneering effort in the attempt to improve rail passenger transportation. The "turbo train" of the late 1960's provides another example of attempts to upgrade intercity rail passenger service. Yet these efforts did not really answer the basic question of what our rail transportation policies concerning passengers ought to be. We entered the 1970's with no comprehensive policy.

In October, 1970, Congress enacted the "Railpax" law, establishing a National Railroad Passenger Corporation. This governmentally sponsored public corporation was designated to become operational May 1, 1971. It is charged with providing "basic" or "essential" intercity rail passenger services (excluding distances of less than 50 miles). The corporation's initial assets came from a $40 million federal grant, contributions of passenger equipment and cash in exchange for stocks by participating railroads, and a federal guarantee of borrowed funds up to $100 million.

The Department of Transportation specifies the essential routes and services. Participating railroads are authorized to operate essential passenger trains under contracts negotiated with Railpax, and are allowed to discontinue all other intercity passenger services if they wish. D.O.T.'s initial specification required services only between 14 major cities, thus allowing abandonment of a large segment of rail passenger service. This recommendation came under immediate attack from several affected communities. Frequent readjustments in D.O.T. specifications may be expected for some time.

Railpax accomplishes two things: it removes railroads from (and puts government into) a money-losing intercity passenger business, and it reduces the amount of available rail passenger services (although hopefully improving the quality of remaining services). As presently conceived, however, it seems to do little toward solving the major problems of intercity passenger transportation (except, perhaps, to shift some "subsidy" burdens from freight services to general taxpayers).

6. What is the most desirable set of priorities in public aids to passenger transportation? This final question encompasses the above five questions, yet it is a separate policy problem in itself. Given that resources for transportation are limited and that choices must be made, what is the proper set of priorities for passenger transportation? Huge amounts have been allocated to highways and freeways during the years since World War II. In spite of this, congestion has increased. Indeed, some suggest that freeways merely accelerate the congestion problem by encouraging greater uses of automobiles and by funneling more vehicles into inadequate city streets and parking spaces.

Other means of passenger transportation have not received large amounts of federal aid. The Secretary of Transportation has been quoted as stating that "We spend approximately as much in six weeks on highways as we have spent in the last six years for mass transit." No substantial sums have been committed to solving the intercity rail passenger problem. Until quite recently, rather small amounts were available for airways and airports. The question of priorities is an obvious one to raise, but not easy to answer.

POLICY CONSIDERATIONS

From even this brief discussion of passenger transportation it should be obvious that no comprehensive national policy for the movement of people exists. Present approaches are split between numerous agencies, many of which are restricted by budgets and by limited objectives. There is a lack of central planning, although no lack of proposed programs. No real national commitment has been made.

Creation of the Department of Transportation was a start in the right direction, and some initial coordinating steps have been taken. Many of D.O.T.'s activities have been concerned with passenger transportation. Perhaps the future will hold a much larger role for D.O.T. in this area, and the initial steps can be translated into concrete operative policy. Additionally, the concern shown in Congress by the numerous proposals to attack the problems of passenger transportation is an encouraging sign. While few proposals have become law, this concern and discussion of the issues may lead to useful developments.

Basically, it is up to our society as a whole to decide what is desirable for passenger transportation. Until the entire society makes its wants, needs, and desires known through political pressures and action, no real passenger transportation policy can be expected. Once we make up our minds, our problems can be solved.

GENERAL SUMMARY

Passenger transportation is uniquely related to numerous ecological, sociological, international, and economic problems. This is partially due to the distinctive nature of passenger transportation, with its predominancy of private carriage, supremacy of air transportation, by-product effects, variability effects, and market complexities. Numerous unanswered policy questions remain. There probably is greater need for policy determination in the area of passenger transportation than in any other transportation area. Great concern exists at various levels, the need for comprehensive and cooperative planning is apparent, and the opportunity for meaningful policy to achieve desirable results, once meaningful policy is established, is very great.

ADDITIONAL READINGS

1. Fabos, Julius, "Highway Design—The Need for Goals and Integrated Environmental Planning," **Transportation Journal,** Vol. 9, No. 2, Winter 1969, pp. 51–59.
2. Farmer, Richard N., "The Economics of Congestion," **Transportation Journal,** Vol. 4, No. 1, Fall 1964, pp. 28–34.
3. Fitch, Lyle C. and Associates, **Urban Transportation and Public Policy.** San Francisco, Calif.: Chandler Publishing Co., 1964, 279 pp.
4. Lansing, John B., **Transportation and Economic Policy.** New York: The Free Press, 1966.
   Chapter 15. "Urban Transportation," pp. 265–301.
5. Meyer, John R., John F. Kain, and Martin Wohl, **The Urban Transportation Problem.** Cambridge, Mass.: Harvard University Press, 1965, 427 pp.
6. Norton, Hugh S., **National Transportation Policy: Formation and Implementation.** Berkeley, Calif.: McCutchan Publishing Corp., 1966.
   Chapter 5. "National Transportation Policy and the Urban Transport Problem," pp. 74–89.
7. Owen, Wilfred, **The Metropolitan Transportation Problem.** Rev. ed. Washington, D.C.: The Brookings Institution, 1966, 266 pp.
8. Owen, Wilfred, "Transportation and the City," **Transportation Journal,** Vol. 6, No. 2, Winter 1966, pp. 24–32.
9. Pell, Claiborne, **Megalopolis Unbound: The Supercity and the Transportation of Tomorrow.** New York: Frederick A. Praeger, Publishers, 1966, 233 pp.
10. Schary, Philip and Robert M. Williams, "Airline Fare Policy and Public Investment," **Transportation Journal,** Vol. 7, No. 1, Fall 1967, pp. 41–49.
11. Smerk, George M. (ed.), **Readings in Urban Transportation.** Bloomington, Ind.: Indiana University Press, 1968, 336 pp.
12. Smerk, George M., "The Urban Mass Transportation Act of 1964: New Hope for American Cities," **Transportation Journal,** Vol. 5, No. 2, Winter 1965, pp. 35–40.
13. Smerk, George M., **Urban Transportation: The Federal Role.** Bloomington, Ind.: Indiana University Press, 1965, 336 pp.

14. Spychalski, John C., "The Diversion of Motor Vehicle-Related Tax Revenues to Urban Mass Transportation: A Critique of Its Economic Tenability," **Transportation Journal,** Vol. 9, No. 3, Spring 1970, pp. 44–50.

15. Taff, Charles A., **Commercial Motor Transportation,** 4th ed. Homewood, Ill.: Richard D. Irwin, Inc., 1969.
Chapter 19. "Intercity Passenger Operations," pp. 429–455.
Chapter 20. "Urban Mass Transit," pp. 456–477.

16. Vickrey, William S., "Congestion Theory and Transport Investment," **American Economic Review,** Vol. LIX, No. 2, May 1969, pp. 251–260.

24

Conflicts in National
Transportation Policy

The conflicts previously emphasized have been between specific groups. While the general public is involved in most of these goal conflicts, this chapter will discuss the conflicts in overall or "national" transportation policy. That is, the aim of this chapter is to identify national policy insofar as possible, discuss the conflicts inherent within this national policy, note proposed solutions to these problems, and indicate areas where a solution might be forthcoming.

IDENTIFICATION OF POLICY

The task of identifying national transportation policy is not as easy as it might at first appear. There are two types or bases of national policy in domestic transportation: the formal statutory policy and the informal institutional policy.

Statutory National Transportation Policy

As noted in Chapter 19, one of the major functions of the legislative process is to establish policy. This is often done by adding a preamble or policy statement to a statute or by setting down a policy within the statute itself. Hence, one way to identify national transportation policy is to see what Congress has said should be included in national transportation policy.

The most comprehensive and most recent formal statutory statement of transportation policy is included in the preamble of the Transportation Act of 1940 which is reproduced on pages 289–290. Since it is important that transportation personnel understand formal national policy, we will analyze that statement from three viewpoints: omissions, carrier-oriented policy, and public-oriented policy.

It should be noted at the outset that while the policy sounds "general" and "national," it does not include air transportation. As described in Chapter 18, air transportation is regulated by the Civil Aeronautics Board and the above policy statement applies only to the Interstate Commerce Commission. A further omission in the policy statement is any reference to private transportation. It should be noted that the statement applies only to modes subject to the Interstate Commerce Act.

Carrier-oriented policy pronouncements are basically in three groups. First, the policy statement sets as a goal the promotion of "safe, adequate, economical and efficient service and sound economic conditions" in transportation and among the carriers. That some of these goals may conflict with each other is not recognized. That is, "safe and adequate" may not always be "economical and efficient." Safety costs money and adequacy presupposes excess capacity to cover peak demands, whereas "economical" connotes least cost and "efficient" might be interpreted as being only enough capacity to handle average needs. The meaning of "sound economic conditions" is vague and may mean whatever the person using the phrase wants it to mean at the time.

Second, the statement says that Congress should encourage "reasonable charges . . . without unjust discrimination, undue preference or advantage or unfair or destructive competitive practices." Here the familiar control of monopoly practices is coupled with minimum-rate control and regulation of competition. These policy aims may well conflict with the goals of "safety and adequacy," "economical and efficient service," and "sound economic conditions" or they may not, depending on the definition or interpretation of these terms. Third, Congress recognized an obligation towards labor and stated that it would encourage the carriers to have "fair wages and equitable working conditions." "Fair" and "equitable" have many meanings and this too could be interpreted in many ways.

The public-oriented policy statements also group themselves into three areas. Oriented as they are toward broad public policy, they too are necessarily vague and ambiguous. First, the policy statement gives the general public goal of "developing, coordinating, and preserving a national transportation system . . . adequate to meet the needs of commerce . . . the Postal Service, and the national defense." These laudable general goals may not always lead to the most "economical and efficient" carrier operation, particularly when it is realized that the needs of commerce, the postal service, and especially national defense may vary considerably depending on conditions, the season, or the general environment. Indeed, "national defense" may call for maintenance of considerable excess capacity at all times.

Second, Congress declared that it would "cooperate with the several states and duly authorized officials thereof." Conflict between state and Federal regulation of transportation will be discussed later. This has always been a problem.

Finally, in perhaps the most ambiguous statement of all, Congress stated that its policy was to provide "fair and impartial regulation of all modes . . . so administered as to recognize and preserve the inherent advantage of each." To be "fair and impartial" is most commendable and would be expected by the

American people. To "recognize and preserve the inherent advantage" of the individual modes is also commendable. It correctly recognizes that each mode has a particular role to play in the whole transportation system. The problem arises, however, when an attempt is made to delineate the "inherent advantage of each."

How can "inherent advantage" be found or measured? If transportation were a competitive industry, the carrier or mode able to transport goods the cheapest would obviously have the "inherent advantage" for that type of traffic. But competition is not allowed to allocate transportation, all costs are not covered by all carriers, minimum rates are regulated so as to prevent "unfair or destructive competitive practices," and entry is controlled so as to preserve "adequate and safe" transportation. Clearly "inherent advantage" is a meaningless term considering the conditions under which transportation operates. In administrative practice, determining "inherent advantage" has proven to be the shoal upon which much of regulation has foundered.

In summary then, the formal statutory national transportation policy, while upholding many high-sounding, commendable, and laudable goals, is contradictory, vague, and indefinable.

Informal Institutional Policy

If the formal statutory transportation policy is vague, ambiguous, and self-contradictory even though written down and enacted by Congress, informal institutional policy is even less specific. Informal and institutional policy comes out of practice and repetition by Congress in various laws as well as certain general economic beliefs and positions. It is possible to summarize informal policy in transportation into four groups or concepts: the ownership concept, the public investment concept, the common-carrier concept, and the exemption concept.

Domestic transportation policy is firmly committed to the concept of private ownership. While ownership of the means of transportation by government has been widespread in other areas of the world, the United States has studiously avoided this path even though the opportunity for government ownership has arisen many times. During World War I, the Federal government seized and operated the railroads. Labor strife has caused other seizures. Defense needs over the years have closely linked the government to all modes of transportation, especially air transportation. The rationale for government ownership has often existed, yet the strong preference for private ownership has always won out. It seems safe to say, then, that one of the informal institutional policies is private ownership of the transportation modes.

Public investment in transportation, however, is another matter. As already noted in Chapter 22, the public has committed itself to providing a portion of the way, to operating the way, to financing some of the operating costs, and to providing some research and development funds for carriers. These types of investment by the public presently are concentrated in the highways, waterways, and airways. Although public ownership is avoided, public investment most certainly is not. The national policy on transportation rests on continuing public investment even though no law or statute so states it.

Third, the common-carrier concept is important in informal institutional transportation policy. The idea that the common carrier is the backbone of the national transportation system is implicitly assumed in practically all policy statements and discussions even though one would be hard put to find a statutory pronouncement to that effect.

Modifying the common carrier concept is the exemptions concept. Informally, national transportation policy has embraced the idea that certain types of transportation should be exempt from economic regulation. A person should be able to move his own goods relatively free of restrictions, for example. Certain types of goods, such as agricultural commodities moving by truck or bulk commodities moving by barge, have been exempt from regulation for various reasons. Additionally, some groups such as agricultural marketing cooperatives, newspaper carriers, and local operators are exempt. While all of these exemptions are explicitly stated in the law, the concept that some groups, commodities, or types of transportation will be treated differently from others is an informal institutional policy.

These informal policies based on private ownership, public investment, common carriage, and exemption shape national transportation policy just as surely as the formal statutory policy. Both must be considered in order to understand national transportation policy. Indeed, these informal policies coupled with the ambiguous and vague formal policies lead to numerous conflicts.

KINDS OF CONFLICTS

Mention has been made of the self-contradictory nature of the formal, statutory, national transportation-policy pronouncements, and conflicts between the informal and the formal policies are self-evident. Added to these conflicts, however, are three broad areas of conflict within national transportation policy. These are philosophical conflicts, regulatory conflicts, and administrative conflicts.

Philosophical Conflicts

The major philosophical conflict in national transportation policy is between the concept of a regulated transportation industry based on the common-carrier concept and the philosophy of free competition. This problem of regulation versus competition is not a new one, and various aspects of it pervade many areas of transportation policy.

The prevailing policy of the United States has been based on the common-carrier idea. Here the transportation firm must hold itself out to serve all customers at all reasonable times and in a nondiscriminatory manner. This is thought to better serve society's needs since transportation is so basic to our economy.

Historically, the decision to base our transportation system on the common carrier is a very old one. Scholars of economic and business history indicate that many of the common-carrier concepts came with the "merchant law" of the late medieval period, and some scholars find evidence of something akin to the common carrier in the commerce of the ancient world. This evidence is based upon the laws of liability where the goods of another person are carried for pay.

The concept of common carriage, however, implies regulation of some type. Common carriers have always operated under various regulations, and the liability provisions noted above are really regulations applied by society to the conduct of those who undertake a public trust. Regulation of charges (rates) by the king or other sovereign and control over the number of firms holding themselves out to serve (entry controls) are also implied by the idea of common carriage.

Equally old is the tradition of competition, the philosophy that individual entrepreneurs should compete or strive against each other to serve the consumer and the general public. While elements of competition can be found in the earliest commercial undertakings, it was not until modern times that this policy pervaded all economic undertakings. This came with the development of the laissez-faire philosophy of minimum regulation or control in the Eighteenth Century.

Applied to transportation, the philosophy of competition and free enterprise holds that anyone should have the right to start any business he pleases. Entry should not be restricted. Once started, the entrepreneur should be allowed to conduct his business affairs in any way he pleases so long as he does not violate the rights of others. No authority should tell him what to charge for his service or when to serve. If he sees an opportunity for gain, he should be allowed to exploit it. By the very act of exploiting these opportunities, he will attract competition and in the struggle, society will be better served than if competition had been controlled. It is obvious that the philosophy of competition and free enterprise is diametrically opposed to the philosophy of regulated common carriers.

The conflict, then, reduces to determining the proper role of competition and the proper role of regulation in transportation. If competition should be allowed in transportation, some of the policy problems would be solved. For example, allocation of resources to the various modes of transportation and between the transportation sector and the nontransportation sector would pose no problem under competition. Resources would flow to the most profitable mode or into transportation relative to nontransportation enterprise according to the most profitable undertaking. Likewise, the problem of coordination between modes of transportation would be lessened. If a coordinated service was more profitable than an uncoordinated one, coordination would take place. Further, the difficult problems of "illegal transportation" would disappear since competition in transportation would call for the abandonment of entry controls. (There would be no illegal transportation.) The whole policy of exemptions would be irrelevant because all carriers would be exempt. Regulation of rates would likewise be less bothersome and perhaps could be abandoned if competition were allowed to play a larger role. Finally, no statement would be necessary about inherent advantage of the various modes. Competition would measure inherent advantage. Only the most efficient mode for each type of traffic would be able to survive.

This is not to say that using the free-enterprise philosophy and competition would solve all the problems of public policy. Competition assumes at least a semblance of equality between competing firms, yet we have noted that the cost characteristics of the various modes of transportation vary markedly. Some modes have a high degree of fixed or constant costs. If rate competition were allowed, these firms could drive down rates tremendously. Under free competition, such rate cutting would drive out rivals and leave the firm with the ability to cut prices most drastically in control. Monopoly abuses might come about under such circumstances. Much of our national regulatory policy has been concerned with the prevention of "destructive competition."

The problem of "adequacy," so painfully evolved and slowly recognized, is not solved by competition; neither are the problems of safety and dependability. The cheapest transportation is not always the most adequate for public needs. Competition between firms of the same mode may result in depressed rates and earnings to the point where facilities deteriorate and society suffers from inadequate transportation. Where the public is a co-user of the facilities (such as highways) or is dependent upon the carrier to protect the shippers' goods, safety and trustworthiness become important. The cheapest transportation is not always the safest or the most trustworthy.

The problem of discrimination also is not solved by competition. It will be recalled that discrimination among classes of goods, places, and shippers was one of the prime reasons why transportation was regulated originally. If free competition were allowed, discrimination would probably be widespread. Transportation facilities are so expensive, particularly where public aid is not available to provide the way, that only a few firms at the most can serve any shipper or city. Sometimes only a single firm gives service. This is not the competition envisioned by the competitive philosophy, of course, but it may be all the "competition" which can exist under the economics of the situation. Discrimination is an ever-present problem.

Of course some of these problems come about only in a few of the modes of transportation. Hence railroads and pipelines because of their cost characteristics might discriminate if left unregulated, while other modes whose entry is economically easier might be prevented from discriminating because of the existence of competition. This calls to mind the familiar distinction between intermodal and intramodal competition already discussed.

The philosophical conflict between regulation and competition is not easily solved. It seems apparent that our transportation system will need a bit of both regulation and competition. The problem becomes one of determining the respective role of competition and the respective role of regulation.

Regulatory Conflicts

Once it is determined that regulation has a role to play, the matter of public policy conflicts must be faced. Within regulation itself at least four conflicts exist. These are conflicts over comprehensiveness, jurisdiction, duplication, and procedure.

Comprehensiveness of Regulation

As noted above, the formal statutory statement of national transportation policy applies only to the Interstate Commerce Commission and the modes of transportation under its jurisdiction. A separate policy applies to the regulation of air transportation administered by the Civil Aeronautics Board. The act establishing the C.A.B. and the regulation of air transportation contains a policy statement which is clearly promotional, as noted in Chapter 18. Remedial aspects are also involved, although it is hard to reconcile these two policy aims. Regulation of other modes of transportation has been based solely on remedial grounds. (Of course, some types of transportation have gone almost completely unregulated, as previously noted.) There are, then, clear conflicts within the framework of regulation on grounds of comprehensiveness of regulation.

Because of these conflicts, proposals have been made from time to time to have a single regulatory agency. While consistency might well call for such an approach, those opposed to a single regulatory agency with comprehensive powers have pointed out that some modes, such as air transportation, developed more recently or are still developing. The argument that regulatory concepts designed for railroads hardly apply to an entirely different industry such as air transportation is likewise heard. The same point could be, and sometimes is, made relative to motor and water transportation, both regulated by the I.C.C. Thus there is a question of consistency even within those modes now regulated by the I.C.C., for it is true that the economic and market characteristics of the I.C.C.-regulated firms vary considerably.

There are also conflicts over the comprehensiveness of regulation of transportation as it now exists and the many nonregulatory aspects of transportation. Public-aid programs greatly affect transportation, especially in highways, airways, and waterways. Certain policies of the Post Office also play a role in the effectiveness of transportation regulation, and military considerations have had a considerable effect.

For many years, transportation matters have been segmented among various governmental agencies without any real coordination. The Department of Transportation, as noted previously, brought together many of these transportation agencies of the federal government under one head. But unfortunately, the Act creating D.O.T. was less comprehensive in coverage than originally proposed. The new Department is a start toward coordination of transportation functions, but only a start.

A most notable omission from the Department of Transportation is the whole matter of water transportation, both inland and maritime. Also proposed, but omitted from the final Congressional action establishing D.O.T., was the authority to develop "standards and criteria for the formulation and economic evaluation of all proposals for the investment of federal funds in transportation facilities or equipment." Both of these omissions prevent the Department of Transportation from fully coordinating all transportation functions at the federal level. Congress was unwilling to delegate these kinds of powers to an Executive agency.

In summary, even though problems of comprehensiveness of regulation and non-regulatory transportation matters exist, Congress has not yet seen fit to bring all transportation regulation under one regulatory agency, to change significantly the exemptions of certain types of transportation, or to give the Department of Transportation strong direct policy powers.

Jurisdiction

There has long been a conflict over which governmental level shall regulate common carriers. As noted in Chapter 16, the states initiated comprehensive regulation in this country. Regulation under the Common Law preceded this state regulation, but it was far from comprehensive. The Federal government was forced into transportation regulation by the Wabash decision of the Supreme Court in 1886. Since that time, the proper role of the Federal and the state governments has been in conflict.

It is easy to say that the Federal government should regulate interstate commerce and that state governments should regulate intrastate commerce, but it is hard to define these terms. The courts have been called upon again and again to decide when interstate commerce (and hence Federal regulation) is involved. The concept of interstate commerce has been an evolving one which over time has increased in scope to the point where many feel there is no room left for state regulation. Some movements wholly within a single state are in interstate commerce, depending on how the order for the goods was placed, the intent of the shipper, and the like. With the further extension of the Shreveport principle in the Transportation Act of 1958 so that it is no longer necessary to segregate intrastate movement and expenses when ascertaining if intrastate rates burden interstate commerce, little except safety regulation under their police powers remains to the states. Of course the policy is inconsistent, for in motor transportation Federal regulatory acts explicitly leave a great deal of room for state regulation.

It is not necessary here to trace the long and interesting history of legal conflict in this area. It is enough merely to point out that conflict as to jurisdiction exists and probably will continue.

Duplication

Because of these two regulatory conflicts of comprehensiveness and jurisdiction, there is likely to be duplication of regulatory effort. The C.A.B., for example, feels that it should regulate the pickup and delivery of air freight by motor carriers since this is a part of the movement by air. At the same time, the I.C.C. may feel that it should also regulate this service since it is surface transportation carried on by motor vehicles.

The I.C.C. regulates interstate motor carriers and grants certificates of public convenience and necessity with authority for them to operate over specified routes and with specified goods. State commissions also grant certificates with similar provisions, however. Some motor carriers have I.C.C. certificates but not state certificates and are thus prohibited from serving some of the very cities they haul through. Freight must go to a terminal point and be hauled back by a properly certificated carrier. Duplication of regulation causes wastefulness in transportation in this instance.

Other examples could be given, but the point is that regulatory conflict exists and regulation is duplicated in many instances.

Procedural

Finally, there is a procedural conflict inherent in regulation. As discussed in Chapter 19, regulatory boards and commissions have substantial powers of fact-finding and, in administering Congressional policy, great powers of interpretation and definition. Indeed they are often referred to as "independent" regulatory commissions since they establish their own precedents, maintain their own bar, have their own procedures, and make economic determinations with but a minimum of judicial or executive interference.

As noted earlier, too, commissions have a peculiar procedure by which they act in the role of the prosecutor in representing the "public," act as the judge in holding hearings before their bar, and finally act as jury in rendering a decision. Many have questioned whether one body can be all three—prosecutor, judge and jury—no matter how objective and expert it may be.

Of course rather careful checks and balances are established and the whole commission, at least in the case of the I.C.C., often operates primarily as an appeal board. Procedure before commissions is rigid and minutely specified with many opportunities for appeal and reconsideration. However, by the very fact that procedure is rigid and specified, a conflict arises. Procedures tend to become institutionalized and are followed for the sake of procedure itself rather than because they lead to better decisions. Hence, regulatory matters may at times be decided more on whether the procedure or ritual was observed than on the justice of the matter.

One of the advantages of regulation over competition is that it expedites decisions. Yet long time lags are built into institutionalized regulatory procedures. While rights of appeal are necessary and just, some time lag develops because the procedure forces it, not because it is needed. Much has been made of the time lag in commission decisions and the necessity of following outdated procedures at a time when speedy justice is required. Thus, some criticize the ironical fossilization and institutionalization of regulatory procedures over time when regulation was initially developed as a speedier and more certain method of control than the competitive market place. Certainly this institutionalization, which seems to come with age and acceptance, is one of the inherent conflicts of regulation.

Administrative Conflicts

In addition to the philosophical and procedural conflicts inherent in regulation, there is a third area of administrative conflicts arising from regulation. Basically this comes from a lack of coordination of two types. These are lack of coordination of nonregulatory agencies with regulatory agencies, and lack of coordination of nonregulatory agencies with other nonregulatry agencies involved with transportation.

Nonregulatory vs. Regulatory Conflicts

We have already mentioned the role of the Department of Transportation in attempting to coordinate all federal transportation activities. But even with this excellent "start" toward coordination, administrative conflicts between regulatory and nonregulatory agencies are common. Four examples of these types of administrative conflicts will illustrate this point.

The Interstate Commerce Commission is charged with regulating water transportation. The Tennessee Valley Authority is charged with promoting water transportation on the Tennessee River as part of the comprehensive area-development plan of the Authority. Promotion and regulation are not easily reconciled; and when two separate agencies are involved, administrative conflict is inevitable.

The I.C.C. is charged with regulating rates in such a way as to maintain an adequate and nondiscriminatory transportation system. At the same time, the General Services Administration is charged with minimizing governmental expenditures as much as possible. The largest single purchaser of transportation is the United States Government. The G.S.A. wants the lowest possible rate and is not concerned with the I.C.C.'s struggle for adequacy. Special rate privileges (Section 22 rates, discussed in Chapter 12) are sought and used by the government and by the G.S.A. While Congress declares that transportation may not discriminate among shippers, it explicitly makes provision for discriminatory low rates for the movement of government goods under these rates. Discrimination is illegal, it seems, unless it is done in favor of the United States Government. Certainly this is an "administrative conflict."

The aims of the antitrust laws and beliefs of our nation are in conflict with the Interstate Commerce Commission's attempts to promote an adequate transportation system by controlling consolidation and merger. Mergers which might add to the efficiency of the national transportation system do not always promote the goals of competition and antitrust. Hence this is another area where administrative conflict between nonregulatory and regulatory policy exists.

The Interstate Commerce Commission controls all interstate movement of freight by motor vehicles except certain exempt goods, notably agricultural items. The Department of Agriculture, representing farm interests, has been most militant in seeing to it that this exemption is maintained and extended. Truck common carriers of agricultural goods are exempt from I.C.C. regulation, as are the vehicles of agricultural marketing cooperatives where certified by the Secretary of Agriculture. Again, inconsistency is involved and administrative conflict between regulatory and nonregulatory agencies comes about.

Enough has been said to illustrate that little coordination between regulatory and nonregulatory agencies exists in transportation matters. This administrative conflict is one of the shortcomings of regulation.

Nonregulatory Interagency Conflicts

Administrative inconsistency and lack of coordination also exists between nonregulatory agencies where transportation is concerned. There is, for instance, no common purchasing policy applied to all governmental agencies purchasing transportation. Although some progress has been made by the military after many years of effort and a common military purchasing policy finally exists, similar coordination has not been achieved for nonmilitary agencies. Each agency proceeds independent of others in transportation matters, and often inefficiencies are involved.

Perhaps more important is the lack of coordination relative to public aid to transportation. No comprehensive plan or agency is involved, and the attempt to give the Department of Transportation powers to coordinate in this area was defeated. For many years substantial aid and development of highways went on with little or no coordination with other agencies, either regulatory or nonregulatory. Even now that this portion of transportation has come under D.O.T., coordination is proving difficult in practice. Waterway improvement is quite divorced from transportation needs, and often is undertaken for reasons of conservation (or as "pork barrel" projects) with little regard to its effects on overall transportation.

The recent interest in the effects of transportation on our environment, discussed in Chapter 3, should give even greater impetus to the need for comprehensive planning and a reduction of nonregulatory conflicts. Actually, there does seem to be more concern for comprehensive thinking about transportation today than ever before. It remains to be seen if these conflicts can be reduced and a more overall view taken.

In general, then, conflicts of many types exist in national transportation policy. It is possible to delineate at least three types of conflicts: philosophical conflicts inherent in competition versus regulation; regulatory conflicts over comprehensiveness, jurisdiction, duplication, and the procedure of regulation; and administrative conflicts developing because of lack of coordination between regulatory and nonregulatory governmental agencies and among nonregulatory agencies.

PROPOSED SOLUTIONS TO CONFLICTS

The policy conflicts noted have been known for some years. It is only in recent times with the changing character of the transportation market, however, that great concern over these conflicts has been evidenced. When railroads were the major means of transportation, the philosophical conflict of competition versus regulation was more easily resolved. The economic characteristics of rail transportation held out little hope for competition to function and regulation was inevitable, or so it seemed. However, with the emergence of the newer types of transportation, a new dimension to competition arose.

Regulatory conflicts are to a marked degree based on the existence of several modes. Under a predominantly rail transportation system with I.C.C. regulation, there was little argument about comprehensiveness or duplication of regulation. While jurisdictional conflicts and procedural problems have always existed, they seem to have intensified over time. Further, administrative conflicts were less important under the conditions existing before the 1930's. The role of the Federal government was much less and therefore the lack of coordination among nonregulatory agencies had less effect. Public aid to transportation after the period of Nineteenth-Century railroad aid, did not become important until the 1920's, thus the lack of coordination between regulatory and nonregulatory agencies was also less important. The same conclusion can be reached by noting that our concern with agricultural problems began in the mid-1920's. Exemptions, Section 22 rates, T.V.A. and water navigation developments, intensified antitrust problems—indeed, practically all the administrative conflicts—have come about since the 1930's.

There was no problem of inherent advantage and coordination or allocation of transportation resources prior to the emergence of competitive modes. Indeed it is correct to say that conflicts in national transportation policy are to a large extent a matter of recent importance which arose with the changing character of the transportation market.

As noted in Chapters 17 and 18, there seems to be a tendency toward social lag in facing up to problems in transportation. These policy problems arose in the late 1920's and in the 1930's, yet little was done about them at the time. To be sure, Congress laid down a "Declaration of National Transportation Policy" in 1940 but, as we have noted above, it was vague, contradictory, and indefinable. Serious lack of coordination at the federal level had existed at least since the 1940's, but it was not until the Department of Transportation was created that any attempt was made at a solution. Even this action can be only partially successful due to the limitations on D.O.T.'s role. Scholars have concerned themselves with all these policy conflicts almost continuously, but public (Congressional) action has been slow.

Recent Reports

Recently a series of studies of national transportation policy has been undertaken by special groups. Some have been done by private agencies such as the study of National Transportation Policy undertaken by Charles Dearing and Wilfred Owen of the Brookings Institution at the request of the First Hoover Commission, published in 1949. Others have been made under the sponsorship of the Department of Commerce and have taken the name of the current Secretary of Commerce. Examples are the Sawyer Report, 1949; Weeks Report, 1955; and Mueller Report, 1960. Congressional Committees have conducted other studies. Best known of these are the Smathers Report, 1958; Kilday Report, 1959; and Doyle Report, 1961. Altogether, seven reports dealing with transportation and its regulation were released in late 1960 and early 1961.

With all these reports and groups studying the problems of national transportation policy, one would think that some excellent solutions would have been proposed. However, there has been no uniformity in their recommendations. Of course, some have been aimed at specific areas of conflict such as public aids, regulatory procedures, lack of administrative coordination, and so forth.

Almost all these reports do suggest, however, that more market competition between modes should be allowed to allocate transportation resources. Most reports have also recognized a role for regulation primarily in the area of protection against monopoly overcharges and abuses. The role of transportation in defense has been emphasized by some reports and used to justify special treatment of some modes of transportation. Administrative conflicts have been recognized in nearly all reports, but solutions proposed have varied all the way from creating a Department of Transportation to advocating a more "flexible" approach.

The Kennedy "Transportation Message"

Perhaps one of the most significant sets of proposals dealing with the problem of transportation was the Transportation Message of President John F. Kennedy in April, 1962 (House Doc. No. 384, 87th Congress, 2nd Session). This message was significant if for no other reason than because it was the first time any President had sent Congress a separate message devoted entirely to transportation. By taking this step, the President signified the importance of transportation problems to the economy. Basically, the Kennedy Message was divided into four parts dealing with intercity transportation, urban transportation, international transportation, and labor relations and research.

The message contains an excellent statement of the importance of transportation to the economy as a whole in its Preamble where the President developed the theme that "an efficient and dynamic transportation system is vital to our domestic economy, productivity, and progress." Along with this idea of need, the message recognized that "a chaotic patchwork of inconsistent and often obsolete legislation and regulation has evolved . . . This patchwork does not fully reflect either the dramatic changes in technology of the past half century or the parallel changes in the structure of competition." Continuing, Mr. Kennedy declared: ". . . transportation is subject to excessive, cumbersome, and time-consuming regulatory supervision that shackles and distorts managerial initiative. Some parts of the transportation industry are restrained unnecessarily; others are promoted or taxed unevenly and inconsistently."

President Kennedy then tried his hand at stating a national transportation policy, as follows:

> The basic objective of our Nation's transportation system must be to assure the availability of the fast, safe, and economical transportation services needed in a growing and changing economy to move people and goods, without waste or discrimination, in response to private and public demands at the lowest cost consistent with health, convenience, national security, and other broad public objectives. Investment or capacity should be neither substantially above nor substantially below these requirements—for chronic excess capacity involves misuse of resources, and lack of adequate capacity jeopardizes progress. The resources devoted to provision of transportation service should be used in the most effective and efficient manner possible; and this, in turn, means that users of transportation facilities should be provided with incentives to use whatever form of transportation provides them with the service they desire at the lowest total cost, both public and private.
>
> This basic objective can and must be achieved primarily by continued reliance on unsubsidized privately owned facilities, operating under the incentive of private profit and the checks of competition to the maximum extent practicable. The role of the public policy should be to provide a consistent and comprehensive framework of equal competitive opportunity that will achieve this objective at the lowest economic and social cost to the Nation.
>
> This means a more coordinated Federal policy and a less segmented approach. It means equality of opportunity for all forms of transportation and their users and undue preference to none. It means greater reliance on the forces of competition and less reliance on the restraints of regulation. And it means that, to the extent possible, the users of transportation services should bear the full costs of the services they use, whether those services are provided privately or publicly.

To implement these policy suggestions, the President recommended specific changes under four headings: equal competitive opportunity under diminished regulation; consistent policies of taxation and users charges; even-handed government promotion of intercity transportation; and protection of the public interest.

To promote "equal competitive opportunity under diminished regulation," the President recommended either extending the bulk commodity exemption, presently applicable to water transportation, to all modes of transportation or repealing the exemption as it now applies solely to barge traffic. He stated that extending this exemption to all carriers was preferred because it would allow competition to act more freely as a natural regulator while repeal of the exemption would increase, not lessen, regulation. Basically the same recommendation was made relative to the agricultural products exemption presently applied to motor carriers. Extend the exemption to all or, failing this, take the exemption away. Coupled with this "extend to all or none" idea was the recommendation that minimum-rate regulation in these areas (bulk commodities and agricultural products) be abandoned, but maximum-rate control (to protect against monopoly) be retained. These proposals were the most drastic and controversial ones made in the message.

The President further recommended maximum-rate control only over intercity passenger fares; repeal of the commodities clause; equal treatment for all using piggyback service, whether carrier or shipper; and Congressional permission for regulatory authorities to allow more experimentation in freight rates, classification, documentation, and coordination. All of these recommendations were aimed at introducing more competition and less regulation into transportation. None were immediately enacted by Congress.

Under "consistent policies of taxation and user charges," the President asked for repeal of the 10 per cent passenger transportation excise tax which had been originally enacted as a wartime tax. He recommended a 5 per cent tax on airline tickets, an extension of the tax on aviation fuel to jet fuel and a 3¢ per gallon tax on fuel in general (noncommercial) aviation. The object here was to recover a portion of the Federal expenditures on airways from the users of the facilities. Likewise, the message recommended a 2¢ per gallon tax on fuel used by water transportation. Finally, he recommended a change in the tax treatment of depreciation by carriers.

Several of these recommendations were subsequently enacted into law. Although great opposition arose to the suggested tax on fuel used on waterways, the rest of the recommendations under this heading were less controversial and were adopted.

Under "evenhanded government promotion of intercity transportation," the President recommended that domestic trunk airlines be declared ineligible for operating subsidies, that other airline and helicopter subsidies be drastically reduced and slowly discontinued, that the "use-it-or-lose-it" policy on feeder airline service to smaller cities be rigorously enforced, and that regional airports or single airports serve adjacent cities where possible. He urged extension of loan guarantee plans in air and rail transportation, urged the Post Office to be more flexible in use of motor carriers for the mails, and urged government agencies to use commercial transportation facilities wherever possible rather than setting up their own facilities. Many of these recommendations were administrative matters which did not require legislation.

Finally, under "protection of the public interest," President Kennedy announced that he had formed an interagency group including the Justice Department to formulate general "guidelines" on merger policy; asked Congress to encourage more through routes and joint rates; requested that the Secretary of Defense and the General Services Administration encourage experimental rate-making and rate simplification; asked Congress to give the I.C.C. powers to enter into cooperative agreements with states relative to enforcement; recommended that all carriers be required to pay reparations, including motor carriers and freight forwarders; and recommended increased penalties on certain violations of regulatory laws. Many of these recommendations were administrative and required little action by Congress.

While we have not discussed the conflicts and background involved in all of the areas discussed by President Kennedy, it is quite evident that the President's message was based on three general approaches: uniformity of regulatory treatment, increased use of competition, and less but more effective regulation. Practically all of the recommendations, executive actions, and suggestions of the message fall into one of these categories.

The Kennedy message also established a "transportation message" pattern which has been followed by other Presidents since that time.

The Johnson "Transportation Message"

In March, 1966, President Lyndon B. Johnson followed the Kennedy precedent with a "transportation message." The Johnson message did not deal with philosophical questions of transportation regulation, but rather with administrative problems of coordination and safety. As has already been noted, Congress responded in October 1966 with the Department of Transportation Act, which went at least part way in meeting the President's suggestions.

The organization and mission of the Department of Transportation already have been discussed in Chapter 19. Other references to D.O.T. as a coordinating agency have been noted earlier in this chapter and need not be repeated here. It remains to be seen, of course, how effective D.O.T. can be in solving the problems of coordination. As a planning agency, the Department has great potentiality in spite of some of the limitations due to its enabling legislation. Under its first head, Secretary Alan Boyd, and increasingly under Secretary John Volpe, D.O.T. became bolder in its approach as time passed. The Department has not moved rapidly, but it has steadily concerned itself more and more with transportation regulatory and policy matters. At this writing, D.O.T. seems destined to become a major voice in transportation matters in the years ahead. But only time will tell if it can solve some of the major conflicts of national transportation policy.

CONCLUSIONS

The special reports as well as the Kennedy Message all call for more competition in transportation. The exact form which this added reliance on competition would take is not always clear. In some cases where this is spelled out such as some of the President's recommendations, the increased reliance on competition could cause future transportation conflicts. We have already noted some of the arguments against a more competitive transportation system where basic economic characteristics are dissimilar or stages of development differ widely. Any introduction of increased competition and less regulation would have to proceed slowly. None of the reports nor the message envision a sudden change in transportation regulation.

More competition would solve some of the philosophical questions. It would likewise help with a partial solution to some regulatory conflicts. Competition could do little to change the administrative conflicts, however. But there seems to be some hope that the Department of Transportation will make at least some progress in this area.

The authors feel that more reliance should be placed on competition, but that regulation has a definite role to play in transportation. By slowly injecting more market forces into selected areas of transportation with a more effective and better organized regulatory structure, domestic transportation should improve and gradually overcome many of the conflicts inherent in the present regulatory system. Certainly the years of study and concern with updating regulation to reflect the transportation system of today must culminate in careful and well-thought-out action by Congress. While the possibility of causing more conflicts is ever present and is a risk in all change, the rewards of a more realistic regulatory and policy structure are potentially great and worth the risk.

GENERAL SUMMARY OF TRANSPORTATION POLICY

Transportation policy has grown like Topsy and has had little overall goal or orientation. To a marked degree, our national policy has been patched up to meet emergencies as they arose. Little advance planning has been done relative to our approach to transportation and a distinct social lag has existed. Our policy has been backward rather than forward looking. Our discussion in the previous chapters has indicated that this has been the general approach in the case of policy concerning unification and integration, labor-management relations, public aids, and national transportation policy in general.

Recent interest in the backward orientation and social-lag problems of national transportation policy holds out great hope that the future may lead to forward-looking, well-thought-out changes in the various policy areas which would help promote a more economical, efficient, and productive transportation system for the national economy.

ADDITIONAL READINGS

1. Arpaia, Anthony F., "Lest the President's Transport Message Become a Scrap of Paper," **Transportation Journal,** Winter 1962, pp. 8–12.

2. Arth, Maurice P., "Federal Transport Regulatory Policy," **American Economic Review,** May 1962, pp. 416–425.

3. Campbell, Thomas C., "Agricultural Exemptions from Motor Carrier Regulation," **Land Economics,** February 1960, pp. 14–25.

4. Conant, Michael, "President Kennedy's Transportation Message and Railroad Survival," **Transportation Journal,** Fall 1962, pp. 16–25.

5. Conant, Michael, **Railroad Mergers and Abandonments.** Berkeley, Calif.: University of California Press, 1964.
Chapter III. "Railroad Consolidations and the Antitrust Laws," pp. 42–68.

6. Dearing, C. L., and Wilfred Owen, **National Transportation Policy.** Washington, D.C.: The Brookings Institution, 1949, pp. 1–440.

7. Doyle, John P., "Transportation at the Crossroads," **Transportation Journal,** Fall 1962, pp. 26–31.

8. Fair, Marvin, "Some Observations on the Theory and Performance of the Independent Regulatory Agencies in Regulating Public Utilities," **I.C.C. Practitioners' Journal,** June 1960, pp. 957–969.

9. Farris, Martin T., "Definitional Inconsistencies in the National Transportation Policy," **I.C.C. Practitioners' Journal,** November–December 1967, pp. 25–33.

10. Gifford, Gilbert L., "Economic Implications of Proposed Changes in Transport Regulation," **Transportation Journal,** Fall 1961, pp. 25–36.

11. Kennedy, John F., **The Transportation System of Our Nation,** Message from the President of the United States, April 5, 1962, House of Representatives, Document No. 384, 87th Congress, 2nd Session.

12. Meyer, John R., Merton J. Peck, John Stenason, and Charles Zwick, **The Economics of Competition in the Transportation Industries.** Cambridge, Mass.: Harvard University Press, 1959.
Chapter IX. "Toward Improved Public and Private Policies in Transportation," pp. 242–276.

13. Miller, Sidney L., Jr., "Federal Regulation of Transportation—A Case of Institutional Frustration," **Transportation Journal,** Winter 1961, pp. 39–41.

14. **National Transportation Policy,** Report of the Committee on Commerce, United States Senate, By Its Special Study Group on Transportation Policies in the United States, Senate Report No. 445, 87th Congress, 1st Session, 1961, ("Doyle Report").

15. Nelson, James C., "Effects of Public Regulation on Railroad Performance," **American Economic Review,** May 1960, pp. 495–505.

16. Nelson, James C., "Government's Role Toward Transportation," **Transportation Journal,** Summer 1962, pp. 15–22.

17. Nightingale, Edmund A., "A Critique of American Transportation Policy Developments," **I.C.C. Practitioners' Journal,** in two parts, April 1963, pp. 891–905, and May 1963, pp. 1004–1020.

18. Norton, Hugh S., **National Transportation Policy: Formation and Implementation.** Berkeley, California: McCutchan Publishing Corporation, 1966.
Part III. "Evaluation and Prospects," pp. 209–243.

19. Pegrum, Dudley F., **Transportation: Economics and Public Policy.** Rev. ed. Homewood, Ill.: Richard D. Irwin, Inc., 1968.
Chapter 17. "Competition and Regulation in Transportation," pp. 422–445.

20. Shinn, Glenn L., "Rate Regulation on Trial," **I.C.C. Practitioners' Journal,** June 1964, pp. 988–992.

21. Williams, Ernest W., Jr., "Public Policy and Research in Transportation," **Transportation Journal,** Winter 1963, pp. 27–33.

22. Williams, Ernest W., Jr., **The Regulation of Rail-Motor Rate Competition.** New York: Harper and Brothers, 1958.
    Chapter 8. "Appraisal of the Commission's Performance," pp. 201–228.

23. Wilson, George W., **Essays on Some Unsettled Questions in the Economics of Transportation.** Bloomington, Indiana: Foundation for Economics and Business Studies, 1962.
    Chapter 1. "The Concept of Inherent Advantage," pp. 5–30.
    Chapter 3. "Inherent Advantage of Rail and Truck," pp. 79–122.

24. Wilson, George W., "The Effect of Rate Regulation on Resource Allocation in Transportation," **American Economic Review,** May 1964, pp. 160–171.

Part Seven

Transportation Aspects of Physical Distribution Administration (Business Logistics)

In previous parts of this book we have considered various aspects of our domestic transportation system—its history and economic significance, its economic characteristics and performance, its services, costs, and rates, its regulation, and our public goals in its operations. In all this our concern has been with the effective use of the system for individual shippers and for the overall public welfare of our profits-oriented, free-enterprise economy.

Even the best physical transportation plant cannot adequately serve our individual and social needs unless it is properly used in physically distributing our products. This calls for a high level of technical and managerial ability on the part of the users. The transportation activities of individual firms must be properly supervised and coordinated with other operations of the firm. Choices must be made among transportation alternatives. New ways of improving transportation efficiency for the firm and, consequently, for the entire economy must be sought constantly.

The complexities of our transportation system have led to the development of a specialized area of management, which we call "traffic management," at the individual-firm level. As transportation conditions and competitive pressures have changed, so has the traffic management function. To efficiently fulfill this function, today's traffic manager must have a broad understanding of the external and internal environment of his business plus general management talent and special knowledge of transportation.

In this part, then, we will view the general nature and scope of the administration of the physical distribution function at the level of the individual firm, with particular emphasis on the role of traffic management in this process. This introduction, together with the earlier portions of this book, is designed to be a taking-off point for those interested in more advanced and technical studies in traffic management or any other phase of physical distribution management. For those interested only in an intelligent layman's or informed businessman's knowledge of the field, on the other hand, this part should lead to a better understanding of the importance of the proper use of transportation in our dynamic economy.

25

Traffic Management's Role in the Decision-Making Mechanism

PHYSICAL DISTRIBUTION AND INDUSTRIAL TRAFFIC MANAGEMENT

Physical distribution is that aspect of production concerned with the movement of goods through space (transportation) and time (storage and warehousing). These movements add to the utility and, thus, to the value of goods, as well as to their cost. A firm's objective in physical distribution, then, is to add as much value as possible with the least increase in cost or to strike a satisfactory or acceptable balance between value-added and cost-added.

The term "physical distribution" often is used to refer in a narrow sense only to outbound movements, with its counterpart—"physical supply"—being used in reference to inbound shipments. As employed in this book, however, unless otherwise specified, a firm's physical distribution process encompasses both inbound and outbound movements and related activities.

Transportation is a necessary component of physical distribution and usually is the most costly part of the process. In fact, until quite recently most firms and individuals acted as if transportation were the only significant element in this process and they viewed transport services only as cost-additive and not as a means of adding value or of reducing nontransport costs. Today, however, it is being recognized more and more that the effective management of a firm's transportation involves interrelationships with other functions such as purchasing, inventory control, production scheduling, warehousing, internal materials handling, package engineering, advertising and sales, plant location, and even broad marketing, product, and customer-relations policies. All of these interrelated activities, then, and perhaps others may properly be included within what we call the physical distribution process.

Evolution of the Traffic Manager

Someone always must control and direct ("manage") transportation. As transportation always has been a necessary element in trade, therefore, it follows that we have had transportation managers for as long as we have had commerce of any kind; in fact, this management must predate even our earliest and simplest forms of organized commerce. But it was not until the development of efficient modern transportation technology which allowed mass production and mass distribution over large geographic areas that full-time specialists in transportation, so-called "traffic managers," became important in industrial and commercial firms using far-flung transportation services. That is, industrial or commercial traffic management became recognized as a separate occupation only after railroads became an important or dominant form of land transport and steamships began to replace sailing vessels during the Nineteenth Century.

In most firms the traffic manager has not ranked high in the management hierarchy. By generally accepted definitions, a manager's functions include the planning, organizing, directing, coordinating, and controlling of some activity or activities. This involves whatever cooperation may be appropriate with other managers plus the follow-up necessary to determine whether or not a job is being satisfactorily performed and authority to take remedial action if it is not. By all definitions a manager is a decision-maker. Judged by these criteria, the vast majority of so-called "traffic managers" of the past and a large number even today cannot properly be classified as high level "managers."

The Early Railroad Era

Traffic management as a distinct occupation came during the pre-regulation railroad era. In those free-wheeling days of the mid-Nineteenth Century and following, railroads had a relatively free hand in setting their rates and services. Discrimination between localities and even between individual customers in a given locality was widespread. Rate advantages or service advantages such as transit privileges not available to competitors were eagerly sought by rival industrial or commercial firms and were just as eagerly granted by fiercely competing railroads.

It is well known that the squeaky wheel gets the grease. Aggressive firms whose transport costs were a large proportion of their total costs or who stood to benefit by service concessions, therefore, were prone to squeak loudly. They hired traffic managers, often former railroad personnel with railroad connections, as their representatives. A major function of these first traffic managers was to obtain favorable rail treatment for their firms either by persuasion or by the potential threat of diverting substantial traffic to other rail lines. Such persons clearly were not "managers" in the accepted definition of that term. Rather, they were more akin to salesmen or lobbyists.

The Regulated Rail Monopoly Era

This situation changed with the coming of effective railroad regulation. Discrimination was outlawed. Rates and services, published in tariffs, were public knowledge and were equally available to all users under substantially similar circumstances. The traffic manager no longer could secure extraordinarily favorable concessions for his firm, at least not legally. Rational economic grounds for choosing among different carriers were limited. For practical purposes, only rail transport was available for large or lengthy movements except in coastal areas and on a few interior routes where water transport managed to survive. And even if alternate rail carriers or routes were available, rates and services generally were identical, or almost so.

In this new environment, the traffic manager became a specialist on rates and routes. His principal stock in trade was the ability to read the increasingly complex and numerous rail freight tariffs. This skill usually was acquired by several years' experience as a rate clerk in a railroad traffic department or by a long apprenticeship in an industrial traffic office or shipping department, perhaps supplemented by correspondence or night-school courses.

Higher echelons of management generally had little knowledge or understanding of the work of the "rather peculiar" fellows in their small offices surrounded by volumes of incomprehensible "rate books." They were looked upon, usually rightly so, as rather narrow specialists or technicians. Their services were recognized as necessary, but were regarded as ranking but little higher than that of shipping clerks. In fact, shipping clerks often were responsible for such "traffic management" as existed in smaller firms or in organizations with relatively low transport costs; and in other cases, the promotional route to traffic manager was up through shipping department ranks.

The major tangible criterion by which higher management usually evaluated the efficiency of the traffic manager was the level of transport costs paid by the firm. If freight charges per unit of product declined, the traffic manager was efficient; if these costs increased without some clearly understandable reason, such as a freight-rate increase or market extension into more distant areas, he might be replaced. It is not surprising, therefore, that the traffic manager's goal generally was to minimize his firm's direct transportation outlays. This clearly was what top management desired. It was probably unusual for a traffic manager to see that the lowest possible transport costs do not always necessarily mean the lowest possible total production costs, and it certainly was exceptional when such an astute traffic manager had the aggressiveness and persuasiveness to convince higher management of this.

The rates-and-routes technician was not completely passive, of course. Often he did represent his firm as a specialist and a special pleader before carriers, carrier associations, and regulatory agencies. These activities frequently did benefit his firm, his industry, or the economy generally by influencing the level of rates and the quantity and quality of services. Obviously, however, these advocate functions did nothing to enhance the traffic manager's status as a manager; rather, they confirmed his status as a specialist and a technician.

In their capacity as specialists, the more effective traffic managers sometimes were called upon for advice on transportation matters by top management or by various functional departments or divisions of their firms. That is, they performed staff duties in addition to handling technical details. Usually, however, the traffic manager's advice, if sought at all in connection with locational, marketing, and production matters, was considered along with advice from several other sources in reaching a decision.

Seldom, if ever, did the traffic manager himself act as a major decision-maker on matters of great importance to the business. Most of his own decisions related to requests for carrier transportation equipment for loading, routing, and documentation of shipments, routine handling of loss and damage claims, freight-bill audits, and the supervision of his small staff of clerks and assistants, if any. Sometimes his responsibilities extended to include some phases of packing, marking, and the actual loading of merchandise aboard rail cars. But at most, the traffic manager's operational decisions were on a par with those of office managers and shipping department foremen.

The Rise of Transport Competition

The emergence of effective intermodal transportation competition, which has developed rapidly since the 1920's, again called for a different type of traffic manager. Many shippers were freed from exclusive dependence upon the rails. The traffic manager in many cases was given a choice between different modes of transport, between common and contract carriers, or even between for-hire and private transport. These alternative services varied considerably in quality and cost. By making the proper choice, a traffic manager might considerably reduce his firm's transport costs, improve customer services, and consequently create good will and retain or generate business for his company, or even influence production schedules and inventory and marketing policies. His decisions, in other words, could significantly affect the prosperity of his firm.

Clearly, under such conditions, the rail rates-and-routes expert alone was not qualified for the traffic manager's role. The old expertise still was necessary, but no longer sufficient. The new role required comprehensive knowledge of the rates and service characteristics of all forms of transportation as well as some knowledge of the effects of various kinds of alternative transport services upon the company's overall operations. The effective traffic manager, in addition to being a technician and a staff specialist, became also something of a generalist and a real decision-making manager. Industrial traffic personnel increasingly came from sources other than railroad rate departments and industrial shipping departments. Even some college graduates (rank heresy to old-line, rail-spawned traffic men) began to infiltrate the mysterious realm of traffic management.

This transformation did not occur overnight. In fact it is still in process. Many of the older generation of traffic managers could not or would not adjust wholeheartedly to the new environment. Even more important, higher management often failed to recognize that a changed technological environment had expanded the horizons of physical distribution and called for a new breed of traffic manager. Consequently, the traffic management function all too often was still regarded as a necessary evil requiring only the services of a narrow specialist whose performance was judged by how effective he was in minimizing direct transport costs. Thus without adequate recognition in status and pay, many traffic managers continued to follow the path of least resistance by doing what had been expected of them historically. This situation still exists in numerous firms.

In the better managed and more progressive companies, however, especially those in which transport costs were a large portion of distribution or total costs, opportunities did increase for the traffic manager. By doing a better job for his firm, he received greater financial rewards and became recognized as a legitimate member of the management team—a low-ranking member, perhaps, but nonetheless a member. His influence on the profitability of the firm was recognized, his decision-making authority was broadened, and his advice was sought more often by top management and by other management officials.

In summary, then, the traffic manager as such is everywhere generally regarded as a technician and staff specialist. In many firms, he is viewed only in this light and typically performs in the manner expected by his superiors. In many other firms, however, and increasingly so, he performs and is seen and rewarded as an important part of the management group in addition to his mysterious specialty.

The "Total Cost" Concept of Physical Distribution Management

During recent years, particularly since the latter 1950's, the advent and growing use of electronic computers, coupled with increasing competitive pressures to produce and distribute goods as efficiently as possible, has focused interest on a "new" concept of "total cost" physical distribution management. That is, widespread interest has developed in the interrelationships between the type of transport used and other production and distribution costs. This development or its application has been variously labeled as "Physical Distribution Management," "Business Logistics," "Rhochrematics" (a combination of Greek words meaning roughly "the science of materials flow"), and by similar terms. In some instances, new managerial titles and departments corresponding to these terms have been created.

Perhaps the only really "new" portion of this concept, at least for those businesses which have long been blessed by good and well-recognized traffic departments, are the new terms themselves. Certainly the "best" traffic managers and higher management officials in the "best managed" businesses have long been aware that minimizing transport costs does not in all circumstances maximize profits. That is, sometimes the use of a higher priced mode, such as air carriage, rather than a lower priced mode, will decrease some other cost or costs considerably more than it increases transport costs, or that providing better customer service through premium transportation sometimes pays off manyfold in good will and increased business volume.

The importance of this so-called new total cost concept should not be minimized, however. Management officials generally, academicians who have shown little interest in transportation for many years, and even some of the "older" or traditional type of traffic managers have been intrigued by it. New and much needed attention and thought have been devoted to the role of transportation in physical distribution. The popular concept of the humdrum activities of the traffic manager have been glamourized. The title of "Physical Distribution Manager" or "Vice-President, Logistics" is likely to carry more popular and corporate prestige than the title of "Traffic Manager." Even more important, the new title and the top-management thinking back of it are likely to result in increased responsibility and authority for its recipient and to attract or develop better managers.

It should be understood, of course, that a new managerial title or a re-named corporate department alone does not improve the efficiency of a business. If the retitled individual continues doing only the same things in the same ways, nothing is benefited except his ego. Physical distribution management includes traffic management, but it is more.

The traffic manager in reality is a purchasing agent, and heads a department devoted to the efficient buying of those transportation services needed by his firm. If he takes into full account the total operational and distribution costs and profits effects of his buying and has the corporate influence or authority to obtain cooperation from other departments or divisions in tailoring transport and other activities into an optimum blend, he is practicing physical distribution management (or business logistics, rhochrematics, etc.) regardless of his title or of the corporate organizational structure. Contrarily, if he does not or cannot obtain the cooperation of other managers (those in charge of such activities as production scheduling, inventory control, purchasing, marketing, and related functions) and of top management itself, he can never be more than a traffic manager.

An increasing number of firms are creating departments and managers of physical distribution. Some of these, unfortunately, are little more than changed labels. But many are managing physical distribution in the best sense by coordinating the activities of the traffic department with the activities of other departments. This of course calls for a physical distribution position in the management structure higher than the position of the traffic manager and the various other departmental managers concerned. Usually to be effective, this means that the manager of physical distribution must have vice-presidential authority (even if not that title) and the ear of top management. Usually no lesser position can bring about the necessary cooperation between departments and managers with traditional sub-optimizing goals.

Figure 29 shows a portion of a simplified corporate organization chart of a manufacturing firm illustrating the control of physical distribution. This chart, while perhaps reasonably representative, does not purport to be "ideal." What is best for one firm is not necessarily best for another. There are almost

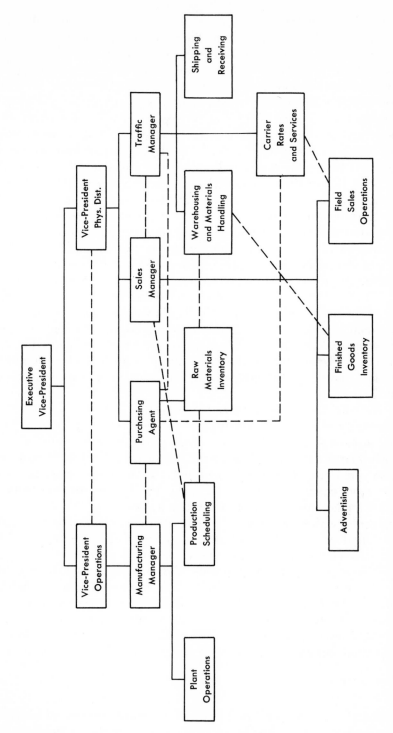

Figure 29: Segment of Organization Chart for Coordinating Physical Distribution Management.

Solid Lines Indicate Line Authority and Responsibility. Broken Lines Show Principal Channels of Interdivisional and Interdepartmental Information and Coordination.

as many organizational forms, formal and informal, as there are individual firms. Specific interrelationships between the traffic department and other departments will be elaborated upon in Chapters 26, 27, and 28.

Many traffic managers have aspired to and some have achieved the position and title of "Vice-President in Charge of Physical Distribution," or some such. The typical well-informed traffic manager's qualifications for such a position certainly are as good as those of the typical manager of marketing or related functional areas, but probably no better. It is essential, of course, that a physical distribution manager be well-versed in transportation, but it is equally essential that he be well-versed in many other phases of his company's activities and of the industry concerned. He must be a "specialist" in general management rather than in a functional area. His subordinate managers will be functional specialists. It is just as likely that a competent manager from a nontransportation area can acquire the transportation understanding necessary for overall physical distribution management as it is that a traffic manager can acquire the necessary grasp of nontransport functions.

In selecting a physical distribution manager, top management in a particular firm will consider many things, of course. These obviously will include the nature of the firm's and the industry's distribution problems, the share of distribution and total costs attributable to transportation, the present corporate organization structure, qualifications of potential candidates for the position (both inside and outside the firm), and perhaps individual personalities, historical intrafirm relationships, and what similar or competing firms have done.

Although information is sketchy and the situation is fluid, it appears that at least a majority of those individuals now bearing the title of Physical Distribution Manager (or similar titles) have been chosen from the ranks of general line managers, that is, from "operations" positions rather than from direct "distribution" positions. Traffic managers and sales managers seem to have contributed about equally to most of the remainder of these positions, with a small number coming from several other functional areas.

In companies without a specifically designated physical distribution manager, such interdepartmental coordination of physical distribution as exists apparently is directed by general management officials in a majority of firms, with traffic departments, sales departments, and purchasing departments (in that order) being next in importance. In many such firms, of course, standing interdepartmental committees or other less formal means of coordination may perform just as effectively as would a formalized organization structure and a titled physical distribution manager. Organization charts and titles do not always guarantee and are not always necessary for an effective level of performance.

Summary

To summarize briefly, the "total cost" management concept of physical distribution represents the latest stage in the evolution of the functions of the traffic manager. Although traffic management has existed in some form as long as traffic itself, the traffic manager's separate position in business organization arose out of the peculiar needs of the early railroad era. As these needs changed with changing institutional and technological environments (regulated rail monopoly, followed by extensive intermodal competition), the traffic manager likewise changed. Finally, the business "cost squeeze" of the 1950's, attributable in part at least to considerable saturation of the pent-up demands of the war years, higher labor costs, and an international increase in productive capacity, efficiency, and competition, forced many firms and industries to search for new methods of cutting cost.

To their surprise, many managements found that greater opportunities for efficiencies existed in proper utilization of transportation than in any other area. Costs of labor, raw materials, and capital in many cases are only slightly under management control, and a great deal of attention has been given to the improvement of production methods and techniques for many years. But the management of transportation from the overall view of profit maximization offered an unexploited new frontier, hence, the interest in the "total cost" management concept of physical distribution and the increasing recognition given to the function of traffic management in this process.

DUTIES AND ORGANIZATION OF THE INDUSTRIAL TRAFFIC DEPARTMENT

Now that we have considered the overall role of the industrial traffic manager in a firm, we can appropriately turn to a more specific examination of how a traffic department may be organized and the nature of its responsibilities. In the following discussion, it is not necessary to assume that the traffic department is or is not a part of a formal structure headed by a Physical Distribution Manager unless the authors so indicate. There is no inherent reason why a traffic manager reporting directly to a Vice-President of Physical Distribution or Logistics should have significantly different responsibilities or a significantly different internal organization in his department than one reporting to some other higher management official.

Traffic Responsibilities

As pointed out above, the traffic manager is a combination of technical expert, staff adviser, and line manager. Almost all line managers have some staff advisory responsibilities, of course, while many staff officials in addition to their research, planning, and recommendation functions also exercise some line authority within their own fields of specialization. Most management officials fall clearly either into the line or the staff division, however, with the other function being relatively minor. This is not generally true of the traffic manager. Instead, he is unique in that he cannot clearly be classified primarily either as a line manager or a staff expert.

Line Duties

Like most managers, line or staff, the traffic manager exercises line control over his subordinates in his own department. His major line responsibility, however, is in the acquiring of transportation services for his company.

Buying appropriate transportation often is a complex activity requiring decisions among many alternatives. The traffic manager must consider all available services and rates of all modes of carriage and even of individual carriers among these various modes from the viewpoint of what best fits his company's need for a specific shipment. As you know, services and rates vary considerably among modes and carriers both at any given time and over periods of time. Likewise, each shipment made by a company may have individual characteristics and needs of its own. Buying the right transportation for a particular movement, therefore, calls for the traffic manager's expertise in transport matters plus an intimate understanding of the general characteristics of his firm and industry, and a detailed knowledge of any peculiarities (physical or otherwise) of a particular shipment.

Purchasing transportation is very different from purchasing groceries in a supermarket. It is true that the grocery shopper may have a bewildering variety of prices, sizes, and labels (supposedly denoting quality) to choose from as does the traffic manager. But here the comparison ceases. The housewife chooses from among what is available to please herself, carts it away, and the transaction is finished. The traffic manager, however, typically spends a large portion of his time in attempting to get something which is not currently on the shelf. That is, by negotiating with individual carriers, carrier associations, or regulatory agencies, individually or through one or more of the associations to which he typically belongs, he actively and often successfully attempts to change prices, quantities, and qualities of transportation.

Further, the traffic manager usually must choose his bundle of transportation services with an eye to what the consignee of a shipment desires. That is, a customer may have peculiar requirements for line-haul or terminal services, or even biases which must be considered. Sometimes sacrifices in terms of immediate convenience and costs to the traffic manager's own firm must be made for the sake of long-run customer good will and repeat orders. Often the traffic department's work is made more difficult (as well as considerably more costly) by promises made by product salesmen who have little if any knowledge of transportation matters pertinent to the product.

In addition to choosing from among the various alternative modes and carriers, the traffic manager must choose a specific route over which the shipment will move, contact the carrier for equipment, and perform the necessary paperwork. He must follow up to see that the ordered equipment actually is received when promised, perhaps supervise loading of the cargo, and see that it is dispatched on schedule. Then he may have to follow up to insure that the cargo arrives on time and in good order or take corrective action if it does not. Finally, he may be responsible for checking the carrier's billing to insure that his company has not been overcharged.

From the foregoing, which is only the briefest thumbnail sketch of the major traffic-management line function, it can be seen that the life of the traffic manager cannot be a dull one. Instead, he is faced with a continuous stream of problems and crises, all important to his company, which require immediate decisions based upon expert knowledge and good judgment. Also, he is responsible for modifying the transportation bundle to more closely fit his company's needs, for actions designed to prevent small transportation problems from growing into large ones, and for taking corrective actions when disaster does strike.

Staff Duties

In addition to line functions, most traffic managers perform a variety of staff or advisory duties. Some of these are routine in nature, perhaps only calling upon the traffic manager's fund of existing technical knowledge for advice on minor operating problems or decisions in other departments or divisions. Some, on the other hand, require extensive special study, research, or experimentation.

For example, if a firm is considering a major capital expenditure for a branch factory or warehouse, the traffic manager may be called upon to make detailed studies of comparative transportation costs of several possible alternate locations. If the firm is considering a move into private carriage as a substitute for or supplement to for-hire services or if it is considering containerization or a major new product line, both technological and comparative cost studies might be required from the viewpoint of transportation. As a staff adviser, of course, the traffic manager would not make final decisions on such matters. His specially developed evidence and advice would be considered along with that of other staff and line officials, with the decision being made by top management or perhaps by a committee made up of the managers most directly involved under delegated authority from top management.

On more routine operational matters which do not require major capital expenditures, the traffic manager's role may vary from providing factual information to the legal department to giving informal advice on relative lot-sizes to the purchasing agent to making special transportation-cost studies for the sales manager. Responsibility for using or not using this material rests with the one requesting it.

In other cases, the traffic manager and some other department head or heads may make joint decisions on operational matters involving their respective areas. This is particularly likely when all the departments concerned are directly responsible to one official such as a Physical Distribution Manager.

Supervision of the Traffic Manager

Traffic management in most firms is ranked as a middle-management position. As such, the traffic manager is responsible either to top management or to some intermediate higher manager. There is no dominant pattern in this chain-of-command structure, however. The traffic department may be autonomous in that it is directly responsible only to the president or senior vice-president who may or may not effectively supervise its operations. It may, on the other hand, report to the head of the marketing, purchasing, or production operations, or even in rare cases to some other official. If the firm has a Physical Distribution Manager or some similar official, of course, the traffic manager normally is under his jurisdiction (see Figure 29).

Logically one might expect that the nature of a firm's product and the relative importance of inbound and outbound transportation costs as a proportion of total costs would determine the organizational position and status of its traffic department. That is, a firm with unusually high transport costs in relation to total costs might have its traffic department directly under top management. A firm with substantial outbound transport costs might place its traffic department within the marketing framework, while one with substantial inbound charges might make the traffic manager subordinate to the purchasing agent or even the production manager.

Reality, however, often confuses logic. In many instances (perhaps too many for efficiency), the organizational position of the traffic department has been determined by historical accident, by the personal capabilities of the traffic manager, by personal preferences or prejudices of top management, by whether or not particular individuals work well or poorly together, or for similar "nonrational" reasons. One of the notable accomplishments of the new interest in total-cost physical distribution management, perhaps, is the introduction of rationality in organization patterns for this function.

Internal Organization of the Traffic Department

A firm's overall philosophy of organization and the nature of its activities set the broad framework within which its traffic department is organized. Within this general framework, then, the specific internal organization geographically and functionally is based upon the peculiar specialized duties of the department.

Geographic Organization

Firms doing business at only one location, of course, do not have any problem of geographic decentralization of the traffic function. Multi-location firms, however, have to choose between centralized or decentralized administration of the traffic function or, more correctly, between the various degrees of possible decentralization. This choice sometimes is exercised by the traffic manager, but usually it is based upon overall company policy. That is, a company which tends toward centralization or decentralization is likely to apply its general policy to its traffic department, but not always. If there is any substantial deviation of the traffic control function from the general pattern, it appears to tend toward centralization.

In a highly decentralized traffic-management operation, the central office staff, perhaps headed by a General Traffic Manager, usually provides technical information, advice, and assistance to Branch or Plant Traffic Managers. In addition, of course, it may promulgate general broad policies, represent the company in rate hearings affecting more than one plant location in differing ways, and perhaps aid in training local traffic personnel. The headquarters office essentially provides staff services for local traffic managers who make most of their own decisions under the general supervision of local plant operating officials.

In slightly more centralized situations, the head office may recruit, assign, or replace local traffic managers subject usually to the concurrence of the pertinent local operating management. Some local traffic managers thus feel that they have two "bosses." In a highly centralized operation, however, the headquarters office may make most of the important decisions such as designating specific carriers and routes or taking action on all but the smallest loss-and-damage claims, thus basically leaving the local traffic manager with the functions of shipping clerk and office manager.

Some large multi-location firms follow an intermediate policy between centralization and decentralization. Some local traffic managers may have a great deal of discretion and authority in making decisions, while others have very little. In some cases, another level of management, perhaps called a Regional or a District Traffic Manager, may be interposed between the General Traffic Manager and Branch Traffic Managers in several areas of a firm's operations.

During recent years, it appears that large multi-location firms have been tending toward more decentralization. This tendency is evident in traffic management, but it does not appear to be advancing as rapidly in this function as in some others.

A discussion of the intrinsic merits of centralization versus decentralization in general is beyond the scope of this book. There are advantages and disadvantages to each, and the merits of each are to some extent dependent upon the overall nature of the particular industry and firm. Also, in a particular situation a decision in favor of centralization or decentralization may be considerably influenced by the supposed capabilities of the persons available to do a desired job.

Some General Traffic Managers or top-management officials feel that they are able to negotiate much more effectively with carriers through centralized control of carrier choice and traffic routing than would be possible if these decisions were made on an uncoordinated basis at many scattered locations. In addition, with firms who sell sizable quantities of their product to carriers, reciprocity may be of considerable importance. Offsetting these factors, of course, are the various disadvantages of local inflexibility in dealing with individual carriers and local transport conditions.

Functional Organization

Traffic departments, like other departments, are organized according to the functions which they are expected to perform. Although these functions do vary to some extent between firms and over time in the same firm, there certainly is much more uniformity in functional than in geographic organization.

The major functions of traffic management have been briefly summarized above and will be discussed in considerably more detail in Chapters 26, 27, and 28. At this point, therefore, we will only refer to Figure 30 which pictures a simplified representative functional organization chart for a medium-sized or large firm's traffic department. This figure may be utilized by the reader in furthering his understanding of the material in the following chapters. It is not presented as the "best" or "most used" form of organization, but merely as a form which is representative of the functions typically performed and of many actual organizations. Depending upon the size of the operation, of course, each of the functions shown might be further subdivided or consolidated.

CARRIER TRAFFIC DEPARTMENTS

This book is not primarily concerned with carrier traffic management as such. It is essential that those engaged in industrial traffic work be acquainted with the organization and functions of their carrier counterparts, however. Most of the day-to-day contact of the shipper with the carrier is through the latter's traffic personnel.

Carriers are in the business of selling transportation services. They necessarily must give customers the services they want at prices they are willing to pay. Further, as the for-hire carriage business is an extremely competitive one, carriers must remain in close touch with shippers both to display their wares and to anticipate and provide required shipper services at competitive prices. These are the functions of the carrier traffic department.

Two clear-cut although necessarily closely related functional divisions exist typically among carrier traffic personnel. One group is concerned primarily with the making and publication of rates. The others essentially are salesmen of the carriers services ("traffic solicitors"). Obviously, rates must be tailored to the needs of users. Thus a close two-way flow of information between solicitors, who are in continuous contact with customers, and rate personnel, who establish the prices at which solicitors must sell the carriers' services, is essential. Lack of close cooperation between these two groups can be disastrous in terms of lost customer good will and business.

There are a host of associated traffic duties related to the primary functions of carrier pricing and selling, of course. These involve such matters as

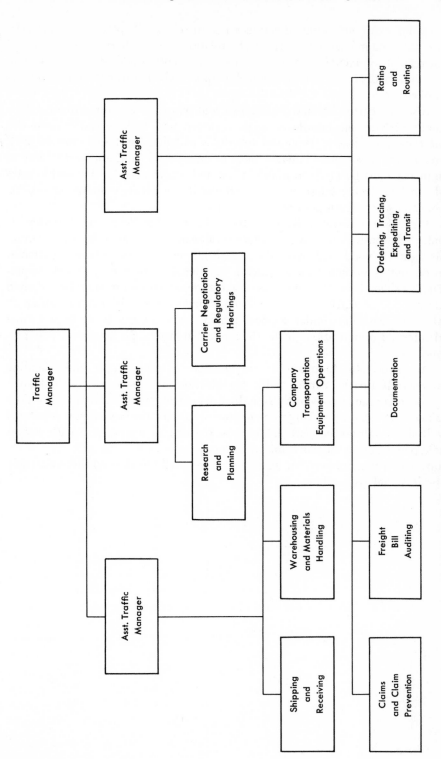

Figure 30: Functional Organization of an Industrial Traffic Department.

special line-haul and terminal services (discussed in Chapter 8), public relations, promotional activities, research, relationships with other carriers and with regulatory agencies, loss and damage prevention and claims settlement, and a variety of similar activities which help to make the transportation bundle complete.

Also, the carrier's traffic department and its operations department which actually delivers the bundle of services priced and sold by traffic personnel must cooperate closely. Promised schedules and delivery times must be met, merchandise losses and damage must be minimized, and the right kind of equipment must be made available when and where needed. Favorable rates and excellent traffic salesmen are worthless if the carrier's operating department cannot or will not perform as promised.

Figure 31 illustrates some of the principal functions and intradepartmental relationships of a representative rail-carrier freight-traffic department. This figure is not based upon the organizational structure of any particular carrier, but is designed as a general functional picture only. With appropriate modifications, the pictured organizational structure may be adapted to any mode of carriage or to any individual carrier. All carriers although performing basically similar services tend to vary the details of their formal and informal organizations to fit their peculiar needs, philosophies, and personnel.

Any successful industrial traffic manager in addition to understanding the general format of carrier traffic organization must have a detailed knowledge of the organizations of those individual carriers with which his firm does business and a close working acquaintanceship with the key carrier personnel involved. A substantial part of his time is spent in negotiating with carrier traffic personnel on an individual day-to-day basis as well as with carrier organizations (rate bureaus, for example) individually or through his own trade or professional associations.

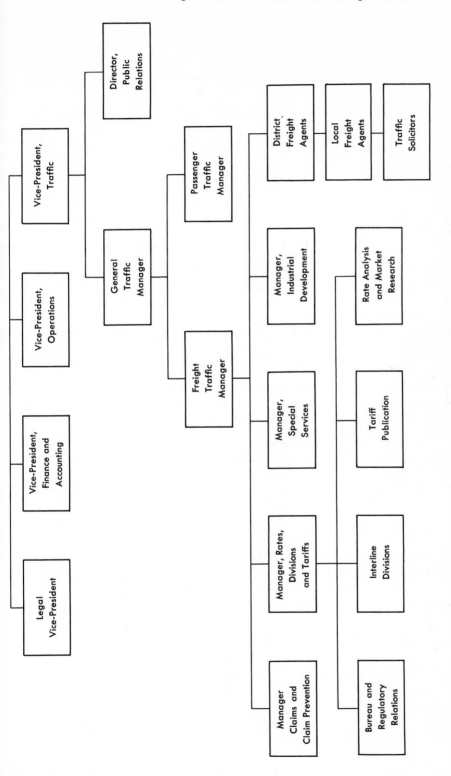

Figure 31: Functional Organization of a Rail Carrier Traffic Department.

ADDITIONAL READINGS

1. Bryan, Leslie A., **Traffic Management in Industry.** New York: The Dryden Press, 1953.
   Chapter 2. "Functions of a Traffic Department," pp. 9–38.
   Chapter 4. "Organization and Administration of a Traffic Department," pp. 55–81.
2. Constantin, James A., **Principles of Logistics Management.** New York: Appleton-Century-Crofts, 1966.
   Chapter 1. "The Scope of Logistics: The External Environment," pp. 1–35.
   Chapter 2. "The Scope of Logistics: The Internal Environment," pp. 36–73.
3. Harper, Donald V., **Basic Planning and the Transportation Function in Small Manufacturing Firms.** Minneapolis, Minn.: University of Minnesota, 1961. 62 pp.
4. Heskett, J. L., Robert M. Ivie, and Nicholas A. Glaskowsky, Jr., **Business Logistics.** New York: Ronald Press Company, 1964.
   Part I. "Scope and Importance of Business Logistics," pp. 3–42.
   Chapter 17. "Organization of Logistics Activities," pp. 479–498.
5. Hille, Stanley J., "Marketing and its Organization in Railroads," **Transportation Journal,** Winter 1966, pp. 33–41.
6. Magee, John F., **Physical-Distribution Systems.** New York: McGraw-Hill Book Company, 1967.
   Chapter 1. "Physical Distribution and the Logistics System Concept," pp. 1–24.
   Chapter 7. "Organization and Management," pp. 166–183.
7. McElhiney, Paul T. and Charles L. Hilton, **Introduction to Logistics and Traffic Management.** Dubuque, Iowa: Wm. C. Brown Company Publishers, 1968.
   Chapter 3. "The Traffic Manager," pp. 23–37.
8. Mossman, Frank H., and Newton Morton, **Logistics of Distribution Systems.** Boston: Allyn & Bacon, Inc., 1965.
   Appendix B. "Constructive and Routine Duties of the Traffic Department," pp. 367–376.
9. Mossman, Frank H. and Newton Morton, **Principles of Transportation.** New York: Ronald Press Company, 1957.
   Part IV. "Transportation Administration," pp. 263–339.
   Chapter 18. "The Role of the Buyer in Transportation," pp. 353–365.
10. Plowman, E. Grosvenor, **Lectures on Elements of Business Logistics.** Stanford, Calif.: Graduate School of Business, Stanford University, 1964.
    Chapter I. "Business Logistics Reviewed," pp. 1–19.
11. Taff, Charles A., **Management of Traffic and Physical Distribution.** 4th ed. Homewood, Ill.: Richard D. Irwin, Inc., 1968.
    Chapter 1. "Conceptual Framework," pp. 1–21.
    Chapter 2. "Organizational Structure," pp. 22–40.
    Chapter 3. "Management and Analytical Methods," pp. 41–71.

26

Traffic Control Decisions
and Activities

The preceding chapter reviewed the evolution of the traffic management function and briefly surveyed its overall role in the managerial and distribution process. This chapter will consider in more detail some (not all, by any means) of the more routine day-to-day activities of traffic management or traffic control decisions as performed by the industrial traffic manager and his assistants. Obviously we cannot go into these operations in infinite detail, but we can at least describe some of the more important types of activities and the reasons back of them. These activities, of course, vary in detail and degree from firm to firm, but in total they account for a good portion of the typical traffic manager's normal functions.

DIRECT DAY-TO-DAY RELATIONSHIPS WITH CARRIERS

A traffic manager is faced with the problem of moving something from its present position to another location and in doing this in a manner and at a cost which will make the greatest contribution to his firm's continued success. This involves a basic decision as to choice of carrier. In his routine activities, the traffic manager may be faced with the choice of private or for-hire carriage, but usually this is not the case. Most often he will simply choose between alternate for-hire carriers. (Chapter 28 will discuss the private versus for-hire alternatives.)

Selecting a Carrier

In selecting a mode of carriage and an individual carrier from that mode, several factors must be considered. Which mode and which individual carrier, assuming that alternatives are available, will best perform the service from the selling firm's viewpoint? from the buying customer's viewpoint? Does the customer have any special needs or preferences, or does the selling firm have a policy regarding how its traffic is allocated among competing carriers? What are the comparative freight rates and associated transport costs of the available carriers? What is the likelihood of loss, damage, or delays en route by the various alternatives? All these and a host of similar related questions must be answered.

This does not imply that conscious and time-consuming decisions are made on all these matters for every shipment. Generally the same types of goods are shipped via the same carriers to the same destination areas or consignees. But explicitly or implicitly choices between carriers do have to be made, and the relative advantages and disadvantages of the various modes and individual carriers must constantly be reviewed as conditions change or as exceptional situations arise.

Equipment Control

After selecting the carrier, the traffic department must see that the proper carrier equipment is made available. A particular piece of equipment—railroad car, truck or trailer, barge—with a certain capacity and of a specified design must be spotted for loading at a given place and time. The traffic manager must inform the carrier of his firm's specific day-to-day needs and follow up to insure that his equipment orders are met. He must know when and with whom his equipment order must be placed and what kind of equipment to accept for his firm's needs if his first-choice equipment is not readily available. This means that he must remain alert to conditions of equipment supply and demand in his industry and geographic area and be familiar with existing and changing equipment technology.

When ordered carrier equipment has been received, it must be promptly and properly loaded and the carrier notified of its availability for movement. Packaging, marking, loading, stowing, and bracing of shipments must conform to minimum carrier standards and rules and must be sufficient to minimize the chances of damage en route. Actual supervision of these activities may or may not be under jurisdiction of the traffic department, but they clearly are traffic control functions. If the traffic manager himself is not directly responsible for their satisfactory performance, he at least must remain well informed in this area in order that those responsible can be advised of weaknesses in present procedures and of potential or actual new developments in techniques.

If carrier equipment is not promptly loaded and started on its way, carrier costs are unnecessarily increased or their revenues lowered. This does not contribute to happy carrier-shipper relationships. Also, it contributes to equipment shortages which at times may severely inconvenience other shippers and even adversely affect the nation's distribution and production activities. For these reasons, additional charges are levied against a shipper who holds carrier equipment for an undue length of time. These are called "demurrage" charges by railroads and "detention" charges in the trucking industry. Traffic managers must know the rules relating to these penalty charges and must schedule equipment ordering and release to minimize them.

Demurrage

Railroad demurrage rules and charges are published in tariffs like other charges. Demurrage charges begin after expiration of the "free time" allowed the shipper or receiver. Normally this is forty-eight hours from the first 7:00 A.M. after the equipment has been made available for loading or unloading, excluding Sundays and holidays. (Once demurrage has started, Sundays and holidays may be chargeable.)

Demurrage charges are a flat daily charge for the time held beyond the free time, but these charges are "progressive," that is, the daily rate becomes higher up to a maximum level as the length of time held increases. Charges may be waived, however, if the shipper or receiver can show that his delay is caused by severe weather conditions which prevent loading or unloading, or by strikes. Also, shippers or receivers are not responsible for demurrage if the carrier "bunches" the arrival of cars in such a manner that normal loading and unloading procedures cannot provide an adequate release of equipment. The user cannot be penalized for the carrier's own shortcomings in performance.

There are two methods of accounting for and paying for demurrage. Under the "straight" method, each car is treated as a unit and stands on its own separate record. Under the "average" plan, users receive "credits" for early release of cars—that is, release before the free time has expired—and "debits" for holding equipment beyond the free time. Then at the end of the month, credits are used to offset debits, and payment is made for the excess debits.

Different demurrage rules, usually allowing considerably more free time, apply to rail shipments held in seaports when the rail movement is merely a part of a longer export or import movement using ocean carriage for a portion of the haul. Also, although water and truck carriers make use of penalty charges for undue holding of equipment, their rules and payments are adapted to their own peculiar circumstances. Truck free time, for example, is considerably shorter than rail free time, being measured in hours instead of days, and truck detention charges are usually considerably higher than rail demurrage charges.

Routing

In addition to ordering the right equipment from the selected carrier, the shipper may wish to instruct the carrier what route the shipment is to follow between origin and destination. This is particularly true in case of rail shipments, where an extremely large number of alternative routes may be available for use on long hauls. But goods must move over some route, and someone must designate that specific route. Usually if there is more than one route, this designation is a function of the traffic department—and often a very important function.

Many firms, particularly smaller ones or those shipping only one or a few products, may ship over the same route or routes to the same customers, thus reducing problems of route determination. In larger organizations shipping a variety of products to a far-flung group of customers, however, the technical aspects of routing (like rate determination) may be a very involved process requiring careful study and the application of elaborate carrier "routing guide" publications or painstaking scrutiny of applicable tariffs. Central traffic offices of large firms often prepare "route cards" or "route sheets" for use of traffic personnel in decentralized local or regional offices.

We cannot go into the technical complexities of routing here. We will consider, rather, why a shipper may prefer to designate the route himself than to leave this to the carrier and the shipper's legal rights to control his routings.

Why a Shipper May Want to Route

By traditional custom and law, a rail shipper has the right to route his shipments. Traffic managers are no more eager to surrender their legal and traditional rights than are any other groups. This right provides traffic solicitors (salesmen) a motive to call upon the traffic manager and treat him kindly in an effort to influence his allocation of traffic between competing carriers over various routes. This, in itself, may be "justification" enough of the right to route for some traffic managers. But there are even better reasons.

Sellers like to please buyers. If a customer prefers that his goods be handled by a particular carrier or a specified group of connecting carriers, the shipper obviously will make every effort to follow the consignee's routing preferences. Also, some routes have lower applicable freight rates between origin and destination than do other possible routes. (Usually, however, if no specific routing is made by the shipper, the carrier is required to use the lowest rated available route for the movement.)

Service and reliability features are of considerable importance in choosing a route. Even though most carrier services may be performed by the originating and the terminating carriers on a multi-line or joint movement, shippers or receivers may have justifiable reasons for preferring some intermediate carriers (and their particular routes) over others. Experience may indicate greater loss and damage to cargoes or less reliability in meeting scheduled delivery dates over some lines and routes than over others. Climatic conditions or anticipated weather changes may also be quite important in influencing the choice of a route for certain types of products.

Some routes permit more rapid delivery to destination than others. A shipper may want his goods to arrive as quickly as possible or at a specific time designated by his customer. On the other hand, the shipper may want his goods to proceed toward their destination slowly either for the convenience of the consignee or to give the shipper sufficient time to complete the selling of goods which may have left the origin still unsold. Also, such useful privileges as diversion, reconsignment, stoppage in transit for further processing, or stoppage for partial unloading or further loading are available only at certain designated points and over particular designated routes. It is the traffic manager's responsibility to route according to these various needs of his company.

It may be, too, that a large shipper will follow the practice of reciprocity, that is, he will give a substantial portion of his carriage business to those carriers who also are good customers for his own product. For example, a steel company given a choice between otherwise equal rail routes might tend to route its shipments over the lines of those carriers who buy most of their steel from it rather than using the facilities of railroads buying from its competitors. The practice of reciprocity is common in all types of businesses and it is perfectly legal as long as it does not result in undue discrimination or preference.

Sometimes, too, a large shipper is able to use his routing rights as a bargaining tool in obtaining more favorable services or rates from carriers. A carrier who knows that a substantial volume of business can be diverted from his own lines to a rival carrier is likely to listen to the shipper's views or grievances with considerable respect. Again, such shipper influence is perfectly legal if not improperly used to the disadvantage of competitors. The desire to control all routing for bargaining purposes is one major reason why this function is often retained in the central traffic office even though many other traffic functions may be decentralized to regional or local offices.

In summary then, exercising the right to route rail shipments, although resulting in much tedious and time-consuming technical work for the traffic department, may be of considerable economic benefit to a shipper.

Legal Aspects of Routing

Shippers are given legal right to route rail movements under Part I of the Interstate Commerce Act. This right is not given under other parts of the Act, but conditions in other forms of transportation do not create such involved problems of routing.

Water and air carriers normally do not engage in a great deal of interline traffic exchange. Shipments by these modes generally move from origin to destination over one route and by one carrier. Interline exchanges are increasing in the trucking industry, but even here such exchanges are relatively unimportant as contrasted with rail interlining. But even when a trucking company accepts a shipper's routing on a Bill of Lading (a transportation contract), it may be held liable for any damages suffered by the shipper as a result of violation of the contract. This comes under the area of contract law, however, rather than under transportation law.

As indicated above, a rail shipper has the legal right to route his shipment. If he does not exercise this right, the carrier must move the shipment over the lowest-priced, or some one of the lowest-priced, available routes. There is an exception, however, in that a carrier cannot be forced to short-haul itself substantially unless to avoid short-haulage would require using an "unreasonably long" route. For example, a given rail carrier accepting a shipment destined to a consignee 1,000 miles distant might have interline connections for that destination at points 100 miles and 500 miles from the origin. In such a case, the originating carrier would normally be entitled to the 500-mile haul. But if the longer haul results in the goods having to be moved 2,000 miles rather than 1,000 miles to reach the destination, the carrier probably could be forced to short-haul itself.

Shipper traffic departments often physically prepare the principal shipping document (Bill of Lading) and insert the desired route and the applicable freight rate. If the shipper inserts the route but does not include the rate, the carrier must follow the designated routing even though it requires a higher rate than some other route. If the shipper specifies the applicable rate but does not include a route, the carrier must move the shipment over the route for which the named rate applies. If there is more than one such route, the carrier may choose the routing. If the shipper's designated route and rate conflict or if the rate shown by the shipper does not apply over any route, the carrier is expected to contact the shipper for clarification. It is not quite clear what the carrier must do in case of such a conflict if the shipper cannot be contacted, but it seems likely that the carrier would be required to use the lowest-rated route possible without substantially short-hauling itself.

Tracing and Expediting

Because of their necessity for tightly planned production or merchandising schedules, consignees often are quite concerned about the location of en-route goods and when these goods will be received. Traffic departments, therefore, often are asked to obtain carrier cooperation in speeding up certain shipments or in determining where shipments presently are in order that their arrival time can be more accurately predicted. This is especially true for railroad carload shipments.

Carriers usually cooperate as much as possible in tracing and expediting, especially if the process is not abused by individual shippers. Some large carriers maintain sizable departments devoted exclusively to these activities. For example, many railroads maintain communications systems which enable them to answer an inquiry concerning the present location of a particular car within minutes or even seconds. And often it is possible to speed up an urgently needed shipment by cutting a car out of a slow train and putting it on a faster one or some similar maneuver. For many shippers and consignees, this is a valuable part of the bundle of transportation services.

Documentation

The Bill of Lading

The Bill of Lading, normally prepared in the shipper's traffic department although legally "issued" by the carrier (acceptance and signature constituting "issuance"), is the most important traffic document both for the shipper and the carrier. This key document has been called the oldest, most widely used, and least read of commercial documents!

The Bill of Lading acknowledges receipt of the goods by the carrier and provides evidence of title to the goods. Even more important, it is the basic contract of carriage between the shipper and carrier, setting forth the rights and responsibilities of each. Like other contracts, its execution requires parties competent to contract, legal purposes, a consideration, and meeting of the minds of the contracting parties.

Historically, the Bill of Lading can be traced back into antiquity where it was used as a "customary" practice by the earliest Mediterranean merchants and sea-traders. It evolved as an important part of the so-called "Law Merchant" of the Medieval and early modern periods, and thus on into contemporary times. Until the present century, however, there was no necessary uniformity in the contractual terms of the document. Each carrier issued its own Bill of Lading containing such contractual terms as it preferred. Carriers might even by terms of the contract escape from their Common Law liability for delivery (see Chapter 7) or drastically limit the amount recoverable by a shipper whose products were lost or damaged by the carrier.

Carriers were prohibited from using Bill of Lading provisions to contract out of their duty of delivery by the Carmack Amendment in 1906. It later developed, however, that carriers still could contract to limit the amount of the shipper's recovery. The First Cummins Amendment in 1915, therefore, prohibited any limitation of liability. This was relaxed somewhat by the Second Cummins Amendment, 1916, which does allow some limitation of liability, although not a release for liability as such, in return for a lower freight rate (except on "ordinary livestock"). This makes possible the use of the so-called "released value" rates (see Chapter 12).

Although the above-named amendments specified what carriers could and could not do contractually in terms of loss and damage liability, they did not require a uniform Bill of Lading. Actually, some railroad and shipper groups attempted to establish a uniform bill during the 1890's, but their success was limited. In 1908 in response to shipper petitions, the Interstate Commerce Commission recommended such action, but it had no power to require it. Congress in 1910 gave the I.C.C. authority to prescribe a uniform Bill of Lading for railroads after appropriate hearings. The hearings started in 1912, but World War I intervened and the I.C.C. did not prescribe the uniform bill until 1922. This 1922 Bill of Lading, although it has been modified to some extent by later I.C.C. action, is essentially the same document now used for all railroad shipments.

Part II of the Interstate Commerce Act gives the I.C.C. about the same regulatory controls of the form of motor carrier Bills of Lading as it has over railroad bills. The Commission has not seen fit to require that motor carrier Bills be standardized, however. But, as the basic laws are similar, the actual contractual contents of rail and truck bills must also be similar, even though they may differ in physical size, shape, and in some wording.

Kinds of Bills of Lading

Bills of Lading may be classified as Government, Livestock, and Commercial. These terms are self-explanatory. That is, the Government Bill is used for governmental shipments, the Livestock Bill for shipping livestock, and the Commercial Bill for the great mass of ordinary business or personal shipments.

The Commercial Bill of Lading may be either a "Domestic" or an "Export" or "Ocean" document. As we are not concerned with foreign ocean transportation in this book, we will simply point out that the ocean variety is quite different from the Domestic Bill. The latter, of course, is most important for most shippers.

The Domestic Commercial Bill of Lading (and the ocean variety too, incidentally) may be either a "straight" or an "order" bill. The latter is a negotiable instrument, that is, it may be endorsed to other parties, and the purchaser of the properly endorsed document acquires title to the goods covered by the document. The "straight" bill, on the other hand, is not negotiable. The difference between the two forms might be thought of as being equivalent to the difference between a personal check "Payable to John Doe" and one "Payable to the Order of John Doe." Carriers, of course, must be very careful in delivering goods consigned under an "order" bill as they may be held liable for misdelivery if they deliver without requiring the presentation of a properly endorsed bill.

The "face" or front side of a uniform Bill of Lading filled out by the shipper or the carrier is fairly self-explanatory. It contains routine operational information such as the names and addresses of the consignor and consignee, routing instructions, the rate, a description of the kinds and quantities of the things shipped, payment method, and similar items. The "fine print" on the back of the bill spells out the contract terms, especially matters of the carrier's liability (or the lack thereof) under various circumstances.

As already mentioned, railroad Bills of Lading are standardized, and truck bills in general are similar in nature although varying in detail and not standardized. Freight forwarders often use the bills of the mode of carriage performing the line-haul movement. REA Express and Air Express shipments move under non-negotiable uniform "Express Receipts." "Airbills" are used for air-freight movements. These are not all uniform, although many are on a voluntary basis. It is probable that the Civil Aeronautics Board has the authority to prescribe a uniform Airbill, but the Board has not found it necessary to do so. Pipelines, operating under different conditions than other for-hire carriers, use a "tender of shipment" form in lieu of a Bill of Lading. The ocean bill, as indicated, is quite different from the domestic variety and is beyond the scope of this book's discussion. Finally, contract carriage is governed by the terms of the individual contract between shipper and carrier.

Although space precludes any further detailed discussion of the Bill of

Lading, the authors feel that this vital shipping document should be thoroughly understood by everyone—shipper or carrier—who is concerned with it in any way. We highly recommend, therefore, that such persons obtain copies of each type of Bill of Lading and study them carefully front and back. They are transportation textbooks in miniature.

Other Traffic Documents

Shipments move on "ways" of paper as well as upon ways of steel, concrete, water, or air. In addition to the often voluminous records needed for strictly internal use, the traffic department is routinely concerned with many other shipping documents such as "arrival notices," "delivery receipts," "freight bills," "inspection reports," "claims reports," and the like. Carriers also struggle with mountains of paper. A key carrier document is the "waybill," made for every shipment, which contains information similar to that on the face of the Bill of Lading and which accompanies the shipment from origin to destination.

One is justified in wondering how transportation was accomplished in earlier and less complex eras when paper was less plentiful and more expensive! The paperwork problem of both shippers and carriers has become so complicated and expensive that various methods are being sought to bring it under control. These methods run the gamut from electronic computers and IBM cards to snap-out carbon insert forms. There is agitation for fewer and more simple forms, but the problem is far from solution.

Traffic Claims

The preparation and collection of claims against carriers and claims prevention is an important traffic management function. Depending upon circumstances, this may be handled almost entirely by the traffic department, or it may be a cooperative effort between traffic and other areas of management. Claims can be divided into two types, namely, those for loss and damage to goods shipped, and reparations and overcharges.

Loss and Damage Claims and Prevention

The liabilites of common carriers for lost or damaged shipments was discussed in Chapter 7. Payments are not made automatically, however. Before an L & D claim is paid, the shipper or receiver (whoever has title to the goods in question) must file and substantiate a claim. The amounts involved often are substantial, perhaps amounting to as much as one billion dollars annually in the economy as a whole.

The filing of claims is governed by statutory law and the transportation contract (Bill of Lading). For example, damage claims generally must be filed with carriers within nine months (six months for express) after delivery of the shipment, and claims for lost shipments must be made within nine months of the "reasonable delivery date" of the good. If the carrier refuses to pay the claim, suit must be brought in a court of law within two years of the date of refusal.

Further, a loss and damage claim must be supported by evidence acceptable in court. Although nothing is specifically prescribed by law as to what is acceptable, supporting evidence customarily includes some kind of standard form plus the Bill of Lading, invoice, and freight bill (preferably original copies) covering the shipment. Other evidence might include inspection reports, appraisal and salvage reports, and photographs.

Clearly, inadequate knowledge of the pertinent rules or laxness in procedures by the traffic manager may be harmful to a firm's efforts to recover for lost or damaged shipments. But recovery of past damages is only part of the story. Efforts to prevent loss and damage from occurring may be of even greater importance.

Lost and damaged shipments are a sheer waste to the nation's economy, resulting both in lost production and in higher freight rates and higher consumer prices. L & D claims are costly to process both for the shipper and the carrier. Even if the claim is paid in full, many man-hours and a considerable amount of paper have been consumed. Very small claims may never be filed, and larger claims may be compromised by underpayment or overpayment to reduce the processing load. Further, damaged or lost merchandise may severely inconvenience consignees, disrupt production or sales schedules, and create problems of lost good will between shippers and receivers, and between both these groups and carriers.

Loss and damage prevention involves a combination of research, education, and supervision on the part both of shippers and of carriers. The cause first has to be discovered. Published statistics indicate that at least two thirds of the loss and damage to shipper goods may be controllable. That is, about one third may be attributable to rough handling by carriers either at terminals or en route. Another one third may be due to improper packaging, marking, or loading by the shipper. The remainder is the result of unknown or uncontrollable factors.

Once the cause is known, devices or procedures must be developed to eliminate or reduce the loss. These techniques then must be thoroughly taught to the actual shipper or carrier personnel engaged in the physical handling and movement process. And continual supervision is required to insure that the techniques are applied. This sounds very elementary. But a large amount of time is spent by carriers and shippers individually and through various associations in trying to "solve" the L & D problem. And losses continue to climb!

Overcharges and Reparations

Overcharge claims are made when a shipper feels that he can demonstrate that he has paid more than the lowest applicable published rate for his shipment. This may be a simple arithmetic mistake, or it may be the result of a rate clerk's error in using tariffs. In principle, this is not a complex process. As you know, a shipper is entitled to pay the lowest published rate. If he pays more and can uncover this and prove it to the carrier, the carrier is legally obligated to make the appropriate refund. Auditing of freight bills, then, is designed to discover overpayments. This function may be performed within the shipping firm, or it may be "farmed out" to independent freight auditors who operate on a percentage-of-recovery commission basis.

Reparations claims are made for a different type of refund. Common carriers are required by law to charge "reasonable" rates. A reasonable rate is called a *lawful* rate. But shippers must pay the published tariff rate, the *legal* rate, which may or may not be a "reasonable" rate. That is, it is possible for a rate to be *legal* but not *lawful.* Or a rate which was reasonable and lawful at one time may with the passage of time become "unreasonably high" and thus not lawful although still legal.

If a shipper can demonstrate to the satisfaction of the I.C.C. or the courts that he has been paying an unreasonably high rate, he is entitled to recover from the carrier the difference between a "reasonable" rate and the rate actually paid for past shipments. These reparations payments cannot be made even if the carrier is willing to pay, however, without a specific order from the I.C.C. or from the courts. Further, reparations awards are governed by a statute of limitations which prevents refunds for back shipments beyond a period of two years for private shippers or three years for government shipments.

A reparations claim must be made according to a prescribed form and procedure, and the shipper must be able to document the amount claimed. Due to court decisions holding that the original Parts II and IV of the Interstate Commerce Act did not provide specifically for reparations, interstate motor carriers and freight forwarders were not liable for reparations until these statutes were changed by Congress in September 1965.

CHANGING THE RATES OR SERVICES ENVIRONMENT

As indicated in the previous chapter, a purchaser of transportation services may directly influence the price and quality of the service he buys. Various kinds of optional carrier services have been described in Part Three of this book, and the procedures for establishing a new rate or changing an existing rate are discussed in Chapter 11.

The traffic manager is his firm's technical expert and direct representative and negotiator in these matters. It is his duty to determine, perhaps in consultation with other departments or divisions, what services or rate changes will be beneficial to his company and whether or not there is a likelihood that these changes can be achieved. Then he has the primary responsibility for preparing and presenting his firm's case to individual carriers, rate bureaus, regulatory agencies, and sometimes even in the courts or before legislative bodies. He may, of course, enlist the aid of various other components of his firm (as sales, purchasing, accounting, legal, etc.), and he may work through shipper organizations such as Shippers Advisory Boards, the National Industrial Traffic League, or his industry trade association.

Some of the desired environmental changes may be nationwide or industry-wide in scope such as general rate decreases, demurrage charges, attempts to curb loss and damage or to influence the building or distribution of transportation rolling stock. Changes in transportation legislation and regulatory procedures or the construction of new highways may be sought. Improvements in carrier technological development or managerial practices may be urged.

Other changes may primarily benefit the traffic manager's own company. These include such things as particular rate decreases, better local supplies and scheduling of rolling stock, the negotiation of transit privileges or average-weight agreements, the building of spur tracks, or improved methods of freight handling by individual carriers. The traffic manager may be called upon to oppose proposed changes that might give his firm's rivals some competitive transportation advantage.

These various attempts to influence the transport environment may be as important to his company as the traffic manager's day-to-day routine activities. In large firms particularly, the General Traffic Manager and perhaps several of his assistants may spend a substantial portion of their time attending meetings and hearings concerned with environmental changes. This necessitates, of course, a considerable amount of research and staff work on the part of subordinate traffic personnel.

OTHER "ROUTINE" ACTIVITIES

Other normal duties of a traffic department include the supervision of the firm's private transportation operations, if any, making arrangements for the personal transportation of company officials traveling on company business, and sometimes handling the details of household goods movements for transferred company personnel. Also, like other managers, the traffic manager must be concerned with the recruitment, supervision, training and development, and promotion of personnel in his department.

SUMMARY

Although not all of the day-to-day traffic control decisions and activities of a typical traffic department have been elaborated upon or even mentioned, the importance of these functions should be clear from the foregoing. If they are done well, the individual firm benefits by lower costs and the efficiency of the nation's production and distribution is improved. If they are done poorly, the firm's costs are unnecessarily high which may lead to its individual disaster, and harm to the overall national economy.

It should be clear, too, that the "routine" of traffic control is not a cut-and-dried process. An infinite variety of problems requiring decisions and implementing action are continually arising. The handling of these problems requires a technically skilled but broadly based individual. In addition to his knowledge of "rates and routes," the effective traffic manager must have a better-than-passing knowledge of economics, psychology, law, and some phases of engineering plus an extensive understanding of his firm, his industry, his customers, his competition, and transportation institutions and technology. And among other characteristics, he must be imaginative, flexible, courageous, and durable.

Traffic control offers both challenges and opportunities. It is an area of business in which much improvement can be made and in which new developments and techniques promise to continue replacing older methods within the foreseeable future. Although its practitioners often go unpraised, its effective performance is vital to the welfare of individual business firms and to the nation's economy.

ADDITIONAL READINGS

1. Bryan, Leslie A., **Traffic Management in Industry.** New York: The Dryden Press, 1953.
   Chapter 9. "Routing of Shipments," pp. 155–168.
   Chapter 20. "Claims," pp. 339–358.
2. Flood, Kenneth U., **Traffic Management,** 2nd ed. Dubuque, Iowa: Wm. C. Brown Co., 1963.
   Chapter 1. "The Buying and Selling of Transportation Service," pp. 1–23.
   Chapter 16. "Shipping Documents," pp. 362–396.
3. Freedgood, Seymour, "Big Dogs, Little Dogs, and the Air Cargo Bone," **Fortune,** October 1964, pp. 122–128 and 194 ff.
4. Grossman, William L., **Fundamentals of Transportation.** New York: Simmons-Boardman Publishing Corp., 1959.
   Chapter XII. "The Selection of a Transportation Alternative," pp. 247–259.
5. Hauk, James G., "Logistics and Physical Distribution Management in the Military," **Transportation Journal,** Vol. 4, No. 2, Winter 1964, pp. 12–19.
6. Heskett, J. L., Robert M. Ivie, and Nicholas A. Glaskowsky, Jr., **Business Logistics.** New York: Ronald Press Company, 1964.
   Chapter 15. "Traffic," pp. 416–444.
7. Schiff, Michael, "Controlling Physical Distribution Costs," **Financial Executive,** April 1963, pp. 13–18.
8. Shutes, George M., "Airfreight from a Marketing Viewpoint," **Journal of Marketing,** October 1960, pp. 39–43.
9. Snyder, Richard E., "Physical Distribution Costs," **Distribution Age,** December 1963, pp. 35–42.
10. Taff, Charles A., **Management of Traffic and Physical Distribution.** 4th ed. Homewood, Ill.: Richard D. Irwin, Inc., 1968.
    Chapter 12. "Routing," pp. 286–310.
    Chapter 13. "Document Processing," pp. 311–341.
    Chapter 16. "Carrier Liability," pp. 391–416.

27

Traffic Management's Relationship to Other Operating Decisions

Traffic management, however broadly or narrowly it may be defined, is directly related to many of a firm's other operational and staff functions. An individual business is a system or an organism. Actions taken in one portion of the firm affect other portions. Things done in the sales department of a business affect the traffic department, and vice versa.

It follows that if a business is to give its best performance, its activities must be effectively coordinated at all levels. Ultimately this is a responsibility of top management, but in practice much of it is done on the initiative of lower-level managers. If these lower-level managers do not understand the need for joint action or are not willing to cooperate with each other, top management may be faced with a serious educational or replacement problem, or the firm may operate at a low level of performance if it survives at all.

We are concerned here only with coordination between the traffic function and other areas of a business. The role of traffic personnel may be only advisory in this coordination or it may involve joint decision-making by traffic and other managers. Whether traffic management's role is decisional or advisory will vary according to the nature of the problem and the traffic manager's status in the organizational hierarchy.

This chapter and the following one will be concerned with the interrelationships between traffic and other departments in firms which have able traffic managers and in which the importance of the traffic function is well understood and appreciated. These conditions, unfortunately, do not exist in all firms. In Chapter 28, we will consider traffic management's advisory role to top management on various problems involving major capital expenditures or major changes in product orientation. The present chapter will consider operational or organizational decisions which normally are handled below the top management level or which do not involve major capital expenditures or significant changes in product policy. Neither this nor the following chapter, of course, will cover all possible areas of interdepartmental relationships or any such relationships in detail.

LEGAL PROBLEMS

Some firms maintain their own legal department. Others have attorneys on retainer, while some seek attorneys only when specific legal problems arise. Other businesses use a combination of these methods. Whatever organizational arrangement is used, however, relationships between a firm's attorneys and its traffic department should be about the same.

Much of the traffic manager's work can be described as quasi-legal in nature. For example, he enters into transportation contracts, files various kinds of claims, and appears before regulatory agencies in rates and services cases for his company. This means that he must have a good working knowledge of the applicable laws and legal procedures. But unless he is himself an attorney, the traffic manager cannot represent his company in a court action. This means that when something goes wrong—a lawsuit arises over a contract, a carrier is sued for nonpayment of a claim, or a court appeal of a regulatory decision is made—the attorneys must take over.

Most attorneys are not transportation experts, however, and even those who are usually have not been involved in the earlier stages of the actions which ultimately are taken to the courts for decision. The traffic department, therefore, assists the attorney in preparing his case by informing him of what has transpired earlier, collecting and assembling pertinent data for his use, and advising him upon the peculiar transportation technicalities of the case. In other words, even though the attorney must present the case in court, actually the attorney and the traffic manager act as a team with each contributing his special knowledge and capabilities to the combined effort.

A wise traffic manager, of course, realizes that almost any of his quasi-legal actions conceivably could lead to a court case and that he must conduct himself accordingly. Careful records must be kept, correct procedures followed, and legal advice sought on any questionable point. Much litigation is prevented by knowing when to seek legal advice and much is won by "building up a record" for the potential use of attorneys if the need arises.

TRANSPORTATION INSURANCE

Insurance is just as real a transportation cost as is any other cost. Typically, however, in firms involved in domestic shipping (as contrasted with ocean shipping), transportation insurance falls into an organizational no-man's-land, not clearly understood and often neglected by both the traffic department and whoever is responsible for handling the firm's major insurance coverages.

Basically there are two kinds of transportation insurance. *Liability* insurance protects the insured from damages caused to others as a result of his actions. *Indemnity* insurance provides protection against losses suffered by the insured himself. Both these kinds of insurance are available and may be quite important to both shippers and carriers. Our present interest is only in shippers' insurance, however.

Transportation Liability Insurance

Liability insurance is primarily of importance to those shippers who use private transportation. This is the "personal liability and property damage" (PL & PD) type of insurance familiar to every automobile owner. If a firm operates a fleet of trucks or other private transportation equipment, this coverage must be provided to protect the company against claims for personal injuries or damages brought by outsiders. It does not cover damages to the firm's own equipment and goods.

Virtually all companies engaged in private transportation have this kind of insurance, although not always in an adequate amount. Its purchase may be handled by the traffic department or it may be handled by some other department or official in the company. In any case, it is closely related to the traffic management function.

Transport Indemnity Insurance

Shippers using private transportation need indemnity protection both against loss and damage to their transportation equipment and to the goods hauled in this equipment. The indemnity need of one using contract carriage will vary depending upon the nature of the carrier's liability under the contract. Those using common carriage may need some form of indemnity protection for goods in the hands of carriers.

As land common carriers have a high degree of liability for goods entrusted to their care, one might wonder why such goods need to be further insured. (The situation is quite different with water carriage where carrier liability is very limited, but marine insurance is beyond the scope of this book.) Actually, many shippers do not carry indemnity protection ("transit insurance") on goods shipped by common carrier. Instead they rely upon the carriers' liabilities for loss and damage (duty of delivery) and assume the risk of any nonrecoverable loss themselves.

But there are several reasons why it is sometimes desirable for a shipper to obtain transit insurance even on goods shipped by land common carriers. 1. The carrier is not liable for an Act of God or an act of the public enemy, and may be exempt from liabiilty on various statutory grounds (see Chapter 7). 2. Even though legally liable, the carrier might not be financially able to pay a large claim, or payment might be delayed for months or years pending a court decision. 3. Shipments may be made under "released rates" which limit the amount necessary to be paid by the carrier. It often is less expensive to ship under a released rate and buy full insurance coverage than to ship under a higher rate with more complete recovery available from the carrier.

In summary, then, transit insurance to indemnify the shipper may be desirable because of the greater likelihood of prompt payment of claims and because it provides more protection. Whether or not this is worthwhile will depend to a considerable extent upon the nature and value of the goods being shipped. Even though there is a likelihood of many small and regular unrecoverable losses, the shipper may be willing and able to absorb these (self-insure). Such losses can be taken into account in pricing the merchandise. On the other hand, the likelihood of loss on a given shipment might be very small, but the value of the shipment might be such that its unrecoverable loss would seriously affect the firm. In such a case, it would be prudent to insure.

Shippers' transit insurance is available in various forms. It may be purchased for a specifically named item or group of items for a single trip, or it may be obtained for any items fitting into a broad general classification for a continuous series of trips. The value of the merchandise shipped may be specifically stated, or the insurance contract may provide that values will be determined upon invoice or market prices (usually with some stated upper limits). Further, this insurance may be obtained either for private or for-hire movements.

The Traffic Manager's Insurance Role

Insurance, like transportation, is a complicated technical field. Normally one would not expect a traffic manager to be an insurance expert any more than one would expect an insurance expert to be highly knowledgeable in transportation matters.

Transportation insurance, however, is only one phase of insurance, and it is equally a phase of transportation. A competent traffic manager should at least know what kinds of transportation insurance are available and what kinds and how much his company needs for its protection. He is, or should be, in a better position than anyone else in his firm to assess the risks inherent in particular shipments, modes, and routes. If his company is not adequately protected in general or on a particular transaction, he should take whatever steps are necessary.

In firms with an insurance department or with some specific official designated to handle all insurance matters, the traffic manager should be responsible for providing the necessary transportation advice or in aiding in the making of insurance decisions. Under other conditions, the traffic manager himself may be responsible for obtaining some or all portions of the necessary transportation insurance.

Where neither the traffic manager nor anyone else has a clear-cut organizational responsibility for transportation insurance and if there is a need for such insurance either on a specific shipment or on a continuous basis, a good traffic manager will apprise top management or his superior of the situation. In insurance matters, transportation as well as other kinds, it is not safe to assume that George is taking care of things. In order to do his job well either as an advisor or as an individual or joint decision-maker, the traffic manager must have a working knowledge of transportation insurance.

PURCHASING AND SALES POLICIES

As inbound and outbound freight costs often are sizable portions of a firm's expenditures, the interrelationships between traffic and purchasing and sales departments perhaps is fairly obvious. The traffic department sometimes is supervised by the Sales Manager or the Purchasing Agent. Ramifications of the traffic function, however, may extend further into buying and selling policies than is observable at first glance. As pointed out, any action or change in one portion of a business organism may cause several reactions or changes elsewhere.

Where, How Much, and When to Buy or Sell

In the past and even to some extent today, those responsible for buying and selling have tended to ignore the traffic management function. Purchasing personnel and salesmen have sub-optimized their own functions by buying or selling wherever, whenever, and whatever quantities seemed most desirable from their individual or departmental viewpoints, or in view of production schedules or inventory limits. The traffic department has been presented with an accomplished agreement and has been expected only to move the goods involved. This is completely contrary to the more recent concept of physical distribution management.

Delivered or laid-down prices, whether for a firm's inbound or outbound goods and regardless of the method of price quotation used, are made up of origin prices plus transportation costs. Even the most sub-optimizing of purchasing agents could readily see that a purchase involving an f.o.b. origin price of $10 per unit plus an inbound freight rate of $2 per unit would be preferable to an f.o.b. origin price of $8 and a $5 transportation cost. Likewise, given the pertinent transportation-cost information, a salesman might recognize that goods sold in one territory are less profitable than those sold in another, but operating within a given territory on a commission basis or being judged by his sales volume, he would probably attempt to sell as much as possible anyway.

One of the most obvious and common interrelationships between traffic and purchasing and sales departments, therefore, is the furnishing by the traffic department of freight rate and other pertinent transportation costs from and to various origins. This enables the purchasing department to choose its supply sources and the sales manager to deploy his sales force and concentrate sales efforts in those geographic areas most profitable to the firm.

It is a little more difficult to show purchasing and sales personnel that the quantities bought and sold in any given transaction may significantly affect the transportation cost and, thus, the firm's profit position. Buyers want to reorder in some predetermined quantity when inventories decline to a certain level or to buy in quantities designed to meet some predetermined production schedule. Salesmen of course prefer to sell large orders, but will sell in small quantities if large orders cannot be obtained. Any exotic traffic gibberish about carload minimums, LTL versus TL, consolidated shipments, incentive rates, and the like, even if understood is likely to be disregarded unless there is considerable respect for and a close working relationship with the traffic department.

The quantities bought and sold or the frequency of transactions, of course, do affect inventory levels, warehousing needs, and sometimes production scheduling. These things, in turn, may directly affect the financial requirements of the company for carrying inventory and the company's customary relationships with its customers and suppliers. No traffic manager would argue that the per-unit volumes and the calendar frequencies of his company's purchases and sales should be adjusted exclusively to the "needs" of his department. Most would agree, however, that transportation factors ought to be considered along with other pertinent needs of the firm and that often significant transportation economies can be achieved by minor adjustments in buying and selling policies without any adverse effects, or with relatively insignificant effects, upon other company operations.

Even if the traffic manager cannot eliminate the expensive small-lot problem, he may be able to work with purchasing and sales personnel to reduce its cost. Instead of shipping each lot individually, the company may use the services of freight forwarders or even consolidate small shipments into volume shipments itself. It may cooperate with other small-lot shippers in the use of a pool car or in forming a cooperative shipping association. Small shipments from or to several different origins or destinations may be arranged through stoppage in transit for partial loading or unloading. An ingenious traffic manager given a modicum of cooperation can find many ways to skin a cat.

Reciprocity

Many companies follow reciprocal buying and selling policies. As pointed out in the previous chapter, this may even extend to the purchase of transportation services. In such cases, the traffic department usually is the affected rather than the initiating department. That is, transportation is bought from those who buy the company's products. By working together on such policies, sales and traffic departments may be able to benefit their firm considerably.

Reciprocity policies may be worked out at the departmental level or the decision may be made by top management. In either case, the traffic manager's advice on such reciprocity policies as affect the choice of a carrier obviously should be sought; and once the decision is made, the traffic manager should cooperate with it insofar as possible as long as the policy is in effect.

INTERNAL WAREHOUSING AND MATERIALS HANDLING

Intraplant movement and storage of raw materials and finished-goods inventories often falls under the supervision of the traffic manager. This logically is a part of the transportation function since plant inventories are merely temporarily at rest in their movement from origin to final destination. Storage and processing can be viewed only as an intermediate step in the transportation process. Further, as the traffic department has responsibilities in getting goods into the plant and in getting them aboard outbound transportation equipment in proper order and on to their destination, it is not at all illogical that this department should handle goods (except for the actual processing or manufacturing operations) while they are within the plant.

We will not discuss the many techniques and mechanical devices used in the internal movement and storage of goods. This is a very comprehensive field in itself and one in which many new developments have brought increased efficiency and promise much more. Each system of intraplant storage and movement must be developed for a particular situation. Thus there are almost as many systems or variations of systems as there are firms and plants. If the traffic manager does have supervisory responsibilities in this area, he will find no shortage of current literature dealing with it.

PACKING, MARKING, AND LOADING

Whether or not the traffic department is responsible for the internal handling of goods, it certainly has a significant responsibility in seeing that outbound shipments are properly packed or packaged, marked, and loaded, Again, these physical operations may or may not be directly under traffic supervision. But if not, close cooperation should be maintained between those who are responsible and the traffic department. As indicated in the previous chapter, perhaps one third of all loss and damage to shipments en route can be traced to improper packing, marking, or loading.

Two things should be kept in mind when packing or packaging goods for shipment. First, the shipment must be protected from the hazards of the voyage. These include such things as climate, rough handling by carriers, and pilferage. Second, packaging adds to costs. The materials used for packaging cost something as does the labor for doing the packing. Further, packaging increases the weight of the shipment and thus adds to the freight bill. The "ideal" packaging is just enough to protect the shipment adequately, but no more.

Classifications, tariffs, and other carrier publications specify minimum packaging requirements for many types of commodities under various conditions. Also, professional "package engineers" or consultants, trade associations, manufacturers of various kinds of packaging materials, and many current journals and periodicals are useful in solving packaging problems. During recent years, much research has gone into developing various kinds of containers, pallets, strapping methods, unitized load devices, and lightweight packaging materials designed to increase protection and reduce costs of shipment. Information on these matters is a part of the traffic managers expert knowledge which should be available to and widely used by whomever actually does the physical packing job.

Very little needs to be said about the marking of shipments except that markings should be correct, clear, and consistent with the information shown on the Bill of Lading. Poorly marked shipments go astray more frequently than well-marked ones; and once shipments have strayed, inadequate markings make it more difficult to locate the shipper or consignee.

Finally, proper loading onto outbound transportation equipment is a traffic function whether or not loading actually is under the supervision of the traffic manager. The loading methods used will depend upon the nature of the goods, the type of packaging, the kind of outbound transportation used, and the physical layout of the plant itself and the kind of materials-handling equipment available.

Proper loading is concerned with protection of the goods shipped, with facilitating their unloading at destination (or partial unloading en route), and with minimizing loading costs (labor and protective dunnage). Shipments must be stowed in the vehicle and braced in a manner to accomplish these objectives.

Loading is another of the traffic manager's areas of expertise and one in which he can draw upon many sources for recent developments. Much of the old expensive hand-loading has been outmoded by mechanical loading using conveyors, chutes, fork-lift equipment, and specially designed carrier vehicles. Also new protective devices such as inflatable rubber dunnage, strapping materials, and even shock-resistant rolling stock are coming into use. Progress in loading efficiency is keeping pace with developments in packaging technology and promises equally great savings in the future. The traffic manager himself (or through cooperative action with or advice to other managers) is responsible for seeing that his firm benefits from these innovations.

GENERAL ORGANIZATONAL AND PERSONNEL POLICIES

Such matters as centralized versus decentralized control, recruitment, promotions, salary-scales, and fringe-benefits policies for employees, and the establishment of broad marketing strategies involve the entire firm. Usually, therefore, decisions on these and similar problems must be made by top management and applied on a reasonably uniform basis.

General policies do affect the operations and efficiency of the distribution process including the traffic management function, however. In addition, the best of general policies are worthless unless they are understood and conscientiously applied by those at the operational level. It is entirely appropriate, therefore, that the opinion and advice of the traffic manager, like that of other concerned managers, be considered by top management in making general policy decisions.

It may not be necessary, of course, that the traffic manager join directly in the Board Room discussions of top policy. His superior may present his views or they may be obtained by memorandum or through informal contacts with top management. Whatever the system of communication, however, a function as important as traffic control should not be ignored in general policy-making. Unfortunately, this is sometimes overlooked by top management.

SUMMARY

In order for a firm to operate effectively as an individual organism, its internal lines of communication must remain open and its activities and decisions must be closely coordinated. Since traffic management and control is a key component in most businesses, it follows that actions taken in many other departments will affect traffic management efficiency. Further, since traffic management is an active rather than a passive component, it is equally true that actions within the traffic department may directly affect the operations of various other departments and thus influence the overall performance of the business.

Although the traffic manager is a specialist in his own area and thus primarily responsible for the firm's traffic-control procedures, he should never forget that the way he does his job may significantly affect the jobs of others. Coordination is not a one-way street. On some matters, the traffic manager should make his decisions with due regard for the advice of other members of management. Some matters may require joint decision-making, while in others the traffic manager's role is purely an advisory one.

Intraorganizational conflict tends to arise most often in situations where joint decisions are necessary, where functional or group goals conflict, or where different groups within an organization interpret the same "factual" data in different ways. Numerous opportunities for such conflict exist in the administration of physical distribution.

Internal conflict, in addition to causing poor or delayed decisions, often leads to a waste of managerial time and abilities. Managers who should be cooperating in an effort to minimize the firm's costs, devote their own and their staffs' energies to making their departments "look good" or to obtaining an advantage over some rival department. Competition within the firm weakens its capability to compete in the market place.

All intraorganizational conflict, of course, cannot be eliminated and perhaps should not be. It should be kept within bounds which minimize its adverse effect on the firm's profits, however. Sometimes this can be accomplished by budgetary control of departmental activities or by guidelines for policy established by top management. Sometimes it is minimized by informal mutual agreements or intrafirm customs concerning the allocation of various types of decisions (who shall have the final say on what) among the potentially competing departments. If all else fails, top management itself may have to act as the final umpire.

There are no villains and heroes in most conflicts. Everyone has problems which he tries to solve in the best way possible. In solving a problem with limited knowledge of its overall implications, however, one may aggravate the problems of others. It is essential, therefore, that a traffic manager be knowledgeable about general conditions and major problems in all areas of his company just as all other managers should have some acquaintance with the traffic function.

ADDITIONAL READINGS

1. Bowersox, Donald J., Edward M. Smykay, and Bernard J. LaLonde, **Physical Distribution Management.** Rev. ed. New York: The Macmillan Co., 1968.
   Chapter 8. "Inventory Allocations," pp. 194–227.
2. Constantin, James A., **Principles of Logistics Management.** New York: Appleton-Century-Crofts, 1966.
   Chapter 10. "Introduction to Inventory Management," pp. 322–335.
3. Cushman, Frank M., **Transportation for Management.** Englewood Cliffs, N.J.: Prentice-Hall, Inc., 1953.
   Chapter 11. "Transportation and Insurance," pp. 425–441.
   Chapter 12. "Warehousing as an Element in the Transportation of Freight," pp. 442–452.
4. Heskett, J. L., Robert M. Ivie, and Nicholas A. Glaskowsky, Jr., **Business Logistics.** New York: Ronald Press Company, 1964.
   Chapter 16. "The Logistics System Concept," pp. 445–476.
5. Little, Wallace I., "A Model for Systems Management of Distribution Functions," **Transportation Journal,** Summer 1968, pp. 48–59.
6. Mossman, Frank H. and Newton Morton, **Logistics of Distribution Systems.** Boston: Allyn & Bacon, Inc., 1965.
   Chapter Eleven. "Distribution Warehousing," pp. 285–310.
   Chapter Twelve. "Inventory Management," pp. 311–348.
7. Stewart, Wendell M., "Physical Distribution: Key to Improved Volume and Profits," **Journal of Marketing,** Vol. 29, No. 1, January 1965, pp. 65–70.
8. Taff, Charles A., **Management of Traffic and Physical Distribution.** 4th ed. Homewood, Ill.: Richard D. Irwin, Inc., 1968.
   Chapter 5. "Inventory Control," pp. 106–128.
   Chapter 6. "Warehousing," pp. 129–155.
   Chapter 7. "Material Handling and Packaging," pp. 156–174.

28

Transportation Advice
on Capital Decisions

The preceding two chapters have dealt with functional business areas wherein the traffic manager makes decisions with or without the advice or consultation of other managers. Several examples were mentioned in which the traffic department played an important advisory role in formulating routine operational policy for his company.

This chapter will continue with traffic's advisory function, emphasizing those nonroutine decisions which call for major capital expenditures. Such decisions usually are made by top management. In making these decisions, top management has the responsibility of calling upon the traffic manager for his expert services in those matters involving transportation. If top management fails to do this or if it is not fully aware of the transportation implications of proposed actions, it is the traffic manager's duty to get the ear of his superiors and save the firm from costly mistakes.

Such an attempt by a traffic manager, even though unsolicited by his superiors, should not be considered presumptuous. Rather, if his advice is pertinent and tactfully presented, it should be highly appreciated. In fact, failure to present pertinent advice whether solicited or not should be regarded as evidence of unfitness of the traffic manager for the position; and if his constructive efforts are not appreciated, he would be well advised to consider other employment.

One area of investment or capial expenditure decision in which the traffic manager's advice would be pertinent is the choice between private and for-hire transportation services. Another might be containerization and often related to this, the type of intraplant materials handling equipment used. The transportation advantages and disadvantages of proposed or existing warehouses or branch plants would be still another area involving transportation, as would a major product innovation. Other situations might be added to this list, but these at least are important and fairly typical types of top-management problems closely related to the traffic management function, and thus worthy of some discussion here.

DECISIONS ON TRANSPORTATION EQUIPMENT EXPENDITURES

Sometimes a shipper's choice of a carrier will be largely determined by his peculiar problems such as his service needs and his location. Often, however, situations may exist in which choices must be made between the use of common, contract, or private carriage, or even some combination of these legal forms as well as between for-hire carriers.

Contract carriage may offer an acceptable alternative to common carriage both in costs and services in some situations. Contract-carrier rates often (although not always, by any means) are lower than common-carrier rates for comparable shipments. Further, by its very nature, contract carriage is a specialized service geared to the individual needs of its particular customer or a few customers. But contract carriers must be assured of a sufficient volume of traffic to make it profitable for them to operate and often must have a back-haul from some source. It usually is not profitable to operate a transportation business which moves goods only in one direction (except oil pipelines, of course).

The alternative to contract carriage for those who are not satisfied with common-carrier services or rates is to go into private carriage. Many firms have done this, especially in motor carriage.

Private Truck Carriage

It is estimated that around 15 per cent of all intercity freight in this country and around two thirds of truck ton-mileage move by private transportation. More than 90 per cent of the nation's truck fleet is owned by private shippers. The trend toward private truck transportation has been upward since World War II, but appears to have accelerated during recent years. Various factors, all basically growing out of dissatisfaction with existing for-hire carrier services or prices, account for this trend.

Transportation costs certainly are an important factor in the switch to private carriage. Private trucking costs, particularly on shorter and intermediate length hauls, often are demonstrably lower than common or contract truck carriage or even rail-carrier rates. In addition, as shipments are handled and transported only by the shipper's own employees, loss and damage (and sometimes packaging expenses) may be less than in for-hire carriage.

Private truck operators have some distinct cost advantages over for-hire operators. They are not obliged to maintain excess capacity. Instead, they may maintain only enough equipment for their normal traffic needs and turn to common carriers for the transport of unusually heavy or peak volumes. Also, they may use their own equipment for hauling merchandise subject to high freight rates, leaving the lower-rated, less profitable traffic for common carriers. Further, they usually do not incur the economic regulatory expense incident to for-hire carriage and may be able to make more efficient use of their labor and operate with lower wage scales than can for-hire carriers. And of course they obtain the transportation "profits" (if any) that otherwise would go to for-hire operators.

A principal cost disadvantage of private truck carriage is the back-haul problem mentioned in connection with contract carriage. Some shippers are able to route and schedule their outgoing trucks in such a manner that inbound supplies and materials can be brought in on the return trip. Others have resorted to legally questionable "gray area" if not outright illegal devices such as buying and selling merchandise not related to their primary business in order to avoid "dead-heading." Without some such arrangement, it is often difficult to justify private truck carriage on a strictly cost basis.

It is also possible that a firm whose principal business is manufacturing, processing, or merchandising may not be able to operate transportation equipment as efficiently as a for-hire carrier even under physically similar conditions. One gains expertise or "know-how" by specialization. More importantly, the manufacturer, considering transportation as a sideline to his major interest, may thus run a loose operation. A for-hire carrier, on the other hand, relying only on transportation profits, would be highly motivated to watch his costs and improve operating efficiency.

It is probable that service factors are more important than potential cost savings in most shippers' decisions to "go private." Common carriers are geared to the needs of a wide and diversified shipping public rather than to the special needs of any individual shipper. Customers often want faster delivery, fewer delays, and different delivery schedules than are available by common carrier between a particular shipper and customer. Thus, in order to remain competitive with other shippers who can and will better please customers, a firm may be forced to abandon common carriage even at the expense of some additional transport cost.

The traffic manager, of course, will seldom be in a position to make the final decision on changing from for-hire to private carriage. This involves capital expenditures as well as changes in the firm's operating patterns and costs. Such decisions properly are made at higher levels. Suggestions or recommendations for changes sometimes come from the traffic department, but probably most often originate from sales personnel.

In presenting top management with comparative estimates of costs and services of for-hire versus private transport, the traffic manager obviously is his company's expert. He may have to conduct detailed cost studies, however. In addition to line-haul operating costs and labor costs, fixed terminal expenses, additional administrative expenses, and depreciation on equipment must be calculated. It is easy to make overly optimistic estimates of the costs of private carriage as many firms have discovered too late.

Although many "average" cost figures are published, it is preferable that cost studies be made in the context of a particular firm's operating environment and peculiarities. Trucking costs vary widely between different sections of the country because of differing labor, fuel, and taxation costs and different operating conditions. They also vary even within the same locality depending upon the type of equipment used, the commodity hauled, and the length of haul.

When the best possible cost estimates have been developed, these can be weighed against the estimated service advantages of private transport. Even then, however, a firm may have alternatives other than private transport. The mere threat of private carriage may be enough to cause for-hire carriers to change their rates and services in ways beneficial to the firm in question. This alternative should always be explored and called to top-management's attention.

Finally, some attention should be given to the broader implications of private versus common carriage. The distribution system upon which much of our economy depends is serviced mainly by common carriers. A large number of shippers cannot possibly rely entirely or even in considerable part on private transportation. It is essential for these shippers and for the general public that our strong common-carrier system be maintained.

Insofar as an overextension of private transportation does tend to erode the overall strength of our established distribution system, it cannot be considered to be completely in the public interest. One cannot and should not expect that a firm in a profit-oriented society neglect its own interests in favor of some ill-defined "public interest" concept. One should expect, however, that responsible management consider this along with other pertinent factors. Such consideration need not be completely altruistic. If its own industry or the economy as a whole suffers, an individual firm is not likely to prosper.

Other Private Transportation Equipment

Many large private shippers, as well as the armed forces, own railroad cars or lease cars from independent car-owning companies. These cars usually are of specialized design to handle some particular type of commodity (as petroleum products, chemicals, fresh or frozen fruits and vegetables, meat, etc.). They usually are assigned to the use of the owning or leasing shipper who pays regular rail freight rates. The car owner, however, receives a mileage allowance (as specified in the applicable tariffs) from the railroads over whose lines the cars move.

Shippers by water often own all or a large part of their required transportation equipment. Many oil companies also, in effect, rely upon private pipeline transport although legally their pipeline operations may be classed as common carriage. There is as yet very little private transportation of freight by air.

The advantages and disadvantages of private transportation or private equipment ownership in these other modes are similar in nature to the advantages and disadvantages of private truck ownership. That is, the shipper may benefit from having the type of equipment most suited for his needs available when he wants it and may possibly (but not always) obtain better service or ship at lower costs. Likewise, the traffic manager's advisory role is to point out to top management the comparative cost and service features of the various alternatives.

CONTAINERIZATION AND INTERNAL MATERIALS HANDLING EQUIPMENT

Considerable ferment has been occurring in the field of containerized shipment during the past few years. The basic idea of containerization is to place several or many small units inside a protective covering which can be handled and shipped as a unit. Actually, a boxcar or a truck van is a "container," but the great present interest is in developing containers which can be hauled aboard a rail car, a truck, an airplane, or a barge or steamship and preferably interchanged between these various modes.

There are many advantages to containerization. Goods are better protected from handling and shipment damage, pilferage, and loss. Packaging expense can be cut, and handling labor can be expedited at lower cost. Some firms have substantially reduced costs and virtually eliminated en route loss and damage by containerization. Carriers also benefit from the more rapid turnaround of equipment and fewer L & D claims, and generally have been very cooperative with shippers in solving container problems and in pushing the movement. A piggyback van is one form of carrier-promoted interchangeable equipment.

Numerous problems arise with containers, however. They are costly and may increase the weight shipped. Both the shipper and the receiver as well as the carrier may have to change their handling techniques. Shipper-owned containers must be returned to their owners, and an empty container occupies as much space and may be almost as costly to handle and transport as a full one. This means that maximum container efficiency requires two-way use, a situation which does not fit the operational pattern of many shippers. (Many carriers own containers, thus "solving" the empty-return problem at least for shippers.)

Several groups are working on the problem of standardizing containers. The "ideal" type sought is a container which can be hauled in multiple units by any mode of carriage. That is, several units might be taken by truck to a railway station and added to several other units to load a flatcar. Then several flatcars might in turn discharge their containers onto a water carrier. At the end of the water movement, the process might be reversed. Such coordination, of course, requires that some standard or uniform size or sizes be adopted to facilitate interchange.

Although containerization is not the answer to all loss and damage and handling problems, it does offer substantial savings under the right conditions. Many shippers cannot containerize and probably never will be able to do so. As the state of technology improves, however, and appropriate institutional and rate adjustments are made, many more shipments will surely move in containers.

Every traffic manager should keep up with developments in this rapidly chang-ing field, or at least with those developments which are of potential use to his firm, and be prepared to give advice and make recommendations to his top management regarding expenditures for this type of equipment.

As indicated above, a switch to containers may involve changing handling methods and obtaining new materials handling equipment. Also, the traffic department itself in many firms is responsible for internal materials handling. In either case, the traffic manager has the responsibility for remaining current on the various types of handling equipment available (both its costs and what it can do to improve his firm's efficiency) and advising his top management as appropriate.

ELECTRONIC COMPUTER EQUIPMENT

Electronic computers are becoming more and more essential in developing information for management control. This is as true in traffic management as in other functional areas. This hardware does not replace the need for thinking or decision-making, as some have believed. Instead it accumulates and processes the data fed into it at almost unbelievable speed and may make it possible for management to see more clearly the differences between various alternatives.

In traffic control, computers have proven to be particularly useful in the preparation and updating of rate and route sheets, in analyzing the comparative costs of movements by different modes, routes, and carriers, and in determining the best locations (from a transportation viewpoint) of branch plants and ware-houses. In addition, of course, these machines can be used to increase the speed and accuracy of various routine clerical operations such as freight-bill auditing. Some current attempts are being made to reduce complex tariffs to computerized form, thus eliminating traditional rate clerk drudgery and making rate quota-tion more reliable and rapid.

Only the largest companies can afford today's expensive computers for ex-clusive use in traffic control. A traffic department, however, can often make good use of computers which are maintained primarily for other purposes. Computer facilities can also be hired on a time-used basis.

Many "old line" traffic managers have been frightened by the advent of computers and the "bright young men" who manipulate them. Apparently some have viewed these new techniques as threats to their positions. Others, however, have taken full advantage of computer techniques to increase their services to their firms and, at the same time, to enhance their own positions in the managerial hierarchy.

Computers are here to stay. They are becoming more versatile, more productive, and better understood. As technology advances, computer prices will make it possible and competition will make it necessary that computer techniques be routinely used in traffic control. The traffic manager, therefore, must dispel any misunderstanding or lack of understanding that he has about this new development.

This is not to say, of course, that traffic managers must necessarily become experts in computer programming and operation. This is a technical field in itself. But every traffic manager worthy of the name should be and soon will be expected to be familiar with what a computer can do (and equally important, what it cannot do) to improve his firm's traffic control performance and to be prepared to advise top management both on the results of computer studies and on the traffic department's needs for computer facilities.

WAREHOUSING AND WAREHOUSE LOCATION

Many persons still think of warehouses as being primarily places of static storage such as basement corners, garages, and attics. Except for such facilities as grain elevators, tank farms, or dockside warehouses which are located adjacent to line-haul transportation facilities, the layman seldom views warehousing as a vital part of our distribution system designed both to improve customer services and reduce transportation costs.

Distribution Functions of Warehousing

Warehousing may be used to reduce transportation costs in many ways. For example, goods can be shipped in large quantities at low rates (CL or TL) from distant production points to warehouses near consuming centers. Then local distribution in small quantities (and at higher LCL or LTL rates) can be made from the local warehouse. Instead of paying higher rates for the entire movement from producer to small consumer, lower bulk rates are used over a portion of the distance.

Warehousing may also enable a seller to supply each of many small buyers with several products. Even if each buyer should purchase in carload lots, a shipment from the producing plant might have to move at higher "mixed carload" rates, that is, at the rates applicable to the highest rated merchandise in the carload shipment. But by shipping straight carloads to a distributing warehouse and mixed carloads for the remainder of the journey, lower rates again are obtained for a portion of the movement.

Pool-car operations, in which several small buyers join together in ordering carload lots of a particular good and thus receive lower freight rates, often use public warehouse services. The shipment may be consigned to the warehouseman who will accept the merchandise, break it up into smaller lots, and deliver to the individual buyers.

It can be seen from these examples that warehousing operations sometimes may be used to reduce transportation costs. The customer-service aspects of warehousing usually are of considerably greater importance than transportation cost-savings features, however. In fact, the total costs of warehousing usually are much greater than any resultant transportation cost savings.

As speed and reliability have improved in transportation and communications, there has been an increasing tendency on the part of retailers to push the burden of maintaining inventories back toward the producer. During the age when messages could not travel faster than a horse and when goods were moved by animal-drawn vehicles, retailers necessarily maintained large stocks of goods and ordered infrequently. Today, however, when orders can be placed on one day and delivered the next from distances several hundred miles away, the retailer can gear his inventories to almost immediate demands. The seller performs the "storage" function. Thus in a competitive situation, the seller must be prepared either by strategically located distribution warehouses or by fast transportation, or both, to make quick delivery upon short notice.

Warehouse space also is necessary at points where commodities are stopped for processing or fabrication in transit. Inbound and outbound daily flows of materials seldom are equal at such points. Raw materials and processed goods usually must be stored temporarily, and transit points may be used as distribution centers for the processed commodity.

Similar temporary storage needs exist where one form of transportation makes connections with another. For example, warehouses in seaport cities act as collection points for small rail or truck shipments awaiting the arrival of steamships for further transportation. Conversely, such warehouses serve as temporary receptacles for large quantities of goods brought in and speedily unloaded by water carriers. Such goods are more gradually dispersed (in smaller volumes) by connecting land carriers. Early railheads connecting rail lines and wagon roads served the same functions. Similar situations still exist where goods must transfer from one mode of domestic carriage to another or where bulk shipments are dispersed or small shipments concentrated.

In summary, then, warehousing is closely tied in with transportation and plays an important role in the dynamic distribution process. Warehousing facilities necessarily come into being at distribution centers, transit centers, where modes of transportation change, and where seasonal production occurs. These facilities serve the needs of buyers, sellers, and transportation firms.

Kinds of Warehouses

A shipper may engage in private warehousing operations by owning or leasing space. Or he may rely upon for-hire public warehouses whose business is storage and related services.

Public warehouses have a legal status similar to that of privately owned public utilities and are actually regulated as public utilities by some state regulatory commissions. In addition to storage and protective services, they may provide a variety of services associated with distribution. They are open to everyone at established tariff charges or negotiated charges.

All public warehouses are subject to the Uniform Warehouse Receipts Act. Two kinds of warehouse receipts, negotiable and non-negotiable, may be issued for goods stored in public warehouses. These receipts might be compared to "order" and "straight" Bills of Lading. That is, the non-negotiable receipt permits delivery only to a specified person or firm, whereas the negotiable receipt permits delivery to the bearer or to the holder of the properly endorsed document. Negotiable warehouse receipts are used both in selling stored goods and in obtaining loans on them. The buyer or lender is protected in that the receipt issued by the warehouseman guarantees that the goods are in his custody and will be surrendered to (and only to) the person holding the receipt.

Field or "custodian" warehousing is a hybrid between the private and public varieties. It permits the issuance of negotiable warehouse receipts covering goods stored on private premises. These goods, even though stored in the owner's building, must actually be in the custody of a public warehouseman. In effect, it is public warehousing brought to the owner's place of business. An owner who wishes to borrow against his stored goods may use this device rather than incurring the expenses of physically moving his goods into a public warehouse.

Warehousing Costs

Warehousing costs, either private or public, may be quite high. They include, of course, capital and operating costs for the facilities as well as administrative and clerical costs. In addition, there are substantial costs involved in holding inventories. Working capital is tied up in stored merchandise; and in addition to physical handling costs, the merchandise may be subject to taxation, spoilage, breakage, theft, and obsolescence. Insurance protection must be provided. It is generally believed that the average annual costs of holding inventories may be as much as 20 to 25 per cent of the value of the goods held.

Faced with such costs and with the trend toward lower inventories on the part of retailers, it is not surprising that producers and intermediate distributors actively seek lower cost alternatives. One such alternative is the substitution of faster and higher priced transportation. That is, warehousing and inventory costs are "traded off" against transportation costs until some optimum balance is reached which reduces total physical distribution costs. This optimum, of course, must take into account the quality of customer service.

Many firms during recent years have made substantial cost reductions by eliminating or reducing the number of their regional distribution warehouses, and thus reducing their inventories. To maintain prompt and reliable customer services, premium transportation such as air carriage is provided from a central warehouse or from only a few locations. The great reductions in inventory holding and warehousing costs much more than offset the consequent increases in transport costs.

Various large firms have reported spectacular savings with no deterioration in customer services, or even improved services, by such actions. Others, however, have found that cost savings were not as great as anticipated, or that customer services and relationships suffered, or both, under centralized distribution. Every firm is an individual. Methods which work well for one may be very unsatisfactory for another. Careful studies of costs and service factors and consideration of the implications of changed methods for other functional areas of the firm should precede any decision to shift from decentralized to centralized distribution or vice versa.

The Traffic Manager's Role in Warehouse Location

Three basic types of questions arise in connection with the location of warehousing facilities. First, are existing services necessary and adequate? Should they be expanded, reduced, or maintained at approximately the present levels? Second, are new warehouses needed? And third, if new warehouses are needed, where should they be located? A related subsidiary question is whether warehousing should be private, public, or field warehousing.

Decisions to change existing warehousing methods may significantly affect all phases of a firm's activities. In addition to customer relations, marketing, transportation, and production operations are involved. The firm's capital structure may be changed, thus calling for different financing methods. Different administrative, inventory handling and control, clerical, accounting, personnel, and labor relations problems may arise. Quite clearly those officials responsible for all these and any other affected activities should be consulted by top management before a decision is reached.

The traffic manager's responsibility is to determine and report the transportation costs and available or obtainable transportation services associated with all of the various alternative methods and locations under consideration. Top management, then, must consider these transportation factors alongside other advantages and disadvantages of the proposed action. Transportation sometimes is an important determinant in the final decision, sometimes not. It does establish limits or boundaries within which the decision must be made, however.

In the pre-computer era, calculating the comparative transportation advantages and disadvantages of even a few alternative locations was a difficult or impossible task. The number of variables which can be handled by mechanical calculation is fairly limited. Today, however, masses of information can be fed into computers and answers received in short order. In fact, not only transportation data, but all kinds of pertinent information may be computerized, thus making it possible to pinpoint the preferable locations with an accuracy undreamed of a few years ago.

The computer does not make the traffic expert or any other functional expert obsolete, however. Instead, it increases his usefulness. If given incomplete or incorrect information, computer-based decisions can lead to horrendous mistakes. The computer clan has a favorite expression, "gigo," meaning "garbage in, garbage out." In developing information for locational or any other types of decisions, the traffic manager must attempt to include all pertinent transportation data in a correct form. The computer must be asked the right questions and given the right information before it can give the right answers.

TRAFFIC MANAGEMENT AND PLANT LOCATION

Whether or not additional plants should be established or where they should be built is another top-management decision requiring transportation advice. Location theory and some aspects of location practice as related to transportation have been discussed in Chapters 14 and 15. Most of the discussion of warehouse location in the preceding section is equally applicable to plant or branch-plant location.

It is not necessary that the foregoing discussions be repeated here. Instead, we have mentioned plant location specifically merely to re-emphasize the importance of traffic management's advisory role in plant-location decisions and to point out that its role and procedures are similar whether the locational problem concerns plant or warehouse facilities.

TRAFFIC MANAGEMENT AND MAJOR PRODUCT INNOVATIONS

Making major product innovations without adequate consideration of transportation factors is as rash as ignoring transportation advice in reaching locational decisions or in deciding to expand marketing activities into new geographical areas. Top management in considering a new product line should never forget that transportation costs are a part of the buyer's price. Thus whether or not a given product can be sold in a particular area or how profitable its sale will be depends upon transportation costs.

Marketing research personnel who determine whether or not a demand exists or can be developed for a new product and engineering personnel who design the product cannot be expected to be knowledgeable on transportation matters. If left to follow their own inclinations, the new product's delivered cost may be unduly high. Traffic personnel, therefore, should be asked several questions about the proposed new item. For example, what mode of transportation is most suitable? Are adequate transportation facilities available into the proposed marketing areas, or if not, can they be obtained? What will be the level of the applicable freight rates, and can more favorable rates be negotiated? What are the applicable freight rates on potentially competitive products? What are the proposed product's loss and damage characteristics and packaging requirements? Are special carrier services needed, and if so, can they be obtained? And at what costs?

The above transportation questions which should be asked about a proposed product innovation are merely suggestive rather than complete. A responsible traffic manager will not content himself with answering only the questions of this type which are asked by his top management or by others concerned with the decision. Others may not know which questions to ask. It is the traffic manager's duty to raise all the pertinent questions and provide the answers.

Many instances could be cited in which minor design changes suggested by traffic managers have greatly reduced transportation costs or in which traffic management's knowledge of service limitations have prevented serious mistakes. An equally large number of examples of firms which have experienced difficulties through failures to seek proper traffic advice could be cited.

SUMMARY

The first chapter of this part briefly identified the concept of physical distribution management and outlined the role of traffic management in this process and in the managerial structure generally. Then we considered in order some of the important functions and decisions of traffic management in its day-to-day operations and some of its routine relationships with other functional areas of the firm. In this chapter, we have presented some of the principal advisory responsibilities of the traffic manager to top management.

In this and the preceding three chapters, in addition to relating the process of physical distribution management to the transportation system and the economy as a whole, we have emphasized the interdependence of all the functional areas of a business firm. Traffic management is an integral part of the functioning of the firm and the economy. Better traffic managers and better uses of their talents lead to more efficiency and better resource allocation in production and distribution, greater profits for the individual firm, and lower consumer prices. Poor traffic management practices waste the firm's and the nation's resources.

ADDITIONAL READINGS

1. Bowersox, Donald J., Edward M. Smykay, and Bernard J. LaLonde, **Physical Distribution Management.** Rev. ed. New York: The Macmillan Co., 1968.
   Chapter 10. "Distribution Warehousing," pp. 246–295.
2. Constantin, James A., **Principles of Logistics Management.** New York: Appleton-Century-Crofts, 1966.
   Chapter 12. "General Merchandise Storage and Warehousing," pp. 364–445.

3. Flood, Kenneth U., **Traffic Management.** 2nd ed. Dubuque, Iowa: Wm. C. Brown Co., 1963.
   Chapter 2. "Company Operated Transport," pp. 24–51.
4. Molloy, William T., "Evaluating the Need for Automatic Data Processing Equipment in Transportation and Traffic Management," **Transportation Journal,** Summer 1969, pp. 43–56.
5. Plowman, E. Grosvenor, **Lectures on Elements of Business Logistics.** Stanford, Calif.: Graduate School of Business, Stanford University, 1964.
   Chapter VI. "Logistical Aspects of Private Carriage," pp. 101–117.
6. Taff, Charles A., **Management of Traffic and Physical Distribution.** 4th ed. Homewood, Ill.: Richard D. Irwin, Inc., 1968.
   Chapter 8. "Locational Factors," pp. 175–191.
   Chapter 17. "Private Transport Operations," pp. 417–437.

Part Eight

Summary and Preview

"What is past is prologue."

William Shakespeare, *The Tempest*

29

The Future of
Domestic Transportation

Where we are today and where we will be tomorrow are, in considerable part, determined by where we were yesterday. We can no more escape our past than we can avoid our future. Although our primary goal in this chapter is to peer into the future, we must do this in the context of the past and the present.

A GLANCE AT THE PAST

Transportation always has been important to mankind. Civilization has advanced as transport has advanced. Rudyard Kipling once said that transportation *is* civilization.

Like development in other arts and sciences, progress in transportation has been relatively slow when viewed in man's entire historical perspective. The human leg has been our primary motive power during most of our existence. The first revolution in transportation occurred when somewhere, by accident or design, someone discovered that animals could be domesticated and made to carry burdens or draw primitive vehicles and that crude sails could be used to propel floating craft capable of carrying persons and cargoes. Apparently a little later, that marvelous invention, the wheel, vastly multiplied transportation capacity just as it multiplied productive capacity.

The first revolution occurred only a few thousands of years ago; relatively speaking, only moments ago on mankind's calendar. The next revolution, however, did not occur until around six hundred years ago. This was marked by improvements in the design and size of ships and sails combined with navigational aids and arts which permitted Western European peoples to break away from sight-of-land sea voyages and spread their culture and commerce to almost all parts of the planet. No other era in history has witnessed such tremendous social and economic changes brought about during such a short period of time by improved transport facilities.

The most recent transportation revolution, which is still in process, was ushered in by the substitution of mechanical motive power for the power of animals and winds. Imaginative persons from the perhaps mythical Icarus to the very real Leonardo da Vinci dreamed of and sometimes even designed "modern" transportation vehicles throughout the ages. But it was not until the development of a practical steam engine patented by James Watt in 1769 that modern transportation could get under way. Steamboats were operating within a generation afterwards, and steam railroads and steamships a little later.

Steam power made the industrial revolution possible both by greatly increasing productive capacity and by making it possible for raw materials to be assembled and products distributed on a mass basis. The second transportation revolution had led to the discovery of the New World. The third permitted the United States to be settled and economically developed within a remarkably short time. Only sixty years after the first steam railroad was operated in this country, the U.S. Census Bureau officially declared that the frontier had ceased to exist.

Technological refinements of the third transportation revolution have progressed rapidly. Within little more than a century after the first practical steam engine, the internal combustion engine was invented and the oil industry began to develop. This made possible automobiles, busses, trucks, and airplanes. Oil replaced coal as fuel for ocean vessels; and following World War II, the coal-burning railroad steam locomotives were rapidly superseded by diesels. Power refinements during recent years have included jet propulsion (used by squids for millions of years) and rockets (whose principles were known by the Chinese two thousand years ago). And atomic power, especially in the area of ocean transportation, seems to have a niche in certain types of services.

In summary, motive power has been the major technological key to transportation development. Vehicles, ways, and institutions have been developed to take advantage of each power breakthrough. Mankind has seen three great transportation revolutions, each consisting of a major change in motive power followed by a long period of refinements. But whereas several thousand years passed between the first and second revolutions, only a few hundred years separated the second and third. The rate of change has been much more rapid following the third revolution and seems to be accelerating. We draw upon all the accumulated body of knowledge and experience of the past, and as this body increases, so does our pace of new ideas and practices.

Transportation developments, of course, do not force corresponding economic and social developments, but changes in transport do permit changes in these other areas, and limitations of transport limit developments elsewhere. For example, we hear a great deal today about the population explosion; but without the earlier transportation explosion, a population explosion would not have been possible.

A VIEW OF THE PRESENT

This book has been primarily concerned with the domestic transportation system of the United States. Despite this system's weaknesses and problems, many of which have been mentioned, it is the finest fruit of mankind's transportation progress to date. By any criteria, we are blessed with the world's most efficient system of transportation and physical distribution.

Why is this so? In part, perhaps, our strength in transportation can be explained by our apparent knack for technology and organization, by geography, and by the resources which have contributed so much to the wealth of our nation. But this is not all. Institutional factors have played a vital role in our transportation development just as they have in other areas of development.

Our political and economic institutions have permitted and encouraged profit-seeking entrepreneurs and managers to exploit technological, organizational, and managerial innovations with relative freedom. The result has been what might be described as a "multi-circuit" system of transportation. That is, we have available many competing alternate routes, modes, and firms from which users can choose. This flexibility of design permits carriage with the least expenditure of operational resources and energy, and with the least likelihood of a blockage of traffic flow due to a breakdown in some component of the system. We benefit by not having all our eggs in one basket.

It is true that the excess capacity inherent in a multi-circuit transport system in contrast with a single-circuit system requires a considerably greater initial investment of resources. But when this investment has been made, and we have made it, the benefits of flexibility and of price and service competition continue indefinitely. Even when additional investment is necessary, it is not necessarily true that expansion should occur only in that mode of carriage which is deemed "most efficient" in the overall sense. Efficiency must be viewed at the margin rather than as an average. The principle of diminishing returns is as important as the principle of economies of scale. Under some conditions, greater use of a so-called "less efficient" form of transport may be economically preferable.

One important part of our present-day regulatory policy is concerned with preserving the "inherent advantages" of competing modes of transportation. Critics sometimes allege that in reality this usually means simply maintaining the status quo. In moments of frustration one may be tempted to believe that if our current regulation had been in effect in 1860, we would today have Pony Express riders competing with jet airplanes in moving mail between California and the East.

Most students of transportation agree that some economic regulation of the industry is desirable. No one can deny, however, that too much regulation or that particularly inflexible regulation tends to stifle experimentation and innovation. Attempts to impose static institutions on dynamic societies inevitably lead to conflict, with resulting disaster either for the institutions or the societies. A key problem in our present transportation regulation, then, is to keep our regulatory institutions reasonably flexible and dynamic. Only by doing this can we continue to enjoy the fruits of advancing technology and managerial ability.

A MURKY GLIMPSE AT MARVELS OF THE FUTURE

The past is history, interesting for what it can explain about the present or lead us to expect in the future. The present is only an instant of time, a transition between past and future, which disappears as we contemplate it. The future is all important. Those thought to have the gift of foreseeing the future have been universally respected since time immemorial.

Forecasting, however, is an inexact and hazardous art. Crystal balls are better for looking backward than forward; and the further one gazes into the future, the more murky the image becomes. But we cannot escape forecasts and their consequences. All future economic planning, like all present economic activity, is necessarily based on forecasts, either explicit or implicit. All of us, whether we realize it or not, are constantly engaged in forecasting and planning our future activities upon our forecasts.

The authors, therefore, are willing to set forth some of their views of the future. We will not attempt to peer one thousand years or even one hundred years into the future, however. Instead, we will confine ourselves to the next two or three decades, a time during which present-day university students may be expected to approach their peak levels of activity in their chosen business and professional careers.

Our predictions are based only upon the continuation of presently existing visible trends in technology, organization, regulation, and physical distribution management. One can speculate but not forecast in a vacuum. For example, we think it highly probable (assuming that hydrogen bombs or other disasters do not destroy the human race) that new transportation revolutions based upon new forms of motive power will come. What this motive power will be—solar energy, anti-gravity or similar "wild" science-fiction power sources, or even undreamed-of sources—no one can say. These new sources may be harnessed within five years or five thousand years. Who knows? What person in 1900 could have predicted that men would be circling the earth in missiles at a height of several hundred miles and actually traveling to the moon during the 1960's? Yet this would have been easier to predict than a revolutionary motive-power source.

Future Technology

Today's travelers and shippers are interested in speed. It seems fairly certain, therefore, that considerable refinements and improvements designed to move people and goods more rapidly will be made. Supersonic jets and "jet busses" capable of carrying hundreds of persons or many tons of cargo, will be used more widely. Rocket-powered missiles may be used to a limited extent for transporting special types of cargo on the earth as well as for travel to the moon.

On the ground, new techniques in safety control may permit much greater speed and bring much greater safety on the highways. Separate ways for freight and people, and electronic control systems, are not inconceivable. Railroad trains can be, and probably will be, operated without crews on board. Automatic rail marshaling or assembling yards and centralized traffic control will be greatly improved and expanded. Mechanized loading and unloading will be stepped up, and containerization will continue to grow. These various differing techniques, of course, will result in modifications of vehicle designs.

Continued rapid improvements in pipeline technology can be expected. Although used now mainly for carrying petroleum and its products, a considerable number of items can be transported by pipeline—crushed coal or ores, wood chips, and grain, for example. Technology in this field is already known and is past the experimental stage.

Mass rapid transportation within major metropolitan areas and between adjacent population centers must and will be improved and expanded. We cannot let automobiles continue to proliferate as they have in the past, otherwise city traffic will completely choke itself. Fast commuter trains or train-like-vehicles utilizing subways and elevated rails in the most congested areas seem to be the only present solution to the plight of many of our larger cities. Endless belt-type conveyer sidewalks may be used in central business districts and to bring people downtown from outlying commuter stations and parking lots.

Hydrofoil vessels, now being used to a slight extent, promise to provide a fast and flexible form of passenger and specialized freight service on inland and protected waterways. The hovercraft or surface-effect vehicle riding on a cushion of air promises even more in the way of versatility. It may be used on water, rails, highways, or even over terrain where no roads exist.

Much of the hard physical labor will be removed from transportation and distribution, but this is not all. Routine clerical and minor administrative tasks will be handled more and more by electronic computers. The "rate clerk" of tomorrow will dial a computer for his classifications, rates, and routes. Traffic documents will be computerized. In fact, we should not be surprised to find shippers' computers "conversing" directly with carrier computers and feeding out their "agreements" to their respective masters.

All of these above-mentioned developments and others are within the capabilities of presently existing technology. The limiting factor is cost. Even though we may be able to do something new and different, the old way may be less expensive. But the old ways are getting increasingly expensive while technological refinements are bringing down the costs of newer techniques. We will adopt the newer methods when they become more profitable, that is, less costly than the older ones.

The broader social costs and resources must be included among the costs of transportation along with individual carrier and customer costs. One important social resource whose consumption results in social costs is space—space for living, working, and recreation.

In our large and relatively thinly populated country, we have been little concerned with space to date. But the supply of land is fixed, and not all land is suitable for agriculture, building, or recreation. Population, on the other hand, continues to increase rapidly. There is a physical and economic limit to the amount of land that we can set aside for transportation. This limit shrinks, while the need for additional transportation expands each time a baby is born.

It is perfectly clear that we cannot continue building surface ways over our most desirable lands indefinitely. Neither can we all take to the air where the saturation point already is dangerously close in many areas. We can and no doubt will postpone the inevitable somewhat by the costly expedient of building underground and elevated ways and by constructing ways across our less desirable lands. But before this, or along with it, economic and social pressures will force us to make maximum utilization of existing ways and facilities.

It appears that more and more of our additional mass commuter traffic and our long and intermediate-haul freight movement must be handled by railroads, the mode most capable of doing this efficiently and with minimum space utilization. We are not predicting that highways and airports will not still be built a generation hence or that Sunday afternoon or rush-hour automobile driving will be less hectic. We are suggesting, however, that cost factors and a frustrated citizenry will see to it that proportionately more traffic moves by rail within the next generation. In fact, we may expect to see rail capacity almost fully utilized again, and perhaps even expanded.

Future Transport Organization and Management

There is little doubt that for-hire transportation companies will become considerably fewer but much larger during the coming generation. Many of these for-hire firms, by one device or another, will evolve into true multi-modal "transportation companies," rather than continuing to exist as railroad, truck, air, water, or pipeline firms. More managerial flexibility and more sophisticated management control techniques and improved technologies will bring increased transport efficiency.

Private transportation will continue to play an important role in our economy, but probably will not grow as rapidly as for-hire transport. Increasingly, the diseconomies of small-unit operations, plus regulatory and user charge restrictions purposely designed to limit the proliferation of privately-operated vehicles, combined with relatively more efficient for-hire transport, will dampen the growth of private carriage.

Overall, the demand for transportation services will continue to keep pace with, or perhaps even exceed, the growth of our Gross National Product. This means that the demand for qualified and versatile transportation managers, professional employees, and skilled technicians will remain strong in the transportation industry, even though the relative numbers of manual and semi-skilled workers in transport may decline.

Future Regulation and Policy

Regulatory institutions, like other social institutions, tend to lag behind environmental changes. Regulations and policies are adopted to deal with present (or past) problem situations. When the problems change, the regulations and policies remain.

Despite lag and slowness, however, institutions do change. During recent years, a general awareness of the need for some changes in transportation policy has developed. We foresee, then, that changes will occur.

We do not predict a freely competitive transportation system. Rather, we foresee some loosening of the restraints on competition within the general framework of existing regulation. Unification, integration, coordination, and cooperation will receive more encouragement and perhaps even some prodding. Various kinds of public aids and promotions will not cease, but will become more selective and will be designed to achieve more specific goals. The application of regulation and policy will not be based completely upon economic and social rationality, but it will be more so than at present.

Regulatory and policy changes of this type will provide a better climate for the utilization and growth of presently known technology and for the birth of new technologies. Transportation and other resources will be better allocated and transport facilities more fully and profitably utilized. The scope of management decision-making will be expanded, thus making good management even more crucial than now. The environmental and social impacts of transportation will be more widely recognized by the public, regulators, and management.

This brave new transportation world will not be accomplished without tribulations, however. Institutional change is never easy. Someone always is hurt. Competitors lose business, communities lose services or prestige, labor loses jobs, and politicians lose votes. But just as the past tells us that better technologies always supersede inferior ones, so it tells us that urgently needed institutional changes cannot be withstood. Fighting change is futile, and ignoring it is worse. We must expect change, try to anticipate its direction and extent, and attempt to adapt to it and minimize its adverse effects.

Future Managers of Physical Distribution

We can anticipate with considerable certainty that the world of tomorrow, in transportation as well as in other areas of endeavor, will be more complex than the world of today. We believe that the role of transportation in tomorrow's world will be equally as important as today and that top management will become increasingly aware of this importance. We trust that transportation will remain free and unnationalized, and we expect that common carriers will continue to be the backbone of our transport system, that railroads will become relatively more important for many kinds of movements, that operating and materials handling techniques will be more efficient, and that more interagency coordination and intra-agency cooperation will exist. Transport firms will be fewer but larger, and regulation will be less restrictive.

We foresee, too, a spreading and increased emphasis upon the total-cost approach to physical distribution. Management will use more electronic processing, operations research, linear programming, and sophisticated market research techniques. Also, although this book has been concerned only with domestic transportation, we feel that international business will grow and that some knowledge of ocean and foreign transportation problems will become increasingly important to the traffic manager or physical distribution manager.

What kind of education should a young person seek then to prepare himself for a career in industrial traffic or physical distribution management? Clearly he must continue to be a specialist and technician in part, but he must also be a generalist and a manager. Opportunities for making great savings for a company by hammering through rate reductions are not as great as formerly, and many time-consuming necessary routine chores can be done more efficiently by computers.

We feel that the manager of the future must have a well-balanced knowledge of all forms of transportation. In addition, he should know a great deal about business administration in general, and in his industry and firm in particular. He should have a good understanding of the social, political, and economic environments within which businesses operate. Obviously, he must be able to adapt to rapid change.

What college courses should our potential manager take? Instead of confining himself to the basic required courses in Business Administration, plus the bare minimum of required science, social science, and humanities courses, and overloading himself with specialized transportation and traffic-management courses, we are firmly convinced that he should broaden himself with a variety of business and nonbusiness courses beyond the introductory level. Mathematics, statistics, computerology, the behavioral sciences, international law, and similar topics should be seriously considered.

As teachers of transportation and at the risk of upsetting old friends in the field of transportation and traffic management, we are willing to go even further. We can even dream of the time when a considerable number of graduates in our field, in addition to their professional toolkits, may be equipped with an above-average acquaintance with such exotic areas as the physical and engineering sciences, American and world history, comparative economic and political systems, art and music, and even languages other than English. Everyone is entitled to dreams, and sometimes they come true.

We end on this optimistic note. We hope that the challenge of the future will inspire our readers to prepare themselves for adapting to and influencing the shape of future events so that a better transportation and physical distribution system in a more livable environment will contribute to a more satisfying life for all.

ADDITIONAL READINGS

1. Barriger, John Walker, **Super-Railroads for a Dynamic Economy.** New York: Simmons-Boardman Publishing Corp., 1955. Pp. xi, 91.
2. Becht, J. Edwin, **A Geography of Transportation and Business Logistics.** Dubuque, Iowa: Wm. C. Brown Company, Publishers, 1970. Chapter 6. "Summary/Conclusion—An Evolving National Transportation and Business Logistics Pattern," pp. 82–92.
3. Brewer, Stanley H., "The Dynamic Nature of Transportation Education," **Transportation Journal,** Summer 1963, pp. 10–15.
4. Carlson, Jack W., "Diffusion of Technology in The United States," **Transportation Journal,** Fall 1968, pp. 5–24.
5. Dillon, Thomas F., "Transportation: Better Service at Lower Cost," **Purchasing,** February 25, 1963, pp. 73–75, 100, 103.
6. Duffy, C. D., "A Standard Transportation Geographic Code," **Papers, Fifth Annual Meeting, Transportation Research Forum,** 1964, pp. 192–201.
7. Farmer, Richard N., "Transportation's Future in the Universities Revisited," **Transportation Journal,** Vol. 2, No. 4, Summer 1963, pp. 23–27.
8. Farris, Martin T., Douglas C. Cochran, Grant M. Davis, and David R. Gourley, "Transportation Education—An Inter-Disciplinary Approach," **Transportation Journal,** Fall 1969, pp. 33–44.
9. Harper, Donald V., "What Next For Transportation Education?" **Transportation Journal,** Spring 1965, pp. 21–28.
10. Heskett, J. L., Robert M. Ivie, and Nicholas A. Glaskowsky, Jr., **Business Logistics.** New York: Ronald Press Company, 1964. Chapter 18. "Logistics and Management," pp. 499–522.
11. Lessing, Lawrence, "The 400-Mph Passenger Train," **Fortune,** April 1965, pp. 124–129, 208, 210, 212, 214, 216, 218.
12. McElhiney, Paul T., "Transportation: A Developing Profession?" **Transportation Journal,** Vol. 4, No. 1, Fall 1964, pp. 14–21.
13. Paden, David L., "Intercity Surface Travel Technology, The Outlook to 1975," **Papers, Fifth Annual Meeting, Transportation Research Forum,** 1964, pp. 49–61.
14. Plowman, E. Grosvenor, "The Intermodality and Cybernetics Keys to Profitable Computerization in Transportation," **Transportation Journal,** Spring 1969, pp. 51–55.
15. Roberts, Merrill J., and Wilbur A. Steger, "Transportation in a Graduate School of Business Curriculum," **Papers, Fifth Annual Meeting, Transportation Research Forum,** 1964, pp. 110–120.
16. Sampson, Roy J., "Transportation's Future in the Universities," **Transportation Journal,** Vol. 2, No. 3, Spring 1963, pp. 7–11.

Index

Abandonment: Act of 1920, 261, 268; Act of 1958, 293–94; motor, 278; railroad, 58, 107, 108, 261, 268, 309, 377

Accessorial line-haul services, 124–27

Accessorial terminal services, 120–22

Accounting regulation, 257, 265, 278, 284, 286

Act to Regulate Commerce of 1887, 252–55, 335

Acts of God, 108–09, 446

Acts of public authority, 109, 446

Acts of public enemy, 109, 446

Acts of shipper, 109

Adams, Walter, 340

Adamson Act of 1916, 259, 347

Adequacy of service, 107, 268, 274, 284–87, 322, 377

Administrative Commissions: C.A.B., 305–07; Federal, 300–07; I.C.C., 300–05; state, 307–09; uniqueness, 300

Agricultural commodities exemption, 278–79, 294, 310, 394, 401, 405

Agricultural location theory, 224–27

Air Commerce Act of 1926, 32, 283, 286

Air Mail Act of 1934, 283–84

Air pollution, 41, 375, 380–81

Air Transport Association of America, 97, 135

Air transportation: air bill, 438; average haul, 63, 75; capital investment, 74, 76–77, 375; characteristics and performance, 74–78; costs, 76–77, 345, 375; coverage, 75–76; employment, 75; fares, 63, 75, 374; freight and express, 77–78; future, 472–73; history, 32–33; interchange of equipment, 132; interline agreement, 134; intermodal competition, 76, 272; intramodal competition, 76, 285; labor relations, 342–53; mergers, 286, 323–40, 336–37; mutual-aid pact, 351; number of firms, 75, 76; operating ratio, 77; passenger miles, 51, 75, 375; promotion, 32, 33, 75, 76, 272, 282–87, 366–68; public service revenues, 75, 76, 367, 405; rail coordination, 137; rates, 75, 77, 285–86; regulation, 75, 76, 282–87; reliability, 75, 76; revenues, 75; routes, 87, 89, 97, 284–85; safety, 283, 284, 286–87; speed, 75, 77, 78; supremacy in passenger transportation, 51, 375; terminal ownership, 123; ton-miles, 51, 75, 78; variability factor, 377–78

Airmail: certificates, 284; contracts, 32, 75, 76, 272, 283, 284, 367, 386; parcel post, 77; revenue needs, 386

Airport-Airways Modernization Act, 386

Airports, 32, 272, 283, 358, 365, 375, 386, 405

Airway congestion, 42, 375, 383

Alabama Midlands Case, 255

Alexander, David, 280

American Railway Union, 347

American Trucking Associations, 135

American Waterways Operators Association, 95, 135

Antitrust conflicts, 330, 332, 333, 335, 400–01

Arbitration Act of 1888, 347

Arpaia, Anthony F., 407

Arth, Maurice P., 408

Association of American Railroads: code of car service rules, 131; code of per diem rules, 131; freight car shortages, 93; interfirm public relations, 135; master car builder rules, 131; public aid estimates, 369; shipper advisory boards, 133

Association of Petroleum Pipelines, 135

Atlantic port differentials, 193, 194
Auditing function, 416, 423, 427, 440–41, 459
Average weight agreements, 121–22

Baltimore and Ohio Railroad, 24, 25
Bankruptcy Act of 1933, 263, 270
Bankruptcy, railroad, 58, 387
Barrett, Colin, 340
Barriger, John W., 340, 477
Basing point pricing, 194, 195
Basing point rates, 187, 195–98, 232
Baumol, William J., 159
Becht, J. Edwin, 102, 477
Belt line railroads, 122, 132
Bigham, Truman C., 15, 37, 140, 205, 265, 297, 319, 353, 371
Bilateral agreements, 384–85
Bill of lading, 438–39, 462
Blanket rates, 187, 198–205, 208, 231
Board of Investigation and Research, 290–91, 362, 365
Board of Mediation and Conciliation, 347
Bonded warehousing, 462
Bowersox, Donald J., 222, 453, 465
Boyle, Gerald T., 116
Brewer, Stanley H., 477
Bryan, Leslie A., 128, 430, 443
Buck v. *Kuykendall*, 274
Bugan, Thomas G., 115
Bulk commodity exemption, 289, 394, 404–05
Bunke, Harvey C., 319
Bureau of Air Commerce, 283, 286
Business Logistics, 13–15; 417–18
Busses: average haul, 63; characteristics and performance, 63–64, 375; fares, 63, 374; number of firms, 64; revenues, 63, 64
By-product effects, 375

Cabotage, 71
Calmus, Thomas W., 159
Campbell, Thomas C., 222, 408

Canals: history, 22–24, 26, 33–35, 70; promotion, 22–23, 34, 357, 359, 366
Capital invested in transportation: air, 74, 365; allocation, 355; highways, 59, 263–64; pipelines, 64; railroads, 52, 53, 361–62; total private, 10–11; water transportation, 69, 365–66
Car service rules, 131, 261
Carlson, Jack W., 477
Carmack Amendment of 1906, 437
Carrier classifications: air, 75–76, bus, 63, 64; freight forwarder, 79; motor, 60, 275–76; rail, 52; water, 69
Carrier traffic management, 426–28
Carter, John P., 199, 205
Caves, Richard E., 297
Central Pacific Railroad, 27
Certificates of public convenience and necessity: air, 284–85; freight forwarder, 292, 303; motor, 276–77, 303, 308, 334–35, 399; rail, 261, 303; state, 274, 308; water, 288, 303
Character of cities, 44, 383–84
Character of neighborhoods, 40, 44, 384
Charter regulation of transportation, 247–48
Cherington, Paul W., 297
Chesapeake and Ohio Canal, 23
Chicago Sanitary Ship Canal, 35
Chicago Switching District, 122
Civil Aeronautics Act of 1938: certificates of public convenience and necessity, 284–85; declaration of policy, 282–83; Grandfather Clause, 284–85; planning, 365; rule of rate making, 285–86
Civil Aeronautics Board: accidents and safety, 76, 286–87; accounts, 286; air freight forwarders, 80; air mail rates, 76; airbill, 438; carrier classifications, 75–76; case load, 307; certificates of public convenience and necessity, 284–85, 405; commissioners, 305, 314; examiners, 307; intramodal competition, 76, 284–85; maximum rates, 286; mergers, 286, 336–37; minimum rates, 286; one carrier principle, 285; organization, 305–06; proceedings, 307;

promotion, 282–83, 284, 405; public service revenue, 76, 367, 405; rule of rate making, 285–86

Civil War and railway expansion, 27

Claims: function, 427; insurance, 445–48, loss and damage, 416, 425, 439–41, 458; overcharge and reparation, 440–41

Class rates, 55, 162, 167, 177

Classification Committee procedures, 163–65, 292–93

Classification: consolidated freight classification, 162–63; development, 162; national motor freight classification, 163, 166; procedures, 163–65; purpose, 161; regulation of, 258, 292–93; uniform freight classification, 162–65

Coast Guard, 316, 319

Cochran, Douglas L., 477

Coggs v. *Bernard,* 108–09

Collective and joint ownership, 135

Combination rates, 134–35, 179

Commerce Clause, 252, 274, 310

Commodities Clause, 257, 264

Commodity competition, 211–12

Commodity movements, 92–98, 100

Commodity rates, 55, 169, 177

Common carrier: duration of liability, 110; duty to avoid discrimination, 103, 111–14, 395; duty to charge reasonable rates, 103, 110–11, 146–47, 395; duty to deliver, 103, 108–10, 395; duty to serve, 103, 106–08, 395; legal service obligations, 104–15; limitations of liability, 109–10; tradition, 356, 394, 395, 457, 475–76

Common costs, 156–57, 191, 334

Common law: duty to avoid discrimination, 103, 111–14, 311, 395; duty to charge reasonable rates, 103, 110–11, 146–47, 253, 311, 395; duty to deliver, 103, 108–10, 311, 395, 438; duty to serve, 103, 106–08, 311, 356, 395; legal basis of regulation, 103, 243, 251, 274; origin of carrier obligations, 103; regulation, 246–47

Compulsory arbitration, 351–52

Compulsory Testimony Act of 1893, 255

Conant, Michael, 115, 340, 372, 408

Concentration of shipments, 118, 126

Congestion, 42–43, 373, 377, 378, 382–84

Congressional committees, 313

Consolidated freight classification, 162–63

Consolidation and merger: Act of 1887, 254, 335; Act of 1920, 261, 269–70, 335; Act of 1940, 291, 335; air carrier, 286, 336–37; antitrust conflicts, 400–01; before regulation, 250, 335; cost savings, 325–27; defined, 129, 324–25; effects, 326–32; increased volume, 327–28; Kennedy message, 405–06; motor carrier, 277–78, 336; obstacles, 332–33; water carrier, 288, 337

Consolidation of shipments, 79, 118

Constantin, James A., 128, 140, 281, 341, 353, 430, 453, 465

Consuming center competition, 209–10

Containerization, 83, 138, 458–59, 473

Continental Trailways, 64

Contract carrier obligations, 115

Cooperation in transportation: aims, 130; collective ownership, 135; definition, 129–30; equipment interchange, 131–32; interline agreements, 134; pools, 130; public relations, 135; ratemaking, 134–35; through billing, 133; through routes and rates, 132–33

Cooperative rate making, 134–35

Coordination of transportation: benefits, 138–39; containerization, 138, 458–59; definition, 129–30, 136, 324–25; express service, 80–81; intermodal, 82–83; obstacles, 139; rail-water, 136; types, 136–38

Corporate form of business, 21, 28, 247–48

Cost allocation, 376

Costs of distribution, 14

Courts: adjudicative role, 311; agricultural commodity exemption, 310; Congressional interpretation, 310; constitutional interpretation, 309–10; enforcement role, 310–11; review of Commission decisions, 255, 311–12

Cowles Plan, 188–89
Cranmer, H. Jerome, 37
Cumberland Road, 21
Cummins Amendments, 437
Cushman, Frank M., 176, 453

Daggett, Stuart, 15, 102, 115, 128, 140, 159, 176, 199, 205, 222, 239, 265, 280, 297, 319, 372
Dartmouth College Case, 248
Davis, Grant M., 320, 477
Dean, Joel, 159
Dearing, C. L., 403, 408
Debs, Eugene, 347
Declaration of National Transportation Policy, 284–85, 289–90, 355, 391–93, 402–03
Demand: aggregate, 150, 152, 153; derived, 152; elasticity, 149–50, 152–54, 189; general, 148–50; individuals, 151–52; modal, 150, 153–54; particular, 150; society, 150–51
Demaree, Allan T., 46
Demurrage and detention, 432–33
Department of Agriculture, 401
Department of Transportation: budget, 319; Coast Guard, 316, 319; employees, 319; Federal Aviation Administration, 76, 287, 294–95, 316, 319, 378, 383; Federal Highway Administration, 316, 319; Federal Railroad Administration, 316, 319; history, 295, 315–16, 317, 397–98, 403, 406; National Highway Safety Bureau, 316, 319; objectives, 295, 316, 398; Office of High Speed Ground Transportation, 386, 387; origin chart, 317; organization, 316, 318; rail passenger transportation, 386, 387–88; St. Lawrence Seaway Development Corp., 316, 319; Urban Mass Transit Administration, 316, 386
Depressed areas, 44–45
Dewey, Ralph L., 115
Dillon, Thomas F., 477
Discrimination: Act of 1920, 261; Act to Regulate Commerce, 253, 414; Air

Carriage Act, 286; Cullom Report, 251–52; definition, 112–13; Freight Forwarder Act, 292; Granger movement, 249–50, 414; Hepburn Act, 256; long and short haul, 249–50, 253, 257, 264, 278, 288; Mann-Elkins Act, 257; Motor Carrier Act, 277; permissible, 113–14; personal, 252, 264, 277, 280, 283, 288; postage stamp plans, 188–89; state motor regulation, 274; types, 112–13; undue, 113–14; Water Carrier Act, 288; Windom Report, 251
Dispersion of shipments, 118–19
Distribution and transportation: general, 7; physical distribution, 13–15, 411–77; transportation geography, 85–102
Distribution cost, 14
Diversion: See Reconsignment and diversion
Documentation function, 427, 436–39
Doyle, John P., 408
Doyle Report: citation, 408; example of Congressional investigation, 313, 403; public aid to transportation, 366–69
Duffy, C. D., 477
Duke Case, 274
Duplication of facilities, 327, 328–29, 332
Duty to avoid discrimination, 103, 111–14, 311, 395
Duty to charge reasonable rates, 103, 110–11, 146–47, 311, 395
Duty to deliver, 103, 108–10, 311, 395
Duty to serve, 103, 106–08, 311, 356, 395

Early road movement, 20–21
Ecology, 41, 43, 378, 380–82
Economies of scale, 325–27, 334
Economic development and transportation, 4, 5, 357, 369
Economic significance of transportation, 4–13
Education for transportation, 476–77
Elasticity of demand, 149–50, 152–54, 189
Elkins Act of 1903, 256, 288

Emergency Transportation Act of 1933, 270, 275
Employee boards, 302
Employment and transportation, 9–10
End-to-end mergers, 327–30, 336–37
Environmental aspects of transportation, 39–43, 380–82
Erdman Act of 1898, 347
Erie Canal, 22–24, 34, 70
Esch Car Service Act of 1917, 261
Esch-Cummins Act of 1920, 259
European capital, 28
Exceptions rates, 165, 167, 177
Executive regulation: power of appointment, 301, 305, 307, 314; power of enforcement, 314; power of investigation, 314; power of recommendation, 315
Exempt carriage: amount, 73, 141; concept, 50, 394; motor carriers, 59, 277–79, 294, 310, 394, 401, 405; water carriers, 73, 289, 394, 404–05
Expediting Act of 1903, 256

Fabos, Julius, 47, 389
Fair, Marvin L., 15, 38, 66, 83, 115, 116, 140, 159, 176, 205, 222, 265, 280, 297, 408
Farmer, Richard N., 389, 477
Farris, Martin T., 340, 408, 477
Featherbedding issue, 350–52
Federal Aid Act of 1916, 30, 271, 363
Federal-Aid Primary system, 363–64
Federal-Aid Secondary system, 271, 363–64
Federal Airport Act of 1946, 365
Federal airways, 32, 365–66
Federal Aviation Administration, 76, 287, 294–95, 316, 319, 378, 383
Federal Coordinator of Transportation, 270, 275, 362
Federal emission standards, 41, 381
Federal guarantee of loans, 293
Federal Highway Administration, 316, 319
Federal highway aid systems, 29–31, 386

Federal interstate highway systems, 31, 59
Federal Power Commission v. *Hope Natural Gas Co.*, 145
Federal Railroad Administration, 316, 319
Fetter, Frank, 224, 233–39
Fishyback transportation, 83, 137
Fitch, Lyle C., 389
Fixed costs: air carrier, 76–77; economies of scale, 325–26; motor, 61; pipeline, 66, 357; pricing, 54–55, 61, 144, 155–59, 190–91, 357, 396; railroad, 54–55, 61, 123, 334, 357; shipper, 152; water carrier, 72
Flood, Kenneth U., 128, 176, 186, 353, 443, 466
Fogel, Robert, 38
Form utility, 14
For-hire carriers, 49–50
Fourth section rates, 183–84, 187, 195–98, 208, 231, 232
Frederick, John H., 297, 372
Freedgood, Seymour, 443
Freight forwarders: average haul, 80; characteristics and performance, 79–80; coordination, 138; documentation, 438; employees, 80; equipment, 80; investment, 79; number of firms, 79; regulation, 79, 292; reparations, 441; revenues, 79; tonnage, 80
Friedlaender, Ann F., 297
Future of transportation, 472–76

Gable, Richard W., 265, 281, 298
General American Transportation Corp., 82
General Services Administration, 400
General significance of transportation, 3–4
Geography and transportation, 16–17, 85–102
Georgia v. *Pennsylvania Railroad*, 173, 292
Gifford, Gilbert L., 408
Gilmore, Harlan W., 102

Glaskowsky, Nicholas A., Jr., 15, 241, 430, 443, 453, 477
Goodrich, Carter, 38
Gourley, David R., 477
Grandfather clause: administrative problems, 280; air carriers, 284–85; control device, 296; freight forwarders, 292; motor carriers, 276–77; water carriers, 288
Granger movement, 248–52, 335
Gravitational models, 237–39
Greenhut, Melvin M., 239, 241
Greyhound Corporation, 64
Grossman, William L., 140, 443
Grounds for court review, 311–12
Guandolo, John, 115
Guarantee of loans, 293, 294, 405

Harbeson, Robert W., 297, 340
Harper, Donald V., 281, 430, 477
Haskell, Robert H., 47
Hastings Plan, 188–89
Hauk, James G., 443
Hay, William W., 102, 128
Healy, Kent T., 340
Hendry, J. G., 340
Henzey, William V., 353
Hepburn Act of 1906, 256, 315
Heskett, J. L., 15, 241, 430, 443, 453, 477
Highway Act of 1916, 30, 271, 363
Highway Act of 1921, 30, 271
Highway congestion, 42, 375, 378, 383
Highway transportation: and the depression, 30–31, 271; Federal regulation, 275–76; history, 20–21, 29–31, 271, 363–64; passenger miles, 51; promotion, 59, 363–64, 386; routes, 94; state aid, 30–31; state regulation, 273–74; system, 59, 363–64; ton-miles, 51, 52; variability effects, 377–78, 382–84
Hille, Stanley J., 430
Hilton, Charles L., 430
Hilton, George W., 298
Hoch-Smith Resolution of 1925, 114, 270
Hoffman, Joseph V., 186

Homestead Act of 1863, 248
Hoover Commission, 35, 314, 403
Hoover, Edgar M., 241
Hope Case Formula, 145
Hudson, William J., 128, 140, 281, 341, 353

Illegal transportation, 280, 396, 456
Illinois Central Railroad, 27
Illinois classification, 162
Illinois and Michigan Canal, 23
Illinois Waterway, 35, 68
Incentive rates, 178–79, 181–82
Industrial location theory, 227–31
Industrial switching, 122
Industrial traffic management: carrier selection, 431–32, 455; centralized or decentralized, 425, 452; claims, 439–41; containerization, 458–59, 473; control decisions, 431–43; demurrage and detention, 433; documentation, 436–42; electronic computer, 459–60, 463–64, 473; equipment control, 432; evolution, 413–21; functions, 413, 426–27; insurance, 445–48, 462; internal organization, 424–26; inventory control, 14, 413, 418, 419, 449, 462; line duties, 422–23; material handling, 14, 450, 458–59; organizational chart, 419, 427; packing, marking, loading, 450–51; plant location, 413, 416, 423, 455, 459, 464; private carriage, 455–58; product innovation, 464–65; purchasing, 14, 445–49; rate negotiations, 441–42; reciprocity, 425, 435, 449; routing, 433–36; sales function, 448–49; staff duties, 423–24; total cost concept, 78, 417–18; tracing and expediting, 436; warehousing, 14, 450, 454, 460–64
Industrywide bargaining, 346, 351
Inherent nature of goods, 109
Inland Waterways Commission, 34
Insurance, 274, 280, 308, 445–48
Integration of transportation: adjusting scale of operation, 326–27, 339–40;

allocation of resources, 331–32; cost savings, 325–27, 330, 339–40; definition, 129–30, 136, 324–25, 339–40; economies of scale, 325–26, 339–40; effects, 328–32, 339–40; goal conflicts, 323–24, 328–30, 336, 339–40; increased volume, 327–28, 339–40; labor decreases, 328–29; long-run effects, 330–32; methods, 324–28, 339–40; national defense, 330; obstacles, 332–40; public policy, 334–35; service decreases, 329–30

Interaction models of locaton, 225–40

Interchange of equipment, 56, 63, 82, 120, 130, 131–32

Intercity freight ton-mles, 51, 52

Intercity passenger miles, 51, 63

Interline agreements, 134

International Air Transport Association, 307, 385

International aspects of passenger transportation, 76, 384–85

Interregional routes, 85–102

Interstate Commerce Act: Act of 1920, 259–62, 335; Act of 1940, 288–91, 335–36; Act of 1958, 293–95, 310; Carmack Amendment, 437; Cummins Amendments, 437; Declaration of National Transportation Policy, 289–90, 355, 391–93; discrimination, 112, 253; Elkins Act, 256, 288; Emergency Transportation Act, 270, 275; Expediting Act, 256; Fourth Section, 183–84, 253–54, 288; freight forwarders, 292; Hepburn Act, 256, 315; Hoch-Smith Resolution, 114, 270; Mann-Elkins Act, 257; Motor Carrier Act, 275–80; original act, 252–54, 335; reasonableness, 146–47, 253, 256; Reed-Bulwinkle Amendment, 135, 173, 292–93; right to route, 434; water carriers, 288–89; weaknesses, 254–55

Interstate Commerce Commission: accounts, 257, 265, 278; anti-trust conflicts, 330, 400–01; authority, 303; bill of lading, 437; car shortages, 93, 258, 261; case load, 302; commis-sioners, 301, 302, 314; cost allocation, 376; establishment, 254, 300; examiners, 302; express companies, 80, 257; freight forwarders, 79, 292; functions, 303; general discrimination, 253, 254, 264, 277, 280, 288; guarantee of loans, 293, 294, 405; joint boards, 279; joint use of terminals, 123–24, 132, 261; long and short haul, 253–54, 264, 278, 288; maximum rates, 256, 258, 277; motor carriers, 275–80; organization, 301–02, 304; per diem rates, 131–32; permits, 276, 288; personal discrimination, 253, 264, 277, 280, 288; piggy-back rules, 136; pipelines, 64, 257; practitioners, 302; proceedings, 302, 399; rail-water coordination, 136; rate bureaus, 173, 292–93; regulatory conflicts, 397–400; reorganization, 302; revenue divisions, 133, 260, 265, 288; review by courts, 255, 311–12; role, 301, 399; safety, 279–80; structure, 301–03; through routes and joint rates, 133, 278, 288; transportation brokers, 81, 276; water carriers, 73, 288–89, 400; weaknesses, 254–55. See also Abandonment, Certificate of Public Convenience and Necessity, Reasonableness of rates

Interstate highway system: aid formula, 363–64; cost, 364; development, 31, 59, 363–64, 386; map, 94

Inventory control function, 14, 413, 418, 419, 449, 461, 462

Isard, Walter, 241

Isolated state of Von Thunen, 225–27

Ivie, Robert M., 15, 241, 430, 443, 453, 477

Jakubauskas, Edward B., 353

James River Canal, 23

Johnson Transportation Mesage, 315, 406

Joint and collective ownership, 135

Joint boards, 279, 308

Joint costs, 156–57

Joint rate, 56, 133, 179

Joint use of terminals, 123–24, 132, 261
Jones Act, 72
Jones, Eliot, 159

Kahn, Fritz R., 116, 281
Kain, John F., 389
Kelly Act of 1925, 32, 272, 283
Koontz, Harold, 265, 281, 298
Kennedy, John F., 315, 350, 404–06
Kennedy Message of 1962, 315
Keyes, Lucile Sheppard, 298
Kilday Report, 403
Knights of Labor, 344

Labor regulation: alternative solutions, 350–53; compulsory arbitration, 351–52; emergency boards, 349–50; goal conflicts, 342–43, 346; history, 262–63, 344, 347–48; Presidential action, 350, 352; Railway Labor Act, 262–63, 347–49; settlement mechanics, 347–50; Transportation Act of 1920, 262–63, 348; voluntary arbitration, 349
LaLonde, Bernard L., 222, 453, 465
Lancaster Pike, 20
Land grants: dollar value, 361–62; rate concessions, 291, 362; settlement of West, 27, 28, 248, 359, 362
Landis Report, 314
Landon, Charles E., 83
Lansing, John B., 389
Launhardt, Wilhelm, 227
Legal and lawful rate concepts, 441
Legal liability, 57, 103, 108–10, 183
Legal service obligations of common carriers: background, 104–06; duration of liability, 110, 446–48; duty to avoid discrimination, 103, 111–14, 311; duty to charge reasonable rates, 110–11, 146–47, 311; duty to deliver, 103, 108–10, 311, 437, 446–48; duty to serve, 103, 106–08, 311; limitations of liability, 109–10, 437, 446–48; origin, 105–06

Legislative regulation: appropriations, 313; delegation of authority, 313; general policy, 312, 391–93; procedures, 313
Leonard, W. N., 341
Lessing, Lawrence, 477
Levy, Lester S., 38
Limitation of liability, 109–10
Line haul costs, 157
Little, Wallace I., 453
Location of cities, 231–33
Location and freight rates, 224–41, 464
Location theory, 224–39
Locational interactions and environment, 39–40
Locklin, D. Philip, 15, 38, 66, 83, 116, 128, 144, 159, 206, 223, 265, 281, 298, 320
Logistics. See Physical distribution
Losch, August, 224, 233–39, 241
Loss and damage: motor carriers, 62; prevention, 440, 458; railroad, 57; routing, 434; water carriers, 74
Lundy, Robert F., 186

McElhiney, Paul T., 116, 430, 477
Magee, John F., 430
McNary-Watres Act of 1930, 283
Mann-Elkins Act of 1910, 257
Market complexity of passenger transportation, 378
Market location theory, 233–39
Marketing and physical distribution, 13–14
Marshall, Arthur M., 354
Mass Transit Trust Fund, 386
Master car builders rules, 131
Materials handling function, 413, 419, 427, 450–51, 458–59
Maximum Freight Rate Case, 255
Maxwell, W. David, 281
Mergers. See Consolidation and merger
Meyer, John R., 159, 389, 408
Miami and Erie Canal, 23
Miller, John M., 116
Miller, Sidney L., Jr., 408

Milwaukee Case, 311
Molloy, William T., 466
Morton, Newton, 15, 116, 128, 140, 154, 176, 223, 241, 341, 430, 453
Morton, Stephen, 38
Moses, Leon F., 223, 280
Mossman, Frank H., 15, 128, 140, 159, 176, 223, 241, 430, 453
Motivation to travel, 378–79
Motor carrier: average haul, 60, 96; bills of lading, 438; capital, 60–61; characteristics and performance, 59–63; claims, 62; coverage, 62; equipment, 60–61; expenses, 61, 123, 345; Federal regulation, 275–80, 399; future, 473–77; interline agreements, 134; intermodal competition, 61–62, 271–72; intramodal competition, 61–62, 273–74; labor relations, 342–53; mergers, 336; number of firms, 60; operating ratio, 61, 66, 72; promotion, 356–57; reliability, 62; reparations, 441; revenues, 60, 61; state regulation, 273–74, 308, 399; taxes, 61; terminal ownership, 123; trailer interchange, 132; wages, 61, 345
Motor Carrier Act of 1935: agricultural commodities exemption, 278–79, 294, 310, 394, 401, 405; carrier classification, 275–76; consolidation and merger, 277, 336; development, 275; entry controls, 276–77, 303, 308; problems, 280; rate controls, 277; regulatory innovations, 278–79; security and accounts, 278; tacking of rights, 328, 336
Mueller Report, 314, 403
Munn v. Illinois, 106, 251, 252

National defense and transportation: air, 282, 358; declaration of national transportation policy, 289–90, 391–93; highways, 364; railroads, 58, 330; vital role, 4, 403
Natonal Highway Safety Bureau, 316, 319
National Industrial Traffic League, 442
National Mediation Board, 263, 348–49

National motor freight classification, 163
National Pike, 21, 359, 363
National Railroad Adjustment Board, 263, 348–49
National Railroad Passenger Corporation, 54, 387–88
National system of interstate and defense highways, 31, 59, 94, 363–64, 386
National transportation policy: administrative conflicts, 400–02; common carrier concepts, 394, 395; declaration, 289–90, 391–93, 402; definition of policy, 291–94; Department of Transportation, 406; exemption concept, 394, 396; inconsistencies, 392–93, 405; informal policy, 393–94; jurisdictional conflicts, 398; Kennedy Message, 403–06; passenger policy questions, 385–88; philosophical conflicts, 394, 397; private ownership, 393, 405; procedural conflicts, 399–400; proposed solutions, 402–06; public investment, 393–94, 405; regulatory conflicts, 397–400, 405; reports, 403; statutory policy, 391–93; urban, 385–88
National Transportation Policy. See Doyle Report
National Transportation Safety Board, 319
Nation's annual freight transportation bill, 9, 10, 141
Nation's annual passenger transportation bill, 9, 11
Nelson, James C., 159, 372, 408
New York State Barge Canal, 34, 35, 68
Newlands Act of 1913, 347
Nicholls, J. A. F., 241
Nightingale, Edmund A., 408
Noise pollution, 42, 375, 380–82
Northern Securities Case, 335
Northwest Ordinance of 1787, 366
Norton, Hugh S., 15, 67, 83, 159, 265, 281, 298, 320, 341, 354, 389, 408

Obligations of common carrier: background, 104–05; duty to avoid discrimination, 110–15; duty to charge reasonable rates, 110; duty to deliver, 108–10; duty to serve, 106–08; origin, 105–06

Office of High Speed Ground Transportation, 386, 387

Ohio and Erie Canal, 23

Oliver, Eli L., 354

Operational interactions and environment, 40–43

Operating Brotherhoods, 344, 351

Order bill of lading, 437, 438, 462

Original cost doctrine, 145

Out-of-pocket costs, 156, 191

Owen, Wilford, 389, 403, 408

Pacific Fruit Express, 82

Packaging requirements, 107, 450–51, 458

Packing function, 416, 432, 450

Paden, David L., 477

Panama Canal Act of 1912, 287

Panic of 1837, 23

Panic of 1873, 250

Parcel post, 81, 305

Passenger transportation: air carriage, 74–77; average journey, 63; busses, 63–64; by-product effect, 375; ecological problems, 380–82; economic consideration, 385–88; fares, 63, 374; international, 76, 384–85; market complexity, 378; predominance of private, 51, 373; sociological problems, 382–84; supremacy of air, 51, 375; variability, 377

Peak traffic problems, 377–78, 382–84

Peck, Merton J., 159, 408

Pegrum, Dudley F., 15, 38, 47, 67, 84, 102, 116, 128, 160, 176, 265, 281, 298, 320, 341, 354, 372, 408

Pell, Claiborne, 389

Pennsylvania Public Works System, 22–23

Penn Central bankruptcy, 58, 387

Per diem rules, 131

Peters, William S., 223

Phillips, Charles F. Jr., 281

Physical distribution: carrier selection, 431–32, 455; control decisions, 431–43; definition, 13, 413; costs, 14; electronic computer, 459–60, 463–64, 473; equipment control, 432; future, 476; inventory control, 14, 413, 418, 419, 449, 462; legal problems, 445; material handling, 14, 450, 458–59; organizational chart, 419, 427; plant location, 413, 416, 423, 455, 459, 464; private carriage, 455–58; product innovation, 464–65; purchasing, 14, 448–49; rate negotiation, 441–42; sales function, 448–49; titles, 14, 417; total cost concept, 78, 417–18; trade-offs, 462; traffic management, 14, 413–29, 431–43, 445–53, 454–65; traffic responsibilities, 14, 421–24; warehousing, 14, 450, 454, 460–64

Physical supply concepts, 413

Pickup and delivery services, 62, 77, 80, 120–21, 208

Piggyback transportation, 56, 82–83, 130, 137–38, 183, 405, 458

Pipelines: average haul, 65; capital, 64, 345; characteristics and performance, 64–66; cooperation, 134; coverage, 64, 65; development, 35–37; documentation, 438; employees, 66, 345; future, 473; intermodal competition, 66, 73; investment, 64, 66; number of firms, 64; operation ratio, 66; rates, 66; regulation, 64–65, 257; revenues, 65; routes, 99, 101; ton-miles, 52, 65, 66; undivided interest, 65, 135

Place utility, 5–7, 114, 413

Plant location function, 413, 423, 459, 464

Plowman, E. Grosvenor, 430, 466, 477

Pollution, 41–42, 373, 380–82

Pool-car service, 126, 460

Pools, traffic and revenue, 130, 134, 264

Post roads, 20

Presidential Railroad Commission, 350

Prices and transportation, 7–9

Private automobile transportation, 51, 373, 374–75

Private car companies, 81–82, 131, 457

Private carriage: Act of 1958, 294;

amount, 141; competition to for-hires, 267–68; concept, 49–50; insurance, 446; motor, 59, 63, 280, 284, 352–53; passenger transportation, 373; traffic management, 422, 431, 446, 454–57; water, 73, 352

Private Truck Council of America, 135

Proceedings and hearings, 302, 304, 307

Producing center competition, 208–09

Production scheduling function, 413, 416, 418, 419, 449

Production and transportation, 5–7, 85–102

Progressive movement, 256

Protective services, 119, 126

Public aid to transportation: airmail subsidy, 367; airways, 364–65, 366, 386; amount, 368–69; effects, 369–71, 376, 379, 386; financing the way, 361–66; goals, 359–61, 388; highways, 363–64, 376, 379, 386; land grants, 359, 361–63; methods, 361–69; operating the way, 366–67; policy, 385–88, 393–94, 401; problem, 355–59, 385–88, 401; promoting competition, 360–61, 366; railroads, 361–63, 387; research, 356–57, 368; supplementing regulation, 360–61; water transportation, 365–66, 367

Public warehousing, 461–62

Pullman strike of 1894, 347

Purchasing function, 413, 418, 419, 422, 424, 448–50

Quality of life, 43, 45, 382–84

Railpax, 54, 387–88

Railroad Boards of Labor Adjustment, 348

Railroad Labor Board, 348

Railroads: abandonment, 58, 107–08, 261, 377; average freight haul, 53, 96; average passenger haul, 63; by-product effect, 375–77; characteristics and performance, 51–59; commodity movements, 96, 98; construction aids, 27–28, 357, 359, 361–63; corporate form, 28; cost allocation, 345, 376; cost characteristics, 54–55; coverage, 56–57; division of revenues, 133, 260; equipment, 52, 131–32; European capital, 28; excess capacity, 58, 371; future, 473–74; intermodal competition, 54, 270–71; intramodal competition, 54, 269–70; labor force, 52; labor relations, 342–53; labor unions, 59, 259, 344; land grants, 27–28, 248, 291, 359, 361–62; mergers, 323–40; number of firms, 52; operating ratio, 54–55, 61, 72; originations by regions, 100; overcapitalization, 28, 258, 262; passenger fares, 63, 75, 374; passenger miles, 51, 53; passenger policy, 387–88; Railpax, 54, 387–88; rate of return, 58; reliability, 57; reparations, 440–41; revenues, 52–53; routes, 53, 91; settlement of West, 27, 88, 359, 360, 369; taxes, 59, 376; terminal ownership, 123; ton-miles, 51, 52; trackage, 26, 29, 51; trunkline, 27

Railroads, transcontinental, 4, 25–29

Railway Express Agency, 80–81, 82, 138, 163, 184, 185, 438

Railway Labor Act of 1926: alternative solutions, 350–53; emergency boards, 349; mechanics of settlement, 348–50; passage, 262–63, 347; voluntary arbitration, 349

Ransom, Roger L., 38

Rate auditing, 416, 423, 427, 440–41, 459

Rate Bureaus, 134–35, 172–75, 292–93

Rate effects: carrier competition, 208; commodity competition, 211–12; consuming center competition, 209–10; economic activity, 207–22; location determinants, 212–22; location of markets, 233–41; location theory, 224–41; producing center competition, 208–09

Rate geography, 85

Rate grouping, 199–205

Rate levels, 144–46, 280

Rate negotiation, 427, 441–42

Rate procedures, 172–75
Rate of return, 144–46
Rate territories, 172–73
Rates: aggregate of intermediary, 180; agreed, 181–82; all-commodity, 178; any-quantity, 178; arbitrary, 179, 195–96; Atlantic Port differential, 193, 194; basing point, 187, 195–98, 232; blanket, 187, 198–205, 208, 231; class, 55, 162, 167, 177; classification, 161–67, 258; combination, 134–35, 179; commodity, 55, 169, 177; contract carrier, 182, 185; cube, 184; cutback, 181; delayed, 184; differential, 179; exceptions, 165, 167, 177; export, 181, 192–94; floating-in, 181; Fourth Section, 183–84, 187, 195–98, 208; functions, 143–46; import, 181, 192–94; incentive, 178–79, 181–82; joint, 56, 133, 179; key point, 200; Land Grant, 291, 362; legal-lawful, 441; local, 179; maximum, 255–56; mileage structures, 189–94; minimum, 179; miscellaneous, 183–86; multiple-car, 178; piggy-back, 183; postage-stamp, 187–89; proportional, 179; released-value, 110, 183, 437, 446; Section 22, 114, 182; space available, 184; structures, 187–206; suspension, 257; tapered, 154, 190–91, 231; terminology, 177–86; through, 132–33, 179; train-load, 178; transit, 180–81; volume, 178; zone, 187, 199–206
Rates and costs, 155–59
Rates and prices, 141
Reasonableness of rates: Act of 1887, 146, 253; common law obligations, 103, 110–11, 146–47; early regulatory experience, 254–55; Hepburn Act, 256–57; lawful rates, 441; Mann-Elkins Act, 257–58
Rebates, 252, 255, 256, 264, 288
Recapture Clause, 260, 264, 269, 270
Reciprocal switching agreements, 122, 132
Reciprocity, 425, 435, 449
Reconsignment and diversion, 124–25, 184, 202–03, 435

Reed-Bulwinkle Act of 1948, 135, 173, 292–93
Regional economic development and transportation costs, 217–222
Regional specialization and transportation: basis of spacial economic activities, 207–222; basis of transportation demand, 150; changes, 98–102; geographic factors, 87, 92, 96; location of production, 6; routes, 92, 96
Regulation of transportation: bankruptcy, 262–63, 270; Buck Case, 274; charter regulation, 247–48; classification, 252, 264; commissions and boards, 299–309, 397–400; Commodities Clause, 257, 264; conflicts, 397–402; contract carriers, 274, 276, 277, 280, 288–89; courts, 309–12; Cullom Report, 251–52; Division of joint rates, 260, 266, 288; dual operations, 278, 289; Duke Case, 274; early weaknesses, 254–55; evolutionary in development, 244, 271, 275, 283–84, 287–89, 292; executive, 313–19; future, 475; Granger Acts, 249–51; inherent advantage, 282, 286, 290, 295, 371, 394–95, 402; insurance, 274, 280, 308; intramodal air, 285; intramodal motor, 271; intramodal rail, 269–70; intrastate rates, 260–61, 264, 279, 294, 308; investigatory commissions, 248, 299; Johnson Message, 315, 406; joint boards, 279, 308; joint use of terminals, 261, 264; judicial review, 311–12; Kennedy Message, 403–06; labor, 262–63, 265, 342–53; legal basis, 250–51, 274; legislative process, 312–13, 391–94; maximum rates, 255, 256, 264, 277, 286, 288, 405; minimum rates, 260, 264, 269–70, 277, 286, 288, 355, 405; monopoly, 244–65, 273, 274, 334; pools, 250, 254, 264, 288, 335; positive control, 259–62, 335–36; promotional era, 246–48; proper role, 393–97; to protect highways, 273; rate bureaus, 292–93; Recapture Clause, 260, 264, 269, 270; safety, 279–80, 282, 283, 286–87; securities, 262, 265, 278, 308;

service regulation, 261, 264; social lag, 245, 272, 402; state certificates, 274, 308; state regulation, 247–51, 273–74, 299–300, 308–09; Wabash Case, 252, 274; Windom Report, 251, 315. See also Abandonments, accounts, agricultural exemption, bulk shipment exemptions, Certificates of Public Convenience and Necessity, consolidation and mergers, Declaration of National Transportation Policy, discrimination, exempt carriage, Grandfather Clause, reasonableness, role of rate making

Regulatory Acts: Act of 1887, 252–54, 335; Act of 1920, 259–62, 325; Act of 1940, 288–91, 335–36; Act of 1958, 293–95, 310; Carmack Amendment, 437; Cummins Amendments, 437; Elkins Act, 256, 288; Emergency Act, 270, 275; Expediting Act, 256; Hepburn Act, 256, 315; Hoch-Smith Resolution, 114, 270; Mann-Elkins Act, 257; Reed-Bulwinkle Amendment, 135, 173, 292–93

Regulatory institutions: commissions and boards, 299–309; courts, 309–12; executive, 313–19; legislative process, 312–13

Reilly, W. J., 238, 239
Released-value rates, 110, 183, 437, 446
Reproduction cost doctrine, 145
Research and planning function, 427
Rhochrematics, 417–18
Richards, Hoy C., 241
Richmond, Samuel B., 298
Ripley, William Z., 335
Roads: early history, 20–21; map, 94; promotion, 59, 271, 363–64; system, 59
Roads, post, 20
Roads, toll, 20–21
Roberts, Merrill J., 15, 37, 140, 160, 205, 265, 266, 297, 319, 353, 371, 477
Rose, Joseph R., 160
Rose, Sanford, 47
Rose, Warren, 298
Routes: geography, 85–86; interregional, 89–90; location, 86–91; map, 82, 91, 94, 95, 97, 99

Routing function, 416, 422, 426, 427, 433–34
Rule of Rate Making: Act of 1920, 259–60, 269–70; Act of 1940, 291; Act of 1958, 294; Civil Aeronautics Act, 285–86; freight forwarder, 292; water transportation, 288
Ruppenthal, Karl M., 160

St. Lawrence Seaway, 34, 71
St. Lawrence Seaway Development Corp., 316, 319
St. Louis-Southwestern Ry. Co. v. U.S., 133
Sampson, Roy J., 38, 102, 160, 206, 320, 341, 477
Sawyer Report, 314, 403
Schary, Philip, 389
Schiff, Michael, 443
Seasonal travel, 382–83
Section 22 Rates, 114, 182, 400
Securities regulation, 262, 265, 278
Segal, Harvey H., 38
Service obligations, 103, 106–08, 437
Sherman Anti-Trust Act of 1890, 130, 335
Shinn, Glenn L., 116, 408
Shipper advisory boards, 133–34, 442
Shippers' associations, 81
Short-run pricing, 155–57
Shreveport Case, 261
Shutes, George M., 443
Side-by-side merger, 326–27, 328–29, 330
Significance of transportation, 3–15
Simler, Norman J., 354
Simpson, John W., 47
Smathers Report, 403
Smerk, George M., 389
Smith, Adam, 85
Smykay, Edward W., 160, 222, 453, 465
Smyth v. *Ames,* 259
Snyder, Richard E., 443
Social Circle Case, 255
Social costs, 39, 40, 42, 43, 45, 383
Sociological aspects of transportation, 44–45, 378, 382–84
Space utility, 14, 413

Spacial economic activity and transportation costs, 207–23

Split deliveries, 178

Spychalski, John C., 298, 390

Standard Time Act, 305

Star, Edward A., 176, 186

State commissions, 307–09, 312–13

State gasoline taxes, 30, 271, 364

State indebtedness, canals, 23, 366

State regulation, 248–51, 273–74

Status symbols, 45

Steger, Wilbur A., 477

Stenason, John, 159, 408

Stephenson Case, 274

Stewart, Wendell M., 453

Stopping-in-transit, 125–26, 178, 434, 449, 461

Storage and elevation, 122

Straight bill of lading, 436, 462

Straszheim, Mahlon R., 298

Street congestion, 42, 373, 375, 377, 378–79, 382–84

Supplemental air carrier, 76, 285

Switching railroads, 52, 122

"Tacking" of rights, 328, 336

Taff, Charles A., 15, 67, 84, 116, 128, 176, 186, 281, 320, 354, 390, 430, 443, 453, 466

Tapered rates, 154, 190–91, 231

Tariffs: class, 165; commodity, 169; definitions, 165; demurrage, 433; exception, 165; format, 169–72; routing, 433–36; service, 169; supplements, 171; types, 165–72

Taxes and transportation, 12

Teamsters' Union, 346, 351

Technology and transportation: air development, 32–33, 356–57; future, 472–74; motor development, 356–57; pipeline, 36; pivotal role in development, 16–17, 356–57, 359, 404; rail development, 24–25; traffic management, 414, 442; water development, 69

Tennessee Valley Authority, 367, 400, 402

Terminals, accessorial services, 120–22; costs, 117, 120, 157–59; effect on rates, 157–59, 190; functions, 118–20; industrial switching, 122; loading and unloading, 121; management, 123; ownership, 123; pickup and delivery, 120–21; size, 117, 123; storage and elevation, 122; weighing and reweighing, 121–22

Texas and Pacific Railroad, 27

Thermal pollution, 41

Through billing, 133

Through rates, 132–33, 179

Through routes, 56, 132–33, 136, 138

Time utility, 5–7, 14, 413

T.O.F.C. service and rates, 56, 82–83, 130, 137–38, 183

Toll roads, 20–21

Total cost concept, 78, 417–21, 476

Tracing and expediting, 126–27, 427, 436

Traffic management. See Industrial traffic management

Trailways System, 64

Transcontinental bus system, 64

Transcontinental railroads, 4, 25–29

Transit insurance, 445–48

Transit privilege: administration, 127, 180–81; commodity competition, 211; defined, 127; location of cities, 232; rates, 180–81; traffic management, 414, 461

Transit rates, 180–81

Transloading, 126

Transportation Act of 1920: abandonment, 261; adequacy, 258–60; car service, 261; division of revenues, 260; extensions, 261; joint use of terminals, 261; labor, 262, 348; level of intrastate rates, 260–61; mergers, 261, 335; minimum rate control, 260; Recapture Clause, 260; Rule of Rate Making, 259–60; terminal regulation, 123–24

Transportation Act of 1940: Certificates of Public Convenience and Necessity, 288; Declaration of National Transportation Policy, 289–90; exemptions, 288–89; mergers, 291, 335; water carriers, 288–89

Transportation Act of 1958: abandonment, 108, 293–94, 309; agricultural

commodities exemption, 293–94, 310; guarantee of loans, 293–94, 367; intrastate rates, 293–94, 398; private transportation, 293–94; Rule of Rate Making, 293–94
Transportation brokers, 81
Transportation and capital investment, 10
Transportation company concept, 324, 334
Transportation and distribution. See distribution and transportation
Transportation and economic development, 4–5, 356, 369, 469–70
Transportation education, 476
Transportation and employment, 9-10
Transportation expenditures: annual total freight, 9, 10; annual total passenger, 9, 11
Transportation of the future, 469–77
Transportation and geography, 16–17, 85–102
Transportation labor: alternative solutions, 350–53; compulsory arbitration, 351–52; emergency boards, 349; employment characteristics, 344–45; goal conflicts, 342–43, 346; industry-wide bargaining, 346; Presidential action, 350; settlement procedure, 348–50; union history, 344; voluntary arbitration, 349
Transportation and national defense. See National defense
Transportation policy conflicts: administrative, 400–02; common carrier concepts, 394, 395; Declaration of National Transportation Policy, 289–90, 391–93, 402; definition, 291–94; Department of Transportation, 406; exemption concept, 394, 396; inconsistencies, 392–93, 405; informal policy, 393–94; jurisdictional, 398; Kennedy Message, 403–06; passenger policy questions, 385–88; philosophical, 394–97; private ownership, 393, 405; procedural, 399–400; proposed solutions, 402–06; public investment, 393–94, 405; regulatory, 397–400, 405; reports, 403; statutory policy, 391–93; urban, 385–88
Transportation and prices, 7–9
Transportation and product innovation, 464–65
Transportation and production, 5–7, 85–102
Transportation and regional specialization. See Regional specialization
Transportation research, 357, 368
Transportation and taxes, 12
Transportation and technology. See Technology and transportation
Travel agents, 379
Travel to work pattern, 377
Treaty of Paris of 1763, 365
Troxel, Emery, 15, 38, 140, 160, 206, 241, 266, 281, 298, 354, 372
Turnpikes, 20–21
Twenty-Vehicle Rule, 277

Ubiquitous raw materials, 228–231
Ulman, Edward L., 102
Unification in transportation: adjusting scale of operation, 326–27, 339–40; allocation of resources, 331–32; cost savings, 325–27, 331, 339–40; definition, 123–30, 324–25, 339–40; economies of scale, 325–26, 339–40; effects, 326–32, 339–40; goal conflicts, 323–24, 328–30, 339–40; increased volume, 327–28, 339–40; labor decreases, 328–29; long-run effects, 330–32; methods, 324–28, 339–40; national defense, 330; obstacles, 332–33; public policy, 333–37; service decreases, 329–30
Uniform freight classification, 162–65
Uniform Warehouse Receipts Act of 1907, 462
Union Pacific Railroad, 27
United States v. Appalachian Electric Co., 366
United States mails: airmail contracts, 32–33, 75, 76, 77, 272, 282–83, 367; certificates, 283–84; highways, 358; Kennedy Message, 405; means of

freight transportation, 77, 81; postage-stamp rate structures, 187–89

United States v. *Milwaukee Railroad,* 311

Urban Mass Transit Administration, 316, 386

Urban passenger transportation, 373–389

Urban redevelopment, 373, 378

Urban transportation and terminals, 117–18

User charges: airports and airways, 365, 386, 405; highway trust fund, 364; investment in way, 361–66, 362, 370–71; Kennedy Message, 405; nonpayment of interest, 358; objectives, 370–71; property tax factor, 358; waterways, 365–66, 405

Utility, place and time, 5–7, 114

Van Metre, Thurman W., 128, 140, 320

Variable costs: air carrier, 76–77; economies of scale, 325–26; motor, 61; pipeline, 66; pricing, 55, 61, 144, 155–59, 190–91; railroad, 54–55, 334; shipper, 152; water carrier, 72

Variability of travel, 377

Vickrey, William S., 390

Von Thunen, 224, 225–227, 228, 231, 233, 234

Wabash Case, 252, 274, 398

Wabash and Erie Canal, 23

Warehouse location, 423, 454, 459, 460–64

Warehousing costs, 462–63

Warehousing function, 14, 419, 427, 450, 460–64

Water pollution, 41–42, 382

Water transportation: capital investment, 69; characteristics and performance, 68–74; coastwise, 68–69, 71–72; commodity movement, 98; costs, 72–74; coverage, 68, 69, 74; equipment, 69; future, 473; Great Lakes, 70–71; history, 17–20, 33–35; intercoastal, 71–72; intermodal competition, 73–74, 271–72; intracoastal, 69, 71–72; liability, 74, 446; mergers, 337; number of firms, 69; operating ratio, 72; passenger miles, 51; promotion, 72–73, 271–72, 357–58, 360, 365–67; regulation, 73, 287–89; revenues, 69; routes, 89, 95; speed, 69, 73; terminal ownership, 123; ton-miles, 52, 69, 72–73

Waybill, 439

Weber, Alfred, 224, 227–31, 233

Weeks Report, 314, 403

Weight and inspection bureaus, 121, 127

Weight losing raw materials, 228–231

Weinstein, Paul A., 354

Welland Canal, 34, 70

Westmeyer, Russell E., 15, 38, 206, 266, 281, 298, 320, 354

Whitehurst, Clinton H., Jr., 372

Wicker, E. R., 38

Williams, Ernest W., Jr., 15, 38, 66, 83, 116, 140, 159, 176, 205, 222, 265, 280, 297, 408

Williams, Robert M., 389

Wilson, George W., 408

Wilson, G. Lloyd, 128, 140

Windom Report, 251, 315

Wisehart, Arthur M., 354

Wohl, Martin, 389

Yaseen, Leonard C., 223

Zwick, Charles, 159, 408